Programming in C: A Practical Approach

Ajay Mittal
Department of Computer Science and Engineering
University Institute of Engineering and Technology (UIET)
Panjab University
Chandigarh

Pearson

ISBN: 978-81-317-2934-2

First Impression, 2010
Nineteenth Impression, 2024
Twentieth Impression, 2025

Published by Pearson India Education Services Pvt. Ltd, CIN: U72200TN2005PTC057128

Head Office: 1st Floor, Berger Tower, Plot No. C-001A/2, Sector 16B, Noida – 201 301,Uttar Pradesh, India.

Registered Office: Featherlite, 'The Address' 5th Floor, Survey No 203/10B, 200 Ft MMRD Road, Zamin Pallavaram, Chennai - 600044

Website: in.pearson.com; Email:companysecretary.india@pearson.com

Digitally printed in India by Trinity Academy for Corporate Training Ltd, New Delhi in the year of 2025.

This book is dedicated to

my mother
Smt. Prem Lata
with deepest gratitude
&
the little angel, my nephew,
Jai Mittal
with love...

About the Author

Ajay Mittal is an Assistant Professor in the Department of Computer Science and Engineering, PEC University of Technology (*formerly Punjab Engineering College*), Chandigarh. He has done M.E. (Computer Science & Engineering) with distinction from Punjab Engineering College. His areas of interest are programming and logic development, algorithm analysis and design, compiler design, computer graphics and computer vision. He is currently doing research in the area of computer vision. He has a number of research papers in national/international journals and conferences to his credit. He has a comprehensive professional experience and has been teaching C language for about a decade. During this span, he has conducted numerous courses on C programming and Advanced C programming.

Contents

About the Author *iv*
Preface *xiii*

1 Data Types, Variables and Constants **1**

1.1 Introduction 2
1.2 C Standards 2
1.2.1 Kernighan & Ritchie (K&R) C Standard 2
1.2.2 ANSI C/Standard C/C89 Standard 2
1.2.3 ISO C/C90 Standard 2
1.2.4 C99 Standard 2
1.3 Learning Programming Language and Natural Language: An Analogy 3
1.4 C Character Set 3
1.5 Identifiers and Keywords 4
1.5.1 Identifiers 4
1.5.2 Keywords 5
1.6 Declaration Statement 5
1.7 Data Types 6
1.7.1 Basic/Primitive Data Types 6
1.7.2 Derived Data Types 6
1.7.3 User-defined Data Types 6
1.8 Type Qualifiers and Type Modifiers 7
1.8.1 Type Qualifiers 7
1.8.2 Type Modifiers 7
1.9 Difference Between Declaration and Definition 7
1.10 Data Object, L-value and R-value 9
1.10.1 Data Object 9
1.10.2 L-value 9
1.10.3 R-value 9
1.11 Variables and Constants 10
1.11.1 Variables 10
1.11.2 Constants 10
1.12 Structure of a C Program 14
1.12.1 Comments 15
1.12.2 Section1: Preprocessor Directive Section 15
1.12.3 Section 2: Global Declaration Section 15
1.12.4 Section 3: Functions Section 16
1.13 Executing a C Program 16

1.14 More Programs for Startup 17
1.15 Summary 22
Exercise Questions 22
Conceptual Questions and Answers 22
Code Snippets 31
Multiple-choice Questions 33
Outputs and Explanations to Code Snippets 36
Answers to Multiple-choice Questions 40
Programming Exercises 40
Test Yourself 45

2 Operators and Expressions **47**

2.1 Introduction 48
2.2 Expressions 48
2.2.1 Operands 48
2.2.2 Operators 48
2.3 Simple Expressions and Compound Expressions 48
2.3.1 Precedence of Operators 49
2.3.2 Associativity of Operators 49
2.4 Classification of Operators 49
2.4.1 Classification Based on Number of Operands 49
2.4.2 Classification Based on Role of Operator 50
2.5 Combined Precedence of All Operators 64
2.6 Summary 66
Exercise Questions 67
Conceptual Questions and Answers 67
Code Snippets 71
Multiple-choice Questions 79
Outputs and Explanations to Code Snippets 81
Answers to Multiple-choice Questions 97
Programming Exercises 97
Test Yourself 102

3 Statements **105**

3.1 Introduction 106
3.2 Statements 106
3.3 Classification of Statements 106
3.3.1 Based Upon the Type of Action they Perform 107
3.3.2 Based Upon the Number of Constituent Statements 108
3.3.3 Based Upon their Role 110
3.4 Summary 137
Exercise Questions 137
Conceptual Questions and Answers 137
Code Snippets 149

Multiple-choice Questions 158
Outputs and Explanations to Code Snippets 160
Answers to Multiple-choice Questions 169
Programming Exercises 169
Test Yourself 180

4 Arrays and Pointers **183**

4.1 Introduction 184
4.2 Arrays 184
4.3 Single-dimensional Arrays 186
4.3.1 Declaration of a Single-dimensional Array 186
4.3.2 Usage of Single-dimensional Array 189
4.3.3 Memory Representation of Single-dimensional Array 190
4.3.4 Operations on a Single-dimensional Array 191
4.4 Pointers 192
4.4.1 Operations on Pointers 194
4.4.2 `void` pointer 200
4.4.3 Null Pointer 201
4.5 Relationship Between Arrays and Pointers 202
4.6 Scaling up the Concept 203
4.6.1 Array of Arrays (Multi-dimensional Arrays) 203
4.6.2 Array of Pointers 209
4.6.3 Pointer to a Pointer 210
4.6.4 Pointer to an Array 210
4.7 Advantages and Limitations of Arrays 211
4.8 Summary 211
Exercise Questions 212
Conceptual Questions and Answers 212
Code Snippets 218
Multiple-choice Questions 224
Outputs and Explanations to Code Snippets 227
Answers to Multiple-choice Questions 238
Programming Exercises 238
Test Yourself 255

5 Functions **257**

5.1 Introduction 258
5.2 Functions 258
5.3 Classification of Functions 259
5.3.1 Based Upon who Develops the Function 259
5.3.2 Based Upon the Number of Arguments a Function Accepts 299
5.4 Summary 302
Exercise Questions 303
Conceptual Questions and Answers 303
Code Snippets 312

Multiple-choice Questions 320
Outputs and Explanations to Code Snippets 322
Answers to Multiple-choice Questions 328
Programming Exercises 328
Test Yourself 337

6 Strings and Character Arrays **339**

6.1 Introduction 340
6.2 Strings 340
6.3 Character Arrays 342
6.4 Reading Strings from the Keyboard 343
6.5 Printing Strings on the Screen 349
6.6 Importance of Terminating Null Character 351
6.7 String Library Functions 352
6.7.1 strlen Function 353
6.7.2 strcpy Function 353
6.7.3 strcat Function 354
6.7.4 strcmp Function 355
6.7.5 strcmpi Function 357
6.7.6 strrev Function 358
6.7.7 strlwr Function 358
6.7.8 strupr Function 359
6.7.9 strset Function 360
6.7.10 strchr Function 361
6.7.11 strrchr Function 362
6.7.12 strstr Function 363
6.7.13 strncpy Function 364
6.7.14 strncat Function 365
6.7.15 strncmp Function 367
6.7.16 strncmpi Function 368
6.7.17 strnset Function 369
6.8 List of Strings 369
6.8.1 Array of strings 370
6.8.2 Array of Character Pointers 371
6.9 Command Line Arguments 373
6.10 Summary 375
Exercise Questions 376
Conceptual Questions and Answers 376
Code Snippets 381
Multiple-choice Questions 388
Outputs and Explanations to Code Snippets 390
Answers to Multiple-choice Questions 400
Programming Exercises 401
Test Yourself 409

7 Scope, Linkage, Lifetime and Storage Classes 411

7.1 Introduction 412
7.2 Scope 412
7.2.1 Determination of Scope of an Identifier 412
7.2.2 Termination of Scope of an Identifier 413
7.2.3 Same Scope 414
7.2.4 Visibility of an Identifier 417
7.3 Linkage 420
7.3.1 External linkage 420
7.3.2 Internal Linkage 422
7.3.3 No Linkage 424
7.4 Storage Duration/Lifetime of an Object 424
7.5 Storage Classes 425
7.5.1 The auto Storage Class 426
7.5.2 The register Storage Class 428
7.5.3 The static Storage Class 429
7.5.4 The extern Storage Class 430
7.5.5 The typedef Storage Class 431
7.6 Dynamic Memory Allocation 432
7.6.1 Memory Leak 436
7.7 Summary 437
Exercise Questions 437
Conceptual Questions and Answers 437
Code Snippets 450
Multiple-choice Questions 458
Outputs and Explanations to Code Snippets 460
Answers to Multiple-choice Questions 469
Programming Exercises 470
Test Yourself 474

8 The C Preprocessor 477

8.1 Introduction 478
8.2 Translators 478
8.3 Phases of Translation 479
8.3.1 Trigraph Replacement 480
8.3.2 Line Splicing 481
8.3.3 Tokenization 481
8.3.4 Preprocessor Directive Handling 482
8.4 Summary 502
Exercise Questions 503
Conceptual Questions and Answers 503
Code Snippets 510
Multiple-choice Questions 518
Outputs and Explanations to Code Snippets 520

Answers to Multiple-choice Questions 528
Programming Exercises 528
Test Yourself 531

9 Structures, Unions, Enumerations and Bit-fields **533**

9.1 Introduction 534
9.2 Structures 534
9.2.1 Defining a Structure 534
9.2.2 Declaring Structure Objects 539
9.2.3 Operations on Structures 543
9.3 Pointers to Structures 554
9.3.1 Declaring Pointer to a Structure 554
9.3.2 Accessing Structure Members Via a Pointer to a Structure 555
9.4 Array of Structures 556
9.5 Structures within a Structure (Nested Structures) 559
9.6 Functions and Structures 561
9.6.1 Passing Each Member of a Structure Object as a Separate Argument 562
9.6.2 Passing a Structure Object by Value 563
9.6.3 Passing a Structure Object by Address/Reference 564
9.7 typedef and Structures 566
9.8 Unions 568
9.9 Practical Application of Unions 571
9.9.1 Calling DOS and BIOS Functions 572
9.9.2 Interrupt Programming 575
9.10 Enumerations 580
9.11 Bit-Fields 586
9.12 Summary 590
Exercise Questions 591
Conceptual Questions and Answers 591
Code Snippets 601
Multiple-choice Questions 610
Outputs and Explanations to Code Snippets 611
Answers to Multiple-choice Questions 617
Programming Exercises 617
Test Yourself 626

10 Files **629**

10.1 Introduction 630
10.2 Files 630
10.3 Streams 631
10.4 I/O Using Streams 633
10.4.1 Opening a Stream 633
10.4.2 Closing Streams 635
10.4.3 Character Input 637
10.4.4 Character Output 638

10.4.5 File Position Indicator 641
10.4.6 End of File and Errors 646
10.4.7 Line Input 648
10.4.8 Line Output 649
10.4.9 Formatted Input 650
10.4.10 Formatted Output 650
10.4.11 Block Input 652
10.4.12 Block Output 652
10.4.13 Stream Buffering and Flushing the Streams 654
10.5 File Type 657
10.6 Files and Command Line Arguments 662
10.7 Summary 663
Exercise Questions 664
Conceptual Questions and Answers 664
Code Snippets 669
Multiple-choice Questions 671
Outputs and Explanations to Code Snippets 671
Answers to Multiple-choice Questions 673
Programming Exercises 674
Test Yourself 678

Appendix A: Number Systems **679**

A.1 Number systems 679
A.2 Number System Conversions 681
A.2.1 Conversion from Decimal Number System to any Other Number System 681
A.2.2 Conversion from Any Other Number System to Decimal Number System 681
A.2.3 Conversion from Binary Number System to Octal and Hexadecimal Number System 682
A.2.4 Conversion from Octal and Hexadecimal Number System to Binary Number System 683

Appendix B: Algorithms and Flowcharts **684**

B.1 Algorithm 684
B.2 Flowcharts 686

Appendix C: Translation Limits **691**

Appendix D: ROM-BIOS and DOS Services **693**

Appendix E: Graphics Programming **709**

E.1 Computer Graphics 709
E.2 Initializing Graphics Mode in Turbo C 3.0 709

E.3 Drawing Basic Shapes 711
E.3.1 Simple Line Drawing 711
E.3.2 Stylish Line Drawing 713
E.3.3 Drawing Other Basic Shapes 716
E.4 Region Filling 717
E.4.1 Filling Regions with Different Patterns and Colors 719
E.5 Pattern Drawing Based on Regular Polygons 721
E.5.1 Drawing Rosettes 723
E.5.2 Swirling Polygons 725
E.6 Motif and Tiling 726
E.7 Viewport and Clipping 728

Appendix F: Answers to Test Yourself Questions **730**

Index *737*

Preface

"Dreams transform into thoughts, thoughts into actions and actions into reality"
—A.P.J. Abdul Kalam

"Until you try, you don't know what you can't do"
—Henry James

Why and How I Wrote this Book

I ventured into the field of C programming as a young novice undergraduate like you about fifteen years back. At that time I had a little programming experience with BASIC, PASCAL and FORTRAN languages. I had heard about the enormous power of C programming language and was fascinated about it. I learnt and practiced it for about five years, and then fortunately had the opportunity to teach it to young engineering students at PEC University of Technology (formerly Punjab Engineering College), Chandigarh. This new assignment changed my perspective a bit; however, my learning and understanding about the language continued to evolve. Gradually, I developed a flair for solving problems faced by students in conceiving and understanding the intricacies of the language. Years of teaching have given me a clear idea about how a student perceives, conceives and understands the language. During these years, I have observed the deficiencies and the weaknesses in the literature available on C language. About two years back, I decided to share my knowledge and experiences with you in the form of a book, which is unique and removes the loopholes in the existing literature on C language. During the past two years, along with the fellows (mentioned in the acknowledgment section), I have worked hard towards the realization of this book on ***Programming in C: A Practical Approach***, which is in your hands right now. It adopts a unique and well-tested practical approach towards learning C language. I am sure that this book will help you in gaining proficiency in C programming. **Happy Learning and All the Best!**

C Programming Language

C is a general-purpose, block-structured, procedural, case-sensitive, free-flow, portable, powerful high-level programming language. The language is so powerful that UNIX, one of the most accepted operating systems, is written in it. It is said that programming languages are 'born', 'age' and eventually 'die'. However, C programming language has only matured from the time it was born. It holds the same relevance as it held when it was developed by Dennis Ritchie at the Bell Telephone Laboratories in 1972.

C Programming: A First Programming Course

Programming in C is introduced into undergraduate professional courses as a first programming course. The course intends to make the students well conversant with the syntax of C programming language and also focuses on the development of logic and problem-solving abilities in the students. The importance of this course can be clearly fathomed from the fact that the knowledge of C programming language is maintained as a pre-requisite for placements in almost all reputed software companies. Good understanding of C language also creates a strong foundation for learning other programming languages like C++, Java, etc.

About the Book

The book *Programming in C: A Practical Approach* adopts a unique and well-tested practical approach towards learning C programming language. The book covers the concepts in a lucid manner for the benefit of novice as well as amateur programmers who are looking for a comprehensive source to increase their skill in C programming. Though the book does not assume prior knowledge in the subject; a basic awareness of the working of computers will make the going easier.

Structure of the Book

The book is structured into ten chapters with six appendices. Emphasis has been laid on the organization and placement of concepts in the chapters so that they can be easily learnt. The principle behind the organization of the concepts in the book is ***gradually decreasing the level of abstraction and thereby increasing the in-depth knowledge***. A link between the listing of a concept and the detailed discussion on the concept is maintained by using forward and backward references.

Chapter 1 provides an introduction to C language along with the chronological listing of its various standards. It starts with the presentation of the common programming vocabulary such as character set, identifiers, keywords, variables, constants and data types. It also makes some forward jumps in the flow of learning and describes how to write, compile and execute simple C programs. Chapter 2 describes operators and how to create expressions using them. A detailed classification in the lines of operators as arithmetic, relational, logical, and bitwise, is presented. It also presents a detailed discussion on how expressions are evaluated and the intricacies involved in this evaluation process. Statements, which form the smallest independent unit within a C program, are discussed in Chapter 3. The classification of statements into executable and non-executable statements, simple statements and compound statements, branching statements and iteration statements is presented in detail.

Chapter 4 deals with the derived data type arrays and pointers. It talks about the interrelationship between arrays and pointers. Chapter 5 introduces functions. Functions help in modularizing the program and the code reuse. It expounds on the concept of recursion in a unique manner. Chapter 6 introduces strings and character arrays. Various string operations using library functions and user-defined functions are presented. The notions of scope, lifetime and linkage are examined in Chapter 7. It also elucidates various storage class specifiers. Chapter 8 analyzes the translators and focuses on a translator known as a preprocessor. Various directives used to control preprocessors are described in detail. Chapter 9 explicates the definition of new data types using structures, unions and enums. The chapter covers bit-fields and interrupt programming, the practical application of unions. Chapter 10 illustrates how input/output can be performed using files.

Appendix A throws light on the number system and the conversion of one number system to another. Appendix B compiles the flowcharts and algorithms pertinent to the topics discussed in the book. Appendix C spells out the translation limits that each compiler conforming to the ANSI/ISO standard must support. Appendix D lists various ROM-BIOS and DOS services.

Appendix E demonstrates graphics programming using Turbo C 3.0. Solutions to all Test Yourself exercises are put together in Appendix F.

Salient Features and Strengths of the Book

The salient features and strengths of the book are:

1. Comprehensive coverage of C programming language. The content of each chapter is clear, lucid and self-explanatory.
2. The theory is reiterated through conceptual questions and their elucidative explanatory answers. The book has an extensive collection of nearly 1000 unique, relevant and conceptual questions. These questions have either been asked by the students during the courses on C programming or have been developed to cover each and every concept of the C programming language.
3. The concepts are explained with the help of programming examples. One of the unique features of the book is the presentation of programming examples with the help of trace arrows and remarks.
4. Simultaneous discussion on the behavior of a program with Borland Turbo C 3.0, Borland Turbo C 4.5 and MS-VC++ 6.0 compilers.
5. Unique and in-depth discussion on structure padding and recursion.

Typographical Conventions

The book tries to keep a consistent style in the use of special or technical terms. The normal text is written in Palatino Linotype regular typeface, whereas the C syntactic terms like reserved words, etc. are written in Agency FB regular typeface. The conceptual questions presented at the end of each chapter are written in *Palatino Linotype italic typeface* for normal text and Agency FB regular typeface for C syntactic terms. The answers to these conceptual questions appear at the same place in Palatino Linotype regular typeface for normal text and Agency FB regular typeface for C syntactic terms. The outputs to the code snippets and answers to multiple-choice questions are present at the end of each chapter using the same typographical conventions. The first occurrence of each technical term is in **bold**.

References to the topics present in other chapters are given in Forward/Backward reference boxes, whereas the references to the topics present in the same chapter are given by providing footnotes.

Web Resources and Feedback

All the source codes are available on the website http://www.pearsoned.co.in/ajaymittal. Constructive comments are most welcomed, and feedback to improve the book will be highly appreciated. Any query may be directly addressed to me at ajaymittal@pec.ac.in.

Acknowledgements

A dream is visualized by a pair of eyes; however, many pairs of hands join together and work hard towards its realization. Throughout the project, I received the much-needed support at all fronts from various people. The list is so exhaustive that I may not be able to enumerate all the names. I express my heartfelt thanks to all who helped me at any point of time during the writing of this book. I would like to specially thank the following persons who have helped me in different ways:

My sincere thanks to *Dr Manoj Dutta*, Director, PEC University of Technology; *Dr Sanjeev Sofat*, Professor and Head, Computer Science and Engineering Department; *Dr Vijay Gupta*, Vice-Chancellor, Lovely Professional University, Ex-Director, Punjab Engineering College; my colleagues *Divya* and *Arvind Kakria* and my friends *Praveen Grewal* and *Naveen Aggarwal* for their unabated support and inspiration.

My students provided helpful insights while working on the drafts of the manuscript: *Mohit Virmani, Deepti Sabani, Akansha Bansal, Subhangi Harsha, Ankit Anand, Amandeep Jakhu* and *Shefali Saroha*. I thank *Mohit* for his thoughtful comments and dedicated efforts in proof reading. His reviews have considerably improved this book.

I am obliged to *Thomas Rajesh, Sachin Saxena, Pradeep Banerjee, M.E. Sethurajan, Jennifer Sargunar, Munish Modi* and other members of the editorial and production teams of Pearson Education for their hard work and vast patience. I am especially thankful to *Jennifer*, who has taken personal interest towards the betterment of the script. I would also like to thank *Showick Thorpe*, who introduced the project to his colleague *Thomas*.

Last but not the least, I express my heartfelt gratitude to my parents *Sh. T.L. Mittal* and *Smt. Prem Lata*, and my brother *Hemraj Mittal* and his wife *Sabina* for their moral support and patience throughout the period of writing the book. My little nephew *Jai Mittal* was my inspiration and played an important role in his own way towards the early completion of the book.

Ajay Mittal

1

DATA TYPES, VARIABLES AND CONSTANTS

Learning Objectives

In this chapter, you will learn about:

- Various features of C language
- Various C's standards
- C's character set
- Identifiers and Keywords
- Rules to write identifier names in C
- Data types, type qualifiers and type modifiers
- Declaration statement
- Difference between declaration and definition
- Length and Range of various data types
- l-value and r-value concept
- Variables and constants
- Classification of constants
- Structure of a C program
- Process of compiling and executing a C program
- Writing simple C programs
- Using printf and scanf functions
- Use of sizeof operator

1.1 Introduction

C is a general-purpose, block-structured, procedural, case-sensitive, free-flow, portable and high-level programming language developed by Dennis Ritchie at the Bell Telephone Laboratories. The selection of 'C' as the name of a programming language seems to be an odd choice but it was named C because it evolved from earlier languages **B**asic **C**ombined **P**rogramming **L**anguage (**BCPL**) and **B**.

In 1967, Martin Richards developed BCPL for writing system software (i.e. operating systems and compilers). Ken Thompson in 1970 developed a stripped version of BCPL and named it B. The language B was used to create early versions of UNIX operating system. Both the languages BCPL and B were 'typeless', and every data object occupied one word in the memory. In 1972, Dennis Ritchie developed C programming language by retaining the important features of BCPL and B programming languages and adding data types and other powerful features to the retained feature set of BCPL and B. The language C was initially designed as a system implementation language for developing system software for the UNIX operating system. Thus, it was widely known as the development language of the UNIX operating system. However, after its popularity, it has spread over many other platforms and is used for creating many other applications in addition to the system software. Thus, nowadays, C is known as a general-purpose language and not only as a system implementation language.

1.2 C Standards

The rapid expansion of C to various platforms led to many variations that were similar but were often incompatible. This was a serious problem for programmers who wanted to develop code that could run on several platforms. This problem led to the realization of the need for a standard. This section lists the formulation of various C standards in the chronological order:

1.2.1 Kernighan & Ritchie (K&R) C Standard

The first edition of 'The C Programming Language' book by Brian Kernighan and Dennis Ritchie was published in 1978. This book was one of the most successful computer science books and has served as an informal standard for the C language for many years. This informal standard was known as '**K&R C**'.

1.2.2 ANSI C/Standard C/C89 Standard

In 1983, a technical committee was created under the American National Standards Institute (ANSI) committee to establish a standard specification of C. In 1989, the standard proposed by the committee was formally approved and is often referred to as **ANSI C**, **Standard C** or sometimes **C89**.

1.2.3 ISO C/C90 Standard

In 1990, the International Organization for Standardization (ISO) adopted the ANSI C standard after minor modifications. This version of the standard is called **ISO C** or sometimes **C90**.

1.2.4 C99 Standard

After the adoption of the ANSI standard, the C language specifications remained unchanged for sometime, whereas the language C++ continued to evolve. To accommodate this evolution of C++, a new standard of C language that corrected some details of ANSI C standard and added more extensive support to it was introduced in 1995. The standard was published in 1999 and is known as **C99**. The C99 standard has not been widely adopted and is not supported by many popular C compilers.

> *i* The text and questions in this book are in accordance to ANSI/ISO standards and are tested on Borland Turbo C (TC) 3.0 compiler for DOS, Borland TC 4.5 compiler for Windows and Microsoft VC++ 6.0 compiler for Windows.

1.3 Learning Programming Language and Natural Language: An Analogy

Writing a C program is analogous to writing an essay. Recall all the stages through which you have undergone in the process of learning how to write an essay in English. Your teacher must have told you:

1. How to create words from letters.
2. How to form sentences using words and grammar.
3. How to organize sentences and create paragraphs.
4. How to arrange paragraphs and write an essay.

In this book, you will learn about:

1. How to create identifiers using the characters available in the character set of C language. This is analogous to creating words in a natural language.
2. How to use identifiers to form expressions, which can be further converted to statements, the smallest logical unit of a program. Forming a statement is analogous to forming a sentence.
3. How to use statements to write functions. Writing a function is analogous to writing a paragraph.
4. How to use functions to create a program. This is analogous to creating an essay from paragraphs.

The above learning objectives are organized in this book as follows:

1. Creating identifier names:	Chapter 1
2. Creating expressions and statements:	Chapters 2 and 3
3. Creating functions:	Chapter 5

Since, I do not want to restrain you from writing programs till Chapter 5, I will make some forward jumps in the flow of learning C programming language. I will introduce you to program writing in this chapter itself, but if something does not seem obvious, I advise you to be a bit patient. The concepts will be clearer when you go through the first few chapters and will be clear by the end of Chapter 5.

1.4 C Character Set

A **character set** defines the valid characters that can be used in a source program or interpreted when a program is running. The set of characters that can be used to write a source program is called a **source character set**, and the set of characters available when the program is being executed is called an **execution character set**. It is possible that the source character set is different from the execution character set, but in most of the implementations of C language, the two character sets are identical.

The basic source character set of C language includes:

1. Letters:
   a. Uppercase letters: A, B, C, ..., Z
   b. Lowercase letters: a, b, c, ..., z
2. Digits: 0, 1, 2, ..., 9
3. Special characters: , . : ; ! " ^ # % ^ & * ( ) { } [ ] < > | \ / _ ~ etc.
4. White space characters:
   a. Blank space character
   b. Horizontal tab space character
   c. Carriage return
   d. New line character
   e. Form feed character

1.5 Identifiers and Keywords

If you know C's source character set, the next step is to write identifiers. This is analogous to writing words in a natural language.

1.5.1 Identifiers

An **identifier** refers to the name of an object. It can be a variable name, a label name,➲ a function name,➲ a typedef name,➲ a macro name➲ or a macro parameter, a tag or a member of a structure, a union or an enumeration.➲

The syntactic rules to write an identifier name in C are as follows:

1. Identifier name in C can have letters, digits or underscores.
2. The first character of an identifier name must be a letter (either uppercase or lowercase) or an underscore. The first character of an identifier name cannot be a digit.
3. No special character (except underscore), blank space and comma can be used in an identifier name.
4. Keywords or reserved words cannot form a valid identifier name.
5. The maximum number of characters allowed in an identifier name is compiler dependent, but the limit imposed by all the compilers provides enough flexibility to create meaningful identifier names.

The following identifier names are valid in C:

`Student_Name, StudentName, student_name, student1, _student`

The following identifier names are not valid in C:

Student Name (due to blank space), Name&Rollno (due to special character &), 1st_student (first character being a digit), for (`for` being a keyword).

---

i It is always advisable to create meaningful identifier names. Meaningful identifier names are easier to read and increase the maintainability of a program. For example, it is better to create an identifier name as `student_name` instead of `snam`.

Forward Reference: Label name (Chapter 3), function (Chapter 5), typedef name (Chapter 7), macro name (Chapter 8), structure, union, enumeration (Chapter 9).

1.5.2 Keywords

Keyword is a reserved word that has a particular meaning in the programming language. The meaning of a keyword is predefined. A keyword cannot be used as an identifier name in C language. There are 32 keywords available in C. Table 1.1 gives a set of keywords present in C language.

Table 1.1 | List of keywords in C

S.No	Keyword	S.No	Keyword	S.No	Keyword	S.No	Keyword
1.	auto	9.	double	17.	int	25.	struct
2.	break	10.	else	18.	long	26.	switch
3.	case	11.	enum	19.	register	27.	typedef
4.	char	12.	extern	20.	return	28.	union
5.	const	13.	float	21.	short	29.	unsigned
6.	continue	14.	for	22.	signed	30.	void
7.	default	15.	goto	23.	sizeof	31.	volatile
8.	do	16.	if	24.	static	32.	while

1.6 Declaration Statement

If you have learnt how to create an identifier name, you should know that every identifier (except label name) needs to be declared before it is used.

An identifier can be declared by making use of the **declaration statement**. The **role** of a declaration statement is to introduce the name of an identifier along with its data type (or just type) to the compiler before its use. The general form of a declaration statement is:

[storage_class_specifier➲][type_qualifier†|type_modifier‡] **type§ identifier** [=value[,...]];

> The terms enclosed within square brackets (i.e. []) are optional and might not be present in a declaration statement. The type, identifier and the terminating semicolon (shown in bold) are the mandatory parts of a declaration statement.

The following declaration statements¶ are valid in C:

int variable;	(type int and identifier name variable present)
static int variable;	(Storage class specifier static, type int and identifier name variable present)
static unsigned int variable;	(Storage class specifier static, type modifier unsigned, type int and identifier name variable present)
static const unsigned int variable;	(Storage class specifier static, type qualifier const, type modifier unsigned, type int and identifier name variable present)
int variable=20;	(type int, identifier name variable and value 20 present)
int a=20, b=10;	(type int, identifier name a and its initial value 20 present, another identifier name b and its initial value 10 present✍)

† Refer Section 1.8.1 for a description on type qualifiers.
‡ Refer Section 1.8.2 for a description on type modifiers.
§ Refer Section 1.7 for a description on types.
¶ These are actually definition statements. Refer Section 1.9 for a description on declaration and definition.

A declaration statement in which more than one identifier is declared is known as a **shorthand declaration statement**. For example, int a=20, b=10; is a shorthand declaration statement. The corresponding **longhand declaration statements** equivalent to this shorthand declaration statement are int a=20; int b=10;. It is important to note that shorthand declaration can only be used to declare identifiers of the same type. In no way can it be used to declare identifiers of different types, e.g. int a=10, float b=2.3; is an invalid statement.

Forward Reference: Storage class specifier (Chapter 7).

1.7 Data Types

If you know how to write a declaration statement, you would probably know that the declaration statement is used to tell the data type (or just type) of an identifier to the compiler before its use.

Data type or just **type** is one of the most important attributes of an identifier. It determines the possible values that an identifier can have and the valid operations that can be applied on it.

In C language, data types are broadly classified as:

1. Basic data types (primitive data types)
2. Derived data types
3. User-defined data types

1.7.1 Basic/Primitive Data Types

The five basic data types and their corresponding keywords available in C are:

1. Character (char)
2. Integer (int)
3. Single-precision floating point (float)
4. Double-precision floating point (double)
5. No value available (void)

1.7.2 Derived Data Types

These data types are derived from the basic data types. Derived data types available in C are:

1. Array type e.g. char[ ], int[ ], etc.
2. Pointer type e.g. char*, int*, etc.
3. Function type e.g. int(int,int), float(int), etc.

Forward Reference: Array type (Chapter 4), pointer type (Chapter 4), function type (Chapter 5).

1.7.3 User-defined Data Types

The C language provides flexibility to the user to create new data types. These newly created data types are called **user-defined data types**. The user-defined data types in C can be created by using:

1. Structure
2. Union
3. Enumeration

Forward Reference: Structure, union, enumeration (Chapter 9).

1.8 Type Qualifiers and Type Modifiers

The declaration statement can optionally have type qualifiers or type modifiers or both.

1.8.1 Type Qualifiers

A **type qualifier** neither affects the range of values nor the arithmetic properties of the declared object. They are used to indicate the special properties of data within an object. Two type qualifiers available in C are:

1. **const**[††] **qualifier:** Declaring an object const announces that its value will not be changed during the execution of a program.
2. **volatile qualifier:** volatile qualifier announces that the object has some special properties relevant to optimization.

1.8.2 Type Modifiers

A **type modifier** modifies the base type to yield a new type. It modifies the range[‡‡] and the arithmetic properties of the base type. The type modifiers and the corresponding keywords available in C are:

1. Signed (signed)
2. Unsigned (unsigned)
3. Short (short)
4. Long (long)

1.9 Difference Between Declaration and Definition

It is very important to know the difference between the terms **declaration** and **definition**. **Declaration** only introduces the name of an identifier along with its type to the compiler before it is used. During declaration, no memory space is allocated to an identifier. **Definition** of an identifier means the declaration of an identifier plus reservation of space for it in the memory. The amount of memory space reserved for an identifier depends upon the data type of the identifier. Identifiers of different data types take different amounts of memory space. The memory space required by an identifier also depends upon the compiler and the working environment used. Table 1.2 lists the length of various data types in DOS and Windows environment.

[††] Refer Section 1.11.2.2 for a description on const qualifier.

[‡‡] Refer Section 1.9 for a description on range modification by type modifiers.

Table 1.2 | Data types and their memory requirements

S.No	Data type	Base/Modified	TURBO C 3.0/DOS	MS VC++ 6.0/WINDOWS
1.	char	Base	1 Byte	1 Byte
2.	int	Base	2 Bytes	4 Bytes
3.	float	Base	4 Bytes	4 Bytes
4.	double	Base	8 Bytes	8 Bytes
5.	signed ⟨data type 1, 2⟩	Modified	⟨same as data type 1, 2⟩	⟨same as data type 1, 2⟩
6.	unsigned ⟨data type 1, 2⟩	Modified	⟨same as data type 1, 2⟩	⟨same as data type 1, 2⟩
7.	short int	Modified	2 Bytes	2 Bytes
8.	long int	Modified	4 Bytes	4 Bytes
9.	long float	Modified	8 Bytes	8 Bytes
10.	long double	Modified	10 Bytes	8 Bytes
11.	void	Base	Object of void type cannot be created	

The data type determines the possible values that an identifier can have. The range of a data type depends upon the length of the data type. Table 1.3 lists the range of various data types in DOS and Windows environment.

Table 1.3 | Range of various data types

S.No	Data type	TURBO C 3.0/DOS	MS VC++ 6.0/WINDOWS
1.	char	–128 to 127	–128 to 127
2.	int	–32768 to 32767	–2,147,483,648 to 2,147,483,647
3.	float	$3.4 * 10^{-38}$ to $3.4 * 10^{38}$	$3.4 * 10^{-38}$ to $3.4 * 10^{38}$
4.	double	$1.7 * 10^{-308}$ to $1.7 * 10^{308}$	$1.7 * 10^{-308}$ to $1.7 * 10^{308}$
5.	signed ⟨data type 1, 2⟩	Same as 1, 2 as by default data types are signed	Same as 1, 2 as by default data types are signed
6.	unsigned char	0 to 255	0 to 255
7.	unsigned int	0 to 65535	0 to 4,294,967,295
8.	unsigned long int	0 to 4,294,967,295	0 to 4,294,967,295
9.	short int	–32768 to 32767	–32768 to 32767
10.	long double	$3.4 * 10^{-4932}$ to $1.1 * 10^{4932}$	$1.7 * 10^{-308}$ to $1.7 * 10^{308}$

i Despite the big difference between the terms declaration and definition, the word declaration is commonly used in place of definition. All the statements written in Section 1.6 are actually definition statements, but I have referred to them as declarations because at that point I just wanted to focus on the name and the type of an identifier.

The statement `int variable=20;` mentioned in Section 1.6 is actually a definition statement because it allocates 2 bytes (or 4 bytes) to `variable` somewhere in the memory (say, at memory location with address 2000) and initializes it with the value `20`. The memory allocation is purely random (i.e. any free memory location will be randomly allocated). This is illustrated in Figure 1.1.

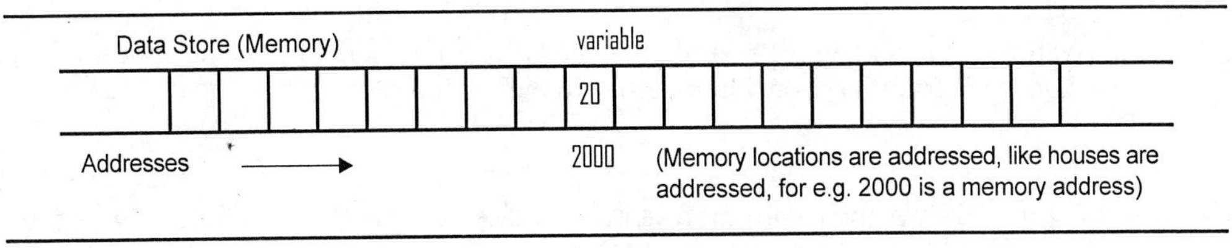

Figure 1.1 | Allocation of memory to variable

If `int variable;` is a definition statement, then how can I declare `variable`?

If you want to actually declare `variable`, write `extern int variable;`. `extern` is a storage class specifier. The keyword `extern` provides a method for declaring a variable without defining it. The `extern` declaration does not allocate the memory.

Forward Reference: Storage class specifier (Chapter 7), `extern` declaration (Chapter 7).

1.10 Data Object, L-value and R-value

You must have known by this time that upon definition, an identifier is allocated some space in memory depending upon its data type and the working environment. This memory allocation gives rise to two important concepts known as the **l-value concept** and the **r-value concept**. These concepts are described below.

1.10.1 Data Object

Data object is a term that is used to specify the region of data storage that is used to hold values. Once an identifier is allocated memory space, it will be known as a data object.

1.10.2 L-value

L-value is a data object locator. It is an expression that locates an object. In Figure 1.1, `variable` is a sort of name given to the memory location 2000. `variable` here refers to l-value, an object locator. The term l-value can be further categorized as:

1. **Modifiable l-value:** A modifiable l-value is an expression that refers to an object that can be accessed and legally changed in the memory.
2. **Non-modifiable l-value:** A non-modifiable l-value refers to an object that can be accessed but cannot be changed in the memory.[¶¶]

l in **l-value** stands for '**left**'; this means that the l-value could legally stand on the left side of an assignment operator.

1.10.3 R-value

R-value refers to 'read value'. In Figure 1.1, `variable` has an r-value `20`.

¶¶ Refer Section 1.11.2.2 to learn how to make an l-value non-modifiable.

> **r** in **r-value** stands for **'right'** or **'read'**; this means that if an identifier name appears on the right side of an assignment operator it refers to the r-value.

Consider Figure 1.1 and the expression `variable=`**`variable`**`+20`. `variable` on the left side of the assignment operator refers to the l-value. **`variable`** on the right side of the assignment operator (in bold) refers to the r-value. **`variable`** appearing on the right side refers to `20`. The number `20` is added to `20` and the value of expression is `40` (r-value). This outcome (`40`) is assigned to `variable` on the left side of the assignment operator, which signifies l-value. The l-value `variable` locates the memory location where this value is to be placed, i.e. at 2000. After the evaluation of the expression `variable=`**`variable`**`+20`, the contents of the memory are shown in Figure 1.2.

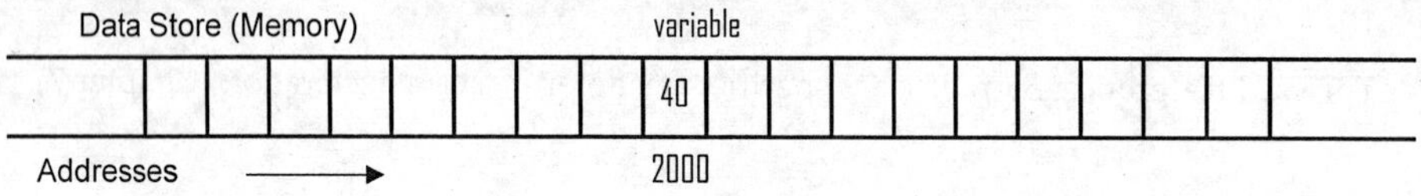

Figure 1.2 | Contents of memory location 2000 after the evaluation of expression `variable=`**`variable`**`+20`

> **Remember it as:**
> The **l-value** refers to the location value, i.e. the location of the object, and the **r-value** refers to the read value, i.e. the value of the object.

> **Forward Reference:** Expressions and operators (Chapter 2).

1.11 Variables and Constants

Variables and **constants** are two most commonly used terms in a programming language.

1.11.1 Variables

A **variable** is an entity whose value can vary (i.e. change) during the execution of a program. The value of a variable can be changed because it has a modifiable l-value. Since it has a modifiable l-value, it can be placed on the left side of the assignment operator. Note that only the entities that have modifiable l-values can be placed on the left side of the assignment operator. The variable can also be placed on the right side of the assignment operator. Hence, it has an r-value too. Thus, a variable has both an l-value and an r-value.

1.11.2 Constants

A **constant** is an entity whose value remains the same throughout the execution of a program. It cannot be placed on the left side of the assignment operator because it does not have a modifiable l-value. It can only be placed on the right side of the assignment operator. Thus, a constant has an r-value only. Constants are classified as:

1. Literal constants
2. Qualified constants
3. Symbolic constants

1.11.2.1 Literal Constant

Literal constant or just **literal** denotes a fixed value, which may be an integer, floating point number, character or a string. The type of literal constant is determined by its value. Literal constants are of the following types:

1. Integer literal constant
2. Floating point literal constant
3. Character literal constant
4. String literal constant

1.11.2.1.1 Integer Literal Constant

Integer literal constants are integer values like -1, 2, 8, etc. The rules for writing integer literal constants are as follows:

1. An integer literal constant must have at least one digit.
2. It should not have any decimal point.
3. It can be either positive or negative. If no sign precedes an integer literal constant, then it is assumed to be positive.
4. No special characters (even underscore) and blank spaces are allowed within an integer literal constant.
5. If an integer literal constant starts with 0, then it is assumed to be in an octal number system, e.g. 023 is a valid integer literal constant, which means 23 is in an octal number system and is equivalent to 19 in the decimal number system.
6. If an integer literal constant starts with 0x or 0X, then it is assumed to be in a hexadecimal number system, e.g. 0x23 or 0X23 is a valid integer literal constant, which means 23 is in a hexadecimal number system and is equivalent to 35 in the decimal number system.
7. The size of the integer literal constant can be modified by using a length modifier. The length modifier can be a suffix character l, L, u, U, f or F. If the integer literal constant is terminated with l or L then it is assumed to be long. If it is terminated with u or U, then it is assumed to be an unsigned integer, e.g. 23l is a long integer and 23u is an unsigned integer. The length modifier f or F can only be used with a floating point literal constant and not with an integer literal constant.

1.11.2.1.2 Floating Point Literal Constant

Floating point literal constants are values like -23.1, 12.8, -1.8e12, etc. Floating point literal constants can be written in a **fractional form** or in an **exponential form**. The rules for writing floating point literal constants in a fractional form are as follows:

1. A fractional floating point literal constant must have at least one digit.
2. It should have a decimal point.
3. It can be either positive or negative. If no sign precedes a floating point literal constant, then it is assumed to be positive.

4. No special characters (even underscore) and blank spaces are allowed within a floating point literal constant.
5. A floating point literal constant by default is assumed to be of type `double`, e.g. the type of `23.45` is `double`.
6. The size of the floating point literal constant can be modified by using the length modifier `f` or `F`, i.e. if `23.45` is written as `23.45f` or `23.45F`, then it is considered to be of type `float` instead of `double`.

The following are valid floating point literal constants in a fractional form:

`-2.5, 12.523, 2.5f, 12.5F`

The rules for writing floating point literal constants in an exponential form are as follows:

1. A floating point literal constant in an exponential form has two parts: the mantissa part and the exponent part. Both parts are separated by `e` or `E`.
2. The mantissa can be either positive or negative. The default sign is positive.
3. The mantissa part should have at least one digit.
4. The mantissa part can have a decimal point but it is not mandatory.
5. The exponent part must have at least one digit. It can be either positive or negative. The default sign is positive.
6. The exponent part cannot have a decimal point.
7. No special characters (even underscore) and blank spaces are allowed within the mantissa part and the exponent part.

The following are valid floating point literal constants in the exponential form:

`-2.5E12, -2.5e-12, 2e10` (i.e. equivalent to 2×10^{10})

1.11.2.1.3 Character Literal Constant

A **character literal constant** can have one or at most two characters enclosed within single quotes e.g. `'A'`, `'a'`, `'\n'`, etc. Character literal constants are classified as:

1. Printable character literal constants
2. Non-printable character literal constants

1.11.2.1.3.1 Printable Character Literal Constant

All characters of source character set except quotation mark, backslash and new line character when enclosed within single quotes form a **printable character literal constant**. The following are examples of printable character literal constants: `'A'`, `'#'`, `'6'`.

1.11.2.1.3.2 Non-printable Character Literal Constant

Non-printable character literal constants are represented with the help of **escape sequences**. An escape sequence consists of a backward slash (i.e. \) followed by a character and both enclosed within single quotes. An escape sequence is treated as a single character. It can be used[§§] in a string like any other printable character. A list of the escape sequences available in C is given in Table 1.4.

---

§§Refer Programs 1-7 and 1-9 for learning the usage of the escape sequences `'\t'` and `'\n'`.

Table 1.4 | List of escape sequences

S.No	Escape sequence	Character value	Action on output device
1.	\'	Single quotation mark	Prints '
2.	\"	Double quotation mark (")	Prints "
3.	\?	Question mark (?)	Prints ?
4.	\\	Backslash character (\)	Prints \
5.	\a	Alert	Alerts by generating a beep
6.	\b	Backspace	Moves the cursor one position to the left of its current position
7.	\f	Form feed	Moves the cursor to the beginning of next page
8.	\n	New line	Moves the cursor to the beginning of the next line
9.	\r	Carriage return	Moves the cursor to the beginning of the current line
10.	\t	Horizontal tab	Moves the cursor to the next horizontal tab stop
11.	\v	Vertical tab	Vertical tab
12.	\0	Null character	Prints nothing

Forward Reference: Refer Question numbers 35–37 and their answers for examples on the usage of escape sequences.

1.11.2.1.4 String Literal Constant

A string literal constant consists of a sequence of characters (possibly an escape sequence) enclosed within double quotes. Each string literal constant is implicitly terminated by a null character (i.e. '\0'). Hence, the number of bytes occupied by a string literal constant is one more than the number of characters present in the string. The additional byte is occupied by the terminating null character. Thus, the empty string (i.e. "") occupies one byte in the memory due to the presence of the terminating null character. However, the terminating null character is not counted while determining the length of a string. Therefore, the length of string "ABC" is 3 although it occupies 4 bytes in the memory.

Forward Reference: Strings and character arrays (Chapter 6).

1.11.2.2 Qualified Constants

Qualified constants are created by using `const` qualifier. The following statement creates a qualified character constant named `a`:

```
const char a='A';
```

Consider a definition statement `int a=10;`. This statement allocates 2 bytes (or 4 bytes, in case of Windows environment) to `a` somewhere in the memory and initializes it with the value `10`. The memory location can be thought of as a transparent box in which `10` has been placed. It is possible to modify the value of `a`. This means that it is possible to open the box and change the value placed in it. Now, consider the statement `const int a=10;`. The usage of the const qualifier places a lock on the box after placing the value 10 in it. Since the box is transparent, it is possible to see (i.e. read) the value placed within the box, but it is not possible to modify the value within the box as it is locked. This is depicted in Figure 1.3.

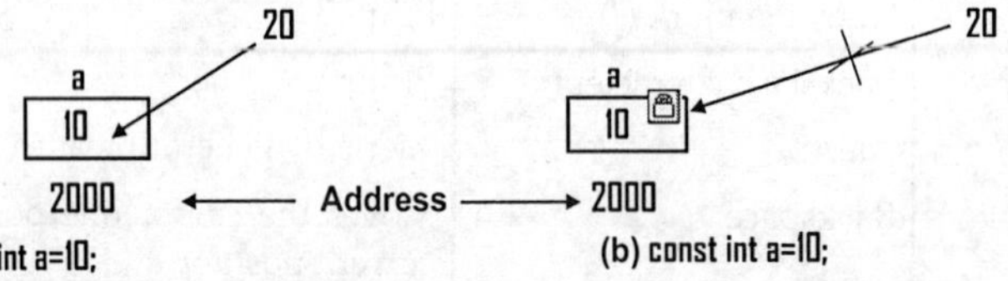

Figure 1.3 | Use of const qualifier

Since qualified constants are placed in the memory, they have l-value. However, as it is not possible to modify them, this means that they do not have a modifiable l-value, i.e. **they have a non-modifiable l-value.**

1.11.2.3 Symbolic Constants

Symbolic constants are created with the help of the define preprocessor directive.➲ For example: `#define PI 3.14124` defines PI as a symbolic constant with value 3.14124. Each symbolic constant is replaced by its actual value during the preprocessing stage.➲

Forward Reference: Preprocessor directives, preprocessing stage (Chapter 8).

1.12 Structure of a C Program

In general, a C program is composed of the following sections:

1. Section 1: **Preprocessor directives**
2. Section 2: **Global declarations**
3. Section 3: **Functions**

Sections 1 and 2 are optional, i.e. they may or may not be present in a C program but Section 3 is mandatory. Section 3 should always be present in a C program. Thus, it can be said that '**A C program is made up of functions**'. Look at the simple program in Program 1-1.

Prog 1-1.c

```
//Comment: First C program
#include<stdio.h>
main()
{
    printf("Hello Readers!!");
}
```

Output window

```
Hello Readers!!
```

Program 1-1 | A simple program that prints "Hello Readers!!"

Program 1-1 on execution[†††] outputs Hello Readers!!. The contents of Program 1-1 are described below.

1.12.1 Comments

Line 1: is a comment. **Comments** are used to convey a message and to increase the readability of a program. They are not processed by the compiler. There are two types of comments:

1. Single-line comment
2. Multi-line comment

1.12.1.1 Single-line Comment

A **single-line comment** starts with two forward slashes (i.e. //) and is automatically terminated with the end of line. Line 1 of Program 1-1 is a single-line comment.

1.12.1.2 Multi-line Comment

A **multi-line comment** starts with /* and terminates with */. A multi-line comment is used when multiple lines of text are to be commented.

1.12.2 Section1: Preprocessor Directive Section

Line 2: #include<stdio.h> is a preprocessor directive statement. The **preprocessor directive section** is optional but you will find it in most of the C programs. In the initial phase of learning, just remember that #include<stdio.h> is a preprocessor directive statement, which includes **st**andard **i**nput/**o**utput (i.e. **stdio**) **h**eader (.h) file. This file is to be included if standard input/output functions like printf or scanf are to be used in a program.
The following points must be remembered while writing preprocessor directives:

1. The preprocessor directive always starts with a pound symbol (i.e. #).
2. The pound symbol # should be the first non-white space character in a line.
3. The preprocessor directive is terminated with a new line character and not with a semi-colon.
4. Preprocessor directives are executed before the compiler compiles the source code. These will change the source code, usually to suit the operating environment (pragma directive) or to add the code (include directive) that will be required by the calls to library functions.

Forward Reference: Preprocessor directives, pragma directive (Chapter 8), library functions (Chapter 5).

1.12.3 Section 2: Global Declaration Section

The **global declaration section** is optional. This section is not present in Program 1-1. In the initial phase of learning, I am not going to use global declarations.

Forward Reference: Global declarations (Chapter 7).

[†††] Refer Section 1.13 to learn how to execute a C program.

1.12.4 Section 3: Functions Section

This section is mandatory and must be present in a C program. This section can have one or more functions. A function named `main` is always required. The functions section (Lines 3–6) in Program 1-1 consists of only one function, i.e. `main` function. Every function consists of two parts:

1. Header of the function
2. Body of the function

1.12.4.1 Header of a Function

The general form of the header of a function is

```
[return_type] function_name([argument_list])
```

The terms enclosed within square brackets are optional and might not be present in the function header. Since the name of a function is an identifier name, all the rules discussed in Section 1.5.1 for writing an identifier name are applicable for writing the function name. Line 3 in Program 1-1 specifies the header of the function `main`, in which the `return_type`➲ and the `argument_list`➲ are not present. The name of the function is `main` and it is a valid identifier name. In the initial phase of learning, I will write functions without specifying a return type and an argument list.

> *i* Writing a function without specifying a return type may lead to the generation of a warning message during the compilation but we can ignore it for the time being.

> **Forward Reference:** `return_type`, `argument_list` (Chapter 5).

1.12.4.2 Body of a Function

The body of a function consists of a set of statements➲ enclosed within curly brackets commonly known as **braces**. Lines 4–6 in Program 1-1 form the body of `main` function. The body of a function consists of a set of statements. Statements are of two types:

1. Non-executable statements➲: For example: declaration statement
2. Executable statements➲: For example: `printf` function call statement

It is possible that no statement is present within the braces. In such a case, the program produces no output on execution. However, if there are statements written within the braces, remember that non-executable statements can only come prior to an executable statement, i.e. first non-executable statements are written and then executable statements are written. The body of `main` function in Program 1-1 has only one executable statement, i.e. `printf` function call statement.

> **Forward Reference:** Statements, executable statement and non-executable statements (Chapter 3).

1.13 Executing a C Program

If you have finished writing the code listed in Program 1-1, follow these steps to execute your program:

1. **Save program:** with .c extension. This will help you in retrieving the code in case the program crashes upon execution.
2. **Compile program:** Compilation can be done by going to the Compile Menu of Borland TC 3.0 and invoking the compile option available in that menu. The shortcut for this step is the Alt+F9 key. If working with Borland Turbo C 4.5, go to the Project Menu and invoke the compile option. It has the same shortcut key. In Microsoft Visual C++ 6.0, go to the Build Menu and invoke the compile option. The shortcut for this is the Ctrl+F7 key. After the compilation, look for errors and warnings. Warnings will not prevent you from executing the program and if there are any, just ignore them for the time being. If there are errors, check that you have written the code properly. There should be no typing mistake and all the characters listed in Program 1-1 should be present as such. If there is no error, Congrats!! you can now execute your program.
3. **Execute/run program:** Execution can be done by going to the Run Menu and invoking the run option in Borland Turbo C 3.0. The shortcut key is Ctrl+F9. In Borland Turbo C 4.5, the program can be executed by going to the Debug Menu and invoking the run option. It has the same shortcut key. In Microsoft Visual C++ 6.0, go to the Build Menu and invoke the run option. The shortcut key for this is Ctrl+F5.
4. **See the output:** If working with Borland Turbo C 3.0, to see the output go to the user screen. This can be done by going to the Window Menu and invoking the user screen option. The shortcut for this step is Alt+F5. In Borland TC 4.5 and Microsoft Visual C++ 6.0, the output screen will automatically pop-up.

1.14 More Programs for Startup

If you have successfully executed Program 1-1 and have gained some confidence, look at some more programs (Programs 1-2 to 1-11). Type the programs as such and compile them. If there are errors, find out the errors and rectify them. After rectification, recompile the programs and execute them to get a practical feel of all the concepts that we have discussed till now.

Line	Prog 1-2.c	Output window
1	//Comment: Case Sensitivity	Linker error **Reasons:** • C Language is case sensitive • Main is not same as main **What to do?** • Replace Main by main in line 3 and then recheck
2	#include<stdio.h>	
3	Main()	
4	{	
5	int valid_name=20;	
6	printf("%d", valid_name);	
7	}	

Program 1-2 | A program that emphasizes the case sensitivity of C language

Prog 1-3.c	Output window

//Comment: Identifier
#include<stdio.h>
main()
{
int 1st_student=20;
printf("%d", 1st_student);
}
	Compilation error
	Reason:
	• 1st_student is not a valid identifier name
	What to do?
	• Replace it everywhere by student1 and then recheck

Program 1-3 | A program that emphasizes the rules to write an identifier name

Line	Prog 1-4.c	Output window
1	`//Comment: Keyword`	Compilation error **Reason:** • if is a keyword. It cannot be used as an identifier name **What to do?** • Replace it everywhere by a valid identifier name and then recheck
2	`#include<stdio.h>`	
3	`main()`	
4	`{`	
5	`    int if=20;`	
6	`    printf("%d", if);`	
7	`}`	

Program 1-4 | A program that emphasizes the fact that keyword is not a valid identifier name

Line	Prog 1-5.c	Output window
1	`//Comment: Semicolon is Terminator`	Compilation error **Reasons:** • A statement in C is terminated with a semicolon • In line 5, declaration (actually definition) statement is not terminated with a semicolon. This leads to the compilation error **What to do?** • Place semicolon at end of line 5 and then recheck
2	`#include<stdio.h>`	
3	`main()`	
4	`{`	
5	`    int valid_name=20`	
6	`    printf("%d", valid_name);`	
7	`}`	

Program 1-5 | A program that emphasizes the fact that statements in C are terminated with a semicolon

Line	Prog 1-6.c	Output window
1	`//Comment: printf function use`	The value is 20
2	`#include<stdio.h>`	
3	`main()`	
4	`{`	
5	`    int valid_name=20;`	
6	`    printf("The value is %d", valid_name);`	
7	`}`	

Program 1-6 | A program that illustrates the use of printf function to print the value of an identifier

Program 1-6 upon execution outputs `The value is 20`. The definition statement in line 5 defines an identifier `valid_name` and initializes it with the value `20`. This value is printed with the help of `printf` function in line 6. The rules for using `printf` function are as follows:

1. The name of `printf` function should be in lowercase.
2. The inputs (or arguments) to `printf` function are given within round or circular brackets, popularly called **parentheses**.
3. At least one input is required, and the first input to `printf` function should always be a string literal or an identifier of type `char*`. ➲

Forward Reference: Pointers (Chapter 4), Character pointer, i.e. `char*` (Chapter 6).

4. The inputs are separated by commas.
5. If values of identifiers are to be printed with the help of `printf` function, the first input to `printf` function should be a **format string**. For example, in Program 1-6, in line 6, "`The value is %d`" is a format string. A **format string** consists of **format specifiers**. For example, line 6

in Program 1-6 consists of a format specifier `%d`. A **format specifier** specifies the format according to which the printing will be done. There is a different format specifier for each data type. Format specifier is written as `%x`, where `x` is a character code listed in Table 1.5.

Table 1.5 | Format specifiers in C language

S.No	Data type	x	Format specifier	Remark
1.	char	c	%c	Single character
2.	int	i	%i	Signed integer
3.	int	d	%d	Signed integer in decimal number system
4.	unsigned int	o	%o	Unsigned integer in octal number system
5.	unsigned int	u	%u	Unsigned integer in decimal number system
6.	unsigned int	x	%x	Unsigned integer in hexadecimal number system
7.	unsigned int	X	%X	Unsigned integer in hexadecimal number system
8.	long int	ld	%ld	Signed long
9.	short int	hd	%hd	Signed short
10.	unsigned long	lu	%lu	Unsigned long
11.	unsigned short	hu	%hu	Unsigned short
12.	float	f	%f	Signed single precision float in form of [-]dddd.dddd e.g. 22.25, -12.34
13.	float	e	%e	Singed single precision float in form of [-]d.dddde[+/-]ddd e.g. -2.3e4, 2.25e-2
14.	float	E	%E	Same as %e, with E for exponent
15.	float	g	%g	Singed value in either e or f form, based on given value and precision
16.	float	G	%G	Same as %g, with E for exponent if e format is used
17.	double	lf	%lf	Signed double-precision float
18.	String type	s	%s	String
19.	Pointer type	p	%p	Pointer

Prog 1-7.c

```
1 //Comment: scanf function use
2 #include<stdio.h>
3 main()
4 {
5     int number;
6     printf("Enter number\t");
7     scanf("%d",&number);
8     printf("The number entered is %d",number);
9 }
```

Output window

```
Enter number	12
The number entered is 12
```

Remarks:

- '\t' present in line 6 is an escape sequence and is used to create tab-spacing
- Observe the tab-space between the string "Enter number" and the value 12 in the output window

Program 1-7 | A program that illustrates the use of scanf function

Program 1-7 upon execution prompts the user to enter a value of `number`. In response, the user enters the value 12. The entered value is then printed by the `printf` function. The `scanf` function is used to take the input just like the `printf` function is used to print the output. The rules for using `scanf` function are as follows:

1. The name of `scanf` function should be in lowercase.
2. The inputs (or arguments) to `scanf` function are given within parentheses.
3. The first input to `scanf` function should always be a format string or an identifier of type `char*`. Ideally, the format string of a `scanf` function should only consist of blank separated format specifiers.

Forward Reference: Refer Question number 14 and its answer to know why the format string of a `scanf` function should only consist of blank separated format specifiers.

4. The inputs are separated by commas.
5. The inputs following the first input should denote l-values. For example, in line 7 of Program 1-7, the second input is `&number`. The symbol `&` is address-of operator and is used to find the l-value of its operand. Thus, `&number` refers to the l-value.

The `scanf` function takes inputs from the user according to the available format specifiers in the specified format string and stores the entered values at the specified l-values. Thus, the `scanf` function specified in line 7 of Program 1-7 takes an integer value (due to `%d` format specifier) and stores it at the l-value (i.e. `&number`).

Forward Reference: Address-of operator, operand (Chapter 2).

Prog 1-8.c

```
//Comment: Add two numbers
#include<stdio.h>
main()
{
    int number1, number2, number3;
    printf("Enter numbers\t");
    scanf("%d %d",&number1, &number2);
    number3 = number1+number2;
    printf("The sum is %d",number3);
}
```

Output window

```
Enter numbers    12 13
The sum is 25
```

Program 1-8 | A program to add two numbers entered by the user

Prog 1-9.c

```
//Comment: Swap two numbers
#include<stdio.h>
main()
{
    int number1, number2, number3;
```

Output window

```
Enter numbers    12 13
Numbers before swap 12 13
Numbers after swap 13 12
```

(Contd...)

```
6    printf("Enter numbers\t");
7    scanf("%d %d",&number1, &number2);
8    printf("Numbers before swap %d %d\n",number1, number2);
9    number3=number1;
10   number1=number2;
11   number2=number3;
12   printf("Numbers after swap %d %d\n",number1, number2);
13 }
```

Remark:

- '\n' present in line 8 is an escape sequence and is used to place a new line character in the output

Program 1-9 | A program to swap two numbers

Prog 1-10.c

```
//Comment: Swap two numbers without using a third number
#include<stdio.h>
main()
{
    int number1, number2;
    printf("Enter numbers\t");
    scanf("%d %d",&number1, &number2);
    printf("Numbers before swap %d %d\n",number1, number2);
    number2=number1+number2;
    number1=number2-number1;
    number2=number2-number1;
    printf("Numbers after swap %d %d\n",number1, number2);
}
```

Output window

```
Enter numbers    12 13
Numbers before swap 12 13
Numbers after swap 13 12
```

Program 1-10 | A program to swap two numbers without using a third number

Prog 1-11.c

```
//Comment: Usage of sizeof operator
#include<stdio.h>
main()
{
    printf("Character takes %d byte in memory\n", sizeof(char));
    printf("Integer takes %d bytes in memory\n", sizeof(int));
    printf("Float takes %d bytes in memory\n", sizeof(float));
    printf("Long takes %d bytes in memory\n", sizeof(long));
    printf("Double takes %d bytes in memory\n", sizeof(double));
}
```

Output window

```
Character takes 1 byte in memory
Integer takes 2 bytes in memory
Float takes 4 bytes in memory
Long takes 4 bytes in memory
Double takes 8 bytes in memory
```

Remark:

- The output of the program may vary with the compiler and the working environment

Program 1-11 | A program to find the size of various data types

Program 1-11 makes the use of sizeof➲ operator to find the size of data types. The specified output is the result of execution using Borland Turbo C 3.0/4.5. If it is executed using MS VC++ 6.0, the size of integer would be 4 bytes.

Forward Reference: sizeof operator (Chapter 2).

1.15 Summary

1. C is a general-purpose, block-structured, procedural, case-sensitive, free-flow, portable, high-level language.
2. There are various C standards: Kernighan & Ritchie (K&R) C standard; ANSI C/Standard C/C89 standard; ISO C/C90 standard; C99 standard.
3. ANSI C and ISO C are the most popular C standards. Most popular compilers nowadays are ANSI compliant.
4. C character set consists of letters, digits, special characters and white space characters.
5. Identifier refers to the name of an object. It can be a variable name, a label name, a typedef name, a macro name, name of a structure, a union or an enumeration.
6. Keyword cannot form a valid identifier name. The meaning of keyword is predefined and cannot be changed.
7. Every identifier (except label name) needs to be declared before its use. They can be declared by using a declaration statement.
8. The declaration statement introduces the name of an identifier along with its data type to the compiler before its use.
9. Data types are categorized as: basic data types, derived data types and user-defined data types.
10. The declaration statement can optionally have type qualifiers or type modifiers or both.
11. A type qualifier does not modify the type.
12. A type modifier modifies the base type to yield a new type.
13. Declaration is different from definition in the sense that definition in addition to declaration allocates the memory to an identifier.
14. Variables have both l-value and r-value.
15. Constants do not have a modifiable l-value. They have an r-value only.
16. C program is made up of functions.
17. C program should have at least one function. A function named `main` is always required.

Exercise Questions

Conceptual Questions and Answers

1. *What method is adopted for locating includable source files in ANSI specifications?*

   For including source files, `include` directive is used. The `include` directive can be used in two forms:
   `#include<name-of-file>`
   or
   `#include"name-of-file"`
   `#include<name-of-file>` searches the prespecified list of directories (names of include directories can be specified in IDE settings) for the source file (whose name is given within angular brackets),

and text embeds the entire content of the source file in place of itself. If the file is not found there, it will show an error 'Unable to include 'name-of-file''.

#include"name-of-file" searches the file first in the current working directory. If this search is not supported or if the search fails, this directive is reprocessed as if it reads #include<name-of-file>, i.e. search will be carried out in the prespecified list of directories. If the search still fails, it will show the error 'Unable to include 'name-of-file''.

> **IDE** stands for **I**ntegrated **D**evelopment **E**nvironment. All the tools (like text editor, preprocessor, compiler and linker) required for developing programs are integrated into one package, known as IDE.

2. *Is there any difference that arises if double quotes, instead of angular brackets are used for including standard header files?*

   If double quotes instead of angular brackets are used for the inclusion of standard header files, the search space unnecessarily increases (because in addition to the prespecified list of directories, the search will unnecessarily be carried out first in the current working directory) and thus, the time required for the inclusion will be more.

3. *Under what circumstances should the use of quotes be preferred over the use of angular brackets for the inclusion of header files, and under what circumstances is the use of angular brackets beneficial?*

   Self-created or user-defined header files should be included with double quotes because inclusion with double quotes makes files to be searched first in the current working directory (where the user has kept self-created header files) and then in the prespecified list of directories. If standard header files are to be included, angular brackets should be used because the standard header files are present in the prespecified list of directories and there is no use of searching them in the current working directory. Usage of double quotes for including standard header files will also work, but will take more time.

4. *'C is a case-sensitive language'. Therefore, does it create any difference if instead of* #include<stdio.h>, #include<STDIO.H> *is used? If no, why?*

   'C is a case-sensitive language' means that the C constructs are case sensitive (i.e. depends upon whether uppercase (like A) or lowercase (like a) is used). The name of the source file specified for inclusion is not a C construct. Whether it will be case sensitive or not depends upon the working environment. In case of DOS and Windows environment, file names are case insensitive. In Unix and Linux environment, file names are case sensitive. So, if working in DOS or Windows environment, <STDIO.H> can be used instead of <stdio.h>, it does not create any difference. But, in case of Unix or Linux environment, it does create a difference.

5. *A program file contains the following five lines of the source code:*

   ```
   #include<stdio.h>
   main()
   {
       printf("Hello World");
   }
   ```

   When the program is compiled, the compiler shows the number of lines compiled to be greater than 5, why it is happening so?

   During the preprocessing stage, #include preprocessor directive (the first line of source code) searches the file stdio.h in the prespecified list of directories and if the header file is found, it (the include directive) is replaced by the entire content of the header file. If the included header file contains another include directive, it will also be processed. This processing is carried out recursively till either no include directive remains or till maximum translation limit is achieved (ISO specifies the nesting level of include files to be at most 15). Hence, one line of source code gets replaced by multiple lines of the header file. During the compilation stage, these added lines will also be compiled; hence, the compiler shows the number of lines compiled to be greater than five.

Forward Reference: Preprocessing stage (Chapter 8).

6. *Is* `int a;` *actually a declaration or a definition?*
   The role of the declaration statement is to introduce the name of an identifier along with its data type (or just type) to the compiler before its use. During the declaration, no memory space is allocated to an identifier. Since `int a;` statement in addition to introducing the name and the type of identifier `a`, allocates memory to `a`, it actually becomes a definition.

7. *How are negative integral numbers stored in C?*
   Internally, numbers are stored in the form of bits (i.e. **b**inary dig**its**) and are represented in the binary number system. In the binary number system, negative numbers are not stored directly. To store both the sign and magnitude of a number, some convention for storage has to be used. In C language, the convention used for storing an integral number is **sign-two's complement representation.**
   What is sign-two's complement representation?
   1. For every integral number, the **M**ost **S**ignificant **B**it (MSB) contains the sign, and the rest of the bits contain the magnitude.
   2. If the sign is positive, the MSB is 0 and if the sign is negative, the MSB is 1.
   3. If the MSB contains bit 0 (i.e. a positive number), the magnitude is in the direct binary representation.
   4. If the MSB contains bit 1 (i.e. a negative number), the magnitude is not in the direct binary representation. The magnitude is stored in two's complement form. To get the value of the magnitude, take two's complement of the stored magnitude.
      How to find two's complement of a binary number?
      Two's complement of a binary number is its one's complement plus one.
      One's complement of a binary number can be determined by negating every bit (i.e. by converting 0's to 1's and 1's to 0's). For e.g. One's complement of 100101 is 011010 (i.e. every bit is negated). Two's complement of 100101 is its one's complement plus one (i.e. 011010 + 1 = 011011). The following tables show how 200 and −200 are stored in memory:

Storage representation of 200:

Sign Bit 16 MSB	Magnitude (MSB is 0, so direct binary representation of 200)														
	Bit 15	Bit 14	Bit 13	Bit 12	Bit 11	Bit 10	Bit 9	Bit 8	Bit 7	Bit 6	Bit 5	Bit 4	Bit 3	Bit 2	Bit 1
0	0	0	0	0	0	0	0	1	1	0	0	1	0	0	0

Storage representation of −200:

Sign Bit 16 MSB	Magnitude (MSB is 1, so magnitude is two's complement representation of 200)														
	Bit 15	Bit 14	Bit 13	Bit 12	Bit 11	Bit 10	Bit 9	Bit 8	Bit 7	Bit 6	Bit 5	Bit 4	Bit 3	Bit 2	Bit 1
1	1	1	1	1	1	1	1	0	0	1	1	1	0	0	0

Integral type consists of integer type and character type.

Forward Reference: Binary number system (Appendix A).

8. *How does the maximum value that an integral data type supports depends upon its size?*

Consider integer data type, taking 2 bytes, i.e. 16 bits in memory. The maximum value it can have is as follows:

Sign Bit 16 MSB	Magnitude (MSB is 0, so direct binary representation)														
	Bit 15	Bit 14	Bit 13	Bit 12	Bit 11	Bit 10	Bit 9	Bit 8	Bit 7	Bit 6	Bit 5	Bit 4	Bit 3	Bit 2	Bit 1
0	1	1	1	1	1	1	1	1	1	1	1	1	1	1	1

Sign Bit = 0 (means number is positive), magnitude is maximum (as all the magnitude bits have maximum value, i.e. 1). The stored number is 32767 (i.e. $2^{15}-1$).

Now, consider character data type (taking 1 byte, i.e. 8 bits in memory). The maximum value it can have is $2^7-1 = 127$. This can be shown as follows:

Sign Bit 8 MSB	Magnitude (MSB is 0, so direct binary representation)						
	Bit 7	Bit 6	Bit 5	Bit 4	Bit 3	Bit 2	Bit 1
0	1	1	1	1	1	1	1

This shows that the maximum value that an integral type can take is directly in relation to its size. That is why, if an integer variable is not able to store a value (e.g. 70000), we switch to `long` integer because `long` integer takes 32 bits in memory. Thirty-one bits will be used for storage of magnitude. Hence, the maximum value (2147483647, i.e. $2^{31}-1$) of `long` integer is far greater than the maximum value of integer (32767, i.e. $2^{15}-1$), which has only 15 bits for the storage of magnitude.

Data type as such does not take any space in memory. Objects associated with the defined identifiers take memory space according to their data types. Wherever it is referred in the text that data type takes some space in memory, it implies that the object of the specified data type takes that much memory space.

9. *What will the output of the following program segment be? (Assume that integer data type takes 2 bytes of memory.)*

```
#include<stdio.h>
main()
{
   int a=32768;
   printf("%d",a);
}
```

The output that this program snippet prints is `-32768`. This can be well understood if one knows how integers are stored in the memory.

If integer type takes 2 bytes in the memory, 32767 is stored as follows:

Sign Bit 16 MSB	Magnitude (MSB is 0, so direct binary representation)														
	Bit 15	Bit 14	Bit 13	Bit 12	Bit 11	Bit 10	Bit 9	Bit 8	Bit 7	Bit 6	Bit 5	Bit 4	Bit 3	Bit 2	Bit 1
0	1	1	1	1	1	1	1	1	1	1	1	1	1	1	1

Now, 32768 is 32767+1. If 1 is added in the above representation:

Sign Bit 16 MSB	Magnitude														
	Bit 15	Bit 14	Bit 13	Bit 12	Bit 11	Bit 10	Bit 9	Bit 8	Bit 7	Bit 6	Bit 5	Bit 4	Bit 3	Bit 2	Bit 1
0	1	1	1	1	1	1	1	1	1	1	1	1	1	1	1
															1
1	**0**	**0**	**0**	**0**	**0**	**0**	**0**	**0**	**0**	**0**	**0**	**0**	**0**	**0**	**0**

The value that comes in the memory is given in bold. The carry generated from Bit 15 has moved into Bit 16 (i.e. sign bit). Now, the sign bit becomes 1 (i.e. number becomes negative). If sign bit is 1, the magnitude of number is stored in two's complement form. The magnitude of number, i.e.

Magnitude (MSB is 1, so magnitude is in two's complement representation)														
Bit 15	Bit 14	Bit 13	Bit 12	Bit 11	Bit 10	Bit 9	Bit 8	Bit 7	Bit 6	Bit 5	Bit 4	Bit 3	Bit 2	Bit 1
0	0	0	0	0	0	0	0	0	0	0	0	0	0	0

is in two's complement form. To get the value of magnitude, take two's complement of two's complemented representation of the magnitude. The magnitude can be found as follows:

		Magnitude														
		Bit 15	Bit 14	Bit 13	Bit 12	Bit 11	Bit 10	Bit 9	Bit 8	Bit 7	Bit 6	Bit 5	Bit 4	Bit 3	Bit 2	Bit 1
Magnitude in two's complement form (Row 1)		0	0	0	0	0	0	0	0	0	0	0	0	0	0	0
One's complement		1	1	1	1	1	1	1	1	1	1	1	1	1	1	1
Two's complement of value in row 1	1	0	0	0	0	0	0	0	0	0	0	0	0	0	0	0

Decimal equivalent of the value obtained is 2^{15} = 32768. The sign was negative, so the number becomes −32768. Hence, whenever the value of an integral data type exceeds the range, the value **wraps around** to the other side of the range.

10. *If a value assigned to an integral variable exceeds the range, the assigned value wraps around to the other side of range. Why?*

    A value greater than the maximum value that the magnitude field can hold makes the sign bit 1, i.e. makes the number negative and it seems like that value has wrapped around to the other side of range; e.g. for character data type, 127 (the maximum value) can be stored as follows:

Sign Bit 8 MSB	Magnitude						
	Bit 7	Bit 6	Bit 5	Bit 4	Bit 3	Bit 2	Bit 1
0	1	1	1	1	1	1	1

If the value is further increased by 1, it becomes as follows:

Sign Bit 8 MSB	Magnitude						
	Bit 7	Bit 6	Bit 5	Bit 4	Bit 3	Bit 2	Bit 1
1	0	0	0	0	0	0	0

The sign bit turns out to be 1. Hence, the number is negative and the magnitude is in two's complement form. To get the value of magnitude, take two's complement of 0000000. It comes out to be 10000000. This is equivalent to 128 and because the sign bit was 1, the value becomes –128 (seems as the value has wrapped around to the other side of the range).

11. *What are l-value and r-value?*

Backward Reference: Refer Section 1.10 for a description on l-value and r-value.

12. *Are nested multi-line comments by default allowed in C? If no, how can nested comments be allowed?*
No, by default nested multi-line comments✍ are not allowed in C. Multi-line comments do not nest, i.e. we cannot have a multi-line comment within another multi-line comment. This happens because after finding /*, which marks the beginning of the multi-line comment, the contents of comments are examined only to find the characters */, which terminates the comment. In the following example:

```
/* comment starts here
...../*nested comment starts here
.....this terminator gets associated with marker of the first line*/
...............this line will not become comment*/
```

In the first line /* is encountered and the multi-line comment starts. Now only */ will be searched. It appears in line 3. This occurrence of */ gets associated with /* of the first line, and the comment is assumed to be finished but some part of the outer comment still persists and this leads to an error.
So in the above example, the portion that gets commented out is given in bold:

/* comment starts here
...../*nested comment starts here
.....this terminator gets associated with marker of the first line*/
...............this line will not become comment*/

Nested comments can be allowed by making changes in IDE settings or by using `pragma` directive.➲ Use `#pragma option -C` to allow nested multi-line comments.

✍ **Comment** is a feature provided by almost all the programming languages. It is used to increase the readability of the program.

Forward Reference: Pragma directive (Chapter 8).

13. *How are real floating-type numbers treated in C?*

    Real floating-type numbers in C, by default, are treated as that of type `double` (i.e. using double precision), so that there should be lesser loss in precision. The following piece of code on execution (using Turbo C 3.0):

```
#include<stdio.h>
main()
{
    printf("%d",sizeof(7.0));
}
```

    prints 8 instead of 4. This is because 7.0 is treated as `double` (double precision) and not as `float` (single precision). To make it `float`, write it as `7.0f`.

14. *The following piece of code is written to get a value from the user:*

```
main()
{
    int number;
    scanf("Enter a number %d",&number);
    printf("The number entered is %d",number);
}
```

    Irrespective of the number that I enter, I get a garbage value. Why?

    This problem is because of the string present inside `scanf` function. The `scanf` function cannot print a string on to the screen. Therefore, **Enter a number** will not be printed. In addition, the entered input should exactly match the format string present inside the `scanf` function. Therefore, if a number say 10 is entered, it does not match with the format string and the output will be garbage. However, if **Enter a number 10** is given in the input, the string in the input exactly matches the format string. The number will take the value 10, and the output will be `The number entered is 10`.

> The **format specifiers** in a format string are generic terms and get matched with any value of the corresponding type. For example, %d gets matched with 10, 20, -23 or any other integer value.

15. *I have written the following piece of code keeping in mind the fact that the format string of* `scanf` *function should only consist of format specifiers. Still, I get a garbage value. Why?*

```
main()
{
    int number;
    printf("Enter a number\t");
    scanf("%d",number);
    printf("The number entered is %d",number);
}
```

    The given piece of code gives a garbage value due to the erroneous use of `scanf` function. Since, the second argument to the `scanf` function is not an l-value of the variable `number`, it will not be able to place the entered value at the designated memory position. The rectified statement can be written as `scanf("%d",&number);`.

16.

```
main()
{
    int a,b;
    printf("Enter two numbers");
```

```
    scanf("%d %d",&a,&b);
    printf("%d + %d = %d\n",a,b,a+b);
    printf("%d / %d= %d\n",a,b,a/b);
    printf("%d % %d=%d\n",a,b,a%b);
}
```

The above piece of code on giving inputs 3 and 4 prints

```
3 + 4 = 7
3 / 4 = 0
3 % %d= 4
```

The last line is not printed correctly. How can I rectify the problem?

This problem can be rectified by using character stuffing. Instead of writing `printf("%d % %d=%d\n",a,b,a%b);` use `printf("%d %% %d=%d\n",a,b,a%b);`.

17. *What will the output of the following code snippet be and why?*

```
main()
{
    char *p="Hello\n";
    printf(p);
    printf("Hello ""Readers!..");
}
```

The output of the code snippet is as follows:

```
Hello
Hello Readers!..
```

The `printf` function requires the first argument to be of `char*` type (i.e. a string); hence, `printf(p)` is perfectly valid and on execution prints `Hello`.

Adjacent string literals get concatenated;➲ hence, `"Hello ""Readers!.."` will get concatenated to form `"Hello Readers!.."`. It will be printed by the next `printf` statement.

> **Forward Reference:** Phase of translation during which the adjacent string literals are concatenated (Chapter 8).

18. *What will the output of the following code snippet be and why?*

```
main()
{
    char *p="Hello\n";
    printf(p"Readers!..");
}
```

There is a compilation error in this code snippet. This error is due to the fact that only adjacent string literals are concatenated. `p` is a variable and is not a string literal. It will not concatenate with the string literal `"Readers!.."`. Hence the error.

19. *What will the output of the following piece of code be?*

```
main()
{
    int a=10,b=5,c;
    c=a/**//b;
    printf("%d",c);
}
```

The output of the code snippet will be `2`. `/**/` is a comment and will be neglected. Hence, the expression becomes `c=a/b`. Its output is `2`.

20. *How are floating point numbers stored in C?*

Institute of Electrical & Electronics Engineers (IEEE) has produced a standard **(IEEE 754)** for floating point numbers. The standard specifies how single precision (4 bytes, i.e. 32 bits) and double precision (8 bytes, i.e. 64 bit) floating point numbers are represented.

An IEEE single-precision floating point number is stored in 4 bytes (32 bits). The MSB is Sign-bit, the next 8 bits are the Exponent bits 'E' and the final 23 bits are the fraction bits 'F'.

<table>
<tr><td>S</td><td>E</td><td>E</td><td>E</td><td>E</td><td>E</td><td>E</td><td>E</td><td>E</td><td>F</td><td>F</td><td>F</td><td>F</td><td>F</td><td>F</td><td>F</td><td>F</td><td>F</td><td>F</td><td>F</td><td>F</td><td>F</td><td>F</td><td>F</td><td>F</td><td>F</td><td>F</td><td>F</td><td>F</td><td>F</td><td>F</td></tr>
<tr><td></td><td colspan="8">8-bits for exponent</td><td colspan="23">23-bits for mantissa (or fraction)</td></tr>
</table>

How is a floating point number stored?

Look at the following example to understand the concept. To store 5.75:

1. **Convert 5.75 from the decimal number system (DNS) to the binary number system (BNS).** The integer part 5 in DNS is equivalent to 101 in BNS.
   The fractional part 0.75 in DNS is equivalent to 0.110 in BNS.
   Therefore, 5.75 in DNS is equivalent to 101.110 in BNS.
2. **The straight binary representation of a floating point number is normalized to make it IEEE 754 compliant.** Normalized numbers are represented in the form of 1.ffffff........ffff (f is binary digit) * 2^p, where p is the exponent. In a normalized number, the integer part is always 1. The decimal point is adjusted by selecting a suitable value of exponent, i.e. p. 101.110 in the normalized form is expressed as 1.01110 * 2^2.

   The value after the decimal point is stored in 23 fraction bits and the integer value is not stored (as it is always 1 in all normalized numbers, so there is no need to store it). So, in 1.01110 * 2^2, only 01110 is stored in 23 bits as fraction.
3. **The exponent is biased with a magic number 127_{10}**, i.e. 127 is added to the exponent to make it 129. The binary equivalent of 129 (i.e. 10000001) is stored in 8 bits reserved for the storage of the exponent.

Thus, 5.75 is stored as follows:

<table>
<tr><td>0</td><td>1</td><td>0</td><td>0</td><td>0</td><td>0</td><td>0</td><td>0</td><td>1</td><td>0</td><td>1</td><td>1</td><td>1</td><td>0</td><td>0</td><td>0</td><td>0</td><td>0</td><td>0</td><td>0</td><td>0</td><td>0</td><td>0</td><td>0</td><td>0</td><td>0</td><td>0</td><td>0</td><td>0</td><td>0</td><td>0</td><td>0</td></tr>
<tr><td>S</td><td>E</td><td>E</td><td>E</td><td>E</td><td>E</td><td>E</td><td>E</td><td>E</td><td>F</td><td>F</td><td>F</td><td>F</td><td>F</td><td>F</td><td>F</td><td>F</td><td>F</td><td>F</td><td>F</td><td>F</td><td>F</td><td>F</td><td>F</td><td>F</td><td>F</td><td>F</td><td>F</td><td>F</td><td>F</td><td>F</td><td>F</td></tr>
<tr><td></td><td colspan="8">8-bits for exponent</td><td colspan="23">23-bits for mantissa</td></tr>
</table>

Why are exponents biased with magic number 127_{10}?

Exponents are biased with magic number 127_{10}, so that floating point numbers can be compared for equality, greater than or less than.

Suppose exponents are not biased with magic number 127_{10}. Instead, sign-two's complement representation is used to store the value of the exponent. If such a representation is used:

2.0, i.e. 1.0 * 2^1 will be stored as follows:

<table>
<tr><td>0</td><td>0</td><td>0</td><td>0</td><td>0</td><td>0</td><td>0</td><td>0</td><td>1</td><td>0</td><td>0</td><td>0</td><td>0</td><td>0</td><td>0</td><td>0</td><td>0</td><td>0</td><td>0</td><td>0</td><td>0</td><td>0</td><td>0</td><td>0</td><td>0</td><td>0</td><td>0</td><td>0</td><td>0</td><td>0</td><td>0</td><td>0</td></tr>
<tr><td>S</td><td>E</td><td>E</td><td>E</td><td>E</td><td>E</td><td>E</td><td>E</td><td>E</td><td>F</td><td>F</td><td>F</td><td>F</td><td>F</td><td>F</td><td>F</td><td>F</td><td>F</td><td>F</td><td>F</td><td>F</td><td>F</td><td>F</td><td>F</td><td>F</td><td>F</td><td>F</td><td>F</td><td>F</td><td>F</td><td>F</td><td>F</td></tr>
<tr><td></td><td colspan="8">8-bits for exponent</td><td colspan="23">23-bits for mantissa</td></tr>
</table>

0.5, i.e. 1.0 * 2^{-1} will be stored as follows:

<table>
<tr><td>0</td><td>1</td><td>1</td><td>1</td><td>1</td><td>1</td><td>1</td><td>1</td><td>1</td><td>0</td><td>0</td><td>0</td><td>0</td><td>0</td><td>0</td><td>0</td><td>0</td><td>0</td><td>0</td><td>0</td><td>0</td><td>0</td><td>0</td><td>0</td><td>0</td><td>0</td><td>0</td><td>0</td><td>0</td><td>0</td><td>0</td><td>0</td></tr>
<tr><td>S</td><td>E</td><td>E</td><td>E</td><td>E</td><td>E</td><td>E</td><td>E</td><td>E</td><td>F</td><td>F</td><td>F</td><td>F</td><td>F</td><td>F</td><td>F</td><td>F</td><td>F</td><td>F</td><td>F</td><td>F</td><td>F</td><td>F</td><td>F</td><td>F</td><td>F</td><td>F</td><td>F</td><td>F</td><td>F</td><td>F</td><td>F</td></tr>
<tr><td></td><td colspan="8">8-bits for exponent</td><td colspan="23">23-bits for mantissa</td></tr>
</table>

Now, if it is checked that whether 2.0 > 0.5, it turns out to be false as 0.5 is stored as a greater value than the value of 2.0.

Now, consider that exponents are biased with the magic number 127_{10}.
2.0 is stored as: Sign Bit = 0, Exponent = 1000 0000 (128 = 1+127), Fraction = 00......0000
0.5 is stored as: Sign Bit = 0, Exponent = 0111 1110 (126 = −1+127), Fraction = 00......0000

It can be shown as follows:

2.0	0	1	0	0	0	0	0	0	0	0	0	0	0	0	0	0	0	0	0	0	0	0	0	0	0	0	0	0	0	0	0	0
0.5	0	0	1	1	1	1	1	1	0	0	0	0	0	0	0	0	0	0	0	0	0	0	0	0	0	0	0	0	0	0	0	0
Value	S	E	E	E	E	E	E	E	E	F	F	F	F	F	F	F	F	F	F	F	F	F	F	F	F	F	F	F	F	F	F	F
		8-bits for exponent								**23-bits for mantissa**																						

2.0 is stored as a greater value than 0.5. Hence, greater than operator will give the correct result.

Conclusion with another example: To find storage representation of 0.4:

1. Convert 0.4 to binary.
   0.4 * 2 = 0.8
   0.8 * 2 = 1.6
   0.6 2 = 1.2
   0.2 * 2 = 0.4
   0.4 * 2 = 0.8; this sequence repeats.
   Therefore, 0.4= **0.01100110011001100**...
2. Normalize **0.0110011001100**... After normalization it can be written as 1.10011001100...$*2^{-2}$.
3. Exponent is biased with the magic number 127. Therefore, the exponent becomes −2+127=125. Its binary equivalent is 0111 1101.
   Hence, 0.4 will be stored as follows:

0	0	1	1	1	1	1	0	1	1	0	0	1	1	0	0	1	1	0	0	1	1	0	0	1	1	0	0	1	1	0	0
S	E	E	E	E	E	E	E	E	F	F	F	F	F	F	F	F	F	F	F	F	F	F	F	F	F	F	F	F	F	F	F
	8-bits for exponent								**23-bits for mantissa**																						

Code Snippets

Determine the output of the following code snippets. Assume that the inclusion of the required header files has been made and there is no prototyping error due to them.

21.
```
main()
{
    printf("%d %d %d %d",72,072,0x72,0X72);
}
```

22.
```
main()
{
    printf("%d %o %x",72,72,72);
}
```

23.
```
main()
{
    printf("%i %i %i %i",72,072,0x72,0X72);
}
```

24.
```
main()
{
    printf("%05d,%5d,%-5d",32,32,32);
}
```

25.
```
main()
{
    printf("%6.3f,%06.3f,%09.3f,%-09.3f,%6.0f,%6.0f",45.6,45.6,45.6,45.6,45.4,45.6);
}
```

26.
```
main()
{
    int a=32768;
    unsigned int b=65536;
    printf("%d %d",a,b);
}
```

27.
```
main()
{
    char a=128;
    unsigned char b=256;
    printf("%d %d\n",a,b);
}
```

28.
```
main()
{
    float a=3.5e38;
    double b=3.5e309;
    printf("%f %lf",a,b);
}
```

29.
```
main()
{
    printf("%d %c",'A','A');
}
```

30.
```
main()
{
    printf("char occupies %d byte\n", sizeof(char));
    printf("int occupies %d bytes\n", sizeof(int));
    printf("float occupies %d bytes", sizeof(float));
}
```

31.
```
main()
{
    printf("bytes occupied by '7'=%d\n",sizeof('7'));
    printf("bytes occupied by 7=%d\n",sizeof(7));
    printf("bytes occupied by 7.0=%d",sizeof(7.0));
}
```

32.
```
main()
{
    printf("%d",sizeof('\n'));
}
```

33. main()
```
{
    printf("%d %c");
}
```

34. main()
```
{
    printf("%d %d %d %d %d\n",sizeof(032),sizeof(0x32),sizeof(32),sizeof(32U),sizeof(32L));
    printf("%d %d %d",sizeof(32.4),sizeof(32.4f),sizeof(32.4F));
}
```

35. main()
```
{
    printf("\nab");
    printf("\bsi");
    printf("\rha");
}
```

36. main()
```
{
    printf("c:\tc\bin");
}
```

37. main()
```
{
    printf("c:\\tc\\bin");
}
```

38. main()
```
{
    printf("hello,world
    ");
}
```

39. main()
```
{
    printf("hello,world\
    ");
}
```

40. main()
```
{
    char *p="Welcome!..""to C programming";
    printf(p);
}
```

Multiple-choice Questions

41. The primary use of C language was intended for

   a. System programming
   b. General-purpose use
   c. Data processing
   d. None of these

42. C is a/an
    a. Assembly-level language
    b. Machine-level language
    c. High-level language
    d. None of these

43. C is a
    a. General-purpose language
    b. Case-sensitive language
    c. Procedural language
    d. All of these

44. Which of the following cannot be the first character of the C identifier?
    a. A digit
    b. A letter
    c. An underscore
    d. None of these

45. Which of the following cannot be used as an identifier?
    a. Variable name
    b. Constant name
    c. Function name
    d. Keyword

46. Which of the following is not a basic data type?
    a. `char`
    b. `float`
    c. `long`
    d. `double`

47. Which of the following is not a type modifier?
    a. `long`
    b. `unsigned`
    c. `signed`
    d. `double`

48. Which of the following is a type qualifier?
    a. `const`
    b. `signed`
    c. `long`
    d. `short`

49. Which of the following is used to make an identifier a constant?
    a. `const`
    b. `signed`
    c. `volatile`
    d. None of these

50. Which of the following have both l-value and r-value?
    a. Variables
    b. Constants
    c. Both variables and constants
    d. None of these

51. Which of the following is not a C keyword?
    a. `typedef`
    b. `enum`
    c. `volatile`
    d. `type`

52. Qualified constant can be
    a. Initialized with a value
    b. Assigned a value
    c. Both initialized and assigned
    d. Neither initialized nor assigned

53. Which of the following is not a valid literal constant?
    a. `'A'`
    b. `1.234`
    c. `"ABC"`
    d. None of these

54. Which of the following is not a valid floating point literal constant?
    a. `+3.2e-5`
    b. `4.1e8`
    c. `-2.8e2.3`
    d. `+325.34`

55. By default, any real constant in C is treated as
    a. A float
    b. A double
    c. A long double
    d. Depends upon the memory model

56. Which of the following is not a valid escape sequence?
    a. \r
    b. \a
    c. \v
    d. \m

57. Escape sequence begins with
    a. /
    b. \
    c. %
    d. -

58. Single-line comment is terminated by
    a. //
    b. End of line
    c. */
    d. None of these

59. The maximum number of characters in a character literal constant can be
    a. 0
    b. 1
    c. 2
    d. Any number

60. Which of the following character is not a printable character?
    a. New line character
    b. Backslash character
    c. Quotation mark
    d. All of these

61. Attributes that characterize variables in C language are
    a. Its name and location in the memory
    b. Its value and its type
    c. Its storage class
    d. All of these

62. In the assignment statement x=x+1; the meaning of the occurrence of the variable x to the left of the assignment symbol is its
    a. Location (l-value)
    b. Value (r-value)
    c. Type
    d. None of these

63. Which one is an example of derived data type?
    a. Array type
    b. Pointer type
    c. Function type
    d. All of these.

64. In C language, which method is used for determining the type equivalence?
    a. Structural equivalence
    b. Name equivalence
    c. Both of these
    d. None of these

65. In the assignment statement x=x+1; the meaning of the occurrence of the variable x to the right of the assignment symbol is its:
    a. Location (l-value)
    b. Value (r-value)
    c. Type
    d. None of these

66. If specific implementation of C language uses 2 bytes for the storage of integer data type, what is the maximum value that an integer variable can take?
    a. 32767
    b. 32768
    c. −32768
    d. 65535

67. If specific implementation of C language uses 2 bytes for the storage of integer data type, then what is the minimum value that an integer variable can take?
   a. –32767
   b. –32768
   c. 0
   d. None of these

68. Which of the following format specifier is used for printing an integer value in octal format?
   a. %x
   b. %X
   c. %o
   d. %i

69. How many bytes are occupied by the string literal constant "xyz" in the memory?
   a. 1
   b. 2
   c. 3
   d. 4

70. The variables and constants of which of the following type cannot be declared?
   a. int**
   b. int(*)[]
   c. void
   d. float

Outputs and Explanations to Code Snippets

21. 72 58 114 114

   Explanation:

   All the outputs are desired in the decimal number system because of %d specifier. Now, 72 is a decimal number, 072 is an octal number equivalent to 58 in the decimal number system, 0x72 and 0X72 are hexadecimal numbers equivalent to 114 in the decimal number system. Hence, the output is 72 58 114 114.

22. 72 110 48

   Explanation:

   72 is to be printed in the decimal (%d specifier), the octal (%o specifier) and the hexadecimal number system (%x specifier). The octal equivalent of 72 is 110 and the hexadecimal equivalent of 72 is 48. Hence, the output is 72 110 48.

23. 72 58 114 114

   Explanation:

   %i specifier is used for integers. By default, it will output integer in the decimal number system as it is the most commonly used number system.

24. 00032, 32,32

   Explanation:

   In the given format string, width specifiers are used along with the format specifiers. Width specifier sets the minimum width for an output value.
   %5d means output will be minimum 5 columns wide and will be right justified.
   %-5d means output will be minimum 5 columns wide and will be left justified.
   %05d means output will be minimum 5 columns wide, right justified, and the blank columns will be padded by zeros.

<table>
<tr><td>0</td><td>0</td><td>0</td><td>3</td><td>2</td><td>,</td><td></td><td></td><td></td><td>3</td><td>2</td><td>,</td><td>3</td><td>2</td><td></td><td></td><td></td></tr>
<tr><td colspan="5">%05d
(*cw = 5, rj, padding of 0's)</td><td></td><td colspan="5">%5d
(*cw = 5, rj)</td><td colspan="6">%–5d
(*cw = 5, - is used for lj)</td></tr>
</table>

***cw is column width, rj is right justified and lj is left justified.**
Hence, the output is 00032, 32,32.

25. 45.600,45.600,00045.600,45.600 , 45, 46

Explanation:

In the given format string, width specifiers and precision specifiers are used along with the format specifiers. Precision specification always begins with a period to separate it from the preceding width specifier.
%6.3f means output is 6 columns wide. 3 is the number of digits after decimal. It is shown as

4	5	.	6	0	0

%06.3f means output is 6 columns wide. 3 is the number of digits after decimal. 0 means blank spaces are to be padded by zeros. It is shown as

4	5	.	6	0	0

%09.3f means output is 9 columns wide. 3 is the number of digits after decimal. 0 means blanks spaces are to be padded by zeros. By default, the output is right justified. It is shown as

0	0	0	4	5	.	6	0	0

%-09.3f means output is 9 columns wide. 3 is the number of digits after decimal. Since – is used, the output will be left justified. Here the output shows blank spaces, and padding by zeros has not been done because only 3 digits can be printed after the decimal. It is shown as

4	5	.	6	0	0			

%6.0f means output is 6 columns wide. 0 is the number of digits after the decimal. Rounding off will take place and 45.4 will be rounded to 45. The output will be

				4	5

%6.0f means output is 6 columns wide. 0 is the number of digits after the decimal. Rounding off will take place and 45.6 will be rounded to 46. It is shown as

				4	6

26. -32768 0

Explanation:

Since the assigned values exceed the maximum value of integer type and unsigned integer type, the values wrap around to the other side of the range. Hence, the outputs are -32768 (minimum value of signed integer) and 0 (minimum value of unsigned integer).

27. -128 0

Explanation:

Since the assigned values exceed the maximum value of character type and unsigned character type, the values wrap around to the other side of the range. Hence, the outputs are -128 (minimum value of signed character) and 0 (minimum value of unsigned character).

28. +INF +INF

Explanation:

Range wraps around only in case of integral data type. Wrap around does not occur in case of float and double data types. In case of float and double data types, if the value falls outside the range +INF or -INF is the output.

> +INF refers to +Infinity and –INF refers to –Infinity.

29. 65 A

Explanation:

Integers and characters together form integral data type and are not separated internally. If characters are printed using %d specifier, it gives the ASCII equivalent of the character. Hence, the output is 65, ASCII code of 'A'. If %c specifier is used, it prints the character, i.e. 'A'.

30. char occupies 1 byte
int occupies 2 bytes
float occupies 4 bytes

Explanation:

sizeof operator outputs the size of the given data type.

31. bytes occupied by '7'=1
bytes occupied by 7=2
bytes occupied by 7.0=8

Explanation:

sizeof operator can also take constant as input and returns the number of bytes required by the data type of that constant as output. 7.0 is a real floating number and will be treated as double type. Hence, sizeof(7.0) gives 8.

32. 1

Explanation:

'\n' is a character, more specifically a new line character. Hence, sizeof operator returns 1, i.e. the size of a character.

33. Garbage

Explanation:

Since format specifiers %d and %c are not linked to any value, they will output garbage. This is only applicable for %d and %c specifiers. If %f specifier is not linked, it leads to abnormal program termination.

34. 2 2 2 2 4
8 4 4

Explanation:

032, 0x32, 32 all are integers in different number systems. 32U is an unsigned integer. Hence, their size is 2. 32L is a long integer of size 4. 32.4 is a real floating-type number and is treated as a double of size 8. 32.4f and 32.4F are float and their size is 4. Hence, the output.

35. ←Blank line

```
hai
```

Explanation:

'\n' is a new line character. Due to '\n', cursor appears in a new line and "ab" gets printed. '\b' is a backspace character. It places the cursor below the character 'b' and "si" gets printed. Therefore, the output becomes "asi". '\r' is a carriage return character. It will make the cursor return to the starting of the same line. The cursor will be placed below 'a'. "ha" gets printed and overwrites "as". Hence, the output becomes "hai".

36. c:	in

Explanation:

'\t' is a tab character and '\b' is a backspace character. Due to '\t' character 'c' gets tab separated from "c:". The output becomes "c:	c". '\b' makes character 'c' to erase and "in" gets printed. Hence, the output becomes "c:	in".

37. c:\tc\bin

Explanation:

The usage of an extra backslash is known as character stuffing. Now '\t' will not be treated as a tab character and will actually get printed. Similarly '\b' will not be treated as a backspace character.

38. Compilation error

Explanation:

String cannot span multiple lines in this way. Hence, the error.

39. hello,world

Explanation:

Each instance of the backslash character (\) immediately followed by a new line character is deleted. This process is known as **line splicing.** Physical source lines are spliced to form logical source lines. Only the last backslash on any physical source line shall be eligible for being part of such a splice.

Physical source lines

```
main()
{
   printf("hello,world\
   ");
}
```

after splicing will form the following logical source lines:

```
main()
{
   printf("hello,world");
}
```

Logical source lines are processed by the compiler. Hence, on execution, hello,world is the output.

Forward Reference: Phase of translation during which line splicing is carried out (Chapter 8).

40. Welcome!..to C programming

Explanation:

Adjacent string literals get concatenated. Hence, "Welcome!..""to C programming" gets concatenated and becomes "Welcome!..to C programming". printf needs first argument to be of char* type. In printf(p) this constraint is satisfied as p is the only argument and is of char* type. Hence, the value of p, i.e. Welcome!..to C programming gets printed.

Answers to Multiple-choice Questions

41. a 42. c 43. d 44. a 45. d 46. c 47. d 48. a 49. a 50. a 51. d 52. a 53. d 54. c 55. b 56. d 57. b 58. b 59. c 60. d 61. d 62. a 63. d 64. a 65. b 66. a 67. b 68. c 69. d 70. c

Programming Exercises

Program 1 | Convert the temperature given in Fahrenheit to Celsius

Algorithm:
Step 1: Start
Step 2: Read the temperature given in Fahrenheit (f)
Step 3: Temperature in Celsius (c) = 5/9*(f–32)
Step 4: Print temperature in Celsius
Step 5: Stop

PE 1-1.c

```
//Convert temperature in Fahrenheit to
//Celsius
#include<stdio.h>
main()
{
    float f,c;
    printf("Enter temperature in Fahrenheit\t");
    scanf("%f",&f);
    c=5.0/9.0*(f-32);
    printf("Temperature in Celsius is %6.2f",c);
}
```

Flowchart depicting the flow of control in program

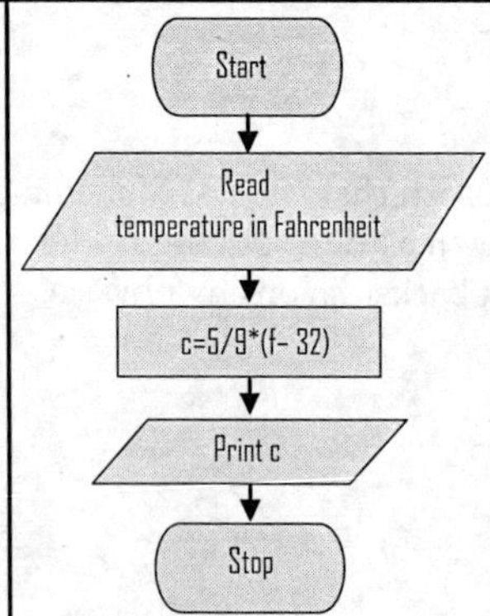

Output window

```
Enter temperature in Fahrenheit   106
Temperature in Celsius is 41.11
```

Flowchart is a graphical representation that depicts the flow of program control.

Forward Reference: Algorithms and Flowcharts (Appendix B).

Program 2 | Find the area and circumference of a circle with radius r

Algorithm:
Step 1: Start
Step 2: Read the radius of circle (r)
Step 3: Circumference cir = 2*22/7*r
Step 4: Area area = 22/7*r*r
Step 5: Print circumference and area
Step 6: Stop

PE 1-2.c

```
//Circumference and area of circle
#include<stdio.h>
main()
{
    float r, cir, area;
    printf("Enter the radius of circle\t");
    scanf("%f",&r);
    cir=2*22.0/7*r;
    area=22.0/7*r*r;
    printf("Circumference of circle is %6.2f\n",cir);
    printf("Area of circle is %6.2f\n",area);
}
```

Flow chart depicting the flow of control in program

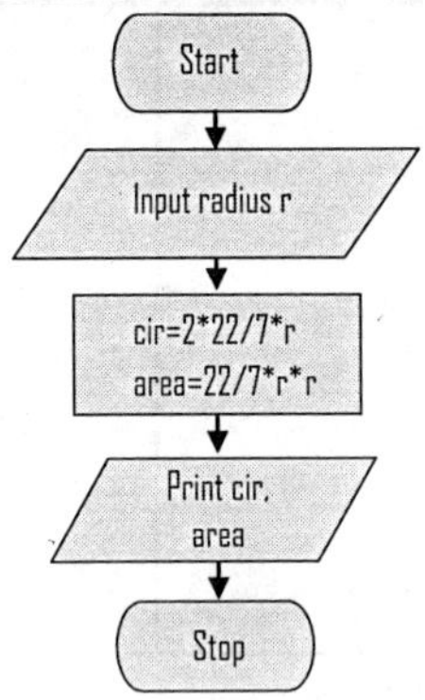

Output window

```
Enter the radius of circle	5
Circumference of circle is 31.43
Area of circle is 78.57
```

Program 3 | Find the average of three numbers

Algorithm:
Step 1: Start
Step 2: Read numbers no1, no2, no3
Step 3: Average avg = (no1+no2+no3)/3
Step 4: Print avg
Step 5: Stop

PE 1-3.c

```
//Average of three numbers
#include<stdio.h>
main()
{
    float no1, no2, no3,avg;
    printf("Enter three numbers\t");
    scanf("%f %f %f",&no1, &no2, &no3);
    avg=(no1+no2+no3)/3;
    printf("Average of numbers is %6.2f\n",avg);
}
```

Flow chart depicting the flow of control in program

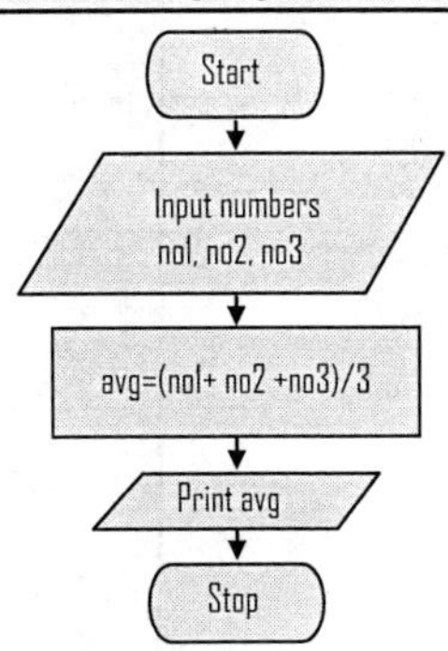

Output window

```
Enter three numbers	12 11 14
Average of numbers is 12.33
```

Program 4 | Simple Interest and the Maturity Amount

Algorithm:
Step 1: Start
Step 2: Read principle (p), rate of interest (roi), time period (t)
Step 3: Interest i = p*roi*t/100
Step 4: Amount amt = p+i
Step 5: Print i, amt
Step 6: Stop

PE 1-4.c

```
//Simple Interest
#include<stdio.h>
main()
{
    float p, roi, t, i, amt;
    printf("Enter principle, rate and time\t");
    scanf("%f %f %f",&p, &roi, &t);
    i=p*roi*t/100;
    amt=p+i;
    printf("Interest is %6.2f\n",i);
    printf("Amount is %6.2f\n",amt);
}
```

Flow chart depicting the flow of control in program

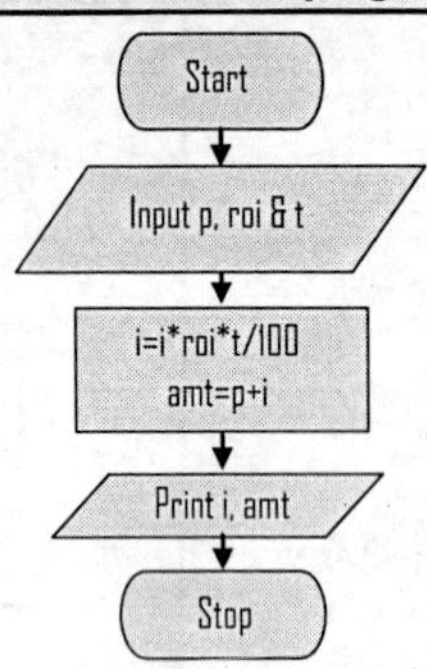

Output window

```
Enter principle, rate and time    1000 7 2
Interest is 140.00
Amount is 1140.00
```

Program 5 | Find area of a triangle whose sides are a, b and c

Algorithm:
Step 1: Start
Step 2: Read sides a, b and c of triangle
Step 3: s = (a+b+c)/2
Step 4: area = sqrt(s*(s–a)*(s–b)*(s–c))
Step 5: Print area
Step 6: Stop

PE 1-5.c

```
//Area of a triangle
#include<stdio.h>
#include<math.h>
main()
{
    float a, b, c, s, area;
    printf("Enter the sides of a triangle\t");
    scanf("%f %f %f",&a, &b, &c);
    s=(a+b+c)/2;
    area=sqrt(s*(s-a) *(s-b) *(s-c));
    printf("Area of triangle is %6.2f sq. units",area);
}
```

Flow chart depicting the flow of control in program

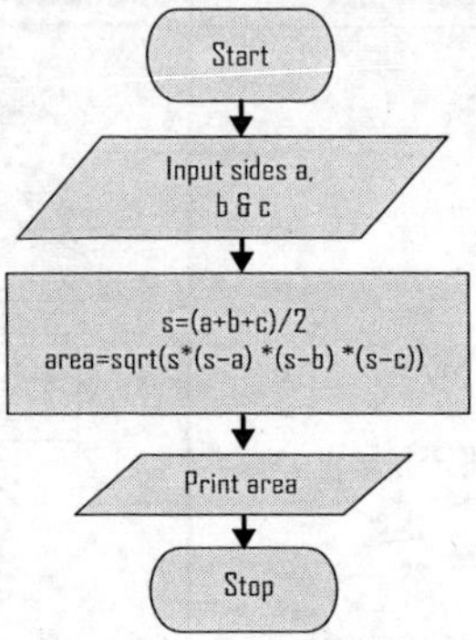

Output window

```
Enter the sides of a triangle    12 5 14
Area of triangle is 29.23 sq. units
```

Program 6 | The velocity of an object is given in km/hr. Write a C program to convert the given velocity from km/hr to m/sec

Algorithm:

Step 1: Start
Step 2: Input the velocity (velk) given in km/hr
Step 3: velocity in m/sec (velm) = velk*5/18
Step 4: Print velocity in m/sec (velm)
Step 5: Stop

PE 1-6.c

```
//Convert units of velocity
#include<stdio.h>
main()
{
    float velk, velm;
    printf("Enter velocity in Km/hr\t");
    scanf("%f",&velk);
    velm=velk*5/18;
    printf("Equivalent velocity is %f m/sec",velm);
}
```

Flow chart depicting the flow of control in program

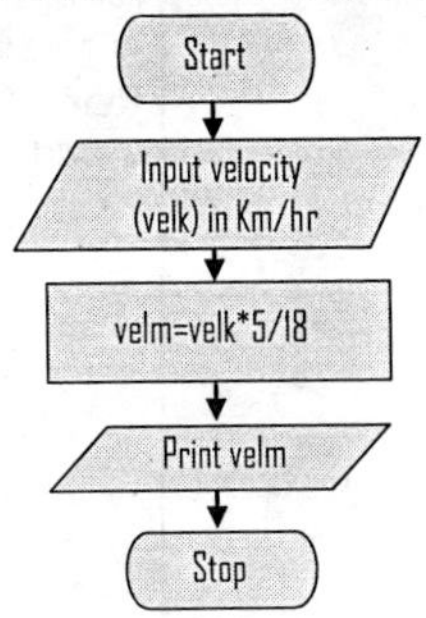

Output window

```
Enter velocity in km/hr    12
Equivalent velocity is 3.333333 m/sec
```

Program 7 | An object undergoes uniformly accelerated motion. The initial velocity (u) of the object and the acceleration (a) are known. Write a C program to find the velocity (v) of the object after time t

Algorithm:

Step 1: Start
Step 2: Input the initial velocity (u) and acceleration (a) of the object in SI units
Step 3: Input the time (t) after which velocity is to be computed
Step 4: Velocity v = u+a*t
Step 5: Print value of velocity (v)
Step 6: Stop

PE 1-7.c

```
//Compute velocity after time t
#include<stdio.h>
main()
{
    float u, v,a, t;
    printf("Enter the value of initial velocity in m/s\t");
    scanf("%f",&u);
    printf("Enter the amount of acceleration\t");
    scanf("%f",&a);
    printf("Enter the time in sec.\t");
    scanf("%f",&t);
    v=u+a*t;
    printf("Velocity after %4.2f sec is %4.2f m/s",t,v);
}
```

Output window

```
Enter the value of initial velocity in m/s    2.4
Enter the amount of acceleration    4
Enter the time in sec.    2
Velocity after 2.00 sec is 10.40 m/s
```

Program 8 | A year approximately consists of 3.156 × 10⁷ seconds. Write a C program that accepts your age in years and convert it into equivalent number of seconds

Algorithm:
Step 1: Start
Step 2: Enter age (age) in years
Step 3: Age in seconds (age_in_sec) = 3.156×10^{7}*age
Step 4: Print equivalent age in seconds (age_in_sec)
Step 5: Stop

PE 1-8.c

```c
//Equivalent age in seconds
#include<stdio.h>
main()
{
    int age;
    float age_in_sec;
    printf("How old are you (years)?\t");
    scanf("%d",&age);
    age_in_sec=3.156E7*age;
    printf("Your age in seconds is %5.2E",age_in_sec);
}
```

Output window

```
How old are you (years)?    18
Your age in seconds is 5.68E+08
```

Remark:

- %E specifier is used to print floating point value in exponent form

Test Yourself

1. Fill in the blanks in each of the following:
   a. The C language was developed by ___________.
   b. An identifier name in C starts with a ___________.
   c. One of the most important attributes of an identifier is its ___________.
   d. `int var;` is a ___________ statement.
   e. ___________ is a data object locator.
   f. Constants do not have ___________ value.
   g. ___________ qualifier is used to create a qualified constant.
   h. Non-printable character constants are represented with the help of ___________.
   i. The first argument of `printf` function should always be a ___________.
   j. Floating point literal constant by default is assumed to be of type ___________.
   k. A C program is made up of ___________.
   l. Every statement in C is terminated with a ___________.
   m. The `printf` function prints the value according to the ___________ specified in the ___________.
   n. The amount of memory that an object of a data type would take can be found by using ___________ operator.
   o. The arguments following the first argument in a `scanf` function should denote ___________.

2. State whether each of the following is true or false. If false, explain why.
   a. C is a case-sensitive language, which means that it distinguishes between uppercase characters and lowercase characters.
   b. An identifier name in C cannot start with a digit.
   c. All the variable names must be declared before they are used in a C program.
   d. Comments play an important role in a C program and are processed by the C compiler to produce an executable code.
   e. Keyword or a reserved word cannot be used as a valid identifier name.
   f. `int a=20, b=30, c;` is an example of a longhand declaration statement.
   g. A type qualifier modifies the base type to yield a new type.
   h. Constants have both l-value and r-value.
   i. A character literal constant can have one or at most two characters enclosed within single quotes.
   j. The `scanf` function can be used to read only one value at a time.

3. Determine which of the following are valid identifier names in C:
   a. main
   b. MAIN
   c. NewStudent
   d. New_Student
   e. a+b
   f. for_while
   g. 123abc
   h. abc123
   i. name&number
   j. _classnumber
   k. _number_

4. Determine which of the following are valid constants:
   a. "ABC"
   b. '#'
   c. Abc
   d. 1,234
   e. –22.124
   f. 1.23E-2.0
   g. 0x2AG
   h. '\r'
   i. 0x23
   j. 23L
   k. –7.0f
5. Identify and correct the errors in each of the following statements:
   a. int a=10, int b=20;
   b. int a=10, float b=2.5;
   c. int a=23u, b=2f;
   d. const int number=100;
      number=500;
   e. printf(1,2,3);
   f. Printf("To err is human");
   g. printf("%d %d" no1, no2);
   h. printf("Humans learn by making mistakes")
   i. scanf("%d %d", no1, no2);
   j. first_value+second_value=sum_of_values

2

OPERATORS AND EXPRESSIONS

Learning Objectives

In this chapter, you will learn about:

- Operands and operators
- Expressions
- Simple expressions and compound expressions
- How compound expressions are evaluated
- Precedence and associativity of operators
- How operators are classified
- Classification based on number of operands
- Unary, binary and ternary operators
- Classification based on role of operator
- Arithmetic, relational, logical, bitwise, assignment and miscellaneous operators
- Rules for evaluation of arithmetic expressions
- Implicit and explicit-type conversions
- Promotions and demotions
- Conditional, comma, sizeof and address-of operator
- Combined precedence of all operators

2.1 Introduction

In Chapter 1, you have learnt about identifiers (i.e. variables and functions specifically printf and scanf functions), constants and data types. In this chapter, I will take you a step forward and tell you how to create expressions from identifiers, constants and operators. Finally, we will look at how expressions are evaluated and the intricacies involved in this evaluation process.

2.2 Expressions

An **expression** in C is made up of one or more operands. The simplest form of an expression consists of a single operand. For example, 3 is an expression that consists of a single operand, i.e. 3. Such an expression does not specify any operation to be performed and is not meaningful. In general, a meaningful expression consists of one or more operands and operators that specify the operations to be performed on operands. For example, a=2+3 is a meaningful expression, which involves three operands, namely a, 2 and 3 and two operators, i.e. = (assignment operator) and + (arithmetic addition operator). Thus, an expression is a sequence of operands and operators that specifies the computation of a value. Let us look at the fundamental constituents of an expression, i.e. operands and operators.

2.2.1 Operands

An **operand** specifies an entity on which an operation is to be performed. An operand can be a variable name, a constant, a function call or a macro➲ name. For example, a=printf("Hello")+2 is a valid expression involving three operands, namely a variable name, i.e. a, a function call, i.e. printf("Hello") and a constant, i.e. 2.

➲ **Forward Reference:** Macros (Chapter 8).

2.2.2 Operators

An **operator** specifies the operation to be applied to its operands. For example, the expression a=printf("Hello")+2 involves three operators, namely function call operator, i.e. (), arithmetic addition operator, i.e. + and assignment operator, i.e. =.

Based on the number of operators present in an expression, expressions are classified as simple expressions and compound expressions.

2.3 Simple Expressions and Compound Expressions

An expression that has only one operator is known as a **simple expression** while an expression that involves more than one operator is called a **compound expression**. For example, a+2 is a simple expression and b=2+3*5 is a compound expression. The evaluation of a simple expression is easier as compared to the evaluation of a compound expression. Since, there is more than one operator in a compound expression, while evaluating compound expressions one must determine the order in which operators will operate. For example, to determine the result of evaluation of the expression b=2+3*5, one must determine the order in which =, + and * will operate. This order determination becomes trivial in the case of evaluation of simple expressions like a+2, as there is only one operator and it has to operate in any case. The order in which the operators will operate depends upon the **precedence** and the **associativity** of operators.

2.3.1 Precedence of Operators

Each operator in C has a **precedence** associated with it. In a compound expression, if the operators involved are of different precedence, the operator of higher precedence operates first. For example, in an expression `b=2+3*5`, the sub-expression `3*5` involving multiplication operator (i.e. *) is evaluated first as the multiplication operator has the highest precedence among =, + and *. The result of evaluation of an expression is an r-value. The sub-expression `3*5` evaluates to an r-value `15`. This r-value will act as a second operand for an addition operator and the expression becomes `b=2+15`. In the resultant expression, the sub-expression `2+15` will be evaluated next as the addition operator (i.e. +) has a higher precedence than the assignment operator (i.e. =). The expression after the evaluation of the addition operator reduces to `b=17`. Now, there is only one operator in the expression. The assignment operator will operate and the value `17` is assigned to `b`.

The knowledge of precedence of operators alone is not sufficient to evaluate a compound expression in case two or more operators involved are of the same precedence. For example, in the expression `b=2*3/5`, the multiplication operator (i.e. *) and the division operator (i.e. /) have the same precedence. The sub-expression `2*3/5` will evaluate to `1` if the multiplication operator operates before the division operator and to `0` if the division operator operates prior to the multiplication operator. To determine which of these operators will operate first, the associativity of these operators is to be considered.

2.3.2 Associativity of Operators

In a compound expression, when several operators of the same precedence appear together, the operators are evaluated according to their **associativity**. An operator can be either left-to-right associative or right-to-left associative. The operators with the same precedence always have the same associativity. If operators are left-to-right associative, they are applied in a left-to-right order, i.e. the operator that appears towards the left will be evaluated first. If they are right-to-left associative, they will be applied in the right-to-left order. The multiplication and the division operators are left-to-right associative. Hence, in expression `2*3/5`, the multiplication operator is evaluated prior to the division operator as it appears before the division operator in the left-to-right order.

Now, let us look at various operators, their classification, precedence and associativity.

2.4 Classification of Operators

The operators in C are classified on the basis of the following criteria:

1. The number of operands on which an operator operates.
2. The role of an operator.

2.4.1 Classification Based on Number of Operands

Based upon the number of operands on which an operator operates, the operators are classified as:

1. Unary operators	A **unary** operator operates on only one operand. For example, in the expression `-3`, `-` is a unary minus operator as it operates on only one operand, i.e. `3`. The operand can be present towards the right of the unary operator, as in `-3` or towards the left of the unary operator, as in the expression `a++`. Examples of unary operators are: `&` (address-of operator), `sizeof` operator, `!` (logical negation), `~` (bitwise negation), `++` (increment operator), `--` (decrement operator), etc.
2. Binary operators	A **binary** operator operates on two operands. It requires an operand towards its left and right. For example, in expression `2-3`, `-` acts as a binary minus operator as it operates on two operands, i.e. `2` and `3`. Examples of binary operators are: `*` (multiplication operator), `/` (division operator), `<<` (left shift operator), `==` (equality operator), `&&` (logical AND), `&` (bitwise AND), etc.
3. Ternary operator	A **ternary** operator operates on three operands. Conditional operator (i.e. `?:`) is the only ternary operator available in C.

2.4.2 Classification Based on Role of Operator

Based upon their role, operators are classified as:

1. Arithmetic operators
2. Relational operators
3. Logical operators
4. Bitwise operators
5. Assignment operators
6. Miscellaneous operators

2.4.2.1 Arithmetic Operators

Arithmetic operations like addition, subtraction, multiplication, division, etc. can be performed by using arithmetic operators. The arithmetic operators available in C are given in Table 2.1.

Table 2.1 | Arithmetic operators

S.No	Operator	Name of operator	Category	-ary of operator	Precedence among arithmetic class	Associativity
1.	+ - ++ --	Unary plus Unary minus Increment Decrement	Unary operators	Unary	Level-I (Highest)	R→L (Right-to-left)
2.	* / %	Multiplication Division Modulus	Multiplicative operators	Binary	Level-II (Intermediate)	L→R (Left-to-right)
3.	+ -	Addition Subtraction	Additive operators	Binary	Level-III (Lowest)	L→R

> The operators within a row have the same precedence, and the order in which they are written does not matter.

The following rules are observed while evaluating arithmetic expressions:

1. The parenthesized sub-expressions are evaluated first.
2. If the parentheses are nested, the innermost sub-expression is evaluated first.
3. The precedence rules are applied to determine the order of application of operators while evaluating sub-expressions.
4. The associativity rule is applied when two or more operators of the same precedence appear in the sub-expression.
5. If the operands of a binary arithmetic operator are of different but compatible types, C automatically applies **arithmetic-type conversion** to bring the operands to a common type. This automatic-type conversion is known as **implicit-type conversion**.The result of the evaluation of an operator will be of the **common type**. The basic principle behind the implicit arithmetic-type conversion is that if operands are of different types, the lower type (i.e. smaller in size) should be converted to a higher type (i.e. bigger in size) so that there is no loss in value or precision. Since a lower type is converted to a higher type, it is said that the lower type is **promoted** to a higher type and the conversion is known as **promotion**. The following are common **arithmetic-type conversions**:
   a. If one operand is `long double`, the other will be converted to `long double`, and the result will be `long double`.
   b. If one operand is `double`, the other will be converted to `double`, and the result will be `double`.
   c. If one operand is `float`, the other will be converted to `float`, and the result will be `float`.
   d. If one of the operands is `unsigned long int`, the other will be converted to `unsigned long int`, and the result will be `unsigned long int`.
   e. If one operand is `long int` and the other is `unsigned int`, then
      i. If `unsigned int` can be converted to `long int`, then `unsigned int` operand will be converted as such, and the result will be `long int`.
      ii. Else, both operands will be converted to `unsigned long int`, and the result will be `unsigned long int`.
   f. If one of the operands is `long int`, the other will be converted to `long int`, and the result will be `long int`.
   g. If one operand is `unsigned int`, the other will be converted to `unsigned int`, and the result will be `unsigned int`.
   h. If none of the above is carried out, both the operands are converted to `int`.

The above-mentioned rules can be **summarized** as:

Binary arithmetic operators can be used in one of the following three different modes:

1. **Integer mode:** If both the operands of a binary arithmetic operator are of integer type, the mode of operation is said to be **integer mode** and the result will be of integer type. For example: the result of `4/3` will be `1` instead of `1.3333`, as integer mode operation results in the value of integer type.

2. **Floating point mode:** If both the operands of a binary arithmetic operator are of floating point type, the mode of operation is said to be **floating point mode** and the result will be of floating point type. For example: the result of 4.0/3.0 will be 1.333333, as the result of floating point mode operation is of floating point type.
3. **Mixed mode:** If one of the operands of a binary arithmetic operator is of integer type and another operand is of floating point type, the mode of operation is said to be **mixed mode**. The operand of integer type is promoted to floating point type and the result will be of floating point type. For example: the result of 4/3.0 will be 1.333333.

Consider Program 2-1.

Prog 2-1.c

```
//Arithmetic expression
#include<stdio.h>
main()
{
    int a;
    a=2*3.25+((3+6)/2);
    printf("The result of evaluation is %d",a);
}
```

Output window

```
The result of evaluation is 10
```

Program 2-1 | A program that illustrates the evaluation of an arithmetic expression

Let us look at how the expression a=2*3.25+((3+6)/2) as specified in Program 2-1 gets evaluated. The innermost parenthesized sub-expression (3+6) gets evaluated first. This sub-expression evaluates to an r-value, i.e. 9. This r-value acts as an operand for the division operator. Now, the expression reduces to a=2*3.25+(9/2). The sub-expression (9/2) gets evaluated next. Since both the operands of the division operator are of integer type, the arithmetic involved is integer arithmetic and thus, the result is an r-value of integer type, i.e. 4 instead of 4.5. The expression becomes a=2*3.25+4. Since the multiplication operator (i.e. *) has a higher precedence than the addition operator (i.e. +) and the assignment operator (i.e. =), the sub-expression 2*3.25 gets evaluated next. In this sub-expression, the arithmetic involved is mixed mode arithmetic as one of the operands is of integer type and the other is of floating point type. The operand 2 is promoted to 2.0. The result of sub-expression 2.0*3.25 turns out to be 6.50. After the evaluation of this sub-expression, the expression gets reduced to a=6.50+4. The sub-expression 6.50+4 involves mixed mode operation and is evaluated to 10.50. Finally, the expression becomes a=10.50. In this expression, the value of floating point type is assigned to a variable of integer type. The operand of floating point type (i.e. 10.50) is automatically converted to an integer type so that it can be assigned to the integer variable a. Since a higher type (i.e. float, bigger in size) is converted to a lower type (i.e. int, smaller in size), it is said that the higher type is **demoted** to the lower type and this conversion is called **demotion**. The method followed during demotion is **truncation**. Thus, 10.50 is demoted (i.e. truncated) to 10 and is assigned to a. This value of a is printed by the printf function.

The important points about the arithmetic operators are as follows:

1. The **unary plus operator** can appear only towards the left side of its operand.
2. The **unary minus operator** can appear only towards the left side of its operand.

3. **Increment operator**
   a. The increment operator can appear towards the left side or towards the right side of its operand. If it appears towards the left side of its operand (e.g. ++a), it is known as the **pre-increment operator**. If it appears towards the right side of its operand (e.g. a++), it is known as the **post-increment operator**.
   b. The increment operator can only be applied to an operand that has a modifiable l-value. If it is applied to an operand that does not have a modifiable l-value, there will be 'L-value required' error. Try executing the code listed in Program 2-2.

Prog 2-2.c

```
//Increment/ Decrement operator's operand
#include<stdio.h>
main()
{
    int a;
    a=++2;
    printf("The result of application of pre-increment operator is %d",a);
}
```

Output window

Compilation error "L-value required"

Reasons:

- Operand of increment/decrement operator should have a modifiable l-value
- 2 is a constant and does not have modifiable l-value

What to do?

- Create a variable b, place value 2 in it and instead of ++2 write ++b

Program 2-2 | A program to illustrate that operand of increment/decrement operator should have a modifiable l-value

   c. ++a or a++ is equivalent to a=a+l.
   d. The **difference between pre-increment and post-increment** lies in the point at which the value of their operand is incremented.
      i. In case of the pre-increment operator, first the value of its operand is incremented and then it is used for the evaluation of expression.
      ii. In case of the post-increment operator, the value of operand is used first for the evaluation of the expression and after its use, the value of the operand is incremented.

The difference between two versions of increment operator is shown in the code listed in Program 2-3.

Prog 2-3.c

```
//Difference between Pre-increment and Post-increment
#include<stdio.h>
main()
{
    int a=2, b=2,c,d;
    c=++a;
    d=b++;
    printf("a=%d, b=%d, c=%d, d=%d",a,b,c,d);
}
```

Output window

a=3, b=3, c=3, d=2

Reasons:

- The value of a is incremented and then it is assigned to c as a is pre-incremented
- The value of b is assigned to d before it is incremented as b is post-incremented

Program 2-3 | A program that illustrates the difference between pre-increment and post-increment

e. Increment operator is a **token**, i.e. one unit. There should be no white-space character between two '+' symbols. If white space is placed between two '+' symbols, they become two unary plus (+) operators. Execute the code listed in Program 2-4 to understand the significance of white-space character.

Prog 2-4.c

```
//++ is a token. Don't place white space in between + symbols
#include<stdio.h>
main()
{
    int a;
    a=+ +2;
    printf("The result of evaluation is %d",a);
}
```

Output window

```
The result of evaluation is 2
```

Remark:

- There will be no compilation error as in Program 2-2 because the expression a=+ +2 does not have an increment operator. Instead it has two unary plus operators, which can be applied on an operand that does not have a modifiable l-value

Program 2-4 | A program that illustrates the significance of white-space character in increment operator

> **Tokens** are the basic building blocks of a source code. Characters are combined into tokens according to the rules of the programming language. There are five classes of tokens: identifiers, reserved words, operators, separators and constants.

4. **Decrement operator**

   a. The decrement operator can appear towards the left side or towards the right side of its operand. If it appears towards the left side of its operand (e.g. `--a`), it is known as the **pre-decrement operator**. If it appears towards the right side of its operand (e.g. `a--`), it is known as the **post-decrement operator**.

   b. The decrement operator can only be applied to an operand that has a modifiable l-value. If it is applied on an operand that does not have a modifiable l-value, there will be a compilation error 'L-value required'.

   c. `--a` or `a--` is equivalent to `a=a-1`.

   d. The **difference between pre-decrement and post-decrement** lies in the point at which the value of their operand is decremented.

      i. In case of the pre-decrement operator, first the value of its operand is decremented and then used for the evaluation of the expression in which it appears.

      ii. In case of the post-decrement operator, first the value of the operand is used for the evaluation of the expression in which it appears and then its value is decremented.

      The difference between two versions of the decrement operator is shown in the code listed in Program 2-5.

   e. Decrement operator is a token, i.e. one unit. There should be no white-space character between two '-' symbols. If white space is placed between two '-' symbols, they become two unary minus (-) operators.

5. **Division operator**

   a. The division operator is used to find the quotient.

Prog 2-5.c

```c
//Diff. between Pre-decrement & Post-decrement operator
#include<stdio.h>
main()
{
    int a=2, b=2,c,d;
    c=--a;
    d=b--;
    printf("a=%d, b=%d, c=%d, d=%d",a,b,c,d);
}
```

Output window

a=1, b=1, c=1, d=2

Reasons:

- The value of a is decremented and then it is assigned to c as a is pre-decremented
- The value of b is assigned to d before it is decremented as b is post-decremented

Program 2-5 | A program that illustrates the difference between pre-decrement and post-decrement

b. The sign of the result of evaluation of the division operator depends upon the sign of both the numerator as well as the denominator. If both are positive, the result will be positive. If both are negative, the result will be positive. If either of the two is negative, the result will be negative. For example: 4/3=1, -4/3=-1, 4/-3=-1 and -4/-3=1. This can be observed by executing the code listed in Program 2-6.

Prog 2-6.c

```c
//Sign of the result of division operator
#include<stdio.h>
main()
{
    printf("Sign of the result of division operator:\n");
    printf("4/3=%d, -4/3=%d\n",4/3,-4/3);
    printf("4/-3=%d, -4/-3=%d",4/-3,-4/-3);
}
```

Output window

Sign of the result of division operator:
4/3=1, -4/3=-1
4/-3=-1, -4/-3=1

Remark:

- The sign of the result of evaluation of the division operator depends upon the sign of the numerator as well as the denominator

Program 2-6 | A program that illustrates the sign of result of division operator

6. **Modulus operator**
   a. The modulus operator is used to find the remainder.
   b. The operands of modulus operator (i.e. %) must be of integer type. Modulus operator cannot have operands of floating point type. Try executing the code listed in Program 2-7.

Prog 2-7.c

```c
//Operands of the modulus operator must be of integer type
#include<stdio.h>
main()
{
    int a;
    a=2%3.0;
    printf("The value of a is %d",a);
}
```

Output window

Compilation error "Illegal use of floating point in the function main"

Reason:

- Operands of modulus operator should be of integer type

What to do?

- Write 3 instead of 3.0 or type cast 3.0 to int by writing (int)3.0

Program 2-7 | A program to illustrate that the operands of modulus operator must be of integer type

c. The sign of the result of evaluation of modulus operator depends only upon the sign of the numerator. If the sign of the numerator is positive, the sign of the result will be positive else negative. For example: 4%3=1, -4%3=-1, 4%-3=1 and -4%-3=-1. This can be observed by executing the code listed in Program 2-8.

Prog 2-8.c

```
//Sign of the result of modulus operator
#include<stdio.h>
main()
{
    printf("Sign of the result of modulus operator:\n");
    printf("4%%3=%d, -4%%3=%d\n",4%3,-4%3);
    printf("4%%-3=%d, -4%%-3=%d",4%-3,-4%-3);
}
```

Output window

```
Sign of the result of modulus operator:
4%3=1, -4%3=-1
4%-3=1, -4%-3=-1
```

Remarks:

- The sign of the result of evaluation of the modulus operator depends only upon the sign of the numerator
- The % sign marks the beginning of format specifier. If it is to be actually printed, use it twice. Refer Question number 16, Chapter 1

Program 2-8 | A program that illustrates the sign of result of modulus operator

2.4.2.2 Relational Operators

Relational operators are used to compare two quantities (i.e. their operands). There are six relational operators in C, which are given in Table 2.2.

Table 2.2 | Relational operators

S.No	Operator	Name of operator	Category	-ary of operator	Precedence among relational class	Associativity
1.	< > <= >=	Less than Greater than Less than or equal to Greater than or equal to	Relational operators	Binary	Level-I	L→R
2.	== !=	Equal to Not equal to	Equality operators	Binary	Level-II	L→R

The important points about the relational operators are as follows:

1. There should be no white-space character between two symbols of a relational operator.
2. The result of evaluation of a relational expression (i.e. involving relational operator) is a boolean constant, i.e. 0 or 1.
3. Each of the relational operators yields 1 if the specified relation is true and 0 if it is false. The result has type int.
4. The expression a<b<c is valid and is not interpreted as in ordinary mathematics. Since the less than operator (i.e. <) is left-to-right associative, the expression is interpreted as (a<b)<c. This means that 'if a is less than b, compare 1 with c, otherwise, compare 0 with c'.
5. An expression that involves a relational operator forms a **condition**. For example, a<b is a condition.

Consider Program 2-9 that illustrates the evaluation of a relational expression.

Prog 2-9.c

```
//Relational operators
#include<stdio.h>
main()
{
    int a;
    a=2<3!=2;
    printf("The value of a is %d",a);
}
```

Output window

The value of a is 1

Remark:

- The expression a=2<3!=2 is interpreted as a=(2<3)!=2. The sub-expression 2<3 is true (i.e. 1). 1!=2 is true (i.e. 1). So, 1 is assigned to a

Program 2-9 | A program that illustrates the use of relational operators

2.4.2.3 Logical Operators

Logical operators are used to logically relate the sub-expressions. The logical operators available in C are given in Table 2.3.

Table 2.3 | Logical operators

S.No	Operator	Name of operator	Category	-ary of operator	Precedence among logical class	Associativity
1.	!	Logical NOT	Unary	Unary	Level-I	R→L
2.	&&	Logical AND	Logical operator	Binary	Level-II	L→R
3.	||	Logical OR	Logical operator	Binary	Level-III	L→R

> **i** In C language, there is no operator available for logical eXclusive-OR (XOR) operation.

The important points about the logical operators are as follows:

1. Logical operators consider operand as an entity, a unit.
2. Logical operators operate according to the truth tables given in Table 2.4.

Table 2.4 | Truth tables of logical operations

AND Operation		
Operand1	Operand2	Result
False	False	False
False	True	False
True	False	False
True	True	True

(a)

OR Operation		
Operand1	Operand2	Result
False	False	False
False	True	True
True	False	True
True	True	True

(b)

NOT Operation	
Operand	Result
False	True
True	False

(c)

3. If an operand of a logical operator is a non-zero value, the operand is considered as true. If the operand is zero, it is considered as false.
4. Each of the logical operators yields 1 if the specified relation evaluates to true and 0 if it evaluates to false. The evaluation is done according to the truth tables mentioned in Table 2.4. The result has type int.
5. The logical AND (i.e. &&) operator and the logical OR (i.e. ||) operator guarantee left-to-right evaluation.
6. Expressions connected by the logical AND (&&) or the logical OR (||) operator are evaluated left to right and the evaluation stops as soon as truthfulness or falsehood of the expression is determined. Thus, in an expression:
   a. E1&&E2, where E1 and E2 are sub-expressions, E1 is evaluated first. If E1 evaluates to 0 (i.e. false), E2 will not be evaluated and the result of the overall expression will be 0 (i.e. false). If E1 evaluates to a non-zero value (i.e. true) then E2 will be evaluated to determine the truth value of the overall expression. The fragment of code in Program 2-10 illustrates the mentioned fact.

Prog 2-10.c

```c
//Logical AND operator
#include<stdio.h>
main()
{
    int i=0,j=1,k=2,l;
    l=i&&j++&&k++;
    printf("Resultant values after evaluation are:\n");
    printf("%d %d %d %d",i ,j,k,l);
}
```

Output window

```
Resultant values after evaluation are:
0 1 2 0
```

Remark:

- The expression l=i&&j++&&k++ is interpreted as l=(i&&j++)&&k++. Since i is false, j++ will not be evaluated and (i&&j++) evaluates to 0 (i.e. false). Since (i&&j++) is false, k++ will not be evaluated and the expression i&&j++&&k++ evaluates to 0, i.e. false. So, 0 is assigned to l

Program 2-10 | A program that illustrates logical AND operation

   b. E1||E2, where E1 and E2 are sub-expressions, E1 is evaluated first. If E1 evaluates to a non-zero value (i.e. true), E2 will not be evaluated and the result of the overall expression will be 1 (i.e. true). If E1 evaluates to 0 (i.e. false) then E2 will be evaluated to determine the truth value of the overall expression. The fragment of code in Program 2-11 illustrates the mentioned fact.

Prog 2-11.c

```c
//Logical OR operator
#include<stdio.h>
main()
{
    int i=0,j=1,k=2,l;
    l=i&&j++||k++;
    printf("Resultant values after evaluation are:\n");
    printf("%d %d %d %d",i ,j,k,l);
}
```

Output window

```
Resultant values after evaluation are:
0 1 3 1
```

Remark:

- The expression l=i&&j++||k++ is interpreted as l=(i&&j++)||k++. Since i is false, j++ will not be evaluated and (i&&j++) evaluates to 0 (i.e. false). Since (i&&j++) is false, k++ needs to be evaluated. k++ evaluates to 2 (i.e. true) and k becomes 3. The overall expression l=i&&j++||k++ evaluates to 1 (i.e. true). So, l=1

Program 2-11 | A program that illustrates logical OR operation

2.4.2.4 Bitwise Operators

The C language provides six operators for bit manipulation. These operators do not consider the operand as one entity and operate on the individual bits of the operands. The bitwise operators available in C are given in Table 2.5.

Table 2.5 | Bitwise operators

<table>
<tr><th>S.No</th><th>Operator</th><th>Name of operator</th><th>Category</th><th>-ary of operator</th><th>Precedence among bitwise class</th><th>Associativity</th></tr>
<tr><td>1.</td><td>~</td><td>Bitwise NOT</td><td>Unary</td><td>Unary</td><td>Level-I</td><td>R→L</td></tr>
<tr><td>2.</td><td><<
>></td><td>Left Shift
Right Shift</td><td>Shift operators</td><td>Binary</td><td>Level-II</td><td>L→R</td></tr>
<tr><td>3.</td><td>&</td><td>Bitwise AND</td><td>Bitwise operator</td><td>Binary</td><td>Level-III</td><td>L→R</td></tr>
<tr><td>4.</td><td>^</td><td>Bitwise X-OR</td><td>Bitwise operator</td><td>Binary</td><td>Level-IV</td><td>L→R</td></tr>
<tr><td>5.</td><td>|</td><td>Bitwise OR</td><td>Bitwise operator</td><td>Binary</td><td>Level-V</td><td>L→R</td></tr>
</table>

The important points about the bitwise operators are as follows:

1. Bitwise operators operate on the individual bits of the operands and are used for bit manipulation.
2. They can only be applied on operands of type `char`, `short`, `int`, `long`, whether `signed` or `unsigned`.
3. The bitwise-AND and the bitwise-OR operators operate on the individual bits of the operands according to the truth tables specified in Table 2.4.
4. The expression `2&3` evaluates to `2` and `2|3` evaluates to `3`. The operations on individual bits of operands (i.e. `2` and `3`) are shown in Figure 2.1.

<table>
<tr><td rowspan="2">Value, operator and result</td><td>Sign bit</td><td colspan="15">Magnitude</td></tr>
<tr><td>Bit 16</td><td>Bit 15</td><td>Bit 14</td><td>Bit 13</td><td>Bit 12</td><td>Bit 11</td><td>Bit 10</td><td>Bit 9</td><td>Bit 8</td><td>Bit 7</td><td>Bit 6</td><td>Bit 5</td><td>Bit 4</td><td>Bit 3</td><td>Bit 2</td><td>Bit 1</td></tr>
<tr><td>2</td><td>0</td><td>0</td><td>0</td><td>0</td><td>0</td><td>0</td><td>0</td><td>0</td><td>0</td><td>0</td><td>0</td><td>0</td><td>0</td><td>0</td><td>1</td><td>0</td></tr>
<tr><td>3</td><td>0</td><td>0</td><td>0</td><td>0</td><td>0</td><td>0</td><td>0</td><td>0</td><td>0</td><td>0</td><td>0</td><td>0</td><td>0</td><td>0</td><td>1</td><td>1</td></tr>
<tr><td>2&3=2</td><td>0</td><td>0</td><td>0</td><td>0</td><td>0</td><td>0</td><td>0</td><td>0</td><td>0</td><td>0</td><td>0</td><td>0</td><td>0</td><td>0</td><td>1</td><td>0</td></tr>
<tr><td>2|3=3</td><td>0</td><td>0</td><td>0</td><td>0</td><td>0</td><td>0</td><td>0</td><td>0</td><td>0</td><td>0</td><td>0</td><td>0</td><td>0</td><td>0</td><td>1</td><td>1</td></tr>
</table>

Figure 2.1 | Bitwise-AND and bitwise-OR operator operating on the individual bits of the operands

5. X-OR operator operates according to the truth table given in Table 2.6.

Table 2.6 | Truth table of X-OR operation

X-OR OPERATION		
Operand1	**Operand2**	**Result**
False	False	False
False	True	True
True	False	True
True	True	False

6. The bitwise NOT operator results in 1's complement of its operand.
7. Left shift by 1 bit is equivalent to multiplication by 2. Left shift by n bits is equivalent to multiplication by 2^n, provided the magnitude does not overflow.
8. Right shift by 1 bit is equivalent to an integer division by 2. Right shift by n bits is equivalent to integer division by 2^n.
9. The expression 4<<1 evaluates to 8 and 4>>1 evaluates to 2. This is shown in Figure 2.2.

Value, operator and result	Sign bit	Magnitude														
	Bit 16	Bit 15	Bit 14	Bit 13	Bit 12	Bit 11	Bit 10	Bit 9	Bit 8	Bit 7	Bit 6	Bit 5	Bit 4	Bit 3	Bit 2	Bit 1
4	0	0	0	0	0	0	0	0	0	0	0	0	0	1	0	0
4<<1=8	0	0	0	0	0	0	0	0	0	0	0	0	1	0	0	0
4>>1=2	0	0	0	0	0	0	0	0	0	0	0	0	0	0	1	0

Figure 2.2 | Left-shift and right-shift operations

2.4.2.5 Assignment Operators

A variable can be assigned a value by using an assignment operator. The assignment operators available in C language are given in Table 2.6.

Table 2.6 | Assignment operators

S.No	Operator	Name of operator	Category	-ary of operator	Precedence	Associativity
1.	=	Simple assignment	Assignment & Shorthand assignment operators	Binary	Level-I	R→L
	*=	Assign product				
	/=	Assign quotient				
	%=	Assign modulus				
	+=	Assign sum				
	-=	Assign difference				
	&=	Assign bitwise AND				
	|=	Assign bitwise OR				
	^=	Assign bitwise XOR				
	<<=	Assign left shift				
	>>=	Assign right shift				

The important points about the assignment operators are as follows:

1. The operand that appears towards the left side of an assignment operator should have a modifiable l-value. If the operand appearing towards the left side of the assignment operator does not have a modifiable l-value, there will be a compilation error 'L-value required'.
2. The shorthand assignment is of the form `op1 op=op2`, where `op1` and `op2` are operands and `op=` is a shorthand assignment operator. It is a shorter way of writing `op1 = op1 op op2`. For example, `a/=2` is equivalent to `a=a/2`.

Forward Reference: Refer Question numbers 53 and 65 and their answers for examples on the usage of a shorthand assignment operator.

3. There should be no white-space character between two symbols of shorthand assignment operators.
4. If two operands of an assignment operator are of different types, the type of operand on the right side of the assignment operator is automatically converted to the type of operand present on its left side. To carry out this conversion, either promotion or demotion is applied.
5. The result of evaluation of an assignment expression is the value that is assigned. For example, in the expression `a=10;`, the value `10` is assigned to `a` and the overall expression evaluates to `10` (i.e. the value that is assigned).
6. The terms assignment and initialization are related but it is important to note the differences between them. They are listed in Table 2.7.

Table 2.7 | Differences between initialization and assignment

S.No	Initialization	Assignment
1.	First time assignment at the time of definition is called initialization. For example: `int a=10;` is initialization of `a`	Value of a data object after initialization can be changed by the means of assignment. For example: Consider the following statements `int a=10; a=20;`. The value of `a` is changed to `20` by the assignment statement
2.	Initialization can be done only once	Assignment can be done any number of times
3.	Qualified constant can be initialized with a value. For example, `const int a=10;` is valid	Qualified constant cannot be assigned a value. It is erroneous to write `a=10;` if `a` is a qualified constant

2.4.2.6 Miscellaneous Operators

Other operators available in C are:

1. Function call operator➲ (i.e. ())
2. Array subscript operator➲ (i.e. [])
3. Member select operator➲
   a. Direct member access operator (i.e. . (dot operator or period))
   b. Indirect member access operator (i.e. -> (arrow operator))
4. Indirection operator➲ (i.e. *)
5. Conditional operator

6. Comma operator
7. sizeof operator
8. Address-of operator (i.e. &)

Forward Reference: Function call operator (Chapter 5), array subscript operator (Chapter 4), member select operator (Chapter 9), indirection operator (Chapter 4).

2.4.2.6.1 Conditional Operator

Conditional operator is the only ternary operator available in C (Table 2.8).

Table 2.8 | Conditional operator

S.No	Operator	Name of operator	Category	-ary of operator	Precedence	Associativity
1.	?:	Conditional operator	Conditional	Ternary	Level-I	R→L

The important points about the conditional operator are as follows:

1. The general form of conditional operator is E1?E2:E3, where E1, E2 and E3 are sub-expressions.
2. The sub-expression E1 must be of scalar type.
3. The sub-expression E1 is evaluated first. If it evaluates to a non-zero value (i.e. true), then E2 is evaluated and E3 is ignored. If E1 evaluates to zero (i.e. false), then E3 is evaluated and E2 is ignored.

Integer and floating types are collectively called **arithmetic types**. Arithmetic types and pointer types are collectively called **scalar types**.

Forward Reference: Refer Question number 33 and its answer for an example on the usage of a conditional operator.

2.4.2.6.2 Comma Operator

The comma operator is used to join multiple expressions together (Table 2.9).

Table 2.9 | Comma operator

S.No	Operator	Name of operator	Category	-ary of operator	Precedence	Associativity
1.	,	Comma operator	Comma	Binary	Level-I	L→R

The important points about the comma operator are as follows:

1. Every instance of a comma symbol is not a comma operator. The commas separating arguments in a function call are not comma operators. If commas separating arguments in a function call are considered as comma operators, then no function could have more than one argument. The commas used in the declaration/definition statement are not considered as comma operators. The commas appearing between the arguments in a function call or commas appearing in a declaration/definition statement are separators.

2. The comma operator guarantees left-to-right evaluation.
3. In expression E1, E2, E3...En, the sub-expressions E1, E2, E3...En are evaluated in left-to-right order. The result and type of evaluation of the overall expression is the value and type of the evaluation of the rightmost sub-expression, i.e. En.
4. The comma operator has least precedence.

The piece of code in Program 2-12 illustrates the use of a comma operator.

Prog 2-12.c

```
//Use of comma operator
#include<stdio.h>
main()
{
    int a,b;
    a=1, 2, 3, 4, 5;
    b=(1, 2, 3, 4, 5);
    printf("Resultant values of a and b are:\n");
    printf("%d %d",a ,b);
}
```

Output window

```
Resultant values of a and b are:
1 5
```

Remarks:

- The precedence of assignment operator is greater than comma operator
- Thus, in the expression a=1,2,3,4,5, the sub-expression a=1 gets evaluated first. Hence, the value assigned to a is 1
- In the expression b=(1,2,3,4,5), the sub-expression 1,2,3,4,5 is parenthesized and will be evaluated first. The result of evaluation of comma operator is the result of evaluation of the rightmost sub-expression, i.e. 5. Thus, (1,2,3,4,5) evaluates to 5 and is assigned to b

Program 2-12 | A program to illustrate the use of comma operator

Forward Reference: Arguments, function (Chapter 5).

2.4.2.6.3 sizeof Operator

The sizeof operator is used to determine the size in bytes, which a value or a data object will take in memory (Table 2.10).

Table 2.10 | sizeof operator

S.No	Operator	Name of operator	Category	-ary of operator	Precedence	Associativity
1.	sizeof	Size-of operator	Unary	Unary	Level-I	R→L

The important points about the sizeof operator are as follows:

1. The general form of a sizeof operator is:
   a. **sizeof expression** or **sizeof (expression)** (For example: sizeof 2, sizeof(a), sizeof(2+3))
   b. **sizeof (type-name)** (For example: sizeof(int), sizeof(int*), sizeof(char))
2. Parentheses should be used if the sizeof operator is applied on a type-name, as indicated in point 1 b) above.
3. The type of result of evaluation of the sizeof operator is int.
4. The operand of the sizeof operator is not evaluated. This fact can be seen by executing the code listed in Program 2-13.

Prog 2-13.c

```c
//sizeof operator
#include<stdio.h>
main()
{
    int a=1,b;
    b=sizeof(++a);
    printf("Resultant values of a and b are:\n");
    printf("%d %d",a,b);
}
```

Output window

```
Resultant values of a and b are:
1 2
```

Remark:

- The operand of sizeof operator is not evaluated. Hence, ++a is not evaluated and thus, the value of a remains unchanged, i.e. 1. The value of a takes 2 bytes in memory (in case of MS-VC++ 6.0, it takes 4 bytes). Thus, the value of b is 2

Program 2-13 | A program to illustrate that operand of sizeof operator is not evaluated

5. The sizeof operator cannot be applied on operands of incomplete type or function type.

Forward Reference: Incomplete type (Chapter 9), function type (Chapter 5).

2.4.2.6.4 Address-of Operator

The address-of operator is used to find the address, i.e. l-value of a data object (Table 2.11).

Table 2.11 | Address-of Operator

S.No	Operator	Name of operator	Category	-ary of operator	Precedence	Associativity
1.	&	Address-of operator	Unary	Unary	Level-I	R→L

The important points about the address-of operator are as follows:

1. The address-of operator must appear towards the left side of its operand.
2. The syntax of using the address-of operator is &operand.
3. The operand of the address-of operator should be a variable or a function designator. The address-of operator cannot be applied to constants, expressions, bit-fields and to the variables declared with register storage class.

Forward Reference: Function designator (Chapter 5), bit-field (Chapter 9), storage class specifier (Chapter 7).

2.5 Combined Precedence of All Operators

Till now, I have described different operators according to their role and have categorized them into various classes like arithmetic operators, relational operators, etc. I have described the precedence of operators within a class (i.e. intra-class precedence). Now, it is the time to consider the precedence of an operator with respect to the operators in other classes (i.e. inter-class precedence). Table 2.11 provides a combined table of precedence.

Table 2.11 | Combined precedence chart

<table>
<tr><th>S.No</th><th>Operator</th><th>Name of operator</th><th>Category</th><th>-ary of operator</th><th>Precedence</th><th>Associativity</th></tr>
<tr><td>1.</td><td>()
[]
->
.</td><td>Function call
Array subscript
Indirect member access
Direct member access</td><td></td><td></td><td>Level-I (Highest)</td><td></td></tr>
<tr><td>2.</td><td>!
~
+
-
++
--
&
*
sizeof</td><td>Logical NOT
Bitwise NOT
Unary plus
Unary minus
Increment
Decrement
Address-of
Deference
Sizeof</td><td>Unary operators</td><td>Unary</td><td>Level-II</td><td>R→L</td></tr>
<tr><td>3.</td><td>*
/
%</td><td>Multiplication
Division
Modulus</td><td>Multiplicative operators</td><td>Binary</td><td>Level-III</td><td>L→R</td></tr>
<tr><td>4.</td><td>+
-</td><td>Addition
Subtraction</td><td>Additive operators</td><td>Binary</td><td>Level-IV</td><td>L→R</td></tr>
<tr><td>5.</td><td><<
>></td><td>Left Shift
Right Shift</td><td>Shift operators</td><td>Binary</td><td>Level-V</td><td>L→R</td></tr>
<tr><td>6.</td><td><
>
<=
>=</td><td>Less than
Greater than
Less than or equal to
Greater than or equal to</td><td>Relational operators</td><td>Binary</td><td>Level-VI</td><td>L→R</td></tr>
<tr><td>7.</td><td>==
!=</td><td>Equal to
Not equal to</td><td>Equality operators</td><td>Binary</td><td>Level-VII</td><td>L→R</td></tr>
<tr><td>8.</td><td>&</td><td>Bitwise AND</td><td>Bitwise operator</td><td>Binary</td><td>Level-VIII</td><td>L→R</td></tr>
<tr><td>9.</td><td>^</td><td>Bitwise X-OR</td><td>Bitwise operator</td><td>Binary</td><td>Level-IX</td><td>L→R</td></tr>
<tr><td>10.</td><td>|</td><td>Bitwise OR</td><td>Bitwise operator</td><td>Binary</td><td>Level-X</td><td>L→R</td></tr>
<tr><td>11.</td><td>&&</td><td>Logical AND</td><td>Logical operator</td><td>Binary</td><td>Level-XI</td><td>L→R</td></tr>
<tr><td>12.</td><td>||</td><td>Logical OR</td><td>Logical operator</td><td>Binary</td><td>Level-XII</td><td>L→R</td></tr>
<tr><td>13.</td><td>?:</td><td>Conditional operator</td><td>Conditional</td><td>Ternary</td><td>Level-XIII</td><td>R→L</td></tr>
</table>

(Contd...)

<table>
<tr><th>S.No</th><th>Operator</th><th>Name of operator</th><th>Category</th><th>-ary of operator</th><th>Precedence</th><th>Associativity</th></tr>
<tr><td>14.</td><td>=
*=
/=
%=
+=
-=
&=

|=

^=

<<=
>>=</td><td>Simple assignment
Assign product
Assign quotient
Assign modulus
Assign sum
Assign difference
Assign bitwise AND
Assign bitwise OR
Assign bitwise XOR
Assign left shift
Assign right shift</td><td>Assignment & Shorthaind assignment operators</td><td>Binary</td><td>Level-XIV</td><td>R→L</td></tr>
<tr><td>15.</td><td>,</td><td>Comma operator</td><td>Comma</td><td>Binary</td><td>Level-XV (Least)</td><td>L→R</td></tr>
</table>

2.6 Summary

1. Operand is an entity on which an operation is performed.
2. Operator specifies the operation to be performed on an operand.
3. Expression is made up of operands and operators.
4. Operands constituting an expression can be identifiers, constants or expressions themselves. The identifiers allowed to constitute an expression are variables, functions and macros. However, label names, typedef name, tags of structure, union or enumeration cannot be a part of an expression. The expressions forming an expression are called **sub-expressions**. An expression that is not a part of another expression is called **full expression**.
5. Based upon the number of operators in an expression, the expressions are classified as simple expressions and compound expressions.
6. Simple expressions have only one operator.
7. There is more than one operator present in a compound expression. To evaluate a compound expression, the order in which the operators will operate is to be determined.
8. The order in which operators operate depends upon the precedence and the associativity of the operators.
9. In a compound expression, if operators of different precedence appear together, the operator of the higher precedence operates first.
10. In a compound expression, if operators of the same precedence appear together, then precedence is not sufficient to determine the order in which operators will operate. The order of evaluation can be determined by looking at the associativity of the operators.
11. If operators are left-to-right associative, the operator that appears first in the left-to-right traversal will operate first.
12. If operators are right-to-left associative, the operator that appears first in the right-to-left traversal will operate first.
13. The operators with the same precedence have the same associativity but vice versa is not true.

14. In an arithmetic expression, if the operands of a binary operator are of a different type, C automatically applies arithmetic-type conversion to bring the operands to a common type. The type of result of the binary operator will also be the common type.
15. Automatic-type conversion is called implicit-type conversion.
16. Type can also be changed by applying explicit-type conversion.
17. Explicit-type conversion is done with the help of a type cast operator, i.e. (). The syntax of using the type cast operator is **(target-type-name) expression**.

Exercise Questions

Conceptual Questions and Answers

1. *I have heard that white-space characters are ignored in C. If I write the statement* `a+ =2;` *in a C program, there is a compilation error. However, if I write it as* `a+=2;` *it works. Why is the blank space (i.e. a white-space character) between + and = not getting ignored?*

   Every white-space character is not ignored in C. White-space characters separating tokens are not significant and are ignored in C. Here, '+=' is a token (i.e. a single unit, one operator). We cannot have white space in between + and =. The occurrence of a white-space character between them makes '+' and '=' two different tokens (i.e. two different operators and both are binary operators). Two binary operators cannot come next to each other without having any operand in between. This leads to an error.
   The following are allowed:

   ```
   1. a        +=        2;
   2. a+=                2;
   3. a                +=2;
   ```

   because white-space characters come in between tokens and not within a token. Similarly, **printf ("Hello");** can be written and will work but **pri ntf("Hello");** will not work because the white-space character does not separate different tokens but comes within a token (i.e. **printf**). Thus, the statement 'White-space characters are ignored in C' can be corrected and refined as 'Non-significant white-space characters are ignored in C'.

2. *I want to check whether a number* b *lies in between numbers* a *and* c. *I have written the following segment of code:*

   ```
   if(a<b<c)
     printf("b lies between a and c");
   else
     printf("b is an outlier");
   ```

   The above segment of code does not work for all test cases. Why? Correct the code so that it starts working as intended.

   The answer to why this code does not work for all test cases lies in understanding how expression a<b<c gets evaluated. In the expression a<b<c, two less than operators (<) are involved. The less than operator is left-to-right associative, thus the expression a<b<c is interpreted as (a<b)<c. a<b is evaluated first. Less than is a relational operator and the outcome of a relational operator is a boolean constant, i.e. 1 (true) or 0 (false). Therefore, a<b can be 1 or 0, depending upon whether a is less than b or not. Then, the result of comparison of a and b gets compared with c. Therefore, instead of b getting compared with c, 0 or 1 gets compared with c. Here lies the fiaw.

Suppose a=2, b=1 and c=5, in a<b<c (i.e. 2<1<5), 2<1 is false, i.e. 0. Therefore, the expression becomes 0<5. 0<5 is true, i.e. 1; hence, the output will be 'b lies between a and c', which is wrong.
Instead of writing a<b<c, the expression should be written as a<b&&b<c. The correct code is:

```
if(a<b&&b<c)
    printf("b lies between a and c");
else
    printf("b is an outlier");
```

In the expression a<b&&b<c (i.e. 2<1&&1<5), 2<1 is false. Therefore, the entire expression evaluates to false and the output is 'b is an outlier'.

3. *A programmer wants to find the average of three numbers. He has written the following piece of code in C:*

```
main()
{
    int a=10,b=12,c=13, average;
    average=a+b+c/3;
    printf("Average is %d",average);
}
```

Does the mentioned piece of code produce the correct result as intended? If no, why?
No, the code does not produce the intended result due to the following reasons:

1. The division operator has a higher precedence than the addition operator. Hence, the expression average=a+b+c/3 is interpreted as average=a+b+(c/3) instead of being interpreted as average=(a+b+c)/3.
2. The type of the variable average is taken as int instead of float.

4. *If the code in the previous question is rectified and rewritten as*

```
main()
{
    int a=10,b=12,c=13;
    float average;
    average=(a+b+c)/3;
    printf("Average is %f",average);
}
```

does this code produce the correct result? If no, why? Rewrite the code, so that it produces the correct result.

Still the code will not produce the correct result. This is due to the fact that in the expression average=(a+b+c)/3, the sub-expression a+b+c will be evaluated first and then it is divided by 3. 10+12+13 turns out to be 35. 35/3 gives 11. (As both 35 and 3 are integers, integer mode arithmetic is applicable. In this mode, the result of evaluation of binary arithmetic operator is an integer.) Now, 11 is assigned to a float variable. Before assigning an integer value to a float variable, the integer value gets promoted (i.e. converted into float). Thus, 11 get promoted to 11.0. Therefore, the average value that gets printed is 11.000000 instead of 11.666667.

The reason behind this problem is the application of integer arithmetic instead of floating point arithmetic. We must do something so that floating point arithmetic or mixed mode arithmetic is applied. To make this happen, any one of the below-mentioned ways can be adopted:

```
1. average=(a+b+c)/3.0;            //←Implicit-type conversion
2. average=(float)(a+b+c)/3;       //←Explicit-type conversion
3. average=(a+b+c)/(float)3;       //←Explicit-type conversion
```

In all the three cases, division is carried out between an int value and a float value. Thus, mixed mode arithmetic is applicable instead of integer arithmetic and the result of computation turns out to be a float value. By using any one of the above three ways, 'Average is 11.666667' gets printed.

5. *The output of the following piece of code turns out to be* 81 *instead of the expected output* 300. *Why does this happen? Suggest possible ways to rectify this problem.*

```
main()
{
    int a=100,b=900,c;
    c=a*b/300;
    printf("The value that c gets is %d",c);
}
```

The expression c=a*b/300 contains three operators, namely assignment operator, multiplication operator and division operator. Multiplication and division operators have the same precedence. The assignment operator has a lesser precedence than these operators. Therefore, multiplication and division operators will be evaluated prior to the assignment operator. Being left-to-right associative, multiplication will be carried out first as the multiplication operator appears towards the left. When 100 and 900 (i.e. both integers) get multiplied, the result turns out to be 90000, which exceeds the range of integer data type. Since the value exceeds the range, wrap around will occur and 90000 will be mapped to 90000−65536 = 24464. Now, this number is divided by 300 to give 81 as the result. Therefore, this problem occurs due to overflow and wrap-around effect.

In order to avoid this problem, we should prevent this overflow and wrap around. This can be done by using range of long integer type instead of integer type. The following alternatives will solve the problem:

1. c=(long)a*b/300;
2. c=a*(long)b/300;

Now, long integer and integer gets multiplied and the result turns out to be a long integer. 90000 is well within the range of long integer type; hence no overflow occurs.

It is very important to note that the following ways do not solve the problem:

1. c=(long)(a*b)/300;
2. c=a*b/(long)300;
3. c=a*b/300L;

This happens because type casting does not prevent overflow in the above-mentioned statements. In 1, first a and b are multiplied. At this stage, overflow occurs and the value becomes 24464. Therefore, there is no benefit now in type-casting it to a long integer. A similar reason applies for 2 and 3.

6. *Why does an assignment operator fail on constants, i.e. why cannot constants be placed on the left side of an assignment operator?*

Assignment operator fails on constants because the assignment operator on its left side expects an operand that has a modifiable l-value. Constants do not have a modifiable l-value and thus cannot be placed on the left side of the assignment operator. If a constant is placed on the left side of the assignment operator, the compiler shows 'L-value required' error.

7. *A programmer wants to find the exponent of a number. He has written the following piece of code:*

```
main()
{
    int x=10,y=2,result;
    result=x^y;
```

```
    printf("The result of exponent operation is %d",result);
}
```

Does the above-mentioned piece of code produce the intended result?

No, the mentioned piece of code does not produce the correct result. There is no operator in C to find the exponent of a number. The ^ operator is a bitwise XOR operator. Hence, the mentioned piece of code finds 'x bitwise-XOR y' instead of 'x exponent y'.

8. *I have read that 'Every statement in C is terminated with a semicolon'. The line number 1 in the given piece of code is terminated with a comma instead of a semicolon. Will this piece of code work? If yes, what would its output be?*

```
main()
{
    printf("Hello"),            //←line 1
    printf("Readers!!..") ;     //←line 2
}
```

As new line characters and comments are ignored during the translation phase by the compiler, the given piece of code:

```
main()
{
    printf("Hello"),            //←line 1
    printf("Readers!!..");      //←line 2
}
```

will be interpreted as

```
main()
{
    printf("Hello"), printf("Readers!!..");
}
```

The interpreted code has only one statement that consists of two comma-separated expressions, i.e. printf("Hello") and printf("Readers!!.."). As the operands of the comma operator are evaluated in left-to-right order, printf("Hello") is evaluated first followed by printf("Readers!.."). Hence, the output of the code would be HelloReaders!!..

9. *From the previous question, I have inferred that semicolons separating two* printf *functions can be replaced by commas. Is my inference correct?*

No. Consider the following piece of code:

```
main()
{
    printf("Hello"); ;printf("Readers!!..");
}
```

The given piece of code on execution prints HelloReaders!!... If the semicolons appearing between the printf functions are replaced by commas, the given code becomes

```
main()
{
    printf("Hello"), ,printf("Readers!!..");
}
```

The resultant code on compilation gives 'Expression syntax error'. This error is due to the fact that two comma operators cannot appear consecutively. There must be an operand in between them. Hence, the drawn inference is not correct.

10. *What will the output of the following code segment be?*

```
main()
{
    int a=10,b=20;
    printf("%d %d\n",a,b);
    a=a*b;
    b=a/b;
    a=a/b;
    printf("%d %d\n",a,b);
    a=a^b;
    b=a^b;
    a=a^b;
    printf("%d %d\n",a,b);
    a=a+b;
    b=a-b;
    a=a-b;
    printf("%d %d\n",a,b);
}
```

The code provides three different ways to swap the contents of two variables without using a temporary variable.

Initially, a=10, b=20. On execution of statements:

a=a*b; //←a will become 200
b=a/b; //←b will become 10
a=a/b; //←a will become 20

Values are swapped.

a=a^b; //←a will become 30
b=a^b; //←b will become 20
a=a^b; //←a will become 10

Values are swapped again.

a=a+b; //←a will become 30
b=a-b; //←b will become 10
a=a-b; //←a will become 20

Values are swapped again.

Hence, the output of the code would be:

```
10 20
20 10
10 20
20 10
```

Code Snippets

Determine the output of the following code snippets. Assume that the inclusion of the required header files has been made and there is no prototyping error due to them.

11.
```
main()
{
    int a;
    a=2*3+4%5-3/2+6;
    printf("%d",a);
}
```

12. main()
```
{
    printf("%d %d %d %d",6/5,-6/5,6/-5,-6/-5);
}
```
13. main()
```
{
    printf("%d %d %d %d",6%5,-6%5,6%-5,-6%-5);
}
```
14. main()
```
{
    int a=12,b;
    printf("%d %d",b,b=a);
}
```
15. main()
```
{
    int a=23,b=12,c=10,d;
    d=c=b=a;
    printf("%d %d %d %d",a,b,c,d);
}
```
16. main()
```
{
    int a=23,b=12,c=10,d;
    d=c+2=b+1=a;
    printf("%d %d %d %d",a,b,c,d);
}
```
17. main()
```
{
    int a=2,b=3,c=1,d;
    d=a<b>c;
    printf("%d",d);
}
```
18. main()
```
{
    int a=3,b=2,c=1,d;
    d=a<b<c-1;
    printf("%d",d);
}
```
19. main()
```
{
    int a=10,b=20,c=30;
    c==a=b;
    printf("%d %d %d",a,b,c);
}
```
20. main()
```
{
    int a=10,b=20,c=30;
    c=a==b;
```

```
    printf("%d %d %d",a,b,c);
}
```

21. main()

```
{
    int a=10,b=20,c=30;
    c==a==b;
    printf("%d %d %d",a,b,c);
}
```

22. main ()

```
{
    int a=012,b=034;
    int x=0x12,y=0x34;
    int c,d,u,v;
    c=a&b;
    d=a|b;
    u=x&y;
    v=x|y;
    printf("%d %d %d %d",c,d,u,v);
}
```

23. main ()

```
{
    int a=012,b=034;
    int x=0x12,y=0x34;
    int c,d,u,v;
    c=a&&b;
    d=a||b;
    u=x&&y;
    v=x||y;
    printf("%d %d %d %d",c,d,u,v);
}
```

24. main()

```
{
    int c=10,d,e;
    d=!c;
    e=~c;
    printf("%d %d",d,e);
}
```

25. main()

```
{
    int c=-4,d=4;
    printf("%d %d %d %d",~c,~d,c^d,~c^~d);
}
```

26. main()

```
{
    int i=10;
    printf("%d",i++*i++);
}
```

27.
```
main()
{
    int i=10,j;
    j=++i++;
    printf("%d %d",i,j);
}
```

28.
```
main()
{
    int i=10,j=11,k,l;
    k=i+++j;
    l=i+++++j;
    printf("%d %d",l,k);
}
```

29.
```
main()
{
    int i=10,j=11,k,l;
    k=i+++j;
    l=i+++ ++j;
    printf("%d %d",l,k);
}
```

30.
```
main()
{
    int i=10,j=11,k,l;
    k=i+++j;
    l=i++ +++j;
    printf("%d %d",l,k);
}
```

31.
```
main()
{
    int x=20,y=35;
    x=y++ + x++;
    y=++y + ++x;
    printf("%d %d",x,y);
}
```

32.
```
main()
{
    int i=100,j=20;
    i++=j;
    printf("%d %d",i,j);
}
```

33.
```
main()
{
    int a=10,b;
    a>=5?b=100:b=200;
    printf("%d",b);
}
```

34. main()
```
{
    int i=0,j=1,k=2,l;
    l=i||j++&&++k;
    printf("%d %d %d %d",i,j,k,l);
}
```

35. main()
```
{
    int i=0,j=1,k=2,l;
    l=i&&j++&&++k;
    printf("%d %d %d %d",i,j,k,l);
}
```

36. main()
```
{
    int i=0,j=1,k=2,l;
    l=++i&&j++&&++k;
    printf("%d %d %d %d",i,j,k,l);
}
```

37. main()
```
{
    int i=0,j=1,k=2,l;
    l=++i||j++&&++k;
    printf("%d %d %d %d",i,j,k,l);
}
```

38. main()
```
{
    int i=0,j=1,k=2,l;
    l=++i&&j++||++k;
    printf("%d %d %d %d",i,j,k,l);
}
```

39. main()
```
{
    int i=0,j=1,k=2,l;
    l=++i&&--j||++k;
    printf("%d %d %d %d",i,j,k,l);
}
```

40. main()
```
{
    int i=0,j=1,k=2,l;
    l=++i&&j--||++k;
    printf("%d %d %d %d",i,j,k,l);
}
```

41. main()
```
{
    int x=4;
    printf("%d %d %d",x,x<<2,x>>2);
}
```

42.
```
main()
{
    int  x=32767;
    printf("%d",x<<1);
}
```
43.
```
main()
{
    int num=3;
    printf("%d",num<<2<<2);
}
```
44.
```
main()
{
    int num=3;
    printf("%d",num<<(2<<2));
}
```
45.
```
main()
{
    int num=5,i=1;
    printf("%d",(num<<i&1<<15)?1:0);
}
```
46.
```
main()
{
    int num=5,i=1;
    printf("%d",(num<<i&&1<<15)?1:0);
}
```
47.
```
main()
{
    float a=0.9;
    int c;
    c=a<0.9;
    printf("%d",c);
}
```
48.
```
main()
{
    float a=0.5;
    int c;
    c=a<0.5;
    printf("%d",c);
}
```
49.
```
main()
{
    float a=0.9;
    int c;
    c=a<0.9f;
    printf("%d",c);
}
```

50. main()
```
{
    int a=0,b=0;
    ++a==0||++b==11;
    printf("%d %d",a,b);
}
```
51. main()
```
{
    int x=4+2%-8;
    printf("%d",x);
}
```
52. main()
```
{
    int i=5;
    i=!i>3;
    printf("%d",i);
}
```
53. main()
```
{
    int a=10,b=70,c;
    c=b=a*=2;
    printf("%d %d %d",a,b,c);
}
```
54. main()
```
{
      printf("%x",-1<<4);
}
```
55. main()
```
{
    int c=- -2;
    printf("%d",c);
}
```
56. main()
```
{
    int c=--2;
    printf("%d",c);
}
```
57. main()
```
{
    int i=5;
    printf("%d %d %d %d %d",i++,i--,++i,--i,i);
}
```
58. main()
```
{
    200;
    printf("%d",200);
}
```

59. main()
```
{
    int i=-1;
    +i;
    printf("%d %d",i,+i);
}
```
60. main()
```
{
    char not;
    not=!2;
    printf("%d",not);
}
```
61. main()
```
{
    int k=1;
    printf("%d==1 is ""%s",k,k==1?"True":"False");
}
```
62. main()
```
{
    const int i=4;
    float j;
    j=++i;
    printf("%d %d",i,++j);
}
```
63. main()
```
{
    int i=5;
    printf("%d",i=++i==6);
}
```
64. main()
```
{
    int i=5,j=10;
    j=i&=j&&10;
    printf("%d %d",i,j);
}
```
65. main()
```
{
    float x,y;
    x=7; y=10;
    x*=y*=y+28.5;
    printf("%f %f",x,y);
}
```
66. main()
```
{
    unsigned int a=0xffff;
    ~a;
    printf("%x",a);
}
```

67.
```
main()
{
    unsigned char i=0x80;
    printf("%d",i<<1);
}
```

68.
```
main()
{
    unsigned a=-1;
    int b;
    printf("%u ",a);
    printf("%u ",++a);
}
```

69.
```
main()
{
    float u=3.5;
    int v,w,x,y;
    v=(int)(u+0.5);
    w=(int)u+0.5;
    x=(int)((int)u+0.5);
    y=(u+(int)0.5);
    printf("%d %d %d %d",v,w,x,y);
}
```

70.
```
main()
{
    int u=3.5,v,w,x,y;
    v=(int)(u+0.5);
    w=(int)u+0.5;
    x=(int)((int)u+0.5);
    y=(u+(int)0.5);
    printf("%d %d %d %d",v,w,x,y);
}
```

Multiple-choice Questions

71. The location of a global variable is bound at
   a. Load time
   b. Procedure entry time
   c. Run time
   d. None of these

72. Which of the following is not an arithmetic operator?
   a. *
   b. +
   c. &
   d %

73. Which of the following is not a bitwise operator?
   a. &&
   b. |
   c. ^
   d. >>

74. Which of the following operators in arithmetic class has the lowest precedence?
   a. %
   b. /
   c. *
   d. +

75. What is the correct way to round off a `float` variable `z` into an integer?

a. `x=(int)(z+0.5)`
b. `x=(z+(int)z+0.5`
c. `x=(int)z+0.5`
d. `x=(int)((int)z+0.5)`

76. Comma operator is a/an

a. Unary operator
b. Binary operator
c. Ternary operator
d. None of these

77. The location of local variables and reference parameter is typically bound at

a. Load time
b. Procedure entry time
c. Run time
d. None of these

78. Evaluation of the expression involving || operator

I. Takes place from left to right
II. Takes place from right to left
III. Stops when one of the operand evaluates to true
IV. Stops when one of the operand evaluates to false

a. I and III
b. III only
c. II only
d. IV

79. Evaluation of the expression involving `&&` operator

I. Takes place from left to right
II. Takes place from right to left
III. Stops when one of the operand evaluates to true
IV. Stops when one of the operand evaluates to false

a. I and III
b. I and IV
c. II only
d. IV

80. Expressions in C can be made from

I. Operands alone
II. Operators alone
III. Operators and operands
IV. None of these

a. I and III
b. III only
c. II only
d. IV

81. What is the fundamental unit of execution in C?

a. Expression
b. Sub-expression
c. Statement
d. Function

82. What is the minimum number of temporary variables required to swap the content of two variables?

a. 1
b. 2
c. 0
d. None of these

83. `int a;` is actually a

a. Declaration
b. Definition
c. Neither a definition nor a declaration
d. None of these

84. The output of the following C code will be as follows:

```
main()
{
```

```
    int a=10,b=20;
    printf("%d %d",a,b);
    a ^=b ^=a ^=b;
    printf("%d %d",a,b);
}
```

a. 10 20 10 20
b. 10 20 20 10
c. 10 10 10 10
d. None of these

85.
```
main()
{
    if(~0 == -1)
    printf("Perfect");
}
```

a. Perfect
b. No output
c. Compilation error
d. None of these

Outputs and Explanations to Code Snippets

11. 15

Explanation:

The expression a=2*3+4%5-3/2+6 gets evaluated as

a=6+4%5-3/2+6
a=6+4-3/2+6
a=6+4-1+6
a=10-1+6
a=9+6
a=15

12. 1 -1 -1 1

Explanation:

The sign of the result of evaluation of division operator depends upon the sign of both the numerator as well as the denominator. If both are positive, the result will be positive. If either is negative, the result will be negative and if both are negative, the result will be positive.

13. 1 -1 1 -1

Explanation:

The sign of the result of evaluation of modulus operator depends upon the sign of numerator only. If the numerator is positive, the result will be positive. If the numerator is negative, the result will be negative.

14. 12 12

Explanation:

The comma operator guarantees left-to-right evaluation, but the commas separating the arguments in a function call are not comma operators. They are considered as separators. If commas separating arguments in a function call are considered as comma operators, then no function could have more than one argument. Hence, these arguments are not guaranteed to be evaluated from left to right. The order of evaluation of arguments in a function call is compiler dependent. In Borland TC 3.0 & Borland TC 4.5, evaluation takes place from right to left. Thus, if the code in the given question is executed using the specified compilers, b=a gets evaluated first and b gets the value 12. The result of the evaluation of the expression b=a turns out to be 12, i.e. the value that is assigned. Therefore, 12 12 gets printed.

Separators are used to separate two tokens. Unlike other programming languages:

- Semicolon in C language is a terminator and not a separator. **Terminator** terminates a statement. Statements in C are terminated with semicolon.
- In C language, the white-space character acts as separator.

Forward Reference: Arguments, function call (Chapter 5).

15. 23 23 23 23

Explanation:

d=c=b=a is a valid expression with no compilation error. The assignment operator is right-to-left associative. Thus, d=c=b=a is interpreted as (d=(c=(b=a))). Thus, first the value of a will be placed in b, then the value of b will be placed in c and then the value of c will be placed in d. Hence, all b, c and d will have a value of a, i.e. 23.

The result of evaluation of an expression is an r-value. Assignment expression is no exception to this rule. The result of evaluation of an assignment expression is the value that is assigned. For example, a=10; assigns 10 to a and the overall expression evaluates to 10 (i.e. the assigned value). As described in the explanation above, the value of b is not assigned to c. Actually, the result of evaluation of expression b=a is assigned to c. However, since the result of evaluation of expression b=a is the same as the value of variable b after assignment, the above explanation is also correct.

16. Compilation error (l-value required error)

Explanation:

c+2 and b+1 are expressions. The result of the evaluation of an expression is an r-value, and the assignment operator cannot have an r-value on its left side. Hence, the placement of c+2 and b+1 on the left side of the assignment operator is erroneous and leads to 'L-value required' error.

17. 0

Explanation:

In expression d=a<b>c, three operators namely, assignment operator (=), less than operator (<) and greater than operator (>) are involved. The precedence of the assignment operator is least and less than operator and greater than operator have the same precedence. < and > operators are left-to-right associative. Thus, less than operator (<) will be evaluated first. a<b, i.e. 2<3 turns out to be true, i.e. 1. Now 1>c, i.e. 1>1 is checked and it turns out to be false, i.e. 0. This is assigned to d. Hence, d got the value 0.

18. 0

Explanation:

Out of =, < and - operators, - operator has the highest precedence. Thus, c-1 will be evaluated first and turns out to be 0. a<b is evaluated then and turns out to be 0 (as 3<2 is false). Then 0<0 is evaluated and turns out to be 0. This outcome is assigned to d. Therefore, d will have the value 0.

19. Compilation error (l-value required)

Explanation:

Out of == and = operator, the equality (==) operator has a higher precedence than the assignment operator. Remember that the assignment operator has a lower precedence than every other operator except the comma operator. The equality operator will be evaluated first. c==a, i.e. 10==30 evaluates to false, i.e. 0. Now, the expression becomes 0=b (i.e. trying to assign a value of b to a constant). It is not allowed, as the assignment operator cannot have a constant (i.e. r-value) on its left side and if it happens (as in this case), there will be 'L-value required' error.

20. 10 20 0

Explanation:

a==b is evaluated first and turns out to be 0. 0 is assigned to c. The values of a and b are not manipulated and remain the same. Hence, the result is 10 20 0.

21. 10 20 30

Explanation:

The equality operator is left-to-right associative. Hence, the expression c==a==b is interpreted as (c==a)==b. The sub-expression c==a is evaluated first and turn out to be 0. Then, 0==b, i.e. 0==20 is evaluated and results in 0. This outcome is not assigned to any variable and will be ignored. Values of a, b and c are not modified anywhere in the function. Hence, the output is 10 20 30.

22. 8 30 16 54

Explanation:

a will be stored in memory as follows:

Sign Bit 16 MSB	Magnitude														
	Bit 15	Bit 14	Bit 13	Bit 12	Bit 11	Bit 10	Bit 9	Bit 8	Bit 7	Bit 6	Bit 5	Bit 4	Bit 3	Bit 2	Bit 1
0	0	0	0	0	0	0	0	0	0	0	0	1	0	1	0

b will be stored in memory as follows:

Sign Bit 16 MSB	Magnitude														
	Bit 15	Bit 14	Bit 13	Bit 12	Bit 11	Bit 10	Bit 9	Bit 8	Bit 7	Bit 6	Bit 5	Bit 4	Bit 3	Bit 2	Bit 1
0	0	0	0	0	0	0	0	0	0	0	1	1	1	0	0

Result of & (Bitwise AND) and |(Bitwise OR) operators is shown in the figure below:

Operator and result	Sign	Magnitude														
	Bit 16	Bit 15	Bit 14	Bit 13	Bit 12	Bit 11	Bit 10	Bit 9	Bit 8	Bit 7	Bit 6	Bit 5	Bit 4	Bit 3	Bit 2	Bit 1
a	**0**	**0**	**0**	**0**	**0**	**0**	**0**	**0**	**0**	**0**	**0**	**0**	**1**	**0**	**1**	**0**
b	**0**	**0**	**0**	**0**	**0**	**0**	**0**	**0**	**0**	**0**	**0**	**1**	**1**	**1**	**0**	**0**
c=a&b=8	0	0	0	0	0	0	0	0	0	0	0	0	1	0	0	0
d=a|b=30	0	0	0	0	0	0	0	0	0	0	0	1	1	1	1	0

x will be stored in memory as follows:

Sign Bit 16 MSB	Magnitude														
	Bit 15	Bit 14	Bit 13	Bit 12	Bit 11	Bit 10	Bit 9	Bit 8	Bit 7	Bit 6	Bit 5	Bit 4	Bit 3	Bit 2	Bit 1
0	0	0	0	0	0	0	0	0	0	0	1	0	0	1	0

`y` will be stored in memory as follows:

Sign Bit 16 MSB	Magnitude														
	Bit 15	Bit 14	Bit 13	Bit 12	Bit 11	Bit 10	Bit 9	Bit 8	Bit 7	Bit 6	Bit 5	Bit 4	Bit 3	Bit 2	Bit 1
0	0	0	0	0	0	0	0	0	0	1	1	0	1	0	0

Result of `&` (Bitwise AND) and `|`(Bitwise OR) operators is shown in the figure below:

Operator and result	Sign	Magnitude (Magnitude is in two's complement representation)														
	Bit 16	Bit 15	Bit 14	Bit 13	Bit 12	Bit 11	Bit 10	Bit 9	Bit 8	Bit 7	Bit 6	Bit 5	Bit 4	Bit 3	Bit 2	Bit 1
`x`	**0**	**0**	**0**	**0**	**0**	**0**	**0**	**0**	**0**	**0**	**0**	**1**	**0**	**0**	**1**	**0**
`y`	**0**	**0**	**0**	**0**	**0**	**0**	**0**	**0**	**0**	**0**	**1**	**1**	**0**	**1**	**0**	**0**
`u=x&y=16`	0	0	0	0	0	0	0	0	0	0	0	1	0	0	0	0
`v=x|y=54`	0	0	0	0	0	0	0	0	0	0	1	1	0	1	1	0

23. `1111`

Explanation:

In C language, a non-zero value is treated as true and zero value is treated as false. Therefore, `012`,`034`, `0x12` and `0x34` are treated as true as all are non-zero values. True `&&` True evaluates to true, i.e. `1`. True `||` True evaluates to true, i.e. `1`. Hence, `1` is assigned to `c`, `d`, `u` and `v`.

24. `0 -11`

Explanation:

! is logical NOT operator and ~ is bitwise NOT operator. Logical NOT operator, i.e. ! operates on its operand considering it as a single entity while bitwise NOT operator, i.e. ~ operates on the individual bits of its operand. In `d=!c`, `c` is `10`, i.e. true. The result of logical negation of true turns out to be false, i.e. `0`. Hence, `d` will have a value of `0`.

The value of `c` (i.e. `10`) will be stored in memory as follows:

Sign Bit 16 MSB	Magnitude														
	Bit 15	Bit 14	Bit 13	Bit 12	Bit 11	Bit 10	Bit 9	Bit 8	Bit 7	Bit 6	Bit 5	Bit 4	Bit 3	Bit 2	Bit 1
0	0	0	0	0	0	0	0	0	0	0	0	1	0	1	0

Bitwise operator (~) negates every bit of `c`. Hence, the result of bitwise negation will be as follows:

Operator and result	Sign Bit 16 MSB	Magnitude of: `c` is in normal binary representation `e` is in two's complement representation														
		Bit 15	Bit 14	Bit 13	Bit 12	Bit 11	Bit 10	Bit 9	Bit 8	Bit 7	Bit 6	Bit 5	Bit 4	Bit 3	Bit 2	Bit 1
`c`	0	0	0	0	0	0	0	0	0	0	0	0	1	0	1	0
`e=~c`	1	1	1	1	1	1	1	1	1	1	1	1	0	1	0	1

Sign bit of e is 1. Therefore, the number e will be negative. Its value can be determined by taking two's complement of the two's complemented representation of its magnitude as shown in the figure below:

	Magnitude (MSB is 1, so magnitude is in two's complement representation)														
	Bit 15	Bit 14	Bit 13	Bit 12	Bit 11	Bit 10	Bit 9	Bit 8	Bit 7	Bit 6	Bit 5	Bit 4	Bit 3	Bit 2	Bit 1
e in two's complement form	1	1	1	1	1	1	1	1	1	1	1	0	1	0	1
Its two's complement	0	0	0	0	0	0	0	0	0	0	0	1	0	1	1

Since sign bit was 1, the value of e will be -11.

25. 3 -5 -8 -8

Explanation:

Operator and result	Sign Bit 16 MSB	Magnitude														
		Bit 15	Bit 14	Bit 13	Bit 12	Bit 11	Bit 10	Bit 9	Bit 8	Bit 7	Bit 6	Bit 5	Bit 4	Bit 3	Bit 2	Bit 1
c=-4	1	1	1	1	1	1	1	1	1	1	1	1	1	1	0	0
d=4	0	0	0	0	0	0	0	0	0	0	0	0	0	1	0	0
~c=3	0	0	0	0	0	0	0	0	0	0	0	0	0	0	1	1
~d=-5	1	1	1	1	1	1	1	1	1	1	1	1	1	0	1	1
c^d=-8 (XOR)	1	1	1	1	1	1	1	1	1	1	1	1	1	0	0	0
~c^~d=-8	1	1	1	1	1	1	1	1	1	1	1	1	1	0	0	0

26. 110

Explanation:

Actually the result of this program snippet is compiler dependent. In the case of a post-increment operator, the value of the operand is used first for the evaluation of expression and **after** its use the value of the operand is incremented. The precise meaning of words '**after**' and '**expression**' is left undefined. Two possible interpretations are as follows:

1. According to the first interpretation, the value of the operand (i.e. i) is incremented after the evaluation of the sub-expression (i.e. i++).
2. According to the second interpretation, the value of the operand (i.e. i) is incremented after the evaluation of full expression (i.e. i++*i++).

If the value is incremented after the evaluation of the sub-expression (i.e. interpretation 1), the expression i++*i++ will be evaluated to 10*11=110. If the value is incremented after the evaluation of full expression (i.e. interpretation 2), the expression i++*i++ will be evaluated to 10*10=100. Different compilers use different interpretations; hence, the result is compiler dependent. In Borland TC 3.0 and Borland TC 4.5 compilers, increment takes place after the evaluation of the sub-expression. Hence, the result is 110.

An expression that is part of another expression is called **sub-expression.** An expression that is not part of another expression is called **full expression.**

27. Compilation error (l-value required)

Explanation:

As the increment operator is right-to-left associative, the expression j=++i++ will be interpreted as j=++(i++). The result of evaluation of sub-expression i++ will be an r-value. This r-value will act as an operand for other increment operator, i.e. pre-increment operator. Thus, the expression reduces to ++(r-value). This reduced expression is erroneous, as increment and decrement operators can only work on operands that have a modifiable l-value. Hence, there will be 'L-value required' error.

28. Compilation error (l-value required)

Explanation:

The tokenizer✍ of C language is greedy in nature. It always tries to create the biggest possible token. Thus, the expression k=i+++j will be treated as k=i++ +j and it is a well-formed expression. The operator ++ will operate first and then operator + will operate. The outcome is assigned to k. In expression l=i+++++j, the tokenizer will divide the operator sequence +++++ into ++ ++ +. Thus, the expression l=i+++++j will be treated as l=i++ ++ +j. The sub-expression i++ will evaluate to an r-value. The second ++ operator cannot operate on an r-value and hence, will lead to 'L-value required' compilation error.

✍ The first phase of a compiler that divides the sequence of input characters into tokens is known as a **tokenizer** or a **lexical analyzer**. C language has **'Greedy Tokenizer'**. It always tries to create the biggest possible token. For example, the sequence of input characters i++-+j will be divided into token sequences i, ++, -, + and j. Consider another example, the sequence of input characters i+++ ++j will be divided into token sequences i, ++, +, ++ and j. Note that the white-space character between two characters is not ignored while tokenizing.

29. 23 21

Explanation:

The expression k=i+++j will be treated as k=i++ +j. First, the value of i is used for the evaluation of sub-expression i++ and then it is incremented by 1. The value of j (i.e. 11) is added to the result of evaluation of i++ (i.e. 10) and the outcome is assigned to k. Therefore, k will be 10+11=21. i will become 11 and j remains 11.

The expression l=i+++ ++j will be treated as l=i++ + ++j. First, the value of i is used for the evaluation of sub-expression i++ and then it is incremented by 1. The value of j will be incremented first and then its value is used for the evaluation of full expression. The result of evaluation of two sub-expressions (i.e. i++ and ++j) is added and is assigned to l. Thus, the value of l becomes 11+12=23. Both i and j become 12 after the evaluation of full expression l=i+++ ++j.

30. Compilation error (l-value required error)

Explanation:

The expression l=i++ +++j will be treated as i++ ++ +j and will give an error due to the reason mentioned in Answer 28.

31. 57 94

Explanation:

In the expression x=y++ + x++, the values of x (i.e. 20) and y (i.e. 35) are used for the evaluation of sub-expressions: y++ and x++. The outcomes of evaluation of these sub-expressions are added, and the result is assigned to variable x (i.e. 20+35=55 and 55 is assigned to x). Then the values of y and x are incremented (i.e. y becomes 36 and x becomes 56). In the next expression, the values of y and x get incremented first (i.e. x becomes 57 and y becomes 37) and then they are used for the evaluation of full expression y=++y + ++x (i.e. y=37+57=94). Hence, x and y become 57 and 94, respectively.

32. Compilation error (l-value required)

Explanation:

In the expression i++=j, the increment operator and the assignment operator are involved. The increment operator ++ has a higher precedence than the assignment operator and will get evaluated first. The result of evaluation of increment operator is an r-value. This r-value lies on the left side of the assignment operator and thus, leads to 'L-value required' error.

33. 100

Explanation:

The expression a>=5 evaluates to true. Hence, the expression b=100 gets evaluated. Value 100 is assigned to variable b and is printed by the next printf statement.

In conditional expression E1?E2:E3, the sub-expression E1 is evaluated first. If it evaluates to a non-zero value (i.e. true), then E2 is evaluated and E3 is ignored. If E1 evaluates to zero (i.e. false), then E3 is evaluated and E2 is ignored.

34. 0 2 3 1

Explanation:

Rules to be followed:

1. The precedence of the logical AND operator (&&) is higher than the precedence of the logical OR (||) operator. The precedence of the logical AND operator and the logical OR operator is only used to parenthesize the expression involving them.
2. The logical AND operator (&&) and the logical OR operator (||) always guarantee left-to-right evaluation irrespective of their precedence.
3. If the first operand of the logical OR operator (||) evaluates to true, the second operand will not be evaluated, as TRUE || anything (true or false) is TRUE.
4. If the first operand of the logical AND operator (&&) evaluates to false, the second operand will not be evaluated, as FALSE && anything (true or false) is FALSE.

Expression l=i||j++&&++k will be treated as l=i||(j++&&++k), as the logical AND operator has a higher precedence than the logical OR operator. The logical AND and logical OR operator guarantee left-to-right execution. Hence, the expression l=i||(j++&&++k) is executed from left to right. The first operand of the logical OR operator (||), i.e. i is 0, i.e. false; hence, the second operand needs to be evaluated to determine the truth value of full expression. The sub-expression j++&&++k starts evaluation. In sub-expression j++, j is post-incremented. The sub-expression j++ evaluates to 1 and the value of j is incremented to 2. Since the first operand of the logical AND operator, i.e. j++ evaluates to 1 (i.e. true), the second operand (i.e. ++k) needs to be evaluated. In sub-expression ++k, k is pre-incremented. The value of k is incremented first and then its value is used for the evaluation of expression. Thus, the value of k used for the evaluation of expression is 3. Therefore, 1&&3 turns out to be 1. Thus, the second operand of the logical OR operator evaluates to 1. Hence, 0||1 will be evaluated and turns out to be 1. The outcome is assigned to l.
Therefore, the values are i=0, j=2, k=3, l=1.

35. 0 1 2 0

Explanation:

Since the logical AND operator is left-to-right associative, the expression l=i&&j++&&++k will be interpreted as l=(i&&j++)&&++k. Recall Rule 4 mentioned in the previous answer. In the sub-expression i&&j++, as the first operand of && operator, i.e. i is 0 (i.e. false), j++ will not be evaluated and the sub-expression i&&j++ evaluates to 0. Due to the same reason, the sub-expression ++k will not be evaluated and the full expression evaluates to 0. 0 is assigned to l. Hence, i=0, j=1, k=2 and l=0.

36. 1 2 3 1

Explanation:

The expression l=++i&&j++&&++k will be interpreted as l=(++i&&j++)&&++k. In the sub-expression ++i&&j++, i is pre-incremented. i becomes 1 and the sub-expression ++i, evaluates to 1. Since the first operand of the && operator evaluates to 1, i.e. true, the sub-expression j++ needs to be evaluated. The sub-expression j++ evaluates to 1 and the value of j becomes 2. As 1&&1 evaluates to 1, the sub-expression ++k will be evaluated. k will become 3. 1&&3 evaluates to 1. Hence, l will get value 1. Therefore, the values are i=1, j=2, k=3, l=1.

37. 1 1 2 1

Explanation:

Since the precedence of the logical AND operator is higher than the logical OR operator, the expression l=++i||j++&&++k will be interpreted as l=++i||(j++&&++k). In the sub-expression ++i, i is pre-incremented. i becomes 1 and the sub-expression ++i evaluates to 1. 1|| anything (0 or 1) is 1. Hence, the sub-expression (j++&&++k) will not be evaluated. The values of j and k remain 1 and 2, respectively. Therefore, the values are i=1, j=1, k=2, l=1.

38. 1 2 2 1

Explanation:

The expression l=++i&&j++||++k will be interpreted as l=(++i&&j++)||++k. In the sub-expression ++i&&j++, i is pre-incremented. i becomes 1 and the sub-expression ++i evaluates to 1. Since the first operand of the logical AND operator evaluates to true, the second operand needs to be evaluated. The sub-expression j++ evaluates to 1 and j is incremented to 2. 1&&1 evaluates to 1. 1 || anything (0 or 1) is 1. Therefore, the sub-expression ++k will not be evaluated and the value of k remains 2. Thus, the expression ++i&&j++||++k evaluates to 1 and is assigned to l. Hence, i=1, j=2, k=2 and l=1.

39. 1 0 3 1

Explanation:

The expression l=++i&&--j||++k will be interpreted as l=(++i&&--j)||++k. In the sub-expression ++i&&--j, i is pre-incremented. i becomes 1 and the sub-expression ++i evaluates to 1. Since the first operand of the logical AND operator evaluates to true, the second operand (i.e. --j) needs to be evaluated. j is decremented to 0 and the sub-expression --j evaluates to 0. Thus, 1&&0 evaluates to 0. As the first operand of the logical OR operator is 0, the sub-expression ++k needs to be evaluated. k becomes 3. 0||3 evaluates to 1 and is assigned to l. Hence, the values are i=1, j=0, k=3 and l=1.

40. 1 0 2 1

Explanation:

The expression l=++i&&j--||++k will be interpreted as l=(++i&&j--)||++k. In the sub-expression ++i&&j--, i is pre-incremented. i becomes 1 and the sub-expression ++i evaluates to 1. Since the first operand of the logical AND operator evaluates to true, the second operand (i.e. j--) needs to be evaluated. The sub-expression j-- evaluates to 1 and j is decremented to 0. 1&&1 evaluates to 1. The first operand of the logical OR operator evaluates to 1, so the second operand need not be evaluated. Hence, ++k will not be evaluated and the value of k remains 2. The expression ++i&&j--||++k evaluates to 1 and is assigned to l. Hence, i=1, j=0, k=2, l=1.

41. 4 16 1

Explanation:

<< is the left shift operator. A shift by 1 bit in the left direction is equivalent to multiplication by 2. A shift by n bits is equivalent to multiplication by 2^n, provided the magnitude does not overflow.

>> is the right shift operator. A shift by 1 bit in the right direction is equivalent to integer division by 2. A shift by n bits is equivalent to integer division by 2^n.

4<<2 is equivalent to $4*2^2 = 4*4 = 16$

4>>2 is equivalent to $4/2^2 = 4/4 = 1$.

> The statement 'A shift by 1 bit in the left direction is equivalent to multiplication by 2' holds true till there is no overflow in the magnitude field of the number. For example, if an integer is stored in 2 bytes, 32767<<2 will not be 65534 because the magnitude field has overflowed.

42. -2

Explanation:

x=32767 will be stored in memory as follows:

Sign Bit 16 MSB	Magnitude														
	Bit 15	Bit 14	Bit 13	Bit 12	Bit 11	Bit 10	Bit 9	Bit 8	Bit 7	Bit 6	Bit 5	Bit 4	Bit 3	Bit 2	Bit 1
0	1	1	1	1	1	1	1	1	1	1	1	1	1	1	1

Shift by 1 bit in left direction will lead to

Sign Bit 16 MSB	Magnitude is in two's complement representation														
	Bit 15	Bit 14	Bit 13	Bit 12	Bit 11	Bit 10	Bit 9	Bit 8	Bit 7	Bit 6	Bit 5	Bit 4	Bit 3	Bit 2	Bit 1
1	1	1	1	1	1	1	1	1	1	1	1	1	1	1	0

Sign bit becomes 1. Hence, the number will be negative and its value can be determined by taking two's complement of two's complemented representation of its magnitude. Two's complement of 111 1111 1111 1110 is 000 0000 0000 0010, i.e. 2. Sign bit was 1, i.e. negative. Hence, the result will be -2.

> A good method to **find two's complement** of a number is:
> 1. Look from the right side in the bits sequence.
> 2. Till 1 is encountered keep the bits sequence same.
> 3. After 1 has been encountered, negate every bit, i.e. 0 to 1 and 1 to 0.
>
> For example, consider number 111 1111 1111 1110 ←
>
> two's complement will be 000 0000 0000 0010

43. 48

Explanation:

Since, the shift operator is left-to-right associative, the expression num<<2<<2 will be interpreted as (num<<2)<<2. The sub-expression num<<2, i.e. 3<<2 evaluates to an r-value 12. This r-value acts as an operand for the second shift operator and the sub-expression 12<<2 evaluates to 48.

44. 768

Explanation:

In expression num<<(2<<2), the sub-expression 2<<2 will be evaluated first. The result of its evaluation will be an r-value, i.e. 8. Then, num<<8 (i.e. 3<<8) will be evaluated and results in 768.

Parenthesized sub-expressions are evaluated first.

45. 0

Explanation:

Since the shift operator has a higher precedence than the bitwise AND (&) operator, the expression (num<<i&1<<15)?1:0) will be interpreted as ((num<<i)&(1<<15))?1:0). First, the operand1 of the conditional operator (i.e. sub-expression num<<i&1<<15) will be evaluated as follows:

Operator and result	Sign bit 16 MSB	Magnitude														
		Bit 15	Bit 14	Bit 13	Bit 12	Bit 11	Bit 10	Bit 9	Bit 8	Bit 7	Bit 6	Bit 5	Bit 4	Bit 3	Bit 2	Bit 1
num=5	0	0	0	0	0	0	0	0	0	0	0	0	0	1	0	1
num<<i=num<<1	**0**	**0**	**0**	**0**	**0**	**0**	**0**	**0**	**0**	**0**	**0**	**0**	**1**	**0**	**1**	**0**
1	0	0	0	0	0	0	0	0	0	0	0	0	0	0	0	1
1<<15	**1**	**0**	**0**	**0**	**0**	**0**	**0**	**0**	**0**	**0**	**0**	**0**	**0**	**0**	**0**	**0**
num<<i&1<<15=0	0	0	0	0	0	0	0	0	0	0	0	0	0	0	0	0

Since the sub-expression num<<i&&1<<15 evaluates to 0, i.e. false, the outcome of the conditional operator will be the result of evaluation of operand3, i.e. 0.

46. 1

Explanation:

The expression (num<<i&&1<<15)?1:0) will be interpreted as ((num<<i)&&(1<<15))?1:0). The sub-expression num<<i&&1<<15 will be evaluated first. The sub-expression num<<i (i.e. 5<<1) evaluates to 10 and the sub-expression 1<<15 evaluates to -32768. Both are non-zero values and non-zero values are considered as true. Also, true&&true is true. Hence, num<<i&&1<<15 evaluates to true, i.e. 1. Since, operand1 of the conditional operator evaluates to true, operand2 (i.e. 1) will be evaluated and results in 1.

47. 1

Explanation:

This question can only be answered after looking at some of the technicalities and intricacies involved in storing floating point numbers. The following facts must be remembered:

1. **Each real floating-type number cannot be represented exactly in memory** (i.e. with infinite **precision).**
   During their storage, some round-off errors occur. Some real floating-type numbers are stored as a greater value and some are stored as a lesser value.
   Execute the given code and have a look at the output:

```
main()
{
  float a=0.4, b=0.9;
  printf("0.4 is stored as %.20f\n",a);
  printf("0.9 is stored as %.20f",b);
}
```

The output of this code turns to be
0.4 is stored as 0.400000005960464478000 (i.e greater value)
0.9 is stored as 0.899999976158142090000 (i.e smaller value)

2. **Floats are stored in 32 bits (1 bit for Sign, 8 bits for Exponents and 23 bits for Fraction).**
   0.9 as a float will be stored in memory as follows:

32	31	30	29	28	27	26	25	24	23	22	21	20	19	18	17	16	15	14	13	12	11	10	9	8	7	6	5	4	3	2	1
0	0	1	1	1	1	1	1	0	1	1	0	0	1	1	0	0	1	1	0	0	1	1	0	0	1	1	0	0	1	1	0
3				F				6				6				6				6				6				6			
S	E	E	E	E	E	E	E	E	F	F	F	F	F	F	F	F	F	F	F	F	F	F	F	F	F	F	F	F	F	F	F
	8-bits for exponent								23-bits for mantissa																						

Backward Reference: Refer Answer number 20 in Chapter 1 to review how float is stored in memory.

3. **Doubles are stored in 64 bits (1 bit for Sign, 11 bits for Exponents and 52 bits for Fraction).**
   To store 0.9 (i.e. 0.11100110011001100110011001100...) as double:
   I. Normalize it. Value becomes 1.1100110011001100...* 2^{-1}
   II. Bias the double exponent with value 1023 like float exponent is biased with 127. Therefore, exponent after biasing becomes -1+1023=1022 i.e. 01111111110 (in binary)
   III. Fractional part is 110011001100110011001100110011...

0.9 as double will be stored in memory as follows:

64	63	62	61	60	59	58	57	56	55	54	53	52	51	50	49	48	47	46	45	44	43	42	41	40	39	38	37	36	35	34	33
0	0	1	1	1	1	1	1	1	1	1	0	1	1	0	0	1	1	0	0	1	1	0	0	1	1	0	0	1	1	0	0
3				F				E				C				C				C				C				C			
S	E	E	E	E	E	E	E	E	E	E	E	F	F	F	F	F	F	F	F	F	F	F	F	F	F	F	F	F	F	F	F
	11-bits for exponent											52-bits for mantissa (Continued in the next table)																			

32	31	30	29	28	27	26	25	24	23	22	21	20	19	18	17	16	15	14	13	12	11	10	9	8	7	6	5	4	3	2	1
1	1	0	0	1	1	0	0	1	1	0	0	1	1	0	0	1	1	0	0	1	1	0	0	1	1	0	0	1	1	0	0
C				C				C				C				C				C				C				D			
F	F	F	F	F	F	F	F	F	F	F	F	F	F	F	F	F	F	F	F	F	F	F	F	F	F	F	F	F	F	F	F
(Continued from the previous table)																															

4. **Last nibble gets rounded off**
   Why is the last nibble (i.e. 4 bits) in double represented by D instead of C?
   This is because of rounding. **C** gets rounded to **D**. This can be confirmed by running the following piece of code:

```
main()
{
  float a=0.9;
  double b=0.9;
  char *p;
  int i;
  p=(char*)&a;
```

```
        printf("Float is stored in memory as:\t");
        for(i=0;i<=3;i++)
        printf("%02X ",(unsigned char)p[i]);
        p=(char*)&b;
        printf("\n Double is stored in memory as:\t");
        for(i=0;i<=7;i++)
        printf("%02X ",(unsigned char)p[i]);
    }
```

The above code gives as output

Float is stored in memory as: 66 66 66 3F
Double is stored in memory as: CD CC CC CC CC CC EC 3F

Why is the output like CD CC CC CC CC CC EC 3F instead of 3F EC CC CC CC CC CC CD?

The output is like this because the Intel family of micro-processors stores numbers in **little-endian format.** Therefore, the least significant byte, i.e. CD gets stored in the lowest memory location and hence gets printed first. The most significant byte, i.e. 3F is stored in the highest memory location and will get printed last.

> In **little-endian format** of storing numbers, the least significant byte is always stored in the lowest numbered memory location, and the most significant byte is stored in the highest.

5. **When float and double are compared, float gets converted into double first. This type of conversion is called promotion. We say that float gets promoted to double.**

   The float value 3F 66 66 66 is promoted to double and becomes:

64	63	62	61	60	59	58	57	56	55	54	53	52	51	50	49	48	47	46	45	44	43	42	41	40	39	38	37	36	35	34	33
0	0	1	1	1	1	1	1	1	1	1	0	1	1	0	0	1	1	0	0	1	1	0	0	1	1	0	0	1	1	0	0
	3				F				E			C				C				C				C				C			
S	E	E	E	E	E	E	E	E	E	E	E	F	F	F	F	F	F	F	F	F	F	F	F	F	F	F	F	F	F	F	F
	11-bits for exponent											52-bits for mantissa (Continued in the next table)																			

32	31	30	29	28	27	26	25	24	23	22	21	20	19	18	17	16	15	14	13	12	11	10	9	8	7	6	5	4	3	2	1
1	1	0	0	0	0	0	0	0	0	0	0	0	0	0	0	0	0	0	0	0	0	0	0	0	0	0	0	0	0	0	0
C				0				0				0				0				0				0				0			
F	F	F	F	F	F	F	F	F	F	F	F	F	F	F	F	F	F	F	F	F	F	F	F	F	F	F	F	F	F	F	F
(Continued from the previous table)																															

   Only 23 fraction bits are available in float. Therefore, when float is promoted to double, the rest of the fraction bits (shown in gray) will be taken as zero. Hence, when 0.9 as float is promoted to double, it becomes 3F EC CC CC C0 00 00 00.

This can be confirmed by running the below-mentioned piece of code:

```
main()
{
  float a=0.9;
  double c;
  int i;
  char *p;
  p=(char*)&a;
  printf("Float value is stored as:\t");
  for(i=0;i<=3;i++)
```

```
        printf("%02X ",(unsigned char)p[i]);
    printf("\n");
    printf("Now float is converted to double\n");
    c=a;
    p=(char*)&c;
    printf("Promoted value is getting stored as:\t");
    for(i=0;i<=7;i++)
        printf("%02X ",(unsigned char)p[i]);
}
```

6. **Comparison of double value and promoted float value**
   Therefore, when this promoted float value (Step No. 5) is compared with the actual double value (Step No. 3) with a less than operator, it results in 1 (i.e. true) because 3F EC CC CC C0 00 00 00 is lesser than 3F EC CC CC CC CC CC CD.

48. 0

Explanation:

0.5 as float will be stored as:

0	0	1	1	1	1	0	1	0	1	1	0	1	1	0	0	1	1	0	0	1	1	0	0	1	1	0	0	1	1	0	0
3				F				0				0				0				0				0				0			
S	E	E	E	E	E	E	E	E	F	F	F	F	F	F	F	F	F	F	F	F	F	F	F	F	F	F	F	F	F	F	F
	8-bits for exponent								23-bits for mantissa																						

0.5 as double will be stored as follows:

64	63	62	61	60	59	58	57	56	55	54	53	52	51	50	49	48	47	46	45	44	43	42	41	40	39	38	37	36	35	34	33
0	0	1	1	1	1	1	1	1	1	1	0	0	0	0	0	0	0	0	0	0	0	0	0	0	0	0	0	0	0	0	0
3				F				E				0				0				0				0				0			
S	E	E	E	E	E	E	E	E	E	E	E	F	F	F	F	F	F	F	F	F	F	F	F	F	F	F	F	F	F	F	F
	11-bits for exponent											52-bits for mantissa (Continued in the next table)																			

32	31	30	29	28	27	26	25	24	23	22	21	20	19	18	17	16	15	14	13	12	11	10	9	8	7	6	5	4	3	2	1
1	1	0	0	0	0	0	0	0	0	0	0	0	0	0	0	0	0	0	0	0	0	0	0	0	0	0	0	0	0	0	0
C				0				0				0				0				0				0				0			
F	F	F	F	F	F	F	F	F	F	F	F	F	F	F	F	F	F	F	F	F	F	F	F	F	F	F	F	F	F	F	F
(Continued from the previous table)																															

The fractional part in both the cases is zero. Therefore, when 0.5 as float is promoted to double, it becomes 3F E0 00 00 00 00 00 00. This promoted value is equal to double value (3F E0 00 00 00 00 00 00). Hence, the less than operator on comparison gives zero.

49. 0

Explanation:

0.9, a double value, is demoted to float and is assigned to a float variable a. 0.9f is also stored as a float. In the expression c=a<0.9f, float is compared with float. Loss of precision is the same in both the demotions. Hence, a<0.9f evaluates to 0 and is assigned to c.

Floating-point literal constant by default is of type double.

Backward Reference: Refer Section 1.11.2.1.2 (Floating Point Literal Constant) in Chapter 1 to review length modifiers.

50. 1 1

Explanation:

The logical OR operator || guarantees left-to-right evaluation. Thus, in the expression ++a==0||++b==11, the sub-expression ++a==0 will be evaluated first. a will be incremented by 1 and the sub-expression ++a evaluates to 1. The sub-expression ++a==0 (i.e. 1==0) evaluates to 0 (i.e. false). As the first operand of the logical OR operator is false, the second operand needs to be evaluated to determine the truth value of the full expression. Thus, the sub-expression ++b==11 will be evaluated. b is incremented by 1 and the expression ++b evaluates to 1. The sub-expression ++b==11 (i.e. 1==11) evaluates to 0, i.e. false. Both the operands of the logical OR operator have evaluated to 0. Thus, the full expression evaluates to zero. This outcome is not assigned to any variable and will be ignored. Hence, the values of a and b that get printed are 1 and 1.

51. 6

Explanation:

In expression 4+2%-8, the modulus operator has the highest precedence. The result of the modulus operator depends only upon the sign of the numerator. Thus, the sub-expression 2%-8 evaluates to 2. This outcome is added to 4 and is assigned to x. Therefore, x will have value 6.

52. 0

Explanation:

As the logical NOT operator (i.e. !) has a higher precedence than the greater than operator (>), it gets evaluated first. The sub-expression !i (i.e. !5) evaluates to 0. This outcome is compared with 3 and the sub-expression 0>3 evaluates to 0 (i.e. false). This outcome is assigned to i.

53. 20 20 20

Explanation:

The assignment operator is right-to-left associative. The sub-expression a*=2 (i.e. a=a*2) is evaluated first. It evaluates to 20 and is assigned to a. The value of a is then assigned to b and b will become 20. The value of b is assigned to c and c will also become 20. Hence, all a, b and c are 20.

54. fff0

Explanation:

-1 will be stored in memory as follows:
MSB will be 1 as the sign is negative. Magnitude will be two's complemented representation of 1, i.e. 111 1111 1111 1111. This value is shifted in the left direction by 4 bits and the outcome of the shift operation is as follows:

<table>
<tr><td rowspan="2">Operator and result</td><td>Sign bit 16 MSB</td><td colspan="15">Magnitude</td></tr>
<tr><td></td><td>Bit 15</td><td>Bit 14</td><td>Bit 13</td><td>Bit 12</td><td>Bit 11</td><td>Bit 10</td><td>Bit 9</td><td>Bit 8</td><td>Bit 7</td><td>Bit 6</td><td>Bit 5</td><td>Bit 4</td><td>Bit 3</td><td>Bit 2</td><td>Bit 1</td></tr>
<tr><td>-1</td><td>1</td><td>1</td><td>1</td><td>1</td><td>1</td><td>1</td><td>1</td><td>1</td><td>1</td><td>1</td><td>1</td><td>1</td><td>1</td><td>1</td><td>1</td><td>1</td></tr>
<tr><td>-1<<4</td><td>1</td><td>1</td><td>1</td><td>1</td><td>1</td><td>1</td><td>1</td><td>1</td><td>1</td><td>1</td><td>1</td><td>1</td><td>0</td><td>0</td><td>0</td><td>0</td></tr>
<tr><td>In Hexadecimal</td><td colspan="4">f</td><td colspan="4">f</td><td colspan="4">f</td><td colspan="4">0</td></tr>
</table>

55. 2

Explanation:

In the expression - -2, both the occurrences of - are instances of unary minus operator. It is right-to-left associative. The rightmost unary minus will first make 2 as -2. Then the second unary minus makes this -2 as 2. Therefore, the result will be 2.

56. Compilation error (l-value required)

Explanation:

-- is not the same as - -. It is one token (i.e. one operator, namely pre-decrement operator). The pre-decrement operator cannot operate on constants and requires an operand that has a modifiable l-value. In the given question, since -- is applied on constant, it shows 'L-value required' error.

57. 4 5 5 4 5

Explanation:

In Borland TC 3.0 and 4.5, arguments of printf function are evaluated from the right. The value of i is 5, so the sub-expression i evaluates to 5. In the sub-expression --i, the value of i is decremented to 4 and the sub-expression evaluates to 4. The sub-expression ++i increments the value of i to 5 and evaluates to 5. In the sub-expression i--, i is post-decremented. The sub-expression evaluates to 5 and then i is decremented to 4. In the sub-expression i++, i is post-incremented, so first the value of i (i.e. 4) will be used and then it is incremented to 5. After the evaluation of values, the printf function prints the values in a left-to-right order according to the given format specifiers. Therefore, the values that get printed are 4 5 5 4 5.

58. 200

Explanation:

200; is a valid statement but does nothing. In the next statement➲ 200 is printed by the printf function.

Forward Reference: Statements (Chapter 3).

59. -1 -1

Explanation:

In expression +i, + is unary plus✍ and will not have any effect on the value of i. It is not the same as ++i. In the next statement, the unmodified value of i gets printed. Hence, -1 -1 is the result.

✍ **Unary plus** does nothing and is known as the **Dummy operator.**

60. 0

Explanation:

2 is considered as true as it is a non-zero value. !TRUE evaluates to false, i.e. 0. The outcome is assigned to the identifier not. This value of the identifier not is printed in the next statement.

61. 1==1 is True

Explanation:

In Borland TC 3.0 and 4.5, arguments of the printf function are evaluated from the right. Thus, expression k==1?"True":"False" is evaluated first. The sub-expression k==1 evaluates to true, hence the result of the conditional operator turns out to be "True". Also, adjacent string literals get concatenated. Hence, "%d==1 is""%s" will get concatenated to form "%d==1 is %s". The integer specifier is matched with k, which has value 1, and the string specifier %s is matched with string "True". Hence, the result that gets printed is "1==1 is True".

62. Compilation error (Cannot modify a constant object)

Explanation:

The expression ++i is erroneous as i is defined as a qualified constant.

Qualified constants do not have a modifiable l-value. Hence, it cannot be used as the operand of an increment/decrement operator.

63. 1

Explanation:

First, the value of i is incremented by 1 and it becomes 6. 6 is compared for equality with 6 and evaluates to true, i.e. 1. This outcome is then assigned to i and gets printed.

64. 1 1

Explanation:

The logical AND operator && has a higher precedence than the assign-bitwise AND operator &=. The sub-expression j&&10 is evaluated first (i.e. 10&&10) and turns out to be true, i.e. 1. The sub-expression i&=1 is equivalent to i=i&1 (i.e. i=5&1). On evaluation it gives 1. Therefore, i will take value 1. This value of i is assigned to j. Hence, both i and j will have value 1.

65. 2695.000000 385.000000

Explanation:

y+28.5 is computed first and turns out to be 38.5. y*=38.5 is computed then and the value of y becomes 385.0. Then, x*=385.0 is computed and the value of x becomes 2695.0. Therefore, the values that get printed are 2695.000000 and 385.000000.

66. ffff

Explanation:

~a does not change the value of a. The value of a remains the same and gets printed as ffff.

67. 256

Explanation:

0x80 is 1000 0000, shifting by 1 bit in the left direction gives 1 0000 0000 and this is equivalent to 256 in decimal.

68. 65535 0

Explanation:

-1 will be stored in memory as follows:

Bit 16	Bit 15	Bit 14	Bit 13	Bit 12	Bit 11	Bit 10	Bit 9	Bit 8	Bit 7	Bit 6	Bit 5	Bit 4	Bit 3	Bit 2	Bit 1
1	1	1	1	1	1	1	1	1	1	1	1	1	1	1	1

i.e. all sixteen 1's. -1 is assigned to a. Therefore, a becomes

	Sign bit 16	Magnitude														
		Bit 15	Bit 14	Bit 13	Bit 12	Bit 11	Bit 10	Bit 9	Bit 8	Bit 7	Bit 6	Bit 5	Bit 4	Bit 3	Bit 2	Bit 1
a=-1	1	1	1	1	1	1	1	1	1	1	1	1	1	1	1	1
++a 1 (carry gets overflowed)	0	0	0	0	0	0	0	0	0	0	0	0	0	0	0	0

a is declared as unsigned. Therefore, the 16th bit is not considered as a sign bit but it is considered as a magnitude bit. Therefore, the value of a that gets printed is 65535. If one is added to a, carry overflows and the result turns out to be 0.

69. 4 3 3 3

Explanation:

In v=(int)(u+0.5), first 3.5+0.5 is evaluated and turns out to be 4.0. This is then type casted to the integer and becomes 4. 4 is then assigned to v.

In w=(int)u+0.5, first u is type casted to the integer, i.e. it becomes 3. Then 0.5 is added to make it 3.5. This value is then assigned to an integer variable. Before assignment, demotion will be carried out. 3.5 will be demoted to 3 and then assigned to w.

In x=(int)((int)u+0.5), x will get a value 3. Instead of implicitly demoting 3.5 to 3 as in the previous case, it is now explicitly type casted to 3.

In y=(u+(int)0.5), first 0.5 is type casted to 0. 0 is added to 3.5 and it comes out to be 3.5. 3.5 after implicit demotion is assigned to an integer variable y. Hence, the value assigned to y will be 3.

> Type casting can be done explicitly by using a type cast operator. The syntax of using a type cast operator is (target-type-name) expression.

70. 3 3 3 3

Explanation:

The identifier u is declared as int. Therefore, 3.5 will be demoted to 3 and will then be assigned to u. Hence, u will have the value 3 instead of 3.5. All the remaining computations are carried out in the same way as in the previous answer.

Answers to Multiple-choice Questions

71. a 72. c 73. a 74. d 75. a 76. b 77. b 78. a 79. b 80. a 81. c 82. c 83. b 84. b 85. a

Programming Exercises

Program 1 | Find one's and two's complement of a number

Algorithm:
Step 1: Start
Step 2: Read the number (num)
Step 3: One's complement (oc) = ~num i.e. negate every bit using bitwise NOT operator
Step 4: Two's complement (tc) = oc+1 i.e. two's complement is one's complement plus 1
Step 5: Print values of oc and tc
Step 6: Stop

PE 2-1.c

```
//One's and Two's complement
#include<stdio.h>
main()
{
    int num, oc, tc;
    printf("Enter number\t");
    scanf("%d",&num);
    oc=~num;
    tc=oc+1;
    printf("One's complement is %d\n",oc);
```

Memory content

num=2

B16	B15	B14	B13	B12	B11	B10	B9	B8	B7	B6	B5	B4	B3	B2	B1
0	0	0	0	0	0	0	0	0	0	0	0	0	0	1	0

oc = -3 (Two's complement representation)

B16	B15	B14	B13	B12	B11	B10	B9	B8	B7	B6	B5	B4	B3	B2	B1
1	1	1	1	1	1	1	1	1	1	1	1	1	1	0	1

Output window

```
Enter number    2
One's complement is -3
Two's complement is -2
```

Remarks:

- ~ is bitwise NOT operator
- The sign bits of oc and tc are 1. Hence, they are negative and are stored in two's-complement representation

(Contd...)

PE 2-1.c	Memory content	Output window
`printf("Two's complement is %d\n",tc);` `}`	tc = -2 (Two's complement representation)	

B16	B15	B14	B13	B12	B11	B10	B9	B8	B7	B6	B5	B4	B3	B2	B1
1	1	1	1	1	1	1	1	1	1	1	1	1	1	1	0

Program 2 | Assuming that bit numbering starts from 1. Write a C program to set a particular bit in a given number

Algorithm:

Step 1: Start

Step 2: Read the number (num)

Step 3: Read the bit number (bit) that is to be set (i.e. to be made 1) in the given number

Step 4: Construct a temporary number such that it has 1 at the bit position that is to be set in the given number and zero elsewhere. Temporary number can be constructed by using left-shift operator as temp=1<<(bit-1)

Step 5: To set the bit in the given number, perform bitwise OR of the number with the constructed temporary number and save result in the number i.e. num=num | temp

Step 6: Print number (num)

Step 7: Stop

PE 2-2.c

```
//Set particular bit in a given number
#include<stdio.h>
main()
{
int num, bit, temp;
printf("Enter number\t");
scanf("%d",&num);
printf("Enter the bit number to be set\t");
scanf("%d",&bit);
temp=1<<(bit-1);
num=num|temp;
printf("Value after setting bit is %d", num);
}
```

Memory content

num=5

B16	B15	B14	B13	B12	B11	B10	B9	B8	B7	B6	B5	B4	B3	B2	B1
0	0	0	0	0	0	0	0	0	0	0	0	0	1	0	1

After setting bit 2, the value of num becomes

B16	B15	B14	B13	B12	B11	B10	B9	B8	B7	B6	B5	B4	B3	B2	B1
0	0	0	0	0	0	0	0	0	0	0	0	0	1	1	1

i.e.7

Output window

```
Enter number    5
Enter the bit number to be set    2
Value after setting bit is 7
```

Program 3 | Assuming that bit numbering starts from 1. Write a C program to negate a particular bit in a given number

Algorithm:

Step 1: Start

Step 2: Read the number (num)

Step 3: Read the bit number (bit) that is to be negated (i.e. to be made 1 if it is 0 and vice-versa) in the given number

Step 4: Construct a temporary number such that it has 1 at the bit position that is to be negated in the given number and zero elsewhere. Temporary number can be constructed by using left-shiftoperator as temp=1<<(bit-1)

Step 5: To negate the bit in the given number, perform bitwise XOR of the number with the constructed temporary number and save result in the number i.e. num=num^temp

Step 6: Print number (num)

Step 7: Stop

(Contd...)

PE 2-3.c

```
//Negate a particular bit in a given number
#include<stdio.h>
main()
{
int num, bit, temp;
printf("Enter number\t");
scanf("%d",&num);
printf("Enter the bit number to be negated\t");
scanf("%d",&bit);
temp=1<<(bit-1);
num=num^temp;
printf("Value after negating bit is %d", num);
}
```

Memory content

num=5

B16	B15	B14	B13	B12	B11	B10	B9	B8	B7	B6	B5	B4	B3	B2	B1
0	0	0	0	0	0	0	0	0	0	0	0	0	1	0	1

After negating bit 2, the value of num becomes

B16	B15	B14	B13	B12	B11	B10	B9	B8	B7	B6	B5	B4	B3	B2	B1
0	0	0	0	0	0	0	0	0	0	0	0	0	1	1	1

i.e.7

num=5

B16	B15	B14	B13	B12	B11	B10	B9	B8	B7	B6	B5	B4	B3	B2	B1
0	0	0	0	0	0	0	0	0	0	0	0	0	1	0	1

After negating bit 3, the value of num becomes

B16	B15	B14	B13	B12	B11	B10	B9	B8	B7	B6	B5	B4	B3	B2	B1
0	0	0	0	0	0	0	0	0	0	0	0	0	0	0	1

i.e.1

Output window

```
Enter number 5
Enter the bit number to be negated 2
Value after negating bit is 7
```

Output window (second execution)

```
Enter number 5
Enter the bit number to be negated 3
Value after negating bit is 1
```

Program 4 | Given two numbers, say val and key. Wherever the bits of number key are 1, set the corresponding bits of number val. Leave all other bits of number val unchanged

Algorithm:

Step 1: Start
Step 2: Read the numbers, val and key
Step 3: val=val | key
Step 4: Print number (val)
Step 5: Stop

PE 2-4.c

```
//Set the corresponding bits
#include<stdio.h>
main()
{
int val, key;
printf("Enter two numbers\t");
scanf("%d %d",&val, &key);
val=val|key;
printf("After setting bits, result is %d",val);
}
```

Memory content

val=4

B16	B15	B14	B13	B12	B11	B10	B9	B8	B7	B6	B5	B4	B3	B2	B1
0	0	0	0	0	0	0	0	0	0	0	0	0	1	0	0

key = 10

B16	B15	B14	B13	B12	B11	B10	B9	B8	B7	B6	B5	B4	B3	B2	B1
0	0	0	0	0	0	0	0	0	0	0	0	1	0	1	0

After setting the corresponding bits, val becomes 14

B16	B15	B14	B13	B12	B11	B10	B9	B8	B7	B6	B5	B4	B3	B2	B1
0	0	0	0	0	0	0	0	0	0	0	0	1	1	1	0

Output window

```
Enter two numbers 4 10
After setting bits, result is 14
```

Output window (second execution)

```
Enter two numbers 4 5
After setting bits, result is 5
```

Program 5 | Given two numbers, say val and key. Wherever the bits of number key are 1, negate the corresponding bits of number val. Leave all other bits of number val unchanged

Algorithm:
Step 1: Start
Step 2: Read the numbers, val and key
Step 3: val=val^key
Step 4: Print number (val)
Step 5: Stop

PE 2-5.c

```c
//Negate the corresponding bits
#include<stdio.h>
main()
{
int val, key;
printf("Enter two numbers\t");
scanf("%d %d",&val, &key);
val=val^key;
printf("After negating bits, result is %d",val);
}
```

Memory content

val = 4

B16	B15	B14	B13	B12	B11	B10	B9	B8	B7	B6	B5	B4	B3	B2	B1
0	0	0	0	0	0	0	0	0	0	0	0	0	1	0	0

key = 5

B16	B15	B14	B13	B12	B11	B10	B9	B8	B7	B6	B5	B4	B3	B2	B1
0	0	0	0	0	0	0	0	0	0	0	0	0	1	0	1

After negating the corresponding bits, val becomes 1

B16	B15	B14	B13	B12	B11	B10	B9	B8	B7	B6	B5	B4	B3	B2	B1
0	0	0	0	0	0	0	0	0	0	0	0	0	0	0	1

Output window

```
Enter two numbers    2 5
After negating bits, result is 7
```

Output window (second execution)

```
Enter two numbers    4 5
After negating bits, result is 1
```

Program 6 | Given two numbers, say val and key. Wherever the bits of number key are 1, reset (i.e. make 0) the corresponding bits of number val. Leave all other bits of number val unchanged

Algorithm:
Step 1: Start
Step 2: Read the numbers, val and key
Step 3: Construct a temporary which is one's complement of the key i.e. temp=~key.
Step 4: val=val&temp
Step 5: Print number (val)
Step 6: Stop

PE 2-6.c

```c
//Reset the corresponding bits
#include<stdio.h>
main()
{
int val, key, temp;
printf("Enter two numbers\t");
scanf("%d %d",&val, &key);
temp=~key;
val=val&temp;
printf("After resetting bits, result is %d",val);
}
```

Memory content

val = 4

B16	B15	B14	B13	B12	B11	B10	B9	B8	B7	B6	B5	B4	B3	B2	B1
0	0	0	0	0	0	0	0	0	0	0	0	0	1	0	0

key = 5

B16	B15	B14	B13	B12	B11	B10	B9	B8	B7	B6	B5	B4	B3	B2	B1
0	0	0	0	0	0	0	0	0	0	0	0	0	1	0	1

After resetting the corresponding bits, val becomes 0

B16	B15	B14	B13	B12	B11	B10	B9	B8	B7	B6	B5	B4	B3	B2	B1
0	0	0	0	0	0	0	0	0	0	0	0	0	0	0	0

Output window

```
Enter two numbers    4 5
After resetting bits, result is 0
```

Output window (second execution)

```
Enter two numbers    2 5
After resetting bits, result is 2
```

Program 7 | Write a C program to multiply a given number with 2^n, without using a multiplication operator. The value of n will be entered by the user

Algorithm:

Step 1: Start
Step 2: Read a number (num).
Step 3: Input the value of n.
Step 4: To multiply number with 2^n, shift the bits of number in left direction n times i.e. res=num<<n
Step 5: Print number (res)
Step 6: Stop

PE 2-7.c

```
//Multiply by 2 raise to the power n
#include<stdio.h>
main()
{
int num, n, res;
printf("Enter number to be multiplied\t");
scanf("%d",&num);
printf("Enter value of n\t");
scanf("%d",&n);
res=num<<n;
printf("Result of multiplication is %d",res);
}
```

Memory content

val = 4

B16	B15	B14	B13	B12	B11	B10	B9	B8	B7	B6	B5	B4	B3	B2	B1
0	0	0	0	0	0	0	0	0	0	0	0	0	0	1	0

res = 16

B16	B15	B14	B13	B12	B11	B10	B9	B8	B7	B6	B5	B4	B3	B2	B1
0	0	0	0	0	0	0	0	0	0	0	1	0	0	0	0

Output window

```
Enter number to be multiplied    2
Enter value of n    3
Result of multiplication is    16
```

Remark:

- Left shift by n bits is equivalent to multiplication by 2^n, provided the magnitude does not overflow

Test Yourself

1. Fill in the blanks in each of the following:

   a. An __________ specifies an entity on which operation is to be performed.
   b. An expression that has only one operator is known as __________.
   c. Assignment operator is __________ associative.
   d. The operands of a modulus operator must be of __________ type.
   e. The result of evaluation of a relational expression is a __________ .
   f. In a compound expression, if operators of different precedence appear together, the operator of __________ precedence operates first.
   g. The order in which operators operate depends upon the __________ and the __________ of the operators.
   h. If the operands of an operator are of different types, C automatically applies __________ to bring the operands to a common type.
   i. The __________ operator returns the number of bytes the operand occupies.
   j. __________ operator has least precedence.

2. State whether each of the following is true or false. If false, explain why.

   a. The operators with the same precedence always have the same associativity.
   b. The multiplication and division operators are left-to-right associative.
   c. The sign of the result of evaluation of the modulus operator depends upon the sign of both the numerator as well as the denominator.
   d. The knowledge of precedence alone is sufficient to evaluate a compound expression.
   e. Conditional operator is a binary operator.
   f. The increment operator can only be applied to an operand that has a modifiable l-value.
   g. The expression `++a` is equivalent to `a+=1`.
   h. In C language, there is no operator available for logical eXclusive-OR (XOR) operation.
   i. Qualified constant cannot be initialized with a value.
   j. The expression `!(x>=y)` is equivalent to the expression `x<y`.

3. Find the result of evaluation for the following expressions:

   a. `5*3/4-2`
   b. `~5+3&&2`
   c. `4-5&&!2`
   d. `2<<2>>2`
   e. `2<<2>2`
   f. `2<3,4,5*3+2`
   g. `5 != 10 && 2 | 3&5`
   h. `2?2^2:2|5`
   i. `3?~2?~5:4:3`
   j. `+2.25+-3.85`

4. Which of the following expressions are valid? If valid, find the result of evaluation of expressions, assuming identifiers `a` and `b` are defined and their values are `a=10` and `b=15`. If invalid, identify the errors.

   a. a+++b=20
   b. a=b==12==b
   c. ++a=23*5-4
   d. b=7.5%2.5

e. 2==3+5+=6
f. 2*3/2.0&3
g. a+++++b
h. ~2~3^4
i. a^=b^=10
j. a&&=10

3

STATEMENTS

Learning Objectives

In this chapter, you will learn about:

- Statements
- How statements are classified
- Non-executable statements and executable statements
- Simple statements and compound statements
- Declaration statement and definition statement
- Null statement and expression statements
- Labeled statements
- Flow control statements
- How to implement decision making
- Selection statements and jump statements
- How to perform iteration
- Iteration statements
- Role of `break` and `continue` statements
- Graphical representation of flow of control

3.1 Introduction

In the last chapter, you have learnt how to form and evaluate expressions. In C language, the expressions do not have any independent existence. To make them exist, they must be converted into statements. A **statement** is the smallest logical entity that can independently exist in a C program. In this chapter, I will tell you how to convert expressions into statements. I will also describe how statements are executed, how to make decisions with the help of branching statements and how to make a set of statements execute a number of times by using iteration statements. Finally, we will look at how various statements can be used in conjunction to perform meaningful tasks.

3.2 Statements

A **statement** is the smallest logical entity that can independently exist in a C program. No entity smaller than a statement, i.e. expressions, variables, constants, etc. can independently exist in a C program unless and until they are converted into statements. The code snippet in Program 3-1 proves the above-mentioned fact.

Line | Prog 3-1.c

```
1  //Expressions cannot exist independently
2  #include<stdio.h>
3  main()
4  {
5      int a;
6      a=2+3
7      printf("Value of a is %d",a);
8  }
```

Output window

Compilation error "Statement missing ; in function main"

Reason:

- Expression in line 6 cannot exist independently. It should be a part of some statement

What to do?

- Convert expression a=2+3 into a statement by terminating it with a semicolon and re-execute the code

Program 3-1 | A program to illustrate that an expression cannot exist independently

A statement in a programming language is analogous to a sentence in a natural language. Just as sentences are terminated with a period (i.e. full stop) in the English language, statements in C language are terminated with a semicolon. When an expression is terminated with a semicolon, it forms an **expression statement**. For example, a=2+3 is an expression. When it is terminated with a semicolon, it forms an expression statement, i.e. a=2+3;. Expression statements are classified according to the type of operator involved in the expression. Since an assignment operator is involved in the expression statement a=2+3;, it can be called an **assignment statement**. Moreover, as an arithmetic operator (+) is also involved in the expression statement a=2+3;, it can also be called an **arithmetic statement**.

3.3 Classification of Statements

Statements in C are classified according to the following criteria:

1. Based upon the type of action they perform
2. Based upon the number of constituent statements
3. Based upon their role

3.3.1 Based Upon the Type of Action they Perform

A statement specifies an action to be performed. Based upon the type of action it performs, the statements in C are classified into the following:

1. Non-executable statements
2. Executable statements

3.3.1.1 Non-executable Statements

Non-executable statements tell the compiler how to build a program. The important points about non-executable statements are listed as follows:

1. These statements help the compiler to determine how to allocate memory, interpret and compile other statements in a program.
2. These statements are intended mainly for the compiler, and no machine code is generated for them. Only executable[†] statements play a role during the execution of a program.
3. The order in which non-executable statements appear in a program is important. When a compiler compiles a program, it scans all the statements from top to bottom. A non-executable statement can only affect the statements that appear below it. Thus, a non-executable statement should appear only before executable statements within a block. [‡]
4. Only non-executable statements can appear outside the body of a function.➲
5. Examples of non-executable statements are function prototypes,➲ global variable➲ declarations, constant declarations and preprocessor directive➲ statements.

Although the separation between executable and non-executable statements is simple and effective, it was rather rigid earlier. This rigidity was relaxed in the C99 standard, and flexibility in terms of freely mixing executable and non-executable statements was provided.

Forward Reference: Function and function prototype (Chapter 5), global variables (Chapter 7), preprocessor directives (Chapter 8).

3.3.1.2 Executable Statements

Executable statements represent the instructions that are to be performed when the program is executed. The important points about executable statements are listed as follows:

1. For an executable statement, some machine code is generated by the compiler.
2. An executable statement can appear only inside the body of a function.
3. The examples of executable statements are assignment statements, branching statements, looping statements, function call statements, etc.
4. A global definition like `const int obj=10;` appears to be an executable statement, but it is a non-executable statement.

The code segment in Program 3-2, if compiled with compilers conforming to pre-C99 standards, illustrates the fact that within a block, non-executable statements can appear only before an executable statement.

[†] Refer Section 3.3.1.2 for a description on executable statements.

[‡] Refer Section 3.3.2.2 for a description on blocks.

Line | Prog 3-2.c

```
1 //Executable and Non-executable statements
2 #include<stdio.h>
3 #include<conio.h>
4 main()
5 {
6     clrscr();
7     int a=10;
8     printf("Value of a is %d",a);
9 }
```

Output window

Compilation error "Declaration is not allowed here"

Remarks:

- Borland TC 3.0 generates this error but some compilers (like Borland TC 4.5 and other latest compilers) do not enforce this constraint and does not produce an error
- File must be saved with .C extension and not with .CPP extension

Reason:

- Line 6 is an executable statement but line 7 is a non-executable statement. If a compiler conforming to pre-C99 standards is used, non-executable statements can appear only before executable statements

What to do?

- Interchange lines 6 and 7 and re-execute the code

Program 3-2 | A program that emphasizes on the order of occurrence of executable and non-executable statements

The code snippet in Program 3-3 illustrates the fact that executable statements can appear only inside the body of a function while non-executable statements can even appear outside the body of a function, i.e. in global scope.

Line | Prog 3-3.c

```
1 //Executable and Non-executable statements
2 #include<stdio.h>
3 #include<conio.h>
4 int a=10;
5 a=a*2;
6 main()
7 {
8     printf("Value of a is %d",a);
9 }
```

Output window

Compilation error "Type name expected"

Reason:

- Line 5 is an executable statement. Executable statements can appear only inside the body of a function, i.e. in local scope. Hence, line 5 leads to the compilation error

What to do?

- Place content of lines 5 after line 7 and re-execute the code

Program 3-3 | A program to show that executable statements can appear only inside the body of a function

3.3.2 Based Upon the Number of Constituent Statements

Based upon the number of constituent statements, statements in C language are classified as follows:

1. Simple statements
2. Compound statements

3.3.2.1 Simple Statements

A **simple statement** consists of a single statement. It is terminated with a semicolon. Examples of simple statements are as follows:

1. `int variable=10;` //←definition statement
2. `variable+5;` //←expression statement
3. `variable=variable+10;` //←assignment statement

3.3.2.2 Compound Statements

A **compound statement** consists of a sequence of simple statements enclosed within a pair of braces. An example of a compound statement is as follows:

```
{                      //← a compound statement consisting of three simple statements
int variable=10;
variable=variable*2;
variable+=5;
}
```

The important points about compound statements are listed below:

1. A compound statement is also known as a **block**.
2. A compound statement need not be terminated with a semicolon. However, if it is terminated with a semicolon, there will be no compilation error but it will be interpreted in a different way.[§]
3. A compound statement can be empty, i.e. there is no simple statement present inside the pair of braces, like {}. An empty compound statement is equivalent to a null[¶] statement, but it cannot act as a terminator for a statement. Figure 3.1 illustrates the interpretation of this fact.

`if(a==b) { }`	Equivalent to →	`if(a==b) ;  //←null statement`	Valid as {} is equivalent to null statement (i.e.;)
`printf("Hello"){}`	Not equivalent to →	`printf("Hello");`	Invalid as {} cannot act as a terminator

Figure 3.1 | Empty compound statement acts as a null statement but not as a terminator

4. A compound statement is treated as a single unit. If there is no jump[††] statement present inside the block, all the constituent simple statements will be executed in a sequence if the program control enters the block.
5. A compound statement can appear at any point in a program wherever a simple statement can appear.
6. In a block, non-executable statements (e.g. declaration statements) should come before executable statements.

[§] Refer Section 3.3.3.2 for a description on how a compound statement terminated with a semicolon is interpreted.

[¶] Refer Section 3.3.3.2 for a description on null statement.

[††] Refer Section 3.3.3.4.1.2 for a description on jump statements.

Curly brackets, i.e. {}, are known as **braces.**

3.3.3 Based Upon their Role

Based upon their role, statements are classified as follows:

1. Declaration statement and definition statement
2. Null statement and expression statement
3. Labeled statements
4. Flow control statements
   a. Branching statements
      i. Selection statements
      ii. Jump statements
   b. Iteration statements

3.3.3.1 Declaration Statement and Definition Statement

The role of a **declaration statement** is to introduce the name of an identifier along with its data type to the compiler before its use. All identifier names (except label names) need to be declared before they are used. During declaration, no memory is allocated to an identifier. The memory space for an identifier can be reserved by using a **definition statement**. The definition statement declares an identifier and also reserves the memory space for it depending upon its data type. For example, `int a;` is a definition statement, which reserves 2 bytes (or 4 bytes) for `a` in the memory. To declare `a`, write `extern int a;`.

Forward Reference: `extern`, storage class specifiers (Chapter 7).

3.3.3.2 Null Statement and Expression Statements

A **null statement** just consists of a semicolon. For example:

```
;        //← is a null statement
```

A null statement is the simplest form of program statement and **performs no operation.** It is just used as a place-holder, i.e. it is used when the syntax of a language construct requires a statement to be present, but the logic of a program does not require it. A null statement is equivalent to an empty compound statement, i.e. {}. A compound statement need not be terminated with a semicolon. However, if it is terminated with a semicolon, it is interpreted as a compound statement followed by a null statement. Figure 3.2 illustrates the interpretation of a compound statement, which is terminated with a semicolon.

Computations in C language are performed with the help of expression statements. An expression terminated with a semicolon forms an **expression statement**. For example:

```
a=2+3;    //← is an expression statement
```

Expression statements like `printf("Hello Readers");` in which the function call operator (i.e. ( )) is involved are called **function call statements** or **function invocations.**

A compound statement terminated with a semicolon	is interpreted as	two statements, i.e. a compound statement followed by a null statement

{
int variable=10;
variable=variable*2;
variable+=5;
};
	Equivalent to	{
		int variable=10;
		variable=variable*2;
		variable+=5;
		}
		;

Figure 3.2 | Interpretation of a compound statement terminated with a semicolon

3.3.3.3 Labeled Statements

Labeled statements are rarely used in isolation. They have practical significance only when they are used in conjunction with branching statements. In the following sub-sections, the syntax of labeled statements is described. Their practical application will be discussed along with the branching statements.[††] Labeled statements are of three types:

1. Identifier-labeled statements
2. Case-labeled statements
3. Default-labeled statements

> *i* Practically, an identifier-labeled statement is used in conjunction with a `goto`[§§] statement. Case-labeled and default-labeled statements are useful only when they are used in conjunction with a `switch`[¶¶] statement.

3.3.3.3.1 Identifier-labeled Statements

The general form of an **identifier-labeled statement** is:

```
identifier: statement
```

The important points about identifier-labeled statements are listed below:

1. The identifier used in an identifier-labeled statement is called a **label name**. For example, in the following identifier-labeled statement, `lab` is the label name:

```
lab: printf ("Labeled statement");
```

2. Unlike other identifiers, i.e. variable names, function names, etc., label names are not explicitly declared by using declaration statements. They are not explicitly declared because:
   a. There is no type associated with them.
   b. No operation is allowed on them. Unlike other identifiers, they cannot be used as an operand in an expression.
3. Label names are implicitly (i.e. automatically) declared by their syntactic appearance, i.e. an identifier followed by a colon and a statement is implicitly treated as a label name.
4. The statement after the label name in an identifier-labeled statement can be any statement, even some another labeled statement. For example, the following statement is an identifier-labeled statement whose constituent statement is another identifier-labeled statement.

[††] Refer Section 3.3.3.4.1 for a description on branching statements.
[§§] Refer Section 3.3.3.4.1.2.1 for a description on `goto` statement.
[¶¶] Refer Section 3.3.3.4.1.1.5 for a description on `switch` statement.

```
label1:        //←An identifier-labeled statement whose
    label2:    //←Constituent statement is another identifier-labeled statement
        printf("Identifier labeled statement's statement is another identifier labeled statement");
```

5. Label name should be unique within a function.
6. Label names do not alter the flow of control.[†††]
7. Identifier-labeled statements have practical significance only when they are used in conjunction with a goto statement.

The piece of code in Program 3-4 illustrates that label names do not impede the flow of control.

Prog 3-4.c

```
//Identifier labeled statements
#include<stdio.h>
main()
{
    label1:
        label2:
            printf("Identifier labeled statement");
}
```

Output window

Identifier labeled statement

Remarks:

- Label names do not alter the flow of control
- label1 followed by label2, followed by the printf statement is one statement. Thus, the mentioned code has only one simple statement

Program 3-4 | A program to illustrate that label names do not alter the flow of control

3.3.3.3.2 Case-labeled Statements

The general form of a **case labeled statement** is:

case constant-expression: statement

The important points about case labeled statements are as follows:

1. A case-labeled statement consists of the keyword case followed by a constant expression (i.e. **case label**), followed by a colon and then a statement. An example of a valid case-labeled statement is as follows:

   case 2: printf("case labeled statement");

2. The case label should be a compile time constant expression of integral type. For example, the following case-labeled statements are valid:

   a. case 2+3: printf("Valid"); //←2+3 is compile time constant expression of int type
   b. case a: printf("Valid"); //←where a is qualified constant of integral type
   c. case 'A': printf("Valid"); //←'A' is a character constant

   The following case-labeled statements are not valid:

   a. case j: printf("Invalid"); //←j is variable and not a constant
   b. case 2.5: printf("Invalid"); //←2.5 is an expression of float type and not of integral type

3. Case-labeled statements can appear only inside the body of a switch[‡‡‡] statement.

[†††] Refer Section 3.3.3.4 for a description on flow of control and flow control statements.
[‡‡‡] Refer Section 3.3.3.4.1.1.5 for a description on switch statement.

4. The constituting statement of a case-labeled statement can be any statement, even some other case-labeled statement with a different case label. For example, a case-labeled statement whose constituent statement is another case-labeled statement having a different case label is as follows:

```
case 1:         //←Case-labeled statement whose
    case 2:     //←Constituent statement is another case-labeled statement
        printf("Case labeled statement's statement is another case labeled statement");
```

3.3.3.3.3 Default-labeled Statements

The general form of a **default labeled statement** is:

default: statement

The important points about default labeled statements are as follows:

1. A default-labeled statement consists of the keyword default followed by a colon and a statement.
2. A default-labeled statement can appear only inside the body of a switch statement.
3. The constituting statement of a default-labeled statement can be any statement except the default-labeled statement. If a default-labeled statement is the constituting statement of another default-labeled statement, it leads to 'Too many default cases' compilation error. For example, the following default-labeled statement is not valid:

```
default:        //←Default-labeled statement cannot have another default-labeled statement
    default:
        printf("This is not valid");
```

3.3.3.4 Flow Control Statements

By default, statements in a C program are executed in a sequential order. The order in which the program statements are executed is known as **'flow of program control'** or just **'flow of control'**. By default, the program control flows sequentially from top to bottom. All the programs that we have developed till now have default flow of control. Many practical situations like decision making, repetitive execution of a certain task, etc. require deviation or alteration from the default flow of program control. The default flow of control can be altered by using **flow control statements.** Flow control statements are of two types:

1. Branching statements
   a. Selection statements
   b. Jump statements
2. Iteration statements

3.3.3.4.1 Branching Statements

Branching statements are used to transfer the program control from one point to another. They are categorized as:

1. Conditional branching: In **conditional branching**, also known as **selection**, program control is transferred from one point to another based upon the outcome of a certain condition. The following **selection statements** are available in C: if statement, if-else statement and switch statement.
2. Unconditional branching: In **unconditional branching**, also known as **jumping**, program control is transferred from one point to another without checking any condition. The following **jump statements** are available in C: goto statement, break statement, continue statement and return statement.

3.3.3.4.1.1 Selection Statements

Based upon the outcome of a particular condition, **selection statements** transfer control from one point to another. Selection statements select a statement to be executed among a set of various statements. The selection statements available in C are as follows:

1. if statement
2. if-else statement
3. switch statement

3.3.3.4.1.1.1 if Statement

The general form of **if statement** is:

```
if(expression)      //←if header
statement           //←if body
```

The important points about an if statement are as follows:

1. An if statement consists of an if header and an if body.
2. An if header consists of an if clause followed by an **if controlling expression** enclosed within parentheses.
3. An if statement is executed as follows:
   a. The if controlling expression is evaluated.
   b. If the if controlling expression evaluates to true, the statement constituting if body is executed.
   c. If the if controlling expression evaluates to false, if body is skipped and the execution continues from the statement following the if statement.
4. The syntax of an if statement permits only a single statement to be associated with if header. Practical applications often require that the execution of two or more statements should depend upon the outcome of a particular condition. In such cases, the dependent statements should be clubbed together to form a compound statement. This concept is clarified with the help of the code snippet listed in Program 3-5 and its corresponding flow chart.

Line	Prog 3-5.c	Flow chart depicting the flow of control in program	Output window

1
2
3
4
5
6
7
8
9
	//if statement
	#include<stdio.h>
	main()
	{
	int a=5, b=10;
	if(a>10 && a>b)
	    printf("a is greater than 10");
	    printf("a is greater than b");
	}
		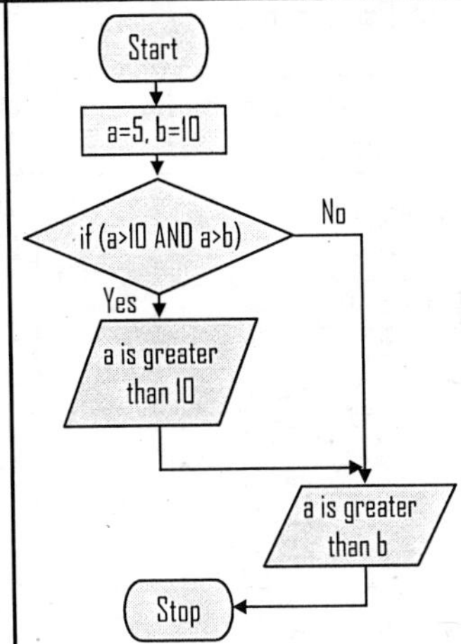	a is greater than b
			Reasons:
			• Only one statement can be associated with if header
			• Irrespective of the indentation made in the program, printf statement in line 8 is not associated with the if header and is not dependent upon the result of evaluation of if controlling expression
			• Statement in line 8 is statement next to if statement and will always be executed irrespective of the outcome of if controlling expression
			What to do?
			• Club statements in lines 7 and 8 into one compound statement as shown in Program 3-6

Program 3-5 | A program to illustrate the execution of if statement

Line	Prog 3-6.c	Flow chart depicting the flow of control in program	Output window

1
2
3
4
5
6
7
8
9
10
11
	//if statement
	#include<stdio.h>
	main()
	{
	int a=5, b=10;
	if(a>10 && a>b)
	{
	    printf("a is greater than 10");
	    printf("a is greater than b");
	}
	}
		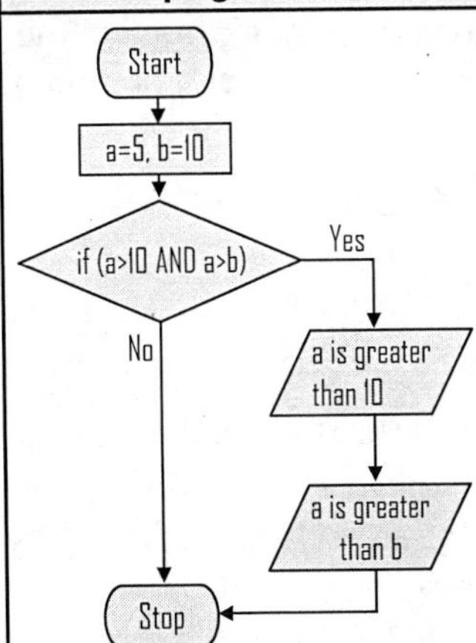	No output
			Reasons:
			• Lines 7–10 constitute a compound statement
			• The execution of both the statements in lines 8 and 9 is dependent upon the result of evaluation of if controlling expression
			• Since the if controlling expression evaluates to false, statements in lines 8 and 9 do not get executed

Program 3-6 | A program to illustrate the execution of if statement

5. No semicolon should be placed at the end of the if header. However, if a semicolon is placed at the end of the if header, there will be no compilation error (although this may

lead to logical error). This is one of the potential logical errors most amateur programmers do. The logical error due to the semicolon placed at the end of the if header is depicted in the code listed in Program 3-7.

Prog 3-7.c	Flow chart depicting the flow of control in program	Output window

//if statement
#include<stdio.h>
main()
{
int a=10, b=20;
if(a==b);
printf("a is not equal to b");
}
	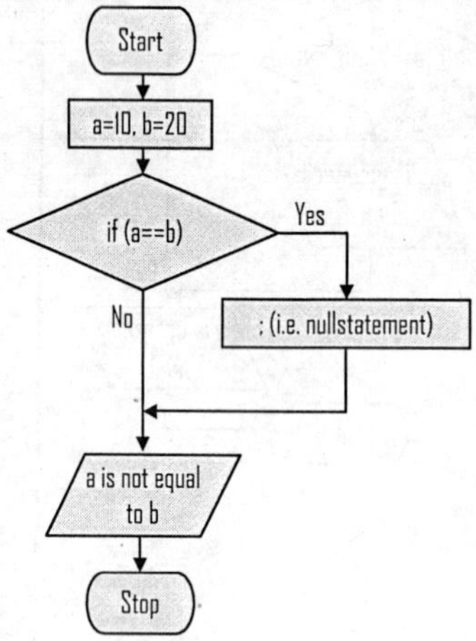	a is not equal to b
		Expected output:
		No output
		Reason for deviation:
		Presence of semicolon at the end of the if header
		How is the listed code interpreted?
		• It is interpreted as:
		if(a==b)
		;
		printf("a is not equal to b");
		• if body is a null statement
		• printf statement is next to the if statement and its execution does not depend upon the outcome of if controlling expression

Program 3-7 | A program to illustrate the effect of the semicolon placed at the end of the if header

3.3.3.4.1.1.2 if-else Statement

Most of the problems require one set of actions to be performed if a particular condition is true, and another set of actions to be performed if the condition is false. To implement such a decision, C language provides an **if-else statement**. The general form of the if-else statement is:

```
if(expression)      //←if-else header
statement1          //←if body
else                //←else clause
statement2          //←else body
```

The important points about an if-else statement are as follows:

1. An if-else statement consists of an if-else header, if body, else clause and else body.
2. An if-else header consists of an if clause followed by an **if-else controlling expression** enclosed within parentheses.
3. An if-else statement is executed as follows:
    a. The if-else controlling expression is evaluated.
    b. If the if-else controlling expression evaluates to true, the statement constituting the if body is executed and the else body is skipped.
    c. If the if-else controlling expression evaluates to false, the if body is skipped and the else body is executed.

d. After the execution of the if body or the else body, the execution continues from the statement following the if-else statement.

The code snippet in Program 3-8 illustrates the use of the if-else statement.

Prog 3-8.c

```
//if-else statement
//Find whether no. is even or odd
#include<stdio.h>
main()
{
int a=11;
if(a%2==0)
    printf("Number a is even");
else
    printf("Number a is odd");
}
```

Flow chart depicting the flow of control in program

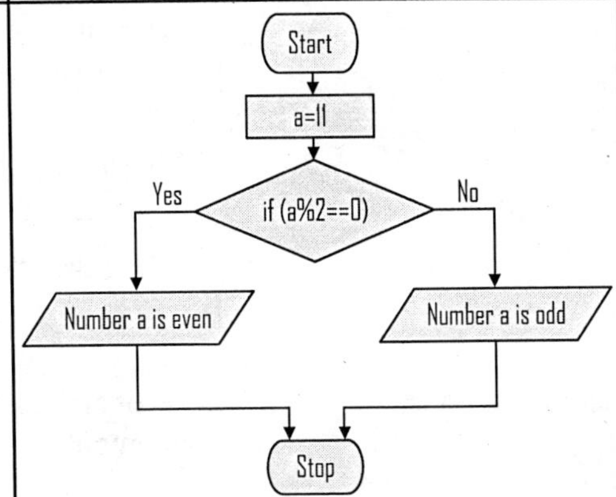

Output window

Number a is odd

Remarks:

- The if-else controlling expression a%2==0 evaluates to false
- The if body is skipped and the else body gets executed

Program 3-8 | A program to illustrate the use of the if-else statement

4. The syntax of if-else statement permits only a single statement to be associated with if clause and else clause. However, this single statement can be a compound statement constituting a number of simple statements. Consider the piece of code in Program 3-9.

Prog 3-9.c

```
1  //if-else statement
2  #include<stdio.h>
3  main()
4  {
5  int a=11;
6  if(a>10)
7      printf("The value of a is %d",a);
8      printf("Value a is greater than 10");
9  else
10     printf("Value a is less than 10");
11 }
```

Output window

Compilation error "Misplaced else in function main"

Reasons:

- Only a single statement can be associated with if clause and else clause
- The mentioned code is interpreted as:

```
if(a>10)                          //←if statement
    printf("The value of a is %d",a);
printf("Value a is greater than 10"); //←statement next to if statement
else                              //←else clause without any matching if clause
    printf("Value a is less than 10");
```

- else clause cannot exist without a matching if clause

What to do?

- Club statements in lines 7 and 8 into one compound statement and re-execute the code

Program 3-9 | A program to illustrate the use of the if-else statement

5. Care must be taken that no semicolon is placed at the end of the if-else header or after the else clause.

3.3.3.4.1.1.3 Nested if Statement

If the body of the if statement is another if statement or contains another if statement (as shown below), then we say that if's are nested and the statement is known as a **nested if statement**. The general form of a nested if statement is:

```
if(expression)
    if statement
```

or

```
if(expression)          //←nested if statement
{       statement
        -------------
        if statement
        -------------
        statement
}
```

(a) Body of an **if** statement is another **if** statement

(b) Body of an **if** statement contains another **if** statement

This nesting can be done up to any level as shown below:

```
if(expression1)
        if(expression2)
                if(expression-n)
                        statement
```

The above structure seems to form a ladder and is known as the **if ladder**.

> The number of levels up to which nesting can be done depends upon the translation limits of the compiler. The translation limits constrain the implementation of language translators and libraries.

Forward Reference: Translation limits mentioned in ANSI specifications (Appendix C).

3.3.3.4.1.1.4 Nested if-else Statement

In a **nested if-else statement**, the if body or else body of an if-else statement is, or contains, another if statement or if-else statement. Program 3-10 illustrates the use of a nested if-else statement to find the greatest of three numbers.

The careless use of a nested if-else statement introduces a source of potential ambiguity referred to as the **dangling else ambiguity**. When **a statement** contains more number of if clauses than else clauses, then there exists a potential ambiguity regarding with which if clause does the else clause properly matches up. This ambiguity is known as **dangling else problem**. The code listed in the column 1 of Table 3.1 suffers from a dangling else problem. The other columns in the table show the two possible interpretations of the code listed in column 1.

Prog 3-10.c	Flow chart depicting the flow of control in program	Output window

//Nested if-else statement
#include<stdio.h>
main()
{
int a, b, c;
printf("Enter three numbers\t");
scanf("%d %d %d",&a,&b,&c);
if(a>b)
{ //←if body starts
    if(a>c)
        printf("%d is greatest", a);
    else
        printf("%d is greatest",c);
}//←if body ends
else
{//←else body starts
    if(b>c)
        printf("%d is greatest",b);
    else
        printf("%d is greatest",c);
}//←else body ends
}
	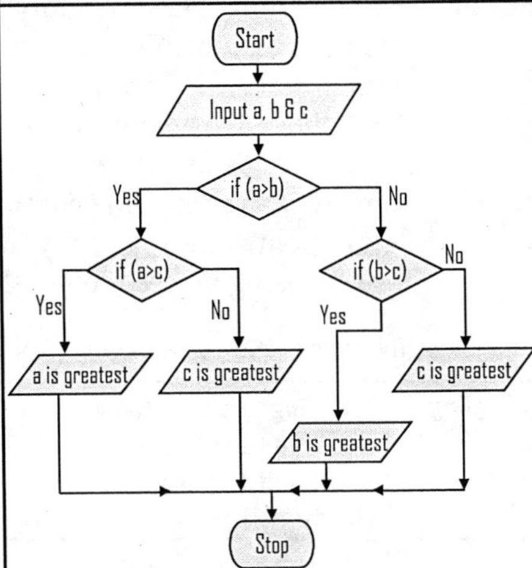	Enter three numbers 1 4 2
		4 is greatest
		Remarks:
		• The program illustrates the use of nested if-else statement
		• Both if body and else body of if-else statement consists of if-else statement

Program 3-10 | A program that uses a nested if-else statement to find the greatest of three numbers

Table 3.1 | The code in column 1 suffers from dangling else ambiguity. Columns 2 and 3 depict the two possible interpretations of the code listed in column 1

Code suffering from dangling else problem (Column 1)	Interpretation-I (Column 2)	Interpretation-II (Column 3)

//Dangling else problem
#include<stdio.h>
main()
{
int a=10, b=20;
if(a==100)
if(b==20)
printf("Match-I");
else
printf("Match-II");
}
	//Interpretation-I
	#include<stdio.h>
	main()
	{
	int a=10, b=20;
	if(a==100)
	    if(b==20)
	        printf("Match-I");
	else
	    printf("Match-II");
	}
		//Interpretation-II
		#include<stdio.h>
		main()
		{
		int a=10, b=20;
		if(a==100)
		    if(b==20)
		        printf("Match-I");
		    else
		        printf("Match-II");
		}

Output	**If interpreted in this way, the output would be:**	**If interpreted in this way, the output would be:**
No output	Match-II	No output

The dangling else problem is solved in two ways:

1. **Implicitly by compiler:** The dangling else ambiguity is implicitly resolved by the compiler by matching the else clause with the last occurring unmatched if, i.e. interpreted in a way as shown in column 3 of Table 3.1. The outputs in columns 1 and 3 are the same. This indicates that the code in column 1 is interpreted in the same way as shown in column 3 of Table 3.1.
2. **Explicitly by user:** The dangling else ambiguity can be explicitly removed by the user by using braces. This is shown in Table 3.2.

Table 3.2 | Dangling else ambiguity removed explicitly by the user

Code suffering from dangling else problem (Column 1)	Dangling else ambiguity removed from the code listed in column 1 by using braces (Column 2)	Dangling else ambiguity removed from the code listed in column 1 by using braces (Column 3)

//Dangling else problem
#include<stdio.h>
main()
{
int a=10, b=20;
if(a==100)
if(b==20)
printf("Match-I");
else
printf("Match-II");
}
	//Dangling else problem
	#include<stdio.h>
	main()
	{
	int a=10, b=20;
	if(a==100)
	{
	    if(b==20)
	        printf("Match-I");
	}
	else
	    printf("Match-II");
	}
		//Dangling else problem
		#include<stdio.h>
		main()
		{
		int a=10, b=20;
		if(a==100)
		{
		    if(b==20)
		        printf("Match-I");
		    else
		        printf("Match-II");
		}
		}

Output	**Output**	**Output**
No output	Match-II	No output

3.3.3.4.1.1.5 switch Statement

A **switch statement** is used to control complex branching operations. When there are many conditions, it becomes too difficult and complicated to use if and if-else constructs. In such cases, the switch statement provides an easy and organized way to select among multiple options, depending upon the outcome of a particular condition. The general form of a switch statement is:

```
switch(expression)        //←switch header
statement                 //←switch body
```

The important points about a switch statement are as follows:

1. A switch statement consists of a switch header and a switch body.
2. A switch header consists of the keyword switch followed by a switch selection expression enclosed within parentheses.

3. The switch selection expression must be of integral type (i.e. integer type or character type).
4. The switch body consists of a statement. The statement constituting a switch body can be a null statement, an expression statement, a labeled statement, a flow control statement, a compound statement, etc.
5. Generally, a switch body consists of a compound statement, whose constituent statements are case-labeled statements, expression statements, flow control statements and an optional default-labeled statement.
6. Case labels of case-labeled statements constituting the body of a switch statement should be unique, i.e. no two case labels should have or evaluate to the same value.
7. There can be at most one default labeled statement within the switch body.
8. A switch statement is executed as follows:
    a. The switch selection expression is evaluated.
    b. The result of evaluation of switch selection expression is compared with the case labels of the case-labeled statements until there is a match or until all the case-labeled statements have been examined.
        i. If the result of evaluation of switch selection expression is matched with the case label of a case-labeled statement, the execution starts from the matched case-labeled statement, and all the statements after the matched case-labeled statement within the switch body gets executed.
        ii. If no case label of case-labeled statements within the switch body matches the result of evaluation of switch selection expression, the execution starts with the default-labeled statement, if it is present, and all the statements after the default-labeled statement within the switch body gets executed.
        iii. If none of the case labels match the result of evaluation of switch selection expression and there is no default-labeled statement present within the switch body, no statement within the switch body will be executed and the execution continues from the statement following the switch statement.

---

i It is a common misunderstanding that only the matched case-labeled statement or the default-labeled statement (if none of the case labels match) gets executed. In fact, the execution begins with the matched case labeled statement or the default labeled statement, and all the statements after the matched case labeled statement or the default labeled statement within the switch body get executed.

The code snippets in Programs 3-11 to 3-13 clarify the points discussed above.

Prog 3-11.c

```
//switch statement
#include<stdio.h>
main()
{
```

Output window

```
This is case option 1
Value of a is 1
This is case option 2
This is default option
```

(Contd...)

Prog 3-11.c

```
int a=1;
switch(a)
{
case 1:
    printf("This is case option 1\n");
    printf("Value of a is %d\n",a);
case 2:
    printf("This is case option 2\n");
default:
    printf("This is default option\n");
}
}
```

Output window

Remarks:

- A switch body consists of four statements and is interpreted as:

```
{
case 1:                              //←Statement 1: case-labeled statement
    printf("This is case option 1\n");
printf("Value of a is %d\n",a);  //←Statement 2: function call statement
case 2:                              //←Statement 3: case-labeled statement
    printf("This is case option 2\n");
default:                             //←Statement 4: default-labeled statement
    printf("This is default option\n");
}
```

- Since case label 1 matches the result of evaluation of switch selection expression, the execution starts from the statement with the case label 1, and all the statements after it within the switch body gets executed

Program 3-11 | A program to illustrate the working of a switch statement

Prog 3-12.c

```
//switch statement
#include<stdio.h>
main()
{
int a=3;
switch(a)
{
case 1:
    printf("This is case option 1\n");
    printf("Value of a is %d\n",a);
default:
    printf("This is default option\n");
case 2:
    printf("This is case option 2\n");
 }
}
```

Output window

```
This is default option
This is case option 2
```

Remarks:

- There is no constraint about the position of a default-labeled statement within the switch body
- Since none of the case labels match the result of evaluation of a switch selection expression, the execution begins with the default-labeled statement
- All the statements after the default-labeled statement within the switch body gets executed

Program 3-12 | A program to illustrate that there is no constraint about the position of a default-labeled statement within the switch body

Prog 3-13.c

```
// switch statement & ranges
#include<stdio.h>
main()
{
char exp='E';
switch(exp)
```

Output window

```
Upper case vowel
```

Remarks:

- A switch body consists of two case-labeled statements. The code is interpreted as:

```
case 'a':     //←Statement 1: case-labeled statement
   case 'e':     //←Constituent statement of case-labeled statement is
```

(Contd...)

```
{
case 'a':
case 'e':
case 'i':
case 'o':
case 'u':
    printf("Lower case vowel\n");
case 'A':
case 'E':
case 'I':
case 'O':
case 'U':
    printf("Upper case vowel\n");
}
}
```

```
    case 'i':  //←another case-labeled statement
        case 'o':
            case 'u':
                printf("Lower case vowel\n");
case 'A':  //←Statement 2: case-labeled statement
  case 'E':
    case 'I':
      case 'O':
        case 'U':
          printf("Upper case vowel\n");
```

- In this way, the switch statement can be used to switch on ranges
- This is only beneficial when the ranges are small
- C language does not support the following ways for switching on ranges:
  - case 'A'-'Z' //←if used, it will be interpreted as case -25 (i.e. ASCII code of 'A'- ASCII code of 'Z')
  - case 'A' to 'Z' //←allowed in Visual Basic but not in C language

Program 3-13 | A program to illustrate the use of a switch statement to switch on ranges

3.3.3.4.1.2 Jump Statements

A **jump statement** transfers the control from one point to another without checking any condition, i.e. unconditionally. The following jump statements are present in C language:

1. goto statement
2. break statement
3. continue statement
4. return statement

3.3.3.4.1.2.1 goto Statement

The **goto statement** is used to branch unconditionally from one point to another within a function. It provides a highly unstructured way of transferring the program control from one point to another within a function. It often makes the program control difficult to understand and modify. Thus, the use of a goto statement is discouraged in powerful structured programming languages like C. The syntactic form of a goto statement is:

```
goto label;
```

The important points about a goto statement are as follows:

1. The goto statement is always used in conjunction with an identifier-labeled statement. Within the body of a function in which the goto statement is present, an identifier-labeled statement with a label name, same as the label name used in the goto statement should be present.
2. The goto statement on execution transfers the program control to an identifier-labeled statement having a label name same as the label name used in the goto statement.

3. The goto statement can be used to make a forward jump as well as a backward jump. If the goto statement is present before its corresponding identifier-labeled statement, the jump made will be known as a **forward jump**. If the goto statement is present after its corresponding identifier-labeled statement, the jump made will be known as a **backward jump**. The forward and backward jumps are shown in Figure 3.3.

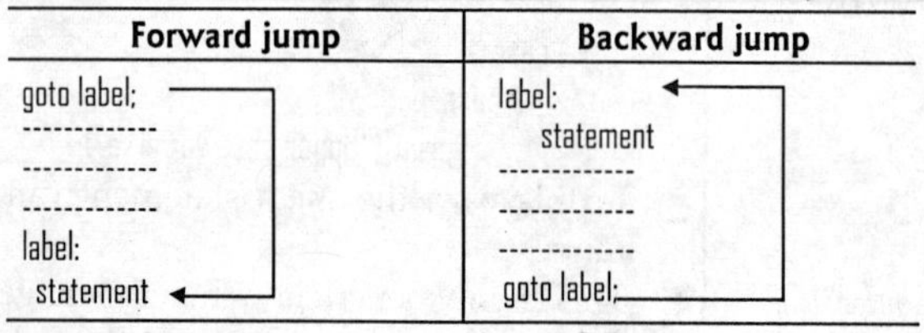

Figure 3.3 | Forward and backward jump

4. There can be two or more goto statements corresponding to an identifier-labeled statement but there cannot be two or more identifier-labeled statements corresponding to a goto statement. The interpretation of this rule is illustrated in Figure 3.4.

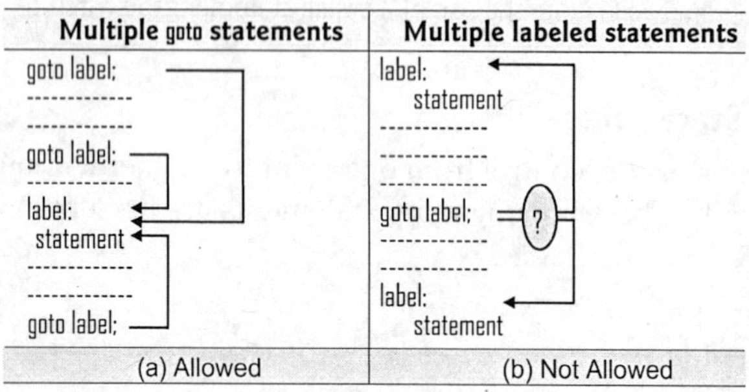

Figure 3.4 | (a) Multiple goto statements corresponding to one identifier-labeled statement are allowed; (b) multiple identifier-labeled statements corresponding to one goto statement are not allowed

5. The goto statement can transfer control anywhere within a function, i.e. it can take control in or out of a nested if statement, nested if-else statement or nested loops. However, a goto statement in no way can take control out of the function in which it is used.

3.3.3.4.1.2.2 break Statement

The syntactic form of a **break statement** is:

```
break;
```

The important points about a break statement are as follows:

1. A break statement can appear only inside, or as a body of, a switch statement or a loop.[§§§] The code snippet listed in Program 3-14 verifies this fact.

[§§§] Refer Section 3.3.3.4.2 for a description on loops.

Prog 3-14.c

```
 1 //break statement
 2 #include<stdio.h>
 3 main()
 4 {
 5 int a=10;
 6 if(a==10)
 7 {
 8     printf("if controlling expression evaluates to true");
 9     break;
10     printf("The value of a is %d",a);
11 }
12 }
```

Output window

Compilation error "Misplaced break in function main"

Reasons:

- The break statement can appear only inside or as a switch/loop body
- The break statement present in line 9 is neither a part of a switch body nor a loop body

What to do?

- Either remove the break statement from if body or place the if statement inside a loop body or a switch body

Program 3-14 | A program to illustrate that the break statement cannot appear outside the switch body or a loop

2. A break statement terminates the execution of the nearest enclosing switch or the nearest enclosing loop. The execution resumes with the statement present next to the terminated switch statement or the terminated loop. The interpretation of this point is illustrated in the code snippet listed in Program 3-15.

Prog 3-15.c

```
//break statement
#include<stdio.h>
main()
{
int a=1;
switch(a)
{
case 1:
    printf("One");
    break;
case 2:
    printf("Two");
    break;
default:
    printf("Default");
}
printf("\nThis statement is next to switch");
}
```

Output window

```
One
This statement is next to switch
```

Remarks:

- The switch body consists of five statements and is interpreted as:

```
{
case 1:              //←Statement 1: case-labeled statement
    printf("One");
break;               //←Statement 2: break statement
case 2:              //←Statement 3: case-labeled statement
    printf("Two");
break;               //←Statement 4: break statement
default:             //←Statement 5: default-labeled statement
    printf("Default");
}
```

- Execution starts from the statement with the case label 1
- Execution of break statement terminates the switch statement and the control immediately transfers to the statement present next to the switch statement, i.e. printf("\nThis statement is next to switch");

Program 3-15 | A program to illustrate the execution of a switch statement

3.3.3.4.1.2.3 continue Statement

The syntactic form of a **continue statement** is:

```
continue;
```

The important points about a continue statement are as follows:

1. A continue statement can appear only inside, or as the body of, a loop.
2. A continue[¶¶¶] statement terminates the current iteration of the nearest enclosing loop. The semantics of the continue statement will be discussed after iteration statements.

3.3.3.4.1.2.4 return Statement

The general forms of a **return statement** are:

```
return;   or              //←Form 1
return expression;        //←Form 2
```

The important points about a return statement are as follows:

1. A return statement without an expression (i.e. Form 1) can appear only in a function whose return type➲ is void.
2. A return statement with an expression (i.e. Form 2) should not appear in a function➲ whose return type is void.
3. A return statement terminates the execution of a function and returns the control to the calling➲ function.

The syntax and semantics of a return statement will be discussed in Chapter 5.

Forward Reference: Functions and their return types, calling function and called function (Chapter 5).

3.3.3.4.2 Iteration Statements

Iteration is a process of repeating the same set of statements again and again until the specified condition holds true. Humans find iterative tasks boring but computers are very good at performing iterative tasks. Computers execute the same set of statements again and again by putting them in a loop. The C language provides the following three **iteration statements**:

1. for statement
2. while statement
3. do-while statement

In general, loops are classified as:

1. Counter-controlled loops
2. Sentinel-controlled loops

3.3.3.4.2.1 Counter-Controlled Loops

Counter-controlled looping is a form of looping in which the number of iterations to be performed is known in advance. Counter-controlled loops are so named because they use a control variable, known as the **loop counter**, to keep a track of loop iterations. The counter-controlled loop starts with the initial value of the loop counter and terminates when the final value of the loop counter is reached. Since the counter-controlled loops iterate a fixed number of times, which is known in advance, they are also known as **definite repetition loops**. There are three main ingredients of counter-controlled looping:

[¶¶¶] Refer Section 3.3.3.4.2.4.2 for a description on the semantics of a continue statement.

1. Initialization of the loop counter.
2. An expression (specifically a condition) determining whether the loop body should be executed or not.
3. An expression that manipulates the value of the loop counter so that the condition in step 2 eventually becomes false and the loop terminates.

Firstly, I will describe the syntax of looping statements available in C language and how they can be used for counter-controlled looping. In Section 3.3.3.4.2.2, I will describe the use of available iteration statements for sentinel-controlled looping.

3.3.3.4.2.1.1 for Statement

Out of all the looping constructs available in C, **for statement** is the most popular one. The general form of a for statement is:

```
for(expression1; expression2; expression3)      //←for header
statement                                       //←for body
```

The important points about a for statement are as follows:

1. The for statement consists of for header and for body.
   Points about for header:
2. The for header consists of the keyword for followed by three expressions separated by semicolons and enclosed within parentheses.
3. All the expressions in the for header are optional and can be skipped. Even if all the expressions are missing, it is mandatory to create three sections by placing two semicolons.
4. Three sections are named as: initialization section, condition section and manipulation section.
   a. **Initialization section:** $expression_1$ constitutes the initialization section. It is used to initialize (i.e. assign a starting value to) the loop counter. If the loop counter has already been initialized, the initialization expression, i.e. $expression_1$ can be skipped. However, a semicolon is necessary and must be placed.
   b. **Condition section:** $expression_2$ forms the condition section. $expression_2$ tests the value of the loop counter. This section determines whether the body of the loop is to be executed or not. In case of infinite loops, the condition section can be skipped.
   c. **Manipulation section:** $expression_3$ is part of the manipulation section. The manipulation expression manipulates the value of the loop counter so that the $expression_2$ present in the condition section eventually evaluates to false and the loop terminates.
5. Care must be taken that the for header is not terminated with a semicolon. If it is terminated with a semicolon, the semicolon is interpreted as a null statement following the for header (i.e. it is treated as for body).
   A point about for body:
6. The syntax of for statement permits only a single statement to be associated with for header. If a number of statements are to be executed repeatedly, the statements should be clubbed together to form a compound statement.
   Execution of for statement:

7. The for statement is executed as follows:
   a. Initialization section is executed only once at the start of the loop.
   b. The expression present in the condition section is evaluated.
      i. If it evaluates to true, the body of the loop is executed.
      ii. If it evaluates to false, the loop terminates and the program control is transferred to the statement present next to the for statement.
   c. After the execution of the body of the loop, the manipulation expression is evaluated.
   d. These three steps represent the first iteration of the for loop. For the next iterations, Steps b and c are repeated until the expression in Step b evaluates to false.

The facts mentioned above are illustrated in Program 3-16.

Prog 3-16.c	Flow chart depicting the flow of control in program	Output window

//Use of for statement to find the
//sum of first n natural numbers
#include<stdio.h>
main()
{
int n, lc, sum=0;
printf("Enter the value of n\t");
scanf("%d",&n);
for(lc=1;lc<=n;lc++)
    sum=sum+lc;
printf("Sum is %d",sum);
}
	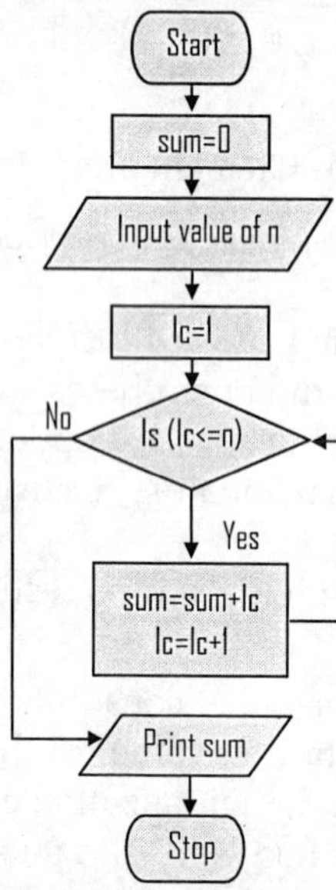	Enter the value of n 10
		Sum is 55

Program 3-16 | A program to illustrate the use of for statement for finding the sum of first n natural numbers

The codes in Table 3.3 are equivalent to the code specified in Program 3-16.

Table 3.3 | Codes equivalent to the code listed in Program 3-16

Equivalent Code-I	Equivalent Code-II	Equivalent Code-III
//Use of for statement to find the sum	//Use of for statement to find the sum	//Use of for statement to find the
// of first n natural numbers	//of first n natural numbers	//sum of first n natural numbers
#include<stdio.h>	#include<stdio.h>	#include<stdio.h>
main()	main()	main()
{	{	{
int n, lc=1, sum=0; **//Initialization of lc**	int n, lc, sum=0;	int n, lc=1, sum=0;
printf("Enter the value of n\t");	printf("Enter the value of n\t");	printf("Enter the value of n\t");

(Contd...)

scanf("%d",&n);
for(;lc<=n;lc++)**//Initialization missing**
    sum=sum+lc;
printf("Sum is %d",sum);
}
	scanf("%d",&n);
	for(lc=1;lc<=n;)**//Manipulation missing**
	    sum=sum+lc++;**//Manipulation of lc**
	printf("Sum is %d",sum);
	}
		scanf("%d",&n);
		for(;lc<=n;)**//Both missing**
		    sum=sum+lc++;
		printf("Sum is %d",sum);
		}

The code snippet in Program 3-17 illustrates the effect of presence of a semicolon at the end of for header.

Prog 3-17.c	Flow chart depicting the flow of control in program	Output window

//Effect of ; at end of for header
#include<stdio.h>
main()
{
int n, lc, sum=0;
printf("Enter the value of n\t");
scanf("%d",&n);
for(lc=1;lc<=n;lc++);
    sum=sum+lc;
printf("Sum is %d",sum);
}
	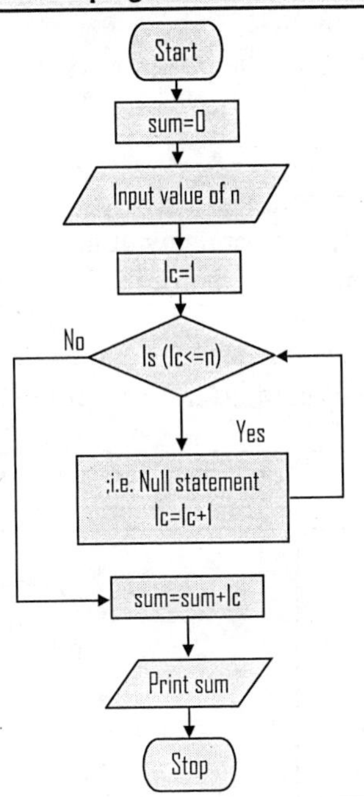	Enter the value of n 10
		Sum is 11
		Remarks:
		• for header is terminated with a semicolon
		• Semicolon is interpreted as null statement and forms the for body
		• The statement sum=sum+lc; is a statement present next to the for statement and thus gets executed only once
		• The value of lc on the termination of loop will be 11
		• This value of lc is added to sum to produce the mentioned output

Program 3-17 | A program to illustrate the effect of a semicolon at the end of a for header

3.3.3.4.2.1.2 while Statement

The general form of a **while statement** is:

```
while(expression)      //←while header
statement              //←while body
```

The important points about a while statement are as follows:

1. The while statement consists of while header and while body.
2. The while header consists of keyword while followed by while controlling expression enclosed within the parentheses.
3. The controlling expression in while header is mandatory and cannot be skipped.

4. The while header should not be terminated with a semicolon. If it is terminated with a semicolon, the semicolon is interpreted as a null statement following the while header (i.e. it is treated as a while body).
5. The syntax of a while statement permits only a single statement to be associated with while header. If a number of statements are to be executed repeatedly, the statements should be clubbed together to form a compound statement.
6. The while statement is executed as follows:
   a. The while controlling expression is evaluated.
      i. If it evaluates to true, the body of the loop is executed.
      ii. If it evaluates to false, the program control is transferred to the statement present next to the while statement.
   b. After executing the while body, the program control returns back to the while header.
   c. Steps a and b are repeated until the while controlling expression in Step a evaluates to false.
7. While making the use of while statement, always remember to initialize the loop counter before the while controlling expression is evaluated and to manipulate the loop counter inside the body of while statement, i.e. before the while controlling expression is evaluated again.

The facts mentioned above are illustrated in Program 3-18.

Line | Prog 3-18.c

```
1   //Use of while statement to find
2   //the factorial of a number
3   #include<stdio.h>
4   main()
5   {
6   int num, lc, fact;
7   printf("Enter number\t");
8   scanf("%d",&num);
9   fact=1;
10  lc=1; //Initialization of loop counter
11  while(lc<=num)
12  {
13      fact=fact*lc;
14      lc=lc+1; //Manipulation of loop counter
15  }
16  printf("Factorial is %d",fact);
17  }
```

Flow chart depicting the flow of control in program

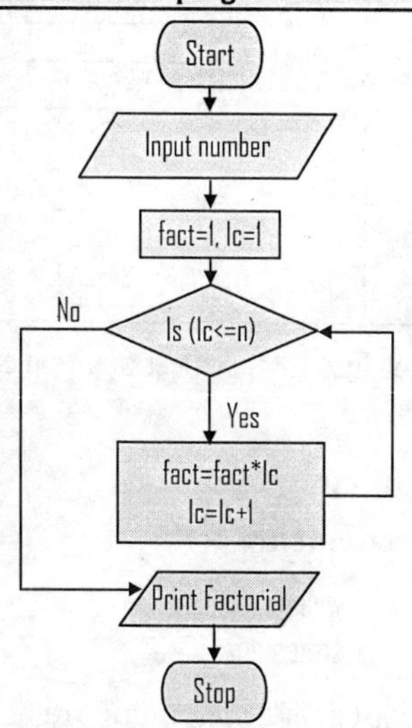

Output window

Enter number 5
Factorial is 120

Remarks:

- Line 9 initializes the value of fact to 1. It is important to initialize fact to 1 else garbage will be the result
- Line 10 provides the initialization of loop counter
- Line 14 manipulates the loop counter

Program 3-18 | A program to find the factorial of a number using while loop

The codes in Table 3.4 are equivalent to the code specified in Program 3-18.

Table 3.4 | Codes equivalent to the code listed in Program 3-18

Equivalent Code-I	Equivalent Code-II	Equivalent Code-III
//Use of while statement to find	//Use of while statemnt to find	//Use of while statement to find
//the factorial of a number	//the factorial of a number	//the factorial of a number
#include<stdio.h>	#include<stdio.h>	#include<stdio.h>
main()	main()	main()
{	{	{
int num, lc=1, fact=1;	int num, lc=1, fact=1;	int num, lc=0, fact=1;
printf("Enter number\t");	printf("Enter number\t");	printf("Enter number\t");
scanf("%d",&num);	scanf("%d",&num);	scanf("%d",&num);
while(lc<=num)	while(lc<=num)	while(lc++<num)
{	fact=fact*lc++;	fact=fact*lc;
fact=fact*lc;	printf("Factorial is %d",fact);	printf("Factorial is %d",fact);
lc=lc+1;	}	}
}		
printf("Factorial is %d",fact);		
}		

3.3.3.4.2.1.3 do-while Statement

The general form of **do-while statement** is:

```
do                      //←do-while header
statement               //←do-while body
while(expression);      //←while clause
```

The important points about a do-while statement are as follows:

1. The do-while statement consists of a do clause, followed by a statement that constitutes do-while body, followed by the while clause consisting of while keyword followed by do-while controlling expression enclosed within parentheses. The while clause is terminated with a semicolon.
2. The controlling expression in a do-while statement is mandatory and cannot be skipped.
3. The syntax of a do-while statement permits only a single statement to be present. If a number of statements are to be executed repeatedly, the statements should be clubbed together to form a compound statement.
4. The do-while statement is executed as follows:
    a. The statement, i.e. body of do-while statement, is executed.
    b. After the execution of a do-while body, the do-while controlling expression is evaluated.
        i. If it evaluates to true, the statement, i.e. do-while body is executed again and Step b is repeated.
        ii. If it evaluates to false, the program control is transferred to the statement present next to the do-while statement.
5. While making the use of a do-while statement, always remember to initialize the loop counter before the do-while statement and to manipulate it inside the body of the do-while statement so that the do-while controlling expression eventually becomes false.
6. The statement, i.e. body of the do-while loop is executed once, even when the do-while controlling expression is initially false.

The code snippet in Program 3-19 illustrates the use of a do-while statement to find the sum of the series 1 + 2 + 3… *n* terms.

Prog 3-19.c	Flow chart depicting the flow of control in program	Output window

//Use of do-while statement to find
//the sum of the series 1+2+3.....n terms
#include<stdio.h>
main()
{
int terms, sum=0, lc=0;
printf("Enter number of terms\t");
scanf("%d",&terms);
do
{
sum=sum+lc;
lc=lc+1;
}
while(lc<=terms);
printf("Sum of series is %d",sum);
}
	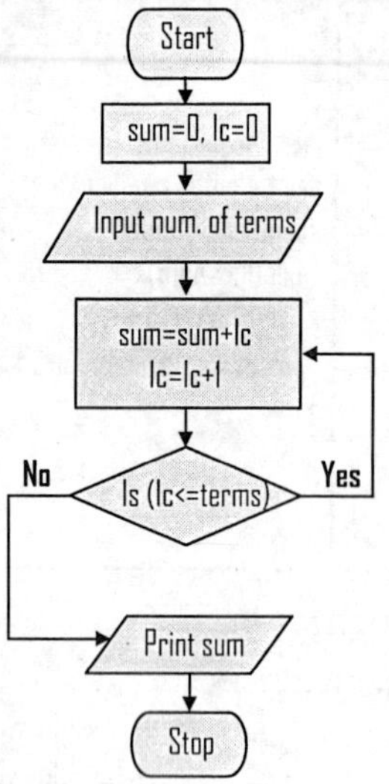	Enter number of terms 5
		Sum of series is 15
		Remarks:
		• Initialize the value of variable sum to 0 else the result will be garbage
		• Look at the position of controlling expression
		• It is present at the end (i.e. exit point) of the loop
		• That is why, do-while is known as **exit-controlled loop**
		• for and while are known as **entry-controlled loops**

Program 3-19 | A program to illustrate the use of a do-while statement

3.3.3.4.2.2 Sentinel-Controlled Loops

In **sentinel-controlled looping**, the number of times the iteration is to be performed is not known beforehand. The execution or termination of the loop depends upon a special value called the **sentinel value**. If the sentinel value is true, the loop body will be executed, otherwise it will not. Since the number of times a loop will iterate is not known in advance, this type of loop is also known as **indefinite repetition loop**.

Consider the problem of finding the maximum and the minimum from a set of numbers. However, the set (i.e. numbers) and the cardinality of set (i.e. how many numbers are there in the set) are not known beforehand; therefore, the user will enter them at the run time. The mentioned problem can be solved by using sentinel-controlled looping as given in Programs 3-20 and 3-21.

Prog 3-20a.c	Prog 3-20b.c	Output window
//while statement for sentinel control	//for statement for sentinel control	Enter number 5
#include<stdio.h>	#include<stdio.h>	Want to enter more y
#include<conio.h>	#include<conio.h>	Enter number 3
main()	main()	Want to enter more y
{	{	Enter number 8
char choice;	char choice;	Want to enter more y
int num, max, min;	int num, max, min;	Enter number -2
printf("Enter number\t");	printf("Enter number\t");	Want to enter more n
scanf("%d",&num);	scanf("%d",&num);	Maximum is 8

(Contd...)

```
max=min=num;
printf("Want to enter more\t");
choice=getche();
while(choice=='y'||choice=='Y')
{
printf("\nEnter number\t");
scanf("%d",&num);
if(num>max)
    max=num;
else
    if(num<min)
        min=num;
printf("Want to enter more\t");
choice=getche();
}
printf("\nMaximum is %d",max);
printf("\nMinimum is %d",min);
}
```

```
max=min=num;
printf("Want to enter more\t");
choice=getche();
for( ;choice=='y'||choice=='Y'; )
{
printf("\nEnter number\t");
scanf("%d",&num);
if(num>max)
    max=num;
else
    if(num<min)
        min=num;
printf("Want to enter more\t");
choice=getche();
}
printf("\nMaximum is %d",max);
printf("\nMinimum is %d",min);
}
```

Minimum is -2

Remarks:

- The loop terminates when the user does not enter the choice 'Y' or 'y'
- choice is the **sentinel value**
- The number of iterations after which the user will say 'no' is not known in advance
- The header file conio.h is to be included for using the function getche
- The function getche is used to get a character from the user. It also outputs, i.e. echoes the entered character onto the screen. The character e in getche stands for echo
- The variant of getche function that is used to get a character from the user without echoing it on the screen is getch function

Program 3-20 | A program to illustrate the use of while statement and for statement for sentinel-controlled looping

Prog 3-21.c

```
//do-while statement for sentinel controlled looping
#include<stdio.h>
#include<conio.h>
main()
{
char choice;
int num, iteration=1, max, min;
do
{
printf("Enter number\t");
scanf("%d",&num);
if(iteration++==1)
    max=min=num;
else
    if(num>max)
        max=num;
    else
        if(num<min)
            min=num;
```

Output window

```
Enter number        5
Want to enter more  y
Enter number        3
Want to enter more  y
Enter number        8
Want to enter more  y
Enter number        -2
Want to enter more  n

Maximum is 8
Minimum is -2
```

Remarks:

- The loop terminates when the user does not enter the choice 'Y' or 'y'
- choice is the sentinel value
- The number of iterations after which the user will say 'no' is not known in advance

(Contd...)

Prog 3-21.c

```
printf("Want to enter more\t");
choice=getche();
printf("\n");
}
while(choice=='y'||choice=='Y');
printf("\nMaximum is %d",max);
printf("\nMinimum is %d",min);
}
```

Output window

Program 3-21 | A program to illustrate the use of a do-while statement for sentinel-controlled looping

3.3.3.4.2.3 Nested Loops

If the body of a loop is, or contains another iteration statement, then we say that the **loops are nested**. An example of a nested for loop is given in Program 3-22.

Prog 3-22.c

```
//Nested for loop
#include<stdio.h>
main()
{
int olc,ilc;
for(olc=1;olc<=4;olc++)
{
    for(ilc=1;ilc<=4;ilc++)
        printf("*");
    printf("\n");
}
}
```

Output window

```
****
****
****
****
```

Remarks:

- olc is the outer loop counter and ilc is the inner loop counter
- The inner loop is responsible for printing 4 stars in a row
- The outer loop is responsible for printing 4 such rows

Program 3-22 | A program to illustrate the use of a nested for loop

3.3.3.4.2.4 Semantics of break and continue Statements

After the discussion of iteration statements, it is time to discuss the use of break and continue statements. The break statement helps in terminating a loop, while the continue statement helps in terminating the current iteration of a loop.

3.3.3.4.2.4.1 Semantics of break Statement

The important points about the usage of a break statement along with loops are as follows:

1. When the break statement present inside a loop is executed, it terminates the loop and the program control is transferred to the statement present next to the loop.
2. When the break statement present inside a nested loop is executed, it only terminates the execution of the nearest enclosing loop. The execution resumes with the statement present next to the terminated loop.
3. There is no constraint about the number of break statements that can be present inside a loop.

The meaning of the above-mentioned points is illustrated in Program 3-23.

Prog 3-23.c

```
//Use of break statement
#include<stdio.h>
main()
{
int i;
for(i=1;i<=10;i++)
{
if(i==5)
    break;
printf("%d ",i);
}
if(i<11)
    printf("\nPremature Termination");
}
```

Flow chart depicting the flow of control in program

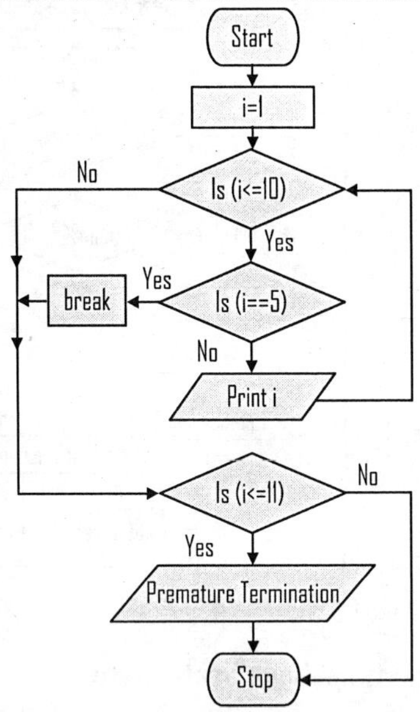

Output window

1 2 3 4
Premature Termination

Remark:

- break statement is used to prematurely terminate the loop

Program 3-23 | A program to illustrate the use of break statement

Program 3-24 illustrates a break statement, which terminates the nearest enclosing loop.

Prog 3-24.c

```
//Use of break statement in nested loops
#include<stdio.h>
main()
{
int olc, ilc;
for(olc=1;olc<=3;olc++)
    for(ilc=1;ilc<=4;ilc++)
    {
    if(ilc==3)
        break;
    printf("%d %d\n",olc,ilc);
    }
}
```

Values of olc and ilc

```
olc=1
    ilc=1   //←prints 1 1
    ilc=2   //←prints 1 2
    ilc=3   //←break executes & terminates the inner loop
olc=2
    ilc=1   //←prints 2 1
    ilc=2   //←prints 2 2
    ilc=3   //←break executes
olc=3
    ilc=1   //←prints 3 1
    ilc=2   //←prints 3 2
    ilc=3   //←break executes
```

Output window

1 1
1 2
2 1
2 2
3 1
3 2

Remarks:

- break statement terminates only the inner loop
- The control still remains inside the outer loop

Program 3-24 | A program to illustrate that break statement terminates the nearest enclosing loop

The use of a break statement in checking whether a number is prime or not is illustrated in Program 3-25.

Prog 3-25.c

```
//Use of break statement to check
//whether a number is prime or not
#include<stdio.h>
main()
{
int num, i;
printf("Enter the number\t");
scanf("%d",&num);
for(i=2;i<num;i++)
    if(num%i==0)
        break;
if(i==num)
    printf("Number is prime");
else
    printf("Number is not prime");
}
```

Flow chart depicting the flow of control

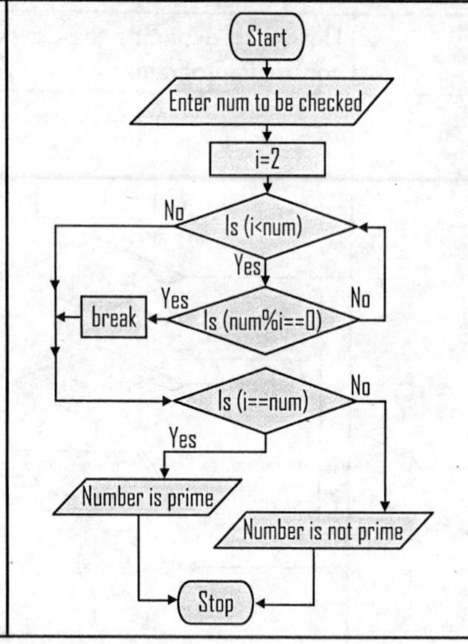

Output window

```
Enter the number   9
Number is not prime
```

Remarks:

- Whether a number is prime or not can be determined by checking whether the number is divisible by any value from 2 to num-1
- When it is found that the number num is divisible by some value of i, there is no need to check the divisibility of num for rest of the values of i

Program 3-25 | A program to check whether a number is prime or not

3.3.3.4.2.4.2 Semantics of continue Statement

The important points about a continue statement are as follows:

1. A continue statement terminates the current iteration of the loop.
2. When a continue statement present inside a nested loop is executed, it only terminates the current iteration of the nearest enclosing loop.
3. On the execution of a continue statement, the program control is immediately transferred to the header of the loop.
4. There is no constraint about the number of continue statements that can be present inside a loop.

The semantics of a continue statement is illustrated in Program 3-26.

Prog 3-26.c

```
//Use of continue statement
#include<stdio.h>
main()
{
int i;
for(i=1;i<=10;i++)
{
if(i%2==0)
    continue;
printf("%d ",i);
}
}
```

Flow chart depicting the flow of control

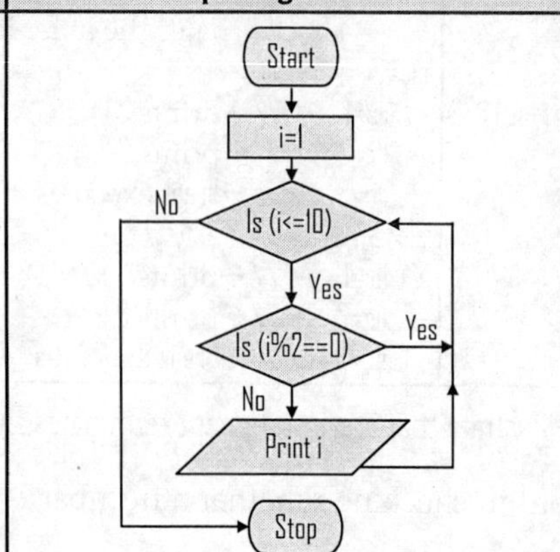

Output window

```
1 3 5 7 9
```

Remark:

- For even values of i, the printf statement will not be executed as the continue statement transfers the control to the header of the loop

Program 3-26 | A program to illustrate the use of a continue statement

3.4 Summary

1. Statement is the smallest logical entity that can independently exist in a C program.
2. No entity smaller than a statement, i.e. expressions, variables, constants, etc. can exist in a C program unless and until they are converted into statements.
3. A single statement is known as a simple statement.
4. A group of single statements can be clubbed together into one statement by enclosing them within braces. A clubbed statement is known as a block or a compound statement.
5. Non-executable statements are meant for the compiler. No machine code is generated for non-executable statements.
6. Only executable statements play a role during the execution of a program. Only for these statements, the machine code is generated.
7. A null statement performs no operation and consists of just a semicolon.
8. An expression statement performs the computation and is formed by terminating an expression with a semicolon.
9. By default, the flow of program control is sequential and it flows from top to bottom.
10. Flow of control needs to be altered to implement decision making and iteration.
11. To alter the default flow of control, flow control statements are used.
12. To implement decision making, selection statements are used.
13. Selection statements are: `if` statement, `if-else` statement, and `switch` statement.
14. Selection statements can be nested.
15. Careless use of nested `if-else` statement may lead to dangling `else` problem.
16. Dangling `else` problem can be implicitly as well as explicitly solved.
17. A `switch` statement is a better alternative to a nested `if-else` statement and is used in the complex decision making.
18. Looping can be performed by using iteration statements.
19. Three iteration statements available in C are: `for` statement, `while` statement and `do-while` statement.
20. A `break` statement is used to terminate the nearest enclosing loop.
21. A `continue` statement is used to terminate the current iteration of the nearest enclosing loop.

Exercise Questions

Conceptual Questions and Answers

1. *What is the smallest logical unit that can independently exist in a C program?*

   Statement is the smallest logical unit that has an independent existence in a C program. No entity smaller than a statement (i.e. expressions, variables and constants, etc.) can exist unless and until they are converted into statements. Consider the following program segment:

```
main()
{
    int a=10,b=20,c;
```

```
    c=a+b                          //← Error: Statement missing ; in function main()
    printf("The value of c is %d",c);
}
```

On compilation, the above-mentioned piece of code gives 'Statement missing ; error'. This error is due to the fact that c=a+b is an expression and not a statement. Expressions cannot independently exist in a C program. To make them exist, they must be converted into statements by terminating them with a semicolon. The following is the rectified code:

```
main()
{
    int a=10,b=20,c;
    c=a+b;                         //←Expression terminated with a semicolon forming a statement
    printf("The value of c is %d",c);
}
```

2. *What is meant by a simple statement and a compound statement?*

   A simple statement consists of a single statement. For example, c=a+b; is a simple statement. A compound statement consists of a sequence of simple statements enclosed within braces. The following is an example of a compound statement:

```
{
    c=a+b;
    a*=2;
    b+3;
}
```

3. *What are executable statements and non-executable statements?*

   Executable statements are the statements that call for a processing action by the computer, such as performing arithmetic, reading data, making decision and so on. Non-executable statements are the statements that provide the information about the nature of data (e.g. declaration statement). Non-executable statements can be placed outside the bodies of functions (i.e. in global scope➲), but executable statements can only be placed within the body of some function (i.e. local scope➲).

Forward Reference: Global and local scope (Chapter 7).

4. *Write a simple C statement to accomplish the following tasks:*
   a. *Assign sum of* x *and* y *to* z *and increment the value of* x *by 1 after the calculation.*
   b. *Decrement the variable* x *by 1 then subtract it from the variable* total.

   a. z=x++ + y;
      Note: Writing z=x++ + y is not valid as it is not a statement. It is an expression.
   b. total-=--x;
      or
      total=total- --x;
      Carefully note the position of white-space character. Writing total=total---x; or total=total-- -x; is not the same as writing total=total- --x;. The difference between them is shown in the table given below:

Column I	Initial values		After execution of statement in Column I	
	total	x	total	x
total-=--x;	15	5	11	4
total=total- --x;	15	5	11	4
total=total-- -x;	15	5	9	5
total=total---x;	15	5	9	5

5. *What is the difference between initialization and assignment?*

   First time assignment at the time of definition is called initialization. Assigning a value to an identifier after initialization will be treated as an assignment. The clear understanding of difference between terms initialization and assignment becomes important when we talk about qualified constants. Consider the following piece of code:

```
main()
{
    const int a=20;   //← Initialization of a qualified constant is valid.
    a=30;             //← Compilation error: Value cannot be assigned to a qualified constant.
}
```

   The above-mentioned code highlights the fact that:
   'We cannot assign a value to a qualified constant but we can initialize it'.

6. *What is null statement and where is it used?*

Backward Reference: Refer Section 3.3.3.2 for a description on null statement.

   A null statement is used when the syntax of a language construct requires a statement to be present but the logic of the program does not require it. Its use is illustrated in the next answer.

7. *How can you print "Hello World" without using a semicolon in a C program?*

   The following code segment prints "Hello World" without using a semicolon.

```
main()
{
    if(printf("Hello World"))
    {}      //←Null statement. Syntax of if statement requires a statement to be present but
}           //  the logic of the program does not require it. Hence, null statement is placed.
```

8. *What is dangling else problem? How is it solved by a compiler and how can it be avoided?*

Backward Reference: Refer Section 3.3.3.4.1.1.4 for the answer to this question.

9. *Why does the following piece of code on compilation gives an error?*

```
main()
{
int a=1;
if(a==1)
    printf("This is if body\n");
```

```
    printf("This statement does not belong to if body");
else
    printf("This is else body");
}
```

The given piece of code on compilation gives 'Misplaced else error.' The source of error can be found by looking at the syntax of an if-else statement. The general form of an if-else statement is:

```
if(expression)          //← if header
statement1              //← if body
else                    //← else clause
statement2              //← else body
```

It should be noted that only one statement can be associated with if clause and else clause. If more than one statement needs to be associated with if clause or else clause, then a block comprising those simple statements must be created. This block of statements, although comprising more than one simple statement, will be treated as a unit, as one statement and can be associated with if clause or else clause. The given piece of code is interpreted as:

```
main()
{
    int a=1;
    if(a==1)
        printf("This is if body\n");          //←Only this statement is associated with if clause
    printf("This statement does not belong to if body");     //←This statement is not in if body
    else        //←else clause is left without any matching if clause and this leads to error
        printf("This is else body");
}
```

To remove this error, club both the simple statements into a compound statement. The rectified code is as follows:

```
main()
{
    int a=1;
    if(a==1)
    {                       //←Compound statement: It will be treated as a unit
        printf("This is if body\n");
        printf("This statement does not belong to if body");
    }
    else                    //←Now the else clause is properly matched with if clause
        printf("This is else body");
}
```

10. *Can the selection expression of a* switch *statement be a string?*

    No, the selection expression of a switch statement cannot be a string. The switch selection expression and case labels must be of integral type. Hence, the switch statement can be used to switch only on integral data types (i.e. character and integer). Consider the following program segment:

```
main()
{
    switch("Hello")
    {
    case "Hello":
        printf("Hello");
```

```
    case "Hi":
        printf("Hi");
    }
}
```

In the above-mentioned piece of code, switch selection expression and case labels (shown in bold) are strings. This is not allowed and thus, the code on compilation gives an error.

11. *Can a* switch *statement have more than one* default *label?*
No, a switch statement cannot have more than one default label. In a switch statement, all the case labels must be unique and at most one default label can be present. The presence of more than one default label or duplicate case labels leads to ambiguity, which results in a compilation error.

12. *Why does the following piece of code on compilation gives an error?*

```
main()
{
int i=65;
switch(i)
{
case 65:
    printf("This statement should get executed\n");
    break;
case 'A':
    printf("A has ASCII code of 65, this statement should get executed\n");
    break;
default:
    printf("Duplicate case labels lead to error\n");
}
}
```

The mentioned piece of code on compilation gives 'Duplicate case in function main' error. This is due to the fact that integers and characters are not treated separately in C language. Characters are stored internally in terms of their ASCII values. Character 'A' has ASCII value 65. So, writing case 'A': is equivalent to writing case 65:. However, case label 65 is already present. Duplicate case labels are not allowed. Hence, this leads to 'Duplicate case in function main' error.

13. *Can we use a* continue *statement within the body of a* switch *statement like we can use a* break *statement within it?*
No, a continue statement can appear only in or as a loop body. A switch statement is a branching statement and not a looping statement. Hence, the continue statement cannot appear inside the body of a switch statement.

14. *Is it mandatory to have* case *labeled or* default *labeled statements within a* switch *body? If the* switch *body does not contain any* case *or* default *labeled statements, will there be a compilation error?*
The general form of a switch statement is:

```
switch(expression)        //←switch header
statement                 //←switch body
```

A switch body consists of a statement. This statement can be a null statement, an expression statement, a labeled statement, a flow control statement, a compound statement, etc. There is no constraint that only labeled statements can form the switch body. Hence, it is not mandatory to have case labeled or default labeled statements within the switch body. The following usages of switch statement (without any case labeled or default labeled statements) are valid:

```
a.  switch(expr);              //←switch body is a null statement
b.  switch(expr)               //←switch body consisting of two function call statements
    {
        printf("Two expression statements");
        printf("This is valid");
    }
c.  switch(expr)               //←switch body has a labeled statement, but the labeled
    {                          //  statement is an identifier labeled statement and not a case labeled
    lab:                       //  or a default labeled statement
    printf("This is also valid");
    goto lab;
    }
```

15. *Can* case *labeled or* default *labeled statement exist outside the* switch *body?*

    No, case labeled statements and default labeled statements can appear only inside the switch body. Placing case labeled statements or default labeled statements outside the switch body leads to 'Case/ Default outside of switch' compilation error.

16. *Why does the following piece of code gives an error on compilation?*

```
main()
{
int exp=2;
switch(exp)
{
case 1:
    int j=2;
    printf("The value of j in case 1 is %d\n",j);
case 2:
    printf("The value of j in case 2 is %d\n",j);
}
}
```

This compilation error is due to the fact that the placement of the definition statement associated with a case or default label is illegal unless it is placed within a statement block. The placement of the definition statement within a statement block is mandatory because if the definition is not enclosed within a statement block, the defined identifier would be visible➲ (i.e. can be used) across the case labels, but is initialized only if the case label within which it is defined is executed. The presence of the statement block ensures that the name is initialized whenever it is visible. In the given piece of code, int j=2; is not placed within a statement block. Hence, there is a compilation error. The compilation error can be removed by placing int j=2; within a statement block.

Forward Reference: Visibility and scope (Chapter 8).

17. *I have tried to rectify the problem in the code mentioned in the previous question. Does the following piece of code compile successfully?*

```
main()
{
int exp=2;
switch(exp)
```

```
{
case 1:
{
    int j=2;
    printf("The value of j in case 1 is %d\n",j);
}
case 2:
    printf("The value of j in case 2 is %d\n",j);
}
}
```

No, the given piece of code does not yet compile successfully. The given piece of code on compilation gives 'Undefined symbol 'j' in function main' error. This error is due to the fact that the identifier j defined within the statement block of case label 1 is visible (i.e. can be used) only inside it. The identifier j is not visible (i.e. does not exist) outside the statement block in which it is defined. Hence, reference to j in the printf statement of case label 2 is not valid and leads to the compilation error.

18. *Why does the following piece of code show just a sequence of zeros in its output?*

```
main()
{
    int number=2;
    while(1)
    {
        printf("%d ",number);
        number*=2;
    }
}
```

The code actually outputs
2 4 8 16 32 64 128 256 512 1024 2048 4096 8192 16384 -32768 0 0 0 0 0 0 0 0 0 0 0 0 0 0 0 0 0 0 0 0 0 0 0 0 0 0 0 0 0 0 0 0 0 0 0 0 0 0 0 0 0 0 0 0 0 0 0 0 0 0...infinite times.
Initially number is two. It is represented in memory as:

Sign Bit 16 MSB	Magnitude													
	Bit 15	Bit 14	Bit 13	Bit 12	Bit 11	Bit 10	Bit 9	Bit 8	Bit 7	Bit 6	Bit 5	Bit 4	Bit 3	Bit 2	Bit 1
0	0	0	0	0	0	0	0	0	0	0	0	0	0	1	0

Multiplying by two makes it four (i.e. equivalent to shifting in left direction by 1 bit).

Sign Bit 16 MSB	Magnitude													
	Bit 15	Bit 14	Bit 13	Bit 12	Bit 11	Bit 10	Bit 9	Bit 8	Bit 7	Bit 6	Bit 5	Bit 4	Bit 3	Bit 2	Bit 1
0	0	0	0	0	0	0	0	0	0	0	0	0	1	0	0

This shifting is continued and after 14 iterations, the number becomes:

Sign Bit 16 MSB	Magnitude													
	Bit 15	Bit 14	Bit 13	Bit 12	Bit 11	Bit 10	Bit 9	Bit 8	Bit 7	Bit 6	Bit 5	Bit 4	Bit 3	Bit 2	Bit 1
1	0	0	0	0	0	0	0	0	0	0	0	0	0	0	0

i.e. -32768. If the shifting is further carried out, the number becomes zero.

Sign Bit 16 MSB	Magnitude														
	Bit 15	Bit 14	Bit 13	Bit 12	Bit 11	Bit 10	Bit 9	Bit 8	Bit 7	Bit 6	Bit 5	Bit 4	Bit 3	Bit 2	Bit 1
0	0	0	0	0	0	0	0	0	0	0	0	0	0	0	0

From this point onwards irrespective of how many times shifting is carried out (i.e. number is multiplied by two), the number remains zero. Hence, from this point onwards, the output will only have zeros.

Now, the speed of processing is so fast that first few outputs will be skipped (cannot be seen in the output as the screen scrolls) and only a sequence of zeros can be seen. If you want to see all the outputs, put some delay mechanism inside the loop. This can be done by using either the function `getch()`, `delay(int)` or `sleep(int)`.

> The function **delay(int)** suspends the execution of the program for a given time interval. The time interval is an integer value and specifies the time in milliseconds. **sleep(int)** is a function equivalent to the `delay` function. The `delay` function is provided in the DOS environment and the `sleep` function is usually available with the WINDOWS environment.

19. *I want to test whether a character entered by the user lies in the range 'A' to 'C' or 'X' to 'Z'. Can I use a* `switch` *statement to do this?*

Yes, a `switch` statement can be used to accomplish it. Use the following piece of code to check whether the character entered lies in the range 'A' to 'C' or 'X' to 'Z'.

```
main()
{
    char ch;
    printf("Enter a character\t");
    scanf("%c",&ch);
    switch(ch)
    {
        case 'A':
        case 'B':
        case 'C':
            printf("The entered character is in range A-C");
            break;
        case 'X':
        case 'Y':
        case 'Z':
            printf("The entered character is in range X-Z");
            break;
        default:
            printf("The entered character is neither in range A-C nor in range X-Z");
    }
}
```

However, this method would not be practical if the ranges are bigger. In case of bigger ranges, usage of `if-else` statements with the involvement of logical operators in the controlling expressions is preferred.

20. *Do labels have scope like variables?*

Yes, labels do have scope like variables. A label name is a type of identifier that has only function scope.➲ It can be used anywhere in the function in which it appears.

Forward Reference: Function scope (Chapter 8).

21. *Can we use a* goto *statement to take control from one function to some other function?*

A goto statement in no way can transfer control from one function to another function. Consider the following piece of code:

```
main()
{
   goto here;
}
other_function()
{
   here:
      printf("The label is in other function");
}
```

The above-mentioned code on compilation gives 'Undefined label here in function main' error. To remove this error, use label here somewhere inside the body of main function.

22. *Can a label be followed by another label or should it be followed by a statement?*

The general forms of labeled statements are:

1. identifier: statement
2. case constant-expression: statement
3. default: statement

After identifier label, case label or default label, there should be a statement. This statement can itself be another labeled statement. Hence, label can follow another label. For e.g.

```
lab:             //←label followed by another labeled statement
   try:
      printf("This is valid");
```

Due to this definition of a labeled statement, the following form of a switch statement is valid:

```
switch(expr)
{
   case 1:
   case 2:
      printf("Case 1 and Case 2");
   case 3: case 4: case 5:
      printf("Case 3,4 and 5");
}
```

23. *Can a label name be the same as a function name or a variable name?*

Yes, label name can be the same as a function name or a variable name. Consider the following piece of code:

```
main()
{
   int i=1;
```

```
main:
    printf("Function name is used as label name\n");
i++;
if(i==2)
    goto i;
goto main;
i:
    printf("Variable name is used as label name\n");
}
```

In the given code, the function name, i.e. main and the variable name, i.e. i are used as label names. The given code on execution gives an output as:

```
Function name is used as label name
Variable name is used as label name
```

24. *Can a reserved word or a keyword like* while, if, *etc. be used as a label name?*

    Reserved words or keywords cannot form valid identifier names. Since label names are identifiers, reserved words or keywords cannot be used as valid label names.

25. *All the identifiers need to be declared before their use. Label names are also identifiers. So, do we need to declare label names?*

    No, label names need not be declared. Label names are identifiers but no type is associated with them. Hence, there is no need to explicitly declare them. Label names are implicitly declared by their syntactic appearance. An identifier followed by a colon and a statement is implicitly treated as a label name.

26. *Is a* goto *statement capable of taking the control in or out of a nested loop?*

    Yes, a goto statement is capable of taking the control in or out of a nested loop. The goto statement is capable of taking control anywhere within a function in which it is used. Consider the following piece of code:

```
main()
{
    int i,j;
    for(i=1;i<5;i++)
        for(j=1;j<5;j++)
        {
            printf("This statement will be executed only once\n");
            goto label;
        }
    label:
        printf("goto statement has taken the control out of nested loop");
}
```

Upon execution, it gives the output as:

```
This statement will be executed only once
goto statement has taken the control out of nested loop
```

27. *Can a single* break *statement be used to terminate a nested loop?*

    No, a single break statement cannot be used to terminate a nested loop. A break statement can only terminate the execution of the nearest enclosing switch or the nearest enclosing loop. Consider the following piece of code:

```
main()
{
    int i,j;
    for(i=1;i<3;i++)
    {
        for(j=1;j<3;j++)
        {
            break;
            printf("This will not get printed");
        }
        printf("This will be executed twice as it is inside outer loop\n");
    }
}
```

The break statement only terminates the inner for loop. The printf statement in the outer for loop executes normally. The above piece of code on execution outputs:

```
This will be executed twice as it is inside outer loop
This will be executed twice as it is inside outer loop
```

28. *What are entry-controlled and exit-controlled loops?*

In **entry-controlled loops**, condition is checked before the execution of body of the loop. The for loop and while loop are examples of entry-controlled loops. In **exit-controlled loops**, the condition is checked after the execution of body of the loop. do-while is an example of an exit-controlled loop. In entry-controlled loops, if the condition is initially false, the body of the loop will not be executed. However, in exit-controlled loops, even if the condition is initially false, the body of the loop will be executed once. Consider the following piece of code:

```
main()
{
    int i=2;
    do
        printf("Condition is false, but this will be printed");
    while(i<1);
}
```

The condition of a do-while loop is initially false; even then "Condition is false, but this will be printed" is the output. This indicates that the body of the exit-controlled loop gets executed once, even if the condition of the loop is initially false.

29. *What are counter-controlled and sentinel-controlled loops?*

Counter-controlled looping is a form of looping in which the number of times the loop will execute is known in advance. The counter-controlled loop starts with the initial value of the loop counter and terminates when the final value of the loop counter is reached. Since a counter-controlled loop iterates a fixed number of times, it is also known as a definite repetition loop. In sentinel-controlled looping, the number of times the loop will execute is not known beforehand. The execution or termination of the loop depends upon a special value called the sentinel value. If the sentinel value is true, the loop body gets executed else not. Since the number of times the loop will iterate is not known in advance, this type of loop is also known as an indefinite repetition loop.

30. *What are the three main ingredients of counter-controlled looping?*

Three main ingredients of counter-controlled looping are:

1. Initialization of the loop counter.
2. A condition determining whether the loop body should be executed or not.
3. An expression that manipulates the value of the loop counter so that the condition in Step 2 eventually becomes false and the loop terminates.

31. *For every usage of a* for *loop, we can write an equivalent* while *loop. So, when should one prefer to use a* for *loop and when should a* while *loop be preferred?*

    A while loop should be preferred over a for loop when the number of iterations to be performed is not known in advance. The termination of the while loop is based on the occurrence of some particular condition, i.e. a specific sentinel value. The usage of a for loop should be preferred when the number of iterations to be performed is known beforehand. In short, a while loop is preferred for sentinel-controlled looping and a for loop is preferred for counter-controlled looping.

32. *Why does the following piece of code on compilation give a compilation error?*

```
main()
{
int i=2;
while(i<10);
{
    printf("The value of i is %d",i);
    if(i==5)
        break;
}
}
```

The given piece of code gives a compilation error due to the fact that the break statement can appear only in or as a switch body or a loop body. Here, the break statement does not appear inside the body of the while loop. The body of the while loop consists of a null statement. To rectify the given code, remove the semicolon present at the end of the while header.

33. *I want to terminate the nearest enclosing loop. Which construct in C provides me this functionality?*

    To terminate the nearest enclosing loop, a break statement can be used. This can be seen by executing the following piece of code:

```
main()
{
    int i,j;
    for(i=0;i<2;i++)
    {
        for(j=0;j<5;j++)
        {
            if(i!=0 || j!=0)
                break;
            printf("This will be printed only once\n");
        }
    printf("This will be printed two times\n");
    }
}
```

34. *I want to terminate the current iteration of the nearest enclosing loop. Which construct in C provides me this functionality?*

    To terminate the current iteration of the nearest enclosing loop, a continue statement can be used. This can be seen by executing the following piece of code:

```
main()
{
    int i,j;
    for(i=0;i<2;i++)
    {
        for(j=0;j<5;j++)
        {
            if(i!=0 || j!=0)
                continue;
            printf("This will be printed only once\n");
        }
    printf("This will be printed two times\n");
    }
}
```

35. *The syntactic form of a* for *loop is as follows:*

    for(expression$_1$;expression$_2$;expression$_3$)
    statement

    What is the order in which expression$_1$, expression$_2$, expression$_3$ and statement get evaluated?

    The order in which the expressions are evaluated is:

    1. expression$_1$ is evaluated before the first evaluation of the controlling expression expression$_2$. expression$_1$ is evaluated only once.
    2. expression$_2$ is the controlling expression and is evaluated every time before the execution of the loop body. If expression$_2$ evaluates to true, the loop (i.e. statement) body will be executed otherwise the control will come out of the loop.
    3. expression$_3$ is evaluated after the execution of the loop body.

Code Snippets

Determine the output of the following code snippets. Assume that the inclusion of the required header files has been made and there is no prototyping error due to them.

36.
```
int a=10,b=20,c;
c=a+b;
main()
{
    printf("Value of c is %d",c);
}
```

37.
```
main()
{
    int a=10,b=20,c;
    c=a+2*b
    printf("The value of c is %d",c);
}
```

38.
```
main()
{
    int a=10,b=20;
    if(a==b)
        printf("a=10,b=20");
```

```
        printf("a and b are not equal");
    }
```

39.
```
main()
{
    int a=10,b=20;
    if(a==b)
    {
        printf("a=10, b=20");
        printf("a and b are not equal");
    }
}
```

40.
```
main()
{
    int a=10,b=20;
    if(a=b)
        printf("a and b are equal");
    else
        printf("a and b are not equal");
}
```

41.
```
main()
{
    int a=10,b=20;
    if(a==b);
        printf("a and b are equal");
    else
        printf("a and b are not equal");
}
```

42.
```
main()
{
    int a=10,b=10;
    if(a==b)
        printf("a and b are equal\n");
    else;
        printf("a and b are not equal\n");
}
```

43.
```
main()
{
    if(1)
        printf("This will always get executed");
    else
        printf("This will never get executed");
}
```

44.
```
main()
{
    if(printf("Hello"))
        printf("Students");
}
```

45. main()
```
{
int a=10,b=20;
if(a==10)
if(b==10)
printf("Value of a and b is 10");
else
printf("Value of a is 10 and b is something else");
}
```

46. main()
```
{
    int a=10,b=20;
    if(a==10)
    {
    if(b==10)
        printf("Value of a and b is 10");
    }
    else
        printf("Value of a is 10 and b is something else");
}
```

47. main()
```
{
    int expr=10;
    switch(expr)
        printf("This is valid but will not get executed");
}
```

48. main()
```
{
    int expr=10;
    switch(expr);
        printf("Tell whether this will get executed or not");
}
```

49. main()
```
{
    float expr=2.0;
    switch(expr)
    {
        case 1: printf("One");
        case 2: printf("Two");
        default: printf("Default");
    }
}
```

50. main()
```
{
    int expr=2,j=1;
    switch(expr)
    {
    case j:
```

```
        printf("This is case 1");
    case 2:
        printf("This is case 2");
    default:
        printf("This is default case");
    }
}
```

51. main()

```
{
    char ch='A';
    switch(ch)
    {
        case 'A':
            printf("Case label is A");
        case "B":
            printf("Case label is B");
    }
}
```

52. main()

```
{
    int expr=1;
    switch(expr)
    {
        case 1: printf("One\n");
        case 2: printf("Two\n");
        default: printf("Three\n");
    }
}
```

53. main()

```
{
    int expr=1;
    switch(expr)
    {
        case 1:
            printf("One\n");
            break;
        case 2:
            printf("Two\n");
            break;
        default: printf("Three\n");
    }
}
```

54. main()

```
{
    int expr=3;
    switch(expr)
    {
        default: printf("Three\n");
```

```
        case 1: printf("One\n");
        case 2: printf("Two\n");
    }
}
```

55. main()

```
{
    int expr=2;
    switch(expr)
    {
        case 1:
            printf("This is case 1");
        case 2-1:
            printf("This is case 2");
    }
}
```

56. main()

```
{
    int i=1,j=3;
    switch(i)
    {
        case 1:
            printf("This is outer case 1\n");
            switch(j)
            {
                case 3:
                    printf("This is inner case 1\n");
                    break;
                default:
                    printf("This is inner default case");
            }
        case 2:
            printf("This is outer case 2");
    }
}
```

57. main()

```
{
    int expr=2;
    switch(expr)
    {
        case 1:
            printf("This is case 1");
            break;
        case 2:
            printf("This is case 2");
            continue;
        default:
```

```
            printf("Default");
        }
    }
```

58. main()

```
    {
        default:
            printf("This is default labeled statement");
        goto default;
    }
```

59. main()

```
    {
        int i=l;
        while(i<=5)
        {
            printf("%d ",i);
            i=i+l;
        }
        printf("\nThe value of i after the loop is %d",i);
    }
```

60. main()

```
    {
        int i=l;
        while(i<=5);
        {
            printf("%d\n ",i);
            i=i+l;
        }
        printf("The value of i after the loop is %d",i);
    }
```

61. main()

```
    {
        int i=l;
        while(i<=5)
            printf("%d ",i);
        printf("The value of i after loop is %d",i);
    }
```

62. main()

```
    {
        int i=l;
        for(    )
        {
            printf("%d",i);
            if(i=5)
                break;
        }
    }
```

63. main()
```
{
    int i;
    for(i=1;i<=32767;i++)
        printf("%d ",i);
}
```

64. main()
```
{
    int i=1;
    for(;;)
    {
        printf("%d ",i);
        if(i==5)
            break;
    }
}
```

65. main()
```
{
    int i=1;
    for(;;)
    {
        printf("%d",i);
        if(i=5)
            break;
    }
}
```

66. main()
```
{
    int i=1;
    for(;i<=5;printf("%d ",i++));
}
```

67. main()
```
{
    int i=1;
    for(;i<=10;i++)
    {
        if(i%2==0)
            continue;
        printf("%d ",i);
    }
}
```

68. main()
```
{
    int i=1;
    loop:
        printf("%d ",i++);
```

```
        if(i==5) break;
        goto loop;
    }
```

69. main()
```
    {
        int i=1;
        loop:
            printf("%d ",i++);
        if(i==5) goto out;
        goto loop;
        out:
        ;
    }
```

70. main()
```
    {
        int i,j;
        for(i=1;i<3;i++)
            for(j=1;j<4;j++)
            {
                if(j==2) break;
                printf("%d %d\n",i,j);
            }
    }
```

71. main()
```
    {
        int i,j;
        for(i=1;i<3;i++)
            for(j=1;j<4;j++)
            {
                if(j==2) continue;
                printf("%d %d\n",i,j);
            }
    }
```

72. main()
```
    {
        int i=3;
        for(;i++=0;)
            printf("%d",i);
    }
```

73. main()
```
    {
        int a=0, b=20;
        char x=1, y=10;
        if(y,x,b,a)
            printf("hello");
    }
```

74. main()
```
{
    int i=0;
    for(;i++;)
        printf("%d",i);
}
```
75. main()
```
{
    int i=0;
    for(;++i;)
        printf("%d",i);
}
```
76. main()
```
{
    int i=3,j=3;
    for(;i<6,j<4;i++,j++)
        printf("%d %d\n",i,j);
}
```
77. main()
```
{
    int i=1;
    while (i<=5)
    {
        printf("%d",i);
        if (i>2)
            goto here;
        i++;
    }
}
other_function()
{
    here:
        printf("The label is in other function");
}
```
78. main()
```
{
    int i=3;
    goto label;
    for(i=0;i<5;i++)
    {
        label:
            printf("%d ",i);
    }
}
```
79. main()
```
{
    int i=5;
```

```
    do
    {
        printf("%d",i);
        i++;
    }while(i<10)
}
```

80. main()

```
{
    int i=5;
    do
    {
        printf("%d",i);
        i++;
    }while(i<0);
}
```

Multiple-choice Questions

81. The smallest independent logical unit in a C program is
    a. Expression
    b. Token
    c. Statement
    d. None of these

82. In C language, statements are terminated with
    a. Period
    b. Semicolon
    c. New-line character
    d. None of these

83. By default, statements in a C program are executed
    a. Randomly
    b. Sequentially in top to bottom order
    c. Sequentially in bottom to top order
    d. None of these

84. `int ival;` is actually a
    a. Declaration statement
    b. Definition statement
    c. Neither a declaration statement nor a definition statement
    d. Declaration as well as a definition statement

85. Sentinel-controlled loop is also known as
    a. Definite repetition loop
    b. Infinite repetition loop
    c. Indefinite repetition loop
    d. None of these

86. Case label inside `switch` body must be
    a. An expression
    b. An integral expression
    c. A constant integral expression
    d. An integer constant

87. Which of the following forms of `for` statement is syntactically valid
    a. `for(;;);`
    b. `for(;;)`
    c. `for(;)`
    d. `for();`

88. The selection expression of `switch` statement must be of
    a. Integer type
    b. Float type
    c. Integral type
    d. String type

89. The C construct that is used to terminate the current iteration of a loop is
   a. break statement
   b. continue statement
   c. return statement
   d. None of these

90. Dangling else is an ambiguity that arises when in a statement the number of else clauses are
   a. Equal to the number of if clauses
   b. Less than the number of if clauses
   c. Greater than the number of if clauses
   d. None of these

91. The C construct that is used to terminate a loop is
   a. break statement
   b. continue statement
   c. return statement
   d. None of these

92. Minimum number of times a do-while loop will be executed is
   a. 0
   b. 1
   c. Cannot be predicted
   d. None of these

93. Which of the following statement is true about continue statement?
   a. It terminates the loop
   b. It terminates the current iteration of the loop
   c. It can be used in or as a switch body
   d. None of these

94. The body of a switch statement must consist of
   a. Case-labeled statements
   b. Default-labeled statements
   c. A statement
   d. Null statement

95. A continue statement can only be used in or as
   a. switch body
   b. Loop body
   c. if body
   d. None of these

96. Labels have
   a. Block scope
   b. Global scope
   c. Function scope
   d. File scope

97. A goto statement cannot take control
   a. Out of nested if-else
   b. Out of a nested loop
   c. Out of a function
   d. None of these

98. Consider the following segment of C code:

```
int j,n;
j=1;
while(j<=n)
    j=j*2;
```

The number of comparison made in the execution of the loop for any n>0 is
   a. ceiling($\log_2$n)+2
   b. n
   c. ceiling($\log_2$n)+1
   d. floor($\log_2$n)+2

99. Consider the following fragment of C code in which i, j and n are integer variables.

```
for(i=n,j=0;i>0;i/=2,j+=1);
```

The value of j after the termination of for loop is
   a. floor($\log_2$n)+1
   b. n/2+1
   c. n
   d. ceiling($\log_2$n)+1

100. Consider the following fragment of C code. How many times will the following loop be executed?

```
x=500;
while(x<=500)
{
    x=x-600;
    if(x<0) break;
}
```

a. 0
b. 100
c. 500
d. 1

Outputs and Explanations to Code Snippets

36. Compilation error

Explanation:

Non-executable statements can be placed outside the body of a function but executable statements can only be placed within the body of a function. c=a+b; is an executable statement and cannot be placed outside the body of a main function. To remove this error, place the statement c=a+b; inside the body of the main function.

37. Compilation error (Statement missing ; in function main)

Explanation:

c=a+2*b is not a statement. It is an expression. No entity smaller than a statement can independently exist in a C program. Hence, the error. To remove this error, convert the expression c=a+2*b into a statement by terminating it with a semicolon.

38. a and b are not equal

Explanation:

printf("a and b are not equal"); does not belongs to if body. It is a statement next to if statement and will always be executed irrespective of the result of evaluation of if controlling expression.

39. No output

Explanation:

The if body is a compound statement consisting of two printf statements. Being a compound statement, it will be treated as a unit, i.e. a single statement. Either all of its constituent statements will be executed or none will get executed depending upon the outcome of the if controlling expression. Here, the if controlling expression evaluates to false. Hence, if body (i.e. printf statements) will not be executed and thus, there is no output.

40. a and b are equal

Explanation:

The controlling expression of if-else statement is a=b. An assignment operator has been used instead of equality operator. The value of b is assigned to a and the value of expression comes out to be 20 (i.e. the assigned value of b). 20 is a non-zero value, i.e. true. If the if-else controlling expression evaluates to true, if body will get executed. Hence, if body (i.e. printf("a and b are equal");) gets executed and a and b are equal is the result.

41. Compilation error (Misplaced else in function main)

Explanation:

This error is due to the presence of a semicolon after the if-else controlling expression. The mentioned code will be interpreted in the following way:

```
main()
{
    int a=10,b=20;
    if(a==b)
        ;                          //←if body is a null statement
    printf("a and b are equal");   //←This statement is next to if statement
    else                           //←else clause is without any if clause
        printf("a and b are not equal");
}
```

To rectify this code, either remove the semicolon or make the null statement and printf("a and b are equal"); statement a single statement by enclosing them within braces.

42. a and b are equal
    a and b are not equal

    Explanation:

    a and b are not equal is a part of the output due to the presence of a semicolon after the else clause. Null statement forms the else body. printf("a and b are not equal"); statement is a statement next to the if-else statement and will always get executed irrespective of the result of the evaluation of if-else controlling expression.

43. This will always get executed

    Explanation:

    The controlling expression of if-else statement is 1. 1 is a non-zero value and is considered as true. Every time you run this program, This will always get executed is the output as if-else controlling expression always evaluates to true.

44. HelloStudents

    Explanation:

    The controlling expression of if statement is evaluated first. Controlling expression of if statement is printf("Hello"). Function calls are valid expressions, so writing if(printf("Hello")) will not lead to any compilation error. The expression gets evaluated and Hello is printed on the screen. The printf function also returns an integer value. The value returned by the printf function is the number of characters it prints. The number of characters in Hello is 5; hence, printf function returns 5. 5 is a non-zero value and is treated as true. As the controlling expression of if statement evaluates to true, if body gets executed and Students is printed on the screen. Hence, the output that gets printed is: HelloStudents.

Forward Reference: Functions and the values returned by them (Chapter 5).

45. Value of a is 10 and b is something else

    Explanation:

    The code suffers from dangling else ambiguity. The ambiguity is implicitly resolved by the compiler and the code is interpreted in the following way:

```
main()
{
    int a=10,b=20;
    if(a==10)
        if(b==10)
            printf("Value of a and b is 10");
```

```
    else
        printf("Value of a is 10 and b is something else");
}
```

The given code has an if statement whose body consists of an if-else statement. The controlling expression of if statement (i.e. a==10) evaluates to true, so its body (i.e. if-else statement) gets executed. The controlling expression of if-else statement (i.e. b==10) evaluates to false, and hence the else body, i.e. printf("Value of a is 10 and b is something else"); gets executed.

46. No output

Explanation:

This code does not suffer from dangling else ambiguity. There is an if-else statement whose if body consists of another if statement and else body consists of a printf statement. The controlling expression of an if-else statement (i.e. a==10) evaluates to true, hence its if body will be executed and else body will be skipped. The if statement present inside the if body of if-else statement starts execution and its controlling expression (i.e. b==10) evaluates to false. Hence, its body will not be executed and thus, nothing gets printed.

47. No output

Explanation:

The switch statement is executed according to the rule mentioned below:
The switch selection expression is evaluated and the result of evaluation of the switch selection expression is compared against the value associated with each case label until either a match is successful or all labels have been examined. If the result of evaluation of the switch selection expression matches the value of a case label, the execution begins from the statement with that case label. The execution continues across case/default boundaries till the end of the switch statement. If there is no match, the execution begins from the statement with the default label if it is present; otherwise the execution of the program continues with the statement following the switch statement.
According to the above-mentioned rule, execution can start only with the matched case labeled statement or the default labeled statement, if it is present. Since the printf statement is neither a matched case labeled statement nor a default labeled statement, it will not be executed. Hence, there will be no output.

48. Tell whether this will get executed or not

Explanation:

Null statement present after the switch controlling expression forms the switch body. The printf statement does not belong to switch body and is a statement present next to the switch statement. This statement will always be executed irrespective of the value of switch selection expression.

49. Compilation error

Explanation:

switch selection expression and case labels must be of integral type. Since in the given code switch selection expression is of float type, there will be a compilation error.

50. Compilation error

Explanation:

Case label must be a compile time constant integral expression. Since in the given code, variable j is used as case label, there is a violation of syntactic rule and this leads to the compilation error.

51. Compilation error

    Explanation:

    Case label must be of integral type, i.e. either integer type or character type. Usage of string as case label (i.e. case "B") is a violation of syntactic rule and leads to the compilation error.

52. One
    Two
    Three

    Explanation:

    A common misunderstanding is that only the statements associated with the matched case label are executed. Rather, execution begins there and continues across case/default boundaries until the end of switch statement is encountered.

53. One

    Explanation:

    The case label 1 gets matched with the value of switch selection expression. Execution begins from the statement with the case label 1. printf("One\n"); gets executed and One is printed on the screen. The execution of statements would have been carried out till the end of switch statement but the break statement is encountered after the printf statement. This break statement terminates the switch statement. Hence, the rest of the case labeled, default labeled and other statements do not get executed. Thus, One is the output.

54. Three
    One
    Two

    Explanation:

    There is no constraint about the position of default labeled statement within the switch body. It can be placed before the case labeled statements, in-between the case labeled statements or after the case labeled statements. Generally, it is placed after the case labeled statements but it can be placed anywhere within the switch body. In the given piece of code, default labeled statement is placed before the case labeled statements. The result of evaluation of switch selection expression is matched with the case labels. Since none of the case labels (i.e. 1 and 2) get matched with the evaluated value of the switch selection expression (i.e. 3), the execution starts from the statement with the default label and is carried out across the case boundaries till the end of the switch statement. Hence, the printf statements associated with case labels 1 and 2 also gets executed.

55. Compilation error

    Explanation:

    The case labels should be unique. Although the case labels in the given piece of code seems to be unique but they are actually the same. The constant expression 2-1 gets evaluated to 1. Since case label 1 is already present, there is 'Duplicate case in function main' error.

56. This is outer case 1
    This is inner case 1
    This is outer case 2

    Explanation:

    The body of the switch statement consists of three statements:

    1. case labeled statement-1
       case 1:

printf("This is outer case 1\n");

2. switch(j) {...}
3. case labeled statement-2

   case 2:

   printf("This is outer case 2\n");

The execution of the statements starts from the statement with the matched case label. Since case label 1 gets matched with the value of the switch selection expression (i.e. value of i), the execution starts with printf("This is outer case 1\n");. The execution from this point is carried out till the end of the switch statement. After the execution of the printf statement, statement 2, i.e. the inner switch statement starts execution. The body of the inner switch also consists of three statements:

1. Case-labeled statement-1

   case 3:

   printf("This is inner case 1\n");
2. break;
3. Default-labeled statement

   default:

   printf("This is inner default case\n");

Since the value of selection expression of the inner switch (i.e. value of j) matches the case label 3, execution starts with printf("This is inner case 1\n");. Execution from this point would have been carried out till the end of the inner switch statement but after the execution of printf statement break statement is encountered. This break statement terminates the execution of the nearest enclosing switch (i.e. inner switch statement). Hence, the default labeled statement is not executed and the control is immediately transferred to the case labeled statement-2 of the outer switch statement. The statement printf("This is outer case 2\n"); gets executed.

This illustrates that there can be a switch statement within the body of another switch statement. Hence, switch statements can be nested.

57. Compilation error: "Misplaced continue in function main()"

Explanation:

A continue statement shall appear only in or as a loop body. It cannot appear in or as a switch body. In the given piece of code, continue is placed inside the switch body. This is a violation of the syntactic rule and leads to the compilation error 'Misplaced continue in function main.'

58. Compilation error

Explanation:

Remember the following syntactic rules:

1. case labeled and default labeled statements can appear only inside the switch statement.
2. case label and default label cannot be used with a goto statement. Only identifier labels can be used with the goto statement.

Since there is violation of both the above-mentioned rules, there are compilation errors:

1. 'Default outside of switch in function main' (Due to violation of rule 1)
2. 'Goto statement missing label in function main' (Due to violation of rule 2)

59. 1 2 3 4 5

    The value of i after the loop is 6

    Explanation:

    The controlling expression (i<=5) is evaluated first and comes out to be true. The body of the loop is executed. 1 gets printed and value of i becomes 2. The controlling expression is evaluated again with the value of i being 2 (i.e. 2<=5). It comes out to be true and 2 gets printed. In this way 3 4 5 gets printed. The value of i becomes 6. The controlling expression (i.e. 6<=5) becomes false and the loop terminates. The value of i when the loop terminates is 6 and gets printed by the next printf statement.

60. No output

    Caution:

    Infinite loop

    Explanation:

    The presence of a semicolon at the end of the while header makes this program to stick into an infinite loop. The controlling expression of a while statement is true and the body of the while statement gets executed. The body of the while statement is a null statement. Null statement produces no output. There is no expression in the body of the while statement that manipulates the value of the loop counter so that the controlling expression eventually evaluates to false. Due to the absence of a manipulating expression, the controlling expression of the while statement always evaluates to true and keeps on executing the null statement. Hence, there will be no output and the program will not terminate as it is trapped inside an infinite loop.

61. 1 1 1 1 1 ...infinite times

    Caution:

    Infinite loop

    Explanation:

    An expression that manipulates the value of the loop counter is missing. The controlling expression of the while statement always evaluates to true. Thus, an infinite loop.

62. Compilation error

    Explanation:

    The general form of for statement is:

    for(expression$_1$;expression$_2$;expression$_3$)

    statement

    All the expressions in for header are optional and can be skipped. Even if all the expressions are missing, it is mandatory to create three sections by placing two semicolons. In the given code, the for header does not have the required sections. Thus, it is syntactically incorrect and leads to a compilation error.

63. 1 2 3 ...32767 -32768 -32767...32767 -32768 -32767...infinite times

    Caution:

    Infinite loop

    Explanation:

    The loop counter i is initialized to 1. The condition i<=32767 (i.e. 1<=32767) evaluates to true. Hence, the loop body gets executed and 1 is printed. The expression i++ gets evaluated and the value of i becomes 2. Condition i<=32767 (i.e. 2<=32767) evaluates to true. The loop body gets executed and 2 is printed. This process is continued till the value 32767 gets printed. Now, when i++ is evaluated, the value of i does not becomes 32768 as 32768 exceeds the range of the integer data type. Instead it becomes -32768 due to the wrap around effect. Thus, the condition i<=32767 (i.e. -32768<=32767) still evaluates to true. Hence, the condition never becomes false and the loop will not terminate.

64. 1 1 1 1...infinite times

Caution:

Infinite loop

Explanation:

for(;;) is syntactically valid and semantically (i.e. logically) it is an infinite loop. Inside the body of for loop, a break statement is present and it seems to be an exit path from the loop. The break statement will only be executed if the value of i becomes 5. Since the body of the for loop contains no expression to manipulate the value of i, the value of i will never become 5 and thus the break statement will never be executed. Hence, 1 will be printed infinite number of times.

65. 1

Explanation:

The initial value of i is 1. No condition is present inside the header of the for loop. Hence, without checking any condition, the body of the loop starts execution. printf("%d",i) gets executed and the value 1 gets printed. The statement present next to the printf statement is an if statement. The controlling expression of if statement is evaluated. The if controlling expression (i.e. i=5) has an assignment operator instead of an equality operator. The value 5 is assigned to i and the if controlling expression evaluates to true. Thus, the body of if statement, i.e. break statement gets executed. The break statement terminates the for loop. Hence, 1 is the output.

66. 1 2 3 4 5

Explanation:

In the given piece of code, condition i<=5 (i.e. 1<=5) evaluates to true. Thus, the body of the for loop, i.e. a null statement gets executed. After the execution of the body, the manipulation section (i.e. printf("%d ",i++)) gets executed. It prints the current value of i (i.e. 1) and then increments the value of i to 2. Again, the condition is checked and the above process is repeated. In this way 2 3 4 5 also gets printed.

67. 1 3 5 7 9

Explanation:

For even values of i, the if controlling expression i%2==0 evaluates to true. The body of the if statement (i.e. continue statement) gets executed. The continue statement on execution, immediately transfers the control to the header of the loop and the rest of the statements in the body of the loop will not be executed for the current iteration. Thus, for the even values of i, printf statement will not be executed.

68. Compilation error

Explanation:

break statement shall appear only in or as a switch body or a loop body. Logically, we have created a loop by using goto statement but since no looping construct (i.e. for, while or do-while) is used, a break statement cannot be placed there. Hence, the compilation error 'Misplaced break in function main' occurs.

69. 1 2 3 4

Explanation:

goto loop; statement is used to create a logical loop and goto out; statement is used to take the control out of this logical loop. The printf statement present inside the logical loop prints the value of i. The value of i is manipulated by the expression i++. When the value of i becomes 5, goto out; takes the control out of the logical loop and the logical loop terminates.

70. 1 1
2 1

Explanation:

Value of i	Condition of outer for loop	Value of j	Condition of inner for loop	Controlling expression of if statement (j==2)	Whether break is executed	Whether printf statement is executed	The values that get printed
1	True	1	True	False	No	Yes	1 1
		2	True	True	Yes	No	
2	True	1	True	False	No	Yes	2 1
		2	True	True	Yes	No	
3	False	Outer for loop is terminated					

71. 1 1
1 3
2 1
2 3

Explanation:

Value of i	Condition of outer for loop	Value of j	Condition of inner for loop	Controlling expression of if statement (j==2)	Whether continue is executed	Whether printf statement is executed	The values that get printed
1	True	1	True	False	No	Yes	1 1
		2	True	True	Yes	No	
		3	True	False	No	Yes	1 3
		4	False	Inner for loop is terminated			
2	True	1	True	False	No	Yes	2 1
		2	True	True	Yes	No	
		3	True	False	No	Yes	2 3
		4	False	Inner for loop is terminated			
3	False	Outer for loop is terminated					

72. Compilation error

Explanation:

++ operator has higher priority than an assignment operator and will get evaluated first. The expression i++ evaluates to an r-value and cannot be placed on the left side of the assignment operator. Thus, i++=0 leads to the compilation error 'L-value required in function main'.

73. No output

Explanation:

The if controlling expression is y,x,b,a. In if controlling expression, the sub-expressions y, x, b and a are separated by comma operators. The comma-separated expressions (i.e. y, x, b and a) are evaluated from left to right and the result of evaluation of full expression is the result of evaluation of the right-most sub-expression (i.e. a). Since a is 0, the value of the entire expression y,x,b,a turns out to be 0. 0 is considered as false and hence the if body will not be executed.

74. No output

Explanation:

i is initialized with 0. The condition of the for loop (i.e. i++) has post-increment operator. This means, firstly the value of i (i.e. 0) is used for the evaluation of expression and then the value of i will be incremented. Thus, the controlling expression of the loop evaluates to 0, i.e. false. Hence, the body of the loop will not be executed and there will be no output.

75. 1 2 ...32767 -32768 -32767...-1

Explanation:

The condition of the for loop has a pre-increment operator. The value of i is incremented first and then used for the evaluation of expression. The value of i first becomes 1 and then is used for the evaluation of the for controlling expression. Since the controlling expression evaluates to true, the body of the loop will be executed and 1 gets printed. The condition is evaluated again, i becomes 2 and gets printed. This process is repeated till 32767 gets printed. Now, when ++i is evaluated, i becomes -32768 instead of 32768 (due to the range wrapping to the other side). This is a non-zero value and will be treated as true and it gets printed. The condition is evaluated again, i becomes -32767 and gets printed. This process is repeated till -1 is printed. After printing of -1, ++i gets evaluated and i becomes 0. 0 is treated as false; hence, the condition of the loop becomes false and the loop terminates.

76. 3 3

Explanation:

The condition of the for loop is an expression i<6,j<4. This expression has two sub-expressions separated by a comma operator. The sub-expressions will be evaluated from left to right but the outcome of the full expression, i.e. i<6,j<4 depends upon the outcome of the right-most sub-expression, i.e. j<4. Hence, till the sub-expression j<4 evaluates to true, the body of the loop will be executed. The initial value of j is 3. The sub-expression j<4 (i.e. 3<4) evaluates to true and the body of the loop will be executed. The value that gets printed is 3 3. After the execution of the body of the loop, the expression i++,j++ gets evaluated. Both i and j become 4. Now the condition j<4 (i.e. 4<4), evaluates to false and the loop gets terminated.

77. Compilation error

Explanation:

A label name is a type of identifier that has only function scope.➲ In function main, goto here; statement is present but there is no label named here. The label here present inside the body of other_function is not visible inside the function main, as label names have only function scope. Hence, the compilation error 'Undefined label here in function main' occurs.

Forward Reference: Scopes, function scope (Chapter 8).

78. 3 4

    Explanation:

    The goto statement is capable of taking the program control in or out of a loop. In the given piece of code, the goto statement is used to transfer the program control inside the for loop. Since the goto statement transfers the control inside the for loop, the initialization expression in the for header will not be executed. Hence, the value of i remains 3 instead of being initialized to 0. After this the for loop works normally and 3 4 gets printed.

79. Compilation error

    Explanation:

    The general form of the do-while statement is:
    ```
    do
    statement
    while(expression);
    ```
    The semicolon after the while controlling expression is a must, else there will be a compilation error 'Statement ; missing'.

80. 5

    Explanation:

    do-while is an exit-controlled loop. The body of the loop will be executed once, even if the controlling condition is initially false. In the given piece of code, the controlling expression is initially false, even then the body of the do-while loop is executed once, and 5 gets printed.

Answers to Multiple-choice Questions

81. c 82. b 83. b 84. b 85. c 86. c 87. a 88. c 89. b 90. b 91. a 92. b 93. b 94. c 95. b 96. c 97. c 98. d 99. a 100. d

Programming Exercises

Program 1 | Check whether a given number is even or odd without using modulus operator

Whether a number is even or odd can be determined by checking its Least Significant Bit (LSB). If the first bit of a number is: (LSB = last bit shown)

- 0, the number is even, e.g. 6, i.e. 0000 0000 0000 0110
- 1, the number is odd, e.g. 13, i.e. 0000 0000 0000 1101

PE 3-1.c

```
//Even or odd without using modulus operator
#include<stdio.h>
main()
{
int num;
printf("Enter the number\t");
scanf("%d",&num);
if((num&1)==0)
    printf("Number %d is even",num);
else
    printf("Number %d is odd",num);
}
```

Output window

```
Enter the number    12
Number 12 is even
```

Program 2 | Check whether a given year is leap or not

A year is a **leap year,** if:

- It is divisible by 4 but not by 100, or
- It is divisible by 400.

PE 3-2.c

```
//Leap year
#include<stdio.h>
main()
{
int year;
printf("Enter the year\t");
scanf("%d",&year);
if(((year%4==0) && (year%100!=0)) || (year%400==0))
    printf("%d is a leap year", year);
else
    printf("%d is not a leap year", year);
}
```

Output window

```
Enter the year    2004
2004 is a leap year
```

Program 3 | Calculate the roots of a quadratic equation

The roots of a quadratic equation $ax^2 + bx + c = 0$ can be obtained by using the expression $x = \frac{-b \pm \sqrt{b^2 - 4ac}}{2a}$, where b^2–$4ac$ is called discriminant.

If $b^2-4ac > 0$, the roots are real and unequal.

If $b^2-4ac = 0$, the roots are real and equal, i.e. $x = \frac{-b}{2a}$.

If $b^2-4ac < 0$, the roots are imaginary, i.e. $x = \frac{-b}{2a} \pm \sqrt{\frac{b^2 - 4ac}{2a}}\, i$.

PE 3-3.c

```
//Roots of a quadratic equation
#include<stdio.h>
#include<math.h>
main()
{
int a, b, c, d;
float r1,r2;
int num;
printf("Enter the coefficients a, b and c\t");
scanf("%d %d %d", &a, &b, &c);
d=b*b-4*a*c;
if(d>0)
{
    r1=(-b+sqrt(d))/(2*a);
    r2=(-b-sqrt(d))/(2*a);
    printf("Roots are real and unequal\n");
```

Output window

```
Enter the coefficients a, b and c    1 4 3
Roots are real and unequal
Roots are: -1.000000 -3.000000
```

(Contd...)

```
    printf("Roots are: %f %f",r1,r2);
}
else if(d==0)
{
    r1= -b/(2*a);
    printf("Roots are real and equal\n");
    printf("Roots are: %f %f",r1,r1);
}
else
    printf("No real roots, roots are imaginary");
}
```

Program 4 | Find the sum of individual digits in a given positive integer number

PE 3-4.c

```
//Find sum of digits of a given number
#include<stdio.h>
main()
{
int num,sum=0,digit;
printf("Enter the number\t");
scanf("%d",&num);
while(num!=0)
{
    digit=num%10;
    sum=sum+digit;
    num=num/10;
}
printf("Sum of digits is %d",sum);
}
```

Output window

```
Enter the number    786
Sum of digits is 21
```

Program 5 | Find the reverse of a given number

PE 3-5.c

```
//Reverse of a given number
#include<stdio.h>
main()
{
int num,reverse=0, digit;
printf("Enter the number\t");
scanf("%d",&num);
while(num!=0)
{
    digit=num%10;
    num=num/10;
    reverse=reverse*10+digit;
}
printf("Reverse is %d", reverse);
}
```

Output window

```
Enter the number    534
Reverse is 435
```

Program 6 | Check whether a given number is a palindrome or not

A number is a **palindrome** if the reverse of the number is equal to the number itself, e.g. 121, 535, etc.

PE 3-6.c

```
//Palindrome
#include<stdio.h>
main()
{
int num, temp, digit, reverse=0;
printf("Enter the number\t");
scanf("%d",&num);
temp=num;
while(temp!=0)
{
    digit=temp%10;
    temp=temp/10;
    reverse=reverse*10+digit;
}
if(num==reverse)
    printf("%d is a palindrome", num);
else
    printf("%d is not a palindrome", num);
}
```

Output window

```
Enter the number    1234
1234 is not a palindrome
```

Output window (second execution)

```
Enter the number    12321
12321 is a palindrome
```

Program 7 | Check whether a given number is perfect or not

An integer is said to be a **perfect number** if its factors (including 1) sum to the number, e.g. 6 is a perfect number as 6=1+2+3, 28 is a perfect number as 28=1+2+4+7+14.

PE 3-7.c

```
//Perfect number
#include<stdio.h>
main()
{
int num, sum=0, i;
printf("Enter the number\t");
scanf("%d",&num);
for(i=1;i<num;i++)
{
    if(num%i==0)
        sum=sum+i;
}
if(num==sum)
    printf("%d is a perfect number", num);
else
    printf("%d is not a perfect number", num);
}
```

Output window

```
Enter the number    28
28 is a perfect number
```

Output window (second execution)

```
Enter the number 23
23 is not a perfect number
```

Program 8 | Print first n perfect numbers

PE 3-8.c

```
//First n perfect numbers
#include<stdio.h>
main()
{
int num=1, sum=0, i, count=1, n;
printf("How many numbers you want to print\t");
scanf("%d", &n);
printf("Perfect numbers are:\n");
while(count<=n)
{
    for(i=1;i<num;i++)
    {
        if(num%i==0)
            sum=sum+i;
    }
    if(num==sum)
    {
        printf("%d\t",num);
        count++;
    }
    num++; sum=0;
}
}
```

Output window

```
How many numbers you want to print    3
Perfect numbers are:
6    28    496
```

Program 9 | Check whether a given number is an Armstrong number or not

A number is said to be an **Armstrong number** if the sum of cube of its digits is equal to the number itself, e.g. 153 is an Armstrong number as $153=1^3+5^3+3^3$, i.e. $153 = 1 + 125 + 27$.

PE 3-9.c

```
//Armstrong number
#include<stdio.h>
main()
{
int num, temp, digit, sum=0;
printf("Enter the number\t");
scanf("%d",&num);
temp=num;
while(temp!=0)
{
    digit=temp%10;
    sum=sum+digit*digit*digit;
    temp=temp/10;
}
if(num==sum)
    printf("%d is an Armstrong number", num);
else
    printf("%d is not an Armstrong number",num);
}
```

Output window

```
Enter the number    153
153 is an Armstrong number
```

Output window (second execution)

```
Enter the number 221
221 is not an Armstrong number
```

Program 10 | Fibonacci series

Fibonacci series is a series in which a term is equal to the sum of the previous two terms. The first term of the series is 0 and the second term is 1.

PE 3-10.c

```
//Fibonacci series:    0 1 1 2 3 5 8 13 21 ...
#include<stdio.h>
main()
{
int n, count=2, a=0, b=1, c;
printf("How many terms do you want to print\t");
scanf("%d",&n);
printf("Fibonacci series:\n");
printf("%d\t%d\t",a,b);
while(count<n)
{
    c=a+b;
    printf("%d\t", c);
    a=b;
    b=c;
    count++;
}
}
```

Output window

```
How many terms do you want to print    5
Fibonacci series:
0    1    1    2    3
```

Program 11 | Find sum of all odd numbers that lie between 1 and n

PE 3-11.c

```
//Sum of odd numbers 1+3+5+7...+n
#include<stdio.h>
main()
{
int n, sum=0, i=1;
printf("Enter the value of n\t");
scanf("%d",&n);
while(i<=n)
{
    if(i%2==1)
        sum=sum+i;
    i++;
}
printf("Sum of odd numbers from %d to %d is %d",1,n,sum);
}
```

Output window

```
Enter the value of n    5
Sum of odd numbers from 1 to 5 is 9
```

Program 12 | Find the sum of series 1+(1+2)+ (1+2+3) +(1+2+3+4)... n terms

PE 3-12a.c

```
//Sum of the given series
#include<stdio.h>
main()
{
int num, i=1, j, sum=0;
printf("Enter the number of terms\t");
```

PE 3-12b.c

```
//Sum of the given series
//Output in a better way
#include<stdio.h>
main()
{
int num, i=1, j, sum=0;
```

Output window PE 3-12a.c

```
Enter the number of terms    3
Sum of the series is 10
```

Output window PE 3-12b.c

```
Enter the number of terms    3
(1)+(1+2)+(1+2+3)= 10
```

(Contd...)

```
scanf("%d",&num);
while(i<=num)
{
    j=1;
    while(j<=i)
    {
        sum=sum+j;
        j++;
    }
    i++;
}
printf("Sum of the series is %d", sum);
}
```

```
printf("Enter the number of terms\t");
scanf("%d",&num);
while(i<=num)
{
    j=1;
    printf("(");
    while(j<=i)
    {
        printf("%d",j);
        sum=sum+j;
        j++;
        if(j<=i)
            printf("+");
        else
            printf(")");
    }
    if(i<num)
        printf("+");
    i++;
}
printf("= %d", sum);
}
```

Program 13 | Find the sum of series $1^2 + 2^2 + 3^2 + \ldots$ n terms

PE 3-13.c

```
//Sum of the given series
#include<stdio.h>
main()
{
int n, i=1, sum=0;
printf("Enter the number of terms\t");
scanf("%d",&n);
while(i<=n)
{
    sum=sum + i*i;
    i++;
}
printf("Sum of series is %d",sum);
}
```

Output window

```
Enter the number of terms    5
Sum of series is 55
```

Program 14 | Find the sum of series 1+1/2+1/3+... n terms

PE 3-14.c

```
//Sum of the given series
#include<stdio.h>
main()
{
int n, i=1;
float sum=0;
printf("Enter the number of terms\t");
scanf("%d",&n);
```

Output window

```
Enter the number of terms    3
Sum of series is 1.833333
```

(Contd...)

PE 3-14.c

```
while(i<=n)
{
    sum=sum + 1/(float)i;
    i++;
}
printf("Sum of series is %f",sum);
}
```

Output window

Program 15	Making use of sine series, evaluate the value of sin(x), where x is in radians

According to sine series: $\sin(x) = x - \frac{x^3}{3!} + \frac{x^5}{5!} - \frac{x^7}{7!} + \ldots \frac{x^n}{n!}$

PE 3-15.c

```
//Evaluate sin(x)
#include<stdio.h>
main()
{
int i=1,n;
float sum, term, x;
printf("Enter the value of x in radians\t");
scanf("%f",&x);
printf("Enter the power of end term\t");
scanf("%d",&n);
sum=0;
term=x;
i=1;
while(i<=n)
{
    sum=sum + term;
    term=(term*x*x*-1)/((i+1)*(i+2));
    i=i+2;
}
printf("Sin of %4.2f is %f",x, sum);
}
```

Output window

```
Enter the value of x in radians    3.14
Enter the power of end term    25
Sin of 3.14 is 0.001593
```

Program 16	Reverse, add and check for palindrome

Problem statement: Take a number, reverse its digits and add the reverse to the original. If the sum is not a palindrome, repeat the procedure with the sum until the result is a palindrome. Write a program that takes a number and gives the resulting palindrome and the number of additions it took to find it.

Test case:

354	807	1515
+ 453	+ 708	+ 5151
807	1515	6666

Result: Palindrome is 6666 and the number of additions to find it is 3.

(Contd...)

PE 3-16.c

```
//Comment: Reverse and Add
#include<stdio.h>
#include<conio.h>
main()
{
int num, temp, reverse=0, add=0, digit;
printf("Enter the number\t");
scanf("%d",&num);
while(1)
{
    temp=num;          //←Save num in temp
    reverse=0;
    while(temp!=0)     //←Find the reverse of temp
    {
        digit=temp%10;
        reverse=reverse*10+digit;
        temp=temp/10;
    }
    if(num==reverse)     //←Is it a palindrome
    {
        printf("\nPalindrome is %d and no. of addition is %d",reverse, add);
        break;
    }
    else                   //←If no, repeat the procedure with sum
    {
        printf("  %d\n",num);
        printf("+ %d\n",reverse);
        num=num+reverse;
        printf("----------\n");
        printf("  %d\n",num);
        printf("-----------\n");
        add++;          //←Keep track of number of additions performed
    }
}
}
```

Output window

```
Enter the number   354
  354
+ 453
----------
  807
----------
  807
+ 708
----------
  1515
----------
  1515
+ 5151
----------
  6666
----------

Palindrome is 6666 and no. of addition is 3
```

Program 17 | Print pyramid of digits as shown below for n number of lines

Pyramid of digits:

```
      1
    2 3 2
  3 4 5 4 3
4 5 6 7 6 5 4
.................................
```

Logic to print the pyramid:

			1			
		2	3	2		
	3	4	5	4	3	
4	5	6	7	6	5	4

(Contd...)

1. Get the number of rows in the pyramid, let it be n.
2. In each row r (where r is the row number) leave (n-r) spaces blank and then print (2r-1) values. The printing of values starts with the row number. The first $\left\lceil \frac{2r-1}{2} \right\rceil$ values are printed by incrementing the previously printed value. The next $\left\lfloor \frac{2r-1}{2} \right\rfloor$ values are printed by decrementing the previously printed value.

PE 3-17.c

```
//Print pyramid of digits
#include<stdio.h>
main()
{
int n, r=1, val, j;
printf("Enter the number of rows in the pyramid\t");
scanf("%d",&n);
while(r<=n)                          //←Print n rows
{
     val=r;                          //←Printing starts with row number
     for(j=1;j<=n-r;j++)
          printf("\t");              //←Print n-r blank spaces
     for(j=1;j<=2*r-1;j++)
          if(j<=(2*r-1)/2)           //←Printing left half of the row
               printf("%d\t",val++);
          else if(j==(2*r-1)/2+1)    //←Printing middle element of row
                    printf("%d\t",val);
               else                  //←Printing right half of the row
                    printf("%d\t",--val);
     printf("\n");
     r++;
}
}
```

Output window

```
Enter the number of rows in the pyramid    4
                  1
             2    3    2
        3    4    5    4    3
   4    5    6    7    6    5    4
```

Program 18 | Print Floyd's triangle

Floyd's triangle:

```
1
2  3
4  5  6
7  8  9  10
..................................
```

Logic to print Floyd's triangle:

1. Get the number of rows in the Floyd's triangle, let it be n.
2. In each row r (where r is the row number), print r values. The printing of values starts with 1. Successive values are printed by incrementing the previously printed values.

(Contd...)

PE 3-18.c

```
//Floyd's triangle
#include<stdio.h>
main()
{i
nt n, r=1, val=1, j;
printf("Enter the number of rows in the triangle\t");
scanf("%d",&n);
while(r<=n)          //←Print n rows
{
     for(j=1;j<=r;j++)              //←Printing a row
          printf("%d\t",val++);    //←Printing values
     printf("\n");                 //←New-line for next row
     r++;
}
}
```

Output window

```
Enter the number of rows in the triangle    4
1
2   3
4   5   6
7   8   9   10
```

Test Yourself

1. Fill in the blanks in each of the following:
   a. The smallest logical entity that can independently exist in a C program is ___________.
   b. Statements in C language are terminated with a/an ___________.
   c. A compound statement is also known as ___________.
   d. The types of labeled statements are ___________, ___________, ___________.
   e. A case label should be a compile time constant expression of ___________ type.
   f. The form of looping in which the number of iterations to be performed is known in advance is called ___________.
   g. The execution or termination of a sentinel-controlled loop depends upon a special value known as ___________.
   h. Sentinel-controlled loop is also known as ___________.
   i. The statements for which no machine code is generated are called ___________.
   j. To alter the default flow of control, ___________ statements are used.
   k. ___________ statement is used to terminate the current iteration of the enclosing loop.
   l. An expression terminated with a semicolon is known as ___________ statement.
   m. ___________ is an exit-controlled loop.
   n. The ___________ statement when executed in a `switch` statement causes immediate exit from it.
   o. Careless use of nested `if-else` statement may lead to ___________ problem.
2. State whether each of the following is true or false. If false, explain why.
   a. Only non-executable statements can appear outside the body of a function.
   b. Null statement performs no operation.
   c. An empty compound statement is equivalent to a null statement.
   d. An entry-controlled loop is executed at least once.
   e. Identifier-labeled statement is a branching statement and alters the flow of control.
   f. A `continue` statement can appear inside, or as a body of `switch` statement or a loop.
   g. Case-labeled statements can appear only inside the body of a `switch` statement.
   h. A `break` statement is used to terminate the current iteration of the loop.
   i. A `switch` selection expression can be of any type.
   j. In an entry-controlled loop, if the body of the loop is executed n times the expression in the condition section is evaluated n+1 times.
3. Write a simple C statement to accomplish each of the following:
   a. Test if the value of the variable `count` is greater than `10`. If so, print "Count is greater than 10".
   b. Assign the value `10` to the variables `a`, `b` and `c`.
   c. Increment the value of variable `var` by `10` and then assign it to variable `stud`.
   d. Test if the least significant bit of the variable `num` is `1`. If so, assign `10` to variable `a` else assign `20` to it.
   e. Find factorial of a number `n` and assign it to variable `fact`.
4. Programming exercise:
   a. Write a C program that prints the integers between 1 and `n` which are divisible by 7. Get the value of `n` from the user.
   b. Write a C program that prints the integers from 1 to `n` omitting those integers which are divisible by 7. Get the value of `n` from the user.
   c. Write a C program that prints the integers between 1 and `n` which are divisible by 3, but not divisible by 4.

d. Write a C program to find the sum of all integers that lie between 1 and `n` and are divisible by 7.
e. Write a C program to evaluate 1×2×3×4×...`n`. Get the value of `n` from the user.
f. Write a C program to print first `n` Armstrong numbers. Get the value of `n` from the user.
g. Write a C program to print first `n` prime numbers. Get the value of `n` from the user.
h. Write a C program to evaluate the following series (Get the value `x` and `n` from the user):

i. $\cos(x) = 1 - \frac{x^2}{2!} + \frac{x^4}{4!} - \frac{x^6}{6!} + \cdots \infty$

ii. $\cosh(x) = 1 + \frac{x^2}{2!} + \frac{x^4}{4!} + \frac{x^6}{6!} + \cdots \infty$

iii. $\exp(x) = 1 + x + \frac{x^2}{2!} + \frac{x^3}{3!} + \frac{x^4}{4!} \cdots \infty$

iv. $e = 1 + \frac{1}{1!} + \frac{1}{2!} + \frac{1}{3!} \ldots + \frac{1}{n!}$

v. $\frac{\pi^2}{6} = 1 + \frac{1}{2^2} + \frac{1}{3^2} + \frac{1}{4^2} \ldots \infty$

i. Write a C program to generate the following patterns (get the number of rows in the pattern from the user):

1.
```
1 2 3 4 5
  1 2 3
    1
```

2.
```
    1
  1 2 3
1 2 3 4 5
  1 2 3
    1
```

4

ARRAYS AND POINTERS

Learning Objectives

In this chapter, you will learn about:

- The limitation of basic data types
- Derived data types: array type and pointer type
- Arrays
- Single-dimensional and multi-dimensional arrays
- Declaration and usage of arrays
- Memory representation of arrays
- Different ways of storing multi-dimensional arrays
- Pointers
- Operations allowed on pointers
- Pointer arithmetic
- void pointer and null pointer
- Relationship between arrays and pointers
- Arrays of pointers
- Pointer to a pointer
- Pointer to an array
- Advantages and limitations of arrays

4.1 Introduction

So far you have learnt about the basic data types, expressions and statements. In the previous chapter, you have learnt the use of iteration statements to perform repetitive tasks like summing first n natural numbers, etc. Consider a problem to find the average of marks secured by five students in a course. A piece of code written for it is given in Program 4-1.

Prog 4-1.c

```c
//Average of marks secured by students
#include<stdio.h>
main()
{
    int marks1=10, marks2=12, marks3=9, marks4=11, marks5=17;
    int sum; float average;
    sum=marks1+marks2+marks3+marks4+marks5;
    average=sum/5.0;
    printf("Average marks secured is %f ",average);
}
```

Output window

```
Average marks secured is 11.800000
```

Program 4-1 | A program to find average marks secured by students

The powerful iteration statements discussed in Chapter 3 have not been used here to sum up the marks secured by the students because the marks are stored in separate variables and it is not possible to access them in a generalized way. Since there are only five students, it is possible to find the average in the above-mentioned manner. Now suppose there are 200 students in a course. For a problem of this scale, it is not feasible to create separate variables for storing the marks and finding the average in the above-mentioned manner. To solve such problems, a method is required that helps in storing and accessing data in a generalized and an efficient manner. The C language provides this method in the form of a derived data type known as **array type** or just **array**.

Consider another real-time problem that requires storing and processing names like "Sam" entered by the user. There is no basic data type available in C that provides this flexibility. A variable of `char` type can be used to store only one character but cannot be used to store all the three characters of the name "Sam". The derived array type provides a solution to this problem. An array enables the user to store the characters of the entered name in a contiguous set of memory locations, all of which can be accessed by only one name, i.e. the array name.

The array type has a close relationship with another derived data type, known as the **pointer type** or just **pointer**. Their relationship is so intimate that they cannot be studied in isolation. In this chapter, I will describe both arrays and pointers. Finally, we will look at the operations that can be applied on them and how to use them to solve problems.

4.2 Arrays

An **array** is a data structure✍ that is used for the storage of homogeneous data, i.e. data of the same type. Figure 4.1 depicts arrays of four different types.

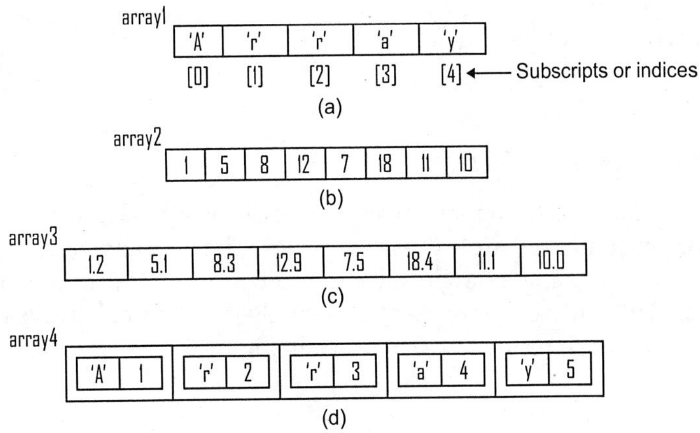

Figure 4.1 | (a) Character array; (b) integer array; (c) float array; (d) array of user-defined type

The important points about arrays are as follows:

1. An **array** is a collection of elements of the same data type. The data type of an element is called **element type**. For example, in Figure 4.1, the element type of array1 is char, array2 is int, array3 is float and array4 is user-defined type.
2. The individual elements of an array are not named. All the elements of an array share a common name, i.e. the **array name**. For example, in Figure 4.1 (a), all the elements of array, i.e. 'A', 'r', 'r', 'a' and 'y' have a common name, i.e. array1.
3. The individual elements of an array are distinguished and are referred to or accessed according to their positions in an array. The position of an element in an array is specified with an integer value known as **index** or **subscript**. Because arrays use indices or subscripts to access their elements, they are also known as **indexed variables** or **subscripted variables**.
4. The array index in C starts with 0, i.e. index of the first element of an array is 0.
5. The memory space required by an array can be computed as (**size of element type**) × (**Number of elements in an array**). For example, in Figure 4.1, array1 takes 1×5, i.e. 5 bytes in the memory, array2 takes 16 bytes (if an integer occupies 2 bytes), array3 takes 32 bytes and array4 takes 15 bytes (if an integer takes 2 bytes) in the memory.
6. Arrays are always stored in contiguous (i.e. continuous) memory locations. For example, in Figure 4.1, if the first element of array1 is stored at memory location 2000, then the successive elements of the array will be stored at the memory locations 2001, 2002, 2003 and 2004. In case of array2, if the first element is stored at memory locations 2000-2001, the next elements will be stored at the memory locations 2002-2003, 2004-2005, and so on.

Data structure is a logical representation of data. It provides systematic mechanisms for storage, retrieval and manipulation of data. Examples of data structures are: **arrays**, stacks, queues, linked lists, trees, etc.

Forward Reference: User-defined data types (Chapter 9).

In general, arrays are classified as:

1. Single-dimensional arrays
2. Multi-dimensional arrays

4.3 Single-dimensional Arrays

A **single-dimensional** or **one-dimensional array** consists of a fixed number of elements of the same data type organized as a simple linear sequence. The elements of a single-dimensional array can be accessed by using a single subscript, thus they are also known as **single-subscripted variables**. The other common names of single-dimensional arrays are **linear arrays** and **vectors**. Single-dimensional arrays are shown in Figure 4.2.

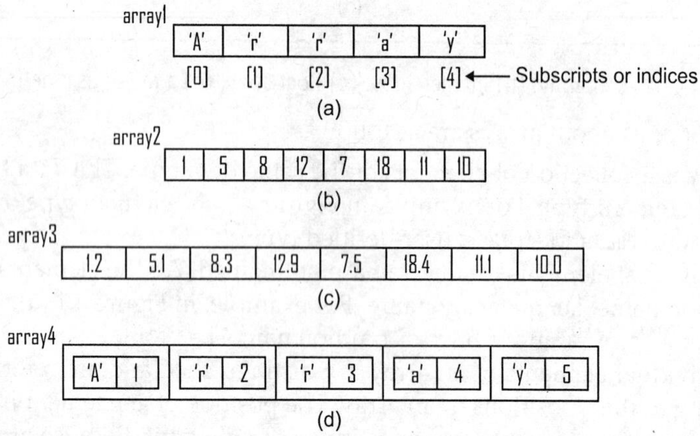

Figure 4.2 | Single-dimensional arrays

There are two aspects of working with arrays:

1. Declaration (i.e. creation) of array
2. Usage (i.e. storing or referring elements) of array

4.3.1 Declaration of a Single-dimensional Array

The general form of a single-dimensional array declaration is:

<storage_class_specifier➲><type_qualifier><type_mod>**type_specifier identifier[**<size_specifier>**]**<=initialization_list<,...>>;

Forward Reference: Storage class specifier (Chapter 7).

The important points about a single-dimensional array declaration are as follows:

1. The terms enclosed within angular brackets (i.e. <>) are optional and might not be present in a declaration statement. The terms shown in bold are the mandatory parts of a single-dimensional array declaration.

2. A single-dimensional array declaration consists of a type specifier (i.e. **element type**), an identifier (i.e. **name of array**) and a size specifier (i.e. **number of elements** in the array) enclosed within square brackets (i.e. []). The following declarations of single-dimensional arrays are valid:

```
int array1[8];    //←array1 is an array of 8 integers               (Integer array)
float array2[5];  //←array2 is an array of 5 floating point numbers (Floating point array)
char array3[6];   //←array3 is an array of 6 characters             (Character array)
```

3. The size specifier specifies the number of elements in an array. The syntactic rules about the size specifier are as follows:

   a. It should be a compile time constant expression of integral type.

   Reasons:

   i. The memory space to an array is allocated at the compile time. The memory requirement of an array depends upon its element type and the number of elements (i.e. size) in it. Hence, the size of an array must be known at the compile time so that memory can be allocated to it.

   ii. The size of an array cannot be expanded or squeezed at the run-time. Thus, size must be a constant expression so that it cannot be changed at the run-time.

   The following declarations of single-dimensional arrays are valid:

```
int array1[3+5];      //←3+5 is a compile time constant expression of int type
float array2[size];   //←where size is a qualified constant of integral type
char array3[size];    //←where size is a symbolic constant of integral type
```

   The following declarations of single-dimensional arrays are not valid:

```
int array1[j];        //← j is a variable and not a constant
int array2[3.5];      //←It is not possible to create an array of 3.5 locations
```

   b. It should be greater than or equal to one.

   Reason: It is not possible to create an array of size zero, i.e. having no element.

   It is allowed to create an array of size 1, i.e. having only one element. Array of size 1 is like a simple variable and does not provide any significant advantage.

   The following declarations of single-dimensional arrays are not valid:

```
int array1[-1];       //← It is not possible to create an array of -1 locations
char array2[0];       //← It is not possible to create an array of 0 locations
```

   c. The size specifier is mandatory if an array is not explicitly initialized, i.e. if an initialization list is not present.

   Reason: If an initialization list is present, it is possible to determine the size of array from the number of initializers in the initialization list. In that case, the size specification becomes optional.

   The following declaration of a single-dimensional array is not valid:

```
int array1[];         //←Here, it is not possible to determine the size of array
                      //← Hence, the amount of memory to be allocated cannot
                      //   be determined
```

4. **Initializing elements of a single-dimensional array:** Like variables can be initialized, similarly the elements of an array can also be initialized. The syntactic rules about the initialization of array elements are as follows:

   a. The elements of an array can be initialized by using an **initialization list**. An initialization list is a comma-separated list of initializers enclosed within braces.

   b. An **initializer** is an expression that determines the initial value of an element of the array.

   c. If the type of initializers is not the same as the element type of an array, implicit type casting will be done, if the types are compatible. If types are not compatible, there will be a compilation error. The code segment in Program 4-2 illustrates this fact.

Prog 4-2.c

```
//Initializers of compatible but different types
#include<stdio.h>
main()
{
    int arr1[]={2.3, 4.5, 6.9};
    float arr2[]={'A','B','C'};
    printf("Elements of arrays are initialized with\n");
    printf("arr1: %d %d %d\n",arr1[0],arr1[1],arr1[2]);
    printf("arr2: %f %f %f\n",arr2[0],arr2[1],arr2[2]);
}
```

Output window

```
Elements of arrays are initialized with
arr1: 2 4 6
arr2: 65.000000 66.000000 67.000000
```

Remarks:

- The element types of the arrays are different from the types of initializers but the types are compatible
- float initializers are demoted and then elements of arr1 are initialized
- char initializers are promoted before initializing the elements of arr2. ASCII values of characters are used

Program 4-2 | A program to illustrate that the initializer's type can be different from the element type of an array

   d. The number of initializers in the initialization list should be less than or at most equal to the value of size specifier, if it is present.

   The following declarations of single-dimensional arrays are valid:

```
int array1[]={1,2,3,4,5}; //←Initialization list {1,2,3,4,5} present
int array2[]={2+3,a+5}; //←Initializers are 2+3 and a+5, where a is an int variable
char array3[6]={'A','r','r','a','y'};   //←Number of initializers is less than the value of
                                        // size specifier
```

   The following declaration of a single-dimensional array is not valid:

```
int array1[2]={1,2,3,4,5}; //← Number of initializers cannot be more than the
                           // value of size specifier
```

   e. If the number of initializers in the initialization list is less than the value of the size specifier, the leading array locations (i.e. occurring first) equal to the number of initializers get initialized with the values of initializers. The rest of the array locations get initialized to 0 (if it is an integer array), 0.0 (if case of floating point array) and '\0' (i.e. null character, if it is an array of character type). The above-mentioned fact is shown in Figure 4.3.

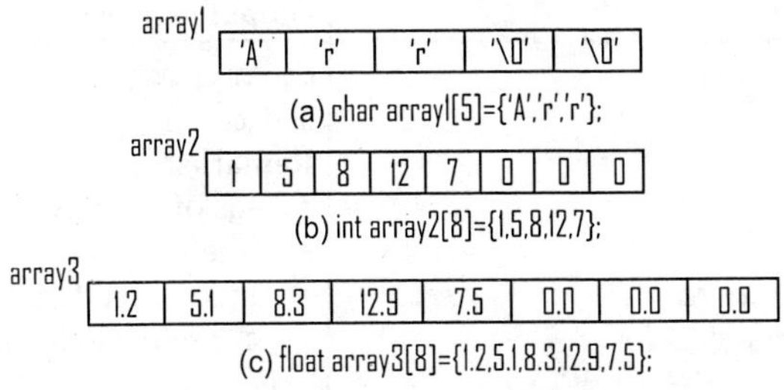

Figure 4.3 | Contents of arrays if the number of initializers is less than their size

4.3.2 Usage of Single-dimensional Array

The elements of a single-dimensional array can be accessed by using a subscript operator (i.e. []) and a subscript. The important points about the usage of single-dimensional arrays are as follows:

1. For accessing the elements of a one-dimensional array, the general form of expression is `E1[E2]`, where `E1` and `E2` are sub-expressions and `[]` is the subscript operator. One of the sub-expressions `E1` or `E2` must be of an array type or a pointer type[†] and the other sub-expression must be of an integral type.
2. The sub-expression of the integral type (i.e. the subscript) must evaluate to a value greater than or equal to `0`.
3. The array subscript in C starts with `0`, i.e. the subscript of the first element of an array is `0`. Thus, if the size of an array is `n`, the valid subscripts are from `0` to `n-1`. However, if the array index greater than `n-1` is used while accessing an element of the array, there will be no compilation error. This is due to the fact that C language does not provide compile time or run-time **array index out-of-bound check**. However, using an out-of-bound index may lead to run-time error or exceptions. Thus, care must be taken to ensure that the array indices are within bounds, i.e. from `0` to `n-1`.

An **array type** is one of the derived data types. It is said to be derived from an element type and if the element type is `T` (where `T` is a generic term and can be `int`, `float`, `char` or any other type), the array type is called '**array of `T`s**'. The construction of an array type from an element type is called '**array type derivation**'. Consider the declaration statement **`int array[5];`** the array type derived from an element type **`int`** is **`int[5]`**.

Forward Reference: Refer Question numbers 17 and 42 and their answers.

The code snippet in Program 4-3 illustrates the use of a singe-dimensional array.

[†] Refer Section 4.4 for a description on pointer type.

Prog 4-3.c

```
//Use of single-dimensional array
#include<stdio.h>
main()
{
    int a[3]={10,20,30};
    printf("Elements of array are:\n");
    printf("%d %d %d",a[0],a[1],a[2]);
}
```

Output window

```
Element of array are:
10 20 30
```

Remarks:

- a is of array type.
- The expression a[0] refers to the first element, a[1] refers to the second element and a[2] refers to the third element of the array

Program 4-3 | A program to illustrate the use of subscript operator

4.3.2.1 Reading, Storing and Accessing Elements of a One-dimensional Array

An iteration statement (i.e. loop) is used for storing and reading the elements of a one-dimensional array. The code snippet in Program 4-4 illustrates a method to read, store and access the elements of a single-dimensional array.

Prog 4-4.c

```
1  //Use of single-dimensional array
2  #include<stdio.h>
3  main()
4  {
5      int marks[200], lc, studs, sum=0;
6      float average;
7      printf("Enter the number of students in class\t");
8      scanf("%d",&studs);
9      printf("Enter marks of students\n\n");
10     for(lc=0;lc<studs;lc++)
11     {
12         printf("Enter marks of student %d\t",lc+1);
13 //Reading and storing elements in a 1-D array
14         scanf("%d",&marks[lc]);
15     }
16     for(lc=0;lc<studs;lc++)
17 //Accessing elements stored in the 1-D array
18         sum=sum+marks[lc];
19     average=(float)sum/studs;
20     printf("\nAverage marks of the class is %f",average);
21 }
```

Output window

```
Enter the number of students in class    5
Enter marks of students

Enter marks of student 1    10
Enter marks of student 2    12
Enter marks of student 3    9
Enter marks of student 4    11
Enter marks of student 5    17

Average marks of the class is 11.800000
```

Remarks:

- The marks of 200 students can be stored in an array named marks. The elements of the array can be accessed in general way by writing marks[lc], where lc ∈ {0....199}
- Although at the runtime marks of only 5 students are entered, the size of array is kept 200 to accommodate the worst case (i.e. 200 students)
- 195 locations are not used. Hence, 195*2=390 bytes of memory got wasted
- In line number 19, integer variable sum is explicitly type casted to float

Program 4-4 | A scalable version of Program 4-1

4.3.3 Memory Representation of Single-dimensional Array

The elements of an array are **stored in contiguous** (i.e. continuous) memory locations. This is depicted in Figure 4.4.

> *i* The mentioned addresses refer to the starting addresses of the elements. The first element in Figure 4.4(c) occupies the memory locations 2000–2003.

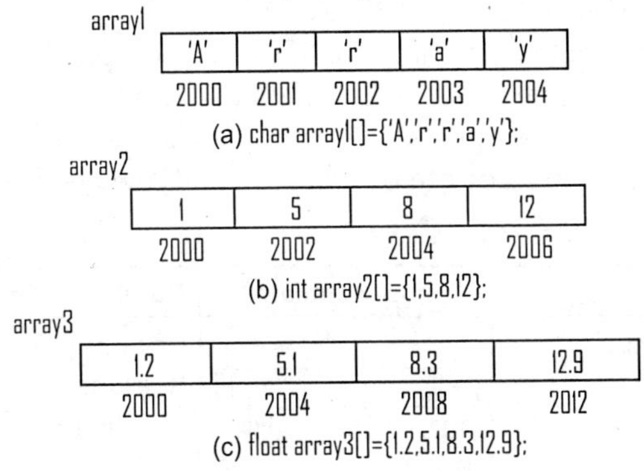

Figure 4.4 | Elements of the array are stored in contiguous memory locations

4.3.4 Operations on a Single-dimensional Array

4.3.4.1 Subscripting a Single-dimensional Array

The only operation allowed on arrays is **subscripting**. Subscripting is an operation that selects an element from an array. To perform subscripting in C language, a subscript operator (i.e. []) is used. The rules for subscripting have already been discussed in Section 4.3.2.

4.3.4.2 Assigning an Array to Another Array

A variable can be assigned to or initialized with another variable but an array cannot be assigned to or initialized with another array. The following statement is not valid and leads to a compilation error:

`array1=array2; //←where array1 and array2 are arrays of the same type and size`

Reason: In C language, the name of the array refers to the address of the first element of the array and is a constant object. It does not have a modifiable l-value. Since it does not have a modifiable l-value, it cannot be placed on the left side of the assignment operator.

To assign an array to another array, each element must be assigned individually. The code segment in Program 4-5 illustrates the mentioned fact.

Prog 4-5.c

```
//Assignment of an array to another array
#include<stdio.h>
main()
{
    int a[3], b[3]={10,20,30};
    printf("Assigning an array to an array:\n");
    a=b;
    printf("Elements of array a are:\n");
    printf("%d %d %d",a[0],a[1],a[2]);
}
```

Output window

Compilation error "L-value required in function main"

Reasons:

- The name of the array a refers to the address of the first element of the array and is a constant object
- It does not refer to a modifiable l-value
- Hence, it cannot be placed on the left side of the assignment operator

What to do?

- Making use of a loop, assign individual elements of array b to the elements of array a by writing a[i]=b[i], where i∈{0,1,2}

Program 4-5 | A program to illustrate that an array cannot be assigned to another array in one step

4.3.4.3 Equating an Array with Another Array

When the operands of an equality operator are of the array type, it always evaluates to false. **Reason:** In C language, the name of an array refers to the address of the first element of the array and the addresses of first elements of two arrays can never be the same. Hence, when the operands of an equality operator are of array type, it always evaluates to false. Program 4-6 illustrates the mentioned fact.

<table>
<tr><th>Prog 4-6.c</th><th>Memory contents</th><th>Output window</th></tr>
<tr>
<td><pre>
//Equality operator & arrays
#include<stdio.h>
main()
{
    int a[3]={10,20,30}, b[3]={10,20,30};
    if(a==b)
        printf("Arrays are equal");
    else
        printf("Arrays are not equal");
}
</pre></td>
<td>a
| 10 | 20 | 30 |
2000 2002 2004
b
| 10 | 20 | 30 |
4000 4002 4004</td>
<td>Arrays are not equal
Reasons:
• The name of arrays a and b refers to the addresses of their first elements, i.e. 2000 and 4000, respectively
• Since the addresses are different, the equality operator evaluates to false, although the contents of the arrays are the same
What to do?
• For checking equality, check the equality of all individual elements</td>
</tr>
</table>

Program 4-6 | A program to illustrate the behavior of equality operator on arrays

To check whether the contents of two arrays are the same or not, check the equality of each individual element.

Programs 4-5 and 4-6 illustrate that the name of an array refers to the address of the first element of the array. An expression of an array type (e.g. the name of array) is automatically converted to an expression of pointer type. This automatic conversion makes the simultaneous discussion of arrays and pointers essential.

4.4 Pointers

A **pointer** is a variable that holds the address of a variable or a function. A pointer is a powerful feature that adds enormous power and flexibility to C language. A pointer variable can be declared as:

[storage_class_specifier][type_qualifier][type_modifier]**type_specifier* identifier**[=l-value[,....]];

The important points about pointers are as follows:

1. The terms enclosed within square brackets (i.e. []) are optional and might not be present in a declaration statement. The terms shown in **bold** are the mandatory parts of a pointer variable declaration.
2. A pointer variable declaration consists of a type specifier (i.e. **referenced type**), **punctuator** * and an identifier (i.e. name of pointer variable). The following declarations are valid:

```
int *iptr;        //←iptr is pointer to an integer
float *fptr;      //←fptr is pointer to a float
char *cptr;       //←cptr is pointer to a character
```

```
const int *ptric;         //←ptric is pointer to an integer constant or constant integer
unsigned int *ptrui;      //←ptrui is pointer to an unsigned integer
```

3. Pointer variable declarations are read from the right side. The punctuator * is read as **'pointer to'**. So the declaration statement `int *iptr;` is read as 'iptr is a pointer to an integer'.

> The concept of pointer declaration is scalable. It is possible to declare a pointer to a variable, which itself is a pointer variable. Such a pointer is known as a **pointer to a pointer.**‡ The declaration statement **int **pptr;** declares a pointer to a pointer and is read as **'pptr is a pointer to a pointer to an integer'**.

4. A pointer variable can hold the address of a variable or a function. In Figure 4.5(a) iptr is an integer pointer and holds the address of an integer variable a. In Figure 4.5(c) pptr is pointer to pointer to an integer and holds the address of an integer pointer iptr, which in turn holds the address of an integer variable val.

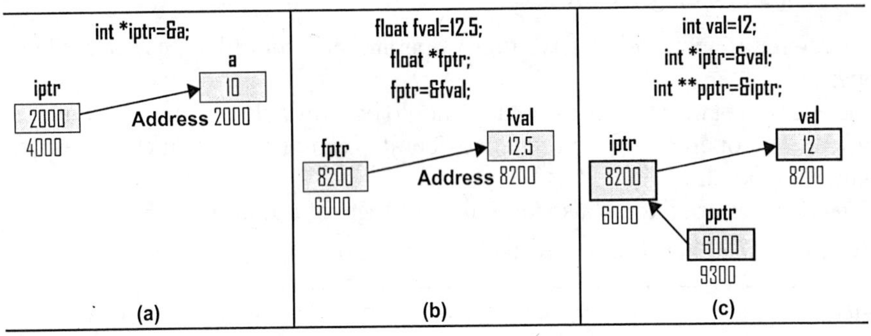

Figure 4.5 | Pointers holding addresses

5. Every pointer variable takes the same amount of memory space irrespective of whether it is a pointer to int, float, char or any other type. This fact is illustrated in the code segment given in Program 4-7.

Prog 4-7.c

```
//Size of pointer variables
#include<stdio.h>
main()
{
    char *cptr;
    int *iptr;
    float *fptr;
    printf("Pointer to character takes %d bytes\n",sizeof(cptr));
    printf("Pointer to integer takes %d bytes\n",sizeof(iptr));
    printf("Pointer to float takes %d bytes\n",sizeof(fptr));
}
```

Output window

```
Pointer to character takes 2 bytes
Pointer to integer takes 2 bytes
Pointer to float takes 2 bytes
```

Remarks:

- The above output is the result of execution using Borland Turbo C 3.0 IDE
- In Borland Turbo C 4.5 or MS-VC++ 6.0 each type of pointer variable takes 4 bytes

Program 4-7 | A program to illustrate that a pointer to any type takes the same amount of memory space

‡ Refer Section 4.6.3 for a description on the pointer to a pointer.

6. The value of a pointer variable is printed with %p format specifier. Since the pointer variables hold addresses, which are unsigned integers, %u format specifier can also be used for printing pointer values. However, the use of %p format specifier is recommended over the use of %u format specifier.

Forward Reference: Pointers to functions (Chapter 5).

4.4.1 Operations on Pointers

The operations allowed on pointers are as follows:

4.4.1.1 Referencing Operation

In **referencing operation**, a pointer variable is made to refer to an object. The reference to an object can be created with the help of a reference operator (i.e. &). The important points about the reference operator are as follows:

1. The reference operator, i.e. & is a unary operator and should appear on the left side of its operand.
2. The operand of the reference operator should be a variable of arithmetic type or pointer type. The operand of the reference operator can also be a function designator, i.e. name of a function.
3. The reference operator is also known as **address-of operator**.

The above-mentioned points are depicted in Figure 4.6.

```
float fval=12.5;     //← fval is a floating point variable initialized with 12.5
  float *fptr;       //← fptr is a pointer to float type
  fptr=&fval;        //← The address-of fval is assigned to fptr. fval is known as
                     //   referenced object and fptr is known as referencing
                     //   object and references fval
```

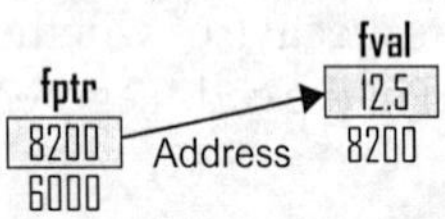

Figure 4.6 | A float pointer referencing a float variable

Integral and floating types are collectively called **arithmetic types**. A **pointer type** describes an object, whose value provides reference to an object of type T. T is a generic term and will be known as **reference type**. It can be int, float, char or any other type. A pointer type derived from the reference type T is called **'pointer to T'**. The construction of a pointer type is called **'pointer-type derivation'**.

Forward Reference: Function designator, pointer to a function (Chapter 5).

4.4.1.2 Dereferencing a Pointer

The object pointed to or referenced by a pointer can be indirectly accessed by dereferencing the pointer. A dereferencing operation allows a pointer to be followed to the data object to which it points. A pointer can be dereferenced by using a dereference operator (i.e. *). The important points about the dereference operator are as follows:

1. The dereference operator (i.e. *) is a unary operator and should appear on the left side of its operand.
2. The operand of a dereference operator should be of pointer type.
3. The dereference operator is also known as **indirection operator** or **value-at operator**.

The code snippet in Program 4-8 illustrates the use of a dereference operator.

Prog 4-8.c

```
//Dereferencing pointers
#include<stdio.h>
main()
{
    int val=12;
    int *iptr=&val;
    int **pptr=&iptr;
    printf("Value is %d\n",val);
    printf("Value by dereferencing iptr is %d\n",*iptr);
    printf("Value by dereferencing pptr is %d\n",**pptr);
    printf("Value of iptr is %p\n",iptr);
    printf("value of pptr is %p\n",pptr);
}
```

Memory

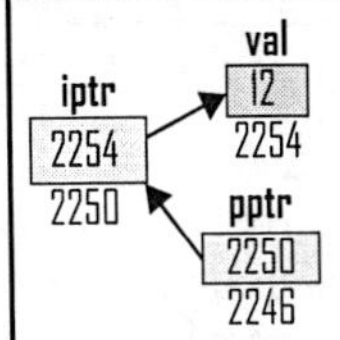

Output window

```
Value is 12
Value by dereferencing iptr is 12
Value by dereferencing pptr is 12
Value of iptr is 2407:2254
Value of pptr is 2407:2250
```

Remarks:

- The printed addresses are in the form of **segment address: offset address**
- The segment address and the offset address are in the **hexa-decimal number system**
- If the memory is assumed to be analogous to a city, the segment address is analogous to a sector number and the offset address is analogous to a house number
- The addresses that you get in the output may be different from the mentioned addresses as the memory allocation is purely random
- val=12, iptr=2254 and ptr=2250
- *iptr=value-at(iptr)=value-at(2254)=12
- **pptr=value-at(value-at(pptr))=value-at(value-at(2250))=value-at(2254)=12

Program 4-8 | A program to illustrate the dereferencing operation

4.4.1.3 Assigning to a Pointer

1. A pointer can be assigned or initialized with the address of an object. A pointer variable cannot hold a non-address value and thus can only be assigned or initialized with l-values. Program 4-9 illustrates this fact.

Prog 4-9.c	Memory contents	Output window

// Invalid assignment to pointer variable
#include<stdio.h>
main()
{
    int val=10;
    int *ptr=val;
    printf("Value of variable is %d\n",val);
    printf("Pointer holds %p\n", ptr);
}
	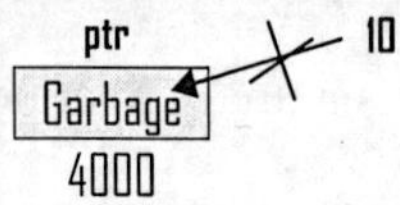	Compilation error "Cannot convert int to int*"
		Reasons:
		• Pointer variables can only hold addresses
		• A pointer variable ptr cannot hold an integer value val
		What to do?
		• Initialize ptr with the address of variable val by writing &val and re-execute the code

Program 4-9 | A program to illustrate that a pointer variable cannot hold a non-address value

> *i* There is an exception to this rule. The constant zero can be assigned to a pointer. For example, int *iptr=0; is valid. Assignment or initialization with zero makes the pointer a special pointer known as the **null pointer.**[§]

2. A pointer to a type cannot be initialized or assigned the address of an object of another type. Program 4-10 illustrates this fact.

Prog 4-10.c	Memory contents	Output window

// Invalid assignment to pointer variable
#include<stdio.h>
main()
{
    int val=10;
    float *ptr=&val;
    printf("Value of variable is %d\n",val);
    printf("Pointer holds %p\n", ptr);
}
	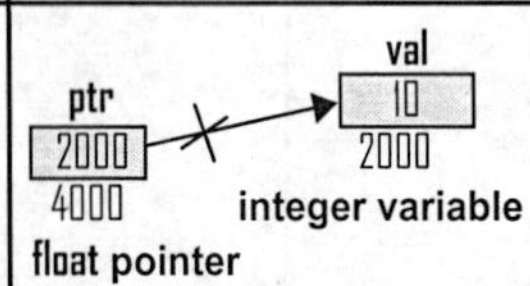
	A float pointer cannot point to an integer variable
		Compilation error "Cannot convert int* to float*"
		Reasons:
		• A pointer variable can only be assigned address of an object of the same type
		• A pointer variable ptr (of type float*) cannot hold the address of an integer variable (i.e. int*)
		What can be done?
		• Explicitly type cast int* to float* by using type cast operator. Write float* ptr=(float*)&val; and then re-execute the code
		Remark:
		• Explicit type casting of pointers may give unexpected results and is not recommended

Program 4-10 | A program to illustrate that a pointer to a type cannot be assigned address of an object of another type

[§] Refer Section 4.4.3 for a description on null pointer.

3. A pointer can be assigned or initialized with another pointer of the same type. However, it is not possible to assign a pointer of one type to a pointer of another type without explicit type casting.

---

i There is an exception to Rules 2 and 3. A pointer to any type of object can be assigned to a pointer of type `void*`¶ but vice-versa is not true. A **`void` pointer** cannot be assigned to a pointer to a type without explicit type casting.

4.4.1.4 Arithmetic Operations (Pointer Arithmetic)

Arithmetic operations can be applied to pointers in a restricted form. When arithmetic operators are applied on pointers, the outcome of the operation is governed by **pointer arithmetic**. The pointer arithmetic rules are mentioned below.

4.4.1.4.1 Addition Operation

1. An expression of integer type can be added to an expression of pointer type. The result of such operation would have the same type as that of pointer type operand. If `ptr` is a pointer to an object, then 'adding 1 to pointer' (i.e. `ptr+1`) points to the next object. Similarly, `ptr+i` would point to the ith object beyond the one the `ptr` currently points to. This is shown in Table 4.1.

Table 4.1 | Addition operation on pointers

S. No	Operator	Type of operand 1	Type of operand 2	Resultant type	Example	Initial value	Final value	How to determine?
1.	Addition operator (+)	Pointer to type T	int	Pointer to type T				Result = initial value of pointer + integer operand*`sizeof` (the reference type T)
	Example1:	`float*`	`int`	`float*`	`ptr=ptr+1`	`ptr=2000`	`2004`	`2000+1*(4)=2004` as `sizeof(float)=4`
	Example2:	`int*`	`int`	`int*`	`ptr=ptr+5`	`ptr=2000`	`2010`	`2000+5*(2)=2010`, if `sizeof(int)=2`
2.	Addition operator (+)	Pointer	Pointer	Not allowed				

2. Addition of two pointers is not allowed.
3. The addition of a pointer and an integer is commutative, i.e. `ptr+1` is same as `1+ptr`.

4.4.1.4.2 Increment Operation

The increment operator can be applied to an operand of pointer type. Table 4.2 depicts the application of an increment operator to an operand of a pointer type.

¶ Refer Section 4.4.2 for a description on `void` pointer.

Table 4.2 | Increment operation on a pointer

S. No	Operator	Type of operand	Resultant type	Example	Initial values	Final values	How to determine?
1.	Increment operator (++)	Pointer to type T	Pointer to type T				**Post-increment:** Result=initial value of pointer **Pre-increment:** Result = initial value of pointer + sizeof (the reference type T) **In both the cases:** Value of pointer=Value of pointer + sizeof (the reference type T)
Example1:	Post-increment	float*	float*	ftr=ptr++	ftr=? ptr=2000	ftr=2000 ptr=2004	
Example2:	Pre-increment	float*	float*	ftr=++ptr	ftr=? ptr=2000	ftr=2004 ptr=2004	

4.4.1.4.3 Subtraction Operation

1. A pointer and an integer can be subtracted. The operation along with examples is shown in Table 4.3.

Table 4.3 | Subtraction operation on pointers

S. No	Operator	Type of operand 1	Type of operand 2	Resultant type	Example	Initial value(s)	Final value	How to determine?
1.	Subtraction operator (-)	Pointer to type T	int	Pointer to type T				Result = initial value of pointer - integer operand *sizeof (the reference type T)
	Example1:	float*	int	float*	ptr=ptr-1	ptr=2000	1996	2000-1*(4)=1996 as sizeof(float)=4
	Example2:	int*	int	int*	ptr=ptr-5	ptr=2000	1990	2000-5*(2)=1990, if sizeof(int)=2
2.	Subtraction operator (-)	Pointer to type T	Pointer to type T	int				Result=(operand1-operand2)/ sizeof (the reference type T)
	Example3:	float*	float*	int	a=p2-p1	p1=2000 p2=2008	2	(2008-2000)/ sizeof(float)= (2008-2000)/4=2

2. Subtraction of integer and pointer is not commutative, i.e. ptr-1 is not the same as 1-ptr. The operation 1-ptr is illegal.
3. Two pointers can also be subtracted. Pointer subtraction is meaningful only if both the pointers point to the elements of the same array. The result of the operation is the difference in subscripts of two array elements. The mentioned rule is described in Table 4.3 and is depicted in Figure 4.7.

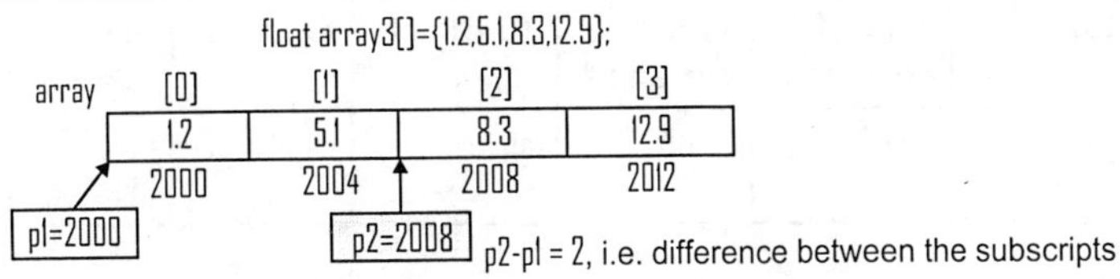

Figure 4.7 | Pointer subtracted from a pointer

4.4.1.4.4 Decrement Operation

The decrement operator can be applied to an operand of pointer type. Table 4.4 depicts the application of a decrement operator to an operand of pointer type.

Table 4.4 | Decrement operation on a pointer

S.No	Operator	Type of operand	Resultant type	Example	Initial values	Final values	How to determine?
1.	Decrement operator (--)	Pointer to type T	Pointer to type T				**Post- decrement:** Result=initial value of pointer **Pre-decrement:** Result = initial value of pointer - sizeof (the reference type T) **In both the cases:** Value of pointer=Value of pointer - sizeof (the reference type T)
Example1:	Post-decrement	float*	float*	ftr=ptr--	ftr=? ptr=2000	ftr=2000 ptr=1996	
Example2:	Pre-decrement	float*	float*	ftr=--ptr	ftr=? ptr=2000	ftr=1996 ptr=1996	

4.4.1.5 Relational (Comparison) Operations

A pointer can be compared with a pointer of the same type or with zero. A comparison of pointers is meaningful only when they point to the elements of the same array. Table 4.5 depicts the comparison of pointers.

Table 4.5 | Relational operations on pointers

S.No	Operator	Type of operand 1	Type of operand 2	Resultant type	Example	Initial values	Final value	How to determine?
1.	Comparison operators (==, !=, <, <=, >, >=)	Pointer to type T	Pointer to type T	int (0 i.e. false or 1 i.e. true)				
	Example1:	float*	float*	int	r=p1!=p2	p1=2000 p2=2008	1	
	Example2:	float*	float*	int	r=p1<p2	p1=2000 p2=2008	1	
	Example3:	float*	float*	int	r=p2>=p1	p1=2000 p2=2008	1	

(Contd...)

S.No	Operator	Type of operand 1	Type of operand 2	Resultant type	Example	Initial values	Final value	How to determine?
	Example4:	float*	float*	int	r=p2==p1	p1=2000 p2=2008	0	

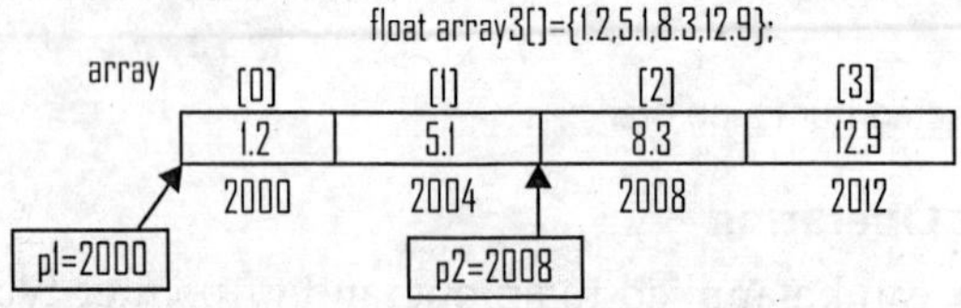

4.4.1.6 Illegal Pointer Operations

The following operations on pointers are not allowed:

1. Addition of two pointers is not allowed.
2. Only integers can be added to pointers. It is not valid to add a float or a double value to a pointer.
3. Multiplication and division operators cannot be applied on pointers.
4. Bitwise operators cannot be applied on pointers.
5. A pointer of one type cannot be assigned to a pointer of another type (except void*) without explicit type casting.
6. A pointer variable cannot be assigned a non-address value (except zero).

The pointer arithmetic discussed above is not applicable to void pointers. However, what actually are void pointers?

4.4.2 void pointer

void is one of the basic data types available in C language. void means nothing or not known. It is not possible to create an object of type void. For example, the following declaration statement is not valid and leads to 'Size of var unknown or zero' compilation error.

```
void var;
```

Although an object of type void cannot be created, it is possible to create a pointer to void. Such a pointer is known as a **void pointer** and has type void*. **void pointer** is a generic pointer and can point to any type of object. Figure 4.8 depicts the mentioned fact.

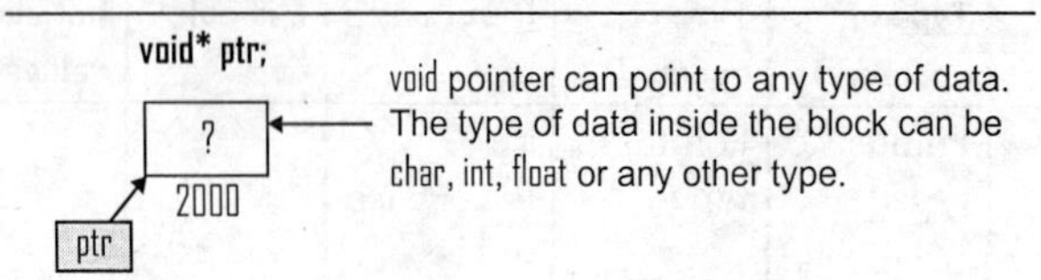

Figure 4.8 | void pointer

4.4.2.1 Operations on void Pointer

The following operations on void pointer are allowed:

1. A pointer to any type of object can be assigned to a void pointer. This is a standard conversion and the compiler will do it implicitly without any explicit type casting. This is shown in Program 4-11.

Line	Prog 4-11.c	Output window
1	`//Assigning a pointer to a void pointer`	int* is implicitly converted to void*
2	`#include<stdio.h>`	**Remarks:**
3	`main()`	• iptr is of int* type
4	`{`	• vptr is of void* type
5	`int a=10;`	• int* implicitly gets converted to void* in line number 7
6	`int *iptr=&a;`	
7	`void *vptr=iptr;`	
8	`printf("int* is implicitly converted to void*");`	
9	`}`	

Program 4-11 | A program to illustrate that pointer to any type implicitly gets converted to void*

2. void pointers can be compared for equality and inequality.

The following operations on void pointers are not allowed:

1. A void pointer cannot be dereferenced.
2. Pointer arithmetic is not allowed on void pointers.

Reason: A void pointer cannot be dereferenced and pointer arithmetic is not applicable on it because the compiler does not know what kind of object the void pointer is really pointing to. Hence, the precise number of bytes to which the pointer refers to is not known. The compiler must know the number of bytes to which a pointer refers to in order to apply dereference operation and pointer arithmetic.

Before the application of dereference operator or arithmetic operator on a void pointer, it must be explicitly type casted to a pointer to a specific type.

4.4.3 Null Pointer

A **null pointer** is a special pointer that does not point anywhere. It does not hold the address of any object or function. It has numeric value 0. The following declaration statement declares nptr as a null pointer:

```
int *nptr=0;
```

The macro or symbolic constant NULL defined in the header files stdio.h, stddef.h, stdlib.h, alloc.h and mem.h can also be used for the creation of a null pointer. The following declaration statement is equivalent to the declaration statement mentioned above:

```
int *nptr=NULL;
```

The important points about null pointers are as follows:

1. When a null pointer is compared with a pointer to any object or a function, the result of comparison is always false.
2. Two null pointers always compare equal.
3. Dereferencing a null pointer leads to a runtime error.

Forward Reference: Macros and symbolic constants (Chapter 8).

4.5 Relationship Between Arrays and Pointers

In C language, **arrays and pointers** are so closely related that they cannot be studied in isolation. They are often used interchangeably. The following relationships exist between arrays and pointers:

1. The name of an array refers to the address of the first element of the array, i.e. an expression of array type decomposes to pointer type. Program 4-12 illustrates this fact.

Prog 4-12.c

```
//Arrays and pointers relationship-1
#include<stdio.h>
main()
{
    int arr[3]={10,15,20};
    printf("First element of array is at %p\n",arr);
    printf("Second element of array is at %p\n",arr+1);
    printf("Third element of array is at %p\n",arr+2);
}
```

Output window

```
First element of array is at 2407:2242
Second element of array is at 2407:2244
Third element of array is at 2407:2246
```

Remarks:

- The name of the array (i.e. arr) refers to the address of the first element of the array and is a constant object
- The expression arr+1 decomposes to pointer type
- Thus, in expression arr+1, the arithmetic involved is pointer arithmetic
- Note that ++arr cannot be written instead of arr+1 as arr is a constant object

Program 4-12 | A program to depict the relationship between arrays and pointers

The name of an array refers to the address of the first element of the array but there are two exceptions to this rule:

a. When an array name is operand of sizeof operator it does not decompose to the address of its first element. Program 4-13 illustrates this fact.

Prog 4-13.c

```
//sizeof operator and arrays
#include<stdio.h>
main()
{
    int array[5]={10,15,20,25,30};
    printf("The result of sizeof operator is %d\n",sizeof(array));
}
```

Output window

```
The result of sizeof operator is 10
```

Remarks:

- The result of the sizeof operator is the size of the complete array (i.e. 5 elements * 2 bytes each = 10 bytes)
- This example clearly indicates that the name of the array is not decomposed into pointer type
- If it would have been decomposed into pointer type, the result would have been 2 as integer pointer takes 2 bytes in the memory (in case of Borland Turbo C 3.0)

Program 4-13 | A program to illustrate the application of the sizeof operator on arrays

b. When an array name is an operand of reference or address-of operator it does not decompose to the address of its first element.

2. In C language, any operation that involves array subscripting is done by using pointers. The expression of form E1[E2] is automatically converted into an equivalent expression of form *(E1+E2). Program 4-14 illustrates this fact.

Line | Prog 4-14.c

```
1 //Arrays and pointers relationship-II
2 #include<stdio.h>
3 main()
4 {
5     int array[3]={10,15,20};
6     printf("Elements are %d %d %d\n",array[0], array[1],array[2] );
7     printf("Elements are %d %d %d\n",*(array+0),*(array+1),*(array+2));
8     printf("Elements are %d %d %d\n",0[array],1[array],2[array]);
9 }
```

Output window

```
Elements are 10 15 20
Elements are 10 15 20
Elements are 10 15 20
```

Remarks:

- E1[E2] is the usual way of subscripting (used in line number 6)
- E1[E2] gets converted to *(E1+E2). The transformed way of subscripting is used in line number 7
- 0[array] used in line number 8 is also valid because 0[array] will automatically be converted to *(0+array), which is equivalent to *(array+0), + being a commutative operation
- *(array+0) is equivalent to array[0]. Hence, 0[array] is equivalent to array[0]

Program 4-14 | A program to depict the relationship between arrays and pointers

4.6 Scaling up the Concept

With all this knowledge at hand, it is the time to scale up the concept and look at array of arrays (i.e. multi-dimensional arrays), array of pointers, pointer to a pointer and pointers to arrays.

4.6.1 Array of Arrays (Multi-dimensional Arrays)

A **2-D array** is an array of 1-D (i.e. single dimensional) arrays and can be visualized as a plane that has rows and columns. Each row is a single-dimensional array. A **3-D array** is an array of 2-D arrays and can be visualized as a cube that has planes. Each plane is a 2-D array. This concept can be scaled up to any level and in general, an **n-D array** is an array of (n-1)-D arrays. Arrays having dimensions higher than three are generally not needed unless and until highly data-extensive applications are to be developed. Therefore, I will restrict the discussion only to three-dimensional arrays.

4.6.1.1 Two-dimensional Arrays

A **two-dimensional array** has its elements arranged in a rectangular grid of rows and columns. The elements of a two-dimensional array can be accessed by using a row subscript (i.e. row number) and a column subscript (i.e. column number). Both the row subscript and the column subscript are required to select an element of a two-dimensional array. A two-dimensional array is popularly known as a **matrix**. Figure 4.9 depicts a two-dimensional array as an array of 1-D arrays.

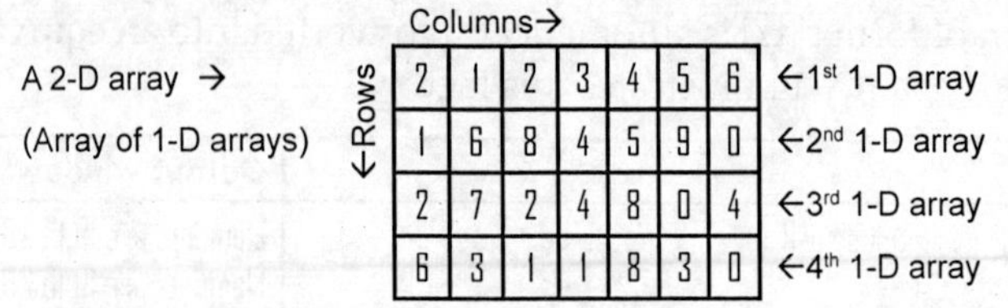

Figure 4.9 | *A two-dimensional array*

4.6.1.1.1 Declaration of a Two-dimensional Array

The general form of a two-dimensional array declaration is:

<sclass_specifier><type_qualifier><type_modifier>**type identifier[**<row_specifier>**][column_specifier]**<=initialization_list<,...>>**;**

The important points about a two-dimensional array declaration are as follows:

1. The terms enclosed within angular brackets (i.e. <>) are optional and might not be present in a declaration statement. The terms shown in bold are the mandatory parts of a two-dimensional array declaration.
2. A two-dimensional array declaration consists of a type specifier (i.e. element type), an identifier (i.e. name of the array), a row size specifier (i.e. number of rows in an array) and a column size specifier (i.e. number of columns in each row). The size specifiers are enclosed within square brackets. The following declarations of two-dimensional arrays are valid:

```
int array1[2][3];       //←array1 is an integer array of 2 rows and 3 columns
float array2[5][1];     //←array2 is a float array of 5 rows and 1 column
char array3[3][3];      //←array3 is a character array of 3 rows and 3 columns
```

3. The row size specifier and column size specifier should be a compile time constant expression greater than zero.
4. The specification of a row size and column size is mandatory if an initialization list is not present. If the initialization list is present, the row size specifier can be skipped but it is mandatory➲ to mention the column size specifier.
5. **Initializing elements of two-dimensional arrays:** Like one-dimensional arrays, the elements of two-dimensional arrays can also be initialized by providing an initialization list.

   The syntactic rules about the initialization of elements of a two-dimensional array are as follows:

   a. The number of initializers in the initialization list should be less than or at most equal to the number of elements (i.e. row size × column size) in the array.
   b. The array locations are initialized row-wise. If the number of initializers in the initialization list is less than the number of elements in the array, the array locations that do not get initialized will automatically be initialized to 0 (if it is an integer

array), 0.0 (in case of a floating point array) and '\0' (i.e. null character if it is an array of character type). The mentioned fact is shown in Figure 4.10.

```
int array[4][7]={2,1,2,3,4,5,6,1,6,8};
```

array Columns→ (←Rows)

2	1	2	3	4	5	6
1	6	8	0	0	0	0
0	0	0	0	0	0	0
0	0	0	0	0	0	0

Figure 4.10 | Initialization of a two-dimensional array

c. The initializers in the initialization list can be braced to initialize elements of the individual rows. If the number of initializers within the inner braces is less than the row size, trailing locations of the corresponding row get initialized to 0, 0.0 or '\0', depending upon the element type of the array. The mentioned fact is shown in Figure 4.11.

```
int array1[4][7]={{2,1},{2,3,4},{5},{6,1,6,8}};
```

array1 Columns→ (←Rows)

2	1	0	0	0	0	0
2	3	4	0	0	0	0
5	0	0	0	0	0	0
6	1	6	8	0	0	0

(a)

```
int array2[4][7]={{2,1},{2,3,4}};
```

array2 Columns→ (←Rows)

2	1	0	0	0	0	0
2	3	4	0	0	0	0
0	0	0	0	0	0	0
0	0	0	0	0	0	0

(b)

Figure 4.11 | Initialization of individual rows of a two-dimensional array

Forward Reference: Refer Question number 58 and its answer to know why it is mandatory to specify column size specifier even if a 2-D array is explicitly initialized.

4.6.1.1.2 Usage of a Two-dimensional Array

The elements of a two-dimensional array can be accessed by using row and column subscripts. The important points about the usage of a two-dimensional array are as follows:

1. An element of a two-dimensional array can be accessed by writing E1[E2][E3], where E1, E2 and E3 are sub-expressions. One of the sub-expressions E1 or E2 must be of an array type or a pointer type, and the other sub-expressions must be of integral type. Program 4-15 illustrates the use of a subscript operator to access the elements of a two-dimensional array.

Prog 4-15.c

```
1  //Two-dimensional arrays
2  #include<stdio.h>
3  main()
4  {
5      int a[2][3]={2,1,3,2,3,4};
6      printf("Elements of array are:\n");
7      printf("%d %d %d\n",a[0][0], a[0][1], a[0][2]);
8      printf("%d %d %d\n",1[a][0], 1[a][1], 1[a][2]);
9  }
```

Memory contents

a	[0]	[1]	[2]
[0]	2	1	3
[1]	2	3	4

Output window

```
Elements of array are:
2 1 3
2 3 4
```

Remarks:

- The general form of an expression for accessing an element of a 2-D array is E1[E2][E3]
- In line number 7, E1 is of array type and E2 is of int type
- In line number 8, E1 is of int type and E2 is of array type
- Both types of usage are valid
- The sub-expression E3 must be of integral type and cannot be of array type

Program 4-15 | A program to illustrate the usage of a two-dimensional array

2. The expression E1[E2][E3] is implicitly converted into an equivalent expression of form *(*(E1+E2)+E3). Program 4-16 illustrates this fact.

Prog 4-16.c

```
// Subscript operator and equivalent conversion to pointer form
#include<stdio.h>
main()
{
    int a[2][3]={2,1,3,2,3,4};
    printf("Use of subscript operator:\n");
    printf("%d %d %d\n",a[0][0], a[0][1], a[0][2]);
    printf("%d %d %d\n",a[1][0], a[1][1], a[1][2]);
    printf("Use of pointer expressions:\n");
    printf("%d %d %d\n",*(*(a+0)+0), *(*(a+0)+1), *(*(a+0)+2));
    printf("%d %d %d\n", *(*(a+1)+0), *(*(a+1)+1), *(*(a+1)+2));
    printf("Use of mixed form of expressions:\n");
    printf("%d %d %d\n",*(a[0]+0), *(a[0]+1), *(a[0]+2));
    printf("%d %d %d\n", *(a[1]+0), *( a[1]+1), *( a[1]+2));
}
```

Output window

```
Use of subscript operator:
2 1 3
2 3 4
Use of pointer expressions:
2 1 3
2 3 4
Use of mixed form of expressions:
2 1 3
2 3 4
```

Remark:

- The expression *(a+i) is equivalent to a[i]. Hence, the expression *(*(a+i)+j) is equivalent to *(a[i]+j), which is further equivalent to a[i][j]

Program 4-16 | A program to illustrate the conversion of a subscript operator into an equivalent pointer form

3. In an expression that involves an array, if the number of subscripts used with the array name is less than the dimensions of the array, the expression refers to an address instead of a value. Program 4-17 illustrates this fact.

Line	Prog 4-17.c	Memory contents	Output window

1
2
3
4
5
6
7
8
9
10
11
12
13
	//Number of subscripts and values
	#include<stdio.h>
	main()
	{
	int a[2][2]={2,1,3,4};
	printf("No subscript used:\n");
	printf("%p\n",a);
	printf("One subscript used:\n");
	printf("%p %p\n",a[0], a[1]);
	printf("Two subscripts used:\n");
	printf("%d %d\n",a[0][0], a[0][1]);
	printf("%d %d\n",a[1][0], a[1][1]);
	}
		a
		Indices [0] [1]
		[0] 2 1
		2234 2236
		[1] 3 4
		2238 2240
			No subscript used:
			234F:2234
			One subscript used:
			234F:2234 234F:2238
			Two subscripts used:
			2 1
			3 4
			Remarks:
			• When no subscript is used, the expression a refers to the starting address of the first element (i.e. first row) of the array
			• When one subscript is used, the expressions a[0] and a[1] refer to the starting address of the first row and the second row, respectively
			• When two subscripts are used, the expressions in line numbers 11 and 12 refer to the value of the corresponding array element

Program 4-17 | A program to illustrate the outcome of an expression that uses lesser subscripts than dimensions

4.6.1.1.2.1 Reading, storing and accessing elements of a 2-D array

The elements can be read and stored in a 2-D array by making use of nested loops. Program 4-18 illustrates the method to read, store and access the elements of a two-dimensional array.

Prog 4-18.c	Output window

// Reading, storing and accessing elements of a two-dimensional array
#include<stdio.h>
main()
{
int a[10][10], olc, ilc, rows, cols;
printf("Enter the number of rows(<10):\t");
scanf("%d",&rows);
printf("Enter the number of cols(<10)\t");
scanf("%d",&cols);
printf("Enter the elements:\n");
for(olc=0;olc<rows;olc++)
for(ilc=0;ilc<cols;ilc++)
scanf("%d",&a[olc][ilc]); //←Reading and storing elements
printf("The entered elements were:\n");
for(olc=0;olc<rows;olc++)
{
for(ilc=0;ilc<cols;ilc++)
printf("%d ",a[olc][ilc]); //←Accessing elements
printf("\n");
}
}
	Enter the number of rows(<10): 2
	Enter the number of cols(<10): 2
	Enter the elements:
	2
	3
	3
	4
	The entered elements were:
	2 3
	3 4
	Remarks:
	• olc is the outer loop counter
	• ilc is the inner loop counter
	• To read and store elements in a 2-D array, a nested loop consisting of two loops is required
	• The outer loop is for getting the rows, and the inner loop is for getting the elements of a row (i.e. columns)

Program 4-18 | A program to illustrate the method of reading, storing and accessing elements of a two-dimensional array

4.6.1.1.3 Memory Representation of a Two-dimensional Array

A 2-D array can be visualized as a plane, which has rows and columns. Although multi-dimensional arrays are visualized in this way, they are actually stored in the memory, which is linear (i.e. one dimensional). Hence, a multi-dimensional array is to be stored in one dimension. There are two ways of doing this:

1. Row major order of storage
2. Column major order of storage

4.6.1.1.3.1 Row Major Order of Storage

In **row major order of storage**, the elements of an array are stored row-wise. **In C language, multi-dimensional arrays are stored in the memory by using row major order of storage.** Figure 4.12 shows the row major order of storage.

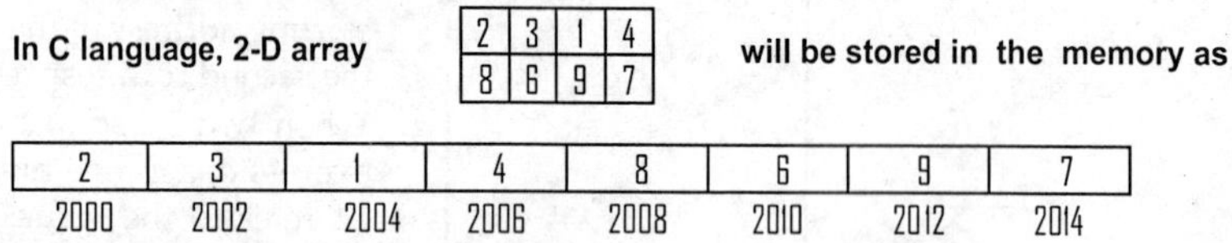

Figure 4.12 | Row major order of array storage

4.6.1.1.3.2 Column Major Order of Storage

In **column major order of storage**, the elements of an array are stored column-wise. Column major order of array storage is used in the languages like FORTRAN, MATLAB, etc. Figure 4.13 shows the column major order of storage.

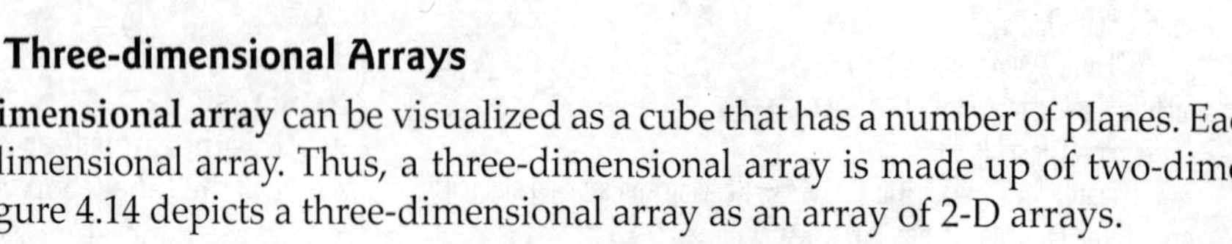

Figure 4.13 | Column major order of array storage

4.6.1.2 Three-dimensional Arrays

A **three-dimensional array** can be visualized as a cube that has a number of planes. Each plane is a two-dimensional array. Thus, a three-dimensional array is made up of two-dimensional arrays. Figure 4.14 depicts a three-dimensional array as an array of 2-D arrays.

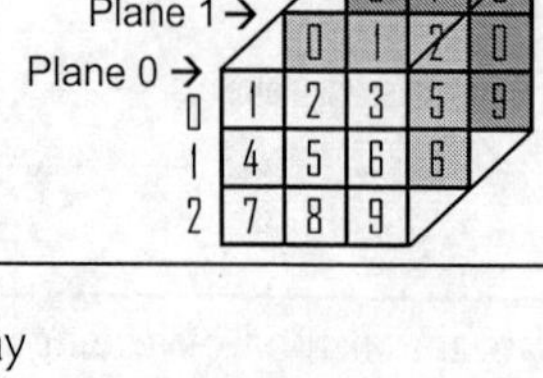

Figure 4.14 | A three-dimensional array

4.6.1.2.1 Declaration of a Three-dimensional Array

The general form of a three-dimensional array declaration is:

<scspec*><type_qual><type_mod>**type identifier[**<plane_specifier>**][row_specifier][column_specifier]**<=init_list<,...>>;

*- scspec means storage class specifier

The important points about a three-dimensional array declaration are as follows:

1. The terms enclosed within angular brackets (i.e. <>) are optional and might not be present in a declaration statement. The terms shown in **bold** are the mandatory parts of a three-dimensional array declaration.
2. A three-dimensional array declaration consists of a type specifier (i.e. element type), an identifier (i.e. name of array), a plane size specifier, a row size specifier and a column size specifier. The size specifiers are enclosed within the square brackets (i.e. []).
3. The plane size specifier, row size specifier and column size specifier should be a compile time constant expression greater than zero.
4. The specification of all size specifiers is mandatory if the elements of an array are not explicitly initialized. If an initialization list is present, the plane size specifier can be skipped but it is mandatory to mention the row size specifier and column size specifier. The general rule is **'While declaring n-D arrays, even if initialization list is present, it is mandatory to specify (n-1) fastest varying specifiers'**. In case of two-dimensional arrays, the column size specifier varies faster as compared to the row size specifier. In case of three-dimensional arrays, column size specifier and row size specifier vary faster than a plane size specifier.
5. **Initializing elements of three-dimensional arrays:** The elements of a three-dimensional array can be initialized in the same way as the elements of a two-dimensional array are initialized, i.e. by providing an initialization list.

4.6.2 Array of Pointers

An **array of pointers** is a collection of addresses. The addresses in an array of pointers could be the addresses of isolated variables or the addresses of array elements or any other addresses. The only constraint is that all the pointers in an array must be of the same type. Program 4-19 illustrates the use of array of pointers.

Prog 4-19.c	Memory contents	Output window

// Array of pointers
#include<stdio.h>
main()
{
    int a=10,b=20, c=30;
    int* arr[3]={&a, &b, &c};
    printf("The values of variables are:\n");
    printf("%d %d %d\n",a,b,c);
    printf("%d %d %d\n",*arr[0],*arr[1],*arr[2]);
}
	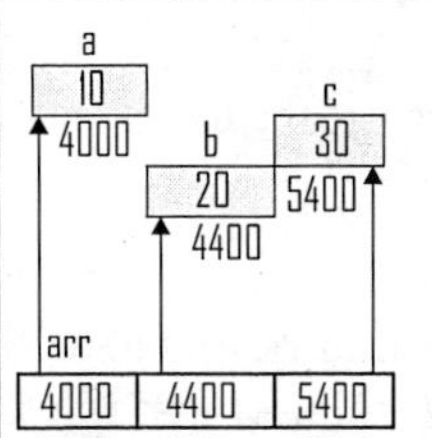	The values of variables are:
		10 20 30
		10 20 30
		Remarks:
		• arr is an array of integer pointers and holds the addresses of variables a, b and c
		• All the variables are of the same type

Program 4-19 | A program to illustrate the use of array of pointers

4.6.3 Pointer to a Pointer

A pointer that holds the address of another pointer variable is known as a **pointer to a pointer**. Such a pointer is said to exhibit multiple levels of indirection. There can be many levels of indirection in a single declaration statement. Consider the code snippet in Program 4-20.

Prog 4-20.c

```
// Pointer to a pointer
#include<stdio.h>
main()
{
    int i=10;
    int *p1=&i;        //←Pointer to int
    int **p2=&p1;   //←Pointer to pointer to int
    int ***p3=&p2; //←Pointer to pointer to pointer to int
    int ****p4=&p3;//←.................concept scales up
    int *****p5=&p4;
    int ******p6=&p5;
    int *******p7=&p6;
    int ********p8=&p7;
    int *********p9=&p8;
    int **********p10=&p9;
    int ***********p11=&p10;
    int ************p12=&p11;
    printf("The values of variables are:\n");
    printf("%d\t",*p1);
    printf("%d\t",**p2);
    printf("%d\t",***p3);
    printf("%d\t",****p4);
    printf("%d\t",*****p5);
    printf("%d\t",******p6);
    printf("%d\t",*******p7);
    printf("%d\t",********p8);
    printf("%d\t",*********p9);
    printf("%d\t",**********p10);
    printf("%d\t",***********p11);
    printf("%d\t",************p12);
}
```

Output window

```
The values of variables are:
10 10 10 10 10 10 10 10 10 10 10 10
```

Remarks:

- The ANSI C standard says that all compilers must handle at least 12 levels of indirection
- Some compilers may support more levels of indirection
- Two levels of indirection are common
- Level of indirection higher than two becomes difficult to understand and visualize
- In an expression, if the number of indirection operators used to dereference a pointer is less than the number of punctuators (*) used to declare the pointer, then the pointer will not be completely dereferenced and the expression refers to an address
- The number of indirection operators required to completely dereference a pointer is equal to the number of punctuators (*) used while declaring it
- For example, in the mentioned code the expression *p2 refers to an address, i.e. address of p1. In the expression **p2, p2 is completely dereferenced and refers to the value of i, i.e. 10

Program 4-20 | A program to illustrate the use of multi-level pointers

4.6.4 Pointer to an Array

It is possible to create a pointer that points to a complete array instead of pointing to the individual elements of an array or isolated variables. Such a pointer is known as a **pointer to an array**. The following declaration statements declare such pointers:

```
int (*p1)[5];            //←p1 is a pointer to an array of 5 integers
int (*p2)[2][2];         //←p2 is a pointer to an integer array of 2 rows and 2 columns
int (*p3)[2][3][4];      //←p3 is a pointer to an integer array having 2 planes. Each plane
                         //←has 3 rows and 4 columns
```

> *i* While declaring pointer to an array, parentheses, i.e. () are used because [] binds more tightly than *. If parentheses are not used, the declaration **int *p1[5];** declares p1 as an array of 5 integer pointers. In the said declaration, p1 becomes an array instead of becoming a pointer because [] binds p1 more tightly than *. To make p1 a pointer to an array of 5 integers, write it as **int(*p1)[5]**. In this declaration, parentheses are used to bind p1 with *.

Program 4-21 illustrates the use of a pointer to an array.

Prog 4-21.c

```
// Pointer to an array
#include<stdio.h>
main()
{
    int arr[2][2]={{2,1},{3,5}};
    int (*ptr)[2]=arr;
    printf("Address of row 1 is %p\n",arr[0]);
    printf("Address of row 2 is %p\n",ptr+1);
    printf("1st element of row 1 is %d\n", arr[0][0]);
    printf("1st element of row 2 is %d\n",ptr[1][0]);

}
```

Memory contents

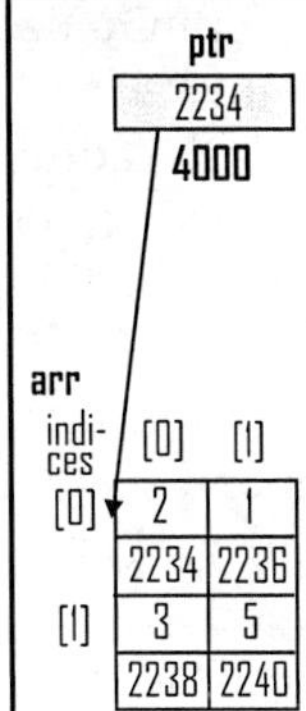

Output window

```
Address of row 1 is 234F:2234
Address of row 2 is 234F:2238
1st element of row 1 is 2
1st element of row 2 is 3
```

Remarks:

- arr refers to the address of the first element of the array
- Elements of a 2-D array are 1-D arrays
- Thus, arr refers to the address of first 1-D array of two integers (i.e. first row)
- The type of arr is int(*)[2]
- Type of ptr is int(*)[2]
- ptr is initialized with the starting address of row 1
- ptr+1 will point to the next row
- As types of arr and ptr are same and both refer to the same address, the expression ptr[1][0] is equivalent to the expression arr[1][0]

Program 4-21 | A program that illustrates the creation and usage of a pointer to an array

4.7 Advantages and Limitations of Arrays

The direct indexing supported by arrays is their biggest advantage. **Direct indexing** means the time required to access any element in an array of any dimension is almost the same irrespective of its location in the array.

The limitations of arrays are as follows:

1. The memory to an array is allocated at the compile time.
2. Arrays are static in nature. The size of an array cannot be expanded or cannot be squeezed at the run time.
3. The size of an array has to be kept big enough to accommodate the worst cases. Therefore, memory usage in case of arrays is inefficient.

4.8 Summary

1. An array is used to store homogeneous data, i.e. data of the same type.
2. All the elements of an array have the same name, i.e. the array name. They are distinguished on the basis of their locations in the array. Locations are specified by using an integer value known as an index or a subscript.

3. Arrays are also known as indexed variables or subscripted variables.
4. Array index in C starts with 0.
5. C does not provide array index out-of-bound check.
6. Arrays are stored in contiguous (i.e. continuous) memory locations.
7. Arrays are classified as single-dimensional arrays and multi-dimensional arrays.
8. Subscript operator is used to access the elements of an array.
9. The array name refers to the address of the first element of the array and is a constant object.
10. An array cannot be assigned to or initialized with another array.
11. If an array is equated with another array, it always evaluates to false.
12. A pointer is a variable that holds the address of a variable or a function.
13. Restricted arithmetic can be applied on pointers. Arithmetic on pointers is governed by pointer arithmetic.
14. Addition of two pointers, addition of a `float` or a `double` value to a pointer, application of multiplication and division operators on pointers are not allowed.
15. `void` pointer is a generic pointer and can point to any type of object.
16. Dereferencing a `void` pointer and applying pointer arithmetic to it is not allowed.
17. Null pointer is a special pointer that does not point anywhere.
18. Dereferencing a null pointer leads to run time error.
19. An n-D array is an array of (n-1)-D arrays.
20. The expression of form `E1[E2]` is implicitly converted to an expression of the form `*(E1+E2)`.
21. In C language, multi-dimensional arrays are stored in the memory by using row major order of storage.

Exercise Questions

Conceptual Questions and Answers

1. *What is a pointer? Where is it used?*

   A pointer is an object➲ that holds the address of another object. A pointer is used to indirectly manipulate the value of an object to which it points.

> **Forward Reference:** Object (Chapter 7).

2. *I know about basic data types in C language but what is pointer type?*

   Apart from basic data types, the C language allows to derive types from the basic data types. These types are called **derived data types**. A pointer type is one of the derived data types.

> **Backward Reference:** Refer Section 4.4 for a detailed description on pointer type.

3. *What will the output of the following piece of code be?*

```
main()
{
    int.*a;
```

```
    float *b;
    char *c;
    printf("%d %d %d", sizeof(a),sizeof(b),sizeof(c));
}
```

The output of the given piece of code is dependent on the execution environment and the compiler used. If the code is executed using Borland TC 3.0 compiler for DOS, it outputs 2 2 2. If the same code is executed using Borland TC 4.5 compiler for Windows or Microsoft VC++ 6.0 compiler, it outputs 4 4 4.

An important point to be noted here is that all pointers take 2 or 4 bytes in the memory (depending upon the execution environment and the compiler used), irrespective of whether they are pointers to int, float, char or some other data type. The difference between pointers of different data types is neither in the representation of the pointer nor in their values. The difference, rather, is in the type of the object being addressed.

4. *Why does the following piece of code on execution using Borland TC 3.0 compiler for DOS outputs 2 1 instead of 2 2 and if executed using Borland TC4.5 compiler for Windows or Microsoft VC++ 6.0 compiler outputs 4 1 instead of 4 4?*

```
main()
{
    char *a,b;
    printf("%d %d",sizeof(a),sizeof(b));
}
```

The code actually gives a correct output. The syntactic rule concerned with the declaration of a pointer states that '**A pointer is declared by prefixing an identifier with punctuator *. In a comma separated declaration list, the punctuator * must precede each identifier intended to serve as a pointer**'.

Thus, in the declaration statement char *a,b;, a is declared as 'pointer to an object of type char' and b is declared as 'data object of type char' and not as a pointer.

5. *The bitwise AND operator (&) and multiplication operator (*) are binary operators. In the following piece of code, these operators are used with only one operand. Even then the code compiles successfully. How is it possible?*

```
main()
{
    int a=10, b=20;
    int *ptr;
    ptr=&a;
    printf("The object to which ptr points has value %d",*ptr);
    ptr=&b;
    printf("The object to which ptr points now has value %d",*ptr);
}
```

The & symbol can be used as a bitwise AND operator and as a reference operator. Similarly, the symbol * can be used as a multiplication operator and as a dereference operator. The particular instance of a symbol corresponds to which operator depends upon the context in which it is used. The context can be determined by looking at:

1. Number of operands
2. Type of operands

The following are the possible combinations:

Symbol	Number of operands	Type of operands	Meaning of arithmetic, scalar and pointer type	Operator
&	Two	Arithmetic type	Integer, float and character	Bitwise AND operator
	One	Scalar type	Arithmetic type and pointer type	Reference operator
*	Two	Arithmetic type	Integer, float and character	Multiplication operator
	One	Pointer type	Pointer to a data type	Dereference operator

The symbol & when used as a reference operator should appear as a prefix unary operator and should be applied on the operands of scalar type that have l-values. The symbol * when used as a dereference operator should appear as a prefix unary operator and should be applied on the operands of the pointer type. In the mentioned piece of code: & symbol refers to the reference operator and * symbol refers to the dereference operator, which are unary operators. Hence the code compiles successfully.

6. *Why does the following piece of code not compile successfully?*

```
main()
{
    int *ptr=10;
    printf("The value pointed to by pointer is %d",*ptr);
}
```

The mentioned piece of code does not compile successfully because of illegal initialization statement whereby a pointer variable ptr is tried to be initialized with an integer value 10. The compiler gives 'Cannot convert int to int*' error because the types int and int* are incompatible and the compiler will not carry out int to int*conversion implicitly. This error can however be removed by making use of explicit type casting and writing the statement as int ptr=(int*)10;. In this statement, the programmer has forcefully converted int to int* and will himself or herself be responsible for the results. This type of explicit type conversion is not recommended.

7. *Can const qualifier be used with pointer types like it can be used with basic data types?*

Yes, const qualifier can be used with pointer types. It is important to understand the use of const qualifier when it is mixed with pointer type. const qualifier can be mixed with pointer type in the following ways:

S.No	Use of const qualifier with pointer type (Column 2)	Meaning of statements in Column 2	What is constant?
1.	const int *ptr	ptr is a pointer to an integer constant	Integer object pointed to by ptr
2.	int const *ptr	ptr is a pointer to a constant integer (same as declaration at S.No. 1)	Integer object pointed to by ptr
3.	int *const ptr	ptr is a constant pointer to an integer	ptr is constant
4.	const int *const ptr	ptr is a constant pointer to an integer constant	Both ptr and the integer object pointed to by ptr are constant
5.	int const *const ptr	ptr is a constant pointer to a constant integer (same as declaration S.No. 4)	Both ptr and the integer object pointed to by ptr are constant

8. *What is pointer arithmetic?*

Backward Reference: Refer Section 4.4.1.4 for a description on pointer arithmetic.

9. *In the expression* *pointer++, *which entity gets incremented: pointer or the value to which the pointer points?*

Dereference operator * and the increment operator ++ are unary operators and unary operators are right-to-left associative. The expression *pointer++ will be interpreted as *(pointer++). Thus, in this expression, the value of the pointer instead of the value pointed by the pointer gets incremented.

10. *I want to print the memory address to which a pointer points. Which format specifier should I use to print it?*

The format specifier used for printing pointers (addresses) is %p. The printed format depends upon which memory model is used. It will either be XXXX:YYYY (segment:offset) or YYYY (offset only).
Consider the following piece of code:

```
main()
{
    int a=10;
    int *ptr=&a;
    printf("The value of pointer is %p",ptr);
}
```

If the code is executed using Borland TC 3.0 compiler for DOS and small memory model, it prints FFF4 (offset address only). If worked with huge memory model, it prints 900E:00FE (segment and offset address).

11. *What is array type and how is it declared?*

Backward Reference: Refer Sections 4.2 and 4.3 for a description on array type.

12. *I want to store an integer value, a* float *value and a character value in an array. Is it possible?*

No, arrays can only be used for storage of homogeneous data (i.e. data of the same type). Arrays cannot be used for storage of heterogeneous data (i.e. data of different types). For storage of heterogeneous data, structures and unions➲ are used.

Forward Reference: Structure and unions (Chapter 9).

13. *How is the declaration* int * a[10] *different from* int (*a) [10]?

While reading C declarations remember that [] binds➲ more tightly than *. In the declaration statement int *a[10]; the identifier name a is bound to [] instead of * and it is read as 'a is an array of 10 integer pointers'. In the declaration statement int (*a)[10];, () is used to bind a to *. Hence, the declaration is read as 'a is a pointer to an array of 10 integers'.

Forward Reference: Refer Section 5.3.1.1.8 on pointers to functions to see that () also binds more tightly than *.

14. *How is an expression involving a subscript operator internally represented?*

The general form of an expression involving a subscript operator is E1[E2], where both E1 and E2 are sub-expressions. One of the sub-expressions E1 or E2 must be of array type or pointer type and the other expression must be of integer type. Every expression of the form E1[E2] automatically gets converted to an equivalent expression of the form *(E1+E2). Hence, the expression E1[E2] is internally represented as *(E1+E2).

Consider the following piece of code:

```
main()
{
    int array[4]={4,5,6,7};
    int *pointer=array;
    printf("%d %d %d\n", array[0],pointer[1],*(array+2), *(pointer+3));
}
```

E1 is of array type (array[0])
E1 is of pointer type (pointer[1])
Transformed form of subscript operator (*(array+2))

The mentioned code on execution outputs:

4 5 6 7

15. *Are the expressions* arr *and* &arr *same, if* arr *is an array of type* T?

No, **the expressions arr and &arr are not the same**. The expression &arr yields 'a pointer to an array of type T' and the expression arr yields 'a pointer to type T'. The expression arr refers to the address of first element of the array and the expression &arr refers to the base address of the entire array. To understand the difference between arr and &arr, consider the following piece of code:

```
main()
{
    int arr[5]={1,2,3,4,5};
    printf("The base address of array is %p or %p\n",arr,&arr);
    printf("After incrementing by one they point to %p and %p",arr+1,&arr+1);
}
```

The code on execution outputs:

```
The base address of array is 1B6F:223A or 1B6F:223A
After incrementing by one they point to 1B6F:223C and 1B6F:2244
```

Increment of one in arr increments it by 2-bytes as it is of type int* while increment of one in &arr increments it by 10-bytes as its type is int(*)[5] (i.e. pointer to an array of 5 integers).

16. *Does the C language provide array index out-of-bound check?*

No, the C language does not provide compile-time or run-time array index out-of-bound check. If an array is declared as T array[size], the maximum valid index is size-1, as array index in C language starts from 0. Nothing stops a programmer from stepping across an array boundary and accessing the array with an index greater than size-1. The program having array index out-of-bound will compile and execute but will access to the memory location that does not belong to the array. This illegal memory access may be fatal and may even crash the program.

17. *Why does the following piece of code on execution give a garbage value?*

```
main()
{
    int array[3]={1,2,3};
    printf("The last element of array is %d",array[3]);
}
```

The mentioned piece of code gives a garbage value because the array index is out-of-bound. The maximum valid array index is 2. Since the array is indexed with 3, reference has been made to the memory location that does not belong to the array (i.e. garbage field). Hence, the code on execution gives a garbage value. Note that in some cases the program may even crash, i.e. terminate.

18. *How will you visualize a multi-dimensional array?*

Backward Reference: Refer Section 4.6.1 for a description on multi-dimensional arrays.

19. *How are multi-dimensional arrays stored in C?*

Backward Reference: Refer Section 4.6.1 for a description on multi-dimensional arrays.

Suppose a three-dimensional array is declared as `int a[3][2][2]={0,0,0,1,2,3,4,5,6,7,8,9};`. It can be visualized as:

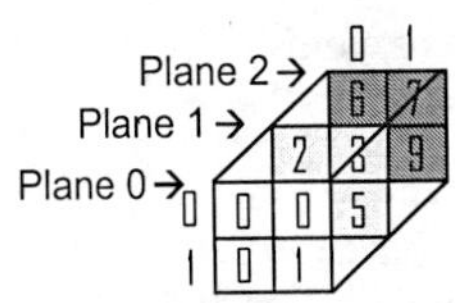

The shown 3-D array will actually be stored in the physical memory as:

a

[0][0][0]	[0][0][1]	[0][1][0]	[0][1][1]	[1][0][0]	[1][0][1]	[1][1][0]	[1][1][1]	[2][0][0]	[2][0][1]	[2][1][0]	[2][1][1]
0	0	0	1	2	3	4	5	6	7	8	9
2000-01	2002-03	2004-05	2006-07	2008-09	2010-11	2012-13	2014-15	2016-17	2018-19	2020-21	2022-23

20. *What would be the result of a* `sizeof` *operator, when it is applied on an array type?*

When the `sizeof` operator is applied on an operand of array type, the result is the total number of bytes occupied by the array.

21. *What is null pointer? Is null pointer same as uninitialized pointer?*

Backward Reference: Refer Section 4.4.3 for a description on null pointer.

No, null pointer is not the same as uninitialized pointer. A null pointer does not point to any object or function, while an uninitialized pointer might point anywhere. The declaration statements `int *ptr=0;` and `int *ptr=NULL;` create a null pointer, named `ptr`, and the declaration statement `int *ptr;` creates an uninitialized pointer.

22. *What is a* `void` *pointer?*

Backward Reference: Refer Section 4.4.2 for a description on `void` pointer.

23. *Why is pointer arithmetic not applicable on* `void` *pointers?*

Pointer arithmetic is not applicable on `void` pointers because the compiler does not know what kind of object the `void` pointer is really pointing to. Before applying an arithmetic operator on `void*`, explicitly type cast `void*` to a pointer to a specific type.

24. *Given the declaration statement,* int array[10],i=2; *what are the types of expressions* array, &array, *array, array[i]*?*

The types of expressions:

array is int*	(i.e. pointer to the first element of array)
&array is int(*)[10]	(i.e. pointer to the entire array)
*array is int	(i.e. value of first element of the array)
array[i] is int	(i.e. value of (i+1)th element of the array)

25. *Given the declaration statement,* int array[10][10],i=2,j=2; *what are the types of expressions* array, &array, *array, array[i], **array, array[i][j]*?*

The types of expressions:

array is int(*)[10]	(i.e. pointer to the first row of array)
&array is int(*)[10][10]	(i.e. pointer to the entire array)
array is int	(i.e. pointer to first element in the first row of array)
array[i] is int*	(i.e. pointer to first element in (i+1)th row of the array)
**array is int	(i.e. value of first element in first row of the array)
array[i][j] is int	(i.e. value of element in (i+1)th row and (j+1)th column of the array)

Code Snippets

Determine the output of the following code snippets. Assume that the inclusion of the required header files has been made and there is no prototyping error due to them.

26.
```
main()
{
    char*p1,p2;
    printf("%d %d",sizeof(p1),sizeof(p2));
}
```

27.
```
main()
{
    printf("%d %d %d",sizeof(char*),sizeof(int*),sizeof(float*));
}
```

28
```
main()
{
    char far *p1, near *p2, huge *p3;
    printf("%d %d %d",sizeof(p1),sizeof(p2),sizeof(p3));
}
```

29.
```
main()
{
    int a=10;
    int *ptr=&a;
    printf("%d %d",++*ptr,*ptr++);
}
```

30.
```
main()
{
    int a=10;
    int *ptr=&a;
    printf("%d %d",*ptr++,++*ptr);
}
```

31. main()
```
{
    int a=10;
    const int *ptr=&a;
    *ptr=50;
    printf("The changed value of pointed object is %d",*ptr);
}
```

32. main()
```
{
    int a=10,b=20;
    int *const ptr=&a;
    *ptr=20;
    printf("The changed value of pointed object a is %d",*ptr);
    ptr=&b;
    *ptr=10;
    printf("The changed value of pointed object b is %d",*ptr);
}
```

33. main()
```
{
    int a=10,b=20;
    const int *const ptr=&a;
    *ptr=20;
    printf("The changed value of pointed object a is %d",*ptr);
    ptr=&b;
    *ptr=10;
    printf("The changed value of pointed object b is %d",*ptr);
}
```

34. main()
```
{
    int *ptr=10;
    printf("The value of pointer is %p",ptr);
}
```

35. main()
```
{
    int *ptr=0;
    printf("The value of pointer is %p",ptr);
}
```

36. main()
```
{
    int *ptr1=0;
    int *ptr2=NULL;
    if(ptr1==ptr2)
        printf("ptr1 becomes a NULL pointer");
    else
        printf("ptr1 does not become a NULL pointer");
}
```

37. main()
```
{
    int arr[ ];
    arr[0]=arr[1]=arr[2]=5;
    printf("%d %d %d",arr[0],arr[1],arr[2]);
}
```
38. main()
```
{
    int size=3;
    int arr[size];
    arr[0]=arr[1]=arr[2]=5;
    printf("%d %d %d",arr[0],arr[1],arr[2]);
}
```
39. main()
```
{
    int a[]={1,2,3};
    printf("%d %d %d",a[0],a[1],a[2]);
}
```
40. main()
```
{
    int a[2]={1,2,3};
    printf("%d %d %d",a[0],a[1],a[2]);
}
```
41. main()
```
{
    int arr[6]={1,2,3,4};
    int i;
    for(i=0;i<6;i++)
    printf("%d ",arr[i]);
}
```
42. main()
```
{
    int arr[3]={1,2,3};
    printf("%d %d %d",arr[1],arr[2],arr[3]);
}
```
43. main()
```
{
    int arr[]={1,2,3};
    arr[0,1,2]=10;
    printf("%d %d %d",arr[0],arr[1],arr[2]);
}
```
44. main()
```
{
    int arr[]={1,2,3,4,5},i;
    arr[1+2]=10;
    for(i=0;i<5;i++)
        printf("%d ",arr[i]);
}
```

45. main()
```
{
    int arr[]={1,2,3,4,5},i;
    arr[2.5+1.5]=10;
    for(i=0;i<5;i++)
        printf("%d ",arr[i]);
}
```
46. main()
```
{
    int array[]={1,2,3,4};
    printf("The number of elements in array are %d",sizeof(array)/sizeof(array[0]));
}
```
47. main()
```
{
    int a=10,b;
    int arr[]={1,2,3}, brr[3];
    printf("Assigning the content of a to b\n");
    b=a;
    printf("Assigning the contents of one array to another\n");
    brr=arr;
    printf("Contents of brr are %d %d %d",brr[0],brr[1],brr[2]);
}
```
48. main()
```
{
    int arr[]={1,2,3},brr[]={1,2,3};
    if(arr==brr)
        printf("Contents of array arr and brr are same\n");
    else
        printf("Contents of array arr and brr are not same");
}
```
49. main()
```
{
    int a[]={1,2,3,4,5};
    int *ptr=a;
    printf("%d %d\n%p %p",*a,*ptr,a,ptr);
}
```
50. main()
```
{
    int arr[]={1,2,3,4,5};
    printf("%p %p\n",arr,&arr);
    printf("%p %p",++arr,++&arr);
}
```
51. main()
```
{
    int arr[]={1,2,3,4,5};
    printf("%p %p\n",arr,&arr);
    printf("%p %p",arr+1,&arr+1);
}
```

52. main()
```
{
    int a[]={1,2,3,4,5};
    printf("%d %d %d %d %d",*a,*(a+0),*(0+a),a[0],0[a]);
}
```
53. main()
```
{
    int *ptr;
    int arr[]={1,2,3,4};
    ptr=arr;
    printf("%d %d",arr[2],ptr[2]);
}
```
54. main()
```
{
    int arr[ ]={2,8,3,4,4,6,7,5};
    int j,*ptr=arr;
    for(j=0;j<5;j++)
    {
        printf(" %d ",*ptr);
        ++ptr;
    }
}
```
55. main( )
```
{
    int j=20;
    int arr[ ] = {10,j,30,40,50},i,*ptr;
    ptr = arr;
    for(i=0; i<5; i++)
    {
        printf("%d ",*ptr);
        ptr++;
    }
}
```
56. main()
```
{
    int arr[2][3]={1,2,3,4};
    printf("%d %d %d %d %d %d",arr[0][0],arr[0][1],arr[0][2],arr[1][0],arr[1][1],arr[1][2]);
}
```
57. main()
```
{
    int arr[2][3]={{1,2},{3,4}};
    printf("%d %d %d %d %d %d",arr[0][0],arr[0][1],arr[0][2],arr[1][0],arr[1][1],arr[1][2]);
}
```
58. main()
```
{
    int arr[][]={1,2,3,4};
    printf("%d %d %d %d %d %d",arr[0][0],arr[0][1],arr[0][2],arr[1][0],arr[1][1],arr[1][2]);
}
```

59. main()
```
{
    int arr[2][][]={1,2,3,4,5,6,7,8};
    int i, j, k;
    for(i=0;i<2;i++)
        for(j=0;j<2;j++)
            for(k=0;k<2;k++)
                printf("%d",arr[i][j][k]);
}
```

60. main()
```
{
    int arr[][3]={1,2,3,4};
    printf("%d %d %d %d %d %d",arr[0][0],arr[0][1],arr[0][2],arr[1][0],arr[1][1],arr[1][2]);
}
```

61. main()
```
{
    int arr[2][2]={1,2,3,4};
    printf("%p %p\n%p %p",&arr[0][0],&arr[0][1],&arr[1][0],&arr[1][1]);
}
```

62. main()
```
{
    int arr[2][3]={1,2,3,4,5,6};
    printf("%d %d %d",arr[1][2],1[arr][2],*(*(arr+1)+2));
}
```

63. main()
```
{
    int arr[2][3]={1,2,3,4,5,6};
    printf("%d %d %d",arr[1][2],1[arr][2],1[2][arr]);
}
```

64. main( )
```
{
    int a[ ] = {0,1,2,3,4};
    int *p[ ] = {a,a+1,a+2,a+3,a+4};
    int **ptr = p;
    printf("%d %p %p %p %p %p\n",**ptr,&ptr,*ptr,*p,p,a);
}
```

65. main()
```
{
    int a[2][2][2]={1,2,3,4,5,6,7,8};
    printf("%p %p %p\n",a,a[0],a[0][0]);
    printf("%p %p %p\n",a,a[1],a[1][1]);
    printf("%d %d",a[0][0][0],a[1][1][1]);
}
```

66. main()
```
{
    void a,b;
    void *ptr;
```

```
    ptr=&a;
    printf("ptr points to a\n");
    ptr=&b;
    printf("ptr now points to b");
}
```

67. main()
```
{
    int a=10;
    int* i_ptr=&a;
    void* v_ptr=i_ptr;
    *i_ptr++;
    *v_ptr++;
    printf("The value of objects pointed to by pointers are %d %d",*i_ptr,*v_ptr);
}
```

68. main()
```
{
    int arr[]={1,2,3,4,5};
    int *ptr=arr;
    ptr=ptr+1;
    printf("The value pointed by ptr is %d",*ptr);
}
```

69. main()
```
{
    int arr[]={1,2,3,4,5};
    int *ptr1=arr;
    int *ptr2=arr+3;
    printf("The result of ptr2-ptr1 is %d",ptr2-ptr1);
}
```

70. main()
```
{
    int array[]={1,2,3,4,5};
    int *ptr1=array;
    int *ptr2;
    ptr2=ptr1*2;
    printf("The value of ptr2 is %p",ptr2);
}
```

Multiple-choice Questions

71. Arrays are used to store the elements of
    a. The same type
    b. Different types
    c. Multiple types
    d. None of these

72. Array index in C language starts from
    a. 1
    b. 0
    c. Any integer value
    d. None of these

73. The size specifier in the array declaration must be

a. An expression
b. A constant expression
c. A constant expression of integral type
d. A constant expression of integral type having a value greater than zero

74. In C language, elements of two-dimensional arrays are stored in

a. Random order
b. Column major order
c. Row major order
d. None of these

75. The elements of an array are stored in

a. Contiguous memory locations
b. Discontinuous memory locations
c. Randomly allocated memory locations
d. None of these

76. If one of the operands of subscript operator is of array type, the other operand of the subscript operator can be

a. An expression
b. An expression of integral type
c. An integral constant only
d. None of these

77. If arr is an array of integers, which of the following expression(s) is equivalent to the expression arr[0]?

a. *arr
b. *(arr+0)
c. 0[arr]
d. All of these

78. Given the declaration statement int arr[5];, the type of expression arr is

a. int*
b. int(*)[5]
c. int*[5]
d. None of these

79. Given the declaration statement int arr[5];, the type of expression &arr is

a. int*
b. int(*)[5]
c. int*[5]
d. None of these

80. Given the declaration statement int arr[5][7];, the linear offset from the beginning of the array to any given element arr[2][3] can be computed as

a. 2*7+3
b. 2+3*5
c. 2*5+3*7
d. None of these

81. Given the declaration statement int array[3][2][2]={1,2,3,4,5,6,7,8,9,10,11,12};, what is the value of array[2][1][0]?

a. 3
b. 5
c. 7
d. 11

82. Given the statement int a[8]={0,1,2,3};, the definition of a explicitly initializes its first four elements. Which one of the following describes how the compiler treats the remaining four elements?

a. The remaining four elements are initialized to zero
b. It is illegal to initialize only a portion of the array
c. C standard defines the particular behavior as implementation dependent
d. None of these

83. In the C language, pointer is

a. Address of a variable
b. An indication of the variable to accessed next
c. A variable for storing address
d. None of these

84. Which of the following is a derived type?
   a. Pointer type
   b. Array type
   c. Function type
   d. All of these

85. Which of the following is a correct way to declare two integer pointers `a` and `b`?
   a. `int* a,b;`
   b. `int *a,*b;`
   c. `int* a,int* b;`
   d. None of these

86. A null pointer points to
   a. No object
   b. Null value
   c. Null character stored at the end of string
   d. None of these

87. Pointer arithmetic cannot be performed on
   a. `void` pointers
   b. Uninitialized pointers
   c. Dangling pointers
   d. None of these

88. Which of the following conversions is carried out implicitly by the compiler?
   a. Conversion of `void` pointer to any other pointer type on assignment
   b. Conversion of integer constant zero into null pointer of desired type on assignment
   c. Conversion of pointer of one type to the pointer of another type on assignment
   d. None of these

89. Given the declaration statement `int* a[2][3][4];`, which of the following definitions and initialization of `p` is valid?
   a. `int* (*p)[3][4]=a;`
   b. `int ****p=a;`
   c. `int* (*p)[2][3][4]=a;`
   d. None of these

90. Given the declaration statement `int const* ptr;`, which of the following objects is constant?
   a. `ptr`
   b. The object pointed to by `ptr`
   c. Both `ptr` and the object pointed to by `ptr`
   d. The given declaration is not valid

91. Given the declaration statement `const int* ptr;`, which of the following objects is constant?
   a. `ptr`
   b. The object pointed to by `ptr`
   c. Both `ptr` and the object pointed to by `ptr`
   d. The given declaration is not valid

92. Given the declaration statement `int* const ptr;`, which of the following objects is constant?
   a. `ptr`
   b. The object pointed to by `ptr`
   c. Both `ptr` and the object pointed to by `ptr`
   d. The given declaration is not valid

93. Given the declaration statement `int const* const ptr;`, which of the following objects is constant?
   a. `ptr`
   b. The object pointed to by `ptr`
   c. Both `ptr` and the object pointed to by `ptr`
   d. The given declaration is not valid

94. In the expression `++*ptr`, the value of which entity gets incremented?
   a. `ptr`
   b The object pointed to by `ptr`
   c. Both `ptr` and the object pointed to by `ptr`
   d. The given expression is not valid

95. In the expression `*ptr++`, the value of which entity gets incremented?
   a. `ptr`
   b. The object pointed to by `ptr`
   c. Both `ptr` and the object pointed to by `ptr`
   d. The given expression is not valid

Outputs and Explanations to Code Snippets

26. 4 1 (If executed using Borland TC 4.5 for Windows or Microsoft VC++ 6.0)
    2 1 (If executed using Borland 3.0 for DOS)

    Explanation:

    Backward Reference: Refer to the explanations given in Answer numbers 3 and 4.

27. 4 4 4 (If executed using Borland TC 4.5 for Windows or Microsoft VC++ 6.0)
    2 2 2 (If executed using Borland 3.0 for DOS)

    Explanation:

    Backward Reference: Refer to the explanation given in Answer number 3.

    sizeof operator yields the size of its operand in bytes. The operand can be an expression or parenthesized name of a type. In the given code, the operands of sizeof operators are parenthesized name of the derived types (i.e. char*, int* and float*).

28. 4 2 4 (If executed using Borland 3.0 for DOS)

    Explanation:

    In DOS, the total amount of memory accessible is 1 MB, i.e. 1 megabyte. The entire block of memory is divided into various segments that are 64 K, i.e. 64 kilobytes in size. There are various segments like Code Segment (CS), Data Segment (DS), Extra Segment (ES), etc.

    The type of pointer to be used for accessing the memory location depends upon whether the memory location to be accessed lies in the same segment or different segments. If the memory location to be accessed lies in the same segment, the access is called **intra-segment access** and if it lies in a different segment then it is called **inter-segment access.**

    If intra-segment access is to be made, pointer of 16-bits is sufficient to refer to all the memory locations (as 2^{16}= 64 K). The 16-bit (2 bytes) pointer that is used for intra-segment access is known as a **near pointer.**

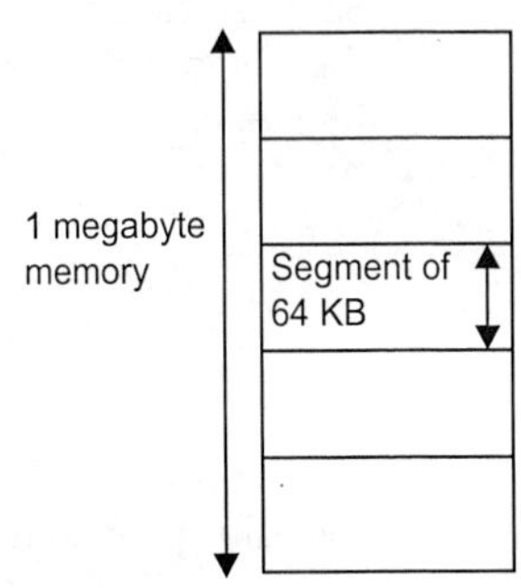

    However, if inter-segment access is to be made, the pointer of 16-bits falls short of its memory addressing capability. Hence, a bigger pointer of 32-bits is used to make inter-segment access. The 32-bit (4 bytes) pointers that are used for inter-segment access are known as **far pointers** and **huge pointers.**

    The far pointer contains a 16-bit segment address and a 16-bit offset address (i.e. address within a segment) while the near pointer has only a 16-bit offset address. huge pointers are essentially far pointers but in a normalized form.

    The concept of far, near and huge pointers is available in DOS, which has less memory accessible. It is not a part of the C standard and is an extension to the language provided by some of the compilers (e.g. Borland Turbo C 3.0). Refer to the compiler documentation before using these non-standardized qualifiers as they might not be supported by all the compilers (e.g. Borland Turbo C 4.5 and MS-VC++ 6.0 compilers do not support these non-standardized extensions).

29. Garbage Value 10

    Caution:

    Program may even abnormally terminate.

Explanation:

Suppose variable a gets allocated at the memory address 2000 and variable ptr gets allocated at the memory address 4000. The variable ptr is initialized with the address of variable a. This can be illustrated as:

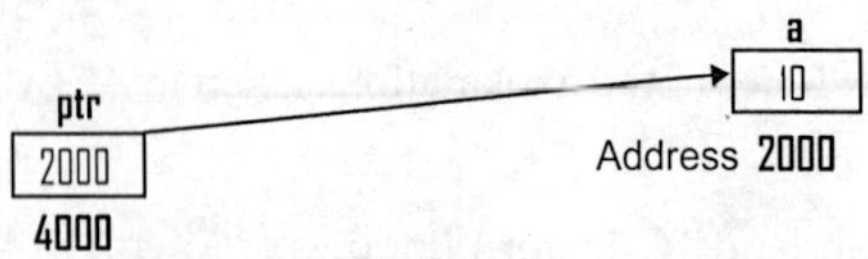

The arguments of printf functions are evaluated from right to left. So, the expression *ptr++ will be evaluated first and will be interpreted as *(ptr++). Due to post-increment, firstly the value of ptr is used for the evaluation of expression and then the value of ptr will be incremented. The expression evaluates to 10 and the value of ptr becomes 2002. This can be illustrated as:

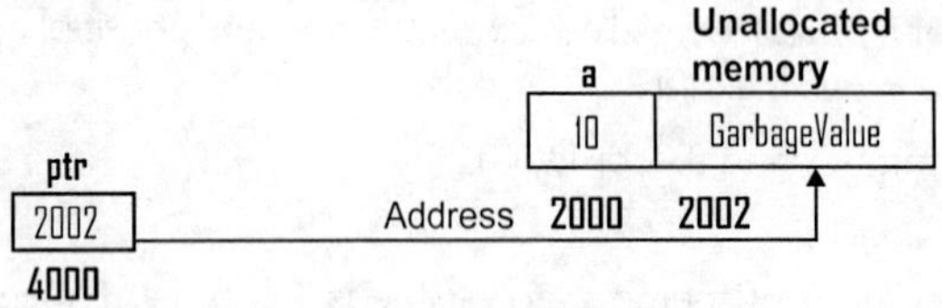

After evaluation of expression *ptr++, the expression ++*ptr will be evaluated. The expression will be interpreted as ++(*ptr). ptr being pointing to an unallocated memory location, i.e. 2002, the behavior of the operation ++(*ptr) is undefined. It will give a garbage value and in extreme cases, the program may even terminate abnormally.

30. 11 11

Explanation:

Suppose variable a gets allocated at the memory address 2000 and variable ptr gets allocated at the memory address 4000. The variable ptr is initialized with the address of variable a. This can be illustrated as:

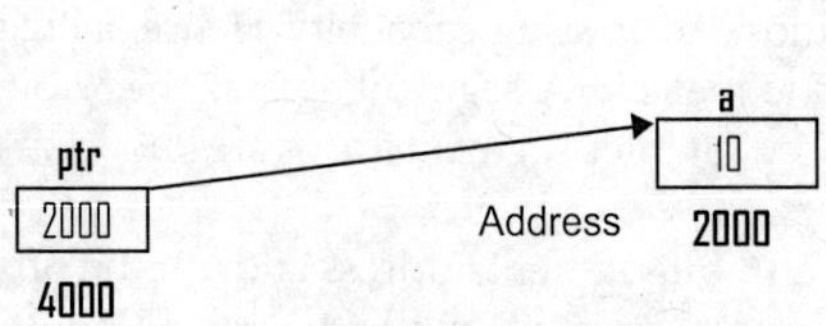

The expression ++*ptr will be evaluated first and will be treated as ++(*ptr). This expression makes the value pointed to by the pointer ptr to increment by 1. This can be shown as:

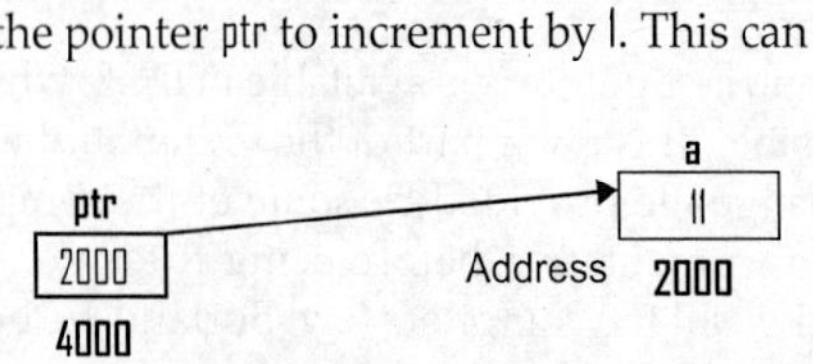

After the evaluation of expression ++*ptr, *ptr++ starts evaluation. The expression *ptr++ will be treated as *(ptr++). Being post-incremented, the value of ptr used for the evaluation of expression will be 2000. The expression evaluates to 11 and the value of ptr becomes 2002.

31. Compilation Error (Cannot modify a constant object)

Explanation:

In the declaration statement const int *ptr=&a;, ptr is declared as 'pointer to a constant integer'. The object to which pointer ptr points is constant and cannot be modified.

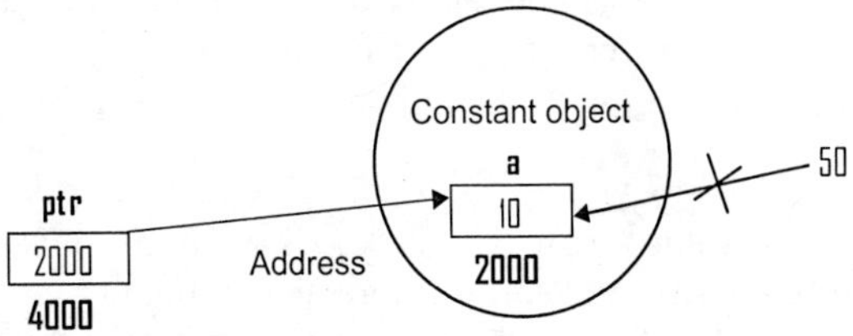

Hence, writing *ptr=50; is not valid and leads to a compilation error.

32. Compilation Error (Cannot modify a constant object)

Explanation:

The declaration statement int *const ptr=&a; declares ptr as 'constant pointer to integer'. Pointer is constant and must point to the same object throughout. It cannot be made to point to a different object throughout the execution of the program.

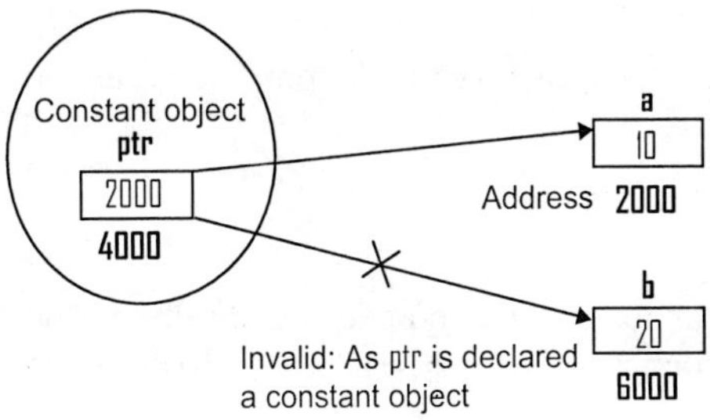

Hence, writing ptr=&b; is invalid and leads to a compilation error.

33. Compilation Error (Cannot modify a constant object)

Explanation:

The declaration statement const int* const ptr=&a; declares ptr as 'constant pointer to a constant integer'. Both the pointer and the object to which the pointer points are constant.

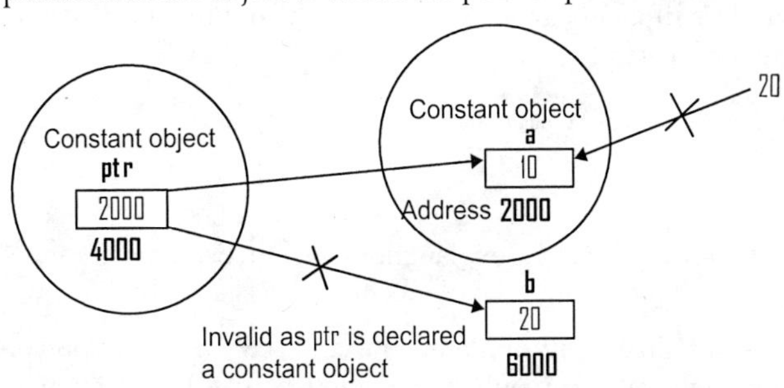

Hence, both the statements *ptr=20; and ptr=&b; are invalid and lead to a compilation error.

34. Compilation error (Cannot convert int to int*)

Explanation:

An integer value 10 is assigned to a pointer variable of type int*. This is not a standard conversion and the compiler will not be able to carry it out implicitly and gives a compilation error 'Cannot convert int to int*'. The error can be removed by explicitly type casting int to int* by writing int*ptr=(int*)10;. However, this conversion is not recommended.

35. The value of pointer is 0000:0000

Explanation:

The conversion of integer value zero to pointer type is standard conversion and is carried out implicitly by the compiler. When a variable or expression of pointer type is initialized, assigned or compared with 0, the constant 0 is implicitly converted into correctly typed null pointer. Hence, there will be no compilation error as in Question number 34.

36. ptr1 becomes a NULL pointer

Explanation:

The integer constant zero is implicitly converted to null pointer of the correct type. NULL is a predefined macro➲ that specifies null pointer value. Hence, in the given code both ptr1 and ptr2 become null pointers. As two null pointers always compare equal, the if condition evaluates to true and 'ptr1 becomes a NULL pointer' gets printed.

Forward Reference: Macros and symbolic constants (Chapter 8).

37. Compilation Error (Size of 'arr' is unknown)

Explanation:

Memory to an array is allocated at the compile time. To allocate the memory, the compiler should be able to determine the number of bytes to be allocated. To determine it, the compiler needs to know:

1. The element type of array
2. The size of array

The size information can be provided by giving:

1. Size specifier (it should be a compile time constant expression), and/or
2. Initialization list (number of initializers in the initialization list determines the size of array)

Since in the declaration statement int arr[]; both the size specifier and the initialization list are not given, the compiler will not be able to determine the number of bytes to be allocated to arr. This leads to a compilation error.

38. Compilation error (Constant expression required)

Explanation:

Backward Reference: Refer the explanation given in Sections 4.2 and 4.3.

Although, size is initialized with a literal constant, size itself is a non-constant object (i.e. it is a variable). Access to its value can only be accomplished at the run time, so it is illegal to use it as an array size specifier. To remove this error, make size a qualified constant by using const qualifier and write it as const int size=3; instead of int size=3;.

39. 1 2 3

Explanation:

The compiler uses the initializers in the initialization list to determine the size of the array and to initialize the array locations.

40. Compilation error (Too many initializers)

Explanation:

The number of initializers in the initialization list cannot be more than the value of the size specifier. They can be less than or at most equal to the value of the size specifier.

41. 1 2 3 4 0 0

Explanation:

If the number of initializers in the initialization list is less than the value of the size specifier, the leading array locations equal to the number of initializers get initialized with the values of initializers. The rest of the array locations get initialized to 0 (if it is an integer array), 0.0 (in case of float array) and '\0', i.e. null character (if array is of character type).

42. 2 3 Garbage Value

Explanation:

In C language, an array index starts from 0 and the maximum value of the valid index is size-1. However, if the index value greater than the maximum valid value is used, there will be no compilation error as C language does not provide an array index out-of-bound check. If array is accessed with an out-of-bound index, the result will be a garbage value. In the extreme case, the program may terminate.

43. 1 2 10

Explanation:

To access an array location, an expression of array type and an expression of integral type are used with a subscript operator. In the statement arr[0,1,2]=10;, arr is an expression of array type and 0,1,2 is an expression of integer type. The expression 0,1,2 evaluates to 2 as the result of the evaluation of a comma operator is the result of evaluation of the right-most sub-expression. Hence, 10 is assigned to arr[2].

44. 1 2 3 10 5

Explanation:

Backward Reference: Refer to the explanation given in Answer number 43.

45. Compilation error (illegal use of floating point)

Explanation:

An expression of float type cannot be used with a subscript operator. Hence, writing a[2.5+1.5] is not valid and leads to a compilation error.

46. The number of elements in array are 4

Explanation:

When the sizeof operator is applied on the operand of an array type, the result is the total number of bytes allocated to the array. So, sizeof(array) results in 8. However, sizeof(array[0]) gives the size of one element of the array, i.e. 2. Hence, sizeof(array)/sizeof(array[0]) results in 4.

47. Compilation Error (L-value required error)

Explanation:

The name of an array refers to the address of the first element of an array and does not have a modifiable l-value. Since it does not have a modifiable l-value, it cannot be placed on the left side of the assignment operator. Hence, writing `brr=arr` is not valid and leads to a compilation error.

48. Contents of array arr and brr are not same

Explanation:

Suppose, the array `arr` gets allocated at the memory location 2000 and `brr` gets allocated at the memory location 4000. This is shown in the figure below:

Since, the name of the array refers to the address of the first element of the array, `arr` refers to 2000 and `brr` refers to 4000. The addresses are not equal (in fact they can never be) and hence, the `printf` statement of the `else` body gets executed to produce the mentioned result.

49. 1 1
1367:21EA 1367:21EA

Explanation:

Backward Reference: Refer to the explanations given in Answer numbers 15 and 20.

The name of type 'array of type T' is implicitly converted to pointer of type 'pointer to T' (with two exceptions). The pointer refers to the address of the first element of the array. Hence, the initialization statement `int *ptr=a;` initializes `ptr` with the address of the first element of the array.

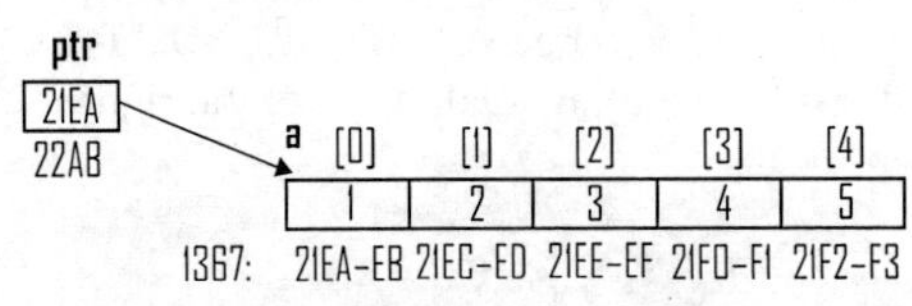

Therefore, `*a` and `*ptr` give the value of the first element of the array, `a` and `ptr` give the address of the first element of the array (i.e. base address of the array).

i The mentioned addresses are in hexadecimal number system.

50. Compilation error (L-value required error)

Explanation:

Backward Reference: Refer to the explanation given in Answer number 15.

The name `arr` refers to the address of the first element of the array and `&arr` refers to the base address of the entire array. Both `arr` and `&arr` are constant objects and do not have a modifiable l-value. The increment operator can operate only on operands that have a modifiable l-value. Hence, the expressions `++arr` and `++&arr` are erroneous.

51. 230F:21EC 230F:21EC
230F:21EE 230F:21F6

Explanation:

Backward Reference: Refer to the explanation given in Answer number 15.

Both the expressions arr and &arr refer to the starting address of the array arr, say 230F:21EC. The expression arr+1 evaluates to 230F:21EE as the type of arr is int* and the sizeof(int*) is 2. The expression &arr+1 evaluates to 230F:21F6 as the type of arr is int(*)[5] and the sizeof(int(*)[5]) is 10.

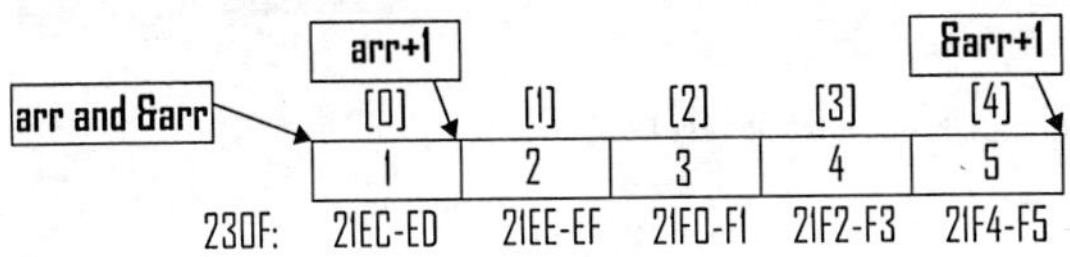

52. 11111

Explanation:

All the expressions *a, *(a+0), *(0+a), a[0] and 0[a] are equivalent and refer to the first element of array, i.e. 1.

53. 3 3

Explanation:

Both the expressions arr[2] and ptr[2] are equivalent to *(arr+2) and *(ptr+2), respectively. Since arr has been assigned to ptr, *(ptr+2) is equivalent to *(arr+2), i.e. 3.

54. 2 3 4 6 5

Explanation:

Since initializers in the initialization list of an integer array are of float type, the initializers will be demoted before initializing array locations. As ptr is initialized with arr, it points to the first element of the array arr. During every iteration of the loop, the value of element pointed to by ptr is printed, and ptr is made to point to the next element of the array arr. In this way, the entire array gets printed.

55. 10 20 30 40 50

Explanation:

Initializers in the initialization list can be pre-defined variables. Hence, writing int arr[]={10,j,30,40,50} is valid as j is a predefined variable having a value of 20.

56. 1 2 3 4 0 0

Explanation:

As the number of initializers in the initialization list is less than the value of the size specifier, the leading array locations equal to the number of initializers get initialized with the values of initializers. The rest of the array locations get initialized to 0. Since multi-dimensional arrays in C are stored in row major order, elements of the array are initialized row by row. Thus, the contents of initialized array will be:

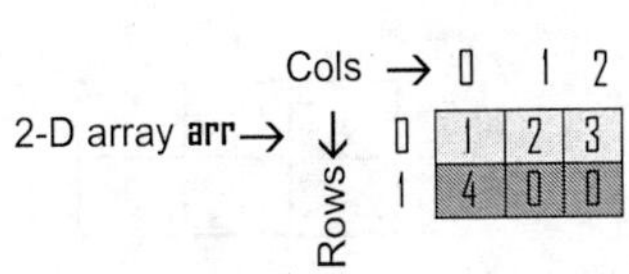

57. 1 2 0 3 4 0

Explanation:

The initializers in the initialization list are bracketed to initialize individual rows. Since the number of initializers within the inner brackets is less than the row size, the last element of each row gets initialized to 0. The contents of the initialized array are as follows:

2-D array **arr** → (Cols →, ↓ Row)

Row \ Cols	0	1	2
0	1	2	0
1	3	4	0

58. Compilation error (Size of type is unknown or zero)

Explanation:

While declaring 2-D arrays, even if the initialization list is present, both the row size specifier and the column size specifier cannot be skipped. In the declaration statement `int arr[][]={1,2,3,4};` there are four initializers, so the number of elements in the array will be at least four. There are three different ways to create an array of four elements:

1. `int arr[1][4]={1,2,3,4}`, i.e. array having one row and four columns, or
2. `int arr[4][1]={1,2,3,4}`, i.e. array having four rows and one column, or
3. `int arr[2][2]={1,2,3,4}`, i.e. array having two rows and two columns

So, the compiler will not be able to determine the number of rows and columns in an array. Since arrays are stored in row major order, if the number of columns in a row of an array is specified, the compiler will be able to determine the number of rows and can create the array. Look at the following declarations and the arrays that get created:

1. `int arr[][4]={1,2,3,4}`

arr	0	1	2	3
0	1	2	3	4

2. `int arr[][2]={1,2,3,4}`

arr	0	1
0	1	2
1	3	4

3. `int arr[][1]={1,2,3,4}`

arr	0
0	1
1	2
2	3
3	4

4. `int arr[][3]={1,2,3,4}` (Number of elements in the array will be greater than 4)

arr	0	1	2
0	1	2	3
1	4	0	0

5. int arr[][5]={1,2,3,4} (Number of elements in the array will be greater than 4)

arr	0	1	2	3	4
0	1	2	3	4	0

59. Compilation error (Size of type is unknown or zero)

Explanation:

"While declaring n-D array, even if initialization list is present, it is mandatory to specify (n-1) fastest varying size specifiers so that compiler can uniquely determine the dimensions and create the array".

In case of 3-D arrays, even if the initialization list is present, it is mandatory to mention both the column size specifier and the row size specifier, as they vary faster as compared to plane size specifier as shown in the figure below. The plane size specifier can be skipped, if the initialization list is present, e.g. the declaration int arr[][2][2]={1,2,3,4,5,6,7,8}; is valid and the compiler will create an array that has two planes, each having two rows and two columns, as shown in the figure below:

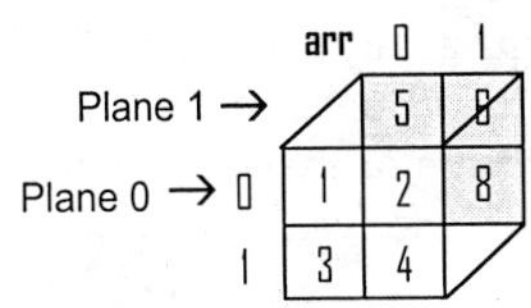

Plane 0				Plane 1			
Row 0		Row 1		Row 0		Row 1	
Col 0	Col 1	Col 0	Col 1	Col 0	Col 1	Col 0	Col 1
a[0][0][0]	a[0][0][1]	a[0][1][0]	a[0][1][1]	a[1][0][0]	a[1][0][1]	a[1][1][0]	a[1][1][1]
1	2	3	4	5	6	7	8
21F8	21FA	21FC	21FE	2200	2202	2204	2206

In the declaration statement present in the given question, the plane size specifier is mentioned but the column size and the row size specifier are not mentioned. Hence, the compiler cannot uniquely determine the dimensions of the array. This leads to a compilation error.

60. 1 2 3 4 0 0

Explanation:

Backward Reference: Refer to the explanations given in Answer numbers 58 and 59.

61. 2367:21EA 2367:21EC
2367:21EE 2367:21F0

Explanation:

The printf statement prints the addresses of array elements. The printed addresses show that the elements of an array are stored in the memory using row major order of storage.

62. 6 6 6

Explanation:

The declaration statement int arr[2][3]={1,2,3,4,5,6}; creates an array as shown in the figure below:

arr	0	1	2
0	1	2	3
1	4	5	6

The expression of form E1[E2][E3] (where one of the sub-expressions E1 or E2 is of array type or pointer type and the other sub-expressions are of integral type) gets converted to expression of form *(*(E1+E2)+E3). Hence, all the expressions arr[1][2], 1[arr][2], *(*(arr+1)+2) are equivalent and refer to the element in row 1 and column 2, i.e. 6.

63. Compilation error (Invalid indirection in function main)

Explanation:

The expression 1[2][arr] gets converted to expression of form *(*(1+2)+arr). Application of dereference operator * on the expression of integer type, i.e. (1+2) is not valid and leads to a compilation error.

64. 0 228F:2202 228F:2208 228F:2208 228F:21F4 228F:2208

Explanation:

Suppose that the defined arrays and the pointer variable have been allocated memory as shown in the figure below. p and a being names of the arrays refer to the address of the first element of the array. Hence, the expressions p and a result in 228F:21F4 and 228F:2208, respectively. Both the expressions *p and *ptr refer to the value at memory address 228F:21F4 and result in 228F:2208. The expression &ptr refers to the address of variable ptr, i.e. 228F:2202. The expression **ptr, refers to value at memory address 228F:2208 and results in 0.

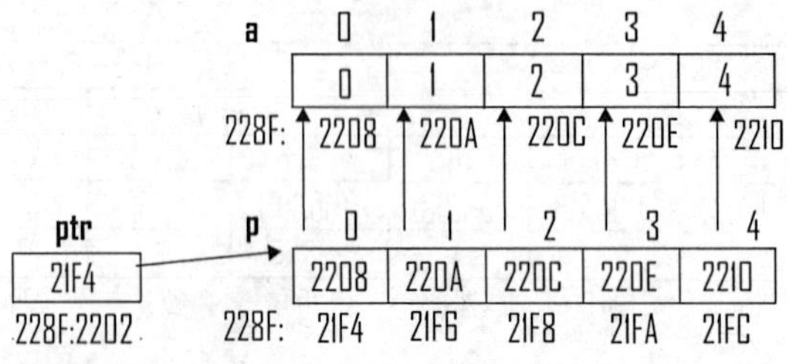

The printf statement prints the values of the evaluated expressions to produce the mentioned result.

---

i As memory allocation is purely random the values of printed addresses may vary, if the code is executed on different machines or at different times.

---

65. 242F:21F8 242F:21F8 242F:21F8
242F:21F8 242F:2200 242F:2204
1 8

Explanation:

In an expression, if the number of subscripts used with an array name is less than the dimensions of the array, then the expression refers to an address. Suppose that array a gets allocated at the memory location 21F8 and is stored in the memory as shown in figure below:

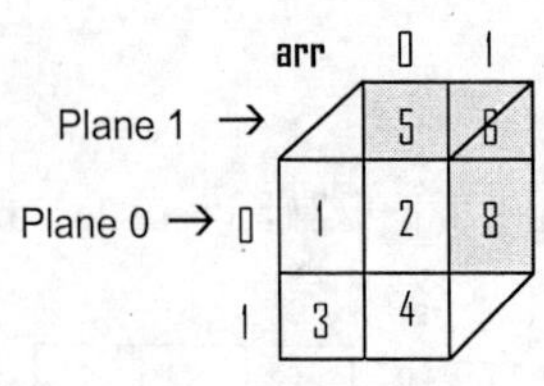

Plane 0				Plane 1			
Row 0		Row 1		Row 0		Row 1	
Col 0	Col 1	Col 0	Col 1	Col 0	Col 1	Col 0	Col 1
a[0][0][0]	a[0][0][1]	a[0][1][0]	a[0][1][1]	a[1][0][0]	a[1][0][1]	a[1][1][0]	a[1][1][1]
1	2	3	4	5	6	7	8
21F8	21FA	21FC	21FE	2200	2202	2204	2206

The expression:

1. a refers to the starting address of the first element of the array (plane 0), i.e. 242F:21F8.
2. a[0] refers to the starting address of plane 0, i.e. 242F:21F8.
3. a[0][0] refers to the address of plane 0 and row 0, i.e. 242F:21F8.
4. a[1] refers to the address of plane 1, i.e. 242F:2200.
5. a[1][1] refers to the address of plane 1 and row 1, i.e. 242F:2204.
6. a[0][0][0] refers to the value at plane 0, row 0 and column 0, i.e. 1.
7. a[1][1][1] refers to the value at plane 1, row 1 and column 1, i.e. 8.

66. Compilation error (Size of a and b is unknown in function main)

Explanation:

Declaring an object of type void is not allowed. Hence, the declaration statement void a,b; is erroneous.

67. Compilation error (Size of type is unknown or zero)

Explanation:

Pointer arithmetic is not allowed on void pointers. Hence, the statement *v_ptr++; is erroneous.

68. The value pointed by ptr is 2

Explanation:

The pointer ptr is initialized with the address of the first element of the array arr. After incrementing it by 1, it points to the next element of the array, i.e. 2. The printf statement prints the value of the element pointed to by the pointer ptr.

69. The result of ptr2-ptr1 is 3

Explanation:

Suppose, the array arr gets allocated at the memory location 2000. ptr1 is initialized with the address of the first element of the array, i.e. 2000 and ptr2 is initialized with the address of arr[3], i.e. 2006. This is depicted in the figure below:

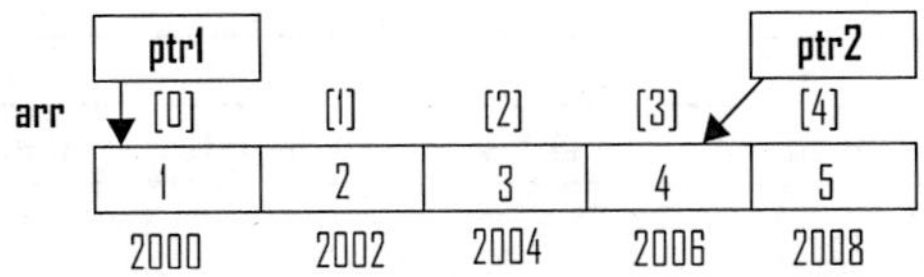

The expression ptr2-ptr1 will be computed as (ptr2-ptr1)/sizeof(int), i.e. (2006-2000)/2=3.

Backward Reference: Refer Section 4.4.1.4.3 for a description on pointer subtraction.

70. Compilation error (illegal use of pointers)

Explanation:

Application of multiplication operator on pointers is not allowed.

Answers to Multiple-choice Questions

71. a 72. b 73. d 74. c 75. a 76. b 77. d 78. a 79. b 80. a 81. d 82. a 83. c 84. d
85. b 86. a 87. a 88. b 89. a 90. b 91. b 92. a 93. c 94. b 95. a

Programming Exercises

Program 1 | Maximum-Minimum: Find the maximum and minimum element in a set of n elements

Algorithm:

Step 1: Start

Step 2: Assign the first array element to two different variables (i.e. max and min) that will hold the maximum and minimum value

Step 3: Loop through the remaining elements, starting from the second element. When a value larger than the present maximum value is found, it becomes the new maximum. Similarly, when a value smaller than the present minimum value is found, it becomes the new minimum

Step 4: After the termination of the loop, print the maximum and minimum values

Step 5: Stop

PE 4-1.c

```
//Maximum and minimum
#include<stdio.h>
main()
{
int elements[20], num, i, max, min;
printf("Enter the number of elements in the set (max. 20)\t");
scanf("%d",&num);
printf("Enter the elements:\n");
for(i=0;i<num;i++)
    scanf("%d",&elements[i]);
max=min=elements[0]; //←Let max and min is the first item
for(i=1;i<num;i++)
    if(elements[i]>max) //←if element[i]>max, then set max=element[i]
        max=elements[i];
    else if(elements[i]<min)   //←else if element[i]<min, then
            min=elements[i];   //← set min=element[i]
printf("Maximum element in the set is %d\n",max);
printf("Minimum element in the set is %d\n",min);
}
```

Output window

```
Enter the number of elements in the set (max. 20) 5
Enter the elements:
12
-3
45
67
8
Maximum element in the set is 67
Minimum element in the set is -3
```

Program 2 | Find arithmetic mean, variance and standard deviation of n elements

Arithmetic mean is given as: $\overline{x} = \dfrac{\sum_{i=1}^{n} x_i}{n}$

Variance is given as: $\sigma_x = \dfrac{\sum_{i=1}^{n}(x_i - \overline{x})^2}{n}$

(Contd...)

Standard deviation is given as: $\sqrt{\frac{\sum_{i=1}^{n}(x_i-\bar{x})^2}{n}}$

PE 4-2.c

```
//Arithmetic mean, variance and standard deviation
#include<stdio.h>
#include<math.h>
main()
{
float elements[20], sum=0.0, mean, var, sd;
int num, i;
printf("Enter the number of elements (max. 20)\t");
scanf("%d",&num);
printf("Enter the elements:\n");
for(i=0;i<num;i++)
    scanf("%f",&elements[i]);
for(i=0;i<num;i++)
    sum=sum+elements[i];
mean=sum/num;
sum=0.0;
for(i=0;i<num;i++)
    sum=sum+(elements[i]-mean)*(elements[i]-mean);
var=sum/num;
sd=sqrt(var);
printf("Arithmetic mean is %f\n",mean);
printf("Variance is %f\n",var);
printf("Standard deviation is %f\n",sd);
}
```

Output window

```
Enter the number of elements(max. 20)    6
Enter the elements:
2.1
2.9
2.3
2.4
1.8
2.5
Arithmetic mean is 2.333333
Variance is 0.115556
Standard deviation is 0.339935
```

Program 3 | Linear Search: Given a list of n elements and a key. Find whether the given key exists in the list or not. If it exists, print its position in the list

Algorithm:

Step 1: Start

Step 2: Read the elements present in the list and store them in an array

Step 3: Read the key to be searched in the list

Step 4: Loop to compare every element in the array with the key. When an equal value is found, print the location where the match has been found. If the loop finishes without finding a match, the search fails and print the message that key is not present in the list

Step 5: Stop

PE 4-3.c

```
//Linear Search
#include<stdio.h>
main()
{
int elements[20], num, i, key, found=0;
printf("Enter the number of elements (max. 20)\t");
scanf("%d",&num);
printf("Enter the elements:\n");
for(i=0;i<num;i++)
```

Output window

```
Enter the number of elements(max. 20)    6
Enter the elements:
12
10
5
-3
14
2
Enter the key that you want to search    -3
```

(Contd...)

PE 4-3.c

```
  scanf("%d",&elements[i]);   //←Read elements in the list
printf("Enter the key that you want to search\t");
scanf("%d",&key);           //←Read the key to be searched
for(i=0;i<num;i++)          //←Loop
  if(elements[i]==key)      //←Comparison of element & key
  {                         //←Key found
       printf("%d exists at location no. %d\n",key, i+1);
       found=1;
  }
if(found==0)                //←Key not found in the list
     printf("%d does not exist in the list",key);
}
```

Output window

```
-3 exists at location no. 4
```

Program 4 | Insertion Sort: Given list of n elements. Arrange them in an ascending order

Principle:

Insertion Sort works on the principle of sorting by insertion. Any given unsorted list can be divided into two lists such that one is sorted and the other is unsorted. For example, the given unsorted list

12	1	8	10	5	3

can be divided into two parts such that one list is sorted and other list is unsorted. The divided list is shown as:

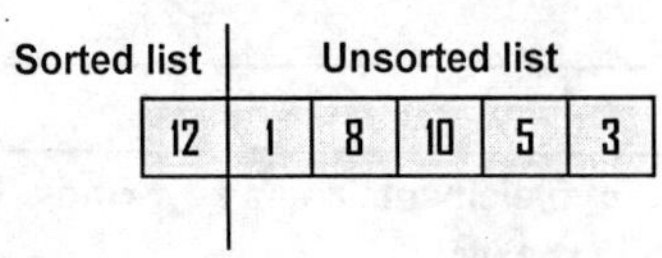

Initially the sorted list consists of zero or one element, as the list containing zero or one element is always sorted and the unsorted list consists of the rest of the elements.

Insertion Sort sorts by removing one element from the unsorted list at a time and inserting it at a proper position in the sorted listed. To make room for the insertion, some of the elements in the sorted list need to be moved. Each iteration of Insertion Sort reduces the size of the unsorted list by one and increases the size of the sorted list by one. Ultimately, the unsorted list will vanish and the entire list will be sorted.

The general procedure of the Insertion Sort is shown in the figure below:

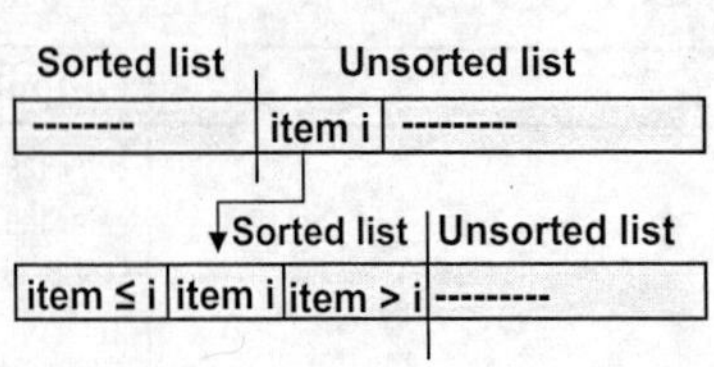

(Contd...)

Insertion Sort sorts the given list as shown below:

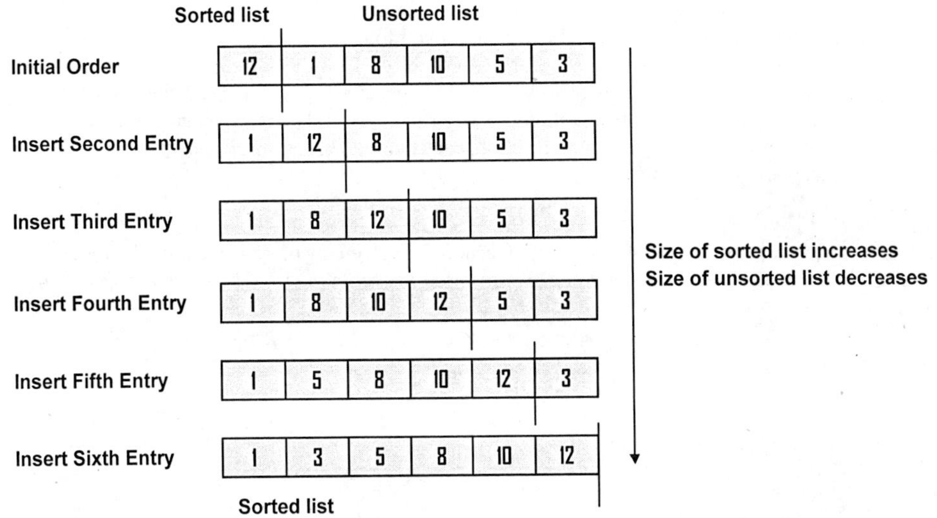

PE 4-4.c

```
//Insertion Sort
#include<stdio.h>
main()
{
int list[20], num, current, i, j;
printf("Enter the number of elements (max. 20)\t");
scanf("%d",&num);    //←Read the number of elements in the list
printf("Enter the elements:\n");
for(i=0;i<num;i++)
    scanf("%d",&list[i]);    //←Read the elements of the list
//←First element is sorted and the rest of the list is unsorted
for(i=1;i<num;i++)
    if(list[i]<list[i-1])          //←Remove element from the unsorted
    {                              //list and place it at proper position
        current=list[i];           //in the sorted list
        for(j=i-1;j>=0;j--)
        {
            list[j+1]=list[j];
                if(j==0||list[j-1]<=current)
                    break;
        }
        list[j]=current;
    }
printf("After sorting, elements are:\n");
for(i=0;i<num;i++)          //←Print sorted list
    printf("%d\n",list[i]);
}
```

Output window

```
Enter the number of elements(max. 20)    6
Enter the elements:
12
10
5
-3
14
2
After sorting, elements are:
-3
2
5
10
12
14
```

Program 5 | Selection Sort: Given a list of n elements. Arrange them in an ascending order

Insertion Sort has one major disadvantage. Insertion of an element removed from the unsorted list into the sorted list requires the elements in the sorted list to be moved to create space for the new element. Consider the insertion of sixth entry in the previous program. Insertion of 3 into the sorted list requires the movement of 5, 8, 10 and 12. These excessive movements become very expensive especially if the elements are very large such as records of employee's personal file or student transcripts. It would be far more efficient if an entry being moved could immediately be placed in its final position. Selection Sort accomplishes this goal and works on the following principle:

Principle:
Selection Sort works on the principle of sorting by selection. The given unsorted list is initially divided into two lists—the sorted list containing no element and the unsorted list containing all the elements. For example, the given unsorted list

can be divided into two parts as:

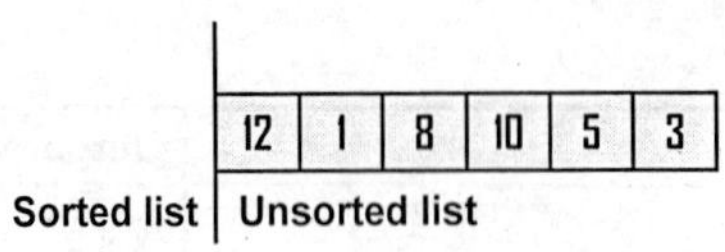

Selection Sort selects the minimum element from the unsorted list and exchanges it with the first element in the unsorted list. The selected element has moved to its final position; hence, the size of the sorted list is increased by one and the size of the unsorted list is decreased by one. This process of selecting the minimum element from the unsorted list, exchanging it with the first element in the unsorted list and then increasing the size of the sorted list and decreasing the size of the unsorted list by one is repeatedly followed till the entire list becomes sorted. The general procedure of Selection Sort is shown in the figure below:

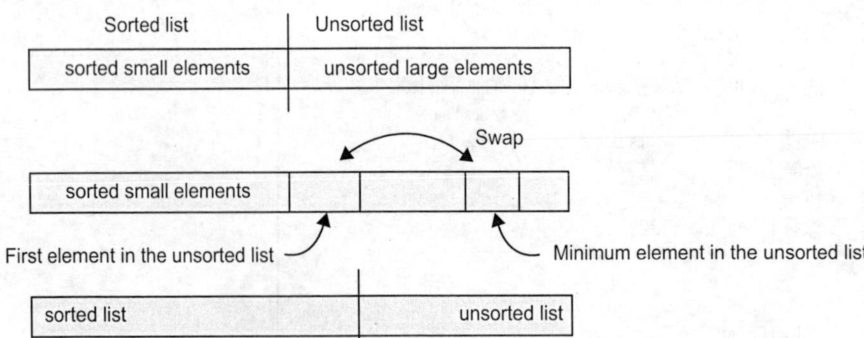

(Contd...)

Selection Sort sorts the given list as shown below:

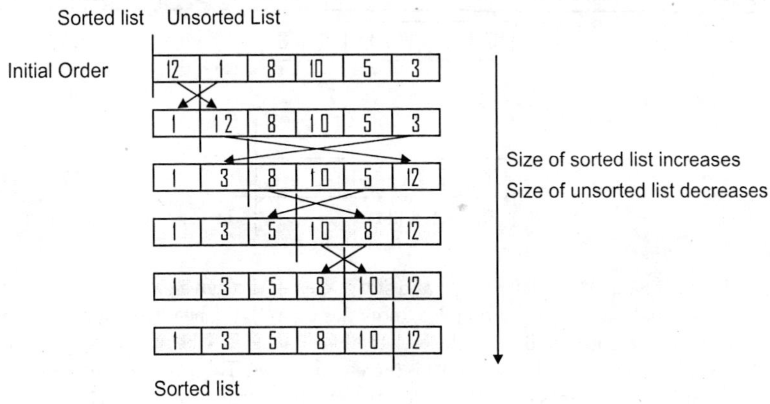

PE 4-5.c

```
//Selection Sort
#include<stdio.h>
main()
{
int list[20], num,min, temp, i, j;
printf("Enter the number of elements (max. 20)\t");
scanf("%d",&num);    //←Read number of elements in the list
printf("Enter the elements:\n");
for(i=0;i<num;i++)
    scanf("%d",&list[i]);    //←Read the elements
for(i=0;i<num-1;i++)         //←Initially entire list is unsorted
{
    min=i;
    for(j=i+1;j<num;j++)    //←Select minimum element in the list
        if(list[j]<list[min])
            min=j;
    { //←Place selected element at 1st position in the unsorted list
    temp=list[min];
    list[min]=list[i];
    list[i]=temp;
    }
}
printf("After sorting, elements are:\n");
for(i=0;i<num;i++)          //←Print sorted list
    printf("%d\n",list[i]);
}
```

Output window

```
Enter the number of elements(max. 20)    6
Enter the elements:
12
10
5
-3
14
2
After sorting, elements are:
-3
2
5
10
12
14
```

Program 6 | Bubble Sort: Given a list of n elements. Arrange them in an ascending order

Principle:

Bubble Sort works on the following observation:

'Bubbles (or lighter elements) rise up in water and heavier elements sink'

The given unsorted list is initially divided into two lists—the sorted list containing no element and the unsorted list containing all the elements. For example, the given unsorted list

(Contd...)

Program 6 | Bubble Sort: Given a list of n elements. Arrange them in an ascending order *(Contd...)*

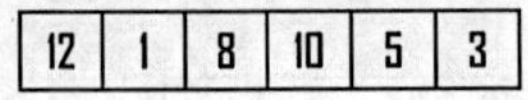

can be divided into two parts as:

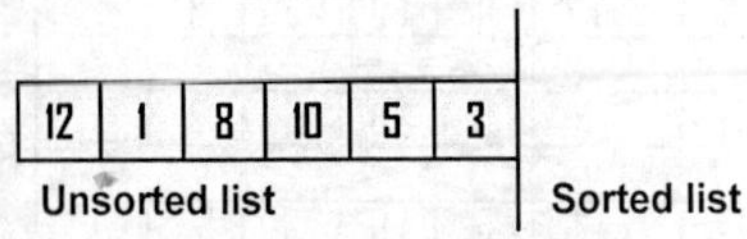

Bubble Sort scans the unsorted list from left to right and swaps elements when a pair of adjacent elements is found to be out of order. After one complete iteration (also known as a **pass**), the heaviest element (i.e. the largest element) is at the right end of the unsorted list, but the earlier elements may still be out of order. The size of unsorted list is decreased by one and the size of the sorted list is increased by one. This process is repeated till the unsorted list vanishes and the entire list becomes sorted. Bubble Sort sorts the given list as shown below:

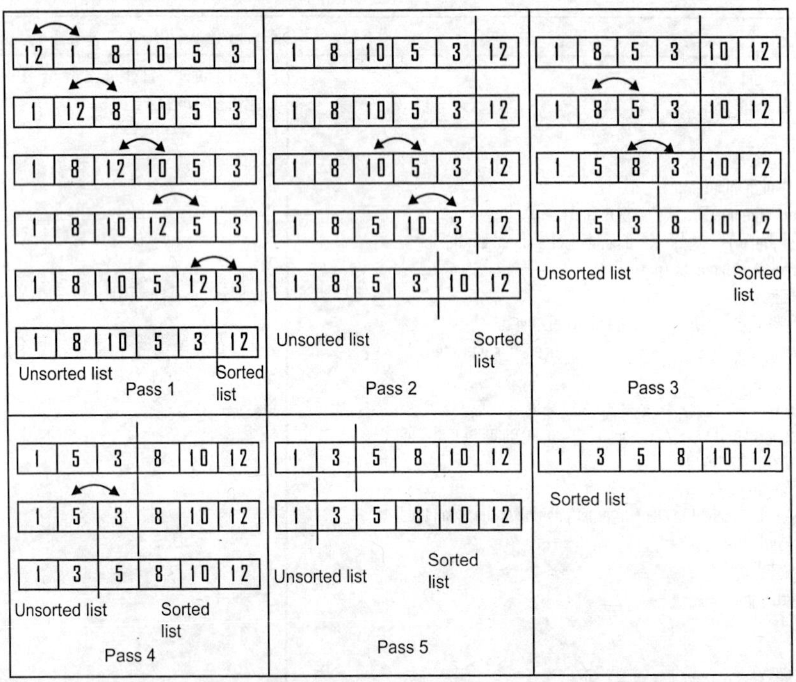

PE 4-6.c

```
//Bubble Sort
#include<stdio.h>
main()
{
int list[20], num,min, temp, i, j;
printf("Enter the number of elements (max. 20)\t");
scanf("%d",&num);          //←Read number of elements in the list
printf("Enter the elements:\n");
for(i=0;i<num;i++)
    scanf("%d",&list[i]);  //←Read the elements
for(i=0;i<num-1;i++)       //←Passes
```

Output window

```
Enter the number of elements(max. 20)    6
Enter the elements:
12
10
5
-3
14
2
After sorting, elements are:
-3
2
```

(Contd...)

```
    for(j=0;j<num-1-i;j++)
        if(list[j]>list[j+1])   //←If elements are out of order, swap them
        {
            temp=list[j];
            list[j]=list[j+1];
            list[j+1]=temp;
        }
printf("After sorting, elements are:\n");
for(i=0;i<num;i++)         //←Print sorted list
    printf("%d\n",list[i]);
}
```

```
5
10
12
14
```

Program 7 | Given two sorted one-dimensional arrays A and B of size m and n, respectively. Merge them into a single-sorted array C that contains every element from arrays A and B in ascending order

PE 4-7.c

```
//Merge two Sorted arrays into one
#include<stdio.h>
main()
{
int A[20], B[20], C[40] ;
int i, j, l, h, m, n;
printf("Enter the number of elements in A (max. 20)\t");
scanf("%d",&m);          //←Read number of elements in A
printf("Enter the elements in sorted order:\n");
for(i=0;i<m;i++)
    scanf("%d",&A[i]);   //←Read the elements
printf("Enter the number of elements in B (max. 20)\t");
scanf("%d",&n);          //←Read number of elements in B
printf("Enter the elements in sorted order:\n");
for(i=0;i<n;i++)
    scanf("%d",&B[i]);   //←Read the elements
i=0; j=0; h=0;
while(i<m || j<n)
{
    if(A[i]<=B[j])
    {
        C[h]=A[i];
        i++;
    }
    else
    {
        C[h]=B[j];
        j++;
    }
    h++;
}
if(i==m)
    for(l=j;l<n;l++)
        C[h++]=B[l];
else if(j==n)
    for(l=i;l<m;l++)
        C[h++]=A[l];
```

Output window

```
Enter the number of elements in A (max. 20)    5
Enter the elements in sorted order:
1 3 5 7 9
Enter the number of elements in B (max. 20)    4
Enter the elements in sorted order:
2 4 6 8
After merging, elements are:
1 2 3 4 5 6 7 8 9
```

(Contd...)

PE 4-7.c	Output window
(continued listing below)	

```
printf("After merging, elements are:\n");
for(i=0;i<m+n;i++)          //←Print merged array C
    printf("%d ",C[i]);
}
```

Program 8 | Matrix addition: Add two matrices of order m × n

PE 4-8.c

```
//Matrix Addition
#include<stdio.h>
main()
{
int mat1[10][10], mat2[10][10], resultant[10][10];
int m, n, row, col;
printf("Enter the order of matrices (max. 10 by 10)\t");
scanf("%d %d",&m, &n);
printf("Enter the elements of matrix-1:\n");
for(row=0;row<m;row++)
{
    for(col=0;col<n;col++)
        scanf("%d",&mat1[row][col]);
}
printf("Enter the elements of matrix-2:\n");
for(row=0;row<m;row++)
{
    for(col=0;col<n;col++)
        scanf("%d",&mat2[row][col]);
}
for(row=0;row<m;row++)
    for(col=0;col<n;col++)
        resultant[row][col]=mat1[row][col]+mat2[row][col];
printf("The result of matrix addition is:\n");
for(row=0;row<m;row++)
{
    for(col=0;col<n;col++)
        printf("%d ",resultant[row][col]);
    printf("\n");
}
}
```

Output window

```
Enter the order of matrices (max. 10 by 10)    3 3
Enter the elements of matrix-1:
1 2 3
4 5 6
7 8 9
Enter the elements of matrix-2:
2 3 4
1 2 3
1 1 0
The result of matrix addition is :
3 5 7
5 7 9
8 9 9
```

Program 9 | Matrix multiplication: Multiply two matrices

Given two matrices A and B

$$A = \begin{bmatrix} A_{11} & A_{12} \\ A_{21} & A_{22} \end{bmatrix} \quad \text{and} \quad B = \begin{bmatrix} B_{11} & B_{12} & B_{13} \\ B_{21} & B_{22} & B_{12} \end{bmatrix}$$

(Contd...)

The result of the matrix multiplication is given as:

$$C_{2\times3} = A_{2\times2}\,B_{2\times3} = \begin{bmatrix} A_{11}B_{11} + A_{12}B_{21} & A_{11}B_{12} + A_{12}B_{22} & A_{11}B_{13} + A_{12}B_{23} \\ A_{21}B_{31} + A_{22}B_{21} & A_{21}B_{12} + A_{22}B_{22} & A_{21}B_{13} + A_{22}B_{23} \end{bmatrix}$$

PE 4-9.c

```
//Matrix Multiplication
#include<stdio.h>
#include<stdlib.h>
main()
{
int mat1[10][10], mat2[10][10], resultant[10][10]={0};
int  m1, n1, m2, n2, i, j, k;
printf("Enter the order of matrix-1 (max. 10 by 10)\t");
scanf("%d %d",&m1, &n1);
printf("Enter the elements of matrix-1:\n");
for(i=0;i<m1;i++)
{
    for(j=0;j<n1;j++)
        scanf("%d",&mat1[i][j]);
}
printf("Enter the order of matrix-2 (max. 10 by 10)\t");
scanf("%d %d",&m2, &n2);
printf("Enter the elements of matrix-2:\n");
for(i=0;i<m2;i++)
{
    for(j=0;j<n2;j++)
        scanf("%d",&mat2[i][j]);
}
if(n1!=m2)
{
    printf("Matrices are not compatible for multiplication\n");
    exit(1);
}
else
{
    for(i=0;i<m1;i++)
        for(j=0;j<n2;j++)
            for(k=0;k<n1;k++)
                resultant[i][j]=resultant[i][j]+mat1[i][k]*mat2[k][j];
}
printf("The result of matrix multiplication is:\n");
for(i=0;i<m1;i++)
{
    for(j=0;j<n2;j++)
        printf("%d ",resultant[i][j]);
    printf("\n");
}
}
```

Output window

```
Enter the order of matrix-1 (max. 10 by 10)    2 3
Enter the elements of matrix-1:
1 2 3
4 5 6
Enter the order of matrix-2 (max. 10 by 10)    3 3
Enter the elements of matrix-2:
2 3 4
1 2 3
1 1 0
The result of matrix multiplication is :
7 10 10
19 28 31
```

Program 10 | Find the sum of principal diagonal elements of a square matrix

The set of elements extending from the upper-left-most corner to the lower-right-most corner in a square matrix are known as **principal diagonal elements.** An element A_{ij} of a square matrix is principle diagonal element if and only if i=j.

PE 4-10.c

```c
//Sum of principle diagonal elements
#include<stdio.h>
main()
{
int matrix[10][10];
int order, sum=0, i, j;
printf("Enter the order of the square matrix(max. 10)\t");
scanf("%d",&order);
printf("Enter the elements of matrix:\n");
for(i=0;i<order;i++)
{
    for(j=0;j<order;j++)
        scanf("%d",&matrix[i][j]);
}
for(i=0;i<order;i++)
    sum=sum+matrix[i][i];
printf("Sum of elements of principal diagonal is %d",sum);
}
```

Output window

```
Enter the order of the square matrix (max. 10)    3
Enter the elements of matrix:
1 2 3
4 5 6
7 8 9
Sum of elements of principal diagonal is 15
```

Program 11 | Matrix transpose: Find the transpose of a given matrix

The **transpose** of the matrix A is another matrix A^T, which can be found by any one of the following actions:

1. Writing the rows of A as the columns of A^T
2. Writing the columns of A as the rows of A^T
3. Reflect A about its main diagonal to obtain A^T(only possible in case of square matrix).

The transpose of an m×n matrix A with elements A_{ij} is an n×m matrix A^T=A_{ji}, 1≤i≤n and 1≤j≤m.

PE 4-11.c

```c
//Matrix Transpose
#include<stdio.h>
main()
{
int matrix[10][10], matrix_transpose[10][10];
int m, n, i, j;
printf("Enter the order of the matrix(max. 10 by 10)\t");
scanf("%d %d",&m, &n);
printf("Enter the elements of the matrix:\n");
for(i=0;i<m;i++)
{
    for(j=0;j<n;j++)
        scanf("%d",&matrix[i][j]);
}
for(i=0;i<n;i++)
```

Output window

```
Enter the order of matrix (max. 10 by 10)    2 4
Enter the elements of matrix:
1 2 3 4
5 6 7 8
Transpose of the matrix is:
1 5
2 6
3 7
4 8
```

(Contd...)

```
    for(j=0;j<m;j++)
        matrix_transpose[i][j]=matrix[j][i];
printf("Transpose of the matrix is:\n");
for(i=0;i<n;i++)
{
    for(j=0;j<m;j++)
        printf("%d ",matrix_transpose[i][j]);
    printf("\n");
}
}
```

Program 12 | Check whether a given square matrix is symmetric or not

A square matrix A is **symmetric** if A=A^T (i.e. the matrix is equal to its transpose).

PE 4-12.c

```
//Symmetric matrix
#include<stdio.h>
main()
{
int matrix[10][10], matrix_transpose[10][10], unequal=0;
int i,j,order;
printf("Enter the order of the square matrix(max. 10 by 10)\t");
scanf("%d",&order);
printf("Enter the elements of the matrix:\n");
for(i=0;i<order;i++)
{
    for(j=0;j<order;j++)
        scanf("%d",&matrix[i][j]);
}
for(i=0;i<order;i++)
    for(j=0;j<order;j++)
        matrix_transpose[i][j]=matrix[j][i];
for(i=0;i<order;i++)
{
    for(j=0;j<order;j++)
        if(matrix[i][j]!=matrix_transpose[i][j])
        {
            unequal=1;
            break;
        }
    if(unequal==1)
        break;
}
if(unequal==0)
    printf("The matrix is symmetric\n");
else
    printf("The matrix is not symmetric\n");
}
```

Output window

```
Enter the order of the square matrix (max. 10 by 10)    3
Enter the elements of matrix:
1 2 3
2 1 4
3 4 1
The matrix is symmetric
```

Program 13 | Upper triangular matrix: Extract the upper triangular matrix from a square matrix

A square matrix in which all the elements below the main (i.e. principal) diagonal are zero is known as **upper triangular matrix** and a square matrix in which all the elements above the main diagonal are zero is known as **lower triangular matrix**.
Upper triangular matrix can be extracted from a square matrix by extracting the elements of principle diagonal and the elements that lie above it.

PE 4-13.c

```
//Extraction of Upper Triangular matrix
#include<stdio.h>
main()
{
int matrix[10][10], ut_matrix[10][10], unequal=0;
int i,j,order;
printf("Enter the order of the square matrix(max. 10 by 10)\t");
scanf("%d",&order);
printf("Enter the elements of the matrix:\n");
for(i=0;i<order;i++)
{
    for(j=0;j<order;j++)
        scanf("%d",&matrix[i][j]);
}
for(i=0;i<order;i++)
    for(j=0;j<order;j++)
        if(i<=j)
            ut_matrix[i][j]=matrix[i][j];
        else
            ut_matrix[i][j]=0;
printf("Upper Triangular matrix is:\n");
for(i=0;i<order;i++)
{
    for(j=0;j<order;j++)
        printf("%d ",ut_matrix[i][j]);
    printf("\n");
}
}
```

Output window

```
Enter the order of the square matrix (max. 10 by 10)    3
Enter the elements of the matrix:
1 2 3
2 1 4
3 4 1
Upper Triangular matrix is:
1 2 3
0 1 4
0 0 1
```

Program 14 | Strictly upper triangular matrix: Check whether a given matrix is strictly upper triangular or not

An upper triangular matrix is **strictly upper triangular** if the elements of the principal diagonal are zero.

PE 4-14.c

```
//Strictly Upper Triangular matrix
#include<stdio.h>
main()
```

Output window

```
Enter the order of the square matrix (max. 10 by 10)    3
Enter the elements of matrix:
0 2 3
```

(Contd...)

```
{
int matrix[10][10], notzero=0;
int i,j,order;
printf("Enter the order of the square matrix(max. 10 by 10)\t");
scanf("%d",&order);
printf("Enter the elements of the matrix:\n");
for(i=0;i<order;i++)
{
    for(j=0;j<order;j++)
        scanf("%d",&matrix[i][j]);
}
for(i=0;i<order;i++)
{
    for(j=0;j<order;j++)
        if(i>=j)
            if(matrix[i][j]!=0)
            {
                notzero=1;
                break;
            }
    if(notzero==1)
        break;
}
if(notzero==1)
    printf("The given matrix is not strictly upper triangular\n");
else
    printf("The given matrix is strictly upper triangular\n");
}
```

```
0 0 4
0 0 0
The given matrix is strictly upper triangular
```

Output window (second execution)

```
Enter the order of the square matrix (max. 10 by 10)    3
Enter the elements of matrix:
6 2 3
0 0 4
2 0 0
The given matrix is not strictly upper triangular
```

Program 15 | Matrix Inverse: Find the inverse of a 3 × 3 matrix

The **inverse** of a square matrix A, is a matrix A^{-1} such that $AA^{-1}=I$, where I is the identity matrix. The matrix A has an inverse if and only if the determinant of A (written as |A|) is not equal to zero. A matrix whose inverse exists is known as **invertible matrix**

Finding the inverse of a matrix using Gauss–Jordan elimination method:

Step 1: Start

Step 2: Read the elements of the matrix A whose inverse is to be found

Step 3: Check whether its determinant is zero or not. If it is zero, print that inverse does not exist and stop, else proceed to Step 4

Step 4: Form the augmented matrix B. It is formed by augmenting the matrix A with an identity matrix of the same dimensions. If the matrix A is of order m × n, the augmented matrix B = [A|I] is of order m × 2n. It consists of two parts: the first part corresponds to A and the second part corresponds to I

Step 5: Apply elementary row operations on the augmented matrix B so that its first part reduces to identity matrix. By performing these row operations, the inverse of the matrix A appears in the second part

Step 6: The matrix augmentation can be undone to retrieve the inverse of the matrix

Step 7: Print the inverse of the matrix

Step 8: Stop

(Contd...)

Example:

$$A = \begin{bmatrix} 2 & 3 & 1 \\ 1 & 1 & 2 \\ 2 & 3 & 4 \end{bmatrix} \quad I = \begin{bmatrix} 1 & 0 & 0 \\ 0 & 1 & 0 \\ 0 & 0 & 1 \end{bmatrix} \quad B = \begin{bmatrix} 2 & 3 & 1 & 1 & 0 & 0 \\ 1 & 1 & 2 & 0 & 1 & 0 \\ 2 & 3 & 4 & 0 & 0 & 1 \end{bmatrix}$$

Step 1: R_1->R_1/B[0][0]

$$B = \begin{bmatrix} 1 & 3/2 & 1/2 & 1/2 & 0 & 0 \\ 1 & 1 & 2 & 0 & 1 & 0 \\ 2 & 3 & 4 & 0 & 0 & 1 \end{bmatrix}$$

Step 2: R_2->R_2-B[1][0]*R_1

$$B = \begin{bmatrix} 1 & 3/2 & 1/2 & 1/2 & 0 & 0 \\ 0 & -1/2 & 3/2 & -1/2 & 1 & 0 \\ 2 & 3 & 4 & 0 & 0 & 1 \end{bmatrix}$$

Step 3: R_3->R_3-B[2][0]*R_1

$$B = \begin{bmatrix} 1 & 3/2 & 1/2 & 1/2 & 0 & 0 \\ 0 & -1/2 & 3/2 & -1/2 & 1 & 0 \\ 0 & 0 & 3 & -1 & 0 & 1 \end{bmatrix}$$

Step 4: R_2->R_2/B[1][1]

$$B = \begin{bmatrix} 1 & 3/2 & 1/2 & 1/2 & 0 & 0 \\ 0 & 1 & -3 & 1 & -2 & 0 \\ 0 & 0 & 3 & -1 & 0 & 1 \end{bmatrix}$$

Step 5: R_1->R_1-B[0][1]*R_2

$$B = \begin{bmatrix} 1 & 0 & 5 & -1 & 3 & 0 \\ 0 & 1 & -3 & 1 & -2 & 0 \\ 0 & 0 & 3 & -1 & 0 & 1 \end{bmatrix}$$

Step 6: R_3->R_3-B[2][0]*R_2

$$B = \begin{bmatrix} 1 & 0 & 5 & -1 & 3 & 0 \\ 0 & 1 & -3 & 1 & -2 & 0 \\ 0 & 0 & 3 & -1 & 0 & 1 \end{bmatrix}$$

Step 7: R_3->R_3/B[2][2]

$$B = \begin{bmatrix} 1 & 0 & 5 & -1 & 3 & 0 \\ 0 & 1 & -3 & 1 & -2 & 0 \\ 0 & 0 & 1 & -1/3 & 0 & 1/3 \end{bmatrix}$$

Step 8: R_1->R_1-B[0][2]*R_3

$$B = \begin{bmatrix} 1 & 0 & 0 & 2/3 & 3 & -5/3 \\ 0 & 1 & -3 & 1 & -2 & 0 \\ 0 & 0 & 1 & -1/3 & 0 & 1/3 \end{bmatrix}$$

(Contd...)

Step 9: $R_2 \to R_2 - B[1][2]*R_3$

$$B = \begin{bmatrix} 1 & 0 & 0 & 2/3 & 3 & -5/3 \\ 0 & 1 & 0 & 0 & -2 & 1 \\ 0 & 0 & 1 & -1/3 & 0 & 1/3 \end{bmatrix}$$

Step 10: Undo the matrix augmentation and print inverse

$$A^{-1} = \begin{bmatrix} 2/3 & 3 & -5/3 \\ 0 & -2 & 1 \\ -1/3 & 0 & 1/3 \end{bmatrix}$$

PE 4-15.c

```c
//Inverse of a matrix
#include<stdio.h>
main()
{
float matrix[3][3], aug_matrix[3][6];
float identity[3][3]={1,0,0,0,1,0,0,0,1};    //←3×3 identity matrix
float c,r, sub, det;
int i,j,order=3,k, row, col;
printf("Enter the elements of 3 by 3 matrix:\n");
for(i=0;i<order;i++)
{
    for(j=0;j<order;j++)
        scanf("%f",&matrix[i][j]);    //←Read the elements of the matrix
}
//←Calculate the determinant of the matrix
det=matrix[0][0]*(matrix[1][1]*matrix[2][2]-matrix[2][1]*matrix[1][2]) -
matrix[0][1]*(matrix[1][0]*matrix[2][2]-matrix[2][0]*matrix[1][2]) +
matrix[0][2]*(matrix[1][0]*matrix[2][1]-matrix[2][0]*matrix[1][1]);
if(det!=0)    //←if determinant is not zero inverse can be found
{
    for(i=0;i<order;i++)    //←augmenting the matrix with identity matrix
        for(j=0;j<order;j++)
        {
            aug_matrix[i][j]=matrix[i][j];
            aug_matrix[i][j+3]=identity[i][j];
        }
//←Elementary row operations
    for(i=0;i<order;i++)
        for(j=0;j<order;j++)
        {
            if(i==j)
            {
//←Implementing Steps 1, 4 and 7 described in the example above
                    c=aug_matrix[i][i];
                    for(k=0;k<6;k++)
                        aug_matrix[i][k]=aug_matrix[i][k]/c;
//←Implementing Steps 2,3,5,6,8 and 9 described in the example above
                for(row=0;row<order;row++)
```

Output window

```
Enter the elements of 3 by 3 matrix:
2 3 1
1 1 2
2 3 4
Inverse of the matrix is:
 0.67    3.00   -1.67
 0.00   -2.00    1.00
-0.33    0.00    0.33
```

(Contd...)

PE 4-15.c	Output window

```
            {
                sub=aug_matrix[row][j];
                for(col=0;col<6;col++)
                if(row!=i)
                {
                    aug_matrix[row][col]-=sub*aug_matrix[i][col];
                }
            }
        }
    }
    printf("Inverse of the matrix is:\n");
    for(i=0;i<order;i++)    //←Printing the inverse of the matrix
    {
        for(j=0;j<order;j++)
            printf("%5.2f ",aug_matrix[i][j+3]);
        printf("\n");
    }
}
else    //←if determinant is zero, print that inverse does not exist
    printf("Inverse does not exist");
}
```

Test Yourself

1. Fill in the blanks in each of the following:
   a. An array is used for the storage of ____________ data.
   b. The array index in C language starts with ____________.
   c. The elements of an array are always stored in ____________ memory locations.
   d. The size specifier in an array declaration must be a compile time expression of ____________ type.
   e. The elements of an array can be accessed by using ____________ operator.
   f. The object pointed to by a pointer can be indirectly accessed by using ____________ operator.
   g. The expression equivalent to the expression `arr[5][4]`, where `arr` is an integer array is ____________.
   h. The biggest advantage of arrays is their ____________ capabilities.
   i. In an expression, if the number of subscripts used with the array is less than the dimensions of the array, the expression always refers to a/an ____________.
   j. The comparison of two null pointers always results in ____________.

2. State whether each of the following is true or false. If false, explain why.

   a. In an array declaration, the number of initializers in the initialization list should be less than or at most equal to the value of size specifier.
   b. The index of an array must be a positive integer greater than zero.
   c. A pointer variable can be initialized with a constant value zero.
   d. A pointer to any type of object can be assigned to a pointer of type `void*` without explicit type casting.
   e. A `void` pointer can be assigned to a pointer variable without explicit type casting.
   f. The name of the array refers to the base address of the complete array.
   g. The size of an array cannot be changed at the run time.
   h. If the size specifier is not mentioned in an array declaration, the size of the array is automatically initialized to a single element.
   i. Multi-dimensional arrays in C are stored in the memory using column major order of storage.
   j. The declaration statement `int* a[10];` declares `a` as a pointer to an integer array of `10` elements.

3. Programming exercises:

   a. Write a C program to find the sum of all the elements of an array.
   b. An array consists of integers. Write a C program to count the number of elements less than, greater than and equal to zero.
   c. Write a C program to check whether a given matrix is skew-symmetric or not.
   d. Write a C program to extract lower-triangular matrix from a square matrix.
   e. Write a C program that returns the position of the largest element in an array.
   f. In a class there are twenty students and each student undergoes five courses. Write a C program to find out the average marks secured by each student and the overall average of the class.

5

FUNCTIONS

Learning Objectives

In this chapter, you will learn about:

- Functions
- Advantages of using functions
- Classification of functions as user-defined functions and library functions
- User-defined functions
- How to declare, define and call functions
- Way of increasing flexibility of functions
- Different ways of supplying inputs to a function
- return statement
- How to provide default inputs to a function
- Recursion and its use to solve problems
- Classification of recursion
- How recursion works
- Tower of Hanoi problem
- Function type and pointers to functions
- Array of function pointers
- Passing arrays and functions to functions
- Commonly used library functions
- Variable argument functions

5.1 Introduction

In the previous chapters, you have seen how to declare identifiers (Chapter 1), how to write expressions (Chapter 2) and how to write statements (Chapter 3). In this chapter, I will tell you how to group these components in a function so that these components can be reused in a program. I will describe the advantages of using functions, how to declare, define and call them. You will be familiarized with the methods of increasing flexibility of a function and different ways of passing inputs to a function. Finally, we will have a discussion about the advanced topics like pointers to functions, arrays of function pointers and passing functions to a function.

5.2 Functions

Most of the computer programs that solve real-world problems are much bigger and complex than the programs presented in the first few chapters. The existing software engineering practices used to develop such complicated programs work on the following principles:

1. **Top-down design, modularization, stepwise refinement and bottom-up development:** According to this principle, a complex problem should be modularized (i.e. divided) into sub-problems that are simpler, manageable and easier to solve as compared to the original problem. If the divided sub-problems are still complex and cannot be easily solved, they are further divided into sub-problems. Each level of division provides a refinement and simplicity to the problem. This process of modularization is carried out till the sub-problems are simple enough and can be easily solved. The solutions for these simple problems are then developed and merged to provide a solution for the overall complex problem. This approach of problem solving is also known as **'divide-and-conquer strategy.'** This strategy is practically followed in real life whereby a senior officer responsible for the execution of a work divides the work among his subordinates. The subordinate officers may further divide the assigned work among their subordinates, get the work done and report back to their senior officer. This hierarchical division of work is shown in Figure 5.1.

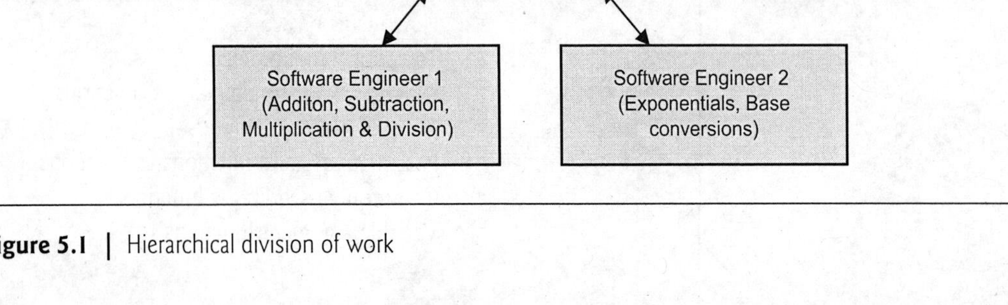

Figure 5.1 | Hierarchical division of work

Thus, in this approach of solution development, a solution to the given problem is thought of at an abstract level. This abstract solution is divided into modules, and each level of division refines the solution by adding details to the divided modules. The process of division is carried out till the divided modules are well defined and simple enough to be generated (i.e. coded). The functionality of each module is kept in a separate function. These functions are relatively independent of each other and interact with each other to provide a solution to the overall problem.

2. **'Don't reinvent the wheel.'** Another important software engineering principle states that **'Don't reinvent the wheel.'** This means that the functionality that has already been developed should be reused instead of being developed again. Functions help a lot in realizing this principle. The commonly required functionality is developed and kept in standard libraries for the use in the form of library functions. In the previous chapters, we have used the input and output functionality by using `scanf` and `printf` library functions. The C standard library provides a rich set of functionality for performing the common mathematical calculations, string and character manipulations, input/output and other useful operations.

The above two software engineering principles give a hint about the importance and the need of functions. Several other advantages of modularizing a program into functions include:

1. Reduction in code redundancy
2. Enabling code reuse
3. Better readability
4. Information hiding
5. Improved debugging and testing
6. Improved maintainability

As already described in Chapter 1, a C program is made up of functions. Functions interact with each other to accomplish a particular task. They are classified according to the following criteria:

1. Based upon who develops the function
2. Based upon the number of arguments a function accepts

5.3 Classification of Functions

5.3.1 Based Upon who Develops the Function

Based upon who develops the function, functions are classified as:

1. User-defined functions
2. Library functions

5.3.1.1 User-defined functions

User-defined functions are the functions that are defined (i.e. developed) by the user at the time of writing a program. The user develops the functionality by writing the body of the function. These functions are sometimes referred to as **programmer-defined functions.** Program 5-1 illustrates the use of user-defined functions `add`, `sub` and `println`.

Line | Prog 5-1.c

```
1  //User defined functions
2  #include<stdio.h>
3  //Function declarations or function prototypes
4  println();
5  int add(int, int);
6  int sub(int x, int y);
7  //main function, the master function
8  main()
9  {
10     int a,b,sum, diff;
11     printf("Enter the values\t");
12     scanf("%d %d",&a, &b);
13 //Function invocations
14 //Asking the workers to do work
15     sum=add(a,b);
16     diff=sub(a,b);
17     println();
18 //Master presents the results returned by workers
19     printf("Result of addition is %d\n",sum);
20     printf("Result of subtraction is %d\n",diff);
21 }
22 //Function definitions
23 println()
24 {
25 printf("------------------------\n");
26 }
27 int add(int a, int b)
28 {
29 return a+b;
30 }
31 int sub(int a, int b)
32 {
33 return a-b;
34 }
```

Output window

```
Enter the values    4 3
------------------------
Result of addition is 7
Result of subtraction is 1
```

Remarks:

- println, add and sub are user-defined functions
- In line numbers 4, 5 and 6, user-defined functions are declared
- In line numbers 23 to 34, they are defined
- In line numbers 15, 16 and 17, they are called
- Line numbers 23, 27 and 31 consist of headers of the functions println, add and sub
- The variables declared in the function headers or function declarations are known as parameters
- In line numbers 6, x and y are the parameter names
- In line numbers 27 and 31, a and b are the parameter names
- The parameters declared inside the function headers are similar to the variables declared inside the body of the function
- **main is also a user-defined function**

Program 5-1 | A program that illustrates the use of user-defined functions

As you have seen in the code snippet in Program 5-1, there are three aspects of working with user-defined functions:

1. Function declaration, also known as function prototype
2. Function definition
3. Function use, also known as function call or function invocation

5.3.1.1.1 Function Declaration

All identifiers (except labels) need to be declared before they are used. As function names are also identifiers, this is true for functions as well. All the functions need to be declared or defined† before they are used (i.e. called‡). The general form of a **function declaration** is:

[return_type] **function_name(**[parameter_list or parameter_type_list]**);**

The important points about the function declaration are as follows:

1. The terms enclosed within the square brackets are optional and might not be present in a function declaration statement. The terms shown in **bold** are the mandatory parts of a function declaration.
2. The function declaration consists of the name of the function along with its return type and parameter list or parameter-type list enclosed within parentheses. Function declaration is also known as **function prototype**. For example, in Program 5-1 the declaration of function `add` in line number 5 consists of **parameter-type list**, and the declaration of function `sub` in line number 6 consists of **parameter list**.
3. Function names are identifiers. All syntactic rules discussed in Section 1.5.1 for writing identifier names are applicable for writing the function names as well. The name of a function is also termed as **function designator**.
4. The specification of the return type is optional. If specified, the return type of a function can be any type (e.g. `char`, `int`, `float`, `int*`, `int**`, `void`, etc.) except array type and function type.§ For example, in Program 5-1 the return type of the function `println` is not specified and the return type of functions `add` and `sub` is `int`.
5. The syntactic rules for writing a parameter-type list and parameter list in a function declaration are as follows:
   a. The **parameter-type list** is a comma-separated list of parameter types. The parameter type can be any type (e.g. `char`, `int`, `float`, `int*`, `int**`, `void`, etc.) except function type. If only a parameter-type list is mentioned, the function declaration is said to have **abstract parameter declaration**.
   b. A parameter name can optionally follow each parameter type. A parameter name should be a valid variable name. If parameter names follow parameter types in a parameter-type list, it becomes a **parameter list**. If the function declaration consists of a parameter list, it is said to have **complete parameter declaration**. For example, in Program 5-1 (in line number 5) function `add` has abstract parameter declaration and (in line number 6) function `sub` has complete parameter declaration.
   c. Using a combination of complete parameter declaration and abstract parameter declaration (i.e. naming some of the parameters and leaving the rest of them unnamed) is also allowed. For example, the following declarations of function `add` are also allowed:

      ```
      int add(int x, int);
      int add(int, int y);
      ```

   d. No two parameter names appearing in the parameter list can be the same.
   e. The shorthand declaration of parameters in the parameter list is not allowed.
6. Function declaration is a statement, so it must be terminated with a semicolon.

† Refer Section 5.3.1.1.2 for a description on function definitions.

‡ Refer Section 5.3.1.1.3 for a description on function calls.

§ Refer Section 5.3.1.1.8 for a description on the function type.

7. A function need not be declared, if it is defined before it is called.

The following function declarations are valid:

1. `add();` //←Return type and parameter list are not present
2. `int add(int,int);` //←int is the return type and int, int is the parameter-type list
3. `int* add(int,float);` //←int* is the return type and int, float is the parameter-type list
4. `int add(int a, int b);` //←Parameter list contains the names of parameters, i.e. a and b
5. `int add(int, int b);` //←Combination of abstract and complete parameter declaration

The following function declarations are not valid:

1. `int add(int a, float a);` //←Both the parameter names are the same
2. `int add&sub(int, int);` //←Name of the function is not valid as it contains the special character &
3. `int add(int a,b);` //←Shorthand declaration of parameters is not allowed
4. `int add(int a, int b)` //←The declaration is not terminated with a semicolon

Function prototypes (i.e. function declarations) are important and their necessity can be seen from two different perspectives:

1. **User perspective** It tells the user how to use a pre-defined or library function.[¶] It tells the user the number of parameters along with their types that a function expects and its return type. This is necessary and sufficient information for a user to use a function. For example, consider the following function prototype:

```
int add(int,int);
```

It tells the user that function add expects two integers and returns the result as an integer. With all this information, the user will be able to use the function add. Function prototype does not provide any information about how the functionality is implemented by the function. We have been able to use the printf function in the previous chapters because we know its prototype. The prototype of the printf function is available in the header file stdio.h. We do not know anything about how printing functionality is implemented by the printf function.

2. **Compiler perspective** It allows the compiler to perform **type checking**. By type checking the compiler ensures that while making a function call, the user provides the correct number and the correct type of arguments. If the number of arguments is not the same as the number of parameters or if their types are not compatible with the types of parameters provided in the function declaration, the compiler issues an error message.

i If some of the parameters are provided with default arguments,[††] the number of arguments in a function call can be lesser than the number of parameters.

[¶] Refer Section 5.3.1.2 for a description on library functions.

[††] Refer Section 5.3.1.1.5 for a description on default arguments.

5.3.1.1.2 Function Definition

Function definition, also known as **function implementation**, means composing a function. Every function definition consists of two parts:

1. Header of the function
2. Body of the function

Thus, defining a function involves composing its header and the body.

5.3.1.1.2.1 Header of a Function

The general form of **header of a function** is:

```
[return_type] function_name([parameter_list])
```

The important points about the function header are as follows:

1. The terms enclosed within the square brackets are optional and might not be present in a function header. The terms shown in bold are the mandatory part of a function header.
2. Unlike function declaration, the header of a function can only have complete parameter declaration. It cannot have abstract parameter declaration or a combination of abstract and complete parameter declaration. The variables declared in the parameter list will receive the data sent by the calling function.[‡‡] They serve as the inputs to the function.
3. No two parameter names appearing in the parameter list can be the same.
4. The shorthand declaration of parameters in the parameter list is not allowed.
5. The return type and the number and the types of parameters in the function header should exactly match the corresponding return type and the number and types of parameters in the function declaration, if it is present. For example, look at the function declarations in line numbers 4, 5 and 6 and function headers in line numbers 23, 27 and 31 in Program 5-1.
6. It is not mandatory to have the same names for the parameters in the function declaration and function definition. For example, in Program 5-1, the names of parameters in the declaration of function `sub` in line number 6 are `x` and `y` while the names of parameters in the header of the function `sub` in line number 31 are `a` and `b`.
7. The header of a function is not terminated with a semicolon.

5.3.1.1.2.2 Body of a Function

The **body of a function** consists of a set of statements enclosed within braces. The body of a function can have non-executable statements⬅ and executable statements.⬅ The non-executable statements can only come before the executable statements. The non-executable statements declare the local variables➡ in the function and the executable statements determine its functionality, i.e. what the function does. A function can optionally have special executable statement known as the `return` statement.[§§] The `return` statement is used to return the result of the computations done in the called function and/or to return the program control back to the calling function.

Backward Reference: Executable and non-executable statements (Chapter 3).

[‡‡] Refer Section 5.3.1.1.3 for a description on calling functions and called functions.

[§§] Refer Section 5.3.1.1.3.3.1 for a description on the `return` statement.

Forward Reference: Local variables (Chapter 7).

5.3.1.1.3 Function Invocation/Call/Use

The call to a function can be well described along with the discussion on the classification of functions. Depending upon their inputs (i.e. parameters) and outputs, functions are classified as:

1. Functions with no input–output
2. Functions with inputs and no output
3. Function with inputs and one output
4. Function with inputs and outputs

5.3.1.1.3.1 Function with No Input–Output

A **function with no input–output** does not accept any input and does not return any result. Since no input is to be given to the function, the parameter list of such functions is empty. Even if the parameter list is empty, the function header must have the empty set of parentheses or with the keyword void.¶¶ These functions have limited functionality and are not flexible (i.e. they cannot be used in a variety of circumstances). Due to their limited functionality they have limited utility too. Consider the snippet in Program 5-2.

	Trace Col. 2	Prog 5-2.c
1		//Function with no input-output
2		#include<stdio.h>
3		//Function declaration
4		printsum();
5		//main function, the master function
6	1 ⇨	main()
7		{
8	2 ⇨	printsum();
9	6 ⇨	}
10		//Definition of function printsum
11	3 ⇨	printsum()
12		{
13	4 ⇨	printf("Sum of 2 and 3 is %d",2+3);
14	5 ⇨	}

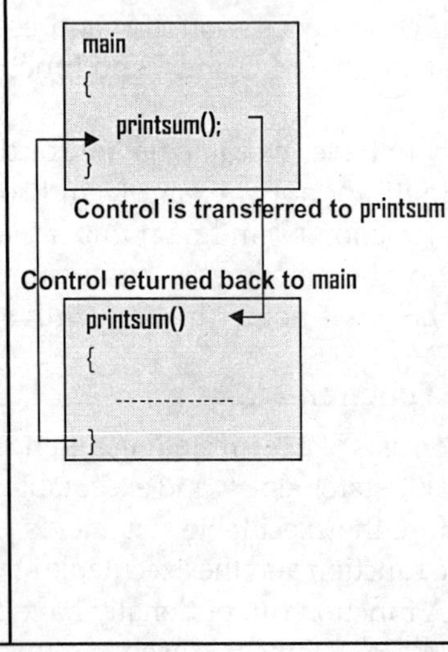

Output window

Sum of 2 and 3 is 5

Warnings (2):

- Function should return a value in function main
- Function should return a value in function printsum

Remarks:

- Ignore the warnings for the time being
- printsum is a function with no input–output
- The order of execution of the statements is depicted in the trace column (i.e. column 2)

Program 5-2 | A program that uses a function with no input–output

The important points about functions with no input–output are as follows:

1. In Program 5-2, the function printsum has no input and does not return any result.
2. The function printsum has been invoked, i.e. called in line number 8. A function with no inputs can be called by writing a **function designator** (i.e. name of the function) fol-

¶¶ Refer Section 5.3.1.1.3.1.1 for a description on void functions.

lowed by a **function call operator,** i.e. ( ). The function designator followed by the function call operator is known as a **function call.**

3. The function that calls a function (i.e. which contains a function call) is known as a **calling function**, and the function that has been called is known as a **called function**. In the given code, `main`✍ is the calling function and `printsum` is the called function.
4. A function call terminated with a semicolon is known as a **function call statement**.
5. After the execution of the function call statement, the program control is transferred to the called function. The execution of the calling function is suspended and the called function starts execution. For example, in Program 5-2, after the execution of the function call statement in line number 8, the program control transfers to line number 11. The order of execution of statements in a program can be checked by tracing✍ the program. The program trace is depicted in column 2. Note the position of trace arrows 2 and 3 in Program 5-2.
6. After the execution of the called function (with no output) is complete, the program control returns to the calling function, and the calling function resumes its execution. In Program 5-2, this is depicted by trace steps 5 and 6 in column 2.

✍ 1. The **execution of C program** always begins with the function `main`. Function `main` need not be explicitly called.
2. Tracing is a debugging technique in which the statements of a program are executed one by one. Non-executable statements are not executed. Hence, during the tracing, the program control does not stop at non-executable statements. Thus, for non-executable statements trace arrows are not shown. The shortcut key for tracing in Borland TC 3.0 and 4.5 is F7. The shortcut key for tracing in MS-Visual C++ 6.0 is F11. Keep on pressing these keys to trace the program.

5.3.1.1.3.1.1 `void` Functions

Program 5-2 on compilation gives a warning message 'Function should return a value.' We have been ignoring this warning since Chapter 1 but now it is the time to know the reason behind this warning and how to remove it.

Every function in C language is supposed to return an integer value. If the return type of a function is not specified, it is assumed to be `int` by default. Thus, in Program 5-2, the return type of the functions `main` and `printsum` is assumed to be `int`. As no `return` statement is used within the body of these functions to return the expected integer value, the compiler gives the warning message 'Function should return a value.'

Removal of warning message

If a function does not return any value, then the return type of the function should be specified as `void` (means nothing). Functions whose return type is `void` are known as **`void` functions.** Reconsider the code snippet mentioned in Program 5-2 with `void` mentioned as the return type of the functions `main` and `printsum`. The modified form of the code listed in Program 5-2 is mentioned in Program 5-3.

Prog 5-3.c

```
//Function with no input-output
#include<stdio.h>
//Function declaration
void printsum();
//main function, the master function
void main()
{
    printsum();
}
//Function definition
void printsum()
{
    printf("Sum of 2 and 3 is %d", 2+3);
}
```

Output window

Sum of 2 and 3 is 5

Remarks:

- As the functions printsum and main do not return any value, void is specified as their return type
- The program now on compilation does not give any warning message
- **Some compilers (e.g. Borland TC 4.5) do not allow void to be specified as return type of the function main. They enforce the return type of the function main to be int**

What to do?

- If Borland TC 4.5 is used, either leave the return type of function main unspecified or specify it as int and place return 0; as the last statement of function main. 0 is an arbitrary value. Any integer value can be used instead of 0

Program 5-3 | A program that uses a void function

The important points about void functions are as follows:

1. A void function does not return any value. Either no return statement should be present inside the body of a void function or if it is present, it should be of the form return;. The return statement of the form[†††] return expression; cannot be used inside the body of a void function. When a return statement of the form return; is placed inside the body of a void function, its execution terminates the execution of the void function and returns the program control back to the calling function. The code snippet in Program 5-4 illustrates this fact.

Line	Trace	Prog 5-4.c
1		//Return statement inside void function
2		#include<stdio.h>
3		//Function declaration
4		void printsum();
5		//Function definitions
6	1 ⇨	void main()
7		{
8	2 ⇨	printsum();
9	7 ⇨	}
10	3 ⇨	void printsum()
11		{
12	4 ⇨	printf("This is a void function\n");
13	5 ⇨	printf("This is a statement before return statement\n");
14	6 ⇨	return;

Output window

This is a void function
This is a statement before return statement

Remarks:

- After the function call in line number 8 gets executed, the program control transfers to line number 10
- This is depicted by trace arrows 2 and 3
- Execution of the function main is suspended and the printsum function starts execution
- After the execution of the return statement in line number 14, the program control returns back to the main function

(Contd...)

[†††] Refer Section 5.3.1.1.3.3.1 for a description on various forms of return statement.

15
16
17
		printf("This is a statement after return statement\n");
		printf("Unreachable code\n");
		}
			• This is depicted by trace arrows 6 and 7
			• The execution of the function printsum is terminated and the main function resumes its execution
			• printf statements in line numbers 15 and 16 remain unreachable

Program 5-4 | A program that illustrates the use of return statement inside void function

2. A void function call expression evaluates to void. Hence, such expressions cannot be placed on the right side of an assignment operator. For example, the expression a=printsum() is erroneous if printsum is a void function. The code snippet in Program 5-5 illustrates this fact.

Line	Prog 5-5.c	Output window

1
2
3
4
5
6
7
8
9
10
11
12
13
	//void function call expression cannot be assigned to a variable
	#include<stdio.h>
	void printsum(void);
	void main(void)
	{
	    int a;
	    a=printsum();
	    printf("The value of a is %d",a);
	}
	void printsum(void)
	{
	    printf("Sum of 2 and 3 is %d",2+3);
	}
		Compilation error "Not an allowed type in function main"
		Remarks:
		• The return type of the function printsum is void
		• An expression of type void cannot be assigned to a variable
		• Hence, the expression a=printsum() in line number 7 is erroneous

Program 5-5 | A program that illustrates the void function call expression, which cannot be assigned to a variable

Also, the keyword void is sometimes placed within parentheses in the function header to signify that the function does not have any input. This is depicted in the code snippet in Program 5-5.

5.3.1.1.3.2 Function with Inputs and No Output

The function printsum developed in Program 5-2 is rigid. Each invocation of the function printsum prints the sum of 2 and 3. It cannot be used to print the sum of different values. The reason behind this rigidity of the printsum function is the lack of inputs to it. A function can be made flexible by adding inputs to it. The modified flexible form of the code listed in Program 5-2 is mentioned in Program 5-6.

The observable points about the code snippet given in Program 5-6 are as follows:

1. The printsum function developed in Program 5-6 is flexible as compared to the printsum function developed in Program 5-2. It can now be used to print the sum of any two integer values.
2. This flexibility is due to the added inputs. The printsum function now accepts two inputs of the integer type.

	Trace	Prog 5-6.c	(Column 4)	Output window
1		//Function with inputs and no output		Enter values of a & b 4 6
2		#include<stdio.h>		Sum of 4 and 6 is 10
3		//Function declaration	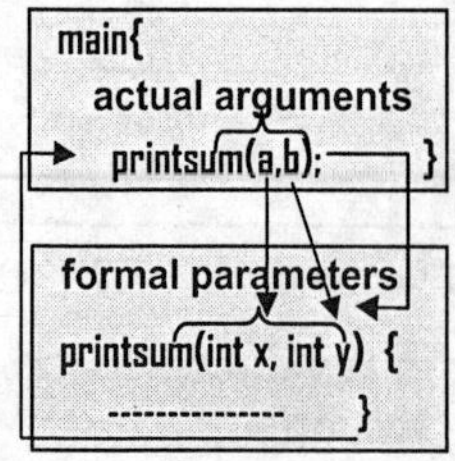	Enter values of a & b again 7 2
4		void printsum(int, int);		Sum of 7 and 2 is 9
5		//Function definitions		**Remarks:**
6	1	void main()		• Function printsum accepts two arguments, i.e. inputs
7		{		• In line number 11, a and b are known as **actual arguments**
8		int a,b;		• In line number 16, x and y are known as **formal parameters**
9	2	printf("Enter values of a & b\t");		• The parameters declared in the function header are like other local variables declared inside the body of a function
10	3	scanf("%d %d",&a,&b);		• After execution of the function call in line number 11, the values of a and b are copied into the variables x and y and the control is transferred to the function printsum
11	4	printsum(a,b);		
12	8	printf("Enter values of a & b again\t");		
13	9	scanf("%d %d",&a,&b);		
14	10	printsum(a,b);		
15	14	}		
16	5, 11	void printsum(int x, int y)		
17		{		
18	6, 12	printf("Sum of %d and %d is %d\n",x,y,x+y);		
19	7, 13	}		

Program 5-6 | A program that uses a function with inputs

3. A function with inputs can be called in a similar way as a function without input is called, i.e. by using a function call operator. Inputs to a function are given by providing comma-separated expressions within the parentheses of the function call operator. For example, the printsum function defined in Program 5-6 can be called in the following ways:

```
printsum(2,3);       //←Inputs are constants 2 and 3
printsum(a,b);       //←Inputs are variables a and b
printsum(a+2,b-3);   //←Inputs are expressions a+2 and b-3
```

4. The expressions that appear within the parentheses of a function call are known as **actual arguments**, and the variables declared in the parameter list in the function header are known as **formal parameters**. For example, in Program 5-6, a and b are actual arguments of printsum function and x and y are the formal parameters.
5. The commas separating the actual arguments in a function call are not comma operators. If commas separating arguments in a function call are considered to be comma operators, then no function could have more than one argument. The commas appearing between the arguments in a function call are just separators.
6. The below-mentioned steps are followed when a function with inputs is invoked:
   a. The actual argument expressions are evaluated.
   b. The program control is transferred to the called function and the result of the evaluation of the actual argument expressions are assigned to the formal parameters on one-to-one basis as shown in column 4 of Program 5-6.

c. The execution of the calling function is suspended and the called function starts the execution.

7. When the execution of the called function (with no output) is complete, the program control returns to the calling function, and the calling function resumes its execution.

Consider the code snippet in Program 5-7, which has a more generalized form of printsum function defined in Program 5-6. The developed printsum function can now print the output in decimal, octal or hexadecimal number system according to the user's requirement.

Prog 5-7.c

```
//Further generalization of printsum
#include<stdio.h>
//Function printsum accepts three inputs
void printsum(int, int, char);
//Function definition
void main()
{
    int a,b;
    char base;
    printf("Enter the values of a & b\t");
    scanf("%d %d",&a,&b);
    printf("Enter base of output(O, D or H)\t");
    flushall();
    scanf("%c",&base);
    printsum(a,b,base);
}
void printsum(int x, int y, char base)
{
    if(base=='d'||base=='D')
        printf("Sum of %d and %d in decimal is %d",x,y,x+y);
    else if(base=='o'||base=='O')
        printf("Sum of %d and %d in octal is %o",x,y,x+y);
    else if(base=='h'||base=='H')
        printf("Sum of %d and %d in hexadecimal is %X",x,y,x+y);
}
```

Output window

```
Enter the values of a & b    2 10
Enter base of output(O, D or H)    H
Sum of 2 and 10 in hexadecimal is C
```

Remarks:

- The flexibility of the function printsum is increased by providing an additional input, i.e. base
- If flushall function is not used before the use of the scanf function, the scanf function might not prompt the user to enter a character
- The function flushall is used to flush, i.e. empty the streams so that the scanf function prompts the user to enter a character

Program 5-7 | A program that uses a more generalized form of the printsum function developed in Program 5-6

Forward Reference: flushall() and streams (refer Question number 15 and its answer, Chapter 6).

5.3.1.1.3.3 Function with Inputs and One Output

The function printsum developed in Programs 5-6 and 5-7 receives inputs but does not return any value, rather it prints the result of the computation. However, the printing of the result of the computation by the called function is not always desired. The result of the computation may be required in the calling function for further processing. The best software engineering practices suggest the following:

1. The developed functions should be kept as general as possible so that they can be used in different situations.
2. Functions should generally be coded without involving any direct I/O operation (i.e. direct use of I/O functions like `printf`, `scanf`, `getch`, etc.). A function should receive inputs in the form of arguments and return the result of computations instead of directly printing it.
3. A function should behave like a 'black box' that receives inputs, and outputs the desired value.

The result of the computations performed inside the called function is returned to the calling function by using the `return` statement.

5.3.1.1.3.3.1 return Statement

The **return statement** is used to return the result of the computations performed in the called function and/or to transfer the program control back to the calling function. There are two forms of the `return` statement:

1. `return;`
2. `return expression;`

The important points about the `return` statement are as follows:

1. **First form of the return statement, i.e. return;:**
   a. This form of the `return` statement is used when a function does not return any value (i.e. inside `void` functions).
   b. It cannot be used inside a function whose return type is not `void`.
   c. It terminates the execution of the called function and transfers the program control back to the calling function without returning any value.
2. **Second form of the return statement, i.e. return expression;:**
   a. This form of the `return` statement returns the function's result along with the program control back to the calling function.
   b. It cannot be placed inside the body of a `void` function and can only appear inside the body of a function whose return type is not `void`.
   c. The expression following the keyword `return` in the `return` statement is known as the **return expression**.
   d. The return expression can be an arbitrarily complex expression and can even have function calls. For example, in the statement `return n*fact(n-1);`, the return expression consists of a call to the function `fact`.
   e. The return expression is evaluated and the result of evaluation of the return expression is returned to the calling function along with the program control.
   f. If the return type of a function and the type of the result of evaluation of a return expression is not the same, the result of evaluation of the return expression is implicitly type casted to the return type of the function, if they are compatible. If they are incompatible, there will be a compilation error. Consider Program 5-8 that makes use of a function to compute the area of a circle.

Prog 5-8.c

```
1  //Area of a circle
2  #include<stdio.h>
3  //Function declaration
4  circle_area(int);
5  //Function definitions
6  void main()
7  {
8      int radius;
9      float area;
10     printf("Enter the radius of circle\t");
11     scanf("%d",&radius);
12     area=circle_area(radius);
13     printf("Area of circle is %f\n",area);
14 }
15 circle_area(int radius)
16 {
17     return 3.1428*radius*radius;
18 }
```

Output window

```
Enter the radius of circle    2
Area of circle is 12.000000
```

Remarks:

- The area of circle that gets printed is 12.000000 instead of the actual value of 12.571200
- This happened because the return type of function circle_area is not mentioned. If the return type of a function is not mentioned, it is assumed to be int by default

Program 5-8 | A program illustrating that the specification of the return type is mandatory if the return type is other than int

The observable points about the code snippet in Program 5-8 are as follows:

i. The area of the circle printed is 12.000000 instead of the actual value 12.571200.
ii. The value of the area actually computed inside the function circle_area is 12.571200 (i.e. a float value) but since the return type of the function is not mentioned, it is assumed to be int (as int is the default return type of a function). The type of result of evaluation of the return expression is not the same as the return type of the function. Thus, as mentioned above, the result of evaluation of the return expression 3.1428*radius*radius, i.e. 12.571200 is type casted (i.e. demoted) to an integer value 12 before being returned. Hence, in the expression area=circle_area(radius), the sub-expression circle_area(radius) evaluates to 12. Since an integer value, i.e. 12 is assigned to a float variable area, it is firstly promoted to 12.000000 and then assigned. This value of area is then printed by the printf function in the next statement, i.e. line number 13.
iii. The precise value of an area can be obtained by specifying the return type of the function circle_area as float. This is shown in the code snippet given in Program 5-9.

Prog 5-9.c

```
//Area of a circle
#include<stdio.h>
//Function declaration
float circle_area(int);
//Function definitions
void main()
{
    int radius;
```

Output window

```
Enter the radius of circle    2
Area of circle is 12.571200
```

Remarks:

- float is specified as the return type of the function circle_area
- The value of area that gets printed is 12.571200 instead of 12.000000 (as printed in Program 5-8)

(Contd...)

Prog 5-9.c

```
    float area;
    printf("Enter the radius of circle\t");
    scanf("%d",&radius);
    area=circle_area(radius);
    printf("Area of circle is %f\n",area);
}
float circle_area(int radius)
{
    return 3.1428*radius*radius;
}
```

Output window

Program 5-9 | A program that illustrates the effect of specification of the return type of a function

3. There is no constraint on the number of return statements that can be placed inside the body of a function. Although, a number of return statements can be placed inside the body of a function, only one of them that appears first in the logical flow of control gets executed. With the execution of this return statement, the program control returns to the calling function and the rest of the statements that appear after this return statement remain unreachable.
4. **'A function can return only one value.'** It is not possible to return more than one value by writing multiple return statements as mentioned in point 3 above or by writing return value1, value2,... valueN;. In this statement value1, value2,... valueN is the return expression, which is evaluated first and then its outcome is returned. The return expression consists of comma operators. The comma operator guarantees left-to-right evaluation and returns the result of the rightmost sub-expression. Hence, the expression value1, value2,... valueN evaluates to valueN and this value is returned. Program 5-10 illustrates this fact.

Prog 5-10.c

```
1  //Attempt to return more than one value
2  #include<stdio.h>
3  //Function declaration
4  int sum_diff(int,int);
5  //Function definitions
6  void main()
7  {
8      int a=10, b=2;
9      printf("Sum is %d\n",sum_diff(a,b));
10     printf("Difference is %d\n",sum_diff(a,b));
11 }
12 int sum_diff(int a,int b)
13 {
14     int sum=a+b;
15     int diff=a-b;
16     return sum,diff;
17 }
```

Output window

```
Sum is 8
Difference is 8
```

Remarks:

- In line number 16, an attempt is made to return values of sum and diff
- However, the return statement can return only one value
- The return statement in line number 16 returns the value of diff, i.e. the value of the rightmost return sub-expression

Program 5-10 | A program illustrating that the return statement cannot return more than one value

As we have seen, it is not possible to return more than one value (without making the use of structures➲) by making use of the return statement. However, it is possible to indirectly return more than one value to the calling function. This indirect method of returning more than one value to the calling function is discussed in the next section.

➲ **Forward Reference:** Structures (Chapter 9).

5.3.1.1.3.4 Function with Inputs and Outputs

More than one value can be indirectly returned to the calling function by making the use of pointers. In fact, the pointers can also be used to pass arguments to a function. Depending upon whether the values or addresses (i.e. pointers) are passed as arguments to a function, the argument passing methods in C language are classified as:

1. Pass by value
2. Pass by address

5.3.1.1.3.4.1 Passing Arguments by Value

The method of passing arguments by value is also known as **call by value.** In this method, the values of actual arguments are copied to the formal parameters of the function. If the arguments are passed by value, the changes made in the values of formal parameters inside the called function are not reflected back to the calling function. The code snippet listed in Program 5-11 illustrates this concept.

Prog 5-11.c

```
//Use of pass by value in swap function
#include<stdio.h>
//Function declaration
void swap(int,int);
//Function definitions
void main()
{
    int a=10,b=20;
    printf("Before swap values are %d %d\n",a,b);
    swap(a,b);
    printf("After swap values are %d %d\n",a,b);
}
void swap(int x, int y)
{
    x=x+y;
    y=x-y;
    x=x-y;
    printf("In swap function values are %d %d\n",x,y);
}
```

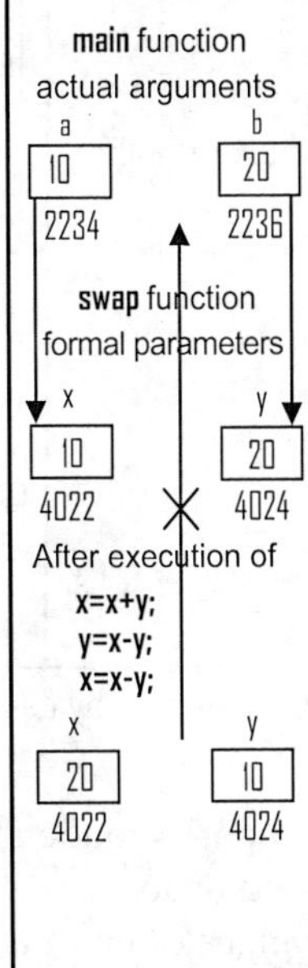

Output window

Before swap values are 10 20
In swap function values are 20 10
After swap values are 10 20

Remarks:

- On the execution of the function call, i.e. swap(a,b);, the values of actual arguments a and b are copied into the formal parameters x and y
- Formal parameters are allocated at separate memory locations
- A change made in the formal parameters is independent of the actual arguments
- On returning from the called function, the formal parameters are destroyed and the access to the actual arguments gives values that are unchanged

Program 5-11 | A program that illustrates pass by value

Analogy: The reason why the changes made in the formal parameters in the called function are not reflected back to the calling function can be understood by looking at this analogy. The main function, i.e. the master function wants to get some changes done in a file from its subordinate worker, i.e. the swap function. The main function got the file (i.e. actual arguments) Xeroxed and has handed over the Xeroxed copy of the file (i.e. formal parameters) to the swap function for changes. The swap function has made changes in the Xeroxed copy and has returned the file back to the main function. On getting the control back, the main function is still referring to the original file and finds that no changes have been made in it. The changes have been made in the Xeroxed copy, so how can the main function find changes in the original file?

5.3.1.1.3.4.2 Passing Arguments by Address/Reference

The method of passing arguments by address or reference is also known as **call by address** or **call by reference**. In this method, the addresses of the actual arguments are passed to the formal parameters of the function. If the arguments are passed by reference, the changes made in the values pointed to by the formal parameters in the called function are reflected back to the calling function. The code snippet listed in Program 5-12 illustrates this concept.

Prog 5-12.c

```
//Use of pass by reference in swap function
#include<stdio.h>
//Function declaration
int swap(int*,int*);
//Function definitions
void main()
{
    int a=10,b=20;
    printf("Before swap values are %d %d\n",a,b);
    swap(&a,&b);
    printf("After swap values are %d %d\n",a,b);
}
int swap(int *x, int *y)
{
  *x=*x+*y;
  *y=*x-*y;
  *x=*x-*y;
  printf("In swap function values are %d %d\n",*x,*y);
}
```

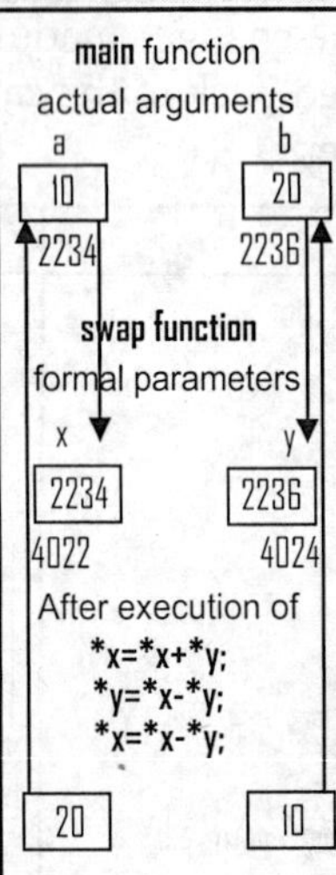

Output window

```
Before swap values are 10 20
In swap function values are 20 10
After swap values are 20 10
```

Remarks:

- Addresses of the actual arguments are passed instead of their values
- Changes made in the called function are actually done in the memory locations of the actual arguments
- On returning from the called function, the formal parameters are destroyed but since the changes were made at the memory locations of the actual arguments, they can still be found there

Program 5-12 | A program that illustrates pass by reference

Analogy: The reason why the changes made in the called function are reflected back to the calling function can be understood by looking at this analogy. The main function, i.e. the master function wants to get some changes done in a file from its subordinate worker, i.e. the swap function. The main function has kept the file (i.e. actual arguments) in a file cabinet (i.e. memory). The main function tells the swap function the changes to be made and the location of the file in the cabinet (i.e. the memory address). The swap function opens up the file cabinet, locates the file, makes changes in it, places it back at the same position in the cabinet and reports to the main function that the work has been done. On getting the control back, the main function opens up the file cabinet, looks at the file and finds the changes made in it.

5.3.1.1.3.4.3 Returning More Than One Value Indirectly

Consider the code listed in Program 5-10, where we tried to return more than one value by making the use of the return statement and failed. I will now illustrate how to return more than one value to the calling function indirectly by making the use of a call by reference. In the code snippet listed in Program 5-13, the called function indirectly returns more than one value to the calling function.

Prog 5-13.c

```
//Indirectly returning more than one value
#include<stdio.h>
//Function declaration
void sum_diff(int,int,int*,int*);
//Function definitions
void main()
{
    int a=10, b=2;
    int sum, diff;
    sum_diff(a,b,&sum,&diff);
    printf("Sum is %d\n",sum);
    printf("Difference is %d\n",diff);
}
void sum_diff(int a,int b, int*sum, int*diff)
{
    *sum=a+b;
    *diff=a-b;
}
```

Output window

```
Sum is 12
Difference is 8
```

Remarks:

- Mixed method of passing arguments is used
- Two arguments, i.e. a and b are passed by value
- Other two arguments, i.e. sum and diff are passed by reference
- The results of the computations made in the called function are stored in the memory locations of the actual arguments (i.e. sum and diff) by making the use of passed addresses
- Actually, sum_diff function does not return any value

Program 5-13 | A program that illustrates the method to indirectly return more than one value by making the use of pass by reference

5.3.1.1.4 Passing Arrays to Functions

Like simple variables, arrays can also be passed to functions. There are two ways to pass arrays to functions:

1. Passing individual elements of an array one by one
2. Passing an entire array at a time

Passing individual elements of an array one by one is similar to passing basic variables. The individual elements of an array can be passed either by value or by reference. However, this way of passing an array is not preferred due to the following reasons:

1. If the number of elements in an array is large, passing the entire array will take a large number of function calls, as one element is passed with each function call. As the function calls are time consuming, this method of passing an array to a function will deteriorate the performance of a program.

2. When the individual elements of an array are passed to the function one by one, the complete array will never be available to the called function for processing at a time. The called function will always have a piecemeal array.

The code segments listed in Program 5-14 illustrate the passing of array elements one by one.

Prog 5-14a.c

```
//Individual elements of array passed
//by value
#include<stdio.h>
int sum_array(int,int);
void main()
{
    int arr[10], nele, lc, sum=0;
    printf("Enter the no. of elements\t");
    scanf("%d",&nele);
    printf("Enter elements of array\n");
    for(lc=0;lc<nele;lc++)
        scanf("%d",&arr[lc]);
    for(lc=0;lc<nele;lc++)
    {
        sum=sum_array(arr[lc],sum);
    }
    printf("Sum is %d",sum);
}
int sum_array(int element, int sum)
{
    return sum+element;
}
```

Prog 5-14b.c

```
//Individual elements of array passed
//by reference
#include<stdio.h>
int sum_array(int*,int);
void main()
{
    int arr[10], nele, lc, sum=0;
    printf("Enter the no. of elements\t");
    scanf("%d",&nele);
    printf("Enter elements of array\n");
    for(lc=0;lc<nele;lc++)
        scanf("%d",&arr[lc]);
    for(lc=0;lc<nele;lc++)
    {
        sum=sum_array(&arr[lc],sum);
    }
    printf("Sum is %d",sum);
}
int sum_array(int* element, int sum)
{
    return sum+*element;
}
```

Output window

```
Enter the no. of elements 5
Enter elements of array
2
4
5
7
1
Sum is 19
```

Remarks:

- Iteration is used to pass the elements of the array one by one
- Number of iterations required to pass n elements of an array to a function is n

Program 5-14 | A program that illustrates the passing of an array element by element

Passing entire array at a time is a preferred way of passing arrays to functions. The entire array is always passed by reference.

The following sections describe the passing of one-dimensional and multi-dimensional arrays to functions.

5.3.1.1.4.1 Passing One-dimensional Arrays to Functions

The syntactic rules to pass one-dimensional arrays to a function are as follows:

1. The actual argument in the function call should only be the name of the array without any subscript.
2. The corresponding formal parameter in the function definition must be of array type or pointer type (i.e. pointer to the first element of the array). If a formal parameter is of array type, it will be implicitly converted to pointer type.
3. The corresponding parameter type in the function declaration should be of array type or pointer type.

The code snippet mentioned in Program 5-15 illustrates the different ways of passing a one-dimensional array to a function.

Line	Prog 5-15a.c (Column 2)	Prog 5-15b.c (Column 3)	Output window
1	//Passing 1-D array	//Passing 1-D array	Enter the no. of elements 5
2	#include<stdio.h>	#include<stdio.h>	Enter elements of array
3	void find_max_min(int[],int);	void find_max_min(int*,int);	2
4	void main()	void main()	4
5	{	{	5
6	int arr[10], nele, lc, sum=0;	int arr[10], nele, lc, sum=0;	7
7	printf("Enter the no. of elements\t");	printf("Enter the no. of elements\t");	1
8	scanf("%d",&nele);	scanf("%d",&nele);	Max is 7
9	printf("Enter elements of array\n");	printf("Enter elements of array\n");	Min is 1
10	for(lc=0;lc<nele;lc++)	for(lc=0;lc<nele;lc++)	**Remarks:** • Passing the entire array at a time is an efficient way of passing a number of values to a function • In column 2, in line number 16, the declared formal parameter arr is of array type • It will be implicitly converted to pointer type • Hence the declaration of arr made in line number 16 in column 2 will be converted to the declaration of arr made in line number 16 in column 3 • The two declarations of arr are equivalent
11	scanf("%d",&arr[lc]);	scanf("%d",&arr[lc]);	
12	find_max_min(arr, nele);	find_max_min(arr, nele);	
13	printf("Max is %d\n",arr[0]);	printf("Max is %d\n",arr[0]);	
14	printf("Min is %d\n",arr[1]);	printf("Min is %d\n",arr[1]);	
15	}	}	
16	void find_max_min(int arr[], int nele)	void find_max_min(int* arr, int nele)	
17	{	{	
18	int lc, max=arr[0], min=arr[0];	int lc, max=arr[0], min=arr[0];	
19	for(lc=1;lc<nele;lc++)	for(lc=1;lc<nele;lc++)	
20	if(arr[lc]>max)	if(arr[lc]>max)	
21	max=arr[lc];	max=arr[lc];	
22	else if(arr[lc]<min)	else if(arr[lc]<min)	
23	min=arr[lc];	min=arr[lc];	
24	arr[0]=max; arr[1]=min;	arr[0]=max; arr[1]=min;	
25	}	}	

Program 5-15 | A program that illustrates the method of passing a one-dimensional array to a function

5.3.1.1.4.2 Passing Two-dimensional Arrays to Functions

The syntactic rules to pass two-dimensional arrays to a function are as follows:

1. The actual argument in the function call should be the name of an array.
2. The corresponding formal parameter in the function definition must be of array type or pointer type (i.e. pointer to the first element of the array).
    a. If the formal parameter is of array type, it is mandatory to specify the column specifier. In general, in case of n-D arrays, if the formal parameter is of array type, it is mandatory to specify (n-1) fastest varying specifiers.
    b. If the formal parameter is of pointer type, it must be a pointer to an element of the two-dimensional array (i.e. one-dimensional array having the number of columns same as the number of columns specified for the two-dimensional array). In general, for n-D arrays, if the formal parameter is of pointer type, it must be a pointer to (n-1)-D array having the size specifications same as the (n-1) fastest varying size specifications for the n-D array.

3. The corresponding parameter type in the function declaration should be a matching array type or pointer type.

The code snippet in Program 5-16 illustrates the passing of a two-dimensional array to a function.

Line | Prog 5-16.c

```
1  //Passing 2-D array
2  #include<stdio.h>
3  void largest_ele(int[][10],int*,int*);
4  void main()
5  {
6      int arr[10][10];
7      int rows, cols, rc, cc;
8      printf("Enter no. of rows in array(<10)\t");
9      scanf("%d",&rows);
10     printf("Enter no. of cols in array(<10)\t");
11     scanf("%d",&cols);
12     printf("Enter elements of array:\n");
13     for(rc=0;rc<rows;rc++)
14         for(cc=0;cc<cols;cc++)
15             scanf("%d",&arr[rc][cc]);
16     largest_ele(arr,&rows,&cols);
17     printf("Largest element is %d\n",arr[rows][cols]);
18     printf("Located in row no. %d\n",rows);
19     printf("Located in column no. %d\n",cols);
20 }
21 void largest_ele(int arr[][10],int *rows, int *cols)
22 {
23     int row=0, col=0, rc=0, cc=0, max=arr[0][0];
24     for(rc=0; rc<*rows;rc++)
25         for(cc=0;cc<*cols;cc++)
26             if(arr[rc][cc]>max)
27             {
28                 max=arr[rc][cc];
29                 row=rc; col=cc;
30             }
31     *rows=row; *cols=col;
32 }
```

Output window

```
Enter no. of rows in array(<10)    3
Enter no. of cols in array(<10)    3
Enter elements of array:
8 4 6
7 9 3
2 1 5
Largest element is 9
Located in row no. 1
Located in column no. 1
```

Remarks:

- In line number 21, the declared formal parameter is of array type
- It will be implicitly converted to pointer type
- The equivalent declaration is int(*)[10], i.e. pointer to one-dimensional array of 10 integers
- It is assumed that the row and column number starts with 0

Program 5-16 | A program to illustrate the method of passing of a two-dimensional array to a function

5.3.1.1.5 Default Arguments

In Section 5.3.1.1.3.2, we have seen how functions can be made flexible by adding inputs to them. Each input adds some flexibility to the function and makes the function more general. However, some inputs are the same in majority of the cases and have special values only in rare circumstances. For example, in Program 5-7, the common base input to the function printsum is 'D', i.e. decimal number system. In rare circumstances, the user wants the output to be in an octal number system or a hexadecimal number system. These general functions are sometimes unwieldy as the values are to be supplied for each argument.

The C language frees the programmer from this difficulty by providing the concept of **default arguments.** A **default argument** is a value that is an appropriate argument value for a parameter in majority of the cases. Consider the code snippet in Program 5-17 that makes the use of default argument for base input in printsum function discussed in Program 5-7.

Line | Prog 5-17.c

```
1  //Default arguments
2  #include<stdio.h>
3  //Function declaration
4  void printsum(int, int, char base='D');
5  //Function definition
6  void main()
7  {
8      printf("Use of default arguments:\n");
9      printf("General conditions:\n");
10     printsum(5,6);
11     printsum(3,4);
12     printf("Rare conditions:\n");
13     printsum(6,9,'H');
14     printsum(6,9,'O');
15 }
16 void printsum(int x, int y, char base)
17 {
18     if(base=='d'||base=='D')
19         printf("Sum of %d and %d in decimal is %d\n",x,y,x+y);
20     else if(base=='o'||base=='O')
21         printf("Sum of %d and %d in octal is %o\n",x,y,x+y);
22     else if(base=='h'||base=='H')
23         printf("Sum of %d and %d in hexadecimal is %X\n",x,y,x+y);
24 }
```

Output window

```
Use of default arguments:
General conditions:
Sum of 5 and 6 in decimal is 11
Sum of 3 and 4 in decimal is 7
Rare conditions:
Sum of 6 and 9 in hexadecimal is F
Sum of 6 and 9 in octal is 17
```

Remarks:

- In line number 4, the parameter base is initialized with the value 'D'
- This initialization makes 'D' as default argument for the parameter base
- A function that provides a default argument for a parameter can be invoked with or without an argument for this parameter
- In line numbers 10 and 11, the function printsum is invoked without specifying an argument for the parameter base
- In line numbers 13 and 14, arguments 'H' and 'O', respectively, are specified as arguments for the parameter base. These values override the default argument value 'D'
- Borland Turbo C 3.0 IDE does not support the use of default arguments

Program 5-17 | A program that illustrates the use of default arguments

The important points about the default arguments are as follows:

1. The arguments can be made default by using initialization syntax within the parameter list during the function declaration. For example, in line number 4 in Program 5-17, the parameter base has been made default by initializing it with 'D'.
2. A function that provides a default argument for a parameter can be invoked with or without an argument for this parameter.
3. However, if an argument is provided, it overrides the default argument value.
4. A function declaration can specify default arguments for all or for a subset of parameters. If the default arguments are specified only for a subset of parameters, then these parameters should be kept on the trailing side. The code snippet in Program 5-18 illustrates this fact.

Line | Prog 5-18.c

```
1  //Default arguments for a subset of parameters
2  #include<stdio.h>
3  //Function declaration
4  int add(int a, int b=12, int c);
5  //Function definitions
6  void main()
7  {
8      add(10,12);
9  }
10 int add(int a, int b, int c)
11 {
12     printf("The result after addition is %d\n",a+b+c);
13 }
```

Output window

Compilation errors
"Default value missing following parameter b".
"Too few parameters in call to 'add(int, int, int)' in function main"

Remark:

- In line number 4, the default argument for the parameter b cannot be specified unless and until the default argument for parameter c is specified

What to do?

- Either specify the default argument for the parameter c or remove the default argument value for the parameter b

Program 5-18 | A program illustrating that the specification of default arguments for a subset of parameters

The code snippet in Program 5-19 is the rectified version of the code listed in Program 5-18.

Line | Prog 5-19.c

```
1  //Default arguments can be specified for parameters that lie on the
2  //trailing side of the parameter list
3  #include<stdio.h>
4  int add(int a, int b=12, int c=8);
5  void main()
6  {
7      add(10);
8      add(10,1);
9  }
10 int add(int a, int b, int c)
11 {
12     printf("The result after addition is %d\n",a+b+c);
13 }
```

Output window

The result after addition is 30
The result after addition is 19

Remarks:

- In line number 4, the default arguments are specified for two trailing parameters b and c
- Since, no default argument is specified for the parameter a, at least one argument is required to invoke the function add
- In line number 8, the argument value 1 overrides the default argument value for the parameter b

Program 5-19 | A program illustrating that the default arguments can be specified for the parameters that lie on the trailing side of the parameter list

5. The default argument should not be specified in the function definition. If the default argument is provided in the parameter list of function definition as well, there will be 'Default argument value redeclared error.' The code snippet in Program 5-20 illustrates this fact.
6. It is not mandatory to have a default argument as a constant expression. Any expression can be used as the default argument. When the default argument is an expression, the expression is evaluated when the function is called. The code snippet in Program 5-21 illustrates this fact.

Prog 5-20.c

```
//Redeclaration of default arguments
#include<stdio.h>
//Function declaration along with the specification of the default
//arguments
int add(int a=12, int b=8);
void main()
{
    add();
    add(10);
    add(10,12);
}
//Function definition with re-specification of the default arguments
int add(int a=12, int b=8)
{
    printf("The result after addition is %d\n",a+b);
}
```

Output window

Compilation error "Default argument value redeclared"

Remark:

- The default arguments are specified in the function declaration, they should not be re-specified in the header of the function definition

What to do?

- Remove default argument values from the header of the function definition

Program 5-20 | A program illustrating that the default arguments should not be re-declared in the header of the function definition

Prog 5-21.c

```
1  //Use of an expression as default argument
2  #include<stdio.h>
3  //Function declarations
4  int sub(int,int);
5  int add(int a=12,int b=sub(3,1));
6  //Function definitions
7  void main()
8  {
9      add();
10     add(10);
11     add(10,12);
12 }
13 int add(int a, int b)
14 {
15     printf("The result after addition is %d\n",a+b);
16 }
17 int sub(int a, int b)
18 {
19     return a-b;
20 }
```

Output window

```
The result after addition is 14
The result after addition is 12
The result after addition is 22
```

Remarks:

- In line number 5, the default argument for the parameter b is an expression sub(3,1)
- Carefully note the order of declaration of function sub and function add
- Before specifying sub as the default argument, it should be either declared or defined
- Change the order of declaration of function sub and function add, i.e. interchange the contents of line numbers 4 and 5 and observe the result of compilation

Program 5-21 | A program that illustrates the use of an expression as the default argument

5.3.1.1.6 Command Line Arguments

We have seen that arguments are given to the functions to increase their flexibility. Since main is also a function, can we give arguments to the function main? The answer to this question is YES! The main function can also accept arguments. The arguments to a called function are supplied from the calling function. However, main is the first function that gets invoked at the program startup. Therefore, how are arguments supplied to the function main? The arguments to the function main are supplied from **command line** and thus, have a special name known as **command line arguments.**

Forward Reference: Command line arguments (Chapter 6).

5.3.1.1.7 Recursion

Recursion is a powerful programming technique that can be used to solve the problems that can be expressed in terms of similar problems of smaller size. For example, consider a problem to find the factorial of a number n. The problem of finding the factorial of n can be expressed in terms of a similar problem of smaller size as $n!=n\times(n-1)!$. Recursion provides an elegant way of solving such problems.

In recursive programming, a function calls itself. A function that calls itself is known as a **recursive function,** and the phenomenon is known as **recursion**. Recursion is classified according to the following criteria:

1. Whether the function calls itself directly (i.e. **direct recursion**) or indirectly (i.e. **indirect recursion**).
2. Whether there is any pending operation on return from a recursive call. If the recursive call is the last operation of a function, the recursion is known as **tail recursion**.
3. Pattern of recursive calls. According to the pattern of recursive calls, recursion is classified as:
   a. Linear recursion
   b. Binary recursion
   c. n-ary recursion

5.3.1.1.7.1 Direct and Indirect Recursion

A function is **directly recursive** if it calls itself, i.e. the function body contains an explicit call to itself. **Indirect recursion** occurs when a function calls another function, which in turn calls another function, eventually resulting in the original function being called again. The functions involved in indirect recursion are known as **mutually recursive functions**. Figure 5.2 illustrates direct and indirect recursion.

Direct recursion	Indirect recursion
A() //←Direct recursive function	A() //←Mutually recursive function A
{	{
------------ //←Statements	------------ //←Statements
------------	B(); //←Function A calls function B
A(); //←Call to itself	------------
------------	}
------------	B() //←Mutually recursive function B
}	{
	------------ //←Statements
	A(); //←Function B calls function A

	}

Figure 5.2 | Direct and indirect recursion

Direct recursive functions are simpler and more elegant as compared to indirectly recursive functions and are most commonly used. The code snippet in Program 5-22 illustrates the use of recursion to find the factorial of a number.

Trace	Prog 5-22.c
	`//Recursion to find the factorial of a number`
	`#include<stdio.h>`
	`//Function declaration`
	`int fact(int);`
	`//Function definitions`
1	`void main()`
	`{`
	`int no, factorial;`
2	`printf("Enter the number\t");`
3	`scanf("%d",&no);`
4	`factorial=fact(no);`
15	`printf("Factorial of %d is %d", no, factorial);`
16	`}`
	`//Definition of directly recursive function fact`
5,8,11	`int fact(int no)`
	`{`
6,9,12	`if(no==1)`
13	`return 1;`
6, 12	`else`
7, 10	`return no*fact(no-1);`
14	`}`

Output window

```
Enter the number 3
Factorial of 3 is 6
```

Remarks:

- The body of the function fact contains call to itself
- Thus, fact is a directly recursive function
- Though recursion is very powerful and highly expressive, it is hard to visualize
- Trace the program and carefully observe the execution of function calls
- Trace arrows in column 2 depicts the order of execution of statements

Program 5-22 | A program that makes the use of a recursive function to find the factorial of a number

The important points about how to develop recursive functions are as follows:

1. Thinking recursively is the first step to solve a problem using recursion.
2. Every recursive solution consists of two cases:
   a. **Base case:** Base case is the smallest instance of problem, which can be easily solved and there is no need to further express the problem in terms of itself, i.e. in this case no recursive call is given and the recursion terminates. Base case forms the **terminating condition** of the recursion. There may be more than one base case in a recursive solution. Without the base case, the recursion will never terminate and will be known as **infinite recursion.** For example, no==1 is the base case of the recursive function fact listed in Program 5-22.

   b. **Recursive case:** In a recursive case, the problem is defined in terms of itself, while reducing the problem size. For example, when fact(n) is expressed as n×fact(n-1), the size of the problem is reduced from n to n-1.
3. Express the solution in the form of base cases and recursive cases. For example, the factorial problem can be expressed as:

$$\text{fact(no)} = \begin{cases} 1 & \text{when no} = 1 \\ \text{no} \times \text{fact(no} - 1) & \text{when no} > 1 \end{cases}$$

Relation of the above form is known as **recurrence relation**.

4. Code for the recurrence relation.

5.3.1.1.7.2 Tail Recursion and Non-tail Recursion

Tail recursion is a special case of recursion in which the last operation of a function is a recursive call. In a tail recursive function, there are no pending operations to be performed on return from a recursive call. Consider the code snippets in Program 5-23 to find the factorial of a number.

Prog 5-23a.c (Column 2)

```
//Non-tail recursive factorial function
#include<stdio.h>
//Function declaration
int fact_norm(int);
void main()
{
    int no, factorial;
    printf("Enter the number\t");
    scanf("%d",&no);
    factorial=fact_norm(no);
    printf("Resultant factorial is %d",factorial);
}
//Non-tail recursive fact function
int fact_norm(int no)
{

    if(no==1)
        return 1;
    else
        return no*fact_norm(no-1);
}
```

Prog 5-23b.c (Column 3)

```
//Tail recursive factorial function
#include<stdio.h>
//Function declaration
int fact_tail(int, int);
void main()
{
    int no, factorial;
    printf("Enter the number\t");
    scanf("%d",&no);
    factorial=fact_tail(no,1);
    printf("Resultant factorial is %d",factorial);
}
//Tail recursive fact function
int fact_tail(int no, int result)
{
    if(no==1)
        return result;
    else
        return fact_tail(no-1,no*result);
}
```

Output window

```
Enter the number 4
Resultant factorial is 24
```

Remarks:

- fact_norm function in column 2 is a non-tail recursive function
- Although the last operation in this function seems to be a recursive function call, it is actually a multiplication operation
- fact_tail function in column 3 is a tail recursive function
- The last operation of this function is a recursive function call

Program 5-23 | Non-tail recursive and tail-recursive versions of function fact

The observable points about the code snippets listed in Program 5-23 are as follows:

1. The function fact_norm listed in Program 5-23a is not tail recursive because there is a pending operation, i.e. multiplication to be performed on return from a recursive call.
2. The function fact_tail listed in Program 5-23b is tail recursive as it has no pending operation on return from a recursive call.
3. Tail recursion is desirable because it eliminates the need to store the result of the computations made in a function before making the tail recursive function call (as there is no operation is to be performed on returning from the tail recursive function). The result of the computations made before tail recursive function call is passed as an argument to the tail recursive function. Due to this, conversion of a non-tail recursive function to a tail recursive function is often required. The method to convert a non-tail recursive function to a tail recursive function is as follows:

    a. A non-tail recursive function can be converted to a tail recursive function by adding one or more auxiliary parameters. For example, result is added as an auxiliary parameter in the definition of function fact_tail.

b. Incorporate the pending operation into the auxiliary parameter in such a way that the non-tail recursive function no longer has a pending operation. For example, the pending operation of multiplication is incorporated into the auxiliary parameter result as no*result.

Consider another application of recursion in finding the terms of a Fibonacci series. In the Fibonacci series, every value is the sum of previous two values. The first two values of the Fibonacci series are 0 and 1. The values 0 1 1 2 3 5 8 13 21 ... form the Fibonacci series. The recurrence relation for finding any term in Fibonacci series is:

$$fib(n) = \begin{cases} 0 & \text{if } n = 1 \\ 1 & \text{if } n = 2 \\ fib(n-1) + fib(n-2) & \text{for } n > 2 \end{cases}$$

Program 5-24a lists the code that uses a non-tail recursive function fib_norm to find a Fibonacci term. The conversion of a non-tail recursive function to a tail recursive function is done in Program 5-24b.

Prog 5-24a.c

```
//Non-tail recursive Fibonacci function
#include<stdio.h>
//Function declaration
int fib_norm(int);
void main()
{
    int n, term;
    printf("Enter term no.\t");
    scanf("%d",&n);
    term=fib_norm(n);
    printf("Fibonacci term is %d",term);
}
//Non-tail recursive function fib_norm
int fib_norm(int n)
{

    if(n==1) return 0;
    if(n==2) return 1;
    return fib_norm(n-1)+fib_norm(n-2);
}
```

Prog 5-24b.c

```
//Tail recursive Fibonacci function
#include<stdio.h>
//Function declaration
int fib_tail(int,int,int);
void main()
{
    int n, term;
    printf("Enter term no.\t");
    scanf("%d",&n);
    term=fib_tail(n,1,0);
    printf("Fibonacci term is %d",term);
}
//Tail recursive version of fib_norm
int fib_tail(int n,int next, int result)
{

    if(n==1) return result;
    return fib_tail(n-1, next+result, next);
}
```

Output window

```
Enter term no. 4
Fibonacci term is 2
```

Remarks:

- fib_norm is a non-tail recursive function as the last operation to be performed in function fib_norm is addition instead of being a recursive call
- fib_norm has two base cases, i.e. when n=1 and when n=2
- fib_tail is the corresponding tail recursive version
- Two auxiliary parameters, i.e. next and result are used
- The pending addition operation in fib_norm is incorporated in the auxiliary parameter of fib_tail as next+result

Program 5-24 | Non-tail recursive and tail recursive functions to find a Fibonacci term

4. Tail recursive functions can be easily transformed into iterative functions to improve the efficiency of a program.

5.3.1.1.7.3 Pattern of Recursive Calls

Based upon the number of recursive calls within a function, the recursion is classified as:

1. Linear recursion
2. Binary recursion
3. n-ary recursion

5.3.1.1.7.3.1 Linear Recursion

The simplest form of recursion is **linear recursion**. A linearly recursive function makes only one recursive call. The function fact discussed in Program 5-22 is a linearly recursive function, as there is only one recursive call within its body. The next section describes how recursion works and how function calls form a linear structure.

5.3.1.1.7.3.1.1 How Recursion Works

Consider the code listed in Program 5-22. Figure 5.3 shows how recursion works to compute the value of factorial of 4.

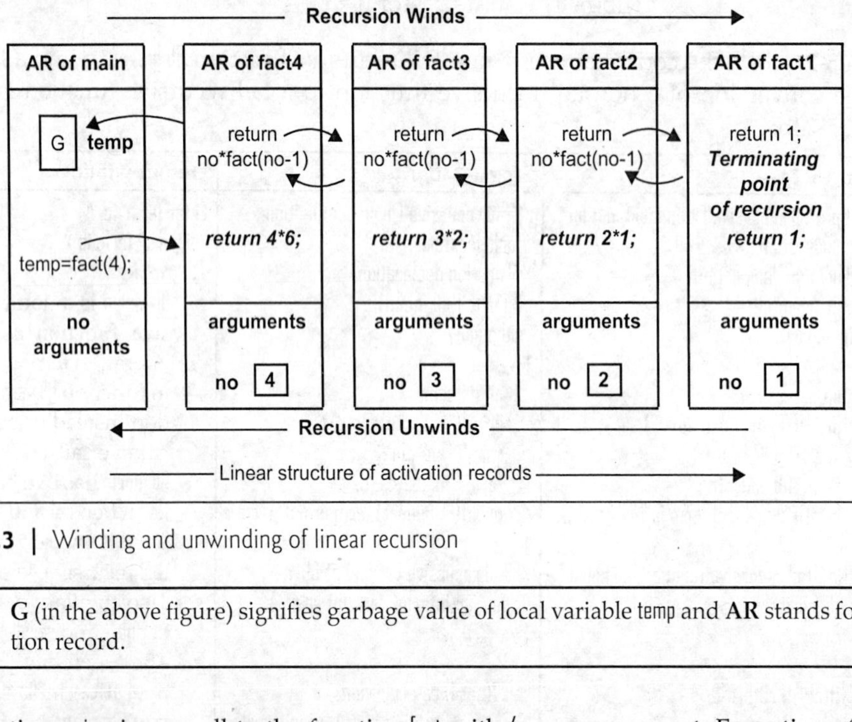

Figure 5.3 | Winding and unwinding of linear recursion

i G (in the above figure) signifies garbage value of local variable temp and **AR** stands for activation record.

The function main gives a call to the function fact with 4 as an argument. Execution of this call creates an activation record✍ for the function fact. The activation record of the function main is packed, placed on the run-time stack,✍ and the activation record of the function fact becomes live. The value of no in the live activation record is 4. Since no≠1 in the current activation, the statement return no*fact(no-1); gets executed. The return expression itself contains a call to the function fact with 3 as an argument. The execution of this function call packs the current activation record of fact, places it onto the run-time stack and creates a new activation record with the value of no as 3 and makes it live. The same process is repeated till the activation record with the value of no as 1 gets created. This part of recursion in which a number of activation records are created and piled up on the run-time stack is known as **winding of recursion**. During the winding of recursion, new activation records keep on getting created. As each activation record requires some memory space, the memory requirement of a program increases during the winding of recursion. If there is no spare memory space for creating the new activation records, the recursion terminates abnormally.

When memory space is available, the winding of recursion terminates when the terminating condition of recursion is reached. In the code snippet listed in Program 5-22, the recursion terminates when the value of no becomes 1. From this point onwards, the recursion starts **unwinding**. During the unwinding process, the called activation returns a value to its calling activation. After returning the value, the activation record of the called activation is destroyed and the memory occupied by it is freed. As shown in Figure 5.3, the last activation returns 1 to the second last activation, which in turn returns 2 to the third last activation and so on. In this way, the first activation of the function fact returns 24 to the function main.

The term **activation** means execution of a function. If a function is executing, it is said to be **active**. In a C program, multiple functions can be active at the same time. For example, suppose function main calls a function fun1, which in turn calls another function fun2. While the function fun2 is executing, the functions main, fun1 and fun2 are all **active**. When the function fun2 completes its execution and returns the program control to the function fun1, only the functions main and fun1 remain active and the function fun2 becomes **inactive**.

Activation of each function requires a separate **activation record**. An activation record refers to the chunk of memory, which holds the following:

1. **Dynamic link:** It points to the activation record of the caller.
2. **Saved state:** It refers to the contents of the program counter and registers when the function is called. It is used to restore the context of the caller function when the program control returns.
3. **Parameters:** They refer to the memory space required by the parameters declared within the header of the function.
4. **Local variables:** They refer to the memory space required by the automatic local variables.
5. **Temporary storage:** It refers to the storage used for evaluating the expressions.

Dynamic link
Saved state
Parameters
Local variable
Temporary storage

An activation record is automatically created when a function starts the execution and is automatically destroyed when a function returns the control to its caller. The activation records for all of the active functions are stored in the region of memory called the **stack**.

Forward Reference: Automatic and local variables (Chapter 7).

5.3.1.1.7.3.2 Binary Recursion

A **binary recursive function** calls itself twice. The fib_norm function listed in Program 5-24a is a binary recursive function. In the binary recursion, the tree of recursive calls is a binary tree. Figure 5.4 depicts the tree of recursive calls for fib_norm(3).

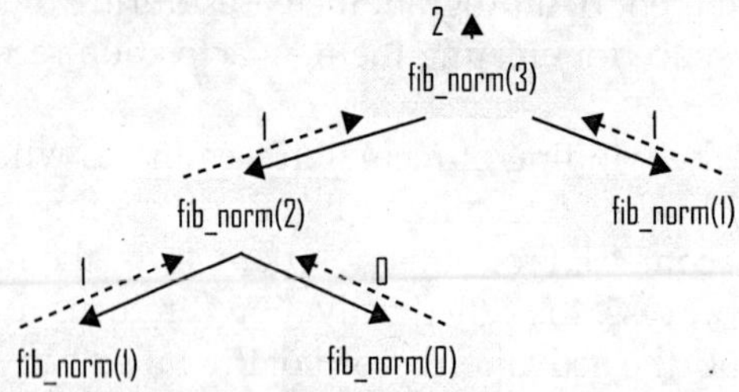

Figure 5.4 | Tree of recursive calls to the function fib_norm

Binary recursion is used in solving some of the important computing problems like:

1. Tower of Hanoi problem
2. Sorting by merge sort
3. Searching by binary search
4. Fibonacci series generation, etc.

> **Binary tree** is a non-linear data structure in which every node of a tree can have at most two children. The tree shown in Figure 5.4 is a binary tree.

5.3.1.1.7.3.2.1 Tower of Hanoi Problem

Tower of Hanoi is one of the classical problems of computer science. The problem states that:

1. There are three stands (Stands 1, 2 and 3) on which a set of disks, each with a different diameter, are placed.
2. Initially, the disks are stacked on Stand 1, in order of size, with the largest disk at the bottom.

The initial structure of Tower of Hanoi with three disks is shown in Figure 5.5.

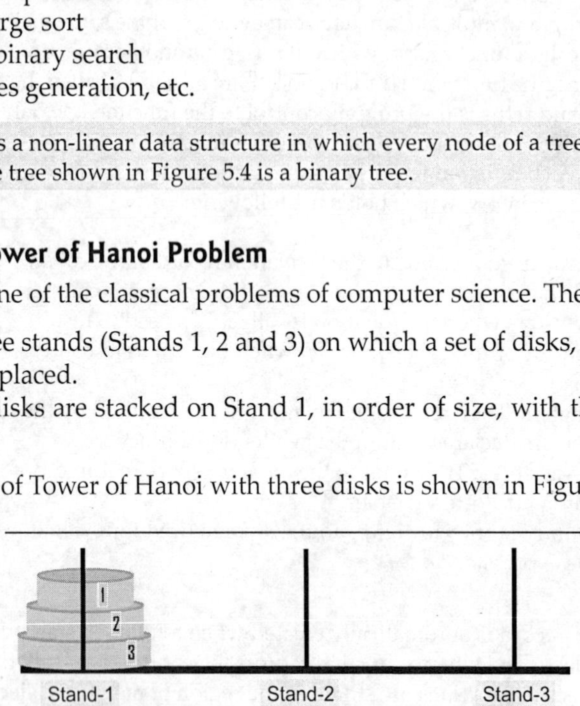

Figure 5.5 | Tower of Hanoi with three disks

The **'Tower of Hanoi problem'** is to find a sequence of disk moves so that all the disks are moved from Stand-1 to Stand-3, adhering to the following rules:

1. Move only one disk at a time.
2. A larger disk cannot be placed on top of a smaller disk.
3. All disks except the one being moved should be on a stand.

'Tower of Hanoi' is tough and computationally expensive. However, the expressive power of recursion can be used to easily formulate a solution to this problem. The general strategy for solving the Tower of Hanoi problem with n disks is shown in Figure 5.6.

1. Move the topmost n-1 disks from Stand-1 to Stand-2.
2. Move the largest disk from Stand-1 to Stand-3.
3. Move n-1 disks from Stand-2 to Stand-3.
4. Final structure.

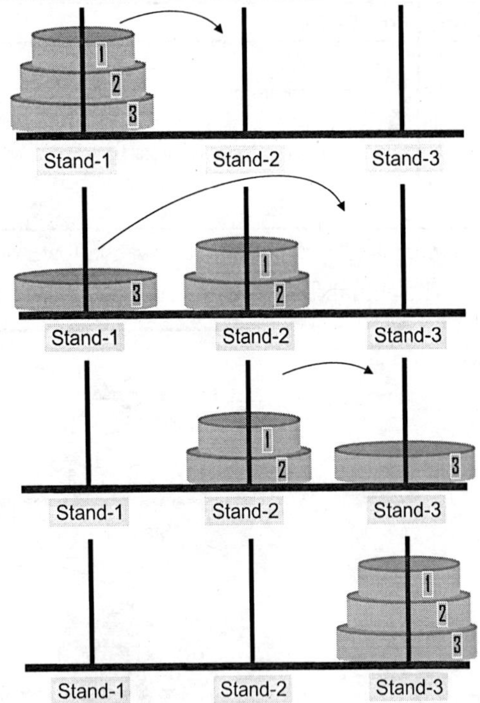

Figure 5.6 | General strategy to solve the Tower of Hanoi problem with three disks

The movement of n-1 disks forms the recursive case of a recursive solution to move n disks. The base case of a solution involves the movement of only one disk. The recurrence relation for solving the Tower of Hanoi problem can be written as:

$$\text{TowerOfHanoi(disks)} = \begin{cases} \text{move the disk} & \text{if disks} = 1 \\ \text{TowerOfHanoi(disks} - 1) & \text{if disks} > 1 \end{cases}$$

The code snippet listed in Program 5-25 solves the Tower of Hanoi problem.

Line	Prog 5-25.c	Output window

1
2
3
4
5
6
7
8
9
10
11
12
13
	#include<stdio.h>
	//Function declaration
	void move(int,int,int,int);
	//Function definitions
	void main()
	{
	    int disks=3;
	    printf("Follow these moves:\n");
	    move(disks,1,3,2);
	}
	void move(int count,int start,int finish,int temp)
	{
	    if(count>0)
		Follow these moves:
		Move disk 1 from 1 to 3
		Move disk 2 from 1 to 2
		Move disk 1 from 3 to 2
		Move disk 3 from 1 to 3
		Move disk 1 from 2 to 1
		Move disk 2 from 2 to 3
		Move disk 1 from 1 to 3
		Remarks:
		• Line number 15 codes step 1 of the general solution shown in Figure 5.6
		• Line number 16 is the base case and codes step 2 of the general solution shown in Figure 5.6

(Contd...)

Line	Prog 5-25.c	Output window
14	`{`	• Line number 17 codes the step 3 of the general solution shown in Figure 5.6 • How disks will be actually moved can be seen by tracing the program and keeping track of argument values to the recursive calls
15	`move(count-1,start,temp,finish);`	
16	`printf("Move disk %d from %d to %d\n",count,start,finish);`	
17	`move(count-1,temp,finish,start);`	
18	`}`	
19	`}`	

Program 5-25 | A program to solve the Tower of Hanoi problem

The actual disk movements are shown in Figure 5.7.

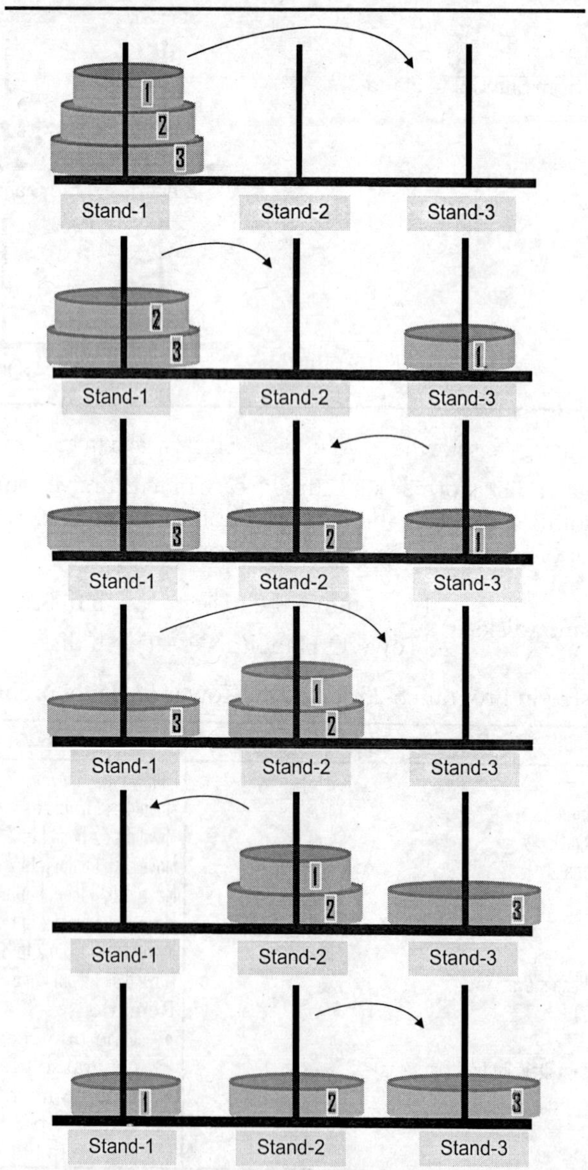

(*Contd...*)

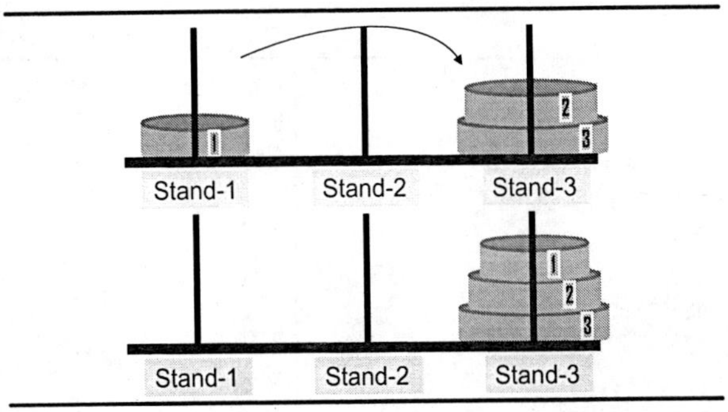

Figure 5.7 | Actual disk movements in solution to the Tower of Hanoi problem with three disks

Binary tree of recursive calls to the `move` function is shown in Figure 5.8.

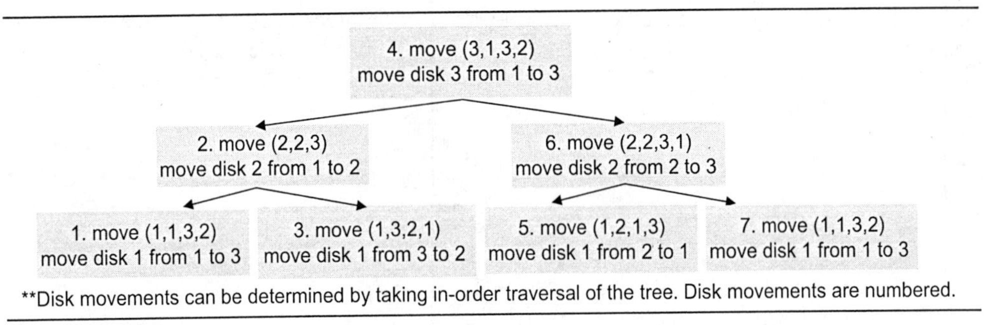

Figure 5.8 | Tree of recursive calls to the function `move`

5.3.1.1.7.3.3 n-ary Recursion

The most general form of recursion is **n-ary recursion** where n is not a constant but some parameter of function. **n-ary recursive** functions are used in generating permutations. The permutations of integers 1, 2 and 3 are as follows:

1	2	3
1	3	2
2	1	3
2	3	1
3	1	2
3	2	1

The code snippet listed in Program 5-26 uses n-ary recursion to print the permutations of integers 1, 2 and 3.

Prog 5-26.c

```
//n-ary recursion
#include<stdio.h>
//Definition of n-ary recursive function
permute(int array[], int parray[],int L,int N)
{
int i,j;
//Base case: Processing the permutations
if(L>N)
{
    for(i=1;i<=N;i++)
        printf("%d ",parray[i]);
    printf("\n");
}
//Recursive Case: Number of case depends upon the parameter
//value N. Number of time recursive calls are given is variable.
else
{
    for(i=1;i<=N;i++)
    {
        if(array[i]==0)
        {
            parray[L]=i;
            array[i]=1;
            permute(array,parray,L+1,N);
            array[i]=0;
        }
    }
}
}
main()
{
    int array[10]={0}, parray[10],n;
    printf("Generating permutations of 1 to n\n");
    printf("Enter the value of n(<10)\t");
    scanf("%d",&n);
    permute(array,parray,1,n);
}
```

Output window

```
Generating permutations of 1 to n
Enter the value of n(<10)    3
1 2 3
1 3 2
2 1 3
2 3 1
3 1 2
3 2 1
```

Remarks:

- permute is an n-ary recursive function
- The number of time recursive calls are given to permute depends upon the value of the parameter n
- Since the parameter n is a variable, the number of recursive calls in the activation of permute varies
- Trace the program to understand it clearly

Program 5-26 | A program that illustrates the use of recursion to print permutations

5.3.1.1.8 Pointers to Functions

Like recursion, pointers to functions provide an extremely interesting, efficient and elegant programming technique. The following concepts allow the creation of a pointer to a function:

1. Like variables, a compiled code upon execution gets some space in the main memory. Thus, a function in the program code is placed at some memory location in the Code Segment.

2. Functions like all other identifiers (except labels) do have a type. **Function type** is one of the derived data types. It consists of return type of the function and types of its parameters. For example, type of a function mult that accepts one integer and one float argument and returns a float value is float(int,float). The construction of a function type from its return type and parameter types is called **'function type derivation'**.
3. It is possible to create a pointer to any type (even void type). Hence, the creation of a pointer to a function type is also possible. A pointer to a function, commonly known as **function pointer,** is a variable that points to the starting address of the function.

Unfortunately, pointers to functions are less frequently used because of their complicated syntax. The following aspects of function pointers must be mastered so that they can be used in a correct way:

1. Declaration of a function pointer
2. Assigning or initializing a function pointer
3. Calling a function using a function pointer

Backward Reference: For a description on Code Segment (CS) refer Answer number 28 (Chapter 4).

5.3.1.1.8.1 Declaration of a Function Pointer

Consider the function fact developed in Program 5-22, which accepts an integer and returns an integer value. The type of function fact is int(int). A pointer to the function type int(int) is declared as:

```
int (*ptr)(int);
```

In the above declaration, ptr is a pointer to a function that accepts an integer and returns an integer value.

While reading C declaration, remember that [] and () bind more tightly than *. Hence, in declaration statement int* ptr(int);, the identifier ptr is bound to () instead of * and is read as: **ptr is a function that accepts an integer and returns an integer pointer**. The () can be used to bind ptr with *. In declaration statement int(*ptr)(int);, () is used to bind ptr with *. Hence, this declaration is read as: **ptr is a pointer to a function that accepts an integer and returns an integer value.**

Table 5.1 mentions some of the functions developed in this chapter, their types and pointers to functions of that type.

Table 5.1 | Pointers to function types

S.No	Function name(s)	Program number	Function type	Pointer to function type
1.	println	5-1	int()	int(*)()
2.	add, sub	5-1	int(int,int)	int(*)(int,int)
3.	printsum, main	5-5	void(void)	void(*)(void)
4.	printsum	5-6	void(int,int)	void(*)(int,int)
5.	printsum	5-7	void(int,int,char)	void(*)(int,int,char)

(Contd...)

6.	circle_area	5-9	float(int)	float(*)(int)
7.	swap	5-12	int(int*,int*)	int(*)(int*,int*)
8.	sum_diff	5-13	void(int,int,int*,int*)	void(*)(int,int,int*,int*)
9.	find_max_min	5-15a	int(int[],int)	int(*)(int[],int)
10.	find_max_min	5-15b	int(int*,int)	int(*)(int*,int)
11	largest_ele	5-16	void(int[][10],int*,int*)	void(*)(int[][10],int*,int*)
12.	f_calling_fs	5-30	void(int,int,int(*)(int,int))	void(*)(int,int,int(*)(int,int))

5.3.1.1.8.2 Assigning or Initializing a Function Pointer

A pointer to a function of type T can be assigned or initialized with the address of a function of type T or with a pointer of the same type. To assign or initialize a function pointer with the address of a function, just place the function designator (i.e. the name of the function) of a suitable and known function on the right side of the assignment operator. In the following statements, the address of the function sub is assigned to the function pointer str:

```
int sub(int,int);
int (*str)(int,int);
str=sub;
```

In the following statements, the function pointer atr is initialized with the address of the function add:

```
int add(int,int);
int(*atr)(int,int)=add;
```

The important points about the function pointer assignment or function pointer initialization are as follows:

1. At the time of function pointer assignment or initialization, the function designator must be known, i.e. declared or defined.
2. The function designator implicitly refers to the starting address of the function. However, the function designator can optionally be preceded by the address-of operator (&) to signify the address of function. The following two statements are equivalent:

```
int (*atr)(int, int)=add;
int (*atr)(int,int)=&add;
```

5.3.1.1.8.3 Calling a Function Using Function Pointer

A function pointer can be used to call a function in any of the following two ways:

1. By explicitly dereferencing it using the dereference operator, i.e. *
2. By using its name instead of the function's name

Program 5-27 illustrates the method of calling a function using the function pointers.

Line	Trace	Prog 5-27.c	Output window
1		`//Calling functions using function pointers`	Calling functions using function pointers: The result of addition is 22 The result of addition is 5 **Remarks:** • Type of function add is int(int,int) • ptr1 and ptr2 are pointers to a function of type int(int,int) • ptr1 is assigned an address of the function add by using the function designator only • ptr2 is assigned an address of the function add by using address-of operator and the function designator • ptr1 and ptr2 both point to the function add • In line number 12, ptr1 is dereferenced and is used to call the function add • In line number 14, ptr2 is used to call the function add without dereferencing it • Trace the program and note the trace arrow numbering
2		`#include<stdio.h>`	
3		`int add(int a,int b);`	
4	1	`main()`	
5		`{`	
6		`//Assigning address by using function designator only`	
7	2	`int (*ptr1)(int,int)=add;`	
8		`//Assigning address by using address-of operator`	
9	3	`int (*ptr2)(int,int)=&add;`	
10	4	`printf("Calling functions using function pointers:\n");`	
11		`//Calling function by dereferencing function pointer`	
12	5	`(*ptr1)(10,12);`	
13		`//Calling by using function pointer name`	
14	9	`ptr2(2,3);`	
15	13	`}`	
16	6,10	`int add(int a, int b)`	
17		`{`	
18	7,11	`printf("The result of addition is %d\n",a+b);`	
19	8,12	`}`	

Program 5-27 | A program that illustrates the method of calling function using function pointers

5.3.1.1.9 Array of Function Pointers

Like arrays of pointers to other types, it is possible to create array of pointers to function type (i.e. array of function pointers). The following declaration statement declares arr as an array of pointers to functions that accept two integers and returns an integer:

```
int (* arr[4])(int,int);
```

The important points about the above declaration and the array of function pointers are as follows:

1. arr is an array of function pointers. Each pointer takes 2 bytes or 4 bytes in the memory depending upon the compiler and the working environment used. Hence, the total memory space allocated to arr will be 8 bytes or 16 bytes. The code snippet in Program 5-28 illustrates this fact.

Prog 5-28.c	Output window

<pre>//Size of array of function pointers
#include<stdio.h>
main()
{
    int (*arr[4])(int,int);
    printf("Memory allocated to arr is %d bytes",sizeof(arr));
}</pre>
	Memory allocated to arr is 8 bytes
	Remarks:
	• Turbo C 3.0 gives the above-mentioned result. If Turbo C 4.5 is used, the result will be 16 bytes
	• The name of an array does not decompose to a pointer type if it is an operand of sizeof operator
	• sizeof operator gives the memory allocated to the complete array

Program 5-28 | A program that finds the size of an array of function pointers

2. Like other arrays, arrays of function pointers can also be initialized by providing an initialization list. The initializers in the initialization list should be function designators of the known functions (i.e. declared or defined) of appropriate type. All the initializing functions should have the same type.
3. The array of function pointers can be used to call functions in a generalized way. The code snippet in Program 5-29 illustrates the initialization of an array of function pointers and the method to call functions in a generalized way.

Prog 5-29.c

```
//Array of function pointers
#include<stdio.h>
//Function declarations
int add(int,int);
int sub(int,int);
int mult(int,int);
int div(int,int);
//Function definitions
main()
{
//Array of function pointers initialized with initialization list
    int (*arr[4])(int,int)={add,sub,mult,div};
    int lc;
    printf("Calling functions using iteration:\n");
//Functions called in a generalized way by using loop
    for(lc=0;lc<4;lc++)
        arr[lc](6,3);
}
int add(int a,int b)
{
    printf("Result of addition of %d and %d is %d\n",a,b,a+b);
}
int sub(int a,int b)
{
    printf("Result of subtraction of %d and %d is %d\n",a,b,a-b);
}
int mult(int a,int b)
{
    printf("Result of multiplication of %d and %d is %d\n",a,b,a*b);
}
int div(int a,int b)
{
    printf("Result of division of %d and %d is %d\n",a,b,a/b);
}
```

Output window

```
Calling functions using iteration:
Result of addition of 6 and 3 is 9
Result of subtraction of 6 and 3 is 3
Result of multiplication of 6 and 3 is 18
Result of division of 6 and 3 is 2
```

Remarks:

- All functions add, sub, mult and div have the same type, i.e. int(int,int)
- These functions accept two integers and return an integer
- arr is an array of 4 function pointers of type int(*)(int,int)
- arr is initialized with an initialization list
- All the initializers are of the same type
- It can also be initialized as: int(*arr[4])(int,int)={&add,&sub,&mult,&div}

Program 5-29 | A program that illustrates the use of array of function pointers

5.3.1.1.10 Passing Function to a Function as an Argument

A function can accept arguments of pointer type. We have seen the application of pointers to pass arrays as arguments to the functions. Pointers can also be used to pass functions to a function. The code snippet in Program 5-30 illustrates the use of pointers to pass functions to a function.

Line	Trace	Prog 5-30.c	Output window
1		`//Passing function to a function as an argument`	Passing functions to a function:
2		`#include<stdio.h>`	Result of addition of 10 and 20 is 30
3		`//Function declarations`	Result of subtraction of 10 and 20 is -10
4		`int add(int,int);`	**Remarks:**
5		`int sub(int,int);`	• The third argument to
6		`//Declaration of function whose third parameter is a function ptr`	the function f_calling_fs is a
7		`void f_calling_fs(int,int,int(*)(int,int));`	function pointer of type
8		`//Function definition`	int(*)(int,int)
9	1	`void main()`	• In line number 13, the ad-
10		`{`	dress of the function add
11	2	`printf("Passing functions to a function:\n");`	is passed to the function
12		`// Third argument in the following function calls is a function designator`	f_calling_fs
13	3	`f_calling_fs(10,20,add);`	• In line number 18, the
14	10	`f_calling_fs(10,20,sub);`	passed argument is used
15	17	`}`	to call the function. Since
16	4,11	`void f_calling_fs(int a, int b, int (*fun)(int,int))`	the address of the func-
17		`{`	tion add has been passed,
18	5,12	`fun(a,b);`	the call fun(a,b) is equiva-
19	9,16	`}`	lent to add(a,b)
20	6	`int add(int a,int b)`	• Similarly, in line num-
21		`{`	ber 14, the function sub is
22	7	`printf("Result of addition of %d and %d is %d\n",a,b,a+b);`	passed to f_calling_fs and
23	8	`return 0;`	on the second execution
24		`}`	of line number 18, it is
25	13	`int sub(int a,int b)`	called
26		`{`	• Trace the program and
27	14	`printf("Result of subtraction of %d and %d is %d\n",a,b,a-b);`	note the trace arrow num-
28	15	`return 0;`	bering
29		`}`	

Program 5-30 | A program that illustrates the passing of functions to a function

5.3.1.2 Library Functions

Library functions or pre-defined functions are the functions whose functionality has already been developed by someone and are available to the user for use. For example, printf and scanf are library functions. There are two aspects of working with library functions:

1. Declaration of library functions
2. Use of library functions

5.3.1.2.1 Declaration of Library Functions/Role of Header Files

We have seen that the user-defined functions need to be declared before they are called. This is true for library functions as well. A library function needs to be declared before it is called. The declarations of library functions are available in their respective header files. To make these declarations accessible in a program file, the corresponding header files are included. For example, the prototype, i.e. the declaration of printf function is available in the header file stdio.h. That is why stdio.h is included before calling the printf function. If the header file containing the declaration of the library function is not included before its use, there will be a compilation error 'Prototype missing.'

5.3.1.2.2 Use of Library Functions

Library functions are used in the same way as user-defined functions, i.e. by using a function call operator. The role and usage of some of the common library functions are listed below.

5.3.1.2.2.1 Library of Mathematical Functions

The mathematical library defines some of the common mathematical functions. The declarations of these mathematical functions are available in the header file **math.h.** Table 5.2 lists the commonly used mathematical functions available in the math library.

Table 5.2 | Mathematical functions available in math library

S.No	Function	Function declaration and use	Role
		Trigonometric functions	
1.	acos	double acos(double x);	Returns arc cosine of x in radians
2.	asin	double asin(double x);	Returns arc sine of x in radians
3.	atan	double atan(double x);	Returns arc tangent of x in radians
4.	atan2	double atan2(double y, double x);	Returns the arc tangent in radians of y/x based on the signs of both values to determine the correct quadrant
5.	cos	double cos(double x);	Returns the cosine of a radian angle x
6.	cosh	double cosh(double x);	Returns hyperbolic cosine of x
7.	sin	double sin(double x);	Returns the sine of a radian angle x
8.	sinh	double sinh(double x);	Returns hyperbolic sine of x
9.	tan	double tan(double x);	Returns the tangent of a radian angle x
10.	tanh	double tanh(double x);	Returns hyperbolic tangent of x
		Exponential, logarithmic and power functions	
11.	exp	double exp(double x)	Returns the value of e raised to the xth power
12.	frexp	double frexp(double x, int *exponent);	frexp splits a double number x into mantissa and exponent. Given x, frexp calculates the mantissa m and exponent n such that x = m*2^n
13,	ldexp	double ldexp(double x, int exponent);	Returns x multiplied by 2 raised to the power of exponent, i.e. returns x*2^n
14.	log	double log(double x);	Returns the natural logarithm (*base e*) of x
15.	log10	double log10(double x);	Returns the common logarithm (*base 10*) of x
16.	pow	double pow(double x, double y);	Returns x raised to the power of y
17.	sqrt	double sqrt(double x);	Returns the square root of x

(Contd...)

Other mathematical functions			
18.	ceil	double ceil(double x);	Returns the smallest integer value greater than or equal to x
19.	fabs	double fabs(double x);	Returns the absolute value of x (a negative value becomes positive, positive value remains unchanged)
20.	floor	double floor(double x);	Returns the largest integer value less than or equal to x
21.	fmod	double fmod(double x, double y);	Calculates x modulo y, i.e. returns the remainder of x divided by y

i The return type of every math library function is double.

5.3.1.2.2.2 Library of Standard Input/Output Functions

The functionality of standard input and output operations is provided by this library. The declarations of these functions are available in the header file stdio.h. stdio is an acronym for standard input output. The common standard input/output functions are printf, scanf, gets,➲ puts,➲ getch, getchar, putch, putchar, etc.

Forward Reference: gets, puts and other input–output functions (Chapter 6).

5.3.1.2.2.3 Library of String Processing Functions

This library consists of functions that are used for string➲ processing. The common string library functions are strcpy, strrev, strcat, strcmp, strcmpi, etc. The declarations of these functions are available in the header file string.h. The role and working of string library functions will be discussed in Chapter 6 after the discussion on character arrays.

Forward Reference: String processing functions (Chapter 6).

5.3.2 Based upon the Number of Arguments a Function Accepts

Based upon the number of arguments a function accepts, functions are classified as follows:

1. Fixed argument functions
2. Variable argument functions

5.3.2.1 Fixed Argument Functions

A function that accepts a fixed number of arguments is called a **fixed argument function**. If the fixed argument function does not specify any default argument, invoking a fixed argument function with a lesser number of arguments than expected leads to a compilation error. A fixed argument function cannot even be invoked by supplying more number of arguments than expected. For example, pow function listed in Table 5.2 expects two arguments of type double. The following invocations of pow function are erroneous:

```
pow();              //←Lesser number of arguments supplied than expected
pow(2.0);           //←Lesser number of arguments supplied than expected
pow(2.0,1.5,1.0);   //←More number of arguments supplied than expected
```

5.3.2.2 Variable Argument Functions

A function that accepts a variable number of arguments is called a **variable argument function**. For example, printf is a variable argument function, which can accept one or more arguments. The type of first argument must be char* and there is no constraint about the type of rest of the arguments. The following calls to printf function are valid:

```
printf("Hello");              //←Only one argument of type char*
printf("%d",2);               //←Two arguments. The type of the first argument is char* and the
                              //  second is int
printf("%s %s","Hi","!!");    //←Three arguments, all of type char*
```

A function that accepts a variable number of arguments can be created by using the macros va_start, va_arg, va_end available in the header file stdarg.h. The piece of code in Program 5-31 illustrates the development of a variable argument function.

Prog 5-31.c

```
//Variable argument functions
//File stdarg.h is to be included for using va_list, va_start, etc.
#include<stdarg.h>
#include<stdio.h>
//Ellipses (i.e. three dots) are used to declare variable argument function
int sum(int no_of_arguments, ...);
//Function definitions
main()
{
    int result;
//Function sum invoked with 4 arguments
    result=sum(3,12,13,14);
    printf("The result of addition of 3 numbers is %d\n",result);
//Function sum invoked with 6 arguments
    result=sum(5,10,20,30,40,50);
    printf("The result of addition of 5 numbers is %d\n",result);
}
//Definition of a variable argument function
int sum(int no_of_arguments,...)
{
    int arg,i=0,total=0;
    va_list ptr;
    va_start(ptr,no_of_arguments);
    arg=va_arg(ptr,int);
    while(i++<no_of_arguments)
    {
        total+=arg;
        arg=va_arg(ptr,int);
    }
    va_end(ptr);
    return total;
}
```

Output window

```
The result of addition of 3 numbers is 39
The result of addition of 5 numbers is 150
```

Program 5-31 | A program that makes use of variable argument functions

The important points about the code listed in Program 5-31 and the variable argument functions are as follows:

1. Since the function sum is 'a fixed number of argument followed by a variable number of argument' function, it is declared as int sum(int no_of_arguments,...);. **Ellipses** (...) are used while declaring a variable argument function.
2. **Role of ellipses:** The number of arguments that can be passed to a variable argument function is not fixed. Hence, while declaring a variable argument function, it is not possible to list the types of all the arguments that might be passed to the function during the function call. The solution to this problem is provided by ellipses. While declaring a variable argument function, ellipses (...) are used in the parameter list. **The presence of ellipses (...) tells the compiler that when the function is called, zero or more arguments may follow and that the type of the arguments is not known.** Ellipses (...) used in the declaration of the variable argument function **suspend the type checking.**
   The prototype/declaration of printf function is int printf(const char*,...);. The prototype says that there can be one or more arguments in the printf function call. The type of first argument would be const char* and the latter arguments can be of any type. Due to ellipses (...) the following uses of printf function are valid:
   1. printf("Hello Readers");
   2. printf("%d %d",2,3);
   3. printf("%d %s %c",2,"Hi",'I');
3. The variable argument functions are developed with the help of macros va_start, va_arg and va_end, declared in the header file stdarg.h. Therefore, the header file stdarg.h is included so that the macros can be used.
4. The header file stdarg.h also declares a type va_list that holds the information needed by the macros va_arg and va_end. A variable ptr of type va_list is declared in the function sum.
5. The macro va_start takes two parameters ptr and lastfix. The type of the first parameter ptr is va_list and lastfix is the last fixed parameter supplied to the variable argument function. The last fixed parameter supplied to the variable argument function sum is no_of_arguments and is of type int. The macro va_start sets ptr to point to the first of the variable arguments being passed to the function.
6. The macro va_arg is used to return the arguments in the variable list. The first time va_arg is used, it returns the first argument in the list. Each successive time va_arg is used, it returns the next argument in the list. The macro va_arg returns the values of type given to it as its second argument (for example, int in the code listed in Program 5-31).
7. The macro va_end should be called after va_arg has read all the arguments. If the macro va_end is not used, the program may show strange and undefined behavior.
8. The order in which the macros va_start, va_arg and va_end should be called is:
   a. va_start must be called before the first call to va_arg or va_end.
   b. va_end should only be called after va_arg has read all the arguments.

Variable argument functions actually have a fixed number of arguments followed by a variable number of arguments.
There should be only three dots, i.e. (...) in **ellipses**. Usage of more than three dots in ellipses leads to a compilation error.
The syntax of **using macros** is similar to the syntax of using functions.

Forward Reference: Macros (Chapter 8).

5.4 Summary

1. Functions help in modularizing a program into smaller simple parts.
2. Functions are classified based upon: (a) who develops the function and (b) the parameter and the return type of the function.
3. Based upon who developed the function, they are categorized as: (a) user-defined functions and (b) library functions.
4. Based upon the parameter and the return type of the function, they are categorized as: (a) functions with no input and no output, (b) functions with inputs but no output, (c) functions with inputs and a single output and (d) functions with inputs and multiple outputs.
5. User-defined functions are defined by the user at the time of writing a program and are also known as programmer-defined functions.
6. There are three aspects of working with user-defined functions: (a) function declaration, (b) function definition and (c) function call.
7. Function definition, also known as function implementation means composing a function. Every function definition consists of two parts: (a) header of the function and (b) body of the function.
8. A function with no input–output does not accept any input and does not return any result.
9. The execution of a C program always begins with the function `main`. It need not to be called explicitly.
10. Functions whose return type is `void` are known as `void` functions. `void` functions do not return any value.
11. While calling a function, the expressions that appear within the parentheses of a function call are known as actual arguments, and the variables declared in the parameter list in the header of function definition are known as formal parameters.
12. The `return` statement is to return the result of computations done in the called function and/or the program control back to the calling function.
13. There are two forms of `return` statement: (a) `return;` and (b) `return expression;`.
14. Depending upon whether values or addresses are passed as arguments to a function, the argument passing methods in C language are classified as: (a) pass by value and (b) pass by reference/address.
15. If arguments are passed by value, the changes made in the values of formal parameters inside the called function are not reflected back to the calling function.
16. If the arguments are passed by reference/address, the changes made in the values pointed to by the formal parameters in the called function are reflected back to the calling function.
17. A function can return only one value by using the `return` statement but it can indirectly return more than one value using the concept of pass by reference/address.
18. When an array is passed as an argument to a function, it implicitly gets converted to a pointer type.

19. The arguments can be made default by using an initialization syntax within the parameter list during the function declaration.
20. The default argument should not be specified in the function definition.
21. Function calling itself is called recursive function and the process is known as recursion.
22. Recursive functions may be: (a) direct recursive/indirect recursive and (b) tail recursive/non-tail recursive.
23. There are three patterns of recursive calls: (a) linear, (b) binary and (c) n-ary.
24. Like recursion, pointers to functions provide an extremely interesting, efficient and elegant programming technique.
25. A pointer to a function, commonly known as the function pointer, is a variable that points to the address of a function.
26. Library functions or pre-defined functions are the functions whose functionality has already been developed by someone and is available to the user for use.
27. The arguments to the function `main` are supplied at the command line and thus have a special name known as command line arguments.

Exercise Questions

Conceptual Questions and Answers

1. *What is a function? What are the advantages of using functions?*

   A function is a group of statements that performs a specific task and is relatively independent of the remaining code. Functions are used to organize programs into smaller and independent units. Several advantages of modularizing the program into functions include:

   1. Reduction in code redundancy
   2. Enabling code reuse
   3. Better readability
   4. Information hiding
   5. Improved maintainability

2. *Do functions have a type like other identifiers? If yes, how is it derived?*

   Yes, functions do have a type like all other identifiers except labels. Function type is one of the derived types and consists of return type of the function and the types of its parameters. For example, the type of a function `mult` that accepts one integer and one `float` parameter and returns a `float` value is `float(int,float)`. The construction of a function type from its return type and parameter types is called 'function type derivation'.

3. *What are the differences between a function declaration and a function definition?*

Backward Reference: Refer Sections 5.3.1.1.1 and 5.3.1.1.2 for a description on function declaration and function definition.

The major differences between a function declaration and a function definition are as follows:

a. A function can only be defined once but can be declared many times.

b. A function can be declared within the body of some other function but cannot be defined within the body of some other function.

c. A function definition can also serve as a function declaration but the vice versa is not true. The function definition serves as a function declaration if it is present before the function call.

d. The function definition can be changed without changing the function declaration but if the function declaration is changed, it becomes necessary to change the function definition.

e. For using (i.e. calling) a function, it is sufficient and necessary to know the function declaration without knowing anything about how it is defined.

4. *What is meant by prototyping a function? Why is a function prototype necessary?*
   The function declaration is also called a function prototype. Hence, function prototyping means declaring a function.

Backward Reference: Refer Section 5.3.1.1.1 for a description on function prototype and its necessity.

5. *'C is a strongly typed language'. What does that mean?*
   'C is a strongly typed language' means that the arguments of every function call are type checked during the compilation. If the compiler detects a type mismatch between the type of an argument and the type of corresponding parameter, an implicit-type conversion is applied if possible. If it is not possible to apply implicit-type conversion, the compiler issues an error message. That is why functions cannot be called until they are declared or defined. The declaration or definition of function is necessary for the compiler to perform the type checking on the arguments of the function call against the function parameter list.

6. *Is it mandatory to specify the same name for the parameters in the declaration and definition of a function?*
   No, it is not mandatory to have the same name for the parameters in the function declaration and the function definition. In fact, it is not even compulsory to write names of the parameters in the function declaration.

Backward Reference: Refer Section 5.3.1.1.1 for a description on abstract parameter declaration and complete parameter declaration.

7. *I want to write a function* `add` *that should add the contents of two integer variables and return their sum. I have made the following declaration for the function:*

```
int add(int vl,v2);
```

   The compiler is not accepting it and is showing an error. Why?

Backward Reference: Refer Section 5.3.1.1.1 (Point 5) for a description on syntactic rules for writing the parameter list and the parameter type list.

   The compiler shows an error due to erroneous parameter list. The shorthand declaration of parameters in the parameter list is not allowed and leads to the compilation error. The rectified declaration for the function can be written as `int add(int vl,int v2);`.

8. *What are user-defined functions and library or pre-defined functions? Is* `main` *a library function or a user-defined function?*

Backward Reference: Refer Sections 5.3.1.1 and 5.3.1.2 for a description on user-defined functions and library functions.

User-defined functions are defined by the user at the time of writing a program. Library functions are the functions whose functionality has already been developed by someone and are available to the user for use.

main is a user-defined function because the functionality to the main function is always added by the user by writing its body.

9. *Why do we include header file(s) in our programs? What is their role?*

Backward Reference: Refer Section 5.3.1.2.1 for a description on the role of header files.

10. *What is meant by the terms actual arguments and formal parameters?*

Backward Reference: Refer Section 5.3.1.1.3.2 (Point 4) for a description on actual arguments and formal parameters.

11. *What are the different ways of passing arguments to a function?*

Backward Reference: Refer Sections 5.3.1.1.3.4.1 and 5.3.1.1.3.4.2 for a description on pass by value and pass by reference.

12. *Does C actually have a pass by reference?*

    No, the C language actually does not have a pass by reference. The C language always passes the argument by value. The call by reference is artificially simulated by passing addresses by value. In a call by reference, the l-values given as actual arguments are copied into the parameters of pointer type.

13. *How are arrays passed to the functions?*

    Arrays are always passed by reference. The word array here means the entire array and not the individual array elements.

Backward Reference: Refer Section 5.3.1.1.4 for a description on passing arrays to functions.

14. *What are the various forms of* return *statement? What is the specific use of each form?*

Backward Reference: Refer Section 5.3.1.1.3.3.1 for a description on return statement.

15. *It is said that 'Function can only return one value'. Can't I return more than one value by writing* return value1, value2, value3;?

Backward Reference: Refer Section 5.3.1.1.3.3.1 (Point 4) to answer this question.

16. *Can a function have more than one* return *statement within its body?*

    Yes, a function can have more than one return statement within its body. There is no constraint about the number of return statements that can be placed within a function's body. For example, the following piece of code is valid:

```
int funct()
{
    return 1;                                   //←Control returns from this point
    printf ("This can never be executed");      //← This point onwards, code is unreachable
    return 2;
    return 3;
    printf("There are multiple return statements");
}
```

Although, a number of return statements can be placed inside the body of a function, only one of them that appears first in the logical flow of control gets executed. With the execution of this return statement, the program control returns to the calling function and the rest of the statements that appear after this return statement remain unreachable.
On compiling the mentioned code, there will be no error, but the compiler issues a warning message 'Unreachable code in function funct'. This warning is due to the fact that the program control returns to the calling function with the execution of the first return statement and can never reach the latter part of the code.

17. *I have developed the following piece of code to compute the area of a circle. It outputs* 78.000000 *instead of the actual value of the area of circle, i.e.* 78.537498. *Why?*

```
circle_area(int);
main()
{
    int rad=5.5;
    float area;
    area=circle_area(rad);
    printf("The area of circle is %f",area);
}
circle_area(int rad)
{
    float area;
    area=3.1415*rad*rad;
    return area;
}
```

Backward Reference: Refer Section 5.3.1.1.3.3.1 (Point 2 (f)) to answer this question.

18. *In the programs that I have written till now, I got a warning message 'Function should return a value'. What does this mean?*
This warning message comes if the return type of a given function is not void, and in the body of the function return statement has not been used to return any value. For example, consider the following piece of code:

```
main()
{
    printf("Warning message");
}
```

The mentioned code on compilation gives a warning message: 'Function should return a value'. There can be three different ways to remove this warning:

```
main()
{
    printf("Warning message");
    return 0;
}
```

Way I

```
void main()
{
    printf("Warning message");
}
```

Way II

```
#pragma warn -rvl
main()
{
    printf("Warning message");
}
```

Way III

A compilation of the above-mentioned codes will not generate a warning message because:

1. Way I returns an integer value.
2. Way II mentions the return type as `void`.
3. Way III configures the compiler using `pragma`➲ directive in such a way that it does not generate 'Function should return a value' warning message.

Forward Reference: `pragma` directive (Chapter 8).

19. *What is the difference between a warning and an error?*

    Warning is only an indicator that something may go wrong but an error is a notification that some mistake (i.e. syntactic violation) has occurred. The compiler can be configured to turn off the display of warning messages but it cannot be stopped from displaying error messages.

20. *Can a return type of a function be an array type or a function type?*

    No. The `return` type of a function shall be `void` or an object type other than an array type and a function type. Arrays and functions are returned to the calling function in the same way as they are passed to the called function, i.e. by the means of pointers. For example, consider the following code snippets:
    In Code I (a), the return type of the function `fun_returning_array` is an array type. The given code on compilation gives an error. Code 1 (b) shows the rectified version of Code I (a) whereby an array `arr` is returned by the means of a pointer, i.e. the address of the first element of the array. In Code II (a), the function `area_of_square` is passed to the function `fun` by the means of a pointer. In Code II (b), the function `fun` returns function `area_of_square` by the means of a pointer.

```
int[3] fun_returning_array();
main()
{
    int *ptr;
    ptr=fun_returning_array();
    printf("%d %d %d",ptr[0],ptr[1],ptr[2]);
}
int[3] fun_returning_array()
{
    int arr[3]={1,2,3};
    return arr;
}
```

Code I (a) (Return type is array type)

```
int* fun_returning_array();
main()
{
    int *ptr;
    ptr=fun_returning_array();
    printf("%d %d %d",ptr[0],ptr[1],ptr[2]);
}
int* fun_returning_array()
{
    int arr[3]={1,2,3};
    return arr;
}
```

Code I (b) (Return type is a pointer)

(Contd...)

<table>
<tr>
<td>

```
int area_of_square(int side)
{
    return side*side;
}
int fun(int (*fun_name)(int))
{
//The parameter fun_name contains the address of function
//area_of_square
    return fun_name(2);
//The function area_of_square is called with argment 2. The
//result returned by the function area_of_square is returned
//by the function fun
}
main()
{
//The function fun is called with the name of function
//area_of_square as an argument
    printf("Area is %d",fun(area_of_square));
}
```

Code II (a)(Function passed to a function)
</td>
<td>

```
int area_of_square(int side)
{
    return side*side;
}
int(*fun())(int)
{
//Function fun accepts no argument. It returns a pointer to
//a function that accepts an integer and returns an integer
    return area_of_square;
}
main()
{
//The function fun is called without any argument. It returns a
//pointer to the function area_of_square. The returned
//pointer is used to call the function area_square with
//argument 2
    printf("Area is %d",fun()(2));
}
```

Code II (b)(Function returned by the means of a pointer)
</td>
</tr>
</table>

21. *What are activation records?*

Backward Reference: Refer Section 5.3.1.1.7.3.1.1 for a description on activation records.

22. *What is recursion? What are the advantages and disadvantages of recursion over iteration?*

Backward Reference: Refer Section 5.3.1.1.7.1 for a description on direct and indirect recursion.

The merits and demerits of recursion over iteration are listed below:

Iteration	Recursion
1. Performance wise, iteration is superior as compared to recursion	1. Performance of recursion is poor as compared to iteration. Recursion involves calling the same function again and again. The execution of a function call is time consuming as the entire state of a calling function needs to be saved before the control is passed to the called function. Therefore, precious computing time is wasted in book-keeping tasks
2. Memory requirement of an iterative function is less as compared to that of a recursive function	2. Recursion involves function calls. Each function call requires creation of an activation record, which takes some memory. The memory required by an activation record is directly proportional to the number of local variables declared within the recursive function.

(Contd...)

	The total memory required by the recursion is equal to the memory taken by all the activation records that exist at some particular instance
3. Infinite iteration will not terminate	3. Infinite recursion will automatically terminate when there is no memory space left for the creation of the activation records
4. Iteration is diffucult to express in some cases	4. One of the major advantages of the recursion is the **ease of expression**. The tasks that are expressible in terms of themselves can be easily coded by using recursive functions. For example, the computation of the factorial of a number. The factorial of a number is equal to the number multiplied by the factorial of the number minus one, i.e. fact(n)=n*fact(n–1)

23. *What is tail recursion?*

Backward Reference: Refer Section 5.3.1.1.7.2 for a description on tail recursion.

24. *How do the declaration statements* `int *func(int);`, `int(*func)(int);` and `int(*func())(int);` *differ from each other?*

    While reading C declarations, remember that [] and () bind more tightly than *. In the declaration statement, `int *func(int);` the identifier name `func` is bound to () instead of * and it is read as: **`func` is a function that accepts an integer and returns a pointer to an integer**. In the declaration statement, `int (*func)(int);` () is used to bound `func` to *. Hence, the declaration is read as: **`func` is a pointer to a function that accepts an integer and returns an integer**. In the declaration statement `int(*func())(int);` the identifier name `func` is bound to inner () instead of * and is read as: **`func` is a function that accepts no argument and returns a pointer to a function that accepts an integer and returns an integer.**

25. *If there is a type mismatch between the type of argument and the type of corresponding parameter, will the compiler apply implicit-type conversion? Is the same applicable if there is a mismatch between the type of value returned and the return type of a function?*

    Yes, if the type of the argument and the corresponding parameter do not match or if the type of value returned does not match the return type of the function, an implicit-type conversion is applied, if possible. If it is not possible to apply an implicit-type conversion, the complier issues an error message.

26. *I have encountered the following piece of code:*

```
int add(int v1,int v2=10);
main()
{
    int result;
    result=add(5);
}
int add(int v1,int v2)
{
    return v1+v2;
}
```

There are two parameter names in the parameter list of the function add. *I have read that if the number of arguments is incorrect or the types of arguments are not compatible with the types of parameters, the compile time error is issued. In the call to function* add *only one argument is given instead of two, but still the code is executing. Why is the compiler not showing an error?*

The compiler does not show an error because v2 is a default argument. A function that provides a default argument for a parameter can be invoked with or without an argument for that parameter. If an argument is not provided, the default argument value is used, but if it is provided it overrides the default argument value.

27. *What are variable argument functions? How are they created?*

Backward Reference: Refer Section 5.3.2.2 for a description on variable argument functions.

28. *A variable argument function can have a variable number of arguments, so it is not possible to list the type and number of all the arguments that might be passed to a function. Therefore, how can I make declaration for a variable argument function, and how is type checking done for a variable argument function?*

Backward Reference: Refer to the role of ellipses mentioned in Section 5.3.2.2 to answer this question.

29. *Are the following declarations equivalent?*
    1. void funct();
    2. void funct(parameter_list,...);
    3. void funct(...);

No, the specified declarations are not equivalent. In declaration 1, funct is declared as a function that accepts no arguments. In declaration 2, funct is declared as a function that at least accepts the arguments of the specific type mentioned in the parameter list. In declaration 3, funct is declared as a function that can take zero or more arguments.

30. *Why does the following piece of code not compile successfully?*

```
test_function()
{
    printf("Control is now in test function");
    return;
}
main()
{
    printf("There is a simple call to a test function");
    test_function();
    printf("Control returns to main after executing test function");
}
```

The code does not compile successfully because the return type of the function test_function is not specified. By default, it would be considered as int. In the body of the function test_function, the first form of the return statement (i.e. return;) is used, but it can only be used if the return type of the function is void. That is why the compiler shows an error. There are two ways of removing this error:

1. Specify the return type of the function test_function as void.
2. Use the second form of return statement (i.e. return expression;) in the body of the function test_function. Write return 0; instead of return;.

31. *I have written the following piece of code:*

```
inc_value(int a)
{
5+return a;
}
main()
{
    int a=10,c;
    c=inc_value(a);
    printf("The incremented value of a returned is %d",c);
}
```

Why is the following piece of code not working?

The code is not working because it is not valid to write 5+return a;. return is a statement and cannot be used as an operand of an operator. Only the expressions can form operands of an operator. Instead of 5+return a; it should have been return 5+a; or return a+5;.

32. *What will the output of the following piece of code be?*

```
main()
{
    printf("%d",sizeof(printf("Hello Readers!!")));
}
```

The output of the code **WILL NOT** be Hello Readers!!2. The given piece of code on execution outputs 2. Remember that the operand of sizeof operator is not evaluated. Thus, when the expression printf("Hello Readers!!") is given to it as an operand, it is not evaluated, and the operator operates on its return type, i.e. int. Thus, the output comes out to be 2. Consider another example:

```
main()
{
    int a=2;
    printf("%d ",sizeof(a+=2));
    printf("%d ",a);
}
```

The mentioned piece of code on execution outputs 2 2 instead of 2 4 because the expression a+=2 is not evaluated.

33. *What will the output of the following piece of code be?*

```
main()
{
    printf("goto statement trying to transfer control to other function");
    goto target_pt;
}
other_funct()
{
    target_pt:
    printf("The target label is present in other function");
}
```

The mentioned piece of code on compilation gives an error 'Undefined label target_pt in function main'. The goto statement can only transfer the control from one point to another within the same function. It cannot take the control from one function to another.

34. *Both the function call statement and the* goto *statement can be used to transfer the control from one point to another. Then, why does the* goto *statement cannot be used to transfer control from one function to another?*

The goto statement cannot be used to take the control from one function to another. Transferring the control from one function to another is not as simple as transferring control within the same function. If a control is to be transferred from one function (i.e. calling function) to another (i.e. called function), the following two additional tasks along with some other activities are to be performed:

1. **Saving all the computations performed in the calling function prior to the function call:** All the computations performed in the calling function prior to the function call need to be saved so that they need not be carried out again upon returning from the called function. To save all the computations performed, all the local variables declared within the calling function are saved before executing the function call. The stored values of the local variables are restored after returning from the called function.
2. **Saving the point of function call:** The point from where the function call is given is saved so that the control can return to the same point after executing the called function. The point of the function call can be saved by taking the dump of content of **registers**, specifically IP register. Instruction Pointer (IP) register is a 16-bit register that points to the memory location of the next statement to be executed. When the control returns from the called function, the content of the Instruction Pointer register is restored so that the statement next to the statement containing the function call gets executed.

Execution of these additional tasks requires some time and that is why function calls are time consuming. Transferring the control within the same function just requires the manipulation of content of the Instruction Pointer and does not require the above tasks to be carried out. Since the goto statement just manipulates the content of the Instruction Pointer and does not carry out the above-mentioned tasks, it cannot be used to transfer the control from one function to another.

35. *Inputs are given to the functions by means of arguments.* main *is also a function. Therefore, can we give inputs to the function* main *by supplying arguments?*

Yes, inputs to the function main can be given by making use of **command line arguments.**

Forward Reference: Command line arguments (Chapter 6).

Code Snippets

Determine the output of the following code snippets. Assume that the inclusion of the required standard header files has been made and there is no prototyping error due to them. Prototypes of user-defined functions are explicitly mentioned, if required.

36.
```
main()
{
    int a;
    a=printf("Hello")+printf("Readers!!");
    printf("\n%d characters printed",a);
}
```

37.
```
main()
{
    int a=10,b=20,c;
    c=add(a,b);
    printf("The result after addition is %d",c);
}
int add(int a, int b)
{
    return a+b;
}
```
38.
```
main()
{
    int add(int,int),a,b;
    a= b=10;
    printf("The result of addition is %d",add(a,b));
}
int add(int a,int b)
{
    return a+b;
}
```
39.
```
int add(int,int);
main()
{
    int a=10,b=10,c;
    c=add(a,b);
    printf("The result after addition is %d",c);
}
int add(int a, int b)
{
    return a+b;
}
```
40.
```
main()
{
    int add(int,int),a,b,c;
    a=10;b=20;
    c=add(a,b);
    printf("The result of addition is %d",add(a,b));
}
int add(int a, b)
{
      return a+b;
}
```
41.
```
main()
{
    int add(int,int),a,b,c;
    a=10; b=20;
    c=add(a,b);
    printf("The result of addition is %d",c);
    int add(int a,int b)
```

```
    {
        return a+b;
    }
}
```

42. void fun(int a)

```
{
    printf("The value of a inside fun is %d\n",a);
}
main()
{
    int a=10,b;
    b=fun(a);
    printf("The value of b after call to fun is %d",b);
}
```

43. fun(int a)

```
{
    printf("The value of a inside fun is %d",a);
}
main()
{
    int a=10,b;
    b=fun(a);
    printf("\nThe value of b after call to fun is %d",b);
}
```

44. fun(int a)

```
{
    printf("The value of a inside fun is %d\n",a);
     a+2;
}
main()
{
    int a=10,b;
    b=fun(a);
    printf("The value of b after call to fun is %d",b);
}
```

45. int add(int,int);

```
main()
{
    int a=10,b=20,c;
    c=add(a,b);
    printf("The result after addition is %d",c);
}
int add(int a, int b)
{
    a+b;
}
```

46. int add(int,int);

```
main()
```

```
{
    int a=10,b=20,c;
    c=add(a,b);
    printf("The result after addition is %d",c);
}
int add(int a, int b)
{
    a+b;
    return;
}
```

47.
```
int add(int a,int b)
{
    return a+b;
}
main()
{
    int c;
    c=add(10);
    printf("The result after addition is %d",c);
}
```

48.
```
int add(int a,int b=12)
{
    return a+b;
}
main()
{
    int c;
    c=add(10);
    printf("The result after addition is %d",c);
}
```

49.
```
int add(int a,int b=12)
{
    return a+b;
}
main()
{
    int c;
    c=add(10,20);
    printf("The result after addition is %d",c);
}
```

50.
```
int add(int a=12,int b)
{
    return a+b;
}
main()
{
    int c;
    c=add(10,20);
    printf("The result after addition is %d",c);
}
```

51.
```
int swap(int a,int b)
{
    a^=b^=a^=b;
    printf("The values of a and b in swap are %d %d\n",a,b);
}
main()
{
    int a=10,b=20;
    printf("This is illustration of pass by value\n");
    printf("The values of a and b before swap are %d %d\n",a,b);
    swap(a,b);
    printf("The values of a and b after swap are %d %d\n",a,b);
}
```

52.
```
int swap(int *a,int *b)
{
    *a^=*b^=*a^=*b;
    printf("The values of a and b in swap are %d %d\n",*a,*b);
}
main()
{
    int a=10,b=20;
    printf("This is illustration of pass by reference or address\n");
    printf("The values of a and b before swap are %d %d\n",a,b);
    swap(&a,&b);
    printf("The values of a and b after swap are %d %d\n",a,b);
}
```

53.
```
int sum_diff(int a,int b)
{
    int sum=a+b;
    int diff=a-b;
    return sum,diff;
}
main()
{
    int a=20,b=10;
    printf("Sum is %d and Difference is %d\n",sum_diff(a,b),sum_diff(a,b));
}
```

54.
```
int sum_diff(int a,int b)
{
    int sum=a+b;
    int diff=a-b;
    return sum, return diff;
}
main()
{
    int a=20,b=10;
    printf("Sum is %d and Difference is %d\n",sum_diff(a,b),sum_diff(a,b));
}
```

55.
```
int sum_diff(int a,int b)
{
    int sum=a+b;
    int diff=a-b;
    return sum;
    return diff;
}
main()
{
    int a=20,b=10;
    printf("Sum is %d and Difference is %d\n",sum_diff(a,b),sum_diff(a,b));
}
```

56.
```
sum_diff(int a,int b,int *sum,int *diff)
{
    *sum=a+b;
    *diff=a-b;
}
main()
{
    int a=20,b=10,sum,diff;
    sum_diff(a,b,&sum,&diff);
    printf("Sum is %d and Difference is %d\n",sum,diff);
}
```

57.
```
fun1()
{
    return printf("Control is in Function1\n");
}
fun2()
{
    return printf("Control is in Function2\n");
}
main()
{
    printf("%d %d",fun1(),fun2());
}
```

58.
```
fun1()
{
    return printf("Control is in Function1\n");
}
fun2()
{
    return printf("Control is in Function2\n");
}
main()
{
    printf("%d",fun1()+fun2());
}
```

59.
```
int fact(int no)
{
    if(no==1)
        return 1;
    else
        return no*fact(no-1);
}
main()
{
    int temp;
    temp=fact(4);
    printf("The value of factorial of 4 is %d", temp);
}
```
60.
```
main()
{
    printf("Infinite Recursion\n");
    main();
}
```
61.
```
check_ptr(int [2][3]);
main()
{
    int arr[2][3]={1,2,3,4,5,6};
    printf("Size of arr in function main is %d\n",sizeof(arr));
    check_ptr(arr);
}
check_ptr(int arr[2][3])
{
    printf("Size of arr in function check is %d",sizeof(arr));
}
```
62.
```
int add(int a,int b)
{
    return a+b;
}
main()
{
    int (*ptr)(int,int);
    ptr=add;
    printf("The result of addition is %d\n",ptr(2,3));
    printf("The result of addition is %d",(*ptr)(2,3));
}
```
63.
```
int add(int a,int b)
{
    return a+b;
}
int sub(int a,int b)
{
    return a-b;
}
int mul(int a,int b)
```

```
{
    return a*b;
}
int div(int a,int b)
{
    return a/b;
}
main()
{
    int (*ptr[4])(int,int)={add,sub,mul,div};
    int i;
    for(i=0;i<4;i++)
        printf("The result of called function %d is %d\n",i+1,ptr[i](10,5));
}
```

64.

```
int add(int,int);
int sub(int,int);
fun(int(*)(int,int));
main()
{
    printf("%d\n",fun(add));
    printf("%d",fun(sub));
}
fun(int (*a)(int,int))
{
    return a(2,3);
}
int add(int a,int b)
{
    return a+b;
}
int sub(int a,int b)
{
    return a-b;
}
```

65.

```
int add(int a,int b){return a+b;}
int sub(int a,int b){return a-b;}
int mult(int a,int b){return a*b;}
int div(int a,int b){return a/b;}
int (*f_returning_fps(int))(int,int);
main()
{
    int i=1, j=3, res1,res2;
    res1=f_returning_fps(i)(15,5);
    printf("Result of operation1 is %d\n",res1);
    res2=f_returning_fps(j)(15,5);
    printf("Result of operation2 is %d\n",res2);
}
int(*f_returning_fps(int a))(int,int)
```

```
{
    int (*arr[4])(int,int)={add,sub,mult,div};
    return arr[a];
}
```

Multiple-choice Questions

66. A function can return
    a. No value
    b. Only one value
    c. Two values
    d. As many values as the user likes

67. By default, the return type of a function is
    a. `char`
    b. `int`
    c. `float`
    d. `void`

68. A function can be
    a. Defined within another function
    b. Declared within another function
    c. Both defined as well as declared within another function
    d. None of these

69. Which of the following can be a possible return type of a function?
    a. Array type
    b. Function type
    c. Pointer type
    d. All of these

70. Which of the following is not a valid parameter type for a function?
    a. Array type
    b. Function type
    c. Pointer type
    d. None of these

71. A function that calls itself within its own body is called
    a. Mutually recursive
    b. Indirect recursive
    c. Direct recursive
    d. None of these

72. The changes made in the parameters in the called function are reflected to the calling function. The probable method of argument passing is:
    a. Pass by value
    b. Pass by reference
    c. Any of pass by value or pass by reference
    d. None of these

73. The method used to pass an array to a function is
    a. Value
    b. Reference
    c. Cannot be passed to functions
    d. None of these

74. Which of the following is a definite advantage of recursion over iteration?
    a. Better execution speed
    b. Saving in memory space
    c. Ease of expression
    d. None of these

75. The declaration statement `int *ptr(int,int);` declares `ptr` to be a
    a. Pointer to a function that accepts two integers and returns an integer
    b. A function that accepts two integers and returns a pointer to an integer
    c. Pointer to an array of two integers
    d. None of these

76. The execution of a program
   a. Always starts with main function
   b. Starts with the function that is defined first
   c. Can start from any function
   d. None of these

77. The type of a function depends upon
   a. Its return type
   b. Types of its parameters
   c. Its return type and types of its parameters
   d. None of these

78. The values given to a function at the time of making the function call are called
   a. Actual arguments
   b. Formal arguments
   c. Formal parameters
   d. None of these

79. The statement that is used to terminate the execution of a function is
   a. break statement
   b. return statement
   c. continue statement
   d. exit function call statement

80. main is a
   a. User-defined function
   b. Library function
   c. Pre-defined function
   d. None of these

81. In the C statement, a=f1(1,2)+f2(2,3)/f3(3,4);, the order in which functions f1, f2 and f3 are called is
   a. f1, f2, f3
   b. f2, f3, f1
   c. f3, f2, f1
   d. Random order

82 In the C statement, a=f1(1,2),f2(2,3),f3(3,4);, the order in which functions f1, f2 and f3 are called is
   a. f1, f2, f3
   b. f2, f3, f1
   c. f3, f2, f1
   d. Random order

83. In the C statement, printf("%d %d %d",f1(1,2),f2(2,3),f3(3,4));, the order in which functions f1, f2 and f3 are called is
   a. f1, f2, f3
   b. f3, f2, f1
   c. Random order
   d. The order is unspecified and is compiler dependent

84. The number of times Infinite recursion is printed by the following C program is

```
main()
{
    printf("Infinite recursion\n");
    main();
}
```

   a. Infinite number of times
   b. 32767 times
   c. Till the run-time stack does not overflow
   d. 65535 times

85. Which of the following is a variable argument function?
   a. printf
   b. puts
   c. gets
   d. strcpy

Outputs and Explanations to Code Snippets

36. HelloReaders!!
    14 characters printed

    Explanation:

    The printf function call is a valid expression. The printf function returns an integer value equal to the number of characters it prints. Hence, printf("Hello") prints Hello and returns 5. Similarly, printf("Readers!!) prints Readers!! and returns 9. The values returned by the printf functions are summed up and the final value is assigned to the integer variable a. The value of a is printed by the next printf statement.

37. Compilation error "Call to undefined function 'add' in function main()"

    Explanation:

    A function needs to be defined or declared before it is called. In the given piece of code, function add is neither defined nor declared before it is called. Hence, the compiler will not be able to perform type-checking and therefore issues an error message.

38. The result of addition is 20

    Explanation:

Backward Reference: Refer the explanation given in Answer number 3.

It is valid to declare a function within the body of some other function. The function add is declared within the body of the function main before its call. Upon invocation, function add returns the result of the addition of the values of a and b, i.e. 20. The returned result is printed by the printf function.

39. The result of addition is 20

    Explanation:

    The only constraint about the place of declaration of a function is that it should be before its call. The declaration can be either in the local scope➲ or in the global scope.➲ In the given piece of code, the function add has been declared in the global scope.

Forward Reference: Local scope and Global scope (Chapter 7).

40. Compilation error

    Explanation:

    Shorthand declaration of the parameters in the parameter list is not allowed and this leads to the compilation error. The rectified declaration of the parameter list is as follows:

    ```
    int add(int a, int b)
    {......}
    ```

41. Compilation error

    Explanation:

Backward Reference: Refer the explanation given in Answer number 3.

A function can be declared but cannot be defined within the body of some other function. In the given piece of code, function `add` is defined within the body of the function `main`. This is not valid and leads to the compilation error.

42. `Compilation error`

Explanation:

Backward Reference: Refer Section 5.3.1.1.3.1.1 (Point 2).

The return type of the function `fun` is `void`. It will not return any value. If it does not return any value, how can the returned value be assigned to `b`? Hence, writing `b=fun(a);` is erroneous and leads to the compilation error.

43. `The value of a inside fun is 10`
`The value of b after call to fun is 31`

Explanation:

The return type of the function `fun` is not specified and by default will be considered as `int`. The function `fun` is expected to return an integer value but no `return` statement is used inside its body to return a value. **If no `return` statement is used inside the body of a function to return a value, then by default it returns the content of the accumulator register (AX). The content of the accumulator register is the result of the last computation.** The `printf` function prints a string and returns a value equal to the number of characters it prints. Therfore, after the execution of `printf` function, the content of the accumulator register will be the value returned by the `printf` function, i.e. `31`. The content of the accumulator register will be returned by the function `fun`, will be assigned to the variable `b` and will be printed later.
Try changing the number of characters in the string given to the function `printf` in the function `fun` and observe the values of `b`.

The content of the accumulator register can be observed by **tracing** the program and looking at its content in the **register window**. In Borland TC 3.0, register window can be opened by going to the Window menu and invoking the Register option. In Borland TC 4.5, register window can be opened by going to the View menu and invoking the Register option.

44. `The value of a inside fun is 10`
`The value of b after call to fun is 12`

Explanation:

Backward Reference: Refer the explanation given in Answer number 43.

The last computation performed in the function `fun` is `a+2`. After the execution of this computation, content of the accumulator would be `12`. As no `return` statement is used in the function `fun`, it returns the content of the accumulator register, i.e. `12`.

45. `The result after addition is 30`

Explanation:

Since no `return` statement is present, the result of the last computation that is present in the accumulator register (i.e. result of `a+b`) is returned.

46. Compilation error

Explanation:

The first form of the return statement (i.e. return;) can only be used if the return type of the function is void. In the given code, the return type of the function add is int, so the second form of the return statement, i.e. return expression; should have been used instead of return;.

47. Compilation error "Too few parameter in call to add(int,int) in function main"

Explanation:

Function add is a fixed argument function and expects two arguments. As it is called with only one argument, i.e. 10, there is a mismatch in the number of arguments and the number of parameters. Therefore, the compiler issues an error message.

48. The result after addition is 22

Explanation:

There will be no compilation error as in Question number 47. If a function provides a default argument for a parameter, then it can be invoked with or without an argument for that parameter. In the given piece of code, the default argument (i.e. 12) is provided for the parameter b. Hence, it is not mandatory to provide an argument for the parameter b.

49. The result after addition is 30

Explanation:

If an argument corresponding to the parameter with the default argument is provided in a function call, it overrides the value of the corresponding default argument. In the given piece of code, function add is called with two arguments, i.e. 10 and 20. The value 20 overrides the default argument value. Hence, the value of b in the function add will be 20. Thus, the value returned by the function add will be 30 and it gets printed by the printf function.

50. Compilation error "Default value missing following parameter a"

Explanation:

A function declaration can specify default arguments for all or for a subset of parameters. If default arguments are specified only for the subset of parameters, then they should be specified for the parameters that lie on the trailing side. Hence, it is not possible to specify the default argument for the parameter a unless and until the default argument for the parameter b is specified.

51. This is illustration of pass by value
The values of a and b before swap are 10 20
The values of a and b in swap are 20 10
The values of a and b after swap are 10 20

Explanation:

Since the values of a and b are passed by value, the changes made in the values of the parameters inside the called function are not reflected to the calling function.

52. This is illustration of pass by reference or address
The values of a and b before swap are 10 20
The values of a and b in swap are 20 10
The values of a and b after swap are 20 10

Explanation:

Since the values of a and b are passed by reference, the changes made in the values pointed to by the parameters inside the called function are reflected to the calling function.

53. Sum is 10 and Difference is 10

Explanation:

A function can return only one value. It seems that return sum,diff; returns the value of both sum and diff. However, it is not true. In the statement return sum,diff;, the return expression sum,diff is evaluated first and then its outcome is returned. The comma operator involved in the expression guarantees left to right evaluation and returns the result of the rightmost sub-expression. Therefore, the return expression sum,diff evaluates to the result of the evaluation of diff. Hence, both the calls to function sum_diff, returns the value of diff, i.e. 10. That is why the output comes out to be Sum is 10 and Difference is 10.

54. Compilation error "Expression syntax in function main"

Explanation:

return is a statement and not an expression. It cannot be used as an operand of any operator. Writing return sum, return diff; is not valid as return statement is an operand of comma operator. It should be either return sum; return diff; or return sum, diff;.

55. Sum is 30 and Difference is 30

Explanation:

A function can have more than one return statement within its body. If more than one return statement is present inside the body of a function, only the return statement that appears first in the logical flow of control gets executed. In the given piece of code, the statement return sum; appears first in the logical flow of control. Therefore, it gets executed and the control along with the value of sum is returned to the calling function, i.e. main. The statement return diff; will never be executed and forms an unreachable part of the code. Hence, both the calls to the function sum_diff, return the value of sum, i.e. 30. That is why the output comes out to be Sum is 30 and Difference is 30.

56. Sum is 30 and Difference is 10

Explanation:

By making the use of the return statement, a function can return only one value. However, it is possible to indirectly get more than one result from a function either by using global variables➲ or pass by reference. In the given piece of code, pass by reference is used to indirectly get two outputs from the function sum_diff.

Suppose, the variables a, b, sum and diff that are local➲ to the function main are allocated at the memory locations 2000, 2002, 2004 and 2006, respectively. The parameters declared in the header of the function sum_diff are local to the function sum_diff and are allocated at separate memory locations, say 4000, 4002, 4004 and 4006 respectively. Note that the type of the variables sum and diff in the function main is int while the type of variables sum and diff in the function sum_diff is int*. The variables a and b are passed by value while the variables sum and diff are passed by reference. The passed values and the execution of statements are shown in the following figure:

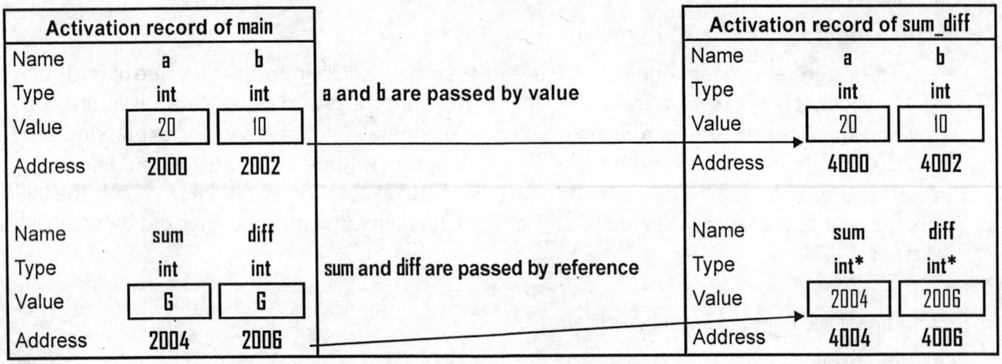

G (in the above figure) means garbage.

The variables in the statement *sum=a+b; refer to the local variables of the function sum_diff. This statement places the result of addition of a and b, i.e. 30 at the memory location 2004, i.e. in the sum variable of the function main. Similarly, *diff=a+b, places the difference of a and b, i.e. 10 at the memory location 2006, i.e. in the diff variable of the function main. In this way, the function sum_diff has indirectly returned two values to the calling function, i.e. main. Thus, reference to the variables sum and diff in the function main after the execution of the function sum_diff gives 30 and 10, respectively, instead of garbage values.

Forward Reference: Local variables and global variables (Chapter 7).

57. Control is in Function2
    Control is in Function1
    24 24

    Explanation:

    The comma operator guarantees left-to-right evaluation, but the commas separating the arguments in a function call are not comma operators. If the commas separating the arguments in a function call are considered as comma operators, then no function could have more than one argument. Hence, arguments are not guaranteed to be evaluated from left to right. The order of evaluation of arguments in a function call is unspecified and is compiler dependent. In Borland TC 3.0 and TC 4.5, the evaluation takes place from right to left.

58. Control is in Function1
    Control is in Funciton2
    48

    Explanation:

    The expression fun1()+fun2() gets evaluated first and the result of its evaluation is printed. The operands of + operator are evaluated from left to right. Hence, the function fun1 is called first and then the function fun2 is called.

59. The value of factorial of 4 is 24

    Explanation:

Backward Reference: Refer Section 5.3.1.1.7.3.1.1 for the answer.

60. Infinite Recursion
Infinite Recursion
Infinite Recursion
Infinite Recursion ...

Caution:

Keeps on printing 'Infinite Recursion' till the run-time stack does not overflow.

Explanation:

The given piece of code, if executed using Turbo C 3.0, keeps on printing 'Infinite Recursion' till the run-time stack does not overflow. The run-time stack overflows when a large number of activation records are stacked up and there is no memory space left for creating and stacking new activation records. Once the run-time stack overflow occurs, the program will terminate. That is why it is said that **'Infinite recursion will automatically terminate but infinite iteration will not'**. Note that in Turbo C 4.5, it is not allowed to call the function main from within the function main.

61. Size of arr in function main is 12
Size of arr in function check is 2 (In Borland Turbo C 4.5 the output will be 4)

Explanation:

arr declared inside the body of the function main is a two-dimensional array of integers having two rows and three columns. The parameter arr declared in the header of the function check_ptr as int arr[2][3] implicitly gets converted to int (*arr)[3], i.e. pointer to an integer array of size 3. That is why, the size occupied by arr in the function main is 12, and in the function check_ptr is 2 (as a pointer takes two bytes in Borland TC 3.0 irrespective of the data to which it points).

62. The result of addition is 5
The result of addition is 5

Explanation:

The declaration statement int(*ptr)(int,int); declares ptr as a pointer to a function that accepts two integers and returns an integer. The assignment statement ptr=add; assigns the starting address of the function add to the pointer ptr. The function add can be invoked by the means of pointer by either writing ptr(2,3); or (*ptr)(2,3);, where 2 and 3 are the values of the arguments to the function add.

63. The result of called function 1 is 15
The result of called function 2 is 5
The result of called function 3 is 50
The result of called function 4 is 2

Explanation:

The declaration statement int (*ptr[4])(int,int)={add,sub,mul,div}; declares ptr as an array of pointers to functions that accepts two integers and returns an integer. It also initializes the array locations with the starting addresses of the functions add, sub, mul and div. These functions are called in the loop by writing p[i](10,5), where 10 and 5 are the arguments to the functions. The functions called for the values of i: 0, 1, 2 and 3 are add, sub, mul and div, respectively. The values returned by these functions are then printed.

64. 5
-1

Explanation:

The declaration fun(int(*)(int,int); declares fun as a function that accepts a pointer to a function that accepts two integers and returns an integer. The return type of fun is not specified and by default would be int. In the function main, fun is called with add as an argument. This means that the starting address of the function add is passed as an argument to the parameter a of the function fun.

Within the body of the function fun, the expression a(2,3), calls the function pointed to by a with 2 and 3 as the arguments. Since a at present points to the function add, the function add is called with the arguments 2 and 3. The value returned by the function add, i.e. 5 is returned by the function fun. Therefore, 5 gets printed. In the next printf statement, the function fun is called with sub as the argument. The starting address of the function sub is passed as an argument to the parameter a of the function fun. The expression a(2,3), calls the function pointed to by a with 2 and 3 as the arguments. Since a now points to the function sub, the function sub is called with the arguments 2 and 3. The value returned by the function sub, i.e. -1 is returned by the function fun and is printed in the function main. Thus, the output.

65. Result of operation1 is 10
    Result of operation2 is 3

    Explanation:

    f_returning_fps is a function that takes an integer and returns a pointer to a function that takes two integers and returns an integer. When the function f_returning_fps is invoked with argument values i=1 and j=3, it returns pointers to the functions sub and div, respectively. The returned pointers are used to invoke the respective functions with argument values 15 and 5. The invoked functions sub and div return integer values 10 and 3, respectively. These returned values are assigned to the variables res1 and res2 and are printed by the printf function.

Answers to Multiple-choice Questions

66. b 67. b. 68. b 69. c 70. b 71. c 72. b 73. b 74. c 75. b 76. a 77. c. 78. a 79. b
80. a 81. b 82. a 83. d 84. c 85. a

Programming Exercises

Program 1 | Devise a C function that checks whether a given number is prime or not and illustrate its use

Line PE 5-1.c

```
//Function to check whether a given number is prime or not
#include<stdio.h>
int prime(int no);    //←Function declaration
main()
{
int num;
printf("Enter the number to be checked:\t");
 scanf("%d", &num);
if(prime(num)==0)
      printf("Number is not prime\n");
else
      printf("Number is prime\n");
}
int prime(int no)    //←Function definition
{
      int i;
      for(i=2;i<no;i++)
            if(no%i==0)       //←Is number divisible by any number from 2 to n-1
                  return 0;   //←if yes, number is not prime, return 0
      return 1;               //←if no, number is prime, return 1
}
```

Output window

```
Enter the number to be checked:   13
Number is prime
```

Output window (second execution)

```
Enter the number to be checked:   18
Number is not prime
```

Program 2 | Devise a C function that sums all the elements of an array. Illustrate its use

PE 5-2.c

```
//Function that sums all the elements of an array
#include<stdio.h>
int sumall(int array[], int num);     //←Function declaration
main()
{
int num, i, result, elements[20];
printf("Enter the number of elements in the array (max. 20):\t");
 scanf("%d", &num);
printf("Enter the elements:\n");
for(i=0;i<num;i++)
    scanf("%d",&elements[i]);
result=sumall(elements, num);
printf("The sum of all the elements of the array is %d",result);
}
int sumall(int array[], int num)     //←Function definition
{
    int i,sum=0;
    for(i=0;i<num;i++)
        sum=sum+array[i];
    return sum;
}
```

Output window

```
Enter the number of elements in the array (max. 20)    5
Enter the elements:
10 2 4 7 11
The sum of all the elements of the array is 34
```

Program 3 | Devise a C function that checks whether two matrices can be multiplied or not. If yes, multiply them. Illustrate the use of the developed function

PE 5-3.c

```
//Matrix Multiplication with the help of functions
#include<stdio.h>
#include<stdlib.h>
int mat_multiply(int mx1[][10], int m1, int n1, int mx2[][10], int m2, int n2, int mx3[][10]);
main()
{
int mx1[10][10], mx2[10][10], mx3[10][10]={0};
int m1, n1, m2, n2, i, j, indicator;
printf("Enter the order of matrix-1 (max. 10 by 10)\t");
scanf("%d %d",&m1, &n1);
printf("Enter the elements of matrix-1:\n");
for(i=0;i<m1;i++)
{
    for(j=0;j<n1;j++)
        scanf("%d",&mx1[i][j]);
}
printf("Enter the order of matrix-2 (max. 10 by 10)\t");
scanf("%d %d",&m2, &n2);
printf("Enter the elements of matrix-2:\n");
for(i=0;i<m2;i++)
{
    for(j=0;j<n2;j++)
        scanf("%d",&mx2[i][j]);
}
```

Output window

```
Enter the order of matrix-1 (max. 10 by 10)   2 3
Enter the elements of matrix-1:
1 2 3
4 5 6
Enter the order of matrix-2 (max. 10 by 10)   3 2
Enter  the elements of matrix-2:
1 2
3 4
5 6
The result of matrix multiplication is:
22 28
49 64
```

Output window (second execution)

```
Enter the order of matrix-1 (max. 10 by 10)   2 3
Enter the elements of matrix-1:
1 2 3
4 5 6
Enter the order of matrix-2 (max. 10 by 10)   2 2
Enter  the elements of matrix-2:
1 2
3 4
Matrices are not compatible for multiplication
```

(Contd...)

PE 5-3.c	Output window

```c
indicator=mat_multiply(mx1, m1, n1, mx2, m2, n2, mx3);
if(indicator==0)
    printf("Matrices are not compatible for multiplication\n");
else
{
printf("The result of matrix multiplication is:\n");
for(i=0;i<m1;i++)
{
    for(j=0;j<n2;j++)
        printf("%d ",mx3[i][j]);
    printf("\n");
}
}
}
int mat_multiply(int mx1[][10], int m1, int n1, int mx2[][10], int m2, int n2, int mx3[][10])
{
    int i, j, k;
    if(n1!=m2)
        return 0;
    else
    {   for(i=0;i<m1;i++)
            for(j=0;j<n2;j++)
                for(k=0;k<n1;k++)
                    mx3[i][j]=mx3[i][j]+mx1[i][k]*mx2[k][j];
            return 1;
    }
}
```

Program 4 | Merge Sort: Given a list of n elements, arrange them in an ascending order using Merge Sort

Divide-and-conquer is an algorithm design strategy. It works as follows:

1. It checks whether the given instance of problem P is small or not. The given instance is said to be small if it can be easily solved.
2. If the given instance is small, solve it and return the solution. Else, follow the next step.
3. Divide the given instance of problem into smaller sub-problems P_1, P_2, P_3....P_n.
4. Solve the smaller sub-problems recursively by applying divide-and-conquer strategy.
5. Combine the solutions for sub-problems P_1, P_2, P_3....P_n into a solution for P.

Merge Sort is a sorting algorithm that is based on divide-and-conquer strategy. Merge sort works as follows:

1. The size of the given list is determined.
2. If it is 0 or 1 (i.e. it is a small problem), then the list is already sorted. Otherwise, for the lists of the size greater than 1, follow the next step.
3. The unsorted list is divided into two halves of approximately equal size (i.e. division of problem P into P_1 and P_2).
4. The divided sub-lists are recursively sorted by applying Merge Sort.
5. The sorted sub-lists are merged back into one sorted list.

For example, Merge sort sorts the given unsorted list L as follows:

L

[0]	[1]	[2]	[3]	[4]	[5]
12	1	8	10	5	3

//←The list L is divided at midpoint into two halves L1 and L2

(Contd...)

L1 | L2

[0]	[1]	[2]	[3]	[4]	[5]
12	1	8	10	5	3

//←The list L1 is further divided at midpoint into two halves L11 and L12

L11 | L12 | L2

[0]	[1]	[2]	[3]	[4]	[5]
12	1	8	10	5	3

//←The list L11 is further divided at midpoint into two halves L111 and L112

L111 | L112 | L12 | L2

[0]	[1]	[2]	[3]	[4]	[5]
12	1	8	10	5	3

//←The lists L111 and L112 are of size 1 and are already sorted. They are merged to form the sorted list L11

L11 | L12 | L2

[0]	[1]	[2]	[3]	[4]	[5]
1	12	8	10	5	3

//←List L12 is of size 1 and is already sorted. The list L11 is also sorted. The sorted lists L11 and L12 are merged to form the sorted list L1

L1 | L2

[0]	[1]	[2]	[3]	[4]	[5]
1	8	12	10	5	3

//←The list L2 is divided at midpoint into two halves L21 and L22

L1 | L21 | L22

[0]	[1]	[2]	[3]	[4]	[5]
1	8	12	10	5	3

//←The list L21 is further divided at midpoint into two halves L211 and L212

L1 | L211 | L212 | L22

[0]	[1]	[2]	[3]	[4]	[5]
1	8	12	5	10	3

//←The lists L211 and L212 are of size 1 and are already sorted. They are merged to form the sorted list L21

L1 | L21 | L22

[0]	[1]	[2]	[3]	[4]	[5]
1	8	12	5	10	3

//←List L22 is of size 1 and is already sorted. The list L21 is also sorted. The sorted lists L21 and L22 are merged to form the sorted list L2

L1 | L2

[0]	[1]	[2]	[3]	[4]	[5]
1	8	12	3	5	10

//←Both the lists L1 and L2 are sorted. They are merged to form the sorted list L

L

[0]	[1]	[2]	[3]	[4]	[5]
1	3	5	8	10	12

(Contd...)

PE 5-4.c

```
//Merge Sort
#include<stdio.h>
int mergesort(int list[], int high, int low);
int merge(int num[], int low, int mid, int high);
main()
{
    int list[20], num, i;
    printf("Enter the number of elements (max. 20)\t");
    scanf("%d",&num);
    printf("Enter the elements:\n");
    for(i=0;i<num;i++)
        scanf("%d",&list[i]);
    mergesort(list, 0, num-1);
    printf("After sorting, elements are:\n");
    for(i=0;i<num;i++)
        printf("%d\n",list[i]);
}
int mergesort(int list[], int low, int high)
{
    int mid;
    if(low<high)
    {
        mid=(low+high)/2;
        mergesort(list, low, mid);
        mergesort(list, mid+1, high);
        merge(list, low, mid, high);
    }
}
int merge(int list[], int low, int mid, int high)
{
    int temp[20], k;
    int h=low, i=low, j=mid+1;
    while((h<=mid) && (j<=high))
    {
        if(list[h]<=list[j])
        {
            temp[i]=list[h];
            h=h+1;
        }
        else
        {
            temp[i]=list[j];
            j=j+1;
        }
        i=i+1;
    }
    if(h>mid)
        for(k=j;k<=high;k++)
        {
            temp[i]=list[k];
```

Output window

```
Enter the number of elements(max. 20)   6
Enter the elements:
12
10
5
-3
14
2
After sorting, elements are:
-3
2
5
10
12
14
```

(Contd...)

```
            i++;
        }
    else
        for(k=h;k<=mid;k++)
        {
            temp[i]=list[k];
            i++;
        }
    for(k=low;k<=high;k++)
        list[k]=temp[k];
    return 0;
}
```

Program 5 | Quick Sort: Given a list of n elements, arrange them in ascending order using Quick sort

Quick Sort is another efficient sorting algorithm that is based on the divide-and-conquer strategy. In Merge Sort, the list was divided at its midpoint into sub-lists that were independently sorted and later merged. In Quick Sort, the division into two sub-lists is made so that the sorted sub-lists do not need to be merged later. This can be accomplished by picking up an element in the list known as the **pivot element**. The elements of the list are rearranged, so that all the elements that are less than the pivot element come towards the left of the pivot element and all the elements greater than the pivot element come after it (i.e. towards its right). This rearrangement is known as **partitioning**. After partitioning, the pivot element is at its final position. The sub-list of lesser elements (i.e. towards the left of pivot element) and greater elements (i.e. towards the right of pivot element) are recursively sorted by using Quick Sort.

Partitioning:

C.A.R. Hoare, the developer of the Quick Sort algorithm, used the following approach to partition a list:

1. Consider the first element of the list as the pivot element.
2. Rearrange the elements of the list so that the pivot element is moved to its final position. This rearrangement can be done as follows:

a. Suppose the given list is:

[0]	[1]	[2]	[3]	[4]	[5]
12	1	8	10	5	3

b. At the end of the list, append an element that is greater than all the elements present in the list.

[0]	[1]	[2]	[3]	[4]	[5]	[6]
12	1	8	10	5	3	∞

c. The first element of the unsorted list is the pivot element. Take two pointers, say i and j. The pointer i points to the pivot element and the pointer j points to the appended largest element.

↓i						↓j
[0]	[1]	[2]	[3]	[4]	[5]	[6]
12	1	8	10	5	3	∞

d. Increment the pointer i, till a value greater than the pivot element is encountered. Decrement the pointer j, till a value smaller than the pivot element is encountered. If the pointer i is towards the left of pointer j (i.e. i<j), swap the values pointed to by them else swap the value pointed to by the pointer j with the pivot element. After this process, the pivot element will be at its final position.

(Contd...)

↓	↓	↓	----------			↓j↓i
[0]	[1]	[2]	[3]	[4]	[5]	[6]
12	1	8	10	5	3	∞

//←The pointer i is moved till element greater than the pivot element is encountered. Since there is no element greater than the pivot element, the pointer i will stop at the appended largest element. If ∞ would have not been appended, the pointer i would have strayed into garbage field.

					j↓	↓i
[0]	[1]	[2]	[3]	[4]	[5]	[6]
12	1	8	10	5	3	∞

//←The pointer j points to the element lesser than the pivot element.

[0]	[1]	[2]	[3]	[4]	[5]	[6]
3	1	8	10	5	12	∞

//←Since pointer j is towards the le of pointer i, swap the pivot element with the element pointed to by j. The pivot element comes to its final position.

The pivot element 12 has moved to its final position. It divides the list into two sub-lists. One containing the elements lesser than the pivot element and one containing elements greater than the pivot element (empty in this case). This clearly indicates that the divided sub-list may have a significantly different size. The divided sub-lists are recursively sorted by using Quick Sort.

PE 5-5.c

```
//Quick Sort
#include<stdio.h>
int quicksort(int list[], int high, int low);
int partition(int num[], int low, int high);
int swap(int list[], int i, int j);
main()
{
    int list[21], num, i;
    printf("Enter the number of elements (max. 20)\t");
    scanf("%d",&num);
    printf("Enter the elements:\n");
    for(i=0;i<num;i++)
        scanf("%d",&list[i]);
    list[num]=10000;
    quicksort(list, 0, num-1);
    printf("After sorting, elements are:\n");
        for(i=0;i<num;i++)
            printf("%d\n",list[i]);
}
int quicksort(int list[], int low, int high)
{
    int pos;
    if(low<high)
    {
        pos=partition(list, low, high+1);
        quicksort(list, low, pos-1);
        quicksort(list, pos+1, high);
    }
}
int partition(int list[], int low, int high)
```

Output window

```
Enter the number of elements(max. 20)   6
Enter the elements:
12
10
5
-3
14
2
After sorting, elements are:
-3
2
5
10
12
14
```

Remark:

- In the given code it is assumed that the elements entered in the array will be less than 10000

(*Contd...*)

```
{
    int v=list[low], i=low, j=high;
    do
    {
        do
        {
            i++;
        }while(list[i]<v);
        do
        {
            j--;
        }while(list[j]>v);
        if(i<j)
            swap(list, i, j);
    }while(i<j);
    list[low]=list[j];
    list[j]=v;
    return j;
}
int swap(int list[], int i, int j)
{
    int temp;
    temp=list[i];
    list[i]=list[j];
    list[j]=temp;
    return 0;
}
```

Program 6 | Binary search: Given a list of n elements arranged in ascending order and a key, find whether the given key exists in the list or not. If it exists, print its position in the list

Binary search is an efficient searching algorithm based on the divide-and-conquer strategy. It is based on the assumption that the elements of the list are arranged in an ascending order. Similar to the linear search, it works by comparing the key with the elements of the list, but with a difference in the pattern of making comparisons.

In the binary search, initially the key is compared with the element present at the middle position of the list. If both are equal, the key is found and the search is finished. If the key is less than the middle element, search the key in the list present towards the left of the middle element. If the key is greater than the middle element, search the key in the list present towards the right of the middle element.

PE 5-6.c

```
//Binary Search
#include<stdio.h>
int binarysearch(int list[], int low, int high, int key);
main()
{
int list[20], num, i, key, low, high, index;
printf("Enter the number of elements (max. 20)\t");
scanf("%d",&num);
printf("Enter the elements in ascending order:\n");
for(i=0;i<num;i++)
```

Output window

```
Enter the number of elements(max. 20)	6
Enter the elements in ascending order:
10
15
32
48
92
128
Enter the key that you want to search	48
48 exists at location no. 4
```

(Contd...)

```
    scanf("%d",&list[i]);          //←Read elements in the list
printf("Enter the key that you want to search\t");
scanf("%d",&key);                  //←Read the key to be searched
index=binarysearch(list, 0, num-1, key);
if(index==-1)
    printf("%d does not exist in the list",key);
else
    printf("%d exists at location no. %d\n",key, index+1);
}
int binarysearch(int list[], int low, int high, int key)
{
    int  mid;
    if(low==high)     //←if low==high, there is only one element
    {
        if(list[low]==key)    //←if that element is equal to key
            return low;       //←return its index
        else                  //←else key is not present in the list
            return -1;        //←return -1 as it is  not a valid index value
    }
    else
    {
        mid=(low+high)/2;   //←middle position is found
        if(list[mid]==key)   //←if element at middle position=key
            return mid;      //←return the index of middle location
        else if(list[mid]>key) //←if key<middle element, search left portion of the list
                return binarysearch(list, low, mid-1, key);
            else                  //←search the right portion of the list
                return binarysearch(list, mid+1, high, key);
    }
}
```

Output window (second execution)

```
Enter the number of elements(max. 20)   6
Enter the elements in ascending order:
10
15
32
48
92
128
Enter the key that you want to search   50
50 does not exist in the list
```

Test Yourself

1. Fill in the blanks in each of the following:
   a. ____________ help in modularizing a program into smaller simple parts.
   b. The execution of a C program always begins with function ____________.
   c. The expressions that appear within the parentheses of a function call are known as ____________.
   d. The two ways of passing arguments to a function are ____________ and ____________.
   e. The variables declared in the parameter declaration list in the function header are known as ____________.
   f. The first argument to the printf function should be of ____________ type.
   g. The return type of each math library function is ____________.
   h. The return type of a function cannot be ____________.
   i. ____________ is a special case of recursion in which the last operation of a function is a recursive call.
   j. By default, the return type of a function is ____________.
   k. Execution of each function requires a separate ____________.
   l. The activation records for all of the active functions are stored in the region of memory called ____________.
   m. The part of recursion in which a number of activation records are created and piled up is known as ____________.

2. State whether each of the following is true or false. If false, explain why.
   a. C is a strongly typed language.
   b. main is a library-defined function.
   c. There can be only one return statement within a function body.
   d. printf is an example of a variable argument function.
   e. The function designator implicitly refers to the starting address of the function.
   f. The return statement is used to terminate the execution of a program.
   g. A function can be defined within the body of another function, and the function defined within another function is known as nested function.
   h. Directly recursive functions are also known as mutually recursive functions.
   i. A function need not be declared, if it is defined before it is called.
   j. The shorthand declaration of parameters in the parameter list is not allowed.
   k. One of the uses of function prototype is in type checking.
   l. If the arguments are passed by reference, the changes made in the values pointed to by the formal parameters in the called function are reflected to the calling function.
   m. A function can return only one value.

3. Programming exercises:
   a. Write a C function that checks whether a given number is even or odd. Illustrate its use.
   b. Write a C function that checks whether a given number is perfect or not. Illustrate its use.
   c. Write a recursive C function to find the sum of individual digits of a given positive integer number.
   d. Write a C function that finds the reverse of a given number.
   e. Write a C function that checks whether a given number is a palindrome or not.
   f. Write a C function that checks whether a given number is an Armstrong number or not.
   g. Write an iterative C function to print the first n terms of a Fibonacci series. Get the value of n from the user.
   h. Write a recursive C function to print the first n terms of a Fibonacci series. Get the value of n from the user. Illustrate its use.

i. Write an iterative C function that finds the value of x^n. Get the values of x and n from the user. Illustrate its use.
j. Write a recursive C function that finds the value of x^n. Get the values of x and n from the user. Illustrate its use.
k. Write a recursive C function that implements linear search. Given a list of n elements and a key. Using the developed function, check whether the given key exists in the list or not. If yes, print the position at which it exists in the list.
l. Write an iterative C function that finds the factorial of a given integer. Use this function to find $^{n}_{r}C = \frac{n!}{r!(n-r)!}$
m. Write a recursive C function that finds the factorial of a given integer. Use this function to find $^{n}_{r}C = \frac{n!}{r!(n-r)!}$
n. Write a C function to evaluate the following series. Use a function to compute the factorials. Get the value x and the number of terms in the series from the user:

   i. $\cos(x) = 1 - \frac{x^2}{2!} + \frac{x^4}{4!} - \frac{x^6}{6!} + \cdots \infty$

   ii. $\cosh(x) = 1 + \frac{x^2}{2!} + \frac{x^4}{4!} - \frac{x^6}{6!} + \cdots \infty$

   iii. $\exp(x) = 1 + x + \frac{x^2}{2!} + \frac{x^3}{3!} + \frac{x^4}{4!} + \cdots \infty$

   iv. $e = 1 + \frac{1}{1!} + \frac{1}{2!} + \frac{1}{3!} + \ldots + \frac{1}{n!}$

o. Write a C function that finds the sum of all the elements of a matrix. Illustrate the use of this function.
p. Write a C function that checks whether a given matrix is symmetric or not. Illustrate its use.
q. Write a C function that finds the sum of elements of the principal diagonal of a matrix. Illustrate the use of this function.
r. Write a C program that extracts the lower-triangular matrix from a square matrix. Illustrate the use of the developed function in a program.
s. Write a C function that finds the largest and the smallest element in a matrix. Illustrate the use of the developed function in a program.
t. Write a C function that swaps the contents of two one-dimensional arrays. Do not use any additional storage space. Illustrate the use of the developed function in a program.
u. Given n boolean variables $x_1, x_2, x_3 \ldots\ldots x_n$. We wish to print all the possible combinations of the truth values that they can assume. For instance, if n is equal to 2, there are four possibilities 00, 01, 10 and 11. Write a C program to accomplish this task.
v. Write a C program to implement ternary search. The ternary search works on the following strategy:
   Given a sorted list of n elements in ascending order. First, test the element at the location n/3 for equality with the given key x. If they are found to be equal, print that the given key is found at the location n/3, else compare it with the element at the location 2n/3. If they are found to be equal, print that the given key is found at location 2n/3, else reduce the size of the list to one-third and search the given key in the reduced list.

6

STRINGS AND CHARACTER ARRAYS

Learning Objectives

In this chapter, you will learn about:

- Strings
- How strings are represented in C language
- The usage of character arrays to store strings
- Null character and its importance in string representation
- How to read strings from the keyboard
- How to print strings on the screen
- Various string operations like copy, compare, concatenate, etc.
- String library functions
- How to store and work with a list of strings
- Command line arguments

6.1 Introduction

The character string is one of the most useful and important data types. You have used the character strings all the way in the previous chapters, but there is still much to learn about them. The C string library provides a wide range of functions for strings like reading, writing, copying, comparing, combining, searching, etc. This chapter will add these capabilities to your programming skills.

6.2 Strings

A **character string literal constant** or just a **string literal** is a sequence of zero or more characters enclosed within double quotes. For example, "GOD Bless!!" is a string literal constant. Knowingly or unknowingly, you have used strings in abundance with the printf function in previous chapters.

The important points about the string literal constants are as follows:

1. String literals are enclosed within double quotes, whereas character literals are enclosed within single quotes, e.g. "A" is a string literal constant while 'A' is a character literal constant.
2. The used double quotes are not part of the string literal and are used only to delimit it.
3. Every string literal constant is automatically terminated by the **null character,** i.e. '\0'.

> The character constant with an ASCII value of zero is known as a **null character** and is written as '\0'.

4. Like other literal constants, string literal constants are also stored in the memory. The characters enclosed within double quotes and the terminating null character are stored in the contiguous memory locations in a similar manner as arrays are stored in the memory. Thus, a string literal constant "GOD Bless!!" will be stored in the memory as shown in Figure 6.1.

G	O	D		B	l	e	s	s	!	!	'\0'
2000	2001	2002	2003	2004	2005	2006	2007	2008	2009	2010	2011

Figure 6.1 | Storage of string literal constant "GOD Bless!!"

5. Unlike other literal constants, the amount of the memory space required for storing a string literal constant is not fixed and depends upon the number of characters present in a string literal.
6. The number of bytes required to store a string literal constant is one more than the number of characters present in it. The additional byte is required for storing the terminating null character. For example, the memory required to store the string literal "xyz" is 4 bytes. The code snippet in Program 6-1 illustrates this fact.

Prog 6-1.c

```
//Memory requirement of string literal
#include<stdio.h>
main()
{
 printf("Memory requirement of \"xyz\" is %d bytes",sizeof("xyz"));
}
```

Output window

Memory requirement of "xyz" is 4 bytes

Remarks:

- Escape sequence \" is used to print double quotes
- The additional byte is required to store the terminating null character

Program 6-1 | A program to illustrate that the memory space required by a string literal constant is one more than the number of characters in it

7. The **length of a string** is defined as the number of characters present in it. The terminating null character is not counted while determining the length of a string. For example, the length of the string literal "xyz" is 3. The code snippet in Program 6-2 verifies this fact.

Prog 6-2.c

```
//Length of string literal
#include<stdio.h>
//string.h header file is to be included for using string library functions
#include<string.h>
main()
{
printf("Length of string literal \"xyz\" is %d characters",strlen("xyz"));
}
```

Output window

Length of string literal "xyz" is 3 characters

Remarks:

- The terminating null character is not counted while determining the length of a string
- strlen is a string library function that determines the length of a string
- The prototype of the strlen function is present in the header file string.h

Program 6-2 | A program to find the length of a string

8. A string literal constant of zero length is known as an **empty string**. The empty string is written as "", i.e. no character enclosed within double quotes. Although an empty string is of zero length, it still takes 1 byte in the memory for the storage of a null character.
9. In C language, **string type** is not separately available, and **character pointers** are used to represent strings. Thus, the type of string literal (e.g. "xyz") is **const char***. The constant pointer refers to the address of the first element of the string. The strings represented and interpreted in this way are known as **C-style character strings**. The code snippet in Program 6-3 illustrates that a string literal decomposes into a pointer (const char*) pointing to the first character of the string.

Prog 6-3.c

```
//C-style character strings are represented by const char*
#include<stdio.h>
main()
{
 printf("The first character of string literal \"xyz\" is %c\n",*"xyz");
 printf("The second character of string literal \"xyz\" is %c",*("xyz"+1));
}
```

Output window

The first character of string literal "xyz" is x
The second character of string literal "xyz" is y

Remarks:

- The type of string literals is const char*
- "xyz" refers to the address of the first element of the string, i.e. the address of x
- Hence, dereferencing "xyz" outputs x

Program 6-3 | A program to illustrate that the string literal constant refers to the address of its first element

10. Since a string literal constant refers to a constant character pointer and does not have a modifiable l-value, only the operations that can be applied on constant pointers can be applied on C-style character strings. The application of any other operator on string literals that cannot be applied on constant pointers leads to 'L-value required' compilation error. The code snippet in Program 6-4 illustrates this fact.

Prog 6-4.c	Output window

//String literal refers to constant character pointer
#include<stdio.h>
main()
{
    printf("The first character of string literal \\"xyz\\" is %c",*"xyz"++);
}
	Compilation error "L-value required"
	Remarks:
	• The expression *"xyz"++ will be interpreted as *("xyz"++)
	• The application of the post-increment operator on "xyz" leads to the compilation error as "xyz" does not have a modifiable l-value

Program 6-4 | A program to illustrate that a string literal constant refers to a constant pointer and does not have a modifiable l-value

11. Since C-style character string is of `const char*` type, it can be assigned to or initialized to a character pointer variable. The following statements are valid:

```
char *string="Strings!!!";
string="Trings!!!";
```

12. Adjacent string literal constants are concatenated. This concatenation is carried out during the preprocessing phase.➲ The code snippet in Program 6-5 illustrates this fact.

Line	Prog 6-5.c	Output window

1
2
3
4
5
6
	//Adjacent string literal constants get concatenated
	#include<stdio.h>
	main()
	{
	    printf("GOD Bless " "us" "!!!");
	}
		GOD Bless us!!!
		Remark:
		• Adjacent string literal constants in line number 5 are concatenated and then printed

Program 6-5 | A program to illustrate that the adjacent string literal constants get concatenated

Forward Reference: Preprocessor directives (Chapter 8).

6.3 Character Arrays

An integer variable can store the value of an integer constant. For example, statement `int a=10;` creates a variable `a` to store an integer constant `10`. Similarly, `float` variables can store floating point constants, and character variables can be used to store character constants. Now, the question that arises here is: 'Can we create a variable that can be used to store a string literal constant?'. The answer to this question is YES! We can create variables of type `char[]` (i.e. **character arrays**) to store string constants.

The general form of a **string variable** or **a character array** declaration is:

```
<s_class_specf><type_qualifier><type_modifier>char identifier[<size_specifier>]<=initialization_list OR string literal>;
```

The important points about string variable declarations are as follows:

1. The terms enclosed within angular brackets (i.e. <>) are optional and might not be present in a declaration statement. The terms shown in **bold** are the mandatory parts of a string variable declaration.
2. Since a string variable is a character array, all the syntactic rules discussed in Chapter 4 for declaring arrays are applicable for declaring string variables as well.
3. The size specification is optional if a string variable is explicitly initialized.
4. The string variable or character array can be initialized in two different ways:

    a. **By using string literal constant:** In the declaration statement `char str[6]="Hello";` the character array or string variable `str` is initialized with a string literal constant `"Hello"`. It will be stored in the memory as shown in Figure 6.2.

    b. **By using initialization list:** The alternate way to initialize a character array is by using a list of character initializers. The declaration statement `char str[6]={'H','e','l','l','o','\0'};` initializes the locations of the character array `str` with character initializers. The character array `str` will be stored in the memory in the same way as shown in Figure 6.2.

```
char str[6]="Hello"; or char str[6]={'H','e','l','l','o','\0'};
str
```

H	e	l	l	o	\0
2000	2001	2002	2003	2004	2005

Figure 6.2 | Two different ways to initialize a string variable or a character array

When a character array is initialized with a list of character initializers, the terminating null character is to be explicitly placed but when it is initialized with a string literal constant, the terminating null character is automatically placed (if the size of the character array is one more than the length of the string literal constant).

Forward Reference: Storage class specifier (Chapter 7).

6.4 Reading Strings from the Keyboard

The user can enter strings and store them in character arrays at the run time in a similar manner as the string literal constants can be stored in the character arrays at the compile time. The methods that can be used to read strings from the user at the run time are as follows:

1. **Using `scanf` function:** The `scanf` function with `%s` format specification can be used to read a string from the user and store it in a character array. The code snippet in Program 6-6 illustrates the use of the `scanf` function to read a string from the user.

Prog 6-6.c

```
//Reading strings using the scanf function
#include<stdio.h>
main()
{
    char name[20];
    printf("Enter your name\t");
    scanf("%s",name);
    printf("Your name is %s",name);
}
```

Output window

```
Enter your name    Sam
Your name is Sam
```

Remark:

- The scanf function automatically terminates the input string with a null character, and therefore the character array should be large enough to hold the input string plus the terminating null character

Program 6-6 | A program to illustrate the use of scanf function to read a string from the user at the run time

The important points about the use of scanf function for reading strings are as follows:

a. The scanf function with %s specifier reads all the characters up to, but not including, the white-space character. For example, in Program 6-6, instead of entering the first name, enter the full name, e.g. "Sam Mine". Even on entering the full name, the output of the program would be "Your name is Sam". This happens because the scanf function reads the characters only up to the first white-space character.
   Thus, scanf function with %s specifier can be used to read single word strings like "Sam" but cannot be used to read multi-word strings like "Sam Mine".
b. The scanf function can be used to read a specific number of characters by specifying the field width. The code snippet in Program 6-7 illustrates the use of a field width specifier.

Prog 6-7.c

```
//Field width specifier and scanf function
#include<stdio.h>
main()
{
    char name[20];
    printf("Enter your name\t");
    scanf("%3s",name);
    printf("Your name is %s",name);
}
```

Output window

```
Enter your name    Samuel
Your name is Sam
```

Remarks:

- If the length of the entered string is more than the specified field width, the number of characters read will be at most equal to the field width
- The scanf function reads all characters up to, but not including, the white-space character even if the value of field width specification is more than the position of first white-space character

Program 6-7 | A program to illustrate the use of a field width specifier and the scanf function

c. The scanf function can also be used to read selected characters by making use of search sets. A **search set** defines a set of possible characters that can make up the string. The rules to write search sets are as follows:
   i. The possible set of characters making up the search set is enclosed within square brackets, e.g. [abcd]. The scanf function reads all the characters up to but not including the one that does not appear in a search set. If a search set [abcd] is used, the scanf function reads the input characters and stops when a character except a, b, c or d is encountered. The code snippet in Program 6-8 illustrates this fact.

Prog 6-8.c

```
//Search set and scanf function
#include<stdio.h>
main()
{
    char name[20];
    printf("Enter your name\t");
    scanf("%[abcd]",name);
    printf("Your name is %s",name);
}
```

Output window

```
Enter your name    daman
Your name is da
```

Remarks:

- Search sets are case sensitive
- If the specified search set is [abcd] and the entered string is Daman, no character will be read, as the character D does not belong to the search set

Program 6-8 | A program to illustrate the use of a search set and the scanf function

ii. If the first character in the bracket is a caret (i.e. ^), the search set is inverted to include all the characters (even white-space characters) except those between the brackets. For example, the search set [^abcd] searches the input for any character except a, b, c and d. The scanf function reads the input characters and stops when the characters a, b, c or d are encountered. The code snippet in Program 6-9 illustrates this fact.

Prog 6-9.c

```
//Inverted search set and scanf function
#include<stdio.h>
main()
{
    char name[20];
    printf("Enter your name\t");
    scanf("%[^abcd]",name);
    printf("Your name is %s",name);
}
```

Output window

```
Enter your name    Neha
Your name is Neh
```

Caution:

- The input will only terminate when any character specified within the brackets is encountered
- Matching process is case sensitive
- Re-execute the code and enter the name in uppercase, i.e. NEHA. The input will not terminate even on pressing enter. Enter character 'a' and then press enter. The input will terminate

Program 6-9 | A program to illustrate the use of inverted search set and the scanf function

The inverted search set can be used with the scanf function to **read a line of text.** The code snippet in Program 6-10 illustrates the use of an inverted search set to read a line of text.

Prog 6-10.c

```
//Reading a line of text using inverted search set
#include<stdio.h>
main()
{
    char line[50];
    printf("Enter a line of text:\n");
    scanf("%[^\n]",line);
    printf("The text you entered is:\n%s",line);
}
```

Output window

```
Enter a line of text:
We can change our destiny!!
The text you entered is:
We can change our destiny!!
```

Remark:

- The inverted search set [^\n] can be used to read the characters till the new line character is encountered

Program 6-10 | A program to illustrate the use of an inverted search set to read a line of text

iii. The search set can be used for including the characters that lie within a particular range. For example, the search set %[d-f] searches the input for any character that lies in the range d to f, i.e. d, e and f.

d. The scanf function automatically terminates the input string with a null character and therefore the character array should be large enough to hold the input string plus the terminating null character.

e. It is not mandatory to use ampersand, i.e. address-of operator (&) with string variable names while reading strings using the scanf function. The reason behind this relaxation is that the scanf function requires an l-value as an argument where it can store the input. Since the string variable is a character array and the name of an array refers to the address of the first element of the array, the string variable name itself refers to the l-value. However, if an address-of operator is used with the string variable name, there will be no problem since it also refers to the same address. The code snippet in Program 6-11 illustrates this fact.

Prog 6-11.c

```
//Usage of address-of operator with
//string variable is not mandatory
#include<stdio.h>
main()
{
    char name[5];
    printf("Enter your name\t");
    scanf("%s",name);
    printf("Your name is %s\n",name);
    printf("Enter your name again\t");
    scanf("%s",&name);
    printf("Your name is %s\n",name);
}
```

Memory contents

name

A	j	a	y	\0
4000	4001	4002	4003	4004

Output window

```
Enter your name     Ajay
Your name is Ajay
Enter your name again     Ajay
Your name is Ajay
```

Remarks:

- Usage of address-of operator while using a string variable with the scanf function is not mandatory
- Both name and &name refer to the same memory address, i.e. 4000

Remember:

- The difference between name and &name is that the type of name is char* while that of &name is char(*)[5]

Program 6-11 | A program to illustrate that the usage of address-of operator with a string variable is not mandatory

2. **Using getchar function:** The getchar function is used to read a character from the terminal, i.e. keyboard. The prototype of the getchar function is int getchar(void); and is available in the stdio.h header file. The getchar function reads a character from the keyboard and returns the ASCII code of the read character. Since a string is a sequence of characters, the getchar function can be called repeatedly to read a string. The code snippet in Program 6-12 illustrates the use of the getchar function to read a string.

3. **Using gets function:** Another convenient way to accept a string from the user at the run time is by using the gets library function. The prototype of the gets function is char* gets(char*); and is available in the stdio.h header file. The gets function accepts a character array or a character pointer as an argument, reads characters from the keyboard until a new line character is encountered, stores them in a character array or

in the memory location pointed by the character pointer, appends a null character to the string and returns the starting address of the location where the string is stored. The code snippet in Program 6-13 illustrates the use of the gets function.

Prog 6-12.c

```
//Iterative use of getchar function to read a string
#include<stdio.h>
main()
{
    char ch, line[50];
    int loc=0;
    printf("Enter a line of text:\n");
    while((ch=getchar())!='\n')
        line[loc++]=ch;
    line[loc]='\0';
    printf("The text you entered is:\n%s",line);
}
```

Output window

```
Enter a line of text:
We can change our destiny!!
The text you entered is:
We can change our destiny!!
```

Program 6-12 | A program to illustrate the use of the getchar function to read a string

Prog 6-13.c

```
1  //Use of gets function to read a string
2  #include<stdio.h>
3  main()
4  {
5      char plang[50];
6      printf("Enter name of a programming language\n");
7      gets(plang);
8      printf("First programming language is %s\n",plang);
9      printf("Enter name of another programming language\n");
10     printf("Second programming language is %s\n",gets(plang));
11 }
```

Output window

```
Enter name of a programming language
Visual Basic
First programming language is Visual Basic
Enter name of another programming language
Visual C#
Second programming language is Visual C#
```

Remarks:

- The gets function can be used to read multi-word strings.
- Since the gets function returns the pointer to the input string, it can be used as an argument within the printf function (as done in line number 10)

Program 6-13 | A program to illustrate the use of the gets function to read a string

The important points about the gets function are as follows:

a. Unlike the scanf function, the gets function reads the entire line of text until a new line character is encountered and does not stop upon encountering any other white-space character.
b. Thus, the gets function is suited for reading multi-word strings.

The important points about the input functions mentioned above are as follows:

a. The input functions are categorized into **buffered input functions** and **unbuffered input functions.**
b. In buffered input, the input given is kept in a temporary memory area known as the **buffer** and is transmitted to the program when the Enter key is pressed. The pressed Enter key is also transmitted to the program in the form of a new line character, which the program must handle. ➲

c. In unbuffered input, the given input is immediately transferred to the program without waiting for the Enter key to be pressed.
d. The difference between buffered and unbuffered input is depicted in Figure 6.3.

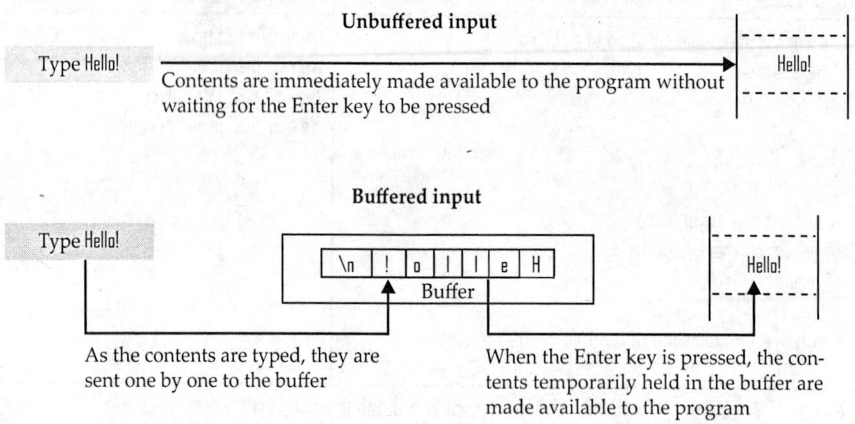

Figure 6.3 | Unbuffered and buffered input

e. The examples of buffered input functions are `scanf`, `getchar` and `gets` function.
f. The examples of unbuffered input functions are `getch` and `getche` function.
g. Program 6-12 can be rewritten using the unbuffered input function `getche` as in Program 6-14.

Prog 6-14.c

```
//Iterative use of getche function to read a string
#include<stdio.h>
#include<conio.h>
main()
{
    char ch, line[50];
    int loc=0;
    printf("Enter a line of text:\n");
    while((ch=getche())!='\r')
        line[loc++]=ch;
    line[loc]='\0';
    printf("\nThe text you entered is:\n%s",line);
}
```

Output window

```
Enter a line of text:
We can change our destiny!!
The text you entered is:
We can change our destiny!!
```

Remarks:

- The prototype of the `getche` function is present in the header file `conio.h`
- The sentinel value to be used for unbuffered input functions like `getche` is '\r', i.e. carriage return character instead of '\n', i.e. new line character that is used for buffered input functions

Program 6-14 | A program to illustrate the use of the `getche` function to read a string

Forward Reference: Refer Question number 15 and its answer to know how a program can handle the transmitted new line character.

6.5 Printing Strings on the Screen

The methods that can be used to print strings on the screen are as follows:

1. **Using printf function:** The printf function can be used to print a string literal constant, the contents of a character array and the contents of the memory locations pointed by a character pointer on the screen in two different ways:
   a. **Without using format specifier:** The printf function can print strings onto the screen without using any format specifier. The code snippet in Program 6-15 illustrates this use.

Line | Prog 6-15.c

```
1  //Printing a string with the help of printf function without using any
2  //format specifier
3  #include<stdio.h>
4  main()
5  {
6      char str[20]="Readers!!"; //Array holding string
7      char* ptr="Dear";          //Character pointer pointing to a string
8      printf("Hello");   // Printing string literal constant
9      printf(ptr)        // Printing string pointed to by a character pointer
10     printf(str);       // Printing contents of character array
11 }
```

Output window

HelloDearReaders!!

Remarks:

- The first argument of the printf function must be of type const char*
- A string literal constant and a string variable name refer to const char*
- Hence, the usage of the printf function as done in line numbers 8, 9 and 10 is perfectly valid

Program 6-15 | A program to illustrate the use of the printf function without a format specifier to print strings

The important points about this type of usage are as follows:

   i. The first argument of the printf function must be of const char* type. Since the string variable name and the string literal constant implicitly decompose into const char*, this type of usage is perfectly valid.
   ii. This type of usage however has a limitation that the contents of only one character array or the contents pointed by only one character pointer can be printed at a time.

   b. **Using %s format specifier:** The second way to print the strings on the screen is by using the printf function along with the %s format specifier. The code snippet in Program 6-16 illustrates this use.

Line | Prog 6-16.c

```
//Printing strings by using printf function along with %s
//format specifier
#include<stdio.h>
main()
{
    char str[20]="Readers!!";
    char* ptr="Dear";
    printf("%s%s%s","Hello", ptr,str);
}
```

Output window

HelloDearReaders!!

Remarks:

- %s specifier is used to print a string literal, the contents of a character array and a string literal pointed to by a character pointer
- Two or more strings can be printed by a single call to the printf function having multiple %s specifiers

Program 6-16 | A program to illustrate the use of the printf function the along with %s specifier to print strings

This type of usage has an advantage that two or more strings can be printed by a single call to the printf function having multiple %s specifiers.

2. **Iteratively printing a string's constituent characters:** A string can be printed by iteratively printing its constituent characters. They can be printed either by using the putchar function or by using the putch function. The prototype of the putchar function is int putchar(int c); and is present in the header file stdio.h. The prototype of the putch function is int putch(int c); and is present in the header file conio.h. The code snippet in Program 6-17 prints the strings by using these functions.

Line | Prog 6-17.c

```
1  //Printing string by iteratively printing its constituent characters
2  #include<stdio.h>
3  #include<conio.h>
4  main()
5  {
6     char str[20]="Hello";
7     char *ptr="Dear";
8     int i=0, j=0 ;
9     while(str[i]!='\0')
10        printf("%c",str[i++]);
11    while(*ptr!='\0')
12        putch(*ptr++);
13    while(*("Readers!!"+j)!='\0')
14    {
15        putchar(*("Readers!!"+j));
16       j++;
17    }
18 }
```

Output window

```
HelloDearReaders!!
```

Remark:

- A character can also be printed by using the printf function and the %c format specifier as shown in line number 10

Program 6-17 | A program to illustrate the printing of a string by printing its constituent characters

3. **Using puts function:** Another convenient way to print the strings on the screen is by using the puts function. The prototype of the puts function is int puts(const char*); and is available in the stdio.h header file. The puts function prints the string on the screen and returns the number of characters printed. The code snippet in Program 6-18 illustrates the use of the puts function to print strings.

Prog 6-18.c

```
//Use of puts function to print a string
#include<stdio.h>
main()
{
    char str[20]="Readers!!";
    char* ptr="Dear";
    puts("Hello");
    puts(ptr);
    puts(str);
}
```

Output window

```
Hello
Dear
Readers!!
```

Remarks:

- The argument to the puts function can be a string literal constant or a character array or a character pointer pointing to a string
- The puts function prints the string and places a new line character after the string

Program 6-18 | A program to illustrate the use of the puts function to print a string

The important points about the usage of the puts function are as follows:

i. It has a limitation that only one string can be printed at one time.
ii. The difference between the puts function and the printf function is that the puts function places a new line character after printing the string, whereas the printf function does not. Compare the outputs of Programs 6-15 and 6-18.

6.6 Importance of Terminating Null Character

The terminating null character in strings is very important. Every string operation checks the presence of the null character to determine the end of a string. Consider the piece of code snippet in Program 6-19 that illustrates the importance of terminating a null character in strings.

Line | Prog 6-19.c

```
1  //Importance of terminating null character
2  #include<stdio.h>
3  #include<string.h>
4  main()
5  {
6      char str[5]={'H','e','l','l','o'};
7      printf("The string is\t");
8      puts(str);
9      printf("Its length is %d",strlen(str));
10 }
```

Memory contents

str

H	e	l	l	o	G	G	G	G	G	\0

4000 4010

Output window

The string is   Hello□¥¤§¶
Its length is 10

Remarks:

- The printf function and the puts function print the characters starting from the memory location pointed to by its argument till the terminating null character is encountered
- In line number 6, the character array str is initialized with a list of characters and the null character is not explicitly placed at its end
- If a character array is not terminated with a null character, the output of the strlen function would be indeterminate and depends upon where the null character is present in the memory
- Thus, the puts function in line number 8 while printing str gives garbage (any arbitrary value) as it starts printing from the memory location pointed to by its argument (i.e. 4000) and keeps on printing till a terminating null character is encountered
- The number of garbage characters in the output depends upon where the first null character is encountered in the memory
- Executing the same code at different times or on different machines may give different outputs (i.e. Hello followed by different and/or different number of garbage characters)
- The strlen function determines the length of the string by counting the number of characters in the string starting from the memory location pointed to by its argument till the null character is encountered. The terminating null character is not counted while determining the length of a string

(Contd...)

Line	Prog 6-19.c	Output window
		• Thus, it is very important to explicitly place the null character at the end when a character array is initialized with the character initializers or when its content are manipulated • The null character is automatically placed at the end of a character array when it is initialized with a string literal constant or when scanf and gets functions are used to read a string from the user

Program 6-19 | A program to illustrate the importance of the terminating null character in the strings

6.7 String Library Functions

The C string library provides a large number of functions that can be used for string manipulations. The commonly used C string library functions are given in Table 6.1.

Table 6.1 | C string library functions

S. No	Function name	Prototype	Role
1.	strlen	int strlen(const char* s);	Calculates the length of a string s
2.	strcpy	char* strcpy(char* dest, const char* src);	Copies the source string str to the destination string dest
3.	strcat	char* strcat(char *dest, const char*src);	Appends a copy of the string src to the end of the string dest
4.	strcmp	int strcmp(const char*sl, const char* s2);	Compares two strings
5.	strcmpi	int strcmpi(const char*sl, const char* s2);	Compares two strings without case sensitivity
6.	strrev	char* strrev(char* s);	Reverses the content of a string s
7.	strlwr	char* strlwr(char* s);	Converts the string to lowercase
8.	strupr	char* strupr(char* s);	Converts the string to uppercase
9.	strset	char* strset(char* s, int ch);	Set all characters in a string s to the character ch
10.	strchr	char* strchr(const char* s, int c);	Scans a string for the first occurrence of a given character
11.	strrchr	char* strrchr(const char* s, int c);	Finds the last occurrence of a character c in the string s
12.	strstr	char* strstr(const char* sl, const char* s2);	Finds the first occurrence of a substring (i.e. s2) in another string (i.e. sl)
13.	strncpy	char* strncpy(char* dest, const char* src, int n);	Copies at the most n characters of the string src to the string dest
14.	strncat	char* strncat(char* dest, const char* src, int n);	Appends at the most n characters of the string src to the string dest

(Contd...)

15.	strncmp	int strncmp(const char* s1, const char* s2, int n);	Compares at the most n characters of two strings s1 and s2
16.	strncmpi	int strncmpi(const char* s1, const char* s2, int n);	Compares at the most n characters of two strings s1 and s2 without case sensitivity
17.	strnset	char* strnset(char* s, int ch, int n);	Sets the first n characters of the string s to the character ch

The following sub-sections illustrate the use of the above-mentioned string library functions along with the development of user-defined functions with the same functionality.

6.7.1 strlen Function

Role: The strlen function is used to find the length of a string.

Input: The input to the strlen function can be a string literal constant or a character array holding a string or a character pointer pointing to a string.

Output: The strlen function returns the length of the string. The terminating null character is not counted while determining the length of the string.

Usage: The code snippets in Program 6-20 illustrate the use of the strlen function and the development of the strlen functionality.

Prog 6-20a.c
Using library function

```
//Finding length of a string
#include<stdio.h>
#include<string.h>
main()
{
    char *ptr="Dear";
    char name[50]="Reader";
    printf("The length of strings:\n");
    printf("Hello is %d\n",strlen("Hello"));
    printf("Dear is %d\n",strlen(ptr));
    printf("Reader is %d\n",strlen(name));
}
```

Prog 6-20b.c
Using user-defined function

```
//Finding length of a string
#include<stdio.h>
int mystrlen(char* s);
main()
{
    char *ptr="Dear";
    char name[50]="Reader";
    printf("The length of strings:\n");
    printf("Hello is %d\n",mystrlen("Hello"));
    printf("Dear is %d\n",mystrlen(ptr));
    printf("Reader is %d\n",mystrlen(name));
}
int mystrlen(char *s)
{
int i=0;
while(*(s+i)!='\0')
    i++;
return i;
}
```

Output window

```
The length of strings:
Hello is 5
Dear is 4
Reader is 6
```

Remarks:

- The strlen function returns the number of characters that precede the terminating null character
- If a terminating null character is not present at the end of a string, the strlen function gives an arbitrary result

Program 6-20 | A program to find the length of a string (a) using a library function and (b) using a user-defined function

6.7.2 strcpy Function

Role: The strcpy function copies the source string to the destination string.

Inputs: A source string and a destination string. The source string can be a string literal or a character array or a character pointer pointing to a string. The destination should be a character array or a character pointer to the memory location in which the source string is to be copied.

Output: The strcpy function copies the source string to the destination and returns a pointer to the destination string.

Usage: The code snippets in Program 6-21 illustrate the use of the strcpy function and the development of the strcpy functionality.

Prog 6-21a.c — Using library function

```
//Copying one string to another
#include<stdio.h>
#include<string.h>
main()
{
    char src[50]="Hello";
    char dest[50];
    puts("Source string is");
    puts(src);
    strcpy(dest,src);
    puts("Destination string is");
    puts(dest);
}
```

Prog 6-21b.c — Using user-defined function

```
//Copying one string to another
#include<stdio.h>
char* mystrcpy(char* dest, const char* src);
main()
{
    char src[50]="Hello";
    char dest[50];
    puts("Source string is");
    puts(src);
    mystrcpy(dest,src);
    puts("Destination string is");
    puts(dest);
}
char* mystrcpy(char* dest, const char* src)
{
int i=0;
while(src[i]!='\0')
{
    dest[i]=src[i];
    i++;
}
//Null character should be explicitly placed at
//the end of the string.
dest[i]='\0';
return dest;
}
```

Output window

```
Source string is
Hello
Destination string is
Hello
```

Remark:

- If the number of characters in the source string is more than the number of characters that the destination can hold, a memory exception may arise

Program 6-21 | A program to copy a string (a) using a library function and (b) using a user-defined function

i The destination character array or the destination memory block to which the character pointer points should be big enough to hold the source string. If they are not big enough, a run time exception may occur. Refer Question number 12 and its answer for more details.

6.7.3 strcat Function

Role: The strcat function concatenates one string with another. It appends a source string to the destination string.

Inputs: The source string to be appended and the destination string to which the source string is to be appended. The first argument of the function strcat can be a character array or a character pointer but should not be a string literal constant.

Output: The strcat function appends a source string to the destination string and returns a pointer to the destination string.

Usage: The code snippets in Program 6-22 illustrate the use of the strcat function and the development of the strcat functionality.

Prog 6-22a.c — Using library function

```c
//Concatenating a string with another
#include<stdio.h>
#include<string.h>
main()
{
    char dest[50]="Hello";
    char src[50]="Readers!!";
    puts("The strings are::");
    puts(dest);
    puts(src);
    strcat(dest,src);
    puts("After concatenation::");
    puts(dest);
}
```

Prog 6-22b.c — Using user-defined function

```c
//Concatenating a string with another
#include<stdio.h>
char* mystrcat(char* dest, const char* src);
main()
{
    char dest[50]="Hello";
    char src[50]="Readers!!";
    puts("The strings are::");
    puts(dest);
    puts(src);
    mystrcat(dest,src);
    puts("After concatenation::");
    puts(dest);
}
char* mystrcat(char* dest, const char* src)
{
int i=0, j=0;
while(dest[i]!='\0')
    i++;
while(src[j]!='\0')
{
    dest[i]=src[j];
    i++;j++;
}
dest[i]='\0';
return dest;
}
```

Output window

```
The strings are::
Hello
Readers!!
After concatenation::
HelloReaders!!
```

Remarks:

- The length of the destination string after concatenation = the length of the destination string before concatenation plus the length of the source string
- The destination should be big enough to hold the destination string plus the source string
- If it is not big enough, the characters of the resulting string would be placed in unreserved memory and may lead to memory violation. Hence memory exception may occur

Program 6-22 | A program to concatenate a string with another (a) using a library function and (b) using a user-defined function

6.7.4 strcmp Function

Role: The strcmp function compares two strings.

Inputs: Two strings str1 and str2 that are to be compared in the form of string literal constants or character arrays or character pointers to the memory locations in which str1 and str2 are stored.

Output: The strcmp function performs the comparison of str1 and str2 character by character, starting with the first character in each string and continuing with the subsequent characters until the corresponding characters differ or until the end of the strings is reached. It returns the ASCII difference of the first dissimilar corresponding characters or zero if none of the corresponding characters in both the strings are different.

Usage: The code snippets in Program 6-23 illustrate the use of the strcmp function and the development of the strcmp functionality.

Prog 6-23a.c
Using library function

```
//Comparing two strings
#include<stdio.h>
#include<string.h>
main()
{
    char str1[20],str2[20];
    int res;
    puts("Enter string 1:");
    gets(str1);
    puts("Enter string 2:");
    gets(str2);
    res=strcmp(str1,str2);
    if(res==0)
        puts("Strings are equal");
    else
        puts("Strings are not equal");
}
```

Prog 6-23b.c
Using user-defined function

```
//Comparing two strings
#include<stdio.h>
int mystrcmp(const char* s1, const char* s2);
main()
{
    char str1[20],str2[20];
    int res;
    puts("Enter string 1:");
    gets(str1);
    puts("Enter string 2:");
    gets(str2);
    res=mystrcmp(str1,str2);
    if(res==0)
        puts("Strings are equal");
    else
        puts("Strings are not equal");
}
int mystrcmp(const char* s1, const char* s2)
{
int i=0;
while(s1[i]!='\0' || s2[i]!='\0')
{
    if(s1[i]!=s2[i])
        return(s1[i]-s2[i]);
    i++;
}
return 0;
}
```

Output window

```
Enter string 1:
Hello
Enter string 2:
Hi
Strings are not equal
```

Output window (second execution)

```
Enter string 1:
Hello
Enter string 2:
Hello
Strings are equal
```

Output window (third execution)

```
Enter string 1:
hello
Enter string 2:
HELLO
Strings are not equal
```

Remarks:

- **strcmp(str1,str2)** returns a value:
- **0** if str1 and str2 are equal, or
- **>0** if str1 is greater than str2, i.e. str1 comes after str2 in lexicographic order (i.e. dictionary order), or
- **<0** if str1 is lesser than str2 i.e. str1 comes before str2, in lexicographic order

Program 6-23 | A program to compare two strings (a) using a library function and (b) using a user-defined function

6.7.5 strcmpi Function

Role: The strcmpi function compares two strings without case sensitivity. The suffix character 'i' in strcmpi stands for ignore case.

Inputs: Two strings str1 and str2 that are to be compared, in the form of string literal constants or character arrays or character pointers to the memory locations in which str1 and str2 are stored.

Output: The strcmpi function performs a comparison of strings str1 and str2 without case sensitivity. It returns the ASCII difference of the first different corresponding characters or zero if none of the corresponding characters in both the strings are different.

Usage: The code snippets in Program 6-24 illustrate the use of the strcmpi function and the development of the strcmpi functionality.

Prog 6-24a.c
Using library function

```
//Comparing two strings without
//case sensitivity
#include<stdio.h>
#include<string.h>
main()
{
    char str1[20],str2[20];
    int res;
    puts("Enter string 1:");
    gets(str1);
    puts("Enter string 2:");
    gets(str2);
    res=strcmpi(str1,str2);
    if(res==0)
        puts("Strings are equal");
    else
        puts("Strings are not equal");
}
```

Prog 6-24b.c
Using user-defined function

```
//Comparing two strings without
//case sensitivity
#include<stdio.h>
int mystrcmpi(const char* s1, const char* s2);
main()
{
    char str1[20],str2[20];
    int res;
    puts("Enter string 1:");
    gets(str1);
    puts("Enter string 2:");
    gets(str2);
    res=mystrcmpi(str1,str2);
    if(res==0)
        puts("Strings are equal");
    else
        puts("Strings are not equal");
}
int mystrcmpi(const char* s1, const char* s2)
{
int i=0;
while(s1[i]!='\0' || s2[i]!='\0')
{
if((s1[i]==s2[i])||(s1[i]-s2[i])==32||(s1[i]-s2[i])==-32)
    i++;
else
    return(s1[i]-s2[i]);
}
return 0;
}
```

Output window

```
Enter string 1:
HELLO
Enter string 2:
hello
Strings are equal
```

Output window (second execution)

```
Enter string 1:
Hello
Enter string 2:
Hi
Strings are not equal
```

Output window (third execution)

```
Enter string 1:
hello
Enter string 2:
HELLO
Strings are equal
```

Remarks:

- The difference between the ASCII values of lowercase letters and their uppercase counterparts is 32
- For example, 'a' has an ASCII value of 97 while 'A' has an ASCII value of 65

Program 6-24 | A program to compare two strings without case sensitivity (a) using a library function and (b) using a user-defined function

6.7.6 strrev Function

Role: The strrev function reverses all the characters of a string except the terminating null character.

Input: A string in the form of a character array or a character pointer or a string literal constant.

Output: The strrev function reverses the string and returns a pointer to the reversed string.

Usage: The code snippets in Program 6-25 illustrate the use of the strrev function and the development of the strrev functionality.

Prog 6-25a.c
Using library function

```c
//Reversing the contents of a string
#include<stdio.h>
#include<string.h>
main()
{
    char str[20];
    puts("Enter a string:");
    gets(str);
    strrev(str);
    puts("After reversal, the string is:");
    puts(str);
}
```

Prog 6-25b.c
Using user-defined function

```c
//Reversing the contents of a string
#include<stdio.h>
char* mystrrev(char* s);
main()
{
    char str[20];
    puts("Enter a string:");
    gets(str);
    mystrrev(str);
    puts("After reversal, the string is:");
    puts(str);
}
char* mystrrev(char* s)
{
int i=0, j=0;
char temp;
while(s[i]!='\0')
    i++;
i--;
while(i>j)
{
    temp=s[i];
    s[i]=s[j];
    s[j]=temp;
    j++;i--;
}
return s;
}
```

Output window

```
Enter a string:
Hello
After reversal, the string is:
olleH
```

Output window (second execution)

```
Enter a string:
Hello Readers
After reversal, the string is:
sredaeR olleH
```

Remarks:

- The strrev function can also be applied on the string literals, i.e. strrev("Hello")="olleH"
- strrev(strrev("String"))="String"
- Reversal of reverse of a string is the string itself

Program 6-25 | A program that reverses contents of a string (a) using a library function and (b) using a user-defined function

6.7.7 strlwr Function

Role: The strlwr function converts all the letters in a string to lowercase.

Input: A string in the form of a character array or a character pointer or a string literal constant.

Output: It returns a pointer to the converted string.

Usage: The code snippets in Program 6-26 illustrate the use of the strlwr function and the development of the strlwr functionality.

Prog 6-26a.c
Using library function

```
//Converting all the characters of a
//string to lower case
#include<stdio.h>
#include<string.h>
main()
{
    char str[20];
    puts("Enter a string:");
    gets(str);
    strlwr(str);
    puts("Lowercase string is:");
    puts(str);
}
```

Prog 6-26b.c
Using user-defined function

```
//Converting all the characters of a
//string to lower case
#include<stdio.h>
char* mystrlwr(char* s);
main()
{
    char str[20];
    puts("Enter a string:");
    gets(str);
    mystrlwr(str);
    puts("Lowercase string is:");
    puts(str);
}
char* mystrlwr(char* s)
{
int i=0;
while(s[i]!='\0')
{
    if(s[i]>=65 && s[i]<=90)
        s[i]=s[i]+32;
    i++;
}
return s;
}
```

Output window

```
Enter a string:
HELLO
Lowercase string is:
hello
```

Output window (second execution)

```
Enter a string:
HELLO READERS!!
Lowercase string is:
hello readers!!
```

Remarks:

- Digits, special characters and white-space characters within the string remain unchanged

Program 6-26 | A program that converts all the characters of a string to lowercase (a) using a library function and (b) using a user-defined function

6.7.8 strupr Function

Role: The strupr function converts all the letters in a string to uppercase.

Input: A string in the form of a character array or a character pointer or a string literal constant.

Output: It returns a pointer to the converted string.

Usage: The code snippets in Program 6-27 illustrate the use of the strupr function and the development of the strupr functionality.

Prog 6-27a.c
Using library function

```
//Converting all the characters of a
//string to uppercase
#include<stdio.h>
#include<string.h>
main()
{
    char str[20];
    puts("Enter a string:");
    gets(str);
    strupr(str);
    puts("Uppercase string is:");
    puts(str);
}
```

Prog 6-27b.c
Using user-defined function

```
//Converting all the characters of a
//string to uppercase
#include<stdio.h>
char* mystrupr(char* s);
main()
{
    char str[20];
    puts("Enter a string:");
    gets(str);
    mystrupr(str);
    puts("Uppercase string is:");
    puts(str);
}
char* mystrupr(char* s)
{
int i=0;
while(s[i]!='\0')
{
    if(s[i]>=97 && s[i]<=122)
        s[i]=s[i]-32;
    i++;
}
return s;
}
```

Output window

```
Enter a string:
hello
Uppercase string is:
HELLO
```

Output window (second execution)

```
Enter a string:
hello readers!!
Uppercase string is:
HELLO READERS!!
```

Remark:

- Digits, special characters and white-space characters within a string remain unchanged

Program 6-27 | A program that converts all the characters of a string to uppercase (a) using a library function and (b) using a user-defined function

6.7.9 strset Function

Role: The strset function sets all characters in a string to a specific character.

Inputs: A string and a character. The string can be in the form of a character array or a character pointer or a string literal constant.

Output: The strset function sets all the characters in the string to the given character and returns a pointer to the string.

Usage: The code snippets in Program 6-28 illustrate the use of the strset function and the development of the strset functionality.

Prog 6-28a.c
Using library function

```
//Setting all the characters of a string to
//a specific character
#include<stdio.h>
#include<string.h>
main()
```

Prog 6-28b.c
Using user-defined function

```
//Setting all the characters of a string to
//a specific character
#include<stdio.h>
char* mystrset(char* s, int ch);
main()
```

Output window

```
Before using strset(), string is:
123456789
After using strset(), string is:
ccccccccc
```

(Contd...)

```
{
    char str[10]="123456789";
    char ch='c';
    puts("Before using strset(), string is:");
    puts(str);
    strset(str,ch);
    puts("After using strset(), string is:");
    puts(str);
}
```

```
{
    char str[10]="123456789";
    char ch='c';
    puts("Before using strset(), string is:");
    puts(str);
    mystrset(str,ch);
    puts("After using strset(), string is:");
    puts(str);
}
char* mystrset(char* s, int ch)
{
int i=0;
while(s[i]!='\0')
{
    s[i]=ch;
    i++;
}
return s;
}
```

Remark:

- All the characters (letters, digits, special characters and white-space characters) within a string are set to a specific character

Program 6-28 | A program that sets all the characters of a string to a specific character (a) using a library function and (b) using a user-defined function

6.7.10 strchr Function

Role: The strchr function scans a string for the first occurrence of a given character.

Inputs: A string and a character to be found in the string. The string can be in the form of a character array or a character pointer or a string literal constant.

Output: The strchr function scans the input string in the forward direction, looking for the specific character. If the character is found, it returns a pointer to the first occurrence of the character in the given string. If the character is not found it returns NULL.

Usage: The code snippets in Program 6-29 illustrate the use of the strchr function and the development of the strchr functionality.

Prog 6-29a.c — Using library function

```
//Scans a string for the first occurrence
//of a given character
#include<stdio.h>
#include<string.h>
main()
{
    char str[20], ch;
    char* ptr;
    puts("Enter a string:");
    gets(str);
```

Prog 6-29b.c — Using user-defined function

```
//Scans a string for the first occurrence
//of a given character
#include<stdio.h>
char* mystrchr(const char* s, int c);
main()
{
    char str[20], ch;
    char* ptr;
    puts("Enter a string:");
    gets(str);
```

Output window

```
Enter a string:
Hello
Enter a character to be found:
e
Located at the index 1
```

Output window (second execution)

```
Enter a string:
Hello
```

(Contd...)

Prog 6-29a.c **Using library function**	Prog 6-29b.c **Using user-defined function**	**Output window**
puts("Enter a character to be found:");	puts("Enter a character to be found:");	Enter a character to be found:
scanf("%c",&ch);	scanf("%c",&ch);	y
ptr=strchr(str,ch);	ptr=mystrchr(str,ch);	Character not found
if(ptr==NULL)	if(ptr==NULL)	**Remark:**
puts("Character not found");	puts("Character not found");	• The terminating null character is also considered to be a part of the string
else	else	
printf("Located at the index %d",ptr-str);	printf("Located at the index %d",ptr-str);	
}	}	
	char* mystrchr(const char* s, int c)	
	{	
	int i=0;	
	while(s[i]!='\0')	
	{	
	if(s[i]==c)	
	return((char*)s+i);	
	i++;	
	}	
	return NULL;	
	}	

Program 6-29 | A program that scans a string for the first occurrence of a given character (a) using a library function and (b) using a user-defined function

6.7.11 strrchr Function

Role: The strrchr function locates the last occurrence of a character in a given string.

Inputs: A string and a character to be found in the string. The string can be in the form of a character array or a character pointer or a string literal constant.

Output: The strrchr function scans the input string in the reverse direction, looking for a specific character. If the character is found, it returns a pointer to the first occurrence of the character in the given string. If the character is not found, it returns NULL.

Usage: The code snippets in Program 6-30 illustrate the use of the strrchr function and the development of the strrchr functionality.

Prog 6-30a.c **Using library function**	Prog 6-30b.c **Using user-defined function**	**Output window**
//Scans a string in the reverse direction	//Scans a string in the reverse direction	Enter a string:
//for the first occurrence of a given	//for the first occurrence of a given	Hello
//character	//character	Enter a character to be found:
#include<stdio.h>	#include<stdio.h>	o
#include<string.h>	char* mystrrchr(const char* s, int c);	Located at the index 4
main()	main()	
{	{	
char str[20], ch;	char str[20], ch;	
char* ptr;	char* ptr;	
puts("Enter a string:");	puts("Enter a string:");	

(Contd...)

Prog 6-30a (continued):

```
    gets(str);
    puts("Enter a character to be found:");
    scanf("%c",&ch);
    ptr=strrchr(str,ch);
    if(ptr==NULL)
    puts("Character not found");
    else
    printf("Located at the index %d",ptr-str);
}
```

Prog 6-30b (continued):

```
    gets(str);
    puts("Enter a character to be found:");
    scanf("%c",&ch);
    ptr=mystrrchr(str,ch);
    if(ptr==NULL)
    puts("Character not found");
    else
    printf("Located at the index %d",ptr-str);
}
char* mystrrchr(const char* s, int c)
{
int i=0;
while(s[i]!='\0')
    i++;
i--;
while(i>=0)
{
    if(s[i]==c)
        return((char*)s+i);
    i--;
}
return NULL;
}
```

Output window (second execution)

```
Enter a string:
Hello
Enter a character to be found:
y
Character not found
```

Output window (third execution)

```
Enter a string:
Hello
Enter a character to be found:
l
Located at the index 3
```

Remark:

- The terminating null character is also considered to be a part of the string

Program 6-30 | A program that scans a string in the reverse direction for the first occurrence of a given character (a) using a library function and (b) using a user-defined function

6.7.12 strstr Function

Role: The strstr function finds the first occurrence of a string in another string.

Inputs: Two strings str1 and str2. The strings can be in the form of a character array or a character pointer or a string literal constant.

Output: The strstr function finds the first occurrence of the string (i.e. str2) in the string (i.e. str1). If the string str2 is found, it returns a pointer to the position from where the string starts. If the string str2 is not found in the string str1, it returns NULL.

Usage: The code snippets in Program 6-31 illustrate the use of the strstr function and the development of the strstr functionality.

Prog 6-31a.c — Using library function

```
//Finding string within a string
#include<stdio.h>
#include<string.h>
main()
{
    char* ptr;
    char str1[20];
    char str2[20]
    puts("Enter a string:");
```

Prog 6-31b.c — Using user-defined function

```
//Finding string within a string
#include<stdio.h>
char* mystrstr(const char* s1, const char* s2);
main()
{
    char* ptr;
    char str1[20];
    char str2[20];
    puts("Enter a string:");
```

Output window

```
Enter a string:
Hello Readers!!
Enter the string to be found:
Read
Found at the index 6
Found in Readers!!
```

(Contd...)

		Output window (second execution)
`gets(str1);`	`gets(str1);`	
`puts("Enter the string to be found:");`	`puts("Enter the string to be found:");`	
`gets(str2);`	`gets(str2);`	Enter a string:
`ptr=strstr(str1,str2);`	`ptr=mystrstr(str1,str2);`	Hello Readers!!
`if(ptr==NULL)`	`if(ptr==NULL)`	Enter the string to be found:
`    puts("String not found");`	`    puts("String not found");`	Student
`else`	`else`	String not found
`{`	`{`	
`printf("Found at the index %d\n",ptr-str1);`	`printf("Found at the index %d\n",ptr-str1);`	
`printf("Found in %s",ptr);`	`printf("Found in %s",ptr);`	
`}`	`}`	
`}`	`}`	
	`char* mystrstr(const char* s1, const char* s2)`	
	`{`	
	`int i=0,j=0,k;`	
	`while(s1[i]!='\0')`	
	`{`	
	`    k=i;`	
	`    while(s2[j]!='\0')`	
	`    {`	
	`        if(s1[k]!=s2[j])`	
	`            break;`	
	`        k++;j++;`	
	`    }`	
	`    if(s2[j]=='\0')`	
	`        return (char*)s1+i;`	
	`    else`	
	`        i++;j=0;`	
	`}`	
	`return NULL;`	
	`}`	

Program 6-31 | A program that finds a string within a string (a) using a library function and (b) using a user-defined function

6.7.13 strncpy Function

Role: The strncpy function copies at the most n characters of a source string to the destination string.

Inputs: A character array or a character pointer to the memory location where the source string is to be copied (i.e. destination), the source string that is to be copied and an integer value that specifies the number of characters of the source string that is to be copied.

Output: The strncpy function copies at the most n characters of the source string to the destination and returns a pointer to the destination string.

Usage: The code snippets in Program 6-32 illustrate the use of the strncpy function and the development of the strncpy functionality.

Line	Prog 6-32a.c Using library function	Prog 6-32b.c Using user-defined function	Output window
1	//Copying at the most n characters of	//Copying at the most n characters of	Enter source string:
2	//a source string to the destination	//a source string to the destination	Hello Readers!!
3	//string	//string	Enter the value of n:
4	#include<stdio.h>	#include<stdio.h>	5
5	#include<string.h>	char* mystrncpy(char* dest, const char* src, int n);	Source string is:
6	main()	main()	Hello Readers!!
7	{	{	Destination string is:
8	char src[50];	char src[50];	Hello
9	char dest[50];	char dest[50];	**Remarks:**
10	int n;	int n;	• If the source string
11	puts("Enter source string:");	puts("Enter source string:");	contains more than n
12	gets(src);	gets(src);	characters, n charac-
13	puts("Enter the value of n:");	puts("Enter the value of n:");	ters are copied and
14	scanf("%d",&n);	scanf("%d",&n);	the null character
15	puts("Source string is:");	puts("Source string is:");	is not placed at the
16	puts(src);	puts(src);	end. The terminat-
17	strncpy(dest,src,n);	mystrncpy(dest,src,n);	ing null character
18	dest[n]='\0';	dest[n]='\0';	is to be explicitly
19	puts("Destination string is:");	puts("Destination string is:");	placed as done in
20	puts(dest);	puts(dest);	line number 18
21	}	}	• If the source string
22		char* mystrncpy(char* dest, const char* src, int n)	is shorter than n
23		{	characters, the termi-
24		int i=0;	nating null charac-
25		while(i<n)	ter is copied into the
26		{	destination string
27		if(src[i]=='\0')	**Try:**
28		{	• Comment line num-
29		dest[i]='\0';	ber 18
30		break;	• Execute the code
31		}	with the same input
32		else	and observe the gar-
33		{	bage characters in
34		dest[i]=src[i];	the output in some
35		i++;	of the executions
36		}	
37		}	
38		return dest;	
39		}	

Program 6-32 | A program that copies at most n characters of a source string to a destination string (a) using a library function and (b) using a user-defined function

6.7.14 strncat Function

Role: The strncat function concatenates a portion of one string with another. It appends at the most n characters of a source string to a destination string.

Inputs: The source string to be appended, the destination string to which the source string is to be appended and the number of characters to be appended. The destination string should be a character array or a character pointer but should not be a string literal constant.

Output: The strncat function appends at the most n characters of the source string to the destination string and returns a pointer to the destination string.

Usage: The code snippets in Program 6-33 illustrate the use of the strncat function and the development of the strncat functionality.

Prog 6-33a.c
Using library function

```
//String Concatenation
#include<stdio.h>
#include<string.h>
main()
{
    char dest[50], src[50];
    int n;
    puts("Enter strings:");
    gets(dest);
    gets(src);
    puts("Enter the value of n:");
    scanf("%d",&n);
    puts("The strings are:");
    puts(dest);
    puts(src);
    strncat(dest,src,n);
    puts("After concatenation:");
    puts(dest);
}
```

Prog 6-33b.c
Using user-defined function

```
//String Concatenation
#include<stdio.h>
char* mystrncat(char* dest, const char* src, int n);
main()
{
    char dest[50], src[50];
    int n;
    puts("Enter strings:");
    gets(dest);
    gets(src);
    puts("Enter the value of n:");
    scanf("%d",&n);
    puts("The strings are:");
    puts(dest);
    puts(src);
    mystrncat(dest,src,n);
    puts("After concatenation:");
    puts(dest);
}
char* mystrncat(char* dest, const char* src,int n)
{
int i=0, j=0,k=1;
while(dest[i]!='\0')
    i++;
while(src[j]!='\0' && k<=n)
{
    dest[i]=src[j];
    i++;j++;k++;
}
dest[i]='\0';
return dest;
}
```

Output window

```
Enter strings:
Hello
Readers!!
Enter the value of n:
7
The strings are:
Hello
Readers!!
After concatenation:
HelloReaders
```

Remarks:

- Unlike strncpy, a terminating null character is always appended to the result
- The maximum number of characters in the destination string after the execution of strncat would be the number of characters in the dest (before execution of strncat)+n+1

Program 6-33 | A program that concatenates at the most n characters of a source string with the destination string (a) using a library function and (b) using a user-defined function

6.7.15 strncmp Function

Role: The strncmp function compares a portion of two strings.

Inputs: Two strings str1 and str2 and the value of n, i.e. the number of characters to be compared.

Output: The strncmp function performs the comparison of str1 and str2, starting with the first character in each string and continuing with the subsequent characters until the corresponding characters differ or until the end of strings is reached or n characters have been compared. It returns the ASCII difference of the first dissimilar corresponding characters or zero if none of the corresponding n characters in both the strings are different.

Usage: The code snippets in Program 6-34 illustrate the use of the strncmp function and the development of the strncmp functionality.

Prog 6-34a.c
Using library function

```
//Comparing a portion of two strings
#include<stdio.h>
#include<string.h>
main()
{
    char str1[20],str2[20];
    int res, n;
    puts("Enter string 1:");
    gets(str1);
    puts("Enter string 2:");
    gets(str2);
    puts("Enter the value of n:");
    scanf("%d",&n);
    res=strncmp(str1,str2,n);
    if(res==0)
      puts("String portions are equal");
    else
      puts("String portions are not equal");
}
```

Prog 6-34b.c
Using user-defined function

```
//Comparing a portion of two strings
#include<stdio.h>
int mystrncmp(const char* s1, const char* s2, int n);
main()
{
    char str1[20],str2[20];
    int res,n;
    puts("Enter string 1:");
    gets(str1);
    puts("Enter string 2:");
    gets(str2);
    puts("Enter the value of n:");
    scanf("%d",&n);
    res=mystrncmp(str1,str2,n);
    if(res==0)
      puts("String portions are equal");
    else
      puts("String portions are not equal");
}
int mystrncmp(const char* s1, const char* s2,int n)
{
int i=0;
while((s1[i]!='\0' || s2[i]!='\0') && i<n)
{
    if(s1[i]!=s2[i])
        return(s1[i]-s2[i]);
    i++;
}
return 0;
}
```

Output window

```
Enter string 1:
Hello
Enter string 2:
Hi
Enter the value of n:
1
String portions are equal
```

Output window (second execution)

```
Enter string 1:
Hello
Enter string 2:
Hello
Enter the value of n:
4
String portions are equal
```

Output window (third execution)

```
Enter string 1:
hello
Enter string 2:
HELLO
Enter the value of n:
3
String portions are not equal
```

Program 6-34 | A program that compares a portion of two strings (a) using a library function and (b) using a user-defined function

6.7.16 strncmpi Function

Role: The strncmpi function compares a portion of two strings without case sensitivity.

Inputs: Two strings str1 and str2 and the value of n, i.e. the number of characters to be compared.

Output: The strncmpi function performs the comparison of str1 and str2 without case sensitivity, starting with the first character in each string and continuing with the subsequent characters until the corresponding characters differ or until the end of strings is reached or n characters have been compared. It returns the ASCII difference of the first different corresponding characters or zero if none of the corresponding n characters in both the strings are different.

Usage: The code snippets in Program 6-35 illustrate the use of the strncmpi function and the development of the strncmpi functionality.

Prog 6-35a.c
Using library function

```
//Comparing a portion of strings
//without case sensitivity
#include<stdio.h>
#include<string.h>
main()
{
    char str1[20],str2[20];
    int res, n;
    puts("Enter string 1:");
    gets(str1);
    puts("Enter string 2:");
    gets(str2);
    puts("Enter the value of n:");
    scanf("%d",&n);
    res=strncmpi(str1,str2,n);
if(res==0)
    puts("String portions are equal");
else
    puts("String portions are not equal");
}
```

Prog 6-35b.c
Using user-defined function

```
//Comparing a portion of strings without
//case sensitivity
#include<stdio.h>
int mystrncmpi(const char* s1, const char* s2, int n);
main()
{
    char str1[20],str2[20];
    int res,n;
    puts("Enter string 1:");
    gets(str1);
    puts("Enter string 2:");
    gets(str2);
    puts("Enter the value of n:");
    scanf("%d",&n);
    res=mystrncmpi(str1,str2,n);
    if(res==0)
      puts("String portions are equal");
    else
      puts("String portions are not equal");
}
int mystrncmpi(const char* s1, const char* s2,int n)
{
int i=0;
while((s1[i]!='\0' || s2[i]!='\0') && i<n)
{
if((s1[i]==s2[i])|| (s1[i]-s2[i])==32|| (s1[i]-s2[i])==-32)
    i++;
else
    return(s1[i]-s2[i]);
}
return 0;
}
```

Output window

```
Enter string 1:
Hello
Enter string 2:
Hi
Enter the value of n:
2
String portions are not equal
```

Output window (second execution)

```
Enter string 1:
Hello
Enter string 2:
Hello
Enter the value of n:
5
String portions are equal
```

Output window (third execution)

```
Enter string 1:
hello
Enter string 2:
HELLO
Enter the value of n:
4
String portions are equal
```

Program 6-35 | A program that compares a portion of two strings without case sensitivity (a) using a library function and (b) using a user-defined function

6.7.17 strnset Function

Role: The strnset function sets the first n characters in a string to a specific character.

Inputs: A string, a character and an integer value n.

Output: The strnset function sets the first n characters in a string to the given character and returns a pointer to the string.

Usage: The code snippets in Program 6-36 illustrate the use of the strnset function and the development of the strnset functionality

Prog 6-36a.c
Using library function

```
//Setting the first n characters of a string
//to a specific character
#include<stdio.h>
#include<string.h>
main()
{
    char str[20], ch;
    int n;
    puts("Enter the string:");
    gets(str);
    puts("Enter the character:");
    scanf("%c",&ch);
    puts("Enter the value of n:");
    scanf("%d",&n);
    puts("Before using strnset(), string is:");
    puts(str);
    strnset(str,ch,n);
    puts("After using strnset(), string is:");
    puts(str);
}
```

Prog 6-36b.c
Using user-defined function

```
//Setting the first n characters of a
//string to a specific character
#include<stdio.h>
char* mystrnset(char* s, int ch, int n);
main()
{
    char str[20], ch;
    int n;
    puts("Enter the string:");
    gets(str);
    puts("Enter the character:");
    scanf("%c",&ch);
    puts("Enter the value of n:");
    scanf("%d",&n);
    puts("Before using strnset(), string is:");
    puts(str);
    mystrnset(str,ch,n);
    puts("After using strnset(), string is:");
    puts(str);
}
char* mystrnset(char* s, int ch, int n)
{
int i=0;
while(s[i]!='\0' && i<n)
{
    s[i]=ch;
    i++;
}
return s;
}
```

Output window

```
Enter the string:
Hello Readers!!
Enter the character:
X
Enter the value of n:
6
Before using strnset(), string is:
Hello Readers!!
After using strnset(), string is:
XXXXXXReaders!!
```

Remark:

- If the length of the string is less than the value of n then the strnset function sets all the characters of the string to the specific character

Program 6-36 | A program that sets the first n characters of a string to a specific character (a) using a library function and (b) using a user-defined function

6.8 List of Strings

In the previous sections, we have seen how to store the strings in character arrays and the functions that can be used to manipulate them. However, real-time applications often require storage and manipulation of a number of strings (i.e. **list of strings**) and not only a single string. A list of strings can be stored in two ways:

1. Using an array of strings
2. Using an array of character pointers

6.8.1 Array of strings

If an application requires the storage of multiple strings, an array of strings can be used to store them. Since a string itself is stored in a one-dimensional character array, the list of strings can be stored by creating an array of one-dimensional character arrays, i.e. two-dimensional character array. Figure 6.4 depicts an array of strings.

A 2-D char array →	R	a	m	a	n	\0		←1st string
(Array of strings)	S	a	m	\0				←2nd string
	V	i	s	h	a	l	\0	←3rd string
	N	e	h	a	\0			←4th string

Figure 6.4 | Array of strings

6.8.1.1 Declaration of Array of strings

The general form of an **array of strings declaration** is:

<sclass_specifier><type_qualifier><type_modifier>**char identifier[**<row_specifier>**][column_specifier]**<=initialization_list>;

The important points about an array of strings declaration are as follows:

1. Array of strings declaration consists of char type specifier, an identifier name, row size specifier and column size specifier. The following declarations are valid:

   ```
   char array1[2][30];    //←array1 can store 2 strings of maximum 30 characters each
   char array2[5][5];     //←array2 can store 5 strings of maximum 5 characters each
   ```

2. All the syntactic rules discussed in Chapter 4 for declaring two-dimensional arrays are applicable for declaring arrays of strings as well.

3. **Initialization of array of strings:** Array of strings can be initialized in two ways:

   a. **Using string literal constants:** Using string literal constants, an array of strings can be initialized as:

   ```
   char str[][20]={
                   "Raman",
                   "Sam",
                   "Vishal",
                   "Neha"
                   };
   ```

   b. **Using a list of character initializers:** Using a list of character initializers, an array of strings can be initialized as:

```
char str[][20]={
                {'R','a','m','a','n','\0'},
                {'S','a','m','\0'},
                {'V','i','s','h','a','l','\0'},
                {'N','e','h','a','\0'}
              };
```

6.8.1.2 Reading List of Strings from the Terminal

A list of strings can be read from the terminal by iteratively calling the `gets` or `scanf` function. Program 6-37 reads a list of strings from the terminal and stores them in an array of strings.

Prog 6-37.c

```
//Reading a list of strings from the terminal
#include<stdio.h>
main()
{
    int i=0,j=0, marks[10], max;
    char students[10][20], ch;
    printf("Enter names of students and their marks:\n");
    while(1)
    {
        scanf("%s %d",students[i], &marks[i]);
        printf("Do you want to enter more(Y/N)\t");
        flushall();
        scanf("%c",&ch);
        if(ch=='Y'||ch=='y')
            i=i+1;
        else
            break;
        if(i==10)
        {
            printf("Cannot hold more names\n");
            break;
        }
    }
    max=0;
    for(j=0;j<i;j++)
        if(marks[j]>marks[max])
            max=j;
    printf("\n%s got maximum marks",students[max]);
}
```

Output window

```
Enter names of students and their marks:
Praveen 89
Do you want to enter more(Y/N)    Y
Ashok 80
Do you want to enter more(Y/N)    Y
Manish 90
Do you want to enter more(Y/N)    Y
Ameet 85
Do you want to enter more(Y/N)    N

Manish got maximum marks
```

Remarks:

- List of strings can be read by iteratively using the `gets` or `scanf` function
- The role of the `flushall` function is to flush (i.e. clear) the contents of all the streams
- Refer Question number 15 for a description on streams and the `flushall` function

Program 6-37 | A program that demonstrates a method to read a list of strings

6.8.2 Array of Character Pointers

An array of strings can also be stored by using an array of character pointers. The starting addresses of strings are stored in an array of character pointers as shown in Figure 6.5.

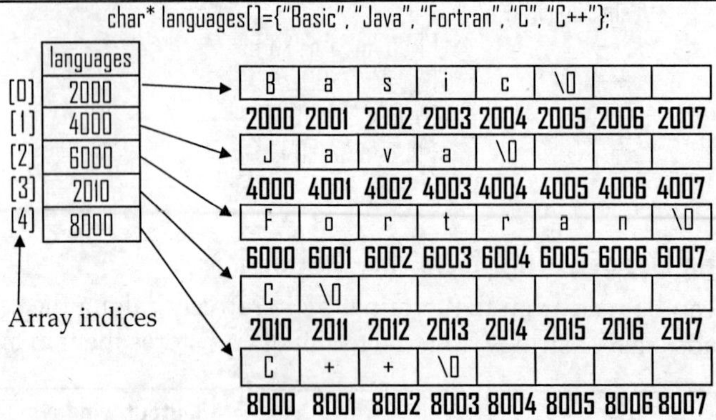

Figure 6.5 | Storing a list of strings using an array of character pointers

6.8.2.1 Use of Array of Character Pointers

Program 6-38 demonstrates the use of an array of character pointers to store a list of strings.

Line | Prog 6-38.c

```
1  //Use of array of character pointers
2  #include<stdio.h>
3  main()
4  {
5  int i,a[4];
6  char* states[]={"Punjab", "Bihar", "Rajasthan", "Gujarat"};
7  char* capitals[]={"Gandhinagar", "Chandigarh", "Jaipur", "Patna"};
8  printf("States\t\t\tCapitals\n");
9  printf("------------------------------------------\n");
10 for(i=0;i<4;i++)
11 printf("%d. %-10s\t\t%d. %s\n",i+1,states[i],i+1,capitals[i]);
12 printf("\nMatch states in Col. 1 with capitals in Col. 2\n");
13 printf("(Enter only Sr. Nos.)\n");
14 printf("------------------------------------------\n");
15 for(i=0;i<4;i++)
16 {
17  printf("Capital of state %d is at\t",i+1);
18  scanf("%d",&a[i]);
19 }
20 printf("------------------------------------------\n");
21 for(i=0;i<4;i++)
22 printf("%-11s is capital of %s\n",capitals[a[i]-1],states[i]);
23 }
```

Output window

```
States              Capitals
------------------------------------------
1. Punjab           1. Gandhinagar
2. Bihar            2. Chandigarh
3. Rajasthan        3. Jaipur
4. Gujarat          4. Patna

Match states in Col. 1 with capitals in Col. 2
(Enter only Sr. Nos.)
------------------------------------------
Capital of state 1 is at    2
Capital of state 2 is at    4
Capital of state 3 is at    3
Capital of state 4 is at    1
------------------------------------------
Chandigarh    is capital of Punjab
Patna         is capital of Bihar
Jaipur        is capital of Rajasthan
Gandhinagar   is capital of Gujarat
```

Remark:

- Lists of strings are stored using arrays of character pointers in line number 6 and 7

Program 6-38 | A program that illustrates the use of an array of character pointers

6.9 Command Line Arguments

In the previous chapter, we have seen that inputs are given to the functions by means of arguments. main is also a function. Therefore, can we give inputs to the function main also by supplying arguments? The answer to this question is YES! Inputs to the function main are given by making use of special arguments known as **command line arguments**.

If you have used DOS, you must have used copy command. The copy command looks like:

copy source_file.txt dest_file.txt

To the copy program, the name of the source file (i.e. source_file.txt) and the name of the destination file (i.e. dest_file.txt) are given as inputs. These inputs are given at the **command line** or **command prompt** and are known **command line arguments.**

C provides a fairly simple mechanism for retrieving command line arguments entered by the user at the command line. To retrieve the command line arguments, the function main should be defined as:

```
main(int argc, char* argv[])        //←Header of the function main
{
//.......Statements.......
//.......Body.....
//.......Statements........
}
```

In the header of the function main, two parameters are given, namely:

1. argc: The parameter argc stands for **argument count** and is of integer type.
2. argv: The parameter argv stands for **argument vector** and is an array of character pointers.

---

i The names of parameters are dummy and can be anything like abc, xyz, etc. but generally the names argc and argv are used.

Suppose that on the command prompt, the user has entered:

```
prog optl opt2 sfile dfile
```

The important points about the given input are as follows:

1. The command line arguments are separated by blank spaces. In the given input, there are five arguments. The name of the program file (actually executable file) will also be counted while determining the argument count.
2. The parameter argc will receive a value equal to the number of arguments specified on the command prompt. In the given example, argc will have the value 5.
3. The first argument is the name of the program file (actually executable file). The file prog.exe should be present in the current working directory.
4. The contents of the parameter argv will be:

```
argv[0]="prog"
argv[1]="optl"
argv[2]="opt2"
argv[3]="sfile"
argv[4]="dfile"
```

The contents of the array argv are shown in Figure 6.6.

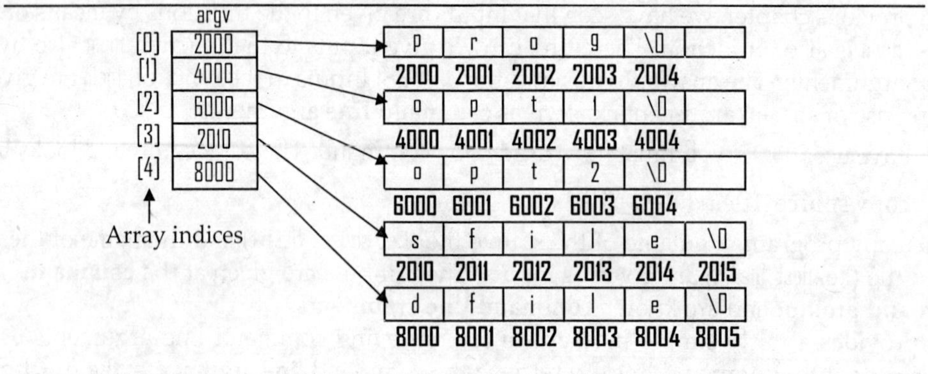

Figure 6.6 | Contents of the array argv

Program 6-39 illustrates the use of command line arguments.

Prog 6-39 mycopy.c

```
//Command line arguments
#include<stdio.h>
main(int argc, char* argv[])
{
    int i=0;
    printf("The number of arguments are %d\n", argc);
    printf("Arguments are:\n");
    for(i=0;i<argc;i++)
        printf("%s\n",argv[i]);
}
```

Command prompt

```
c:\tc\bin>mycopy source.txt dest.txt
The number of arguments are 3
Arguments are:
c:\tc\bin>mycopy.exe
source.txt
dest.txt
```

Program 6-39 | A program that illustrates the use of command line arguments

To execute Program 6-39, follow these steps:

1. Save the program with .c extension. Suppose the name given to the program file is mycopy.c.
2. Compile the program and check for compilation errors.
3. If there are no errors, build an executable file by invoking Make or Build all option in the Compile Menu of Turbo C 3.0 or by invoking Make all or Build all option in the Project menu, if using Turbo C 4.5. By default, the name of the executable file would be the same as the name of the program file. However, if a different name is given to the executable file, note it.
4. Observe the name and path of the directory in which the executable file is created.
5. Invoke the command prompt. Change the directory and make the current working directory the same as the directory in which the executable file was created.

6. Execute the program by writing the name of the executable file followed by blank separated arguments, e.g. `mycopy source.txt dest.txt`
7. If using Turbo C 3.0, the other way to execute Program 6-39 is by providing arguments from the IDE. Invoke `Arguments...` option is available in the Run Menu. Provide the arguments and execute the program. Note that if using this option, all the arguments except the name of the program file are to be provided. The name of the program is used by default and should not be specified.

Practically, the command line arguments are used in the applications that involve file handling.

Forward Reference: Files and file handling (Chapter 10).

6.10 Summary

1. A string literal is a sequence of zero or more characters enclosed within double quotes.
2. A string literal is automatically terminated by a null character.
3. A null character has an ASCII value of 0 and is written as '\0'.
4. Due to this additional null character, a string constant takes 1 byte more than the number of characters present in the string.
5. String literals are stored in character arrays.
6. In C language, string type is not separately available and character pointers are used to represent a string.
7. The type of string literal constants is `const char*`. The constant pointer refers to the address of the first character of the string.
8. Strings can be read from the keyboard by using `scanf` and `gets` functions.
9. The `scanf` function is used for reading single-word strings while the `gets` function can be used for reading multi-word strings.
10. Strings are printed on the screen by using `printf` and `puts` functions.
11. The `printf` function does not place a new line character after printing the string but the `puts` function places a new line character after printing the string.
12. The C string library provides a rich set of functionality to manipulate strings in the form of library functions like `strcpy`, `strcmp`, `strcat`, `strrev`, etc.
13. Real-time applications often require storage and processing of a number of strings at a time. A list of strings can be stored by using an array of strings or by using an array of character pointers.
14. The `main` function can also take string inputs from the command line. The arguments given to the function `main` from the command line are known as command line arguments.

Exercise Questions

Conceptual Questions and Answers

1. *What is a null character?*

   A character constant with an ASCII value of zero is known as the null character and is written as '\0'.

2. *What is a character string literal constant? How is it written and stored in the memory?*

Backward Reference: Refer Section 6.2 for a description on character string literal constants.

3. *What can the maximum number of characters in a character literal constant be?*

   The character constant can be one (e.g. 'A') or two (e.g. '\n') characters long. Hence, the maximum number of characters in a character literal constant can be two.

4. *What would be the size of the following arrays:*

```
char str1[]= "Hello";
char str2[]={'H','e','l','l','o'};
```

   The character array str1 is initialized with a character string literal constant "Hello". Since a character string literal constant is terminated by a null character '\0', the contents stored in the character array str1 will be (say array is allocated at 2000):

	str1					
	H	e	l	l	o	\0
Memory addresses →	2000	2001	2002	2003	2004	2005

   The character array str2 is initialized with the five initializers in the initialization list. Hence, the contents of str2 will be (say array is allocated at 4000):

	str2				
	H	e	l	l	o
Memory addresses →	4000	4001	4002	4003	4004

   Therefore, the size of array str1 is 6 and that of str2 is 5.

5. *What are the different ways to print character arrays?*

   The following code illustrates four different ways to print character arrays:

```
main()
{
    char character_array[]="Example";
    int i;
    printf(character_array);                    //← Way 1
    printf("\n%s\n",character_array);           //← Way 2
    puts(character_array);                      //← Way 3
    for(i=0;character_array[i]!='\0';i++)       //← Way 4
        printf("%c",character_array[i]);
}
```

   In way 1, the character array is printed without using any format specifier. The first argument of the printf function must be of type const char* and the array name character_array is implicitly converted to pointer type char*. Since the types const char* and char* are compatible, the compiler implicitly converts char* to const char*. Therefore, this usage is perfectly valid. This type of usage however has a limitation that only one character array can be printed at a time.

In way 2, the character array is printed by using a %s format specifier. This type of usage has an advantage that many character arrays can be printed by a single call to the printf function by using multiple %s specifiers. For example:

```
main()
{
    char character_array1[]="Hello";
    char character_array2[]="Readers";
    printf("%s %s",character_array1,character_array2);
}
```

In way 3, the puts function is used to print the character array. The difference between the puts and printf function is that the puts function places a new line character at the end, while the printf function does not do so.

In way 4, a for loop is used to print all the characters of the array character_array one by one.

6. *Is the declaration* char str[6]="Hello" *same as* char *str="Hello"?

   No, the declaration char str[6]="Hello"; is not the same as char *str="Hello";. The first declaration statement declares str to be a character array of size six and initializes the elements of array str with the characters of the string literal constant "Hello". However, the second declaration statement declares str to be a pointer to the character type and initializes it with the base address of string "Hello". The difference between the two declarations is shown in the figure below:

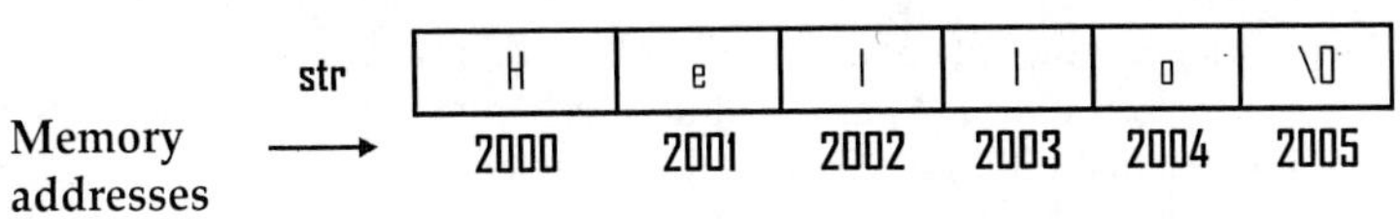

(a) char str[6]="Hello";

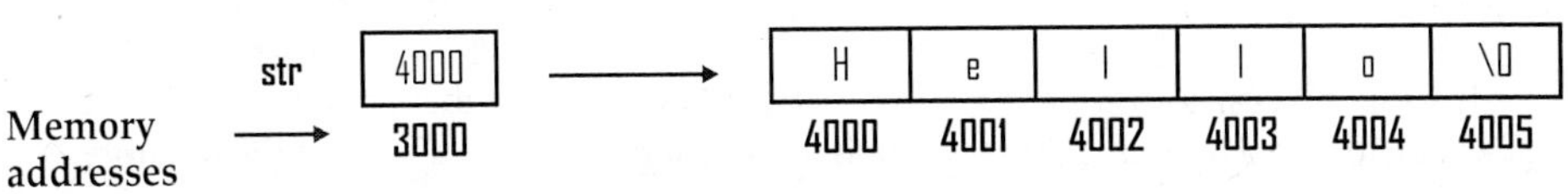

(b) char *str="Hello";

   Another difference is that the first declaration statement allocates six bytes of the memory space to str, while the second declaration allocates two bytes to str (since it is a pointer).

---

i It is very important to note that arrays are not pointers, although they are very closely related and sometimes have similar usage. For example, it is valid to write puts(str) and printf(str), where str is either declared by (a) or (b) as shown in the figure above.

---

7. *The following piece of code on execution gives some garbage. Why?*

```
main()
{
    char str[5]="Hello";
    puts(str);
}
```

The puts function outputs a sequence of characters (i.e. a string) on the screen. The output starts from the character pointed to by the pointer argument and is carried out till the null character is encountered.

The declaration char str[5]="Hello"; creates a character array of five locations and initializes the locations with the characters 'H', 'e', 'l', 'l' and 'o'. The array does not have the space to accommodate the null character. The array allocation and the memory contents are shown in the figure below:

	Array str					Unallocated memory				
str	H	e	l	l	o	G	G	G	G	G
Memory addresses →	**2000**	**2001**	**2002**	**2003**	**2004**	**2005**	**2006**	**2007**	**2008**	...

The function call puts(str) prints the characters starting from location 2000 till the null character is encountered. Since the character array str does not have the terminating null character, the output will be **Hello followed by some garbage characters.** The number of garbage characters depends upon where the null character (i.e. 0 value) is encountered in the memory. Execution of the same code at different times or on different machines may give a different number of garbage characters.

8. *Will the following piece of code also give some garbage as the previous code does?*

```
main()
{
    char *str="Hello";
    puts(str);
}
```

No, the mentioned piece of code outputs Hello and does not give any garbage character. The declaration char* str="Hello"; creates str as a 'pointer to character' and initializes it with the base addresses of string literal constant "Hello". This can be depicted as:

str	4000	→	H	e	l	l	o	\0
Memory addresses →	**2000**		**4000**	**4001**	**4002**	**4003**	**4004**	**4005**

The function call puts(str) starts printing the characters from the memory location 4000 till the null character is encountered. Since there is a null character '\0' available at the memory location 4005, the output will be Hello only without any garbage.

9. *Why does the following piece of code not work? Rectify it.*

```
main()
{
  char string[15]="Hello Readers";
  strcat(string,'!');
  puts(string);
}
```

The following piece of code on compilation gives 'Cannot convert char to char*' error. The error is due to the fact that the strcat function expects two arguments of type char* (i.e. both the arguments should be strings). In the function call, strcat(string,'!'); the second argument is a character (i.e. of type char) and is not a string (i.e. of type char*). The conversion from type 'char to char*' is not a standard conversion, hence, the compiler will not carry it out implicitly and flags it as an error. The rectified call to the strcat function is strcat(string,"!");.

10. *What is the difference between* strchr *and* strrchr *functions?*

Backward Reference: Refer Sections 6.7.10 and 6.7.11 for a description on strchr and strrchr functions.

11. *Describe the behavior of the* scanf *function when applied on strings.*

Backward Reference: Refer Section 6.4 for a description on the behavior of the scanf function when applied on strings.

12. *The following piece of code compiles successfully. However, on execution gives an exception. Why? Rectify it.*

```
main()
{
    char *str;
    printf("Enter a string\t");
    gets(str);
    printf("The string entered was\t");
    puts(str);
}
```

The given code on execution gives an exception because before calling the gets function we have not allocated sufficient memory space to store the string entered by the user. There will be no compilation error because the gets function has no way to check whether the memory space pointed to by str is allocated or not.

The following are the rectified pieces of equivalent code:

Rectified code 1

```
#include<stdio.h>
main()
{
    char str[10];
    printf("Enter a string\t");
    gets(str);
    printf("The entered string was\t");
    puts(str);
}
```

Rectified code 2

```
#include<stdio.h>
#include<alloc.h>
main()
{
    char *str=(char*)malloc(10);
    printf("Enter a string\t");
    gets(str);
    printf("The entered string was\t");
    puts(str);
}
```

In the rectified code 1, str has been declared to be a character array of size 10. Hence, 10 bytes are allocated to str at the compile time. In the rectified code 2, the **malloc** (i.e. memory allocate) function is used to allocate 10 bytes of memory. malloc function returns a void pointer to the allocated memory space. The void* is type casted to char* and is assigned to str, i.e. str is made to point to the allocated memory space.

Some of the compilers like GNU GCC compiler, Borland Turbo C 3.0, etc. may not generate an exception, if the uninitialized pointer like str is used with the gets function.

13. *What would be the output of the following piece of code?*

```
main()
{
    char str[10]="ab\n\tcd";
```

```
    printf("Size of string is %d",strlen(str));
}
```

The given piece of code on execution outputs:

Size of string is 6

Character sequences like \n are interpreted at the compile time. When a backslash and an adjacent character n appear in a character constant or a string literal constant, they are immediately translated into a single new line character, i.e. one token. Similar translations also occur for other character escape sequences like \t, \b, \r, etc.

Hence, the string literal constant "ab\n\tcd" has six characters namely 'a', 'b','\n', i.e. new line character, '\t,' i.e. tab character, 'c' and 'd'.

14. *Consider the following piece of code:*

```
main()
{
    char str[10];
    gets(str);
    printf("Size of string is %d",strlen(str));
}
```

What would the output of the mentioned piece of code be, if the user entered the same string as in the previous question, i.e. "ab\n\tcd"*?*

On execution of the code, if the user enters the string "ab\n\tcd", the output of the code would be:

Size of string is 8

The output of this code is different from the output of the previous question because of the fact that when strings are taken from the user or read from a file at the run time, no interpretation of character sequences like \n, \t, etc. is performed. '\' and 'n' are treated as separate characters and are not transformed into single characters. The same is true for other escape sequences.

Hence, the string "ab\n\tcd" entered by the user at the run time has eight characters namely 'a', 'b','\', 'n', '\', 't', 'c' and 'd'.

15 *Consider the following piece of code:*

```
main()
{
    char str1[20],str2[20];
    printf("This code demonstrates two different ways to read strings\n");
    printf("Enter string 1\t");
    scanf("%s",str1);
    printf("Enter string 2\t");
    gets(str2);
    printf("\nThe strings entered were\n");
    puts(str2);
    puts(str1);
}
```

On execution, the code does not use the prompt to enter string 2 and directly starts printing the strings. Why?

The reason behind this behavior can be understood by learning how input and output are done in C. All the input and output in C are done with **streams.** A **stream** can be thought of as a buffer from which a sequence of data elements is made available during input or to which a sequence of data elements is written during output. The figure shown below depicts how input and output are done by means of input and output streams.

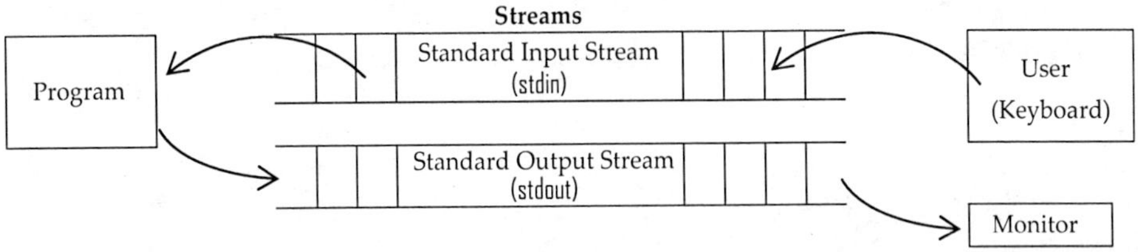

All the input functions like scanf, gets, getc etc. read from the **standard input stream** stdin and prompt the user to enter the data only if the stream is empty. If the stream already contains data or some characters, the input function will not prompt the user and silently retrieves the already available characters from the stream.
Suppose on execution of the given code, the user typed Hello and pressed the Enter key. The contents entered into the standard input stream are shown in the figure below.

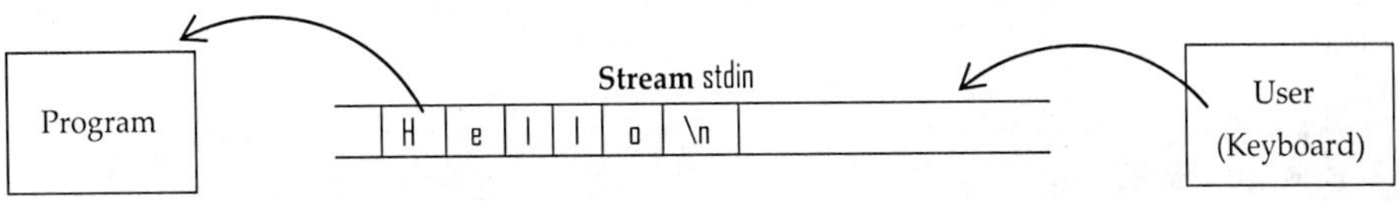

The scanf function retrieves all the characters from stdin up to but not including the white-space character. Hence, after the execution of the function call scanf("%s",str1);, Hello is removed from stdin and is stored in str1 but the new line character still remains in the stream stdin. The call to the function gets(str2); finds the new line character in the stream. That is why it does not prompt the user to make input. It silently removes that new line character from stdin and stores it in str2.
This problem can be solved by removing the new line character from the stdin stream before giving call to the gets function. This can be done either by calling function flushall(); or fflush(stdin);. The rectified piece of code is as follows:

```
main()
{
   char str1[20],str2[20];
   printf("This code demonstrates two different ways to read strings\n");
   printf("Enter string 1\t");
   scanf("%s",str1);
   printf("Enter string 2\t");
   flushall();  //flushall(); flushes all the streams
                //or fflush(stdin); flushes only stdin stream.
   gets(str2);
   printf("\nThe strings entered were\n");
   puts(str2);
   puts(str1);
}
```

Code Snippets

Determine the output of the following code snippets. Assume that the inclusion of the required header files has been made and there is no prototyping error due to them.

16.
```
main()
{
   char str1[]= "Strings";
   char str2[]={'S','t','r','i','n','g','s'};
```

```
        puts(str1);
        puts(str2);
    }
17. main()
    {
        char str[]="Strings";
        int i;
        for(i=0;str[i];i++)
        printf("%c",str[i]);
    }
18. main()
    {
        printf("%d %d",sizeof('A'),sizeof("A"));
    }
19. main()
    {
        char str1[]="Hello";
        char *str2="Hello";
        printf("%d %d\n",sizeof(str1),sizeof(str2));
        printf("%d %d",sizeof(*str1),sizeof(*str2));
    }
20. main()
    {
        char str[]="Characters";
        printf("%d %d",strlen(str) ,sizeof(str));
    }
21. main()
    {
        char str1[]="Hello";
        char str2[]="Readers!";
        printf("Hello ""Readers!""\n");
        puts("Hello ""Readers!");
        printf("%s %s",str1,str2);
    }
22. main()
    {
        char str1[]="Hello";
        char str2[]="Readers!",
        puts(str1,str2);
    }
23. main()
    {
        char str1[]="Hello";
        char str2[]="Readers!";
        puts((str1,str2));
    }
24. main()
    {
        char *str;
```

```
    str="Hello","Readers!";
    puts(str);
}
```

25. main()

```
{
    char *str;
    str=("Hello","Readers!");
    puts(str);
}
```

26. main()

```
{
    char str1[]="Hello";
    char str2[]="Readers!";
    printf(str1,str2);
}
```

27. main()

```
{
    char str[]="HelloReaders!";
    printf("%s %s %s",&str[5],&5[str],str+5);
}
```

28. main()

```
{
    char str[]="Hello Readers!";
    printf("%c %c %c",str[6],6[str],*(str+6));
}
```

29. main()

```
{
    printf("Hello Readers!"+6);
}
```

30. main()

```
{
    putchar("Hello Readers!"[6]);
    putchar(6["Hello Readers!"]);
}
```

31. main()

```
{
    printf("The size of string is %d\n",sizeof("Hello Readers!"));
    printf("The string is allocated memory starting at %p",&"Hello Readers!");
}
```

32. main()

```
{
    char str1[]="Strings!";
    char str2[]="Strings!";
    if(str1==str2)
        printf("Strings are same!!");
    else
        printf("Strings are different!!");
}
```

33. main()
```
{
    char str1[]="Strings!";
    char str2[]="Strings!";
    if(strcmp(str1,str2)==0)
        printf("Strings are same!!");
    else
        printf("Strings are different!!");
}
```
34. main()
```
{
    char str1[]="strings!";
    char str2[]="STRINGS!";
    if(strcmp(str1,str2)==0)
        printf("Strings are same!!");
    else
        printf("Strings are different!!");
}
```
35. main()
```
{
    char str1[]="strings!";
    char str2[]="STRINGS!";
    if(strcmpi(str1,str2)==0)
        printf("Strings are same!!");
    else
        printf("Strings are different!!");
}
```
36. main()
```
{
    if(strcmp("Strings","Strings\0"))
        printf("Strings are different!!");
    else
        printf("Strings are same!!");
}
```
37. main()
```
{
    char str1[]={'S','t','r','i','n','g','s'};
    char str2[]="Strings";
    if(strcmp(str1,str2))
        printf("Strings are different!!");
    else
    printf("Strings are same!!");
}
```
38. main()
```
{
    char format[]="%d\n";
    format[1]='c';
```

```
    printf(format,65);
}
```

39. main()

```
{
    char format[]={37,111,32,37,120,0};
    printf(format,format[0],format[1]);
}
```

40. main()

```
{
    char str1[]="Strings";
    char str2[10];
    str2=str1;
    puts(str1);
    puts(str2);
}
```

41. main()

```
{
    char src[]="Strings";
    char dest[10];
    strcpy(dest,src);
    puts(src);
    puts(dest);
}
```

42. main()

```
{
    char dest[]="Visual Basic";
    char src[]="C++";
    puts(strcpy(&dest[7],src));
}
```

43. main()

```
{
    char dest[]="Visual Basic";
    char src[]="C++";
    strcpy(&dest[7],src);
    puts(dest);
}
```

44. main()

```
{
    char dest[]="Visual Basic";
    char src[]="Visual C++";
    strcpy(&dest[7],&src[7]);
    puts(dest);
}
```

45. main()

```
{
    if(printf("\0"))
        printf("Characters");
    else
```

```
        printf("Strings");
    }
```

46. main()

```
    {
        char cities[][11]={"Delhi","Chandigarh","Noida"};
        int i;
        for(i=0;i<3;i++)
            puts(cities[i]);
    }
```

47. main()

```
    {
        char languages[5][20]={"Visual Basic","Java","Fortran","C","C++"};
        int i; char *t;
        t=languages[3];
        languages[3]=languages[4];
        languages[4]=t;
        for (i=0;i<=4;i++)
            printf("%s\n",languages[i]);
    }
```

48. main()

```
    {
        char *languages[]={"Basic","Java","Fortran","C","C++"};
        int i; char *t;
        t=languages[3];
        languages[3]=languages[4];
        languages[4]=t;
        for (i=0;i<=4;i++)
            printf("%s\n",languages[i]);
    }
```

49. main()

```
    {
        char lang[5][20]={"Visual Basic","Java","Fortran","C","C++"};
        int i; char *t;
        t=lang[0];
        while(*t++!=32);
            for(i=0;i<5;i++)
            {
                puts(lang[0]);
                strcpy(t,lang[i+1]);
            }
    }
```

50. main()

```
    {
        int i,len;
        char *ptr="String";
        len=strlen(ptr);
        for(i=0;i<len;i++)
```

```
    {
        puts(ptr);
        ptr++;
    }
}
```

51.
```
string_manipulation(char[][]);
main()
{
    char arr[][10]={"Hello","Students"};
    string_manipulation(arr);
    printf("%s %s",arr[0],arr[1]);
}
string_manipulation(char arr[][])
{
    strcpy(arr[1],"Readers!!");
}
```

52.
```
string_manipulation(char(*)[10]);
main()
{
    char arr[][10]={"Hello","Students"};
    string_manipulation(arr);
    printf("%s %s",arr[0],arr[1]);
}
string_manipulation(char (*arr)[10])
{
    strcpy(arr[1],"Readers!!");
}
```

53.
```
string_manipulation(char[][10]);
main()
{
    char arr[][10]={"Hello","Students"};
    string_manipulation(arr);
    printf("%s %s",arr[0],arr[1]);
}
string_manipulation(char arr[][10])
{
    strcpy(arr[1],"Readers!!");
}
```

54.
```
char[20] print_string()
{
    char str[20]="Strings!!";
    return str;
}
main()
{
 puts(print_string());
}
```

55.
```
main(int argc,char*argv[])
{
    int i;
    printf("The argument count is %d\n",argc);
    printf("The content of argument vector i.e. array is\n");
    for(i=0;i<argc;i++)
        printf("%s\n",argv[i]);
}
```

Suppose the name of the program file is ques55.c *and the executable file* ques55.exe *is invoked from the command prompt as follows:*

c:\>ques55 Hello Readers!!

Multiple-choice Questions

56. The maximum number of characters in a character literal constant can be

   a. One
   b. Two
   c. Three
   d. As many as the user likes

57. The size occupied by a string literal constant in the memory is

   a. One more than the number of characters in the string
   b. Same as the number of characters in the string
   c. One less than the number of characters in the string
   d. None of these

58. The value returned by the strlen function when a string literal constant is given to it as an argument is

   a. One more than the number of characters in the string argument
   b. Same as the number of characters in the string argument
   c. One less than the number of characters in the string argument
   d. None of these

59. String literal constants are terminated by

   a. New line character
   b. Carriage return character
   c. Null character
   d. None of these

60. The ASCII code of the null character is

   a. 32
   b. 27
   c. 13
   d. 0

61. The output of the statement printf("%d","123456"[1]); is

   a. 1
   b. 2
   c. 50
   d. None of these

62. The output of the statement printf("%s","123456"+1); is

   a. 123456
   b. 123457
   c. 23456
   d. None of these

63. The correct way to compare two string literal constants "Hello" and "Hi" is

   a. "Hello"="Hi"
   b. "Hello"=="Hi"
   c. strcmp("Hello","Hi")
   d. None of these

64. The output of the statement puts("\0ABCD\0"); is

a. ABCD
b. No output
c. \0ABCD
d. Compilation error

65. The result of evaluation of the expression strcmp("Hello","Hi"); will be

a. 0
b. 4
c. –4
d. None of these

66. The correct statement to copy a string literal constant "Hello" to a character array str is

a. str="Hello";
b. strcpy(str,"Hello");
c. strcpy("Hello",str);
d. None of these

67. Adjacent string literal constants

a. Are always concatenated
b. Are treated as two separate tokens
c. Leads to compilation error
d. None of these

68. The invocation of the function call strcat("Hi","Readers!!"); leads to

a. HiReaders!!
b. Compilation error
c. Run-time exception
d. None of these

69. The invocation of the function call puts("Hi","Readers!!"); leads to

a. HiReaders!!
b. Compilation error
c. Run-time exception
d. None of these

70. The invocation of the function call puts("Hi""Readers!!"); leads to

a. HiReaders!!
b. Compilation error
c. Run-time exception
d. None of these

71. The output of the following program file ques71.c, if executed from the command line as ques71 1 2 3, is

```
main(int argc, char* argv[])
{
    int val;
    val=argv[1]+argv[2]+argv[3];
    printf("%d",val);
}
```

a. 6
b. 123
c. Compilation error
d. None of these

72. The output of the following program file ques72.c, if executed from the command line as ques72 1 2 3, is

```
#include<stdlib.h>          //←atoi function converts string to an integer and its
                            //←prototype is in stdlib.h
main(int argc, char* argv[])
{
    int val;
    val=atoi(argv[1])+atoi(argv[2])+atoi(argv[3]);
    printf("%d",val);
}
```

a. 6
b. 123
c. Compilation error
d. None of these

73. The output of the following program file ques73.c, if executed from the command line as ques73 1 2, is

```
main(int argc, char* argv[])
{
    char str[10];
    strcpy(str,argv[1]);
    strcpy(str,argv[2]);
    printf("%s",str);
}
```

a. 1
b. 2
c. 12
d. None of these

74. The output of the following program file ques74.c, if executed from the command line as ques74 1 2, is

```
main(int argc, char* argv[])
{
    char str[10];
    strcpy(str,argv[1]);
    strcat(str,argv[2]);
    printf("%s",str);
}
```

a. 1
b. 2
c. 12
d. None of these

75. Which of the following is true about argv?

a. It is an array of character pointers
b. It is a pointer to an array of character pointers
c. It is an array of characters
d. None of these

Outputs and Explanations to Code Snippets

16. Strings
Strings! ¥¤§¶

Explanation:

As the character array str1 is initialized with the character string literal constant, str1[7] will be a null character. However, as the character array str2 is initialized with a list of characters, i.e. 'S', 't', 'r', 'i', 'n', 'g' and 's', no terminating null character is placed in it. Hence, the puts function while printing str2 gives garbage as it prints from the memory location pointed to by its argument till the terminating null character is encountered.

17. Strings

Explanation:

The for loop is used to print the elements of character array str one by one. The loop terminates when the value of i becomes 7 and str[i] evaluates to 0 (i.e. the ASCII value of null character). for(i=0;str[i];i++) is equivalent to writing for(i=0;str[i]!='\0';i++).

18. 1 2

Explanation:

'A' is a character constant and characters take one byte in the memory. "A" is a string literal constant and string literal constants are terminated by a null character, i.e. '\0'. So "A" is actually made up of two characters, i.e. 'A' and '\0'. Hence, sizeof("A") comes out to be 2.

19. 6 2
    1 1

    Explanation:

    str1 is a character array of 6 locations while str2 is a pointer to character. Hence, size of str1 and str2 would be 6 and 2, respectively (in Borland TC 3.0 for DOS), and 6 and 4 (in Borland TC 4.5 for Windows or Microsoft Visual C++ 6.0). The usage of * with str1 and str2 dereferences them to a character and hence, sizeof(*str1) and sizeof(*str2) would be 1 and 1.

20. 10 11

    Explanation:

    The strlen function computes the length of a string given to it as an argument. The strlen function does not count the null character while computing the length of the string. It returns the number of characters that precedes the terminating null character. On the other hand, the sizeof function also counts the memory required by the null character while computing the number of memory bytes occupied by the string.

21. Hello Readers!
    Hello Readers!
    Hello Readers!

    Explanation:

    Adjacent character string literal constants are concatenated. Hence, writing "Hello ""Readers!""\n" is equivalent to writing "Hello Readers!\n". The printf function outputs this character string literal constant onto the screen. The puts function also does the same with a difference that it places the new line character at the end. Hence, there is no requirement of the new line character in the string given to puts. The last call to the printf function uses %s specifiers to output the contents of the character arrays str1 and str2.

22. Compilation error "Extra parameter in call to puts"

    Explanation:

    The puts function expects only one argument of char* type while in the call puts(str1,str2); two arguments of type char* are provided. Hence, there is an extra parameter in the function call, which is the source of error.

23. Readers!

    Explanation:

    The argument of the puts function is an expression (str1,str2). Now, the instance of the comma symbol separating str1 and str2 in the expression (str1,str2) is treated as a comma operator. The comma operator guarantees left-to-right evaluation and returns the result of the rightmost sub-expression. Therefore, the expression (str1,str2) evaluates to str2. Hence, the string Readers! gets printed.

24. Hello

    Explanation:

    The string literal constant refers to the address of its initial element except in the cases when it is an operand of the sizeof operator or the unary & operator. Hence, "Hello" and "Readers!" refer to the starting addresses of the strings "Hello" and "Readers!". In the expression, str="Hello","Readers!", the assignment operator has a higher priority as compared to the comma operator. Hence, the assignment operator is evaluated first and the starting address of the string literal constant "Hello" is assigned to str. In the next statement, the string pointed to by str is printed by the puts function. Hence, "Hello" is the output.

25. Readers!

Explanation:

The use of parentheses makes the comma operator to be evaluated first. The comma operator returns the result of the rightmost sub-expression. Therefore, in the expression str=("Hello","Readers!"), the starting address of the string "Readers!" is assigned to str. In the next statement, the string pointed to by str is printed by the puts function. Hence "Readers!" is the output.

26. Hello

Explanation:

On compilation, the given code does not produce a compilation error as the code of Question number 22 does. This is due to the fact that printf is a variable argument function. It can take a variable number of arguments while puts can only take one argument. Examples when the printf function takes 1, 2 and 3 arguments are as follows:

```
printf("Hello Readers");    //← Only one argument
printf("%d",2);             //← Two arguments
printf("%d %d",2,3);        //← Three arguments
```

The following important points should also be remembered:

1. The comma symbol appearing in a printf function call is not treated as a comma operator.
2. The printf function expects the first argument to be a string (commonly known as a format string). It actually prints only the first argument while the other arguments available in the printf function replace the format specifiers in the first string, if they are present. If no format specifiers are present in the format string, the arguments following the first argument are ignored.

Hence, the output of printf(strl, str2); is Hello, as the string strl does not contain a format specifier.

27. Readers! Readers! Readers!

Explanation:

The declaration statement char str[]="HelloReaders!"; allocates str, say at the memory location 2000. The contents of the array are shown in the figure below:

	[0]	[1]	[2]	[3]	[4]	[5]	[6]	[7]	[8]	[9]	[10]	[11]	[12]	[13]
str	H	e	l	l	o	R	e	a	d	e	r	s	!	\0
	2000	2001	2002	2003	2004	2005	2006	2007	2008	2009	2010	2011	2012	2013

The printf function prints the sequence of characters from the address given as an argument till null character is encountered. All the expressions &str[5], &5[str] and str+5 evaluate to 2005. Therefore, the printing starts from the character present at the location 2005 and is carried out till a null character is encountered.

28. R R R

Explanation:

The expressions str[6], 6[str] and *(str+6) refer to the seventh character of the array str, i.e. R.

29. Readers!

Explanation:

Suppose the string literal constant "Hello Readers!" is allocated the memory space from the address 2000 to 2014 as depicted in the figure below:

[0]	[1]	[2]	[3]	[4]	[5]	[6]	[7]	[8]	[9]	[10]	[11]	[12]	[13]	[14]
H	e	l	l	o		R	e	a	d	e	r	s	!	\0
2000	2001	2002	2003	2004	2005	2006	2007	2008	2009	2010	2011	2012	2013	2014

String literal constant refers to the address of its initial element except in the cases when it is an operand of the sizeof operator or the unary & operator. Hence, the expression "Hello Readers!" evaluates to 2000, and the expression "Hello Readers!"+6 evaluates to 2006. When the expression "Hello Readers!"+6 is given as an argument to the printf function, the printf function starts printing the characters from 2006 till a null character is encountered. Hence, the output comes out to be Readers!.

30. RR

Explanation:

The function putchar outputs the character given to it as an argument on the screen. Suppose the string "Hello Readers!" is allocated the same memory location as in Answer number 29.

In the first call to the function putchar, the argument is an expression "Hello Readers!"[6]. This expression gets converted to the form *("Hello Readers!"+6). The expression *("Hello Readers!"+6) evaluates to *(2000+6), i.e. *(2006), i.e. R (refer to the explanation given in Answer number 29). Similarly, 6["Hello Readers!"] evaluates to R.

Backward Reference: Refer to the explanation given in Answer number 14 (Chapter 4).

31. The size of string is 15
The string is allocated memory starting at 2A4F:00AD

Explanation:

The string literal constant expression does not decompose into the pointer to its initial element when it is an operand of the sizeof operator or the unary & operator.

32. Strings are different!!

Explanation:

In the expression str1==str2, str1 and str2 are the names of character arrays and refer to the addresses of their first elements. Since the addresses of the first element of two arrays can never be the same, the expression str1==str2 evaluates to false and Strings are different!! is the output.

33. Strings are same!!

Explanation:

strcmp(str1,str2) performs a comparison between str1 and str2, starting with the first character in each string and continuing with the subsequent characters until the corresponding characters differ or until the end of strings is reached. It returns the ASCII difference of the first dissimilar corresponding characters or zero if none of the corresponding characters in both the strings are different.

For example, when strcmp function is applied on the strings str1 (say strings) and str2 (say sonia) shown in the figure below, it returns 116-111 (i.e. ASCII code of 't' – ASCII code of 'o') = 5.

	str1	s	t	r	i	n	g	s	\0
Memory addresses	→	2000	2001	2002	2003	2004	2005	2006	2007

	str2	s	o	n	i	a	\0
Memory addresses	→	4000	4001	4002	4003	4004	4005

strcmp(str1,str2) returns a value equal to:

- 0 if str1 and str2 are equal, or
- >0 if str1 is greater than str2, i.e. str1 comes after str2 in lexicographic order, or
- <0 if str1 is lesser than str2, i.e. str1 comes before str2 in lexicographic order.

In the given question, str1 and str2 being the same, the expression strcmp(str1,str2)==0 evaluates to true as the strcmp function returns 0. Hence, Strings are same!! is the output.

34. Strings are different!!

    Explanation:

    The strcmp function when used to compare str1 and str2 returns 115-83 (i.e. ASCII code of 's'-ASCII code of 'S') = 32. The returned value is not equal to zero. Hence, the expression strcmp(str1,str2)==0 evaluates to false and Strings are different!! is the output. Note that the strcmp function considers the case sensitivity of the characters while comparing the strings.

35. Strings are same!!

    Explanation:

    The strcmpi function compares the strings without case sensitivity. The character i in the strcmpi function stands for ignore case.

36. Strings are same!!

    Explanation:

    Suppose, the character string literal constants "Strings" and "Strings\0" are allocated the memory space at the addresses 2000 and 4000 as shown in the figure below:

	S	t	r	i	n	g	s	\0
Memory addresses →	2000	2001	2002	2003	2004	2005	2006	2007

	S	t	r	i	n	g	s	\0	\0
Memory addresses →	4000	4001	4002	4003	4004	4005	4006	4007	4008

The function call strcmp("Strings","Strings\0") compares characters of both the strings one by one until the corresponding characters differ or until the end of the strings is reached. In the given piece of code, the function call terminates by comparing the null characters located at the locations 2007 and 4007 and returns 0. Hence, Strings are same!! is the output.

37. Strings are different!!

    Explanation:

    Suppose that the character array str1 gets allocated at the memory address 2000 as shown in the figure below. The first seven elements of the character array str1 are initialized with the characters 'S', 't', 'r', 'i', 'n', 'g' and 's', and the memory locations following 2006 contain garbage values.

	[0]	[1]	[2]	[3]	[4]	[5]	[6]					
str1	S	t	r	i	n	g	s	G	G	G	G	
	2000	2001	2002	2003	2004	2005	2006	2007	2008	2009	2010	...

G (in the above figure) means garbage value.

The contents of the character array str2 allocated at the memory address 4000 are shown in the figure below:

	[0]	[1]	[2]	[3]	[4]	[5]	[6]	[7]				
str2	S	t	r	i	n	g	s	\0	G	G	G	G
	4000	4001	4002	4003	4004	4005	4006	4007	4008	4009	4010	...

The function strcmp(str1,str2) returns the ASCII difference of the first dissimilar corresponding characters or zero if there is no dissimilarity. The first dissimilarity in str1 and str2 is in the characters located at 2007 and 4007, respectively. Hence, the function strcmp returns the difference between garbage value G and 0 (i.e. the ASCII code of the null character). There is high probability that this garbage value is a non-zero value, and hence Strings are different!! is the output. However, by chance, if the garbage value located at 2007 is 0 (which has lesser probability), then the output will be Strings are same!!.

38. A

Explanation:

The contents of the character array format after initialization are shown in the figure below:

	[0]	[1]	[2]	[3]
format	%	d	\n	\0
	2000	2001	2002	2003

After the execution of the assignment statement format[1]='c'; the contents of the character array format become:

	[0]	[1]	[2]	[3]
format	%	c	\n	\0
	2000	2001	2002	2003

Writing printf(format,65); is equivalent to writing printf("%c\n",65);. Printing of integer value 65 is done according to the %c format specifier; hence A is the output (since 65 is the ASCII value of 'A').

39. 45 6f

Explanation:

The character array format is initialized with an initialization list consisting of integer values. If the initialization list of a character array consists of integer values, then the locations of the array are initialized with the characters whose ASCII values are equivalent to the integer values in the initialization list. The characters having an ASCII value of 37 is '%', 111 is 'o', 32 is ' ', (i.e. blank space), 120 is 'x' and 0 is '\0', i.e. null character. The initialized contents of the character array format are shown in the figure below:

	[0]	[1]	[2]	[3]	[4]	[5]
format	%	o		%	x	\0
	2000	2001	2002	2003	2004	2005

Now, printf(format,format[0],format[1]); prints the value of format[0] (i.e. 37) and format[1] (i.e. 111) according to %o and %x format specifiers, respectively. Hence, the output comes out to be 45 and 6f as the octal equivalent of 37 is 45 and the hexadecimal equivalent of 111 is 6f.

40. Compilation error "L-value required"

Explanation:

str2 is the name of the character array and is a constant object. It cannot be placed on the left side of an assignment operator. Hence, writing str2=str1 is not valid and gives 'L-value required' error.

41. Strings
Strings

Explanation:

The strcpy(dest,src); copies the string pointed by src into the memory location pointed to by dest. The copying terminates after the terminating null character of src has been copied to dest. The strcpy function returns the starting address of the memory location where the string has been copied. Thus, after the execution of the function call strcpy(dest,src); both str and dest contain "Strings", and their contents are printed using the puts function.

42 C++

Explanation:

The contents of the character array dest and src are shown in the figure below:

	[0]	[1]	[2]	[3]	[4]	[5]	[6]	[7]	[8]	[9]	[10]	[11]	[12]
dest	V	i	s	u	a	l		B	a	s	i	c	\0
	2000	2001	2002	2003	2004	2005	2006	2007	2008	2009	2010	2011	2012

	[0]	[1]	[2]	[3]
src	C	+	+	\0
	4000	4001	4002	4003

The function call strcpy(&dest[7],src); copies the contents of the source string src to the memory locations starting from 2007, i.e. &dest[7]. The contents of dest after the function call are as follows:

	[0]	[1]	[2]	[3]	[4]	[5]	[6]	[7]	[8]	[9]	[10]	[11]	[12]
dest	V	i	s	u	a	l		C	+	+	\0	c	\0
	2000	2001	2002	2003	2004	2005	2006	2007	2008	2009	2010	2011	2012

The strcpy function returns the address of the memory location where the string has been copied. Hence, strcpy(&dest[7],src); returns 2007. The puts prints the sequence of characters starting from the memory location 2007 till a null character is encountered. Hence, C++ is the output.

43. Visual C++

Explanation:

Backward Reference: Refer to the explanation given in Answer number 42

44. Visual C++

Explanation:

Backward Reference: Refer to the explanation given in Answer number 42.

45. Strings

Explanation:

The printf function returns an integer value equivalent to the number of characters printed. Printing of the null character using the printf function returns zero. Hence, Strings is the output.

46. Delhi
Chandigarh
Noida

Explanation:

The content of a two-dimensional character array cities is shown in the figure below:

cities	[0]	[1]	[2]	[3]	[4]	[5]	[6]	[7]	[8]	[9]	[10]
[0]	D	e	l	h	i	\0					
	2000	2001	2002	2003	2004	2005	2006	2007	2008	2009	2010
[1]	C	h	a	n	d	i	g	a	r	h	\0
	2011	2012	2013	2014	2015	2016	2017	2018	2019	2020	2021
[2]	N	o	i	d	a	\0					
	2022	2023	2024	2025	2026	2027	2028	2029	2030	2031	2032

Referring to a two-dimensional array with only one subscript gives the starting address of a row. Hence, the expression cities[0] refers to the starting address of the first row, i.e. 2000, and cities[1] refers to the starting address of the second row, i.e. 2011. The function call puts(cities[i]), prints the strings in the first, second and third rows.

47 Compilation error "L-value required"

Explanation:

Referring to a two-dimensional array with only one subscript refers to the starting address of the row and is a constant object. The C compiler will not allow its manipulation. Hence, writing languages[3]=languages[4] is not valid and leads to 'l-value required' compilation error.

48. Basic
Java
Fortran
C++
C

Explanation:

languages is an array of character pointers and is initialized with the base addresses of the string literal constants "Basic", "Java", "Fortran", "C" and "C++". Contiguous memory (say from the memory address 1000-1009) is allocated to the array languages while the string literal constants are placed randomly in the memory. This is depicted in the figure below:

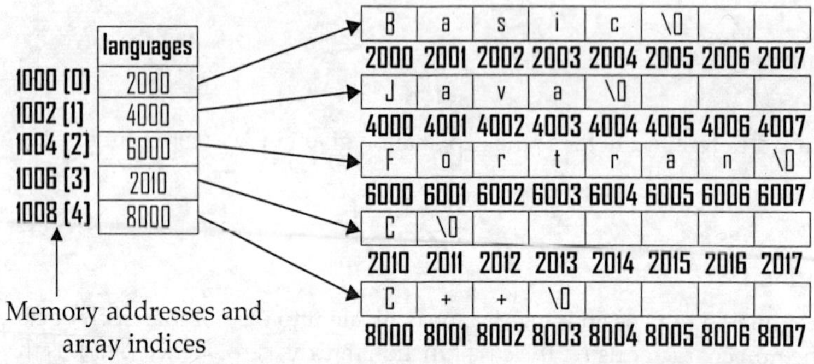

The statements t=languages[3];, languages[3]=languages[4]; and languages[4]=t; swap the values of languages[3] and language[4]. After the execution of these statements, the contents of array languages are as depicted in the figure below:

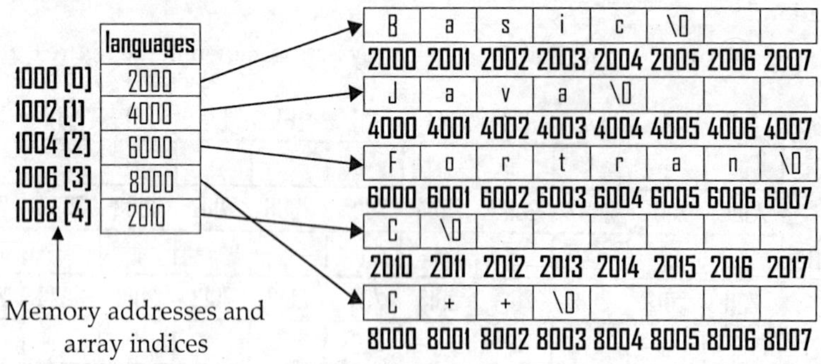

Thus, the printing of the strings pointed by the content of the array languages yields the mentioned result.

49. Visual Basic
    Visual Java
    Visual Fortran
    Visual C
    Visual C++

    Explanation:

    The content of the two-dimensional character array lang is shown below:

lang	[0]	[1]	[2]	[3]	[4]	[5]	[6]	[7]	[8]	[9]	[10]	[11]	[12]
[0]	V	i	s	u	a	l		B	a	s	i	c	\0
	2000	2001	2002	2003	2004	2005	2006	2007	2008	2009	2010	2011	2012
[1]	J	a	v	a	\0								
	2013	2014	2015	2016	2017	2018	2019	2020	2021	2022	2023	2024	2025
[2]	F	o	r	t	r	a	n	\0					
	2026	2027	2027	2028	2029	2030	2031	2032	2033	2034	2035	2036	2037
[3]	C	\0											
	2038	2039	2040	2041	2042	2043	2044	2045	2046	2047	2048	2049	2050
[4]	C	+	+	\0									
	2051	2052	2053	2054	2055	2056	2057	2058	2059	2060	2061	2062	2063

The character pointer t, say, gets allocated at 4000. After the execution of the assignment statement t=lang[0]; t starts pointing to the starting address of the first row of the character array lang. After the execution of while(*t++!=32); statement, t points to the location next to the blank space (ASCII value 32) in the first row of lang, i.e. 2007. Each iteration of the for loop with the loop counter value i prints the content of lang[0] and copies the strings in the row i+1 at the memory location pointed by t, i.e. 2007.

50. String
    tring
    ring
    ing
    ng
    g

    Explanation:

    Suppose the character pointer ptr and the character string literal constant "String" are allocated the memory space as shown in the figure below. Since is initialized with the character string literal constant, it points to the starting address of the string literal, i.e. 4000.

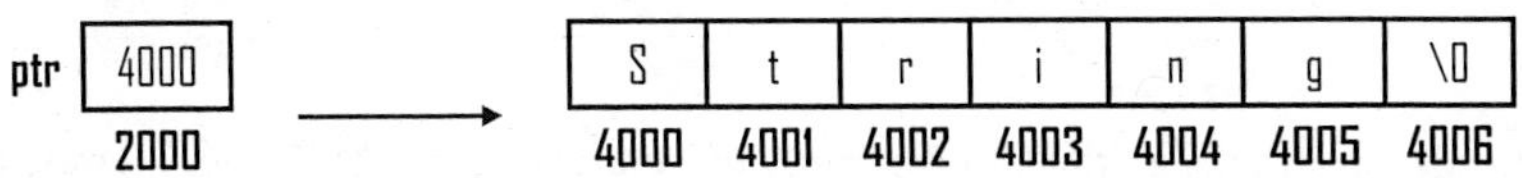

    Every iteration of the for loop prints a string being pointed by ptr and increments the contents of the pointer ptr.

51. Compilation error

    Explanation:

    Backward Reference: Refer the explanation given in Answer number 59 (Chapter 4).

    While declaring a two-dimensional array, both the row size and column size cannot be left blank. It is mandatory to mention the column size specifier. Hence, the declaration string_manipulation(char [][]); is not valid. It can be rectified by mentioning the column size specifier as string_manipulation(char [][10]);. The same should also be done in the function header.

52. Hello Readers!!

    Explanation:

    The two-dimensional character array arr is passed by reference to the string_manipulation function. Suppose the array arr (local to the function main) gets allocated at the memory location 2000. The name arr declared in the function header string_manipulation is of type pointer to the character array of size 10 and is local to the function string_manipulation. Suppose it gets allocated at the memory location say 4000. The name of a two-dimensional array refers to the starting address of the first row of the array. Therefore, the function call string_manipulation(arr); passes 2000, i.e. the starting address of the first row of the array to the function string_manipulation. This is shown in the figure below:

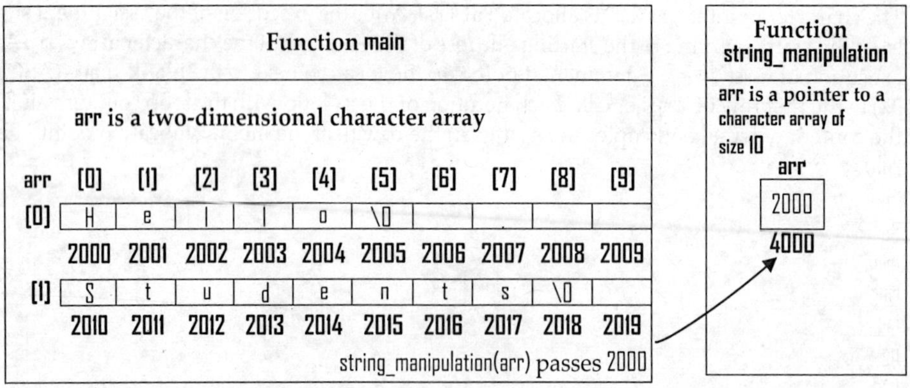

The call to the function strcpy inside the body of function string_manipulation copies the string "Readers!!" at arr[1], i.e., 2010 (because arr is a pointer to a character array of size 10). Thus, the string "Readers!!" overwrites the string "Students" present in the second row of the character array arr. That is why when arr[0] and arr[1] are printed, the output comes out to be Hello Readers!!.

53. Hello Readers!!

    Explanation:

    The parameter declaration char arr[][10] gets implicitly converted to char(*arr)[10]. Thus, the mentioned code becomes equivalent to the code given in Question number 52.

Backward Reference: Refer to the explanation given in Answer number 52 for the output.

54. Compilation error

    Explanation:

    The return type of a function cannot be an array type. Since the return type of the function print_string is an array type, i.e. char [20], the compiler issues an error message.

55. The argument count is 3
    The content of argument vector i.e. array is
    c:\ques55.exe
    Hello
    Readers!!

    Explanation:

Backward Reference: Refer to the explanation given in Section 6.9.

Arguments in command line are separated by blank spaces. Since there are two blank spaces, the total number of command line arguments is three. Note that the name of the program file (actually executable file) is also counted while determining the argument count. argv[0] points to c:\>ques55.exe, argv[1] points to Hello and argv[2] points to Readers!!. Therefore, these strings get printed.

Answers to Multiple-choice Questions

56. b 57. a 58. b 59. c 60. d 61. c 62. c 63. c 64. b 65. c 66. b 67. a 68. c
69. b 70. a 71. c 72. a 73. b 74. c 75. a

Programming Exercises

Program 1 | Input a string and find the number of vowel(s) present in the string

PE 6-1.c

```
//Number of vowels in a string
#include<stdio.h>
main()
{
char string[200];
int count=0, i=0;
printf("Enter a string:\n");
gets(string);
while(string[i]!='\0')
{
    switch(string[i])
    {
        case 'A':
        case 'E':
        case 'I':
        case 'O':
        case 'U':
        case 'a':
        case 'e':
        case 'i':
        case 'o':
        case 'u':
            count++;
    }
    i++;
}
if(count==1)
  printf("One vowel is present in the string");
else
  printf("%d vowels are present in the string", count);
}
```

Output window

```
Enter a string:
There is nothing more beautiful in the world than a healthy wise old man- Yutang
25 vowels are present in the string
```

Program 2 | Input a string and count the number of occurrences of a particular character in the string

PE 6-2.c

```
//Count number of occurrences of a particular character in the string
#include<stdio.h>
main()
{
    char string[200], ch;
    int count=0, i=0;
    printf("Enter a string:\n");
    gets(string);
    printf("Enter the character:\t");
    scanf("%c",&ch);
    while(string[i]!='\0')
    {
        if(string[i]==ch)
```

Output window

```
Enter a string:
Nature, time and patience are three great physicians- Bohn
Enter the character: e
In the given string, e occurred 8 times
```

(Contd...)

PE 6-2.c

```
            count++;
        i++;
    }
    printf("In the given string, %c occurred %d times\n",ch, count);
}
```

Output window

Program 3 | Input a string and count the number of blank spaces in the string

PE 6-3.c

```
//Number of blank spaces
#include<stdio.h>
main()
{
    char string[200], ch;
    int count=0, i=0;
    printf("Enter a string:\n");
    gets(string);
    while(string[i]!='\0')
    {
        if(string[i]==' ')
            count++;
        i++;
    }
    printf("Number of blank spaces in the given string are %d", count);
}
```

Output window

```
Enter a string:
People resent a joke if there is some truth in it- Tagore
Number of blank spaces in the given string are 11
```

Program 4- Input two strings of equal length from the user and determine how many times the corresponding positions in two strings hold exactly the same characters

PE 6-4.c

```
//Number of same characters at the corresponding positions in two strings
#include<stdio.h>
#include<string.h>
#include<stdlib.h>
main()
{
    char str1[30], str2[30];
    int length1, length2, count=0, i;
    printf("Enter two strings of equal length\n");
    printf("Enter first string:\t");
    gets(str1);
    printf("Enter second string:\t");
    gets(str2);
    length1=strlen(str1);
    length2=strlen(str2);
    if(length1!=length2)
    {
        printf("The entered strings are of different lengths\n");
        exit(1);
    }
```

Output window

```
Enter two strings of equal length
Enter first string:     choice
Enter second string:    chance
Corresponding positions hold same characters 4 times
```

Output window (second execution)

```
Enter two strings of equal length
Enter first string:     very
Enter second string:    much
Corresponding positions hold same characters 0 times
```

Output window (third execution)

```
Enter two strings of equal length
Enter first string:     life
Enter second string:    lovely
The entered strings are of different lengths
```

(Contd...)

```
    else
    {
        for(i=0;i<length1;i++)
            if(str1[i]==str2[i])
                count++;
        printf("Corresponding positions hold same characters %d times", count);
    }
}
```

Program 5 | Input a string and display the alternate characters of the string

PE 6-5.c

```
//Printing alternate characters of a string
#include<stdio.h>
main()
{
    char str[200], altchars[200];
    int i=0, length, j=0;
    printf("Enter a string:\n");
    gets(str);
    length=strlen(str);
    while(i<length)
    {
        altchars[j]=str[i];
        i=i+2;
        j=j+1;
    }
    altchars[j]='\0';
    printf("Alternate characters in the string are:\n");
    puts(altchars);
}
```

Output window

```
Enter a string:
Hatred is preferable to the friendship of fools
Alternate characters in the string are:
Hte speeal otefinsi ffos
```

Program 6 | Input a string and display the alternate characters of the string in the reverse order

PE 6-6.c

```
//Printing alternate characters of a string in the reverse order
#include<stdio.h>
#include<string.h>
main()
{
    char str[200], altchars[200];
    int i=0, length, j=0;
    printf("Enter a string:\n");
    gets(str);
    length=strlen(str);
    i=length-1;
    while(i>=0)
    {
        altchars[j]=str[i];
        i=i-2;
```

Output window

```
Enter a string:
Harmony in character gains goodwill even from strangers
Alternate characters of the string in reverse order are:
senrsmr eelido na ecrh iyorH
```

(Contd...)

PE 6-6.c

```
        j=j+1;
    }
    altchars[j]='\0';
    printf("Alternate characters of the string in reverse order are:\n");
    puts(altchars);
}
```

Output window

Program 7 | Input a multi-word string and find out the number of words in the string

PE 6-7.c

```
//Number of words in a string
#include<stdio.h>
#include<string.h>
main()
{
char str[200];
int i=0, count=0;
printf("Enter a string:\n");
gets(str);
while(str[i]!='\0')
{
    if(str[i]==' ')
        count++;
    i++;
}
printf("Number of words in the string are %d\n",count+1);
}
```

Output window

```
Enter a string:
A man should be educated enough to know that education alone is not enough
Number of words in the string are 14
```

Program 8 | Input a string and check whether the given string is a palindrome or not

PE 6-8.c

```
//To check whether a given string is a palindrome or not
#include<stdio.h>
#include<string.h>
main()
{
    char str[200], rev[200];
    printf("Enter a string:\t");
    gets(str);
    strcpy(rev,str);
    rev=strrev(str);
    if(strcmp(str,rev)==0)
        printf("The given string is a palindrome");
    else
        printf("The given string is not a palindrome");
}
```

Output window

```
Enter a string: NITIN
The given string is a palindrome
```

Output window (second execution)

```
Enter a string: Hello
The given string is not a palindrome
```

Program 9 | Input a string and count the number of occurrences of a particular word in the string

PE 6-9.c

```
//Counting the number of occurrences of a particular word in a string
#include<stdio.h>
#include<string.h>
main()
{
    char str[200], word[20], temp[20];
    int i=0, j=0, count=0;
    printf("Enter a string:\n");
    gets(str);
    printf("Enter the word:\t");
    gets(word);
    while(str[i]!='\0')
    {
        while(str[i]!=' ' && str[i]!='\0')
        {
            temp[j]=str[i];
            j++; i++;
        }
        temp[j]='\0';
        if(str[i]!='\0')
        {
            i++; j=0;
        }
        if(strcmp(temp,word)==0)
            count++;
    }
  if(count==0)
    printf("The word \"%s\" does not exist in the string", word);
  else
    printf("The word \"%s\" exists %d times in the string", word, count);
}
```

Output window

```
Enter a string:
Fools are not aware of their own faults although they are known to all
Enter the word:     are
The word "are" exists 2 times in the string
```

Output window (second execution)

```
Enter a string:
You must not expect everything exactly to your taste
Enter the word:     are
The word "are" does not exist in the string
```

Program 10 | Input a string and count the number of occurrences of a particular string in the string

PE 6-10.c

```
//Counting the occurrences of a particular string in the string
#include<stdio.h>
#include<string.h>
main()
{
    char str1[200], str2[200], temp[20];
    int i=0, j=0,k=0, count=0;
    printf("Enter a string:\n");
    gets(str1);
    printf("Enter the string to be searched:\t");
    gets(str2);
    while(str1[i]!='\0')
    {
        k=0;
        while(str2[k]!='\0')
```

Output window

```
Enter a string:
Try not to become a man of success but rather to be a man of value
Enter the string to be searched:     a man of
String "a man of" exists 2 times
```

Output window (second execution)

```
Enter a string:
Try not to become a man of success but rather to be a man of value
Enter the string to be searched:     civil society
String "civil society" doesnot exist in the given string
```

(Contd...)

PE 6-10.c

```
        {
            if(str1[j]==str2[k])
                j++, k++;
            else
            {
                j=i+1;
                break;
            }
            if(str2[k]==0)
                count++;
        }
        if(str2[k]==0)
            i=j;
        else
            i++;
    }
    if(count==0)
    printf("String \"%s\" doesnot exist in the given string\n", str2);
    else
    printf("String \"%s\" exists %d times\n", str2, count);
}
```

Output window

Program 11 | A class consists of a number of students whose names are entered in a random order. Display the names of all the students that start with a particular character

PE 6-11.c

```
//Displaying the names of students starting with a particular character
#include<stdio.h>
#include<string.h>
main()
{
    char names[40][30], firstchar;
    int num, i;
    printf("How many students are there in the class:\t");
    scanf("%d",&num);
    printf("Enter the names of students:\n");
    for(i=0;i<num;i++)
    gets(names[i]);
    printf("\nEnter the first character of student's name:\t");
    scanf("%c",&firstchar);
    printf("Students whose names starts with %c are:\n",firstchar);
    for(i=0;i<num;i++)
        if(names[i][0]==firstchar)
            puts(names[i]);
}
```

Output window

```
How many students are there in the class:    10
Enter the names of students:
Abhay Singh
Neha Singla
Jasraj Singh
Aditya Raina
Tarun Kumar
Amol Sood
Joydeep Chandra
Tushar Sharma
Rajini Bansal
Sam

Enter the first character of student's name:    A
Students whose names starts with A are:
Abhay Singh
Aditya Raina
Amol Sood
```

Program 12 | A class consists of a number of students whose names are entered in a random order. Display the names in a sorted order

PE 6-12.c

```
//Displaying the names of students in a sorted order
 #include<stdio.h>
#include<string.h>
main()
{
    char names[40][30], current[30];
    int num, i,j;
    printf("How many students are there in the class:\t");
    scanf("%d",&num);
    printf("Enter the names of students:\n");
    for(i=0;i<num;i++)
    gets(names[i]);
    for(i=1;i<num;i++)    //← Insertion Sort
    if(strcmp(names[i],names[i-1])<0) //←equivalent to if(names[i]<names[i-1])
    {
        strcpy(current,names[i]); //←equivalent to current=names[i]
        for(j=i-1;j>=0;j--)
        {

                strcpy(names[j+1],names[j]); //←eq. to names[j+1]=names[j]
                if(j==0||(strcmp(names[j-1],current)<0))
                    break;
        }
    strcpy(names[j],current);
    }
    printf("\nAfter sorting, names of students are:\n");
    for(i=0;i<num;i++)         //←Print sorted list
        puts(names[i]);
}
```

Output window

```
How many students are there in the class:    10
Enter the names of students:
Abhay Singh
Neha Singla
Jasraj Singh
Aditya Raina
Tarun Kumar
Amol Sood
Joydeep Chandra
Tushar Sharma
Rajini Bansal
Sam

After sorting, names of students are:
Abhay Singh
Aditya Raina
Amol Sood
Jasraj Singh
Joydeep Chandra
Neha Singla
Rajini Bansal
Sam
Tarun Kumar
Tushar Sharma
```

Program 13 | Chandigarh Housing Board has released a list of successful applicants in the preliminary draw of lots. Find out whether a given name is in the list or not

PE 6-13.c

```
//Searching a name in the list
 #include<stdio.h>
#include<string.h>
main()
{
char applicants[40][30], name[30];
int num, i,found=0;
printf("The list of draw is of how many applicants?\t");
```

Output window

```
The list of draw is of how many applicants?    10
Enter the names:
Abhay Singh
Neha Singla
Jasraj Singh
Aditya Raina
Tarun Kumar
Sam
```

(Contd...)

PE 6-13.c

```c
scanf("%d",&num);
printf("Enter the names:\n");
for(i=0;i<num;i++)
gets(applicants[i]);
printf("\nEnter name to be searched:\t");
gets(name)
for(i=1;i<num;i++)   //← Linear search
    if(strcmp(applicants[i],name)==0)
        found=1;
if(found==1)
printf("Name \"%s\" appears in the list of successful applicants");
else
printf("Name \"%s\" does not appear in the list of successful applicants");
}
```

Output window

```
Amol Sood
Joydeep Chandra
Tushar Sharma
Rajini Bansal

Enter the name to be searched:    Sam
Name "Sam" appears in the list of successful applicants
```

Program 14 | Count the number of sentences, words and characters in a given paragraph

PE 6-14.c

```c
//Counting the number of sentences, words and characters in a given paragraph
 #include<stdio.h>
main()
{
char paragraph[1000];
int i=0, sentence=0, word=0, chs=0;
printf("Enter the text:\n");
scanf("%[^\n]", paragraph);
while(paragraph[i]!='\0')
{
    switch(paragraph[i])
    {
        case '!':
        case '.':
        case '?':
            sentence++;
            chs++;
            break;
        case ' ':
        case '\t':
            chs++;
            word++;
            break;
        default:
            chs++;
    }
    i++;
 }
printf("\nNumber of sentences in paragraph are %d\n", sentence);
printf("Number of words in paragraph are %d\n", word+1);
printf("Number of characters in paragraph are %d\n", chs);
}
```

Output window

```
Enter the text:
Hello! How are you? Where were you? I have been looking
for all these days.

Number of sentences in paragraph are 4
Number of words in paragraph are 15
Number of characters in paragraph are 75
```

Test Yourself

1. Fill in the blanks in each of the following:
   a. A string literal constant of zero length is called ____________.
   b. Every string literal in C is terminated by ____________.
   c. The amount of memory taken by an empty string literal is ____________.
   d. The type of string literal is ____________.
   e. A string literal constant is always enclosed within ____________.
   f. Adjacent string literals are ____________.
   g. The `scanf` function uses ____________ format specification to read a string from the user.
   h. ____________ string library function is used to compare two strings without case sensitivity.
   i. The ____________ character is used to invert the search set.
   j. ____________ function is used to read a character from the keyboard.
   k. Inputs to function `main` are given by making use of special arguments known as ____________.

2. State whether each of the following is true or false. If false, explain why.
   a. The length of a string literal constant is equal to the number of characters present in it.
   b. The length of an empty string literal constant is one.
   c. The amount of the memory space required for storing a string literal constant is not fixed and depends upon the number of characters present in the string literal.
   d. The number of bytes required to store a string literal is equal to the number of characters present in it.
   e. It is not mandatory to use ampersand (i.e. address-of operator) with string variable names while reading string using the `scanf` function.
   f. Unlike the `scanf` function, the `gets` function reads the entire line of text until a new line character is encountered and does not stop upon encountering any other white-space character.
   g. The `printf` function can print a string on the screen without using any format specifier.
   h. If the character array to be printed does not have a terminating null character, the output would be the content of the character array followed by some garbage character.
   i. It is not mandatory to have the first argument of the `printf` function to be of `const char*` type.
   j. The string library function `strrev` reverses all the characters of a string including the null character.
   k. It is not possible to initialize a character array with a string literal constant.
   l. A list of strings can be stored by using a two-dimensional character array.

3. Programming exercises:
   a. A certain piece of text is entered. By mistake, at some places two or more spaces are placed between two words. Write a C program that removes these extra spaces between the words.
   b. Without using inbuilt string library functions, write a C program to check whether a given string is a palindrome or not.
   c. Write a C program to find the longest word in a given string. Also print the length of the word.
   d. Write a C program to read a text and omit all occurrences of a particular word in the text.
   e. Write a C program to read a text and omit all occurrences of a particular string in the text.
   f. Write a C program to read a text. Implement the find and replace functionality. The find functionality will find a given substring in the text, and the replace function will replace the found substring with a given string.

7

SCOPE, LINKAGE, LIFETIME AND STORAGE CLASSES

Learning Objectives

In this chapter, you will learn about:

- Scope and visibility of an identifier
- Local variables and global variables
- Linkage
- Different types of linkages in C
- The lifetime of an object
- Different storage classes
- How to allocate memory at the run time

7.1 Introduction

In the previous chapters, we have learnt about how to declare variables within a function and have seen that the amount of memory allocated to a variable depends upon its data type. We have restricted our discussion to the declaration of variables within a function (i.e. local variables) and have not discussed about the global variables (i.e. variables declared outside all the function definitions). The issues like scope, visibility, storage class and linkage of a variable were not included in the discussion. In this chapter, we will discuss these key issues in detail.

7.2 Scope

The **scope** of an identifier is a region of the program within which the identifier is visible (i.e. it can be used). In C language, the following four types of scopes are defined, which determine the visibility of an identifier:

1. File scope or global scope
2. Block scope or local scope
3. Function prototype scope
4. Function scope

7.2.1 Determination of Scope of an Identifier

The scope of an identifier (except label) is determined by the position of its declaration. The scope of a label is determined by the position of its appearance. The rules to determine the scope of an identifier are as follows:

1. If a declaration statement that declares an identifier (except label) appears outside all the functions and their parameter lists, the identifier has **file scope** or **global scope**. Such a declaration statement is called **global declaration**, and the identifier is said to be **global** or **external identifier**.
2. If a declaration statement that declares an identifier (except label) appears inside a block (i.e. within an opening brace and its associated closing brace) or within a list of parameter declarations in a function definition, the identifier has **block scope** or **local scope**. Such a declaration is known as **local declaration** and the identifier is said to be **local to the block** in which it is declared, or **local to the function** if it appears within the list of parameter declarations in a function definition.
3. If a declaration statement that declares an identifier (except label) is a part of a list of parameter declarations in a function prototype, the identifier has **function prototype scope**.
4. A label is the only kind of identifier that always has **function scope**. It can be used anywhere within the function in which an identifier-labeled statement specifying the label name appears.

Consider the piece of code in Program 7-1 that makes the use of various identifiers. Based upon the position of their declarations, the scopes of the identifiers have been determined and are specified in column 3.

Prog 7-1.c (Column 2)	Scopes (Column 3)	Output window
//Identifiers and their scopes		Enter two numbers 12 13 Sum is 25 Diff is -1 **Remarks:** • Since the declarations of the identifiers a and b appear within the function prototype, they have function prototype scope • The identifier diff appears outside the bodies of all the functions and their parameter lists. Hence, it has file or global scope • The identifiers no1, no2 and sum appear within the definition of the function main, so they have local scope and are said to be local to the function main • The identifiers f and g appear within the list of parameter declarations in the definition of the function sum_diff, hence, they have local scope and are local to the function sum_diff • The identifier sum has local scope • The identifier label has function scope, since label names always have function scope
#include<stdio.h>		
int sum_diff(int a, int b);	//←a and b have function prototype scope	
int diff;	//←diff has file scope or global scope	
main()		
{		
int no1,no2,sum;	//←no1, no2 and sum have block scope or	
printf("Enter two numbers\t");	// local scope	
scanf("%d %d",&no1, &no2);	// They are said to be local to the function	
sum=sum_diff(no1,no2);	// main	
printf("Sum is %d\n",sum);		
printf("Diff is %d\n",diff);		
}		
int sum_diff(int f, int g)	//←f and g have block scope or local scope	
{	// f and g are local to the function sum_diff	
int sum;	//←sum has block scope or local scope	
if(f!=g)	// It is said to local to the function	
goto label;	// sum_diff	
else		
{		
sum=2*f;		
diff=0;		
return sum;		
}		
label:	//←label has function scope	
sum=f+g;		
diff=f-g;		
return sum;		
}		

Program 7-1 | A program that illustrates the concept of scope determination

7.2.2 Termination of Scope of an Identifier

The termination of scope of an identifier is determined by the following rules:

1. **File scope** terminates with the end of the source file (commonly known as **translation unit**).
2. **Block scope** terminates with the end of the associated block (i.e. with the closing brace of the block).

3. **Function prototype scope** terminates with the end of the function declaration (i.e. function prototype).
4. **Function scope** terminates with the closing brace of the function definition.

7.2.3 Same Scope

Two identifiers have the **same scope** if and only if their scopes terminate at the same point. The piece of code in Program 7-2 illustrates the concept of the same scope.

Prog 7-2.c

```
//Concept of the same scope
#include<stdio.h>
fun();
int c;
main()
{
    int a,b;
    printf("a and b have the same scope\n");
    printf("They have local scope\n");
    fun();
}
int d;
fun()
{
    printf("c and d have the same scope\n");
    printf("They have global scope\n");
}
```

Output window

```
a and b have the same scope
They have local scope
c and d have the same scope
They have global scope
```

Remark:

- Although identifiers c and d are declared at different places, they have the same scope since their scopes terminate at the same point

Program 7-2 | A program that illustrates the concept of the same scopes

7.2.3.1 Declaration and Definition of an Identifier within the Same Scope and Different Scopes

In the previous chapters, we have seen the difference between the terms declaration and definition. **Declaring** a variable means describing its type to the compiler without allocating any memory space to it. **Defining** a variable means declaring it, plus allocating memory space to it. In general, we say that `int a;` is a declaration statement although it is a definition statement. To actually make it a declaration, prefix `extern` storage class specifier† and write it as `extern int a;`. The keyword `extern` provides a method for declaring an identifier without defining it. The `extern` specification does not cause any memory space to be allocated.

In a C program, it is possible to declare an identifier with a same name and type more than once in the same scope (i.e. one scope). An identifier can have many identical declarations in the same scope. The word identical means that the type of identifier in all the declarations should be equivalent.

> **Two types are equivalent** if they contain the same set of type specifiers, taking into account that some specifiers can be implied by others. For example, `long` alone implies `long int`. Thus, the types `long` and `long int` are equivalent.

† Refer Section 7.5 for a description on storage class specifiers.

The piece of code in Program 7-3 demonstrates that multiple identical declarations in the same scope are allowed.

Line	Prog 7-3.c	Output window

1
2
3
4
5
6
7
8
9
	//Multiple identical declarations in the same scope
	#include<stdio.h>
	main()
	{
	    extern int a;
	    extern int a;
	    printf("The value of a is %d",a);
	}
	int a=20;
		The value of a is 20
		Remarks:
		• The identifier a is declared twice (in line numbers 5 and 6)
		• The extern declaration does not allocate any memory space
		• It only provides information about the type of the identifier and tells the compiler that the definition of the identifier will be available elsewhere in the program
		• The identifier a is defined in line number 9
		• It is mandatory to define an identifier used in a program
		Try:
		• Comment line number 9 and try to execute the code. Look at the errors

Program 7-3 | A program illustrating that there can be multiple identical declarations of an identifier in the same scope

If there are multiple declarations of an identifier in a scope, the type of the identifier in all the declarations must be the same. If the type of an identifier in the declarations is not the same, there will be 'Type mismatch in re-declaration of identifier name' compilation error. The piece of code in Program 7-4 illustrates this fact.

Line	Prog 7-4.c	Output window

1
2
3
4
5
6
7
8
9
	//The types in multiple declarations must be identical
	#include<stdio.h>
	main()
	{
	    extern int a;
	    extern float a;
	    printf("Non-identical declarations in same scope\n");
	    printf("The value of a is %d",a);
	}
		Compilation error "Type mismatch in re-declaration of 'a' in function main"
		Remark:
		• The type of identifier a in the declarations made in line numbers 5 and 6 are not identical, which is the source of error
		What to do?
		• Make the type of identifier a in both the declarations identical
		Can the program be executed now?
		• No, the program on execution gives linker error 'Undefined symbol _a in module'
		• From the perspective of the compiler, there is no error and the compilation stage will succeed
		• Since there is no definition of the identifier a, the linker will not be able to link the declaration with the definition of a and this leads to a linker error
		What to do?
		• Define a

Program 7-4 | A program illustrating that the type of an identifier in multiple declarations must be identical

Although it is possible to declare an identifier more than once in the same scope, it is not allowed to define an identifier more than once in the same scope. Each object[‡] (identifier) must have only one definition in a scope. This is known as **one definition rule**. For objects with no linkage[§] (i.e. local variables), this rule applies separately to each block. For objects with internal linkage (refer footnote[§]), this rule applies separately to each translation unit (i.e. file). For objects with external linkage (refer footnote[§]), it applies to the entire program (which can have more than one file).

Backward Reference: Data object (Chapter 1).

The piece of code in Program 7-5 illustrates the application of one definition rule.

Line	Prog 7-5.c	Output window
1	//Multiple definitions in the same scope	Compilation error "Multiple declaration for 'a' in function main" **Remarks:** • According to one definition rule, there can be only one definition of an identifier in a scope • Although there are multiple definitions, the compiler message indicates multiple declarations since the term declaration is commonly used in place of definition • It is pertinent to mention that the specified error is irrespective of the initialized values **What to do?** • Remove either of the definitions made in line numbers 5 or 6
2	#include<stdio.h>	
3	main()	
4	{	
5	int a=10;	
6	int a=20;	
7	printf("The value of a is %d",a);	
8	}	

Program 7-5 | A program that illustrates the application of one definition rule

Although it is not allowed to define an identifier more than once in the same scope, it is possible to define an identifier with the same name more than once, if the definitions lie in different scopes. In such a case, all of them refer to separate objects. The piece of code in Program 7-6 illustrates this fact.

Line	Prog 7-6.c	Output window
1	//Multiple definitions of an identifier in different scopes	The value of a & b in line 6 is 10 20
2	#include<stdio.h>	The value of a & b in line 9 is 20 30
3	int a=10, b=20;	The value of a & b in line 12 is 30.500000 40

(Contd...)

[‡] Refer Section 7.4 for a description on object.

[§] Refer Section 7.3 for a description on linkage.

```c
main()
{
    printf("The value of a & b in line 6 is %d %d\n",a,b);
    {
        int a=20, b=30;
        printf("The value of a & b in line 9 is %d %d\n", a,b);
        {
            float a=30.5; int b=40;
            printf("The value of a & b in line 12 is %f %d\n", a,b);
        }
    }
}
```

Remarks:

- The identifier a is defined thrice in the program, even then there is no compilation error because the definitions are present in different scopes
- One definition rule states that only one definition of an identifier can be present in a scope

Program 7-6 | A program illustrating that multiple definitions of an identifier can be present in different scopes

In Program 7-6, we have seen that it is possible to define identifiers with the same name (having same type or different types) in different scopes. However, it is not possible to declare an identifier with the same name but different types in different scopes. Even if the declarations are present in different scopes, the type of identifiers in multiple declarations must be identical. The piece of code in Program 7-7 illustrates this fact.

Prog 7-7.c

```c
//Multiple declarations in different scope
#include<stdio.h>
extern int a;
main()
{
    extern float a;
    printf("This is not allowed");
}
```

Output window

Compilation error "Type mismatch in re-declaration of 'a' in function main"

Remark:

- The type of identifiers must be identical in all the declarations, whether they lie in the same scope or different scopes

Program 7-7 | A program illustrating that the type of an identifier must be identical in all the declarations irrespective of the scope in which the declaration is present

7.2.4 Visibility of an Identifier

An identifier is **visible** (i.e. can be used) only in the portion of a program encompassed by its scope. The **visibility of an identifier** (except label) begins from the point of its declaration till the termination of its scope. The visibility of a label name is within the function in which the identifier-labeled statement specifying the label name appears, i.e. within the opening and the closing brace of the function definition in which it appears.

Consider the piece of code in Program 7-8 that makes use of various identifiers. The regions of the program in which the identifiers are visible are shown in column 3 in Figure 7.1.

Code window

```
//Visibility of an identifier
#include<stdio.h>
int func(int a, int b);
int c;
main()
{
    int d;
    //...Statements
}
int e;
int func(int f, int g)
{
    int h;
    //...Statements
    label:
    //...Statements
    goto label;
}
```

Visibility region (Column 3)

- a and b are visible only within function prototype
- d is visible from this point till the end of the function main
- e is visible from this point till the end of the file, including the function func. It is not visible inside the function main
- f, g, h and label are visible only within the function func
- c is visible from this point onwards till the end of the file. It is visible in the functions main and func

Figure 7.1 | Visibility of an identifier

An identifier cannot be used outside the region in which it is visible. If it is used, it leads to a compilation error. The piece of code in Program 7-8 illustrates this fact.

Prog 7-8.c

```
1  //An identifier used outside its scope
2  #include<stdio.h>
3  void func();
4  main()
5  {
6      int a=20;
7      printf("The value of a in main is %d\n",a);
8      func();
9  }
10 void func()
11 {
12     printf("The value of a in func is %d",a);
13 }
```

Output window

Compilation error "Undefined symbol 'a' in function func"

Remarks:

- The identifier a declared (actually defined) in line number 6 has a local scope and is visible only inside the function main
- The usage of identifier a in the function func is not valid since it is not visible there

What to do?

- Either define a in the global scope so that it is visible in both the functions main and func or re-define identifier a in the function func

Program 7-8 | A program illustrating that an identifier cannot be used outside of the region in which it is visible

7.2.4.1 Shadowing and Name Resolution

When an identifier with a same name is defined in different scopes, all the definitions refer to separate objects. Now when the identifier is used in an expression, it should be determined as to which object this usage of identifier refers to. The principle of shadowing helps in determining the object to which a particular usage of an identifier refers to. **Shadowing** states that the definition of an identifier in the immediate scope (i.e. present or current scope) shadows (i.e. hides, supersedes) the definitions of the identifier present in the enclosing scope.

Name resolution is a process by which a name (i.e. an identifier) used in an expression is associated with a declaration. It uses the principle of shadowing and works as follows:

1. The declaration of a name is searched in the immediate scope. If the declaration is found, the name is resolved and is associated with the declaration.
2. If the declaration is not found, the enclosing scope is searched. If the declaration is found, the name is resolved and is associated with the declaration.
3. If the declaration is still not found, the process in Step 2 is repeated until either a declaration is found or the global scope has been searched.
4. If the global scope has been searched and no declaration has been found, the use of the identifier name is flagged as an error.

---

i In some places, the word declaration is used in place of definition. The places where declaration actually means definition can be determined by the context.

The piece of code in Program 7-9 illustrates the principle of shadowing and name resolution.

Line | Prog 7-9.c

```
1  //Shadowing and name resolution
2  #include<stdio.h>
3  int a=10;    //←identifier a defined in file/global scope
4  main()
5  {
6      printf("The value of a in line 6 is %d\n",a);
7      {
8          int a=20; //←This definition of a shadows the definition
9                    //    of a present in the global scope
10         printf("The value of a in line 10 is %d\n",a);
11         {
12             float a=30.5;//←This definition of a shadows the definition of a
13                          // present in the global scope and the enclosing block scope
14             printf("The value of a in line 14 is %f\n",a);
15         }
16     }
17 }
```

Output window

```
The value of a in line 6 is 10
The value of a in line 10 is 20
The value of a in line 14 is 30.500000
```

Remarks:

- To resolve the usage of the identifier a in line number 6, the immediate scope is searched. Since there is no declaration of a in the immediate scope, the enclosing scope, i.e. global scope is searched. The declaration of a is found and the usage of a in line number 6 is associated with this declaration (actually definition). Hence, the value of a in line number 6 is 10
- To resolve the usage of identifier a in line number 10, the immediate scope, i.e. block scope is searched. The declaration of a is found in line number 8 and the usage of a is resolved with this declaration. Hence the value of a in line number 10 is 20
- Similarly, the usage of a in line number 14 is resolved with the declaration present in the immediate block scope at line number 12

Program 7-9 | A program that illustrates shadowing and name resolution

7.3 Linkage

Linkage is a process by which the identifiers declared in different scopes, or in the same scope more than once, are made to refer to the same data object or the function. There are three different types of linkage:

1. External linkage
2. Internal linkage
3. No linkage

7.3.1 External linkage

The C language allows a program to be spread across two or more files, compiled separately and then linked together. In a program that consists of a set of translation units (i.e. files) and libraries; each declaration of a particular identifier with an external linkage denotes the same object or the function. An identifier with an external linkage can be used anywhere within a multi-file program.

The linkage of an identifier can be made external by using **extern** storage class specifier in the declaration statement. All the global variables and functions by default have external linkage. The code snippet in Program 7-10 illustrates the use of identifiers with an external linkage.

Prog 7-10 one.c

```
1 //External linkage
2 #include<stdio.h>
3 fun();
4 main()
5 {
6 extern int a;
7 printf("In main value of a is %d",a);
8 fun();
9 }
```

two.c

```
int a=20;
fun()
{
printf("In fun value of a is %d",a);
}
```

Project window new10.prj

Files
- one.c
- two.c

Output window

```
In main value of a is 20
In fun value of a is 20
```

Remarks:
- By default, all the global variables and the functions have external linkage
- Global variable a and the function fun defined in two.c have external linkage
- The linkage of the identifier a declared in line number 6 in one.c is made external by using extern storage class specifier
- The declaration of a in line number 6 and the use of function fun in line number 8 in the file one.c refers to the definitions in the file two.c
- Although a is defined in the file two.c, it is mandatory to declare the identifier a in the file one.c before its usage

Program 7-10 | A program that illustrates the usage of external linkage

Figure 7.2 Illustrates the execution of the multi-file program using Turbo C 3.0.

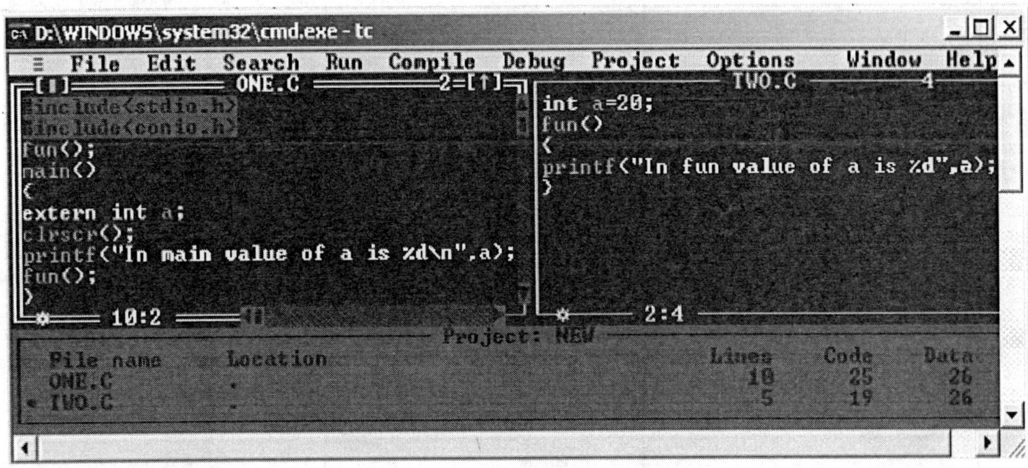

(a) Edit window

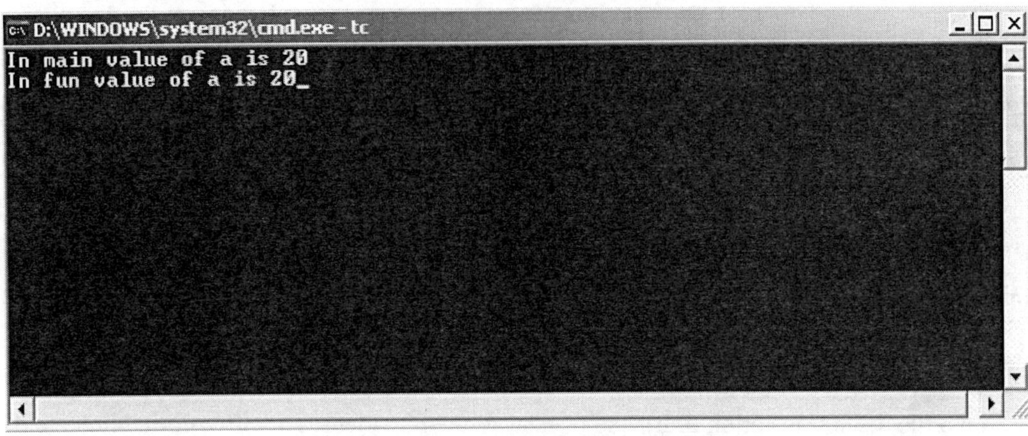

(b) User screen

Figure 7.2 | Snapshots of the multi-file program and its execution using Turbo C 3.0

The objects with an external linkage are accessible within all the translation units of a program and hence must be uniquely defined. Multiple definitions of an identifier with external linkage in different translation units lead to linker errors. The piece of code in Program 7-11 illustrates this fact.

Prog 7-11 one.c	two.c	Project window newll.prj

//Usage of objects with external linkage
//in multiple translation units
#include<stdio.h>
fun();
main()
	int a=20;
	fun()
	{
	printf("The value of a in func is %d",a);
	}
		Files
		• one.c
		• two.c

(Contd...)

Prog 7-11 one.c	two.c	Output window

{
extern int a;
printf("The value of a in main is %d",a);
fun();
}
int a=10;
		Linker error "_a defined in module one.c is duplicated in module two.c"
		Remarks:
		• The files one.c and two.c are compiled separately and there is no compilation error
		• The identifier a is defined in both the files one.c and two.c
		• Since both the definitions have external linkage, they will be visible across the program. These duplicate definitions lead to the linker error
		What to do?
		• Either remove the definition made in one.c, or
		• Change the linkage of a in two.c from external to internal so that it is accessible only within two.c
		• Refer Section 7.3.2 to know how to change the linkage of global variables and functions from external to internal

Program 7-11 | A program illustrating that objects with external linkage are accessible within all the translation units of a program

7.3.2 Internal Linkage

Within a file (i.e. a translation unit), each declaration of an identifier with internal linkage denotes the same object or the function. The object and the function are unique to that translation unit. Such objects and functions can only be accessed in the translation unit in which they are defined and are not accessible in other translation units.

The linkage of an identifier can be made internal by using **static** storage class specifier in the declaration statement. The code snippet in Program 7-12 illustrates the use of identifiers with an internal linkage.

Prog 7-12 one.c	two.c	Project window new12.prj

//Usage of internal linkage
#include<stdio.h>
fun();
	static int a=20;
	fun()
	{
		Files
		• one.c
		• two.c

(Contd...)

		Output window

main()
{
extern int a;
printf("In main value of a is %d",a);
fun();
}
int a=10;
	printf("In fun value of a is %d",a);
	}
		In main value of a is 10
		In fun value of a is 20
		Remarks:
		• The linkage of identifier a defined in two.c is made internal by using the static storage class specifier
		• The identifier a defined in two.c is accessible only within two.c and hence does not duplicate the definition of identifier a present in one.c
		• The function fun defined in two.c still has external linkage and, therefore, is accessible from one.c
		Try:
		• Make the linkage of function fun internal so that it is not accessible from one.c
		• To make the linkage of function fun internal, write the header of the function fun as static fun() in the file two.c
		• Look for the errors that creep in by changing the linkage of the function fun defined in two.c

Program 7-12 | A program that illustrates the usage of internal linkage

Figure 7-3 illustrates the execution of Program 7-12 by using Turbo C 3.0.

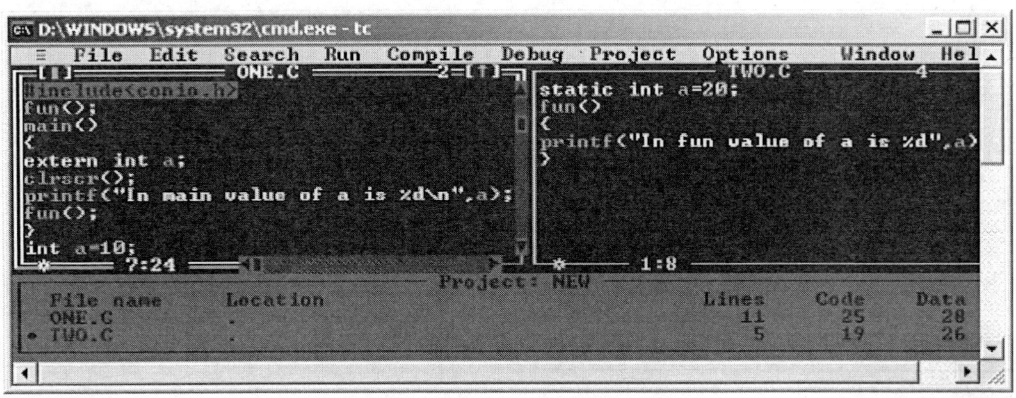

(a) Edit window

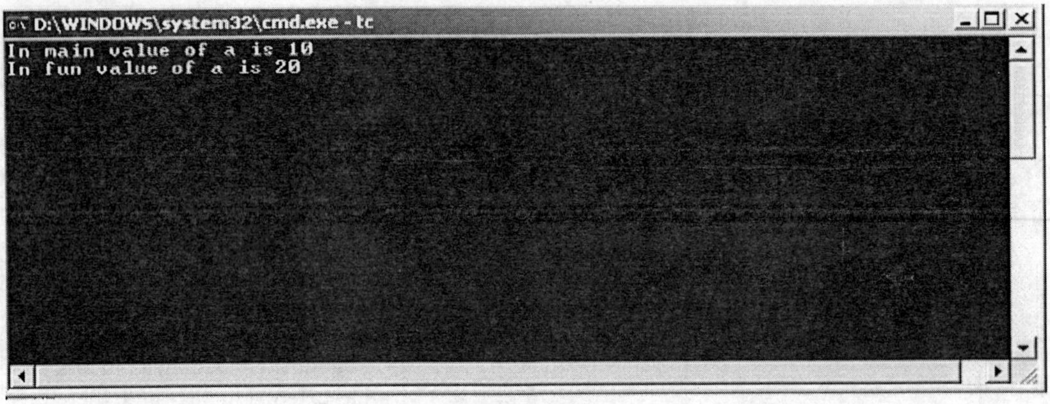

(b) User screen

Figure 7.3 | Snapshots of Program 7-12 and its execution using Turbo C 3.0

7.3.3 No Linkage

By default, all the identifiers with block scope or function prototype scope have no linkage. Each of the declared identifier (except functions) with no linkage refers to a separate object. Functions can have internal linkage or external linkage only. They cannot have no linkage.

7.4 Storage Duration/Lifetime of an Object

An identifier denotes an object. Whenever an identifier is declared (actually defined), some storage space depending upon the type of an identifier is reserved by the compiler. For example, upon encountering the declaration statement `int variable=20;`, the compiler reserves 2 bytes (or 4 bytes in Turbo C 4.5) of storage space. Upon execution, the reserved storage space is allocated. The allocated memory space is denoted as an **object** (specifically data object). This is shown in Figure 7.4.

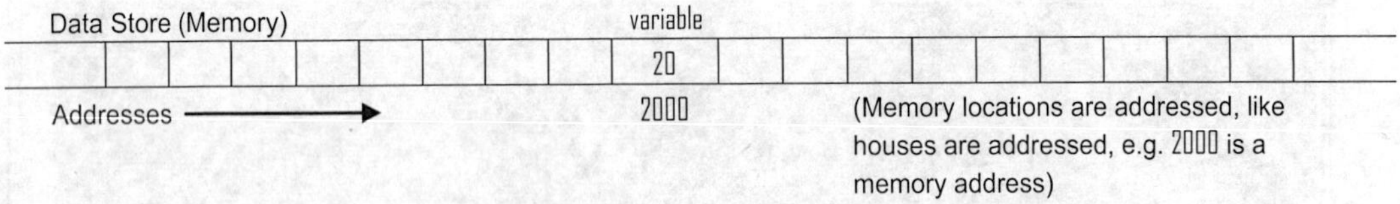

Figure 7.4 | Data object `variable` allocated at the memory location 2000

i Object exists only at the run time, i.e. at the time of execution of the program.

The duration for which the storage space is reserved depends upon the **storage duration** of the object. The storage duration of an object determines its **lifetime**. Thus, the **lifetime of an object** is a portion of the program execution during which the memory space is guaranteed to be reserved for it. Throughout the lifetime of an object, it has a constant address and it retains its last stored value. The lifetime of an object and the scope of an identifier are related but are entirely different concepts. Ideally, **the scope of an identifier should be a subset of the lifetime of an object** it denotes; otherwise, it would be possible to refer to an identifier even after its denoted storage space goes away. If an object is referred outside of its lifetime, its behavior would be undefined.

In C language, there are three types of lifetime:

1. **Static (or global):** An object (i.e. a function or a variable) with static or global lifetime exists and has a value throughout the execution of a program. All the objects associated with the functions and global identifiers have static or global lifetime.
2. **Automatic (or local):** Objects with automatic or local lifetime are allocated new storage space each time the execution control passes to the block in which their associated identifiers are defined. When the program control moves out of the block, the objects associated with the identifiers defined within the block cease to exist and no longer have meaningful values. All the objects associated with the local identifiers by default have automatic or local lifetime.
3. **Allocated:** The lifetime of an allocated object extends from the time of their allocation until deallocation. The allocation is done with the help of memory allocation functions like **malloc**, **calloc** or **realloc**.¶ The deallocation can be done by calling the library function named **free**. The malloc, calloc or realloc functions allocate the memory at the run time. The allocation of memory made at the run time is known as **dynamic memory allocation** (refer footnote¶), in contrast to the **static memory allocation**, in which the memory is allocated (actually reserved) at the compile time.

7.5 Storage Classes

Every identifier not only has a data type but also has a storage class. To fully define an identifier, one needs to mention not only its data type, but also its **storage class**. If any storage class is not specified in a declaration statement, the compiler assumes the default storage class depending upon the scope in which the declaration is made. The **storage class** of an identifier determines:

1. Where the object associated with the identifier would be stored (in the memory or CPU registers).
2. What the initial value of the object associated with the identifier would be (if the identifier is not initialized in the declaration statement).
3. Whether the object associated with the identifier would have static (global) or automatic (local) lifetime.
4. What the linkage of a function or an identifier would be.

The storage class of an identifier can be specified with the help of a **storage class specifier**. The storage class specifier is prefixed in a declaration statement declaring an identifier associated with the object. The C language provides the following storage class specifiers:

1. auto
2. register
3. static

¶ Refer Section 7.6 for a description on malloc, calloc, realloc functions and dynamic memory allocation.

4. extern
5. typedef

The general syntax of a declaration statement is:

[**storage_class_specifier**][type_qualifier | type_modifier] datatype identifiername [=value[, ...]];

For example, the declaration statement static int a;, associates static storage class with the object identified by a.

The important points about the usage of storage class specifiers in a declaration statement are as follows:

1. At most one storage class specifier can be specified in a declaration statement. For example, the declaration statement auto register int a; is erroneous as two storage class specifiers, i.e. auto and register have been used in the declaration statement.
2. The storage class specifier that can be used in a declaration statement depends upon the scope in which the declaration is made. The exact meaning of each storage class specifier depends upon:
    a. Whether the declaration appears in the global scope or local scope.
    b. Whether the identifier being declared is a variable or a function.

The following sections present the use of various storage class specifiers in detail.

7.5.1 The auto Storage Class

The important points about the **auto** storage class are as follows:

1. By default, an object whose identifier has block scope or local scope (i.e. declared within a block) has auto storage class.
2. The storage class specifier auto specifies that the declared data object (i.e. variable) will be stored in the main memory.
3. It specifies that the declared object will have automatic (local) lifetime. The object will come into existence from the point of its declaration and remains into existence till the program control remains within the block in which it is declared. The code snippet in Program 7-13 illustrates this fact.

Trace	Prog 7-13.c	Output window
	//Existence of auto variables	The value of a is 10 The value of b is 20 Here b is not visible The value of a is 10 **Remarks:** • To look at the value of the variable a and b at various trace steps, add watch on a and b • The procedure to add watch in Turbo C 3.0 is: o Go to Debug Menu by pressing 'Alt+d' o Go to watch option by pressing 'w' o Press 'Enter' to add watch on variable a o Repeat the entire procedure to add watch on variable b
	#include<stdio.h>	
1	main()	
	{	
2	auto int a=10	
3	printf("The value of a is %d\n",a);	
	{	
4	int b=20;	
5	printf("The value of b is %d\n",b);	
	}	
6	printf("Here b is not visible\n");	
7	printf("The value of a is %d",a);	
8	}	

(Contd...)

			o The shortcut key to add watch is 'Ctrl+F7' • The procedure to add watch in Turbo C 4.5 is: o Go to Debug Menu by pressing 'Alt+d' o Go to watch option by pressing 'w' o The shortcut for the first two steps (i.e. for opening watch option directly) is Ctrl+F5 o Enter the expression on which watch is to be placed i.e. variable a o Repeat the entire procedure to add watch on variable b • After adding watch, start tracing and open watch window to observe the value of a and b. • To open the watch window, go to the window menu by pressing 'Alt+w' and then select the watch option by pressing 'w'
			Watch window
			At trace step 1: Undefined symbol 'a' Undefined symbol 'b'
			At trace step 2: a=-29011 (i.e. Garbage value as a is yet not initialized) Undefined symbol 'b' (b is not yet defined as the program control has not yet entered the block in which it is declared)
			At trace step 3: a=10 Undefined symbol 'b'
			After trace step 3, i.e. At trace step 4: a=10; b=657 (i.e. Garbage value as b is not yet initialized)
			At trace step 5: a=10 b=20
			At trace step 6: a=10 Undefined symbol 'b' (Now b does not exist as the program control came out of the block in which it is declared)
			After trace step 8: Undefined symbol 'a' Undefined symbol 'b'

Program 7-13 | A program illustrating that the auto objects have automatic lifetime

4. The variables declared with auto storage class specification are not implicitly initialized. A variable declared with auto storage class specification has to be explicitly initialized, otherwise it will have a garbage value.
5. It is not possible to specify auto storage class specifier in the declarations that are made in the global scope. The piece of code in Program 7-14 illustrates this fact.

Prog 7-14.c

```
//auto storage class specifier
#include<stdio.h>
auto int a;
main()
{
    printf("Enter the value of a");
    scanf("%d",&a);
    printf("The entered value is %d",a);
}
```

Output window

Compilation error "Storage class 'auto' is not allowed here"

Remark:

- Since the scope of an identifier should be a subset of the lifetime of its object, auto (i.e. local) cannot be the lifetime of an object that has a global scope

Program 7-14 | A program illustrating that auto storage class specifier cannot be used in the declarations made in the global scope

6. The variables declared with auto storage class specification have no linkage.

7.5.2 The register Storage Class

The important points about the register storage class are as follows:

1. The register storage class suggests that the access to the declared object should be as fast as possible.
2. The object of an identifier for which the register storage class has been specified is stored in central processing unit (CPU) register instead of being stored in random access memory (RAM) or the main memory, if possible. The CPU register is a scarce resource and provides faster access than memory. If it is not possible to spare a CPU register to store an identifier; the identifier will be stored in RAM and the register specification is simply treated as auto specification.
3. The storage class specifier register specifies that the declared object will have automatic (i.e. local) lifetime. Hence, the register storage class specifier cannot be used in the declarations made in the global scope.
4. The variables declared with register storage class specification are not implicitly initialized. A variable declared with register storage class specification has to be explicitly initialized, otherwise it will have a garbage value.
5. The variables declared with register storage class specification have no linkage.
6. It is not possible to compute the address of an object whose identifier is declared with register storage class specifier. If address-of operator (i.e. &) is applied to an object declared with storage class register, the compiler will issue an error message. The piece of code in Program 7-15 illustrates this fact.

Prog 7-15.c

```
//register storage class specifier and the address of an identifier
#include<stdio.h>
main()
{
    register int a=200;
    printf("The value of a is %d\n", a);
    printf("The address of variable a is %p",&a);
}
```

Output window

Compilation error "Must take address of a memory location"

Remarks:

- It is not possible to compute the address of a variable declared with register storage class specification
- Note that some compilers ignore the register storage class specifier and store objects in the memory as an auto object. In such a case, there will be no compilation error and the address of the allocated memory space will be printed

Program 7-15 | A program illustrating that it is not possible to compute the address of an object whose identifier is declared with a register storage class specifier

8. The register storage class is commonly used for loop counters to improve the performance of a program.

7.5.3 The static Storage Class

The important points about the static storage class are as follows:

1. The storage class specifier static specifies that the declared object will have static (i.e. global) lifetime.
2. It specifies that the declared object will be stored in the main memory.
3. It can be used both with the identifiers declared in the local scope (i.e. local identifiers) as well as in the global scope (i.e. global identifiers).
4. The variables declared with static storage class specification are implicitly initialized. If a variable declared with static storage class specification is not explicitly initialized, its object will be implicitly initialized to 0 if it is of int type, 0.0 if it is of float type and '\0' if it is of char type.
5. If a static variable is present inside the local scope, the associated object is initialized only once. The object will not be reinitialized even if the program control re-enters the block in which the variable is declared. Thus, the value of static variables persists between the function calls. The piece of code in Program 7-16 illustrates this fact.

Prog 7-16.c

```
//The value of static variables persists between the function calls
#include<stdio.h>
fun(int i);
main()
{
int i=0;
for(i=0;i<5;)
    fun(++i);
}
```

Output window

The value of a on entry to fun on execution no. 1 is 10
The value of a after increment is 11
The value of a on entry to fun on execution no. 2 is 11
The value of a after increment is 12
The value of a on entry to fun on execution no. 3 is 12
The value of a after increment is 13
The value of a on entry to fun on execution no. 4 is 13
The value of a after increment is 14
The value of a on entry to fun on execution no. 5 is 14
The value of a after increment is 15

(Contd...)

Prog 7-16.c

```
fun(int i)
{
    static int a=10;
    printf("The value of a on entry to fun on execution no. %d is %d\n", i, a);
    printf("The value of a after increment is %d\n",++a);
}
```

Output window

Remarks:

- The value of variable a persists between the function calls
- The variable a is initialized only once, i.e. when the function fun is called for the first time

Program 7-16 | A program illustrating that the value of static variables persists between the function calls

6. The static storage class specifier can also be used to modify the linkage of an identifier:
   a. The global identifiers by default have external linkage. If static specifier is used in the declaration of a global identifier, the identifier will have internal linkage instead of external linkage.
   b. When static storage class specifier is used with the local identifiers, the local identifiers will have internal linkage instead of no linkage.
7. The static storage class specifier cannot be used in parameter declaration either in the function declaration or in the function definition. The piece of code in Program 7-17 illustrates this fact.

Prog 7-17.c

```
//static storage class specifier
#include<stdio.h>
int add(static int a, static int b)
{
return a+b;
}
main()
{
int c=add(2,3);
printf("The value of c is %d",c);
}
```

Output window

Compilation error "Storage class static is not allowed here"

Remark:

- The usage of static storage class specifier is not allowed in the parameter declaration either in the function declaration or in the function definition

Program 7-17 | A program illustrating that a static storage class specifier cannot be used in the parameter declaration either in the function declaration or in the function definition

7.5.4 The extern Storage Class

The important points about the **extern** storage class are as follows:

1. Identifiers declared in the global scope, by default, have extern storage class.
2. The storage class specifier extern is used to declare a variable without defining it.
3. However, if a variable is initialized, the extern declaration becomes a definition. For example, extern int a; is a declaration but extern int a=200; is a definition. The initialization is possible only if the declaration is done in the file or global scope.
4. An extern variable cannot be initialized if a declaration statement is written within the block or local scope. The piece of code in Program 7-18 illustrates this fact.

Prog 7-18.c	Output window

//extern storage class specifier
#include<stdio.h>
main()
{
    extern int a=200;
    printf("The value of a is %d",a);
}
	Compilation error "extern variable cannot be initialized in function main"
	"Undefined symbol 'a' in function main"
	Remarks:
	• The extern storage class can only be used with the objects that have external linkage
	• Since local variables have no linkage, extern cannot be used in the declaration statement present in the local scope

Program 7-18 | A program illustrating that an extern variable cannot be initialized if the declaration is done in the block scope or local scope

5. The extern storage class specifier is used to specify that an object is defined with external linkage elsewhere in a program.
6. The extern storage class specifier cannot be used in the parameter declaration either in the function declaration or in the function definition. The piece of code in Program 7-19 illustrates this fact.

Prog 7-19.c	Output window

//extern storage class specifier
#include<stdio.h>
int add(extern int a, extern int b)
{
return a+b;
}
main()
{
int c=add(2,3);
printf("The value of c is %d",c);
}
	Compilation error "Storage class extern is not allowed here"
	Remark:
	• The function parameters can only have auto or register storage class

Program 7-19 | A program illustrating that extern storage class specifier cannot be used in the parameter declaration either in the function definition or declaration

7.5.5 The typedef Storage Class

The important points about the typedef storage class are as follows:

1. The typedef storage class specifier is used for syntactic convenience only.
2. typedef is used for creating a synonym or an alias for a known type.
3. The syntax of writing a typedef declaration is:

```
typedef known-type-T synonym-name;
```

   where T is a generic term and can be int, float, char or any other type.

The code snippet in Program 7-20 illustrates the use of typedef storage class.

Prog 7-20.c

```
1 //typedef storage class specifier
2 #include<stdio.h>
3 main()
4 {
5 typedef char* cp;
6 cp c;
7 printf("The size of character pointer c is %d bytes",sizeof(c));
8 }
```

Output window

The size of character pointer c is 2 bytes

Remarks:

- After creating a synonym name cp using typedef, it is possible to refer to the type char* by writing cp
- The declaration in line number 6, declares a variable c of type char*
- If executed using Borland TC 4.5, the size of the character pointer would be 4 bytes

Program 7-20 | A program that illustrates the use of typedef storage class specifier

4. Note that typedef does not introduce a new type. It only creates a synonym for the known type.

Table 7.1 summarizes the features of a variable defined with the described storage class specifications.

Table 7.1 | Summary of storage classes

S.No	Storage class	Storage	Initial value	Lifetime	Linkage
1.	auto	Memory	Garbage	Automatic	No
2.	register	CPU registers	Garbage	Automatic	No
3.	static	Memory	Zero	Static	Internal
4.	extern	Memory	Zero	Static	External
5.	typedef	Used for syntactic convenience only			

7.6 Dynamic Memory Allocation

The allocation of memory at the run time (i.e. as a program executes) is known as **dynamic memory allocation**. In C language, memory can be dynamically allocated by calling malloc, calloc or realloc functions. The prototypes of these functions are available in the header files alloc.h or malloc.h. The functions that are used for dynamic memory allocation are as follows:

1. **The malloc function:**

   The syntax of malloc function is:

   ```
   void* malloc(size_t size);
   ```

   The important points about the malloc function are as follows:

   i. The malloc function allocates the memory space for an object whose size is specified by the parameter size.

   ii. size_t is not a type. It is a synonym for the type unsigned int. The type definition for size_t is available in the header files alloc.h and malloc.h.

iii. The allocated space will not be initialized. The value of the allocated space will be undetermined (i.e. garbage).
iv. The dynamically allocated memory is allocated from heap.
v. The malloc function returns a void pointer (i.e. void*) to the allocated space, if successful.
vi. If unsuccessful in making the allocation, it returns a null pointer.

✍ Before using malloc, calloc or realloc functions, include header file alloc.h or malloc.h if you are using Borland Turbo C 3.0 or Borland Turbo C 4.5 and malloc.h if you are using Microsoft Visual C++ 6.0.

The piece of code in Program 7-21 illustrates the use of the malloc function.

Prog 7-21.c (Trace steps: 1 at main(), 2 at float *ptr;, 3 at ptr=..., 4 at *ptr=30.25;, 5 at printf, 6 at })

```
//Use of malloc function
#include<stdio.h>
#include<malloc.h>
main()
{
    float *ptr;
    ptr=(float*)malloc(sizeof(float));
    *ptr=30.25;
    printf("The value within block is\n%f",*ptr);
}
```

Memory contents

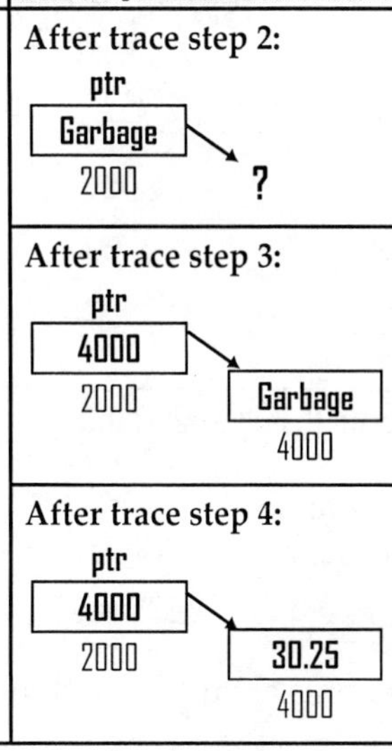

Output window

The value within block is
30.250000

Program 7-21 | A program that illustrates the use of the malloc function

2. **The calloc function:**
The syntax of the calloc function is:

```
void* calloc(size_t n, size_t size);
```

The important points about the calloc function are as follows:

i. The calloc function allocates the memory space for an array of n objects, each of whose size is specified by the parameter size.
ii. All the bits in the allocated memory space are initialized to zero.
iii. The function returns a void pointer (i.e. void*) to the allocated memory space, if successful.
iv. If the memory space cannot be allocated, a null pointer is returned.

The piece of code in Program 7-22 illustrates the use of the calloc function.

Trace	Prog 7-22.c
	//Use of calloc function
	#include<stdio.h>
	#include<malloc.h>
1	main()
	{
2	int *ptr,i;
3	ptr=(int*)calloc(3,sizeof(int));
4,6,8,10	for(i=0;i<=2;i++)
5,7,9	*(ptr+i)=10*(i+1);
11,13,15,17	for(i=0;i<=2;i++)
12,14,16	printf("The value at the index %d is %d\n",i,*(ptr+i));
18	}

Memory contents

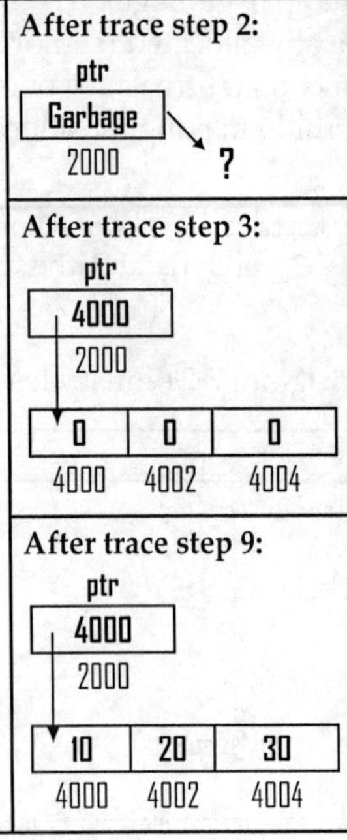

Output window

The value at the index 0 is 10
The value at the index 1 is 20
The value at the index 2 is 30

Program 7-22 | A program that illustrates the use of the calloc function

3. **The realloc function:**
   The syntax of the realloc function is:

```
void* realloc(void *ptr, size_t size);
```

The important points about the realloc function are as follows:

i. The realloc function deallocates the old object pointed by ptr and returns a pointer to a new object that has the size specified by the parameter size.
ii. The major use of the realloc function is to resize the dynamically allocated object (especially an array).
iii. The content of the new object shall be the same as that of the old object prior to deallocation, if the new object is greater in size than the old object. Any bytes in the new object beyond the size of the old object have undetermined values (i.e. garbage values).
iv. If ptr given to the realloc function is a null pointer, the realloc function behaves like the malloc function.
v. If the second argument (i.e. size) passed to the realloc function is zero, it behaves like a free function.
vi. If ptr does not match a ptr earlier returned by a malloc, calloc or realloc function, or if space has been deallocated by call to the free or realloc function, its behavior is undefined.
vii. If the memory for the new object cannot be allocated, the old object is not deallocated and its value remains unchanged.
viii. The realloc function returns a void pointer (i.e. void*) to the new object, or a null pointer if the new object cannot be allocated.

The piece of code in Program 7-23 illustrates the use of the realloc function.

Trace	Prog 7-23.c
	//Use of realloc function
	#include<stdio.h>
	#include<malloc.h>
1	main()
	{
2	int *ptr,i;
3	ptr=(int*)calloc(3,sizeof(int));
4,6,8,10	for(i=0;i<=2;i++)
5,7,9	ptr[i]=10*(i+1);
	//ptr[3] is illegal
11	ptr=(int*)realloc(ptr,5*sizeof(int));
12	ptr[3]=23;
13	ptr[4]=84;
14,16,18,20,22,24	for(i=0;i<=4;i++)
15,17,19,21,23	printf("Value at index %d is %d\n",i,*(ptr+i));
25	realloc(ptr,0); //equivalent to free(ptr)
26	}

Memory contents

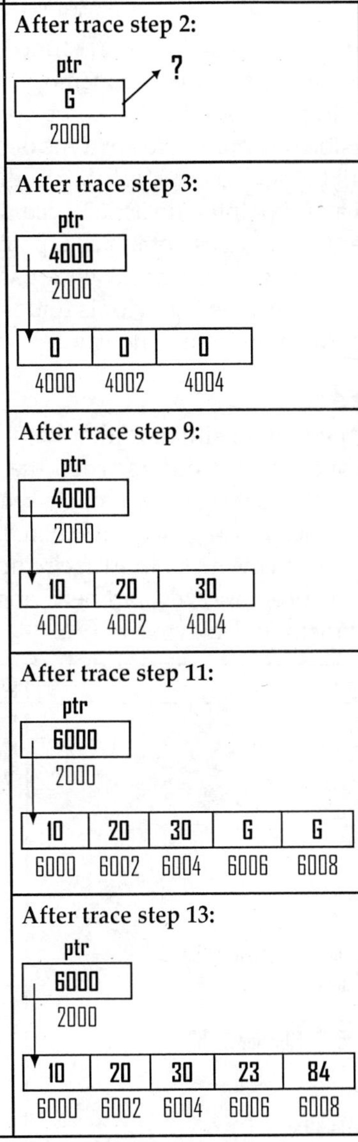

Output window

```
Value at index 0 is 10
Value at index 1 is 20
Value at index 2 is 30
Value at index 3 is 23
Value at index 4 is 84
```

Program 7-23 | A program that illustrates the use of the realloc function

Since malloc, calloc and realloc functions return a void pointer, the returned pointer must be type casted to the appropriate type before use.

The lifetime of dynamically allocated objects extends from the time of their allocation until deallocation. The deallocation is automatically done with the termination of a program or can be done by giving a call to the function free.

4. **The free function:**

   The syntax of the free function is:

   ```
   void free(void* ptr);
   ```

   The important points about the free function are as follows:

   i. The free function causes the memory space pointed to by ptr to be deallocated.

   ii. Pointer to any type of object can be passed as an argument to the free function. The conversion of a pointer to any type of object to a void pointer is a standard conversion and will be carried out implicitly without any explicit type cast.

   iii. If ptr is a null pointer, no action occurs.

   iv. If the argument does not match a pointer earlier returned by the calloc, malloc or realloc functions or if the memory space has already been deallocated by a call to free or realloc functions, the behavior is undefined.

   v. The free function returns no value.

7.6.1 Memory Leak

Memory leak is a common situation that happens when the dynamic memory allocation is used without proper care. It occurs when the dynamically allocated memory is no longer needed but it is not freed. If we continuously keep on allocating the memory without freeing it for reuse, the entire heap storage will be exhausted. After this, it will not be possible to allocate any memory space from the heap. In such circumstances, the memory allocation functions will start failing and the program will start behaving unexpectedly. The piece of code in Program 7-24 suffers from memory leak.

Prog 7-24.c

```c
//Memory leak
#include<stdio.h>
#include<malloc.h>
#include<string.h>
void lcase(char* Uname)
{
    char *Lname;
    int i=0;
    Lname=(char*)malloc(strlen(Uname)+1);
    while(*(Uname+i)!='\0')
    {
        *(Lname+i)=*(Uname+i)+32;
        i++;
    }
    *(Lname+i)='\0';
    printf("Name in Lower Case is %s\n",Lname);
    //←To avoid memory leak, place free(Lname); here
}
main()
{
    char name[]="SAM";
    printf("Name in Upper Case is %s\n",name);
    lcase(name);
}
```

Output window

```
Name in Upper Case is SAM
Name in Lower Case is sam
```

Remarks:

- The mentioned piece of code converts an uppercase string into lowercase
- The code suffers from memory leak
- The memory has been allocated in the function lcase by giving a call to the malloc function but it is not freed
- This dynamically allocated memory has allocated lifetime, i.e. it exists till it is not freed by giving a call to the function free or till the program does not terminate
- Thus, the allocated memory exists even after the program control returns from the function lcase
- If the function lcase is called larger number of times in the function main, the entire heap storage will be exhausted and the program will start behaving unexpectedly
- To rectify the problem, use free function at the end of lcase function to free the allocated memory for reuse

Program 7-24 | A program that suffers from memory leak

7.7 Summary

1. The scope of an identifier is a region of the program within which the identifier is visible (i.e. it can be used).
2. There are four types of scopes, namely file scope or global scope, block scope or local scope, function prototype scope and function scope.
3. Two identifiers have the same scope if and only if their scopes terminate at the same point.
4. The keyword `extern` provides a method for declaring an identifier without defining it.
5. An identifier can have many identical declarations in the same scope.
6. It is not allowed to define an identifier more than once in the same scope.
7. One definition rule states that each object must have only one definition in a scope.
8. It is possible to define an identifier with the same name more than once if the definitions lie in different scopes.
9. Shadowing states that the definition of an identifier in the immediate scope shadows/supersedes the definitions of the identifier present in the enclosing scope.
10. Name resolution is a process by which a name used in an expression is associated with a declaration or a definition.
11. Linkage is a process by which the identifiers declared in different scopes or in the same scope more than once can be made to refer to the same data object or function.
12. Lifetime of an object is the portion of the program execution during which the storage is guaranteed to be reserved for it.
13. To fully define an identifier, we also need to specify its storage class.
14. There are five storage classes, namely `auto`, `register`, `static`, `extern` and `typedef`.
15. Allocation of the memory at the run time is called dynamic memory allocation.
16. The memory can be allocated dynamically by using the `malloc`, `calloc` or `realloc` functions.
17. The `free` function is used to deallocate the memory allocated by `malloc`, `calloc` or `realloc` functions.
18. Careless allocation of the memory at the run time leads to memory leak.

Exercise Questions

Conceptual Questions and Answers

1. *What is meant by the scope of an identifier? What are the different types of scopes available in C language?*

   The scope of an identifier is a region of the program within which the identifier is visible (i.e. it can be used). C defines four scopes that determine the visibility of an identifier:

   1. File scope or global scope
   2. Block scope or local scope
   3. Function prototype scope
   4. Function scope

Backward Reference: Refer Section 7.2 for a description on the scope of an identifier.

2. *How can I determine whether an identifier has file scope, block scope, function scope or function prototype scope?*

Backward Reference: Refer Section 7.2.1 for a description on the determination of the scope of an identifier.

3. *How can I determine the region of the program in which an identifier is visible?*

Backward Reference: Refer Sections 7.2.4 and 7.2.2 to determine the visibility of an identifier.

4. *When is the scope of two identifiers said to be the same?*

Backward Reference: Refer Section 7.2.3 for a description on the same scope.

5. *What is the difference between declaring a variable and defining a variable?*

Backward Reference: Refer Sections 7.2.3.1 and 7.5.4 for a description on the difference between declaring a variable and defining a variable.

6. *Is it possible to declare an identifier with a same name and type more than once in the same scope?*

   Yes, it is possible to declare an identifier with a same name and type more than once in the same scope.

Backward Reference: Refer Section 7.2.3.1 to find the answer to this question.

7. *Can we define an identifier with a same name more than once in the same scope? Can we define an identifier with a same name in different scopes? If identifiers with a same name are defined in different scopes, do they refer to one object or different objects?*

   No, it is not possible to define an identifier with a same name more than once in the same scope, but it is possible to define an identifier with a same name in different scopes. If identifiers with a same name are defined in different scopes, they refer to different objects.

Backward Reference: Refer Section 7.2.3.1 to find the answer to this question.

8. *Is it possible to declare an identifier with a same name but a different type in different scopes?*

Backward Reference: Refer Section 7.2.3.1 to find the answer to this question.

9. *What is meant by shadowing?*

Backward Reference: Refer Section 7.2.4.1 for a description on shadowing.

10. *What is meant by name resolution?*

Backward Reference: Refer Section 7.2.4.1 for a description on name resolution.

11. *What is meant by linkage? What are the different kinds of linkages available in C language?*

Backward Reference: Refer Section 7.3 for a description on linkage.

12. *What is meant by the lifetime of an identifier? Is it the same concept as the scope of an identifier? If no, how is it different from the scope?*

    The lifetime of an identifier (actually object) is a portion of the program execution during which the storage is guaranteed to be reserved for it. Throughout its lifetime, it has a constant address and it retains its last stored value. The lifetime of an identifier and the scope of an identifier are related but are entirely different concepts. Ideally, the scope of an identifier should be a subset of the lifetime of an object it denotes; otherwise, it would be possible to refer to an identifier even after its denoted storage goes away. If an identifier is referred outside of its lifetime, its behavior would be undefined.

13. *In C language, what are the various types of lifetime that an object can have?*

Backward Reference: Refer Section 7.4 for a description on lifetime of an object.

14. *If I want to specify the lifetime of an object, how can I specify it?*

    The lifetime of an object can be specified with the help of a storage class specifier.

Backward Reference: Refer Section 7.5 for a description on storage classes and storage class specifiers.

15. *What are the differences between* `static` *local variable and global variable?*

    The key differences between a `static` local variable and a global variable are:

    1. A `static` local variable has block/local scope while a global variable has file/global scope.
    2. A `static` local variable has internal linkage while a global variable has external linkage.

    The key similarity between a `static` local variable and a global variable is that both have static/global lifetime.

16. *Can a variable be declared in a header file? Can it be defined in a header file?*

    A variable that is to be accessed from more than one file can and should be declared in a header file. However, such a variable must be defined only in one source file. Variables can be, but should not be defined in the header files because the header files can be included in multiple source files, which would cause multiple definitions of a variable and thus lead to an error.

17. *Is it possible to declare a* `static` *variable without defining it?*

    No, it is not possible to declare a `static` variable without defining it. Consider the following statement:

    `static int a;` //←This is a definition and not a declaration as memory space is allocated to `a`

    If we do not want to allocate memory space to the identifier `a`, the storage class specifier `extern` should be used. However, it is not possible to use both the storage class specifiers `static` and `extern` at the same time. Hence, it is not possible to declare a `static` variable without defining it.

18. *It is said that 'Functions and global variables have external linkage. A global variable or a function defined in one source file can be used in another source file in a multi-file program'. How can I do this?*

    Consider a program that consists of two source files `one.c` and `two.c`. The source file `two.c` contains the definition of an identifier `ident1` and a function `fun`. These definitions are used in another source file `one.c` of the program. Since the global variables and the function have external linkage, this usage is allowed. The following code snippets illustrate this type of usage using Codeblocks, the open source, cross-platform IDE:

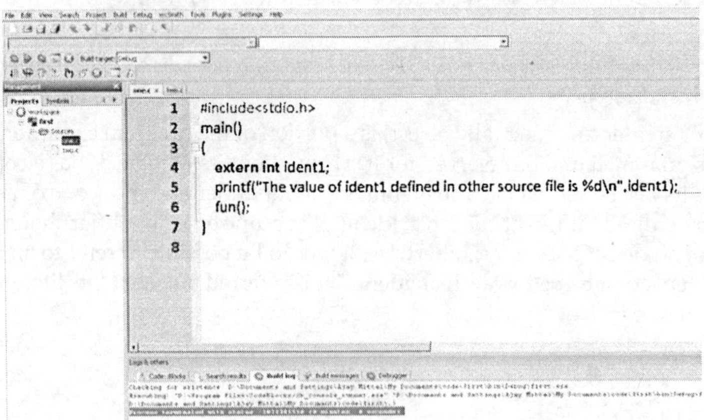

(a) one.c

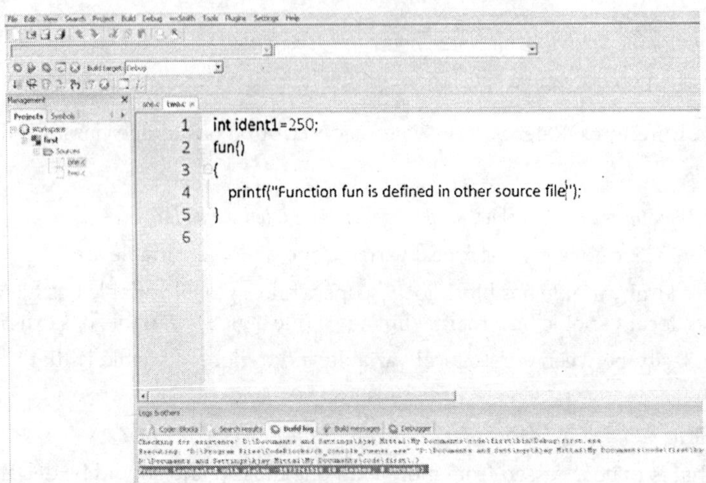

(b) two.c

The given piece of code on execution outputs:

```
The value of ident1 defined in other source file is 250
Function fun is defined in other source file
```

Backward Reference: Refer Section 7.3.1 to learn how to execute a multi-file program using Turbo C 3.0.

19. *What is the effect of storage class specifier* static *when applied on function definition/declaration and global identifiers?*

    The storage class specifier static when applied on a function definition/declaration and global identifiers, changes their linkage from external to internal, i.e. they can now be used only within the same source file and not within the other source files. Consider the same code as in the previous answer except that the definition of the identifier and the function has been made static by specifying static storage class specifier in the source file two.c.

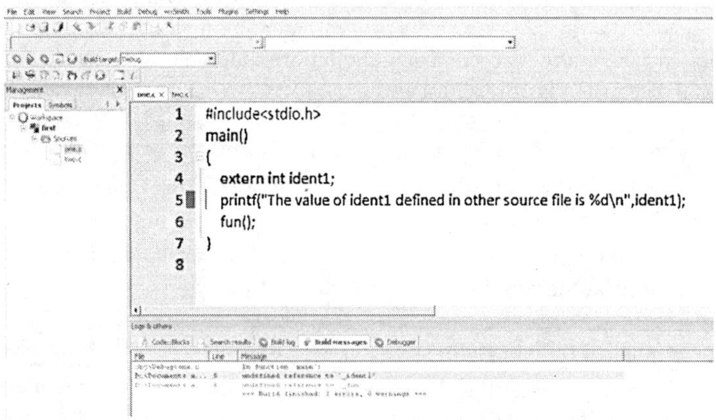

(a) one.c

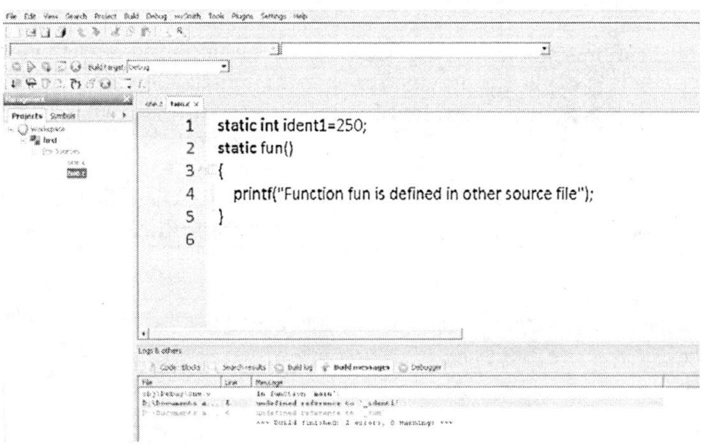

(b) two.c

On execution, there are two linker errors: 'Undefined reference to 'identl'' and 'Undefined reference to 'fun''. These errors are due to the fact that identl and fun have internal linkage as static storage class specifier has been used. They can now only be used within the same source file (i.e. two.c) and not within any other source file (i.e. one.c).

20. *When should the* register *storage class specifier be used? Does using the* register *storage class specifier guarantee to improve the performance of a program?*

    The register storage class specifier hints to the compiler that the variable will be heavily used and should be kept in the CPU register, if possible, so that it can be accessed faster. However, since the CPU registers are limited in number and some registers can hold only specific type of data (such as floating point numbers), the number of register storage class specifiers that will actually have any effect depends upon the machine on which the program will be executed. Also, in some cases, it might actually be slower to keep a variable in a register because that register will then become unavailable for other purposes, or because the variable is not used enough to justify the overhead of loading and storing it in CPU register.

Therefore, when should the register storage class specifier be used?

The answer is never, with most modern compilers. Modern C compilers are so advanced that they usually make better decisions than the programmer about which variables should be stored in the registers. In fact, many compilers actually ignore the register storage class specifier, which is perfectly legal, because it is only a hint and not a directive.

21. *What is meant by initialization and assignment? What are the different types of initializations?*

First time assignment at the time of definition is called **initialization.** Assigning a value to an identifier after initialization is treated as **assignment**. Initialization is classified according to two criteria:

1. Whether it is done by the system or by the user (implicit/explicit initialization).
2. Whether it is done at the run time or at the compile time.

Implicit/explicit Initialization	Run-time/compile-time initialization
1. In an initialization statement, if the value of initialization is implicitly provided by the system and not by the user, then it is known as **implicit initialization**. Only extern and static variables are guaranteed to be implicitly initialized.	1. In an initialization statement, if the value of initialization can be determined at the compile time, then it is called **compile-time initialization**.
2. In an initialization statement, if the value of initialization is explicitly provided by the user, then it is known as **explicit initialization**.	2. In an initialization statement, if the value of initialization can only be determined at the run time, then it is called **run-time initialization**.

For example:
static int a; //←Implicitly initialized
int a=20; //←Explicit initialization
	For example:
	int a=20; //←Compile-time initialization
	int a=sqrt(4); //←Run-time initialization

22. *I know that a case label should be a constant expression of integral type. I have written the following piece of code. The compiler is not accepting it and is showing an error* "Constant expression required", *although I have made* lab, *a constant by using* const *qualifier. Why?*

```
main()
{
    const int lab=sqrt(4);
    int expr=2;
    switch(expr)
    {
        case lab:
            printf("Initializations are of two types");
        case 3:
            printf("Case labels should be constant expression known at the compile time");
    }
}
```

The statement 'case label should be a constant expression of integral type' is correct but incomplete. A further refinement states that 'Case label should be a compile-time constant expression of integral type'. This means that the value of the expression should be known at the compile time. In the mentioned code, the initialization is a run time initialization, so the value of initializer can only be determined at the run time. This is not allowed for case labels and hence leads to a compilation error.

23. *Do all the variables need to be initialized explicitly?*

    No, all the variables need not be initialized explicitly. The variables that are defined outside all functions (i.e. in file/global scope with external or internal linkage) and the variables defined inside a function with internal linkage (i.e. with `static` storage class specifier) are implicitly initialized with a base value, if not initialized explicitly. For example, integers are implicitly initialized with `0`, `float` with `0.0`, `char` with `'\0'`, if explicit initializers are not given. It is important to note that even if `static` variables are present inside block/local scope, they are initialized only once.

    The variables defined inside a function with no linkage (i.e. `auto` variables or `register` variables) will have undefined values (i.e. garbage values), if they are not explicitly initialized. If they are not initialized, the user should make sure that they are assigned some value before they are used.

24. *Where are the variables stored in the memory?*

    Depending upon their lifetime, variables are stored in one of the following three memory regions:

    1. Variables that are defined outside all the functions (i.e. in file/global scope with an external or an internal linkage) and the variables defined inside a function with internal linkage (i.e. with `static` storage class specifier) exist for the lifetime of a program's execution. These variables are stored in a **data segment**. A data segment is a fixed size area in the memory set aside for these variables.

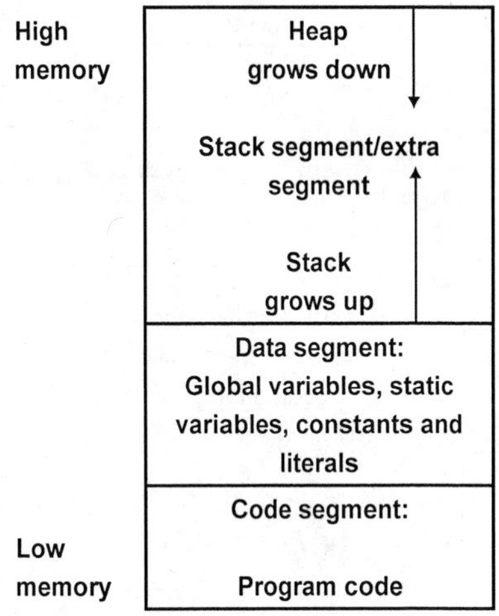

    2. Variables that are defined inside the block/local scope without using the `static` storage class specifier (i.e. `auto` variables) come into existence when the program control enters the block of code containing them and they cease to exist when the program control leaves that block of code. These variables are stored in a **stack**. A stack is an area of memory that starts out small and grows automatically up to some predefined limit. The stack is kept in the region of memory known as the **stack segment**.
    3. The third type of memory area is used not to actually store the variables but to store the objects pointed to by pointer variables. This type of memory area is used to store the objects that have allocated lifetime. This memory area is known as a **heap**. A heap is another area that starts out small and grows, but it grows only when there is an explicit call to some memory allocation functions like `malloc`, `calloc` or `realloc`. The heap, like the stack, has a limit on how much it can grow. The heap can share memory segment either with the stack or the data segment or can have its own segment (i.e. extra segment).

25. *What is dynamic memory allocation? What are the differences between dynamic memory allocation and static memory allocation?*

The allocation of memory at the run time (i.e. as the program executes) is known as **dynamic memory allocation**. In C, memory can be allocated dynamically by calling malloc, calloc or realloc functions. The allocation of memory at the compile time is called **static memory allocation**.

Static memory allocation	Dynamic memory allocation
1. Static memory is allocated automatically by the compiler when the definition statements are encountered.	1. Dynamic memory is allocated only when there is an explicit call to malloc, calloc or realloc functions.
2. To make static memory allocation, the amount of the memory space to be reserved should be known at the compile time.	2. In dynamic memory allocation, the amount of the memory space to be reserved can be given at the run time.
3. Since the amount of memory to be allocated is determined in advance at the compile time, this type of memory allocation may sometimes lead to memory wastage especially in the case of arrays.	3. Since the amount of memory to be allocated can be given at the run time, the memory is allocated as per the requirements, and memory wastage can be avoided.
4. Memory allocated at the compile time has static or automatic lifetime.	4. Memory allocated at the run time has allocated lifetime.
5. This allocation is done either from a data segment or a stack.	5. This allocation is done from the heap.
6. Static memory allocation is faster as compared to dynamic memory allocation.	6. Dynamic memory allocation is slower as compared to static memory allocation.

26. *How can I dynamically allocate and deallocate the memory?*

Backward Reference: Refer Section 7.6 for a description on dynamic memory allocation.

27. *The mentioned code on execution outputs* "Hello Readers!!".

```
#include<alloc.h>
/*Note: In all the questions that have a call to malloc, calloc or realloc functions, include header file alloc.h or malloc.h if you are
using Borland Turbo C 3.0 or Borland Turbo C 4.5 and malloc.h if you are using Microsoft Visual C++ 6.0*/
main()
{
    char *str;
    str=(char*)malloc(20);
    strcpy(str,"Hello Readers!!");
    puts(str);
}
```

I know that the prototype of the malloc *function is* void*malloc(size_t size);. *In the mentioned code, an integer is given as an argument to the* malloc *function instead of an argument of type* size_t. *Even then the compiler is not showing an error* 'Unable to convert int to size_t'. *Why?*

The compiler does not show an error because size_t is not a type. It is just a synonym for the type unsigned int. The type definition for size_t is available in the header files alloc.h and malloc.h. To verify it, open the header files alloc.h or malloc.h and search for size_t. You will find a statement typedef unsigned size_t;, which declares size_t as a synonym for the type unsigned int.

In the given piece of code, 20 (i.e. an integer) is given as an input argument to the function malloc, while it actually expects an unsigned int. The compiler can implicitly type cast int to unsigned int, both types being compatible. Thus, the given code is free from errors.

Thus, it will be wrong to say that int and size_t are compatible types because size_t is actually not a type.

28. *What is memory leak?*

Backward Reference: Refer Section 7.6.1 for a description on memory leak.

29. *What is the biggest advantage of using arrays and what is the biggest disadvantage of using statically allocated arrays?*

The biggest advantage of using arrays is the direct addressing scheme supported by the arrays. **Direct addressing** means that any location of an array can be directly accessed by using an index (subscript) value. The time required to access any value is the same irrespective of the location of the value. The biggest disadvantage of using statically allocated arrays is that the static memory allocation most of the times leads to memory wastage.

Consider the following scenario that illustrates how static memory allocation leads to memory wastage. Suppose there are 200 students in a class of computing course. The instructor of the course wants to store the marks of all the students and has created a statically allocated array of type float. Since he or she actually does not know the number of students who are actually going to appear in the examination beforehand, he or she has to keep the size of the array as 200 (i.e. equal to the maximum number of students). This statically allocated array will take 800 bytes in the memory. However, suppose on the exam day, 25 students could not make it for the examination and remain absent. Thus, only 175 locations out of 200 allocated locations are actually used and 100 bytes of the memory space gets wasted.

30. *How can I allocate a one-dimensional array dynamically?*

A one-dimensional array can be allocated dynamically by using malloc or calloc memory allocation functions. Consider the following piece of code that makes use of the calloc/malloc function to dynamically create a one-dimensional array:

```
#include<stdio.h>
#include<alloc.h>
#include<stdlib.h>   //←The prototype of the exit function is present in the header files stdlib.h and process.h
main()
{
   int *array, size, i;
   printf("Enter the size of array that you want to create\t");
   scanf("%d",&size);
   array=(int*)malloc(size*sizeof(int));
   //array=(int*)calloc(size,sizeof(int));   //←Instead of the previous statement, this statement can also be used
   if(array==NULL)
   {
      printf("Memory allocation function failed, memory space could not be allocated");
      exit(1);
   }
   else
      printf("Congrats!! array of size %d created successfully\n",size);
```

```
    for(i=0;i<size;i++)
        array[i]=10*(i+1);
    printf("Elements of array are\n");
    for(i=0;i<size;i++)
        printf("%d ",array[i]);
    free(array);
}
```

31. *Can a two-dimensional array be dynamically allocated in the same way as a one-dimensional array?*

Yes, a two-dimensional array can be dynamically allocated using the malloc or calloc function, but creating a two-dimensional dynamic array is a bit more complicated than creating a one-dimensional dynamic array.

If the number of columns in the two-dimensional array to be created is known, the following code illustrates its dynamic creation and use:

```
#include<stdio.h>
#include<alloc.h>
#include<stdlib.h>    //←or #include<process.h>
#define NCOLS 3
main()
{
    int (*array)[NCOLS];
    int NROWS, i, j;
    printf("Enter the number of rows of two-dimensional dynamic array\t");
    scanf("%d",&NROWS);
    array=(int(*)[NCOLS])malloc(NROWS*NCOLS*sizeof(int));
    //array=(int(*)[NCOLS])calloc(NROWS, NCOLS*sizeof(int));
    if(array==NULL)
    {
        printf("Memory allocation function failed, memory space could not be allocated");
        exit(1);
    }
    else
        printf("Congrats!! array of size %d*%d created successfully\n",NROWS,NCOLS);
    for(i=0;i<NROWS;i++)
        for(j=0;j<NCOLS;j++)
            array[i][j]=i+j;
    printf("\n\nThe contents of array are:\n\n");
    for(i=0;i<NROWS;i++)
    {
        for(j=0;j<NCOLS;j++)
            printf("%d",array[i][j]);
        printf("\n");
    }
    free(array);
}
```

In the above-mentioned code, the two-dimensional dynamic array is used in the same way as a two-dimensional static array is used, i.e. by using two subscript operators.

If the number of columns in a two-dimensional array is not known, the following code illustrates its dynamic creation and use. Note that by this method, the dynamic two-dimensional array cannot be used in the same way as the two-dimensional static array.

```
#include<stdio.h>
#include<alloc.h>
#include<stdlib.h>    //←or #include<process.h>
main()
{
   int *array;
   int NROWS,NCOLS, i, j;
   printf("Enter the number of rows and columns of two-dimensional dynamic array\t");
   scanf("%d %d",&NROWS,&NCOLS);
   array=(int*)malloc(NROWS*NCOLS*sizeof(int));
   //array=(int*)calloc(NROWS, NCOLS*sizeof(int));
   if(array==NULL)
   {
      printf("Memory allocation function failed, memory space could not be allocated");
      exit(1);
   }
   else
      printf("Congrats!! array of size %d*%d created successfully\n",NROWS,NCOLS);
   for(i=0;i<NROWS;i++)
      for(j=0;j<NCOLS;j++)
         array[i*NCOLS+j]=i+j;
   printf("\n\nThe contents of array are:\n\n");
   for(i=0;i<NROWS;i++)
   {
      for(j=0;j<NCOLS;j++)
         printf("%d",array[i*NCOLS+j]);
         printf("\n");
   }
   free(array);
}
```

32. *The number of rows and the number of columns of a two-dimensional array to be created is not known in advance. They will be entered by the user at the run time. The user only knows to access the elements of a two-dimensional array using two subscripts, like* arr[i][j] *if* arr *is of array type. How should the user create a two-dimensional dynamic array so that he or she should be able to use it too?*

    If the number of rows and the number of columns of a two-dimensional array are not known in advance, it can still be dynamically created in such a way so that it can be used like a normal two-dimensional static array, i.e. using two subscripts. The following code illustrates this fact:

```
#include<stdio.h>
#include<alloc.h>
#include<stdlib.h>    //←or #include<process.h>
main()
{
   int **array;
   int NROWS,NCOLS, i, j;
   printf("Enter the number of rows and columns of two-dimensional dynamic array\t");
```

```
    scanf("%d %d",&NROWS,&NCOLS);
    array=(int**)malloc(NROWS*sizeof(int*));
    if(array==NULL)
    {
        printf("Memory allocation function failed, memory space could not be allocated");
        exit(1);
    }
    for(i=0;i<NROWS;i++)
    {
        array[i]=(int*)malloc(NCOLS*sizeof(int));
        if(array[i]==NULL)
        {
            printf("Memory allocation function failed, memory space could not be allocated");
            exit(1);
        }
    }
    printf("Congrats!! array of size %d*%d created successfully\n",NROWS,NCOLS);
    for(i=0;i<NROWS;i++)
        for(j=0;j<NCOLS;j++)
            array[i][j]=i+j;
    printf("\n\nThe contents of array are:\n\n");
    for(i=0;i<NROWS;i++)
    {
        for(j=0;j<NCOLS;j++)
            printf("%d",array[i][j]);
        printf("\n");
    }
    free(array);
}
```

33. *Can the size of a statically and dynamically allocated array be increased? If yes, how?*

    It is not possible to increase the size of a statically allocated array. However, the size of a dynamically allocated array can be increased using the realloc function. The following code illustrates how to increase the size of a dynamically allocated array:

```
#include<stdio.h>
#include<alloc.h>
#include<stdlib.h>    //←or #include<process.h>
main()
{
    int *array, size,newsize, i;
    printf("Enter the size of array that you want to create\t");
    scanf("%d",&size);
    array=(int*)malloc(size*sizeof(int));
    //array=(int*)calloc(size,sizeof(int));    //←This statement can also be used instead of previous statement
    if(array==NULL)
    {
        printf("Memory allocation function failed, memory space could not be allocated");
        exit(1);
    }
```

```
    else
        printf("Congrats!! array of size %d created successfully\n",size);
    for(i=0;i<size;i++)
        array[i]=10*(i+1);
    printf("\n\nElements of array are\n");
    for(i=0;i<size;i++)
        printf("%d ",array[i]);
    printf("\nDue to increased requirement, size of array needs to be increased\n");
    printf("\nEnter the new size of the array\t");
    scanf("%d",&newsize);
    array=(int*)realloc(array,newsize*sizeof(int));
    if(array==NULL)
    {
        printf("The size of array cannot be increased, resize operation failed");
        exit(1);
    }
    else
        printf("Congrats!! The size of array increased from %d to %d\n",size,newsize);
    for(i=size;i<newsize;i++)
        array[i]=10*(i+1);
    printf("\n\nElements of array are\n");
    for(i=0;i<newsize;i++)
        printf("%d ",array[i]);
    free(array);
}
```

34. *What are the problems associated with the usage of global variables?*

There are certain problems associated with the usage of global variables. The global variables should be used with caution and should always be carefully documented. The major problems associated with using global variables are:

1. The name of a global variable may clash with a name of global variables defined in the libraries or in other source files. This name-clashing problem is called the **global namespace pollution problem**.
2. The global variables are visible (i.e. they can be used) within all the functions of a program. All the functions can change the value of global variables. This makes debugging, testing and maintenance of the code difficult.

35. *The global objects are visible to all the functions of a program. That means various functions of a program can communicate by using global objects. Then, why don't we fully rely on global objects as a method of communication between functions?*

We do not full rely on global objects as a method of communication between functions because:

1. Usage of global objects pollutes the global namespace and this may lead to name conflicts.
2. The global objects can be manipulated in any function. Any function can accidentally or maliciously manipulate the global object. This accidental or malicious manipulation cannot be prevented if global objects are used and is very difficult to find out. This makes testing and debugging difficult for the programs that make excessive use of global objects.

Code Snippets

Determine the output of the following code snippets. Assume that the inclusion of the required header files has been made and there is no prototyping error due to them.

36.
```
int var=100;
fun()
{
    printf("The value of var in fun is %d\n",var);
}
main()
{
    printf("The value of var in main is %d\n",var);
    var=var+200;
    fun();
}
```

37.
```
int var=100;
fun()
{
    int var=50;
    printf("The value of var in fun is %d\n",var);
}
main()
{
    printf("The value of var in main is %d\n",var);
    var=var+200;
    fun();
}
```

38.
```
fun()
{
    int var=100;
    printf("The value of var in fun is %d\n",var);
}
main()
{
    printf("The value of var in main is %d\n",var);
    var=var+200;
    fun();
}
```

39.
```
fun(int var)
{
    printf("The value of var in fun is %d\n",var);
}
main()
{
    int var=100;
    printf("The value of var in main is %d\n",var);
    fun(var/2);
}
```

40.
```
fun()
{
    lab:
        printf("Labels have function scope");
}
main()
{
    goto lab;
}
```

41.
```
int var=100;
main()
{
    extern int var;
    extern int var;
    printf("The value of var is %d",var);
}
```

42.
```
int var=200;
int var=250;
main()
{
    printf("Multiple definitions");
}
```

43.
```
auto int var=200;
main()
{
    printf("The value of var is %d",var);
}
```

44.
```
main()
{
int exp=1,j=10;
switch(exp)
{
case 1:
{
    int j=2;
    printf("The value of j in case 1 is %d\n",j);
}
case 2:
    printf("The value of j in case 2 is %d\n",j);
}
}
```

45.
```
main()
{
    extern int var;
    printf("The value of var is %d",var);
}
```

46.
```
main()
{
    extern int var;
    printf("The value of var is %d",var);
}
int var=200;
```

47.
```
main()
{
    extern int var;
    printf("The value of var is %d",var);
    int var=200;
}
```

48.
```
extern int var=200;
main()
{
    printf("The value of var is %d",var);
}
```

49.
```
main()
{
    extern int var=200;
    printf("The value of var is %d",var);
}
```

50.
```
function(static int para)
{
    printf("The value of parameter is %d",para);
}
main()
{
    int var=200;
    printf("The value of var is %d",var);
    function(var);
}
```

51.
```
int var;
main()
{
    printf("If not initialized, the value of global variable will be %d",var);
}
```

52.
```
main()
{
    int var;
    printf("If not initialized, the value of local variable will be %d",var);
}
```

53.
```
main()
{
    static int var;
    printf("If not initialized, the value of static local variable will be %d",var);
}
```

54.
```
main()
{
    static extern int var;
    printf("The value of var is %d",var);
}
```

55.
```
int a=200;
main()
{
    int b=300;
    printf("The values in outer block of main are %d %d\n",a,b);         //←line 1
    {
        int a=400;
        printf("The values in inner block of main are %d %d\n",a,b);     //←line 2
    }
    printf("The values back in outer block of main are %d %d\n",a,b);    //←line 3
}
```

56.

one.c	two.c

extern_function();
main()
{
    extern int var;
    printf("The value of external var is %d\n",var);
    extern_function();
}
	int var=200;
	extern_function()
	{
	    printf("Function in other translation unit");
	}

57.

one.c	two.c

static_function();
main()
{
    extern int var;
    printf("The value of external var is %d",var);
    static_function();
}
	static int var=200;
	static static_function()
	{
	    printf("Function in other translation unit");
	}

58.

one.c	two.c

int var=200;
function()
{
    printf("Function in same translation unit");
}
main()
{
    printf("The value of external var is %d",var);
    function();
}
	int var=200;
	function()
	{
	    printf("Function in other translation unit");
	}

59.
```
fib_term()
{
    int a=0,b=1;
    int c;
```

```
    c=a+b; a=b; b=c;
    return c;
}
main()
{
    int count=0,i;
    printf("First five terms of Fibonacci series are:\n");
    for(i=0;i<5;i++)
        printf("%d ",fib_term());
}
```

60.
```
fib_term()
{
    static int a=0,b=1;
    int c;
    c=a+b; a=b; b=c;
    return c;
}
main()
{
    int count=0,i;
    printf("First five terms of Fibonacci series are:\n");
    for(i=0;i<5;i++)
        printf("%d ",fib_term());
}
```

61.
```
main()
{
    int i=5;
    printf("The value of i is %d\n",i--);
    if(i)
        main();
}
```

62.
```
main()
{
    static int i=5;
    printf("The value of i is %d\n",i--);
    if(i)
        main();
}
```

63.
```
main()
{
    int i;
    for (i=0; i<3; i++)
    {
        int x = 0;
        static int y = 0;
        printf("x=%d, y=%d\n", x++, y++);
    }
}
```

64.
```
int *j;
func()
{
    static int i=10;
    j=&i;
}
main()
{
    func();
    printf("The value of i in function func is %d",*j);
}
```

65.
```
main()
{
    int *j;
    {
        int i=10;
        j=&i;
    }
    printf("The value of i is %d",*j);
}
```

66.
```
main()
{
    int* ptr;
    ptr=malloc(sizeof(int));
    *ptr=200;
    printf("The value of allocated object is %d",*ptr);
}
```

67.
```
main()
{
    int* ptr;
    ptr=(int*)malloc(sizeof(int));
    *ptr=200;
    printf("The value of allocated object is %d",*ptr);
}
```

68.
```
main()
{
    int* ptr;
    ptr=(int*)malloc(sizeof(int));
    printf("If not assigned a value, the allocated object has %d",*ptr);
}
```

69.
```
main()
{
    int* ptr;
    ptr=(int*)calloc(1,sizeof(int));
    printf("If not assigned a value, the allocated object has %d",*ptr);
}
```

70. main()
```
{
    int *ptr;
    ptr=(int*)malloc(256*256-1);
    if(ptr==NULL)
        printf("Memory allocation fails");
    else
        printf("Memory allocation successful");
}
```

71. main()
```
{
    int *ptr;
    ptr=(int*)malloc(256*256L-1);
    if(ptr==NULL)
        printf("Memory allocation fails");
    else
        printf("Memory allocation successful");
}
```

72. main()
```
{
    int *ptr;
    ptr=(int*)malloc(256*256L);
    if(ptr==NULL)
        printf("Memory allocation fails");
    else
        printf("Memory allocation successful");
}
```

73. main()
```
{
    char *ptr;
    ptr=(char*)malloc(6);
    strcpy(ptr,"Hello");
    puts(ptr);
    strcat(ptr,"Readers!!");
    puts(ptr);
}
```

74. main()
```
{
    char *ptr1;
    ptr1=(char*)malloc(6);
    strcpy(ptr1,"Hello");
    puts(ptr1);
    ptr1=(char*)realloc(ptr1,15);
    strcat(ptr1,"Readers!!");
    puts(ptr1);
}
```

75.
```
main()
{
    typedef int i;
    i var=200;
    printf("The value of variable var is %d",var);
}
```
76.
```
main()
{
    typedef static int i;
    i var=200;
    printf("The value of variable is %d",var);
}
```
77.
```
main()
{
    typedef char* cp;
    cp i,j;
    printf("The size of i and j is %d %d",sizeof(i),sizeof(j));
}
```
78.
```
char* print_string()
{
    char str[]="Strings!!";
    puts(str);
    return str;
}
main()
{
    puts(print_string());
}
```
79.
```
char* print_string()
{
    static char str[]="Strings!!";
    puts(str);
    return str;
}
main()
{
    puts(print_string());
}
```
80.
```
char * print_string()
{
    char *str="Strings!!";
    puts(str);
    return str;
}
main()
{
    puts(print_string());
}
```

Multiple-choice Questions

81. The difference between variable declaration and variable definition is that
    a. Declaration allocates memory for a variable while definition does not
    b. Variable can be defined many times but can be declared only once
    c. Definition allocates memory for a variable while declaration does not
    d. None of these

82. The region of the program in which an identifier will be visible is determined on the basis of
    a. Scope of the identifier
    b. Lifetime of the identifier
    c. Storage class of the identifier
    d. None of these

83. The region of the program in which the storage for an identifier is guaranteed to be reserved is determined on the basis of
    a. Scope of the identifier
    b. Lifetime of the identifier
    c. Storage class of the identifier
    d. None of these

84. The identifier declared outside of all the functions and their parameter lists have
    a. Global scope
    b. Local scope
    c. Function scope
    d. Function prototype scope

85. The statement `int a;`
    a. Defines an identifier `a`.
    b. Declares an identifier `a`
    c. Neither defines nor declares an identifier `a`. It is erroneous
    d. None of these

86. The statement `extern int a;`
    a. Is a definition of identifier `a`
    b. Is a declaration of identifier `a`
    c. Is both a declaration as well as a definition of identifier `a`
    d. None of these

87. The statement `extern int a=200;`, if present in global scope
    a. Defines an identifier `a`
    b. Declares identifier `a`
    c. It is erroneous to initialize `extern` variable in global scope
    d. None of these

88. The statement `extern int a=200;`, if present in local scope
    a. Defines an identifier `a`
    b. Declares identifier `a`
    c. It is erroneous to initialize `extern` variable in local scope
    d. None of these

89. The ideal relationship between the scope and the lifetime of an identifier is that
    a. Scope of an identifier should be a subset of lifetime of an identifier
    b. Lifetime of an identifier should be a subset of scope of an identifier
    c. Scope of an identifier should be the same as the lifetime of an identifier
    d. None of these

90. The lifetime of global variables by default is
    a. Static
    b. Automatic
    c. Allocated
    d. None of these

91. The global variables by default have
    a. External linkage
    b. Internal linkage
    c. No linkage
    d. None of these

92. The local variables by default have
    a. External linkage
    b. Internal linkage
    c. No linkage
    d. None of these

93. The lifetime of local variables by default is
    a. Static
    b. Automatic
    c. Allocated
    d. None of these

94. The lifetime of an object can be specified with the help of
    a. Type specifier
    b. Storage class specifier
    c. Format specifier
    d. None of these

95. The lifetime of an local identifier can be changed from automatic to static by using
    a. An `extern` specifier
    b. An `auto` specifier
    c. A `static` specifier
    d. None of these

96. The linkage of global variable can be changed from external to internal by using
    a. An `extern` specifier
    b. An `auto` specifier
    c. A `static` specifier
    d. None of these

97. The maximum number of storage class specifiers in a declaration statement can be
    a. Only one
    b. Two
    c. Any number
    d. None of these

98. The memory space to local variables is allocated from
    a. Stack
    b. Heap
    c. Data segment
    d. None of these

99. The correct way to deallocate dynamically created one-dimensional array `arr` is
    a. `free(arr);`
    b. `free(arr[0]);`
    c. `free(*arr);`
    d. None of these

100. The `typedef` specifier is used to
    a. Create a new type
    b. Create a synonym for a known type
    c. Rename a known type
    d. None of these

101. The statement `int x=0x23|0x56;` has
    a. Compile time initialization
    b. Run-time initialization
    c. Compile time error
    d. None of these

102. The statement `int x=sqrt(4);` has
    a. Compile time initialization
    b. Run-time initialization
    c. Compile time error
    d. None of these

103. The `static` variables of `int` type are implicitly initialized to
    a. `0`
    b. Undetermined value (i.e. garbage value)
    c. `static` variables can only be assigned a value but cannot be initialized
    d. None of these

104. The operator that cannot be applied on variables defined with `register` storage class specifiers is

a. `sizeof`
b. Address-of
c. Logical negation
d. None of these

105. While resolving name, the declaration of the name is first searched in

a. Immediate scope
b. Global scope
c. Enclosing scope
d. None of these

Outputs and Explanations to Code Snippets

36. `The value of var in main is 100`
`The value of var in fun is 300`

Explanation:

Two things to be kept in mind while determining the output of this code snippet are:

1. Whether some declaration of the name is visible at the point of its usage. If no declaration is visible at the point of usage of the name, there will be a compilation error.
2. With which definition of the name, the present usage of the name is resolved and associated.

In the given code snippet:

1. The global declaration of the identifier `var` is visible inside both the functions `main` and `fun`. Hence, there will be no compilation error.
2. Since there is no local definition of the identifier `var` in the function `main`, the name `var` used inside the function `main` is resolved and associated with the global definition having value `100`. This is printed and later `var` is modified to `300`. In the function `fun` also, no local definition of the identifier `var` is present. Hence, the name `var` used inside the function `fun` is also resolved with the same global definition of `var`, having the changed value `300`. This value is printed inside the function `fun`.

37. `The value of var in main is 100`
`The value of var in fun is 50`

Explanation:

In the given code snippet:

1. The global declaration of identifier `var` is visible inside the function `main`. Since there is no local definition of the identifier `var` in the function `main`, the identifier name `var` used inside the function `main` is resolved and is associated with the global definition having the value `100`. This is printed and later `var` is modified to `300`.
2. However, in the function `fun`, a local definition of the identifier `var` is present. This local definition of `var` shadows the global definition of the identifier `var`. Hence, the name `var` used inside the function `fun` is resolved with the local definition of `var` and not with the global definition of the identifier `var`. The local identifier `var` has the value `50`. This value is printed in the function `fun`.

38. `Compilation error "Undefined symbol 'var' in function main"`

Explanation:

Although the identifier `var` has been declared inside the function `fun`, it is not visible inside the body of the function `main`. As no declaration of the identifier `var` is visible at the point of its usage in the function `main`, there will be a compilation error.

39. `The value of var in main is 100`
`The value of var in fun is 50`

Explanation:

The identifier var defined as a parameter in the definition of the function fun has block/local scope and can be legally used only inside the body of the function. The function fun has been called by value inside the function main. Hence, the parameter var obtains the value 50 as a result of argument passing and this value of var is printed inside the function fun.

40. Compilation error "Undefined label 'lab' in function main"

Explanation:

A label has function scope, i.e. it is visible only inside the body of the function in which it is declared (note that a label name need not to be declared separately. Its syntactic appearance, i.e. label name followed by a colon and a statement serves as a declaration for the label). In the given code snippet, the label name lab declared inside the function fun is not visible inside the function main. In the function main, there is no separate declaration of the label lab. Hence, the usage of the label name lab in the goto statement remains unresolved and leads to a compilation error.

41. The value of var is 100

Explanation:

The identifier var has been declared twice in the block/local scope. It is legal to declare an identifier with the same name and type more than once in the same scope. No definition of identifier var is present inside the local scope. The usage of the identifier var inside the function main is resolved with the global definition having the value 100. This value of var is printed by the printf function.

42. Compilation error "Variable 'var' is initialized more than once"

Explanation:

An identifier cannot be defined more than once in the same scope. Two definitions of the identifier var in file/global scope leads to the compilation error.

43. Compilation error "Storage class 'auto' is not allowed here"

Explanation:

The scope, i.e. visibility of an identifier should be a subset of its lifetime. Thus, auto (i.e. local) cannot be the lifetime of an object that has global scope. Hence, the usage of the auto storage class specifier in the declaration made in the global scope leads to the compilation error.

44. The value of j in case 1 is 2
The value of j in case 2 is 10

Explanation:

When an identifier is referenced, the immediate scope in which the name is used is searched. If a declaration is found, the name is resolved and the value is used. If it is not found, the enclosing scope is searched. This process continues, until either a declaration is found or a global scope has been searched. If the latter occurs and no declaration is found for the name, the use of name is flagged as an error. Reference of j used in the printf statement of case label 1 is resolved by j declared in the immediate scope and the resolved value of j will be 2. The reference of j in the printf statement of case label 2 is resolved by j declared in the function scope and the resolved value of j will be 10. The resolved values of j are printed by the respective printf statements.

45. Linker error "Undefined symbol _var in module"

Explanation:

The identifier var is declared using the extern storage class specifier. The storage class specifier extern promises that somewhere in the program the identifier will be defined and has external linkage. The promise is not being fulfilled is detected at the time of linking, when the linker checks all the modules (i.e. the source files and the linked objects) to find that the identifier var has not been defined anywhere in the program. As far as compilation is concerned, the code does not show any error.

46. The value of var is 200

Explanation:

The identifier var is declared using the extern storage class specifier. Later, it is defined and has external linkage. The usage of identifier var inside the function main is resolved with the external definition and the value 200 is printed.

47. Compilation error "Multiple declaration for 'var' in function main"

Explanation:

The identifier var is declared using the extern storage class specifier. The definition corresponding to this declaration can have external linkage but cannot have no linkage. Since the identifier var is defined in the block/local scope, it has no linkage. This is not allowed and leads to the compilation error.

48. The value of var is 200

Explanation:

The extern specifier is used to declare a variable without defining it. However, if the variable is initialized, the extern declaration becomes a definition. Hence, extern int var=200; becomes a definition. The usage of identifier var in the function main is resolved with this definition of var. Thus, the value of var printed by the printf function inside the function main is 200.

49. Compilation error "extern variable cannot be initialized in function main"

Explanation:

The extern variable cannot be initialized if the declaration statement is written within the block/local scope. The error is due to the fact that the extern storage class can only be used with the objects that have external linkage. Since local variables have no linkage, extern cannot be used in the declaration statement present in the local scope.

50. Compilation error "Storage class 'static' is not allowed here"

Explanation:

The static storage class specifier cannot be used in the parameter declaration either in the function declaration or in the function definition. Hence, declaring the parameter para as static in the function definition leads to the compilation error.

51. If not initialized, the value of global variable will be 0

Explanation:

Identifiers with external linkage (i.e. global variables) or with internal linkage (i.e. static variables) are implicitly initialized with a base value, i.e. 0 for int, 0.0 for float and '\0' for char. In the given code snippet, var is a global identifier of int type. Hence, it is implicitly initialized to 0 and its value is printed inside the function main.

52. If not initialized, the value of local variable will be 19125

Explanation:

A variable defined inside a function with no linkage (i.e. auto variable or register variable) will have an undefined value (i.e. garbage value), if it is not initialized explicitly. If it is not initialized, the user should make sure that it is assigned some value before it is used. In the given code, the local identifier var is neither initialized nor assigned any value before its use. Hence, the value of the variable var printed inside the function main is a garbage value. Note that this value may vary from system to system and on different executions.

53. If not initialized, the value of static local variable will be 0

Explanation:

The identifiers with internal linkage (i.e. static variables) are implicitly initialized with a base value, i.e. 0 for int, 0.0 for float and '\0' for char. Hence, the local static identifier var is initialized to 0. This value of var gets printed.
Note that the scope of the identifier var is still local, i.e. it is visible only inside the function main, the lifetime is global, i.e. the storage is reserved till the program executes and the initialization is carried out only once.

54. Compilation error "Too many storage classes in declaration in function main"

Explanation:

At most one storage class specifier can be mentioned in a declaration statement. Two storage class specifiers, i.e. static and extern have been used in the declaration statement static extern int var;. This is a violation and on compilation leads to an error.

55. The values in outer block of main are 200 300
The values in inner block of main are 400 300
The values back in outer block of main are 200 300

Explanation:

The variable a is defined in the global scope and has the value 200. The variable b is defined in the local scope (say outer block scope) of the function main. In line 1, the occurrence of a is resolved with the global definition of a and the occurrence of b is resolved with the local (i.e. in outer block scope) definition of b. Hence, the values of a and b that get printed are 200 and 300, respectively.

After line 1, another block scope starts (say inner block scope) and that too has a definition of variable a. The present definition of a has the value 400. The usage of a in line 2 refers to the definition present in the immediate scope (i.e. in inner block scope), having the value 400. Since b is also used in line 2, its definition is searched in the immediate scope (i.e. the inner block scope). Since no definition of variable b is found in the inner block scope, the enclosing scope (i.e. outer block scope) is searched for the definition of b. The definition of variable b is present in the outer block scope and, hence, the usage of variable b in line 2 is resolved with this definition having the value 300. Thus, the values of a and b printed in line 2 are 400 and 300, respectively.

After line 2, the inner block scope ends. The usage of the variable a in line 3 is again resolved with its definition present in the global scope and the variable b is resolved with its definition present in the immediate scope (i.e. outer block scope). Hence, the values of a and b that get printed are 200 and 300, respectively.

56. The value of external var is 200
Function in other translation unit

Explanation:

All the global variables and functions by default have external linkage. An identifier with external linkage can be used anywhere within a multi-file program. In the given code, the usage of the identifiers var and extern_function in the source file one.c is resolved with their definitions present in the source file two.c.

57. Linker errors "Undefined symbol _var" & "Undefined reference to _static_function"

Explanation:

The identifiers var and static_function defined in the source file two.c will have internal linkage because the storage class specifier static has been used. The identifier with an internal linkage can be used only within the same translation unit in which it is defined and not across multiple translation units. Thus, the usage of the identifiers var and static_function in the source file one.c cannot be resolved with the static definition of identifiers var and static_function made in the source file two.c. Also, no other definition of the identifiers var and static_funciton is available. Hence, the usage of the identifiers var and static_function remains unresolved and leads to a linker error.

58. Linker errors "Multiple definition of _var" & "Multiple definition of _function"

Explanation:

Since the identifiers var and function are defined in the source file one.c in the file/global scope, they will have external linkage. No other definition of these identifiers with external linkage should be present in the same translation unit. In other translation units, there can be a definition of the same identifiers with internal linkage, but not with external linkage, else there will be multiple definition error. In the given piece of code, the identifiers var and function are redefined with external linkage in the source file two.c. Thus, there are multiple definition errors. To rectify the problem, either remove the definitions from the source file two.c or make their linkage internal by using the static storage class specifier. The use of static prevents the clash of definitions made in the source file two.c with the definitions present in the source file one.c.

59. First five terms of Fibonacci series are:
    1 1 1 1 1

Explanation:

Every time the program control enters a function block, the auto local variables defined (i.e. defined without using static specifier) inside the block and the parameter list of the function are created and initialized. Being local to the function block, these auto variables exist till the program control remains inside the function block. As the program control leaves the function block, all the auto local variables defined inside the function block are destroyed.

In the given piece of code, when the program control enters the block of the function fib_term, the local variables a, b and c are created and the variables a and b are initialized to 0 and 1, respectively. After the execution of the statements c=a+b; a=b; b=c;, the value of the variables, a, b and c will be 1, 1 and 1. This value of the variable c is returned using the return statement. As the control leaves the function block, all the local variables i.e. a, b and c are destroyed and the memory occupied by them is freed. The value returned by fib_term function, i.e. 1 is printed in the function main.

When the function fib_term is called again, the local variables a, b and c are created again. The variables a and b are initialized again to 0 and 1, respectively. The whole process mentioned above is repeated and the value of c is computed as 1, which is returned by the function fib_term to the function main. Hence, every time the function fib_term is called, it returns 1.

60. First five terms of Fibonacci series are:
    1 2 3 5 8

Explanation:

Every time the program control enters a function block, the auto local variables defined (i.e. defined without using static specifier) inside the block and the parameter list of the function are created and initialized. The static variables defined (i.e. defined by using the storage class specifier static specifier) inside a function block are created only once (i.e. during the first call to the function). The auto local variables exist till the control remains inside the function body but the static local variables exist till the program terminates. As the auto local variables are destroyed on the return from the function, they are created and initialized every time a function is recalled. As the static variables persist and do not get destroyed on the return from a function, these variables are created and initialized only once (i.e. during the first call to a function). These variables retain their values during the function calls.

In the given piece of code, when the function fib_term is called for the first time, the variables a, b and c are created. The variables a and b are initialized to 0 and 1, respectively. After the execution of the statements c=a+b; a=b; b=c;, the values of the variables a, b and c will be 1, 1 and 1. This value of variable c is returned using the return statement. As the control leaves the function block, the auto local variable, i.e. c is destroyed and the memory occupied by it is freed. The static variables a and b are not destroyed. The value returned by the fib_term function, i.e. 1 is printed in the main function.

When the function fib_term is called again, i.e. second time, the auto local variable c is created again but the static local variables a and b already persist. Since the values, i.e. 1 and 1 already persist in the static local variables a and b, they are not initialized now. The statements c=a+b; a=b; b=c; are executed and the value of variables a, b and c becomes 1, 2 and 2. The value of c, i.e. 2 is returned to the function main and c is destroyed.

In this manner, every time the function fib_term is called, it uses the persisting values of a and b to compute the value of c.

61. The value of i is 5
    The value of i is 5
    The value of i is 5
    ....Till stack does not overflow

    Explanation:

    The variable i is an auto local variable. It is defined and initialized to 5 every time the function main is called. In the body of the function main, the value of i, i.e. 5 is printed and then it is decremented to 4. The control expression of the if statement, i.e. i evaluates to true (as i=4) during each call to the function main. Hence, main is called again and again and the recursion becomes infinite. This infinite recursion will automatically terminate when there is no stack space to create any more activation records (i.e. when the stack overflows). Note that some compilers like Borland Turbo C 4.5 do not allow the function main to be called from any function in the program and gives a compilation error.

62. The value of i is 5
    The value of i is 4
    The value of i is 3
    The value of i is 2
    The value of i is 1

    Explanation:

    The variable i is a static local variable. It is defined and initialized only once, i.e. during the first invocation of the function main. The later invocations of the function main use the persisting value of i. Therefore, in the given piece of code, during the first invocation of the function main, the variable i is defined and initialized to 5. This value of i is printed and then it is decremented to 4. The control expression of the if statement then evaluates to true, and the recursive call is given to the function main.

During this call, i.e. second call, the variable i is not defined and not initialized again. The persisting value of i, i.e. 4 is used. This value of i is printed and i is decremented to 3. The control expression of the if statement evaluates to true, and the recursive call is given to the main function again. The above process is repeated with the persisting values of i and the above-mentioned output is the result.

63. x=0, y=0
    x=0, y=1
    x=0, y=2

    Explanation:

    During each execution of the body of the for loop, the variable x is defined again and initialized to 0 as its storage class is auto. However, the variable y is defined and initialized only once, i.e. during the first execution of the body of the for loop as its storage class is static. Hence, during every execution of the body of the for loop, the value of the variable x is not preserved, but the value of the variable y is preserved.

64. The value of i in function func is 10

    Explanation:

Backward Reference: Refer Section 7.5.3 for a description on static storage class.

65. The value of i is 10

    Caution:

    This code may give a memory exception.

    Explanation:

    The identifier j is defined in the local scope (say outer block) of the function main. The identifier i is defined in the further nested scope (say inner block). The identifier j is even visible inside the inner block. In the inner block, the variable j is assigned the address of the variable i. As soon as the program control comes out of the inner block, the variable i is destroyed and the memory occupied by it is freed. However, the pointer j still points to the memory location where i was stored.

    The pointer that points to an unallocated or freed memory location is known as a **dangling pointer**. Hence, j is a dangling pointer. Dereferencing a dangling pointer may sometimes (less probable) lead to memory exception. It is with high probability that the user will get the correct result. This is due to the reason that although the memory is deallocated, the contents remain there unless and until the location is allocated to some other object and is then modified.

66. Compilation error "Unable to convert 'void*' to 'int*'"

    Explanation:

    The malloc function is used to allocate a memory block that can hold any (i.e. generic) type of data. If successful, the malloc function returns a generic pointer (i.e. void*) to the allocated block because it does not know what type of data will be stored in the allocated block. Depending upon the type of data stored in the allocated memory block, this void pointer must be type casted to an appropriate type. In the given piece of code, a memory block is allocated to hold the integer data, but the void pointer is not type casted to an appropriate type before being assigned to ptr. Hence, there is a compilation error. To rectify the code, type cast void* returned by the malloc function to int* before assigning it to ptr.

67. The value of allocated object is 200

Explanation:

Backward Reference: Refer the explanation given in Answer number 66.

68. If not assigned a value, the allocated object has 19073

Explanation:

The value of the memory space allocated by the malloc function is undetermined, i.e. garbage. Hence, the given code prints a garbage value.

69. If not assigned a value, the allocated object has 0

Explanation:

The value of the memory space allocated by the calloc function is automatically initialized to zero.

70. Memory allocation fails (if using Borland Turbo C 3.0)

or

Memory allocation successful (Microsoft Visual C++ 6.0)

Explanation:

The input argument of the malloc function is 256*256-1.
If working with compilers that allocate 2 bytes to an integer like Turbo C 3.0, the result of the evaluation of 256*256-1 comes out to be -1. This is due to the fact that 256*256 becomes 65536, which exceeds the maximum value of integer data type, i.e. 32767. If a value exceeds the maximum value of the integer data type, there is wrap-around effect. After wrap around, 65536 will be mapped to 0 and 256*256-1 becomes -1. Hence, the value of the input argument given to the malloc function is -1. The input to the malloc function must be greater than zero as it is not possible to allocate a memory block of size zero or lesser than 0 bytes. Thus, the malloc function fails in the given code and returns a NULL pointer. Since ptr is a NULL pointer, the if expression evaluates to true, and the if body of the if-else statement gets executed and 'Memory allocation fails' gets printed.

If working with compilers that allocate 4 bytes to an integer like Microsoft Visual C++ 6.0, the result of evaluation of 256*256-1 comes out to be 65535. This is due to the fact that the maximum value of the integer data type if it is of size 4 bytes is 2147483647. Hence, there will be no wrap-around effect. The malloc function allocates the memory block of size 65535 bytes successfully and returns a pointer to it. Thus, ptr is not a null pointer. The expression of the if-else statement evaluates to false, the else body gets executed and 'Memory allocation successful' gets printed. Note that if using Microsoft Visual C++ 6.0, include file malloc.h instead of alloc.h.

71. Memory allocation successful

Explanation:

Even if you are working with compilers like Turbo C 3.0, the result of the evaluation of 256*256L-1 comes out to be 65535. This is because of 256L being a long integer. The result of 256*256L comes out to be 65536, which lies within the permissible range of long integers. Hence, no wrap around will occur as in Answer number 70. The expression 256*256L-1 evaluates to 65535. The malloc function allocates the memory block of size 65535 bytes successfully and returns a pointer to it. Thus, ptr is not a null pointer. The expression of the if-else statement evaluates to false, the else body gets executed and 'Memory allocation successful' gets printed. Note that sometimes you may get an output as 'Memory allocation fails'. This happens when the compiler is not able to allocate such a large chunk of memory space.

72. Memory allocation fails (If working in DOS environment i.e. using Borland Turbo C 3.0 or Borland Turbo C 4.5)
    or
    Memory allocation successful (If working in Windows environment i.e. using MS VC++ 6.0)

    Explanation:

    The maximum size of the memory block that can be allocated using the malloc function depends upon the environment in which you are working. The maximum size of memory block that can be allocated with the help of the malloc function in DOS environment is 65535 bytes i.e. 64 KB-1. If the memory block of size greater than 65535 bytes, is to be allocated, the function farmalloc can be used.

---

i Some of the latest compilers do not support the farmalloc function.

---

73. Hello
    HelloReaders!!

    Caution:

    The code may sometimes give memory exception.

    Explanation:

    The function malloc is used to allocate a memory block of 6 bytes. The function strcpy is used to place the string "Hello" in the allocated memory block. The allocated memory block is big enough to successfully accommodate the five characters of the string "Hello" and a terminating null character. The function strcat concatenates the string "Readers!!" with the string "Hello". Now, the memory block cannot fully accommodate the string "HelloReaders!!". Hence, some of the characters are written into the unallocated memory space. This access to the unallocated memory space may sometimes lead to an exception or abrupt program termination. However, it is highly probable that the user will get the correct result.

74. Hello
    HelloReaders!!

    Explanation:

    The function malloc is used to allocate a memory block of 6 bytes. The function strcpy is used to place the string "Hello" in the allocated memory block. The allocated memory block is big enough to successfully accommodate the five characters of the string "Hello" and a terminating null character, but it is not big enough to accommodate the string "HelloReaders!!". If the string "HelloReaders!!" is placed in the memory block of present size, some of the characters of the string will be written into the unallocated memory space. This may lead to an abnormal behavior. Hence, the realloc function is used to resize the memory block and to make it big enough so that it can hold the string "HelloReaders!!". After resizing the memory block, the string "Readers!!" is concatenated with the string "Hello" already present in the reallocated memory block. Since the entire string is accommodated into the reallocated memory block, there will be no abnormal behavior.

75. The value of variable var is 200

    Explanation:

    The typedef storage class specifier is used for creating a synonym name i for the type int. After this statement, the synonym name i can be used in the place of the type int. Hence, the initialization statement i var=200; is equivalent to int var=200;.

76. Compilation error "Two many storage classes in declaration in function main"

    Explanation:

    Only one storage class specifier can be used in a declaration statement. In the declaration statement typedef static int i;, two storage class specifiers, namely typedef and static are specified. This leads to a compilation error.

77. The size of i and j is 2 and 2

    Explanation:

    The declaration statement cp i,j; creates two variables i and j to be of type cp. However, cp is an alias name for the type char*. Hence, the type of both the variables i and j is char*. Thus, the size taken by both of them is 2 and 2 (if using Borland Turbo C 3.0), 4 and 4 (if using Borland Turbo C 4.5 or MS VC++ 6.0).

78. Strings!!
    öå¥¢¤¨Í (Garbage)

    Explanation:

    The character array str is local to the function print_string. It has automatic (i.e. local) lifetime. Memory space is allocated to str as the program control enters the function print_string and encounters its declaration statement. It remains into existence till the program control remains within the function. As the control comes out of the function, the character array str will be destroyed and the memory allocated to it is freed.

    In the function print_string, the call to the puts function prints "Strings!!". The next statement returns str (i.e. the address of the first element of str) to the function main. An attempt to print the string by the means of the returned pointer in the function main will print garbage because the memory location to which str points has been deallocated. Hence, the printf function outputs garbage.

79. Strings!!
    Strings!!

    Explanation:

    The character array str has been declared as static. It has static (i.e. global) lifetime. After its creation, it remains into existence till the end of the program. The attempt to print the string by the means of the returned pointer in the function main will print "Strings!!" because the character array str, being static, still exists although the function print_string has terminated.

80. Strings!!
    Strings!!

    Explanation:

    The character pointer str is local to the function print_string. It is stored on the stack and has automatic (i.e. local) lifetime. The character pointer str is initialized with the address of the first element of the string literal "Strings!!". **The string literal "Strings!!" is stored in the data segment and has static (i.e. global) lifetime.** After its creation, it will remain into existence till the program terminates.

    In the function print_string, the call to the puts function prints "Strings!!". The next statement returns str (i.e. the address of the first element of str) to the function main. As the program control returns to the function main, the character pointer str is destroyed but the memory location whose address has been returned to the function main still exists as it has static lifetime. Thus, an attempt to print the string by the means of the returned pointer in the function main will print "Strings!!".

Answers to Multiple-choice Questions

81. c 82. a 83. b 84. a 85. a 86. b 87. a 88. c 89. a 90. a 91. a 92. c 93. b
94. b 95. c 96. c 97. a 98. a 99. a 100. b 101. a 102. b 103. a 104. b 105. a

Programming Exercises

Program 1 | An instructor of a computing course wants to store and find the average of marks of all the students appearing in an examination. As he or she does not know how many students will appear on the examination day, he or she does not want to create a static array and waste the memory space. Solve his or her problem by creating a dynamic array, storing the marks of the students and finding the average

PE 7-1.c

```
//Dynamic Array
#include<stdio.h>
#include<alloc.h>
#include<stdlib.h>
main()
{
    int *array, num, i, sum=0;
    float avg;
    printf("How many students have appeared in the examination?\t");
    scanf("%d",&num);
    array=(int*)malloc(num*sizeof(int));
    if(array==NULL)
    {
        printf("Memory allocation failed. Program cannot proceed\n");
        exit(1);
    }
    else
    {
        printf("Enter the marks of %d students:\n",num);
        for(i=0;i<num;i++)
            scanf("%d",(array+i));
        for(i=0;i<num;i++)
            sum+=*(array+i);
        avg=(float)sum/num;
        printf("Sum of marks of all the students is %d\n",sum);
        printf("Average of marks secured are %f",avg);
    }
}
```

Output window

```
How many students have appeared in the examination?    5
Enter the marks of 5 students:
12
14
21
16
8
Sum of marks of all the students is 71
Average of marks secured are 14.200000
```

Program 2 | Two matrices are to be multiplied but their size is not known in advance. The size and the elements of the matrices will be entered by the user at the run time. Making use of dynamic memory allocation, create the matrices and find the result of their multiplication

PE 7-2.c

```
//Dynamic two-dimensional array
#include<stdio.h>
#include<alloc.h>
#include<stdlib.h>
main()
{
    int *mat1, *mat2, *resultant;
```

Output window

```
Enter the order of first matrix:
2 3
Enter the order of second matrix:
3 3
Enter the elements of first 2*3 matrix:
1 2 3
4 5 6
```

(Contd...)

```
    int rows1, cols1, rows2, cols2, i, j, k;
    printf("Enter the order of first matrix:\n");
    scanf("%d %d", &rows1, &cols1);
    printf("Enter the order of second matrix:\n");
    scanf("%d %d", &rows2, &cols2);
    if(cols1!=rows2)
    {
        printf("Matrix multiplication is not compatible\n");
        exit(1);
    }
    else
    {
        mat1=(int*)malloc(rows1*cols1*sizeof(int));
        mat2=(int*)malloc(rows2*cols2*sizeof(int));
        resultant=(int*)calloc(rows1, cols2*sizeof(int));
        if(mat1==NULL||mat2==NULL||resultant==NULL)
        {
            printf("There is some problem in memory allocation\n");
            exit(1);
        }
        else
        {
            printf("Enter the elements of first %d*%d matrix:\n", rows1, cols1);
            for(i=0; i<rows1; i++)
            {
                for(j=0; j<cols1; j++)
                    scanf("%d",&mat1[i*cols1+j]);
                printf("\n");
            }
            printf("Enter the elements of second %d*%d matrix:\n", rows2, cols2);
            for(i=0; i<rows2; i++)
            {
                for(j=0; j<cols2; j++)
                    scanf("%d",&mat2[i*cols2+j]);
                printf("\n");
            }
            for(i=0; i<rows1; i++)
                for(j=0;j<cols2;j++)
                    for(k=0;k<cols1;k++)
                        resultant[i*cols2+j]+=mat1[i*cols1+k] * mat2[k*cols2+j];
            printf("The result of matrix multiplication is:\n");
            for(i=0; i<rows1; i++)
            {
                for(j=0; j<cols2; j++)
                    printf("%d ",resultant[i*cols2+j]);
                printf("\n");
            }
            free(mat1); free(mat2); free(resultant);
        }
    }
}
```

```
Enter the element of second 3*3 matrix:
2 3 4
1 2 3
1 1 0
The result of matrix multiplication is:
7 10 10
19 28 31
```

Program 3 | Making the use of recursion and static variables, print the first n terms of Fibonacci series

PE 7-3.c

```
//Fibonacci Series
#include<stdio.h>
#include<conio.h>
int fib(int num);
main()
{
    int terms;
    printf("Enter the number of terms that you want to print:\t");
    scanf("%d",&terms);
    printf("%d terms of Fibonacci series are:\n");
    fib(terms);
}
fib(int num)
{
    static int a=0;
    static int b=1;
    static int i=0;
    static int c;
    if(i==0)
    {
        printf("%d ",a);
        i++;
    }
    if(i==1)
    {
        printf("%d ",b);
        i++;
    }
    if(i<num)
    {
        c=a+b;
        a=b;
        b=c;
        printf("%d ",c);
        i++;
        fib(num);
    }
}
```

Output window

```
Enter the number of terms that you want to print:    10
10 terms of Fibonacci series are:
0 1 1 2 3 5 8 13 21 34
```

Program 4 | Making use of recursion and static variables, print the sum of the first n natural numbers

PE 7-4.c

```
//Sum of first n natural numbers
#include<stdio.h>
#include<conio.h>
int sum(int);
int main()
{
int num;
```

Output window

```
Enter the number of natural numbers that you want to sum up:    10
The sum of 10 natural numbers is 55
```

(Contd...)

```
printf("Enter the number of natural number that you want to sum up:\t");
scanf("%d",&num);
printf("The sum of first %d natural numbers is %d", num, sum(num));

}
int sum(int num)
{
    static int i=1;
    static int result=0;
    result=result+i;
    i++;
    if(i<=num)
        sum(num);
    return result;
}
```

Program 5 | Two strings are entered by the user. Dynamically create an array that holds the result of concatenation of the entered strings

PE 7-5.c

```
//String concatenation
#include<stdio.h>
#include<alloc.h>
#include<string.h>
int main()
{
    char str1[50], str2[50], *resultant;
    int length1, length2;
    printf("Enter first string:\t");
    gets(str1);
    printf("Enter second string:\t");
    gets(str2);
    length1=strlen(str1);
    length2=strlen(str2);
    resultant=(char*)malloc(length1+length2+1*sizeof(char));
    strcpy(resultant, str1);
    strcat(resultant, str2);
    printf("Concatenated string is %s", resultant);
}
```

Output window

```
Enter first string:     Hello
Enter second string:    Readers
Concatenated string is HelloReaders
```

Test Yourself

1. Fill in the blanks in each of the following:
   a. The region of the program within which an identifier is visible is determined by its ___________.
   b. ___________ is the only kind of identifier that always has function scope.
   c. The keyword ___________ provides a method for declaring an identifier without defining it.
   d. One definition rule states that ___________.
   e. The principle of shadowing states that ___________.
   f. ___________ is a process by which a name used in an expression is associated with a declaration.
   g. All the global variables and functions by default have ___________ linkage.
   h. The linkage of an identifier can be made internal by using ___________ storage class specifier in the declaration statement.
   i. All the identifiers with block scope or function prototype scope by default have ___________ linkage.
   j. Function can have ___________ or ___________ linkage but cannot have ___________ linkage.
   k. The portion of program execution during which the memory space of an object is guaranteed to be reserved is known as ___________.
   l. Objects with ___________ lifetime are allocated new storage each time the execution control enters the block in which their associated identifiers are defined.
   m. The allocation of memory space made at the run time is known as ___________.
   n. An object with block scope by default has ___________ storage class.
   o. ___________ storage class specifier is used to create a synonym for a known type.

2. State whether each of the following is true or false. If false, explain why.
   a. The scope of an identifier is determined by the position of its declaration.
   b. Function scope terminates with the end of function declaration.
   c. It is possible to define an identifier with a same name and type more than once in the same scope.
   d. It is possible to define an identifier with a same name more than once, if the definitions lie in different scopes.
   e. It is possible to declare identifiers with a same name but different types in different scopes.
   f. At most one storage class specifier can be specified in a declaration statement.
   g. The variables declared with `auto` storage class specification are implicitly initialized.
   h. It is not possible to specify an `auto` storage class specifier in the declarations that are made in the global scope.
   i. It is not possible to apply address-of operator to an identifier declared with `register` storage class specifier.
   j. The variables declared with `static` storage class specification are implicitly initialized to zero.
   k. The values of `auto` variables persist between the function calls.
   l. `size_t` is a type.
   m. The value of the memory space allocated by using the `malloc` function is implicitly initialized to zero.
   n. Careless allocation of memory at the compile time leads to memory leak.

3. Programming exercises:

   a. Two matrices are to be added but their size is not known in advance. The size and the elements of the matrices will be entered by the user at the run time. Write a C program that makes the use of dynamic memory allocation to create the matrices and find the result of their addition.
   b. Write a C program that makes use of dynamic memory allocation to create and store a matrix and find its inverse.
   c. Write a C program that makes use of a recursive function and `static` variables to find the factorial of a given number.
   d. Write a C program that dynamically creates two string arrays to hold strings entered by the user. Concatenate the strings and store the resulting string in the first array. Resize the first array using `realloc`.

8

THE C PREPROCESSOR

Learning Objectives

In this chapter, you will learn about:

- Translators and their classification
- Phases of translation
- Trigraph replacement, line splicing and tokenization
- Macros and its types
- Token replacement and token pasting
- Predefined macros
- Source file inclusion and line control directive
- `error` directive
- `pragma` directive
- Null directive

8.1 Introduction

In the previous chapters, you have developed several programs using C language, which is a high-level language. However, you will be surprised to know that the computer (i.e. the machine) cannot understand high-level languages. It can only understand machine-level languages, which are in the form of 1's and 0's. Humans do not want to write programs in machine-level languages because they are difficult to read and modify, more error prone and difficult to debug. Therefore, **translators**, which convert a high-level language program into an equivalent machine-level language program, are used to enable humans to write programs in high-level languages and at the same time make it possible to execute them on machines. The concept of translators can be understood by looking at the story board given below:

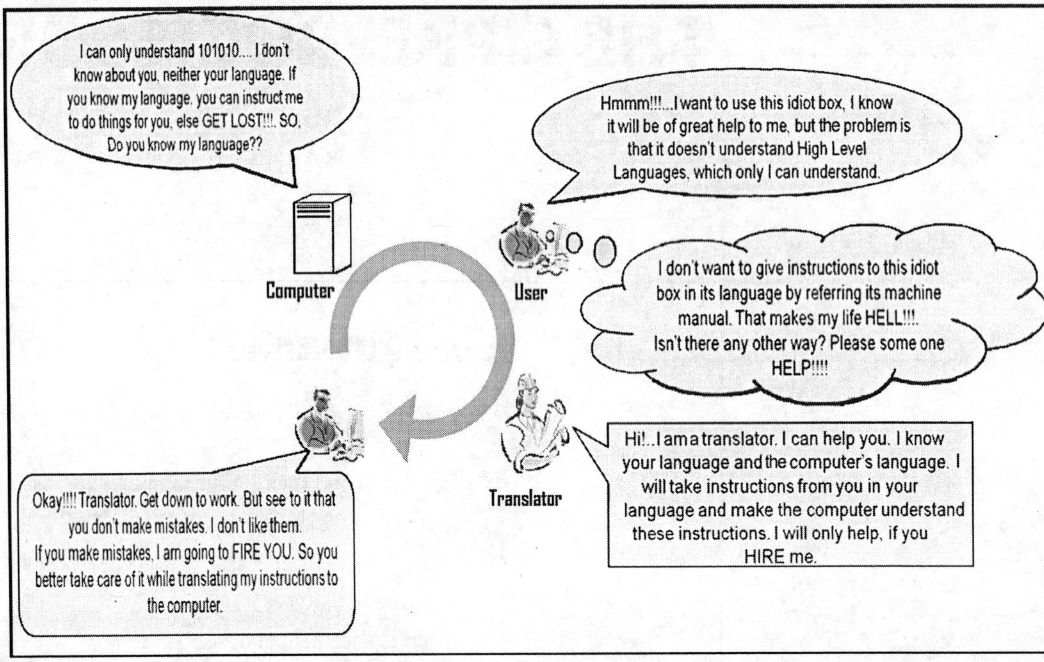

You should also know that **compiler** is not the only translator that works before the execution of a program. The **preprocessor** is another translator that works and processes the source code before it is given to the compiler. It operates under the control of commands known as **preprocessor directives**. In this chapter, I will tell you how the preprocessor directives are written, various preprocessor directives and the precautions one must take while using them.

8.2 Translators

A **translator** is a program that takes a program written in a language called the **source language** as an input and converts it into an equivalent program in another language called the **target language**. Translators are classified according to the classes of their source and target languages. The classification of translators according to the classes of their source and target languages is shown in Table 8.1.

Table 8.1 | Classification of translators according to their source and target languages

S.No	Source language Input	Name of Translator Output	Target language
1.	High-level language	Preprocessor	High-level language
2.	High-level language	Compiler	Low-level language (i.e. assembly-level language or machine-level language)
3.	Assembly-level language	Assembler	Machine-level language
4.	High-level language	Interpreter	Machine-level language

The **preprocessor** is a translator that converts a program written in one high-level language into an **equivalent** program written in another high-level language. For example, a preprocessor converts the code written in C into an equivalent program in simplified C language. The **compiler** converts a program written in a high-level language into an equivalent program either in an assembly-level language or a machine-level language. If the output of the compiler is an assembly language program, an **assembler** is required to further convert it into the machine code. An **interpreter** is a translator that converts the statements written in a high-level language program into equivalent statements in a machine-level language one by one on the fly.

8.3 Phases of Translation

The conversion of a source program file into an executable file is done in eight conceptual steps known as **phases of translation**. The eight phases of translation are:

1. Trigraph sequences are replaced by their single character equivalents. This phase is carried out by the preprocessor and is called **trigraph replacement**.
2. Each instance of a backslash character (i.e. \) immediately followed by a new-line character is deleted by the preprocessor. This process is known as **line splicing**.

Backward Reference: Refer Question numbers 38 and 39 (Chapter 1) and their answers for examples on line splicing.

3. The source file is decomposed into preprocessing tokens and a sequence of white-space characters. Each comment is replaced by a single-space character and new-line characters are retained. Whether a sequence of white-space characters other than a new-line character is to be replaced by a single-space character or not is implementation defined. This phase is carried out by the preprocessor and is called **tokenization**.
4. The preprocessor directives are executed and macros are expanded. This is known as **directive handling** and **macro expansion**. After their execution, all the preprocessor directives are then deleted.
5. Escape sequences in character constants and string literals are converted to their character equivalents.
6. Adjacent string literals are concatenated.
7. Each preprocessing token is converted into a token. White-space characters separating tokens are no longer significant and are removed. The resulting tokens are syntactically and semantically analyzed and translated into an object code by the compiler.

8. All external object and function references are resolved. All the required libraries are linked together to satisfy an external reference not defined in the current program. This phase is carried out by the linker, and the output of this phase is an executable file ready for the execution.

The first four phases of translation need an explicit description and are described in the following sections in detail. The working of the rest of the phases is clear from the above-mentioned text and will be clearer in the further course of discussion.

8.3.1 Trigraph Replacement

A **character set** defines the valid characters that can be used in a source program or interpreted when a program is running. The set of characters that can be used to write a source program is called a **source character set**, and the set of characters available when the program is executing is called an **execution character set**. It is possible that the source character set is different from the execution character set.

There are a number of character sets that exist. For example, ISO 646, ASCII, EBCDIC, ISO8859, ISO8859-1, ISO8859-2,…, ISO8859-16, etc. A character that exists in one character set might not exist in some other character set.

To write C programs using character sets that do not contain all of C's punctuation characters, ANSI allows the use of nine trigraph sequences in the source file. A **trigraph sequence** is a sequence of three characters, the first two of which are question marks and the third character should belong to the given set of characters {=, (, /,), ', <, !, >, -}. Trigraph sequences are replaced by their corresponding character equivalents during the first phase of translation (i.e. **trigraph replacement**). Table 8.2 lists the valid trigraph sequences and their character equivalents.

Table 8.2 | Trigraph sequences and their character equivalents

S.No	Trigraph sequence	Character equivalent
1.	??=	#
2.	??(	[
3.	??/	\
4.	??)	]
5.	??'	^
6.	??<	{
7.	??!	|
8.	??>	}
9.	??-	~

No other trigraph sequence is recognized. A question mark (?) that does not begin the above-mentioned trigraph sequences remains unchanged during the translation.

Some compilers support an option to turn the recognition of trigraphs off or disable the trigraphs by default, and they require an option to turn them on. Some issue warning messages when they encounter trigraph sequences in the source files. Borland supplies a separate trigraph processor (TRIGRAPH.EXE) with Turbo C 3.0 and 4.5. This file is present in the BIN folder of the Turbo C installation and is only used when the trigraph processing is desired.

The objective behind supplying a separate trigraph processor is to maximize the speed of compilation.

8.3.2 Line Splicing

During the preprocessing stage, each instance of a backslash character (i.e. \) immediately followed by a new-line character is deleted. This process is known as **splicing**. Physical source lines present in the source program are spliced to form logical source lines. Only the last backslash on any physical source line is eligible for being a part of such a splice. Consider Figure 8.1.

Physical source lines of code (Column 1)		Logical source lines of code (Column 2)		Output (Column 3)

main()
{
printf("Hello World\
");
}
	Line splicing →	main()
		{
		printf("Hello World");
		}
			After execution →	Hello World

Figure 8.1 | Line splicing

Column 1 contains the physical source lines of the code. After the preprocessing stage, the physical source lines are spliced to form logical source lines of the code, as mentioned in column 2 in Figure 8.1. Logical source lines are processed by the compiler during phase 7 of translation. The output produced on the execution of the logical source lines of the code listed in column 2 is shown in column 3 in Figure 8.1.

8.3.3 Tokenization

A **preprocessing token** is the smallest indivisible element of C language in the translation phases from 3 to 6. The categories of the preprocessing tokens are: header names, identifiers, preprocessing numbers, character constants, string literals, punctuators and a single non-white-space character. A **token** is the smallest indivisible element of C language in the translation phases 7 and 8. The categories of tokens are: keywords, identifiers, constants, string literals and punctuators (i.e. operators, separators or terminator). For example, the operator `+=` is one token.

C's **tokenizer** is greedy in nature. It always tries to create the biggest possible token. If an input stream of characters has been parsed into tokens up to a given character, the next token is the longest sequence of the characters that could constitute a token. For example, the program fragment `x+++++y` is parsed as `x ++ ++ + y`, which violates a constraint on the increment operator and leads to a compilation error. If the tokenizer would have been intelligent instead of being greedy and parses the mentioned fragment as `x ++ + ++ y`, it would have been a valid expression.

Backward Reference: Refer Question number 28 (Chapter 2) and its answer to see the greedy nature of C's tokenizer.

8.3.4 Preprocessor Directive Handling

The preprocessor is controlled by directives known as **preprocessor directives,** which are not a part of C language. A **preprocessor directive** consists of various preprocessing tokens and begins with a # (pound) symbol. The important points for writing a preprocessor directive are as follows:

1. The pound symbol (#) should either be the first character in a source file or the first non-white-space character in a line.
2. A new-line character ends the preprocessor directive.
3. The white-space characters that can appear between the preprocessing tokens within a preprocessing directive are a single-space character or a horizontal tab-space character (i.e. white-space characters like new-line, vertical tab and form feed are not allowed).
4. The preprocessor directives can appear anywhere in a program but are generally placed at the beginning of a program before the function main or before the beginning of a particular function.

Table 8.3 illustrates the application of the rules mentioned above for writing an include directive.

Table 8.3 | Rules for writing the preprocessor directives

S.No	Preprocessor directive	Valid or invalid?
1.	#include<stdio.h>	**Valid**, pound symbol is the first character in the source file
2.	#include <stdio.h>	**Valid,** white-space characters (only space and horizontal tab) can appear within a preprocessor directive
3.	#include<conio.h>	**Valid**, pound symbol is the first non-white-space character in a line
4.	a#include<string.h>	**Invalid**, as pound symbol is not the first non-white-space character in a line
5.	#include<math.h> #include<stdarg.h>	**Invalid**, as the first preprocessor directive is not terminated with a new-line character and the second preprocessor directive's pound symbol is not the first non-white-space character
6.	#include <dos.h>	**Invalid**, as a white-space character between preprocessing tokens within a preprocessing directive cannot be a new-line character

The various preprocessor directives available in C language are as follows:

1. Macro replacement directive (#define, #undef)
2. Source file inclusion directive (#include)
3. Line directive (#line)
4. Error directive (#error)
5. Pragma directive (#pragma)
6. Conditional compilation directives (#if, #else, #elif, #endif, #ifdef, #ifndef)
7. Null directive (# new-line)

8.3.4.1 Macro Replacement Directives

A **macro** is a facility provided by the C preprocessor, by which a token can be replaced by the user-defined sequence of characters. Macros are defined with the help of the define directive. The identifier name immediately following the define directive is called the **macro name**. Macro names are generally written in upper case.

8.3.4.1.1 Types of Macro

There are two types of macros:

1. Macro without arguments, also called **object-like macros.**
2. Macro with arguments, also called **function-like macros.**

8.3.4.1.1.1 Object-like Macros

An **object-like macro** is also known as a **symbolic constant**. It is defined as:

```
#define macro-name replacement-list
```

The important points about object-like macros are as follows:

1. The define directive causes each subsequent instance of the macro name to be replaced by the replacement list of preprocessing tokens present in the definition of the macro.
2. The replacement list can even be empty.
3. The object-like macro name must be a preprocessing identifier. During the translation phases 3 to 6, keywords are not recognized separately and are treated as identifiers. Hence, they can also be used as a macro name, e.g. the following object-like macro definition is perfectly valid:

```
#define int char
```

Forward Reference: Refer Question numbers 44 and 45 and their answers for the appropriate usage of a macro name.

4. There shall be a white-space character (blank-space character or horizontal tab space character) between the macro name and the replacement list in the definition of an object-like macro.

The piece of code in Program 8-1 illustrates the use of an object-like macro.

Prog 8-1.c	After the preprocessing stage	Output window

//Object-like macro
#include<stdio.h>
#define PI 3.142
main()
{
int rad=5;
printf("Area of circle is %f",PI*rad*rad);
}
	//The content of the header file stdio.h
	//replaces the include directive and is
	//placed here
	main()
	{
	int rad=5;
	printf("Area of circle is %f",3.142*rad*rad);
	}
		Area of circle is 78.550000
		Remarks:
		• PI is an object-like macro
		• During the preprocessing stage, each subsequent instance of PI is replaced by its replacement list (i.e. 3.142)

Program 8-1 | A program that illustrates the definition and the use of an object-like macro

8.3.4.1.1.2 Function-like Macros

A macro with arguments is called a **function-like macro**. Its usage is syntactically similar to a function call and it can be defined as:

```
#define macro-name(parameter-list) replacement-list
```

The piece of code in Program 8-2 illustrates the use of a function-like macro.

Prog 8-2.c	After the preprocessing stage	Output window

//Function-like macro
#include<stdio.h>
#define SQR(x) (x*x)
main()
{
int side=5;
printf("Area of square is %d",SQR(side));
}
	//The content of the header file stdio.h
	//replaces the include directive and is
	//placed here
	main()
	{
	int side=5;
	printf("Area of square is %d",(side*side));
	}
		Area of square is 25
		Remarks:
		• Each time a function-like macro name is encountered, the macro name is replaced by the replacement list
		• The parameters present in the replacement list of macro definition are replaced by the actual arguments present in the macro invocation

Program 8-2 | A program that illustrates the definition and the use of a function-like macro

> *i* The white-space characters preceding or following the replacement list are not considered as a part of the replacement list for either form of macro (i.e. object-like or function-like).

During the preprocessing stage, the macro names are expanded and are replaced by their replacement lists. This process is known as **macro expansion**. Macro expansion is purely textual. If proper care is not taken while defining macros, they might lead to unexpected results.

8.3.4.1.2 Common Macro Pitfalls

Macros can create problems if they are not defined and used carefully. The common macro pitfalls are described in subsequent sections.

8.3.4.1.2.1 Magical White Space

1. There should be a white-space character (blank-space character or horizontal tab-space character) between the macro name and the replacement list in the definition of an object-like macro. The piece of code in Program 8-3 illustrates the effect of the violation of the above-mentioned rule.

Prog 8-3.c	Output window
//Magical white-space character #include<stdio.h> #define PI=3.1428 main()	Compilation error "Expression syntax in function main" **Remarks:** • The code is not working due to the erroneous definition of the object-like macro PI

(Contd...)

{
printf("The value of constant PI is %f",PI);
}
	• There should be a white-space character between the macro name and the replacement list in the definition of an object-like macro instead of the character '='
	What to do?
	• Rectify the macro definition as #define PI 3.1428

Program 8-3 | A program that illustrates the significance of a white-space character between the macro name and its replacement list

2. There should be no white-space character between the macro name and the left parenthesis of parameter list in the definition of a function-like macro. The piece of code in Program 8-4 illustrates the effect of the violation of the above-mentioned rule.

Prog 8-4.c	Output window

//Magical white-space character
#include<stdio.h>
#define CUBE (x) x*x*x
main()
{
printf("Cube of 5 is %d",CUBE(5));
}
	Compilation error "Undefined symbol x in function main"
	Remarks:
	• Due to a white-space character between the macro name CUBE and the left parenthesis of the parameter list in the macro definition, CUBE will be treated as an object-like macro and not as a function-like macro
	• After the macro expansion, the expression CUBE(5) will become (x) x*x*x(5)
	• The preprocessed code on compilation gives the specified error
	What to do?
	• Remove the white-space character between the macro name and the left parenthesis in the macro definition. Re-execute the code and check the result

Program 8-4 | A program illustrating that there should be no white-space character between the macro name and the left parenthesis of the parameter list

8.3.4.1.2.2 Operator Precedence Problems

1. In the definition of a macro, the replacement list must always be parenthesized to protect any lower precedence operator in it from a higher precedence operator in the surrounding expression. The piece of code in Program 8-5 illustrates the effect of the violation of the above-mentioned rule.

Prog 8-5.c	Output window

//Operator precedence problem-I
#include<stdio.h>
#define DOUBLE(x) x+x
main()
{
int result, x;
printf("Enter the value of x\t");
scanf("%d",&x);
	Enter the value of x 3
	Value of result is 18
	Expected result:
	Value of result is 30
	Remarks:
	• Macro expansion is purely textual
	• Macros are expanded during the preprocessing stage before the compilation stage

(Contd...)

Prog 8-5.c	Output window

result=5*DOUBLE(x);
printf("Value of result is %d",result);
}
	• Thus, after the preprocessing stage, the expression result=5*DOUBLE(x) becomes result=5*x+x
	• Since the multiplication operator has a higher precedence than the addition operator, it will operate first
	• Thus, the result of the expression comes out to be 18 instead of 30
	What to do?
	• Parenthesize the replacement list to protect the lower precedence operator (i.e. addition operator) in it from the surrounding higher precedence operator (i.e. multiplication operator)
	• Re-define the macro as: #define DOUBLE(x) (x+x) and re-execute the code

Program 8-5 | A program that illustrates an operator precedence pitfall in the macro definition

2. In the definition of a function-like macro, all the occurrences of parameters in the replacement list must be parenthesized to protect any low precedence operator in the actual arguments from the rest of the macro expansion. The piece of code in Program 8-6 illustrates the effect of the violation of the above-mentioned rule.

Prog 8-6.c	Output window

//Operator precedence problem-II
#include<stdio.h>
#define SQR(x) (x*x)
main()
{
int val=2, result;
result=SQR(val+1);
printf("Result is %d",result);
}
	Result is 5
	Expected result:
	Result is 9
	Remarks:
	• After the preprocessing stage, the expression result=SQR(val+1) becomes result=val+1*val+1 (i.e. result=2+1*2+1)
	• Since the multiplication operator has a higher precedence than the addition operator, it will get evaluated first. Thus, the expression evaluates to 5
	• Since the lower precedence operators in the actual arguments are not protected from the rest of the macro expansion, the program gives an unexpected result
	What to do?
	• Parenthesize all the parameters in the replacement list
	• Redefine the macro as: #define SQR(x) ((x)*(x)) and re-execute the code

Program 8-6 | A program that illustrates an operator precedence pitfall in the macro definition

8.3.4.1.2.3 Arguments with a Side-effect

1. While calling a function-like macro, the argument should not be an expression with a side-effect.

> A **side-effect** is a modification of a data object or a file. Modifying an object, modifying a file or calling a function that does any of these operations are all side-effects. The evaluation of an expression may also produce side-effects. For example, the evaluation of the expression result=value++ has side-effects as it modifies the data objects, namely result and value. The assignment operator,

(Contd...)

increment operator and decrement operator have side-effects. The side-effects of evaluations should be complete at certain specified points in the execution sequence known as **sequence points.**

A **sequence point** is a point in the program execution sequence at which all the side-effects of the previous evaluations are complete and no side-effects of subsequent evaluations have taken place. The semicolon marks a sequence point, i.e. all the changes made by assignment operators, increment operators and decrement operators in a statement must take place before the program control proceeds to the next statement.

The piece of code in Program 8-7 illustrates the call to a function-like macro whose argument is an expression with a side-effect.

Line	Prog 8-7.c	Output window

1
2
3
4
5
6
7
8
9
	//Arguments with side-effect
	#include<stdio.h>
	#define SQR(x) (x*x)
	main()
	{
	int val=2, result;
	result=SQR(++val);
	printf("Result is %d",result);
	}
		Result is 16
		Expected result:
		Result is 9
		Remarks:
		• Function-like macro call text replaces all the occurrences of the parameters in the replacement list with the actual arguments. **The actual arguments are not evaluated before being replaced**
		• Thus, after the preprocessing stage, the expression result=SQR(++val) becomes result=++val*++val and evaluates to 16
		• If SQR would have been defined as a function, the result would have been 9 because **in a function call the actual arguments are evaluated before being passed to the function**
		What to do?
		• Eliminate the side effect from the argument of SQR and write the statement in line number 6 as:
		++val;
		result=SQR(val);

Program 8-7 | A program to illustrate that an argument to a function-like macro should not be an expression with a side-effect

8.3.4.1.2.4 Undesirable Semicolon

1. Avoid the use of a semicolon in and at the end of a macro definition. The code snippet in Program 8-8 illustrates the effect of the presence of a semicolon in a macro definition.

Prog 8-8.c	Output window

//Effect of the use of a semicolon in the macro definition
#include<stdio.h>
#define SWAP(a,b) a=a+b; b=a-b; a=a-b
main()
{
int a=20, b=10;
	Compilation error "Misplaced else in function main"
	Remarks:
	• During the preprocessing stage, the macro SWAP is expanded and is replaced by multiple statements (i.e. a=a+b; b=a-b; a=a-b;)

(Contd...)

Prog 8-8.c

```
printf("Swap the values of a and b only if a is greater\n");
if(a>b)
    SWAP(a,b);
else
    printf("Values are not swapped\n");
printf("Resultant values of a and b are %d %d",a,b);
}
```

Output window

- Only the first statement (i.e. a=a+b;) forms the if body. The other two statements will be considered as the statements next to the if statement
- The else clause remains unmatched and leads to "Misplaced else error"
- It is recommended to use commas instead of using semicolons in the macro definition

What to do?

- Redefine the macro as:
  `#define SWAP(a,b) a=a+b, b=a-b, a=a-b`

Program 8-8 | A program that illustrates the effect of the use of a semicolon in a macro definition

The code snippet in Program 8-9 illustrates the effect of the presence of a semicolon at the end of a macro definition.

Prog 8-9.c

```
//Effect of the use of semicolon at the end of macro definition
#include<stdio.h>
#define CUBE(x) ((x)*(x)*(x));
main()
{
int a=2, b=8;
if(CUBE(a)==b)
    printf("Cube of a is equal to b\n");
else
    printf("Cube of a is not equal to b\n");
}
```

Output window

Compilation error

Remark:

- The semicolon at the end of the macro definition after the macro expansion forms an ill-formed expression and leads to a compilation error

What to do?

- Remove the semicolon present at the end of the macro definition
- Re-execute the code and check the result

Program 8-9 | A program that illustrates the effect of the use of a semicolon at the end of a macro definition

8.3.4.1.3 Stringification/Token Replacement

In a function-like macro definition, if the replacement list consists of a parameter immediately preceded by a '#' preprocessing token, then during the preprocessing stage, the preprocessor replaces both the '#' preprocessing token and the parameter with a single character string literal (which contains the spelling of the argument corresponding to the parameter). Since # and parameter are replaced by a single character string literal, it is known as **token replacement**. In addition, as # preprocessing token converts the argument corresponding to a parameter into a string literal, # is known as **stringizing operator** and the operation is known as **stringification**. The code snippets in Programs 8-10 and 8-11 illustrate the use of a stringizing operator.

Prog 8-10.c

```
//Token replacement or stringification
#include<stdio.h>
#define STR(x) #x
main()
{
printf(STR(Token replacement));
}
```

After the preprocessing stage

```
//The content of the header file stdio.h
//replaces the include directive and is
//placed here
main()
{
printf("Token replacement");
}
```

Output window

Token replacement

Program 8-10 | A program that illustrates the use of a stringizing operator

Prog 8-11.c	After the preprocessing stage	Output window

//Token replacement or stringification
#include<stdio.h>
#define STR(x) #x
main()
{
char str[20]=STR(Token replacement);
puts(str);
}
	//The content of the header file stdio.h
	//replaces the include directive and is
	//placed here
	main()
	{
	char str[20]="Token replacement";
	puts(str);
	}
		Token replacement

Program 8-11 | A program that illustrates the use of a stringizing operator

The important points about token replacement are as follows:

1. White-space characters between the argument's preprocessing tokens become a single-space character in the replaced character string literal constant. The piece of code in Program 8-12 illustrates this fact.

Prog 8-12.c	After the preprocessing stage	Output window

//Token replacement or stringification
#include<stdio.h>
#define STR(x) #x
main()
{
char str[20]=STR(Token   replacement);
puts(str);
}
	//The content of the header file stdio.h
	//replaces the include directive and is
	//placed here
	main()
	{
	char str[20]="Token replacement";
	puts(str);
	}
		Token replacement

Program 8-12 | A program illustrating that during stringification, white-space characters between the argument's preprocessing token are replaced by a single-space character

2. White-space characters before the first preprocessing token and after the last preprocessing token composing the macro's argument are deleted. The piece of code in Program 8-13 illustrates this fact.

Prog 8-13.c	After the preprocessing stage	Output window

//Token replacement or stringification
#include<stdio.h>
#define STR(x) #x
main()
{
char str[20]=STR(Token replacement   );
puts(str);
}
	//The content of the header file stdio.h
	//replaces the include directive and is
	//placed here
	main()
	{
	char str[20]="Token replacement";
	puts(str);
	}
		Token replacement

Program 8-13 | A program illustrating that during stringification, white-space characters at the start and at the end of an argument's preprocessing token are deleted

3. The original spelling of each preprocessing token in the argument is retained in the character string literal constant, except a '\' character is inserted before each '"' and '\' character. The piece of code in Program 8-14 illustrates this fact.

Prog 8-14.c	After the preprocessing stage	Output window
//Token replacement or stringification	//The content of the header file stdio.h	White "space" character
#include<stdio.h>	//replaces the include directive and is	
#define STR(x) #x	//placed here	
main()	main()	
{	{	
char str[30]=STR(White "space" character);	char str[30]="White \"space\" character";	
puts(str);	puts(str);	
}	}	

Program 8-14 | A program that illustrates the insertion of '\' character during stringification

8.3.4.1.4 Concatenation/Token Pasting

In an object-like macro definition, if in the replacement list, a ## preprocessing token appears between two tokens, both the tokens are pasted to form one token. In a function-like macro definition, if in the replacement list, a ## preprocessing token appears between two parameters, the parameters will be replaced by the corresponding arguments, and the arguments will be glued and pasted to form one token. Since, two tokens are pasted (or concatenated) to create one token, it is known as **token pasting** or **token concatenation** or just **concatenation**, and the operator ## is known as the **concatenation operator**. The code snippets in Program 8-15 illustrate token pasting in an object-like macro.

Prog 8-15.c	After the preprocessing stage	Output window
//Token pasting in an object-like macro	//The content of the header file stdio.h	Value of xy is 10
#include<stdio.h>	//replaces the include directive and is	
#define var x##y	//placed here	
main()	main()	
{	{	
int var=10;	int xy=10;	
printf("Value of xy is %d",xy);	printf("Value of xy is %d",xy);	
}	}	

Program 8-15 | A program that illustrates token pasting in an object-like macro

The code snippets in Program 8-16 illustrate token pasting in a function-like macro.

Prog 8-16.c	After the preprocessing stage	Output window
//Token pasting in a function-like macro	//The content of the header file stdio.h	Value of var1 is 10
#include<stdio.h>	//replaces the include directive and is	
#define PASTE(x,y) x##y	//placed here	
main()	main()	
{	{	
int PASTE(var,1)=10;	int var1=10;	
printf("Value of var1 is %d",var1);	printf("Value of var1 is %d",var1);	
}	}	

Program 8-16 | A program that illustrates token pasting in a function-like macro

The following points must be remembered while using token pasting:

1. A ## preprocessing token shall not occur at the beginning or at the end of the replacement list for either form of the macro definition (i.e. object-like macro or function-like macro).
2. ## is one token. There should be no white-space character between two # characters.

8.3.4.1.5 Predefined Macros

The ANSI C standard defines several macros for the use in C language. The macros that are already defined in C language are known as **predefined macros.** These macros can be used without defining them. They cannot be redefined and hence, these macro names cannot appear immediately after define and undef directive.

The predefined macros recognized by ANSI-compliant compilers are as follows:

1. **__FILE__**: The __FILE__ macro expands to the name of the current file in the form of a string constant. The piece of code in Program 8-17 illustrates the use of __FILE__ macro.

Prog 8-17.c	Output window
//__FILE__ macro	The name of current file is 8-17.c
#include<stdio.h>	
main()	
{	
printf("The name of current file is %s", __FILE__);	
}	

Program 8-17 | A program that illustrates the application of the predefined __FILE__ macro

2. **__LINE__**: The __LINE__ macro expands to the current line number in the source file. The expanded line number is a decimal integer constant. The line number can be altered with the help of the line directive.[†] The piece of code in Program 8-18 illustrates the use of __LINE__ macro.

Prog 8-18.c	Output window
//__LINE__ macro	Current line number is 5
#include<stdio.h>	**Remark:**
main()	• Place two blank lines before the printf statement and re-execute the code to notice the change in the output
{	
printf("Current line number is %d", __LINE__);	
}	

Program 8-18 | A program that illustrates the application of the predefined __LINE__ macro

3. **__DATE__**: The __DATE__ macro expands to the compilation date of the source file in the form of a string constant. The expanded string constant is 11 characters long and is of the form "Mmm dd yyyy". The important points about __DATE__ macro are as follows:

   a. The name of the month will be three characters long with the first character being in uppercase.
   b. The name of the month is the same as generated by the asctime library function declared in the header file time.h.
   c. If the value of day of the month is less than 10, it is padded with space on the left (i.e. the first character of dd is a space character). Some of the compilers, e.g. Turbo C 3.0 output zero padded value of the day, if it is less than 10.

[†] Refer Section 8.3.4.3 for a description on line directive.

The piece of code in Program 8-19 illustrates the use of __DATE__ macro.

Prog 8-19.c

```
//__DATE__ macro
#include<stdio.h>
main()
{
printf("Date of compilation is %s", __DATE__);
}
```

Output window (using Turbo C 3.0)

```
Date of compilation is Apr 02 2009
```

Output window (using Turbo C 4.5)

```
Date of compilation is Apr  2 2009
```

Program 8-19 | A program that illustrates the application of the predefined __DATE__ macro

4. __TIME__: This macro expands to a string constant that describes the time at which the C pre-processor is being invoked. The expanded string constant is eight characters long and is of the form "hh:mm:ss". The piece of code in Program 8-20 illustrates the use of __TIME__ macro.

Prog 8-20.c

```
//__TIME__ macro
#include<stdio.h>
main()
{
printf("Time of preprocessing is %s", __TIME__);
}
```

Output window (using Turbo C 4.5)

```
Time of preprocessing is 18:56:55
```

Program 8-20 | A program that illustrates the application of the predefined __TIME__ macro

5. __STDC__: This macro expands to 1, if the compiler conforms to ANSI C and ISO C standards. Some compilers may not support this macro. For example, this macro is not supported by Turbo C 3.0. The piece of code in Program 8-21 illustrates the use of __STDC__ macro.

Prog 8-21.c

```
//__STDC__ macro
#include<stdio.h>
main()
{
if(__STDC__==1)
printf("This compiler conforms to ANSI and ISO C standards");
else
printf("This compiler does not comply with ANSI and ISO C standards");
}
```

Output window (using Turbo C 4.5)

```
This compiler conforms to ANSI and ISO C standards
```

Program 8-21 | A program that illustrates the use of the predefined __STDC__ macro

The important points about the predefined macros are as follows:

1. The ANSI predefined macros start and end with two underscores. There should not be a white-space character between the underscores.
2. The predefined macro name cannot appear immediately following a `define` directive. Also, a predefined macro cannot be undefined using an `undef` directive.‡ The piece of code in Program 8-22 illustrates this fact.

‡ Refer Section 8.3.4.1.6 for a description on the `undef` directive.

Prog 8-22.c	Output window (Turbo C 3.0)

//Predefined macros
#include<stdio.h>
#define __TIME__ 10
#undef __DATE__
main()
{
printf("define and undefine directives cannot be used with predefined macros");
}
	Compilation errors
	"Define directive needs an identifier"
	"Bad undef directive syntax"

Program 8-22 | A program to illustrate that it is not allowed to redefine and undefine a predefined macro

Some implementations provide additional predefined macros. Whether a predefined macro is supported by a specific implementation or not can be checked by referring to its documentation. The common implementation defined macros are:

1. **__cplusplus**: This macro is defined when C++ compiler is in use. It can be used to test whether C compiler or C++ compiler is used.
2. **NULL**: The NULL macro is defined in the header files stdio.h and stddef.h. It represents a null pointer value. The NULL pointer is defined as (void*)0. The null pointer created with the help of NULL does not point to any object or function and is not the same as the uninitialized pointer, which might point anywhere.
3. **EOF**: The EOF macro is defined in the header file stdio.h. This macro represents an integer value that is returned when end-of-file is encountered.

Forward Reference: Use of EOF macro (Chapter 10).

8.3.4.1.6 undef Directive

The undef preprocessor directive causes the specified identifier to be no longer defined as a macro name. The general form of the undef preprocessor directive is:

```
#undef identifier
```

The piece of code in Program 8-23 illustrates the use of the undef directive.

Prog 8-23.c	Output window

//undef directive
#include<stdio.h>
#define VER 2.2
#undef VER
main()
{
printf("Current version of software is %f",VER);
}
	Compilation error "Undefined symbol 'VER' in function main"

Program 8-23 | A program that illustrates the use of the undef directive

The important points about the undef directive are as follows:

1. If the identifier specified with the undef directive is not currently defined as a macro name, it is ignored.
2. The identifier specified with the undef directive cannot be the name of a predefined macro.
3. A macro can be redefined anywhere in the program. The most recent definition of the macro is considered while expanding the macro. If the redefinition of the macro is not identical (i.e. the redefined macro definition is not exactly the same as the first definition of the macro), the compiler will issue a warning message 'Redefinition of 'macroname' is not identical'. It is not compulsory to undefine a macro before redefining it. The code snippet in Program 8-24 illustrates the above-mentioned facts.

Prog 8-24.c

```
//Redefining a macro
#include<stdio.h>
#define DOUBLE 2
#define DOUBLE(x) (2*x)
main()
{
printf("Double of 2 is %d", DOUBLE(2));
}
```

Output window

Double of 2 is 4

Warning:

Redefinition of 'DOUBLE' is not identical

Remarks:

- The macro DOUBLE is redefined without undefining it
- It is not mandatory to undefine a macro before redefining it
- After the redefinition of DOUBLE as a function-like macro, it is not possible to use it as an object-like macro, i.e. as a symbolic constant
- Usage of DOUBLE as a symbolic constant instead of a function-like macro leads to a compilation error
- The macro definitions will not be considered identical if:
  - o one of the macro is an object-like macro and the other is a function-like macro
  - o both are object-like macros but they have different replacement lists
  - o both are function-like macros but they have different parameter lists or replacement lists

Program 8-24 | A program that illustrates the redefinition of a macro

8.3.4.1.7 Scope of Macro Definitions

The identifier defined as a macro can be used from the point of its definition till a corresponding undef directive is encountered or (if it is not encountered) till the end of the translation unit (i.e. file). Unlike the scope of other identifiers (i.e. variables, labels, etc.), the scope of a macro name is independent of the block structure. The piece of code in Program 8-25 illustrates this fact.

Line | Prog 8-25.c

```
1  //Scope of macro definitions
2  #include<stdio.h>
3  main()
4  {
5  printf("Macro MAC and variable var are not yet defined\n");
6  printf("They cannot be used here\n");
7  {
8  #define MAC 10
9  int var=10;
10 printf("Value of MAC=%d, var=%d\n",MAC, var);
11 }
12 //Here variable var is inaccessible
13 printf("Macro MAC can be used here but variable var cannot\n");
14 printf("Value of MAC outside the block is %d\n",MAC);
15 #undef MAC
16 printf("Macro MAC cannot be used now onwards");
17 }
```

Output window

```
Macro MAC and variable var are not yet defined
They cannot be used here
Value of MAC=10, var=10
Macro MAC can be used here but variable var cannot
Value of MAC outside the block is 10
Macro MAC cannot be used now onwards
```

Remarks:

- Macro defined inside the block (line number 8) is used outside the block (line number 14). It shows that the scope of macro definition is independent of the block structure
- Usage of macro name after it has been undefined (using #undef) leads to a compilation error

Program 8-25 | A program that illustrates the concept of scope of macro definitions

8.3.4.2 Source File Inclusion Directive

The source file inclusion directive include tells the preprocessor to replace the directive with the content of the file specified in the directive. The include directive is generally used to include the header files, which contain the prototypes of the library functions and the definitions of the predefined constants. The source file inclusion directive include can be written in three different ways:

1. #include <name-of-file>: #include<name-of-file> searches the prespecified list of directories (names of include directories can be set in IDE settings) for the source file (whose name is given within angular brackets), and text embeds the entire content of the source file in place of itself. If the file is not found there, it will show the error 'Unable to include 'name-of-file''.
2. #include "name-of-file": #include"name-of-file" first searches the file in the current working directory. If this search is not supported or if the search fails, this directive is reprocessed as if it reads #include<name-of-file>, i.e. the search will be carried out in the prespecified list of directories. If the search still fails, it will show the error 'Unable to include 'name-of-file''.
3. #include token-sequence: #include token-sequence searches the file as in Point 1 or in Point 2 depending upon the form of the directive to which it matches after the preprocessing token sequence is processed.

The piece of code in Program 8-26 illustrates the use of the third form of the include directive.

Line | Prog 8-26.c

```
//Source file inclusion directive
#define STR(x) #x
#include STR(stdio.h)
```

Output window

```
Third form of source file inclusion directive
```

(Contd...)

Prog 8-26.c	Output window
main()	
{	
printf("Third form of source file inclusion directive");	
}	

Program 8-26 | A program that illustrates the use of the source file inclusion directive

8.3.4.3 line Directive

The line directive is used to reset the line number and the file name as reported by __LINE__ and __FILE__ macros. The line directive is used for the purpose of error diagnostics. The line directive has two forms:

1. #line constant: The line directive of this form causes the compiler to ascertain that the line number of the next source line is equal to the decimal integer constant specified in the directive. It has no effect on the file name as reported by the __FILE__ macro.
2. #line constant "filename": The line directive of this form causes the compiler to ascertain that the line number of the next source line is given by the decimal integer constant and the current file is named by the identifier filename specified in the directive.

The piece of code in Program 8-27 illustrates the use of the line directive.

Line	Prog 8-27.c	Output window
1	//line directive	Line no. is 5, Filename is 8-27.c
2	#include <stdio.h>	Now, Line no. is 200, Filename is 8-27.c
3	main()	Atlast, Line no. is 100, Filename is Abc.c
4	{	**Remarks:**
5	printf("Line no. is %d, Filename is %s\n", __LINE__, __FILE__);	• In line number 6, the line directive assigns 200 as the line number to the next line
6	#line 200	
7	printf("Now, Line no. is %d, Filename is %s\n", __LINE__, __FILE__);	• In line number 8, the line directive assigns 100 as the line number to the next line and changes the file name to "Abc.c"
8	#line 100 "Abc.c"	
9	printf("Atlast, Line no. is %d, Filename is %s\n", __LINE__, __FILE__);	
10	}	

Program 8-27 | A program that illustrates the use of the line directive

8.3.4.4 error Directive

The error directive causes the preprocessor to generate the customized diagnostic messages and causes the compilation to fail. The error directive has the following forms:

1. #error: This directive causes the preprocessor to issue an error without any message.
2. #error token-sequence: This directive causes the preprocessor to issue an error message that includes the text specified by the token sequence.

The error directive is often used➲ with conditional compilation directives.§ The code segment in Program 8-28 illustrates the use of the error directive.

§ Refer Section 8.3.4.6 for a description on conditional compilation directives.

Prog 8-28.c

```
//error directive
#include <stdio.h>
#error This is a customized error message
main()
{
printf("Use of error directive cause the compilation to fail");
}
```

Output window

```
Compilation error
Fatal 8-28.C 3: Error directive: This is a customized error message
```

Program 8-28 | A program that illustrates the use of the error directive

Forward Reference: Refer Question number 25 and its answer for the usage of the error directive.

8.3.4.5 pragma Directive

The pragma directive is used to specify diverse options to the compiler. The options are specific for the compiler and the platform used. The pragma directive configures some of the compiler options that can otherwise be configured from the command line. Note that all options of the compiler cannot be configured using the pragma directive. An unrecognized pragma directive is ignored without an error or a warning message. It is strongly recommended to use the pragma directive after referring to the compiler documentation. The pragma directive is written as:

```
#pragma token-sequence
```

The commonly used forms of the pragma directive are as follows:

1. #pragma option: It is written as #pragma option [options...]. The common options that can be used with Turbo C 3.0 and the DOS environment are given in Table 8.4.

Table 8.4 | Some of the pragma options available with Turbo C 3.0

S.No	Option	Role
1.	-C	Allows nested comments
2.	-C-	(Default) Does not allow the nesting of comments
3.	-G	Causes the compiler to bias its optimization in favor of speed over size
4.	-G-	(Default) Causes the compiler to bias its optimization in favor of size over speed
5.	-r	(Default) Enables the use of register variables
6.	-r-	Suppresses the use of register variables
7.	-a	Forces structure members to be aligned on machine-word boundary.
8.	-a-	(Default) Results in byte alignment

Forward Reference: Byte alignment and machine-word alignment (Chapter 9).

Program 8-29 illustrates the use of the pragma option -C.

Prog 8-29.c

```
//Nested multi-line comments
#include <stdio.h>
main()
{
/*Start of Outer Comment
  /*Inner Comment*/
End of Outer Comment*/
printf("By default nested comments are not allowed");
}
```

Output window

```
Compilation error
```

Rectified code

```
//Nested multi-line comments
#include <stdio.h>
#pragma option -C
main()
{
/*Start of Outer Comment
  /*Inner Comment*/
End of Outer Comment*/
printf("By default nested comments are not allowed\n");
printf("pragma option -C makes them allowed");
}
```

Output window

```
By default nested comments are not allowed
pragma option -C makes them allowed
```

Program 8-29 | A program that illustrates the use of pragma option -C to allow nested comments

2. #pragma warn: The #pragma warn can be used to turn on, off or toggle the state of warnings. The #pragma warn can be written as:

#pragma warn +www	(Turns on the warning with character code www)
#pragma warn -www	(Turns off the warning with character code www)
#pragma warn .www	(Toggles the state of warning with character code www)

The character codes for specific warnings can be determined by referring to the compiler documentation. The common warning character codes that can be used with the pragma directive in Turbo C 3.0 are given in Table 8.5.

Table 8.5 | Some of the warning codes that can be used with the pragma directive in Turbo C 3.0

S.No	Warning code	Warning
1.	dup	Redefinition of 'macro' is not identical
2.	voi	void functions may not return a value
3.	rvl	Function should return a value
4.	par	Parameter 'parameter' is never used
5.	pia	Possibly incorrect assignment
6.	rch	Unreachable code
7.	aus	'Identifier' is assigned a value that is never used

The code snippets in Program 8-30 illustrate the use of #pragma warn to suppress the common warnings mentioned above.

Prog 8-30.c

```c
//Suppression of warning messages
#include <stdio.h>
#define PI 2
#define PI 4
main()
{
int a=10;
if(a=PI)
    printf("The value of PI is %d",PI);
return 1;
    printf("This is unreachable statement");
}
```

Modified code

```c
//Suppression of warning messages
#include <stdio.h>
#pragma warn -dup
#pragma warn -pia
#pragma warn -rch
#pragma warn -rvl
#pragma warn -aus
#define PI 2
#define PI 4
main()
{
int a=10;
if(a=PI)
    printf("The value of PI is %d",PI);
return 1;
    printf("This is unreachable statement");
}
```

Output window (Prog 8-30.c)

```
The value of PI is 4
```

Warnings(5):

```
Redefinition of PI is not identical
Possibly incorrect assignment in function main()
Unreachable code in function main()
Function should return a value in function main()
'a' is assigned a value that is never used in function main()
```

Output window (Modified code)

```
The value of PI is 4
```

Warnings(0)

Remark:

- All the warnings are suppressed by using the pragma directive

Program 8-30 | A program that illustrates the use of pragma directive to suppress various warnings

3. `#pragma startup` and `#pragma exit`: The `#pragma startup` and `#pragma exit` directives can be used to execute a function before and after the execution of the function `main`. These directives can be written as:

```
#pragma startup function-name
#pragma exit function-name
```

The piece of code in Program 8-31 illustrates the use of `#pragma startup` and `#pragma exit` directives.

Prog 8-31.c

```c
//pragma startup and pragma exit directives
#include <stdio.h>
function_before_main()
{
printf("This will be executed before main\n");
}
function_after_main()
{
printf("This will be executed after main\n");
}
```

Output window

```
This will be executed before main
This is main function
This will be executed after main
```

Remarks:

- The output indicates that the function `function_before_main` is executed before, and the function `function_after_main` is executed after, the execution of the function `main`

(Contd...)

Prog 8-31.c	Output window

#pragma startup function_before_main
#pragma exit function_after_main
main()
{
printf("This is main function\n");
}
	• The functions function_before_main and function_after_main must be defined before being used with the pragma directives
	• The function function_before_main can set up some prerequisites for the function main, and function_after_main can perform some clear up tasks

Program 8-31 | A program that illustrates the use of pragma startup and pragma exit

8.3.4.6 Conditional Compilation Directives

Conditional compilation means that a part of a program is compiled only if a certain condition comes out to be true. The available conditional compilation directives are as follows:

#if, #ifdef, #ifndef, #else, #elif, #endif

The syntax of using the conditional compilation directives is listed in Table 8.6.

Table 8.6 | Syntax and semantics of the conditional compilation directives

S.No	Conditional compilation directive	Syntax	Semantics
1.	#if-#endif	#if constant-exp statements-set #endif	The compiler compiles the statements-set only if the constant expression evaluates to true
2.	#if-#else-#endif	#if constant-exp statements-set1 #else statements-set2 #endif	If the constant expression evaluates to true, the statements-set1 will be compiled, else the statements-set2 will be compiled
3.	#if-#elif-#endif	#if constant-exp1 statements-set1 #elif constant-exp2 statements-set2 #endif	Statements-set1 will be compiled if the constant expression1 evaluates to true. The statements-set2 will be compiled only if the constant expression1 evaluates to false and constant expression2 evaluates to true
4.	#ifdef-#endif	#ifdef identifier statements-set #endif	Statements-set will be compiled only if the identifier is a predefined macro name or has been previously defined as a macro with define preprocessor directive without an intervening undef directive with the same identifier name
5.	#ifdef-#else-#endif	#ifdef identifier statements-set1 #else statements-set2 #endif	Statements-set1 will be compiled only if the identifier is a predefined macro name or has been previously defined as a macro name with define preprocessor directive without an intervening undef directive with the same identifier name. Otherwise, statements-set2 will be compiled

(Contd...)

6.	#ifdef-#elif-#endif	#ifdef identifier statements-set1 #elif constant-exp statements-set2 #endif	Statements-set1 will be compiled only if the identifier is a predefined macro or has been previously defined as a macro with define preprocessor directive without an intervening undef directive with the same identifier name. Statements-set2 will be compiled if no macro with the name as specified by the identifier has been defined, and the constant expression evaluates to true. If the macro has not been previously defined and the constant expression evaluates to false, no statements-set will be compiled
7.	#ifndef-#endif	#ifndef identifier statements-set #endif	Statements-set will be compiled if no macro with the name as specified by the identifier has been previously defined
8.	#ifndef-#else-#endif	#ifndef identifier statements-set1 #else statements-set2 #endif	Statements-set1 will be compiled if no macro with the name as specified by the identifier has been previously defined. Otherwise, statements-set2 will be compiled
9.	#ifndef-#elif-#endif	#ifndef identifier statements-set1 #elif constant-exp statements-set2 #endif	Statements-set1 will be compiled only if no macro with a name as specified by the identifier has been previously defined. Statements-set2 will be compiled if a macro with the name as specified by the identifier is a predefined macro or has been defined with define directive without an intervening undef directive with the same identifier name and the constant expression evaluates to true. If the macro has been defined and the constant expression evaluates to false, no statements-set will be compiled

The important points about the use of conditional compilation directives are as follows:

1. The conditional compilation preprocessor directives can appear anywhere in the program.
2. The statements set can be empty, can have preprocessor directives and/or C statements.

The piece of code in Program 8-32 illustrates the use of conditional compilation directives.

Prog 8-32.c

```
//Conditional compilation directives
#include <stdio.h>
#define EMBEDDED
#ifndef EMBEDDED
    #error This code is meant for embedded systems only
#endif
main()
```

Output window

Embedded systems are used in real time applications

(Contd...)

Prog 8-32.c	Output window

```
{
#ifdef EMBEDDED
  printf("Embedded systems are used in real time applications\n");
#else
  This part of program will not be compiled
  Put code meant for Non-embedded systems
#endif
}
```

Program 8-32 | A program that illustrates the use of conditional compilation directives

8.3.4.7 Null Directive

A null directive is of the form:

```
# new-line
```

The null directive has no effect.

8.4 Summary

1. A translator is a program that converts a program written in a source language to an equivalent program in a target language.
2. Translators are classified according to the classes of their source and target languages.
3. According to classes of their source and target languages, translators are classified as preprocessors, compilers, assemblers and interpreters.
4. The preprocessor is a translator that is invoked prior to the compiler.
5. The preprocessor is controlled by the commands known as preprocessor directives, which are not a part of C language.
6. There are eight phases of translation to convert a source program file into an executable file.
7. Trigraph replacement is the first phase of translation. During this phase, the trigraph sequences are replaced by their single-character equivalents.
8. During the second phase of translation, known as line splicing, each an instance of a backslash character immediately followed by a new-line character is deleted by the preprocessor.
9. The third phase of translation is tokenization, during which the source file is decomposed into the preprocessing tokens and a sequence of white-space characters.
10. During the fourth phase of translation, the preprocessor directives are executed and the macros are expanded.
11. A preprocessor directive always begins with a # (pound) symbol.
12. A macro is a facility provided by a C preprocessor, by which a token can be replaced by the user-defined sequence of characters.
13. Two types of macros can be created: object-like macros and function-like macros.
14. Object-like macro is also known as a symbolic constant.
15. Function-like macro is a macro with arguments.
16. A function-like macro is said to be safe, if it behaves like a function call.
17. Macros can create problems if they are not defined and used carefully.

18. The preprocessing token # is known as a stringizing operator.
19. The preprocessing token ## is used for token pasting.
20. Conditional compilation directives are used for conditional compilation. It means that a part of a program is compiled only if a certain condition comes out to be true.
21. Conditional compilation directives are: `#if`, `#ifdef`, `#ifndef`, `#else`, `#elif`, `#endif`.

Exercise Questions

Conceptual Questions and Answers

1. *What are translators and how are they classified?*

Backward Reference: Refer Section 8.2 for a description on translators.

2. *What are the various stages a program undergoes before execution?*

The various stages a program undergoes before execution are:
1. Translation
2. Loading

The various parts of translation are:
1. Preprocessing
2. Compilation
3. Linking

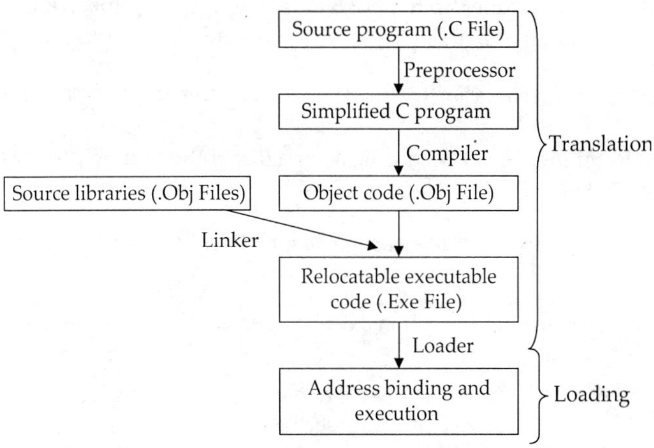

3. *What are the various phases of translation?*

Backward Reference: Refer Section 8.3 for a description on phases of translation.

4. *What is a trigraph sequence and a digraph sequence?*

Backward Reference: Refer Section 8.3.1 for a description on trigraph sequences.

Digraph sequences are a pair of characters that get replaced by their character equivalent. Similar to a trigraph processor, a separate digraph processor is required for processing the digraph sequences. The following table lists the valid digraph sequences and their character equivalents:

S.No	Digraph sequence	Character equivalent
1.	<:	[
2.	:>	]
3.	<%	{
4.	%>	}
5.	%:	#
6.	%:%:	##

The major difference between trigraph sequences and digraph sequences is that trigraphs are replaced within string literals but digraph sequences are not.

5. *What is line splicing?*

Backward Reference: Refer Section 8.3.2 for a description on line splicing.

6. *What is the difference between a token and a processing token?*

Backward Reference: Refer Section 8.3.3 for a description on token and preprocessing token. Also refer Question number 1 (Chapter 2) and its answer.

7. *How are preprocessor directives written? List the various preprocessor directives available in C.*

Backward Reference: Refer Section 8.3.4 for a description on preprocessor directives and the rules to write them.

8. *What is a macro? What are object-like macros and function-like macros? How are they defined?*

Backward Reference: Refer Section 8.3.4.1 to answer this question.

9. *The following lines of code are written in a source file:*

```
#define EMPTY                //←line number 1
EMPTY #include <stdio.h>     //←line number 2
```

Can you say that line number 2 is a preprocessor directive?

Line number 2 begins with a macro name EMPTY. Since line number 2 does not begin with a pound symbol (#), it will not be said as a preprocessor directive

10. *Why is the following piece of code not working?*

```
#define PI=3.1417
main()
{
    printf("The value of constant PI is %f",PI);
}
```

The following piece of code is not working due to the erroneous definition of the object-like macro PI. There should be a white-space character between the macro name and the replacement list in the definition of the object-like macro PI instead of the character '='. The rectified piece of code is written as

```
#define PI 3.1428571
main()
{
    printf("The value of constant PI is",PI);
}
```

11. *I have read that 'An identifier should be declared before it is used, else there will be a compilation error'. The identifier* PI *has not been declared in the following piece of code but still the code gets executed and the compiler does not show any error. Why?*

```
#define PI 3.1417
main()
{
    printf("The value is %f", PI);
}
```

The compiler does not show any error because the compiler does not find any token PI as it has already been replaced by the replacement list 3.1417 during the preprocessing stage. After the preprocessing stage and macro expansion, the processed code handed over to the compiler will be

```
main()
{
    printf("The value is %f", 3.1417);
}
```

Since this code does not contain any instance of the token PI, there is no requirement to declare it.

12. *I have written the following piece of code:*

```
#define square(x) x*x
main()
{
    float result;
    result=1.0/square(2);
    printf("Result is %f",result);
}
```

I was expecting the output of the code to be 0.250000*, but on execution, the code outputs* 1.000000*. Why? How can I rectify it?*

Remember that macro expansion is purely textual. Macros are expanded during the preprocessing stage before the compilation stage. This fact is illustrated by the code segments listed below:

Before the preprocessing stage	After the preprocessing stage

#define square(x) x*x
main()
{
    float result;
    result=1.0/square(2);
    printf("Result is %f",result);
}
	
	main()
	{
	    float result;
	    result=1.0/2*2; //←Macro expanded
	    printf("Result is %f",result);
	}

After the macro expansion is carried out during the preprocessing stage, the expression `result=1.0/square(2);` becomes `result=1.0/2*2;`. Since the division operator and the multiplication operator have the same precedence and are left-to-right associative, the division is carried out first and then the multiplication is done. Thus, the result comes out to be `1.000000`. The given piece of code can be rectified by **parenthesizing the macro's replacement list to protect any lower precedence operators present in it from the higher precedence operators present in the surrounding expression.** The rectified code is given below:

```
#define square(x) (x*x)
main()
{
    float result;
    result=1.0/square(2);
    printf("Result is %f",result);
}
```

The mentioned rectified code on execution outputs: `Result is 0.250000`

13. *I have defined the macro in the way suggested in the answer of the previous question and have written the following piece of code:*

```
#define square(x) (x*x)
main()
{
    int number=2,result;
    result=square(number+1);
    printf("Square of 3 is %d",result);
}
```

Still the code does not work as intended and outputs `5` *instead of* `9`. *Why? How can I rectify it?*

After macro expansion is done during the preprocessing stage, the given piece of code becomes:

```
main()
{
    int number=2,result;
    result=(number+1*number+1);
    printf("Square of 3 is %d",result);
}
```

The expression `result=(number+1*number+1);` evaluates to `5` instead of the expected value `9` because the multiplication operator has a higher precedence than the addition operator. The given piece of code can be rectified **by parenthesizing all the occurrences of the parameters in the macro's replacement list to protect any low precedence operators in the actual arguments from the rest of the macro expansion.** The rectified code is given below:

```
#define square(x) ((x)*(x))
main()
{
    int number=2,result;
    result=square(number+1);
    printf("Square of 3 is %d",result);
}
```

The mentioned rectified code on execution outputs: `Square of 3 is 9`

14. *If I define the macro* `square` *as suggested in the answer of the previous question and call it in an expression, can I safely assume that my code will work correctly as if it were an expression statement consisting of a function call?*

If the macro square is defined in the way suggested in Answer number 13, still it cannot be safely assumed that an expression containing a call to the macro square is the same as if it is an expression containing a call to a function that returns the squared value of its input parameter. Consider the following pieces of code and the differences in the results of their executions:

Code-I Macro version	Code-II Function version

`#define square(x) ((x)*(x))`
`main()`
`{`
`    int i=2,result;`
`    result=square(++i);`
`    printf("The value of result is %d",result);`
`}`
	`int square(int x){`
	`return x*x; }`
	`main()`
	`{`
	`    int i=2,result;`
	`    result=square(++i);`
	`    printf("The value of result is %d",result);`
	`}`

The execution of code-I, i.e. macro version outputs: The value of result is 16.
The execution of code-II, i.e. function version outputs: The value of result is 9.
The macro square exhibited this type of behavior because its argument is an expression (i.e. ++i) with a side-effect.

15. *What are the points that one should keep in mind while defining macros?*

Backward Reference: Refer Section 8.3.4.1.2 for a description on common macro pitfalls. Also refer Question numbers 10, 12, 13, 14, 48, 54, 55 and 56 and their answers.

16. *What are the differences between function-like macros and functions?*

Although function-like macros and functions appear to be the same, they are actually not. The major differences between function-like macros and functions are as follows:

Function-like macros	Functions
1. The replacement list of function-like macros is just text replaced during the preprocessing stage every time the macro name is encountered. There is no argument passing and no control is transferred.	1. In a function call, the control is passed to the called function along with the arguments, the calculations are made in the called function and their value is returned to the calling function.
2. Since the control is not actually transferred, the time required in making a function call is saved. Thus, the use of function-like macros provides a better performance as compared to functions.	2. As the control transfers to and fro between the called function and the calling function, some of the time gets wasted in making the function call. Thus, the use of functions and their calls slow down the program.
3. Since the macro name is text replaced by the replacement list during the preprocessing stage, the use of macros will increase the program size. This increases the code redundancy.	3. Functions use the same piece of code again and again. Hence, they avoid code redundancy and this is the main benefit of using functions.
4. Thus, the use of macros makes the program run faster but increases the program size.	4. Thus, the use of the function makes the program smaller and compact but it deteriorates the program's speed.

17. *I have encountered the following piece of code that makes use of an object-like macro* PI. *When I try to execute the code, it gives an error* 'Undefined symbol PI'. *Why?*

```
#define PI 3.141
#undef PI
main()
{
    int rad=2;
    printf("Area of circle is %f",PI*rad*rad);
}
```

The given piece of code on compilation gives an error 'Undefined symbol PI' due to the usage of undef directive. The symbol PI has been defined as an object-like macro but as it has been undefined with the undef directive before its use; therefore, the preprocessor will not be able to make the macro replacement. That is why, the compiler shows the error.

18. *What is meant by token replacement and token pasting?*

Backward Reference: Refer Sections 8.3.4.1.3 and 8.3.4.1.4 for a description on token replacement and token pasting.

19. *Is macro replacement carried out within a string literal constant?*

No replacement is carried out if a name identical to the macro name appears as a part of a string literal constant or as a part of some other name. For example, consider the following piece of code:

```
#define LINE 100
main()
{
    int MAXLINE=25;
    printf("The length of LINE is %d", MAXLINE);
}
```

The mentioned piece of code on execution prints: The length of LINE is 25. No replacement is carried out for the name LINE that appears as a part of the string literal or as a part of the name MAXLINE.

20. *What are the various ways in which a source file inclusion directive can be written?*

Backward Reference: Refer Section 8.3.4.2 to answer this question.

21. *What method is adopted for locating the includable source files in ANSI specifications?*

According to ANSI specifications:

(1) **#include<name-of-file>** searches a prespecified list of directories (names of include directories can be set in IDE settings) for the source file (whose name is given within angular brackets), and text embeds the entire content of the source file in place of itself. If the file is not found there, it will show error 'Unable to include name-of-file'.

(2) **#include"name-of-file"** first searches the file in the current working directory. If this search is not supported or if the search fails, this directive is reprocessed as if it reads #include<name-of-file>, i.e. search will be carried out in a prespecified list of directories. If the search still fails, it will show the error 'Unable to include name-of-file'.

(3) **#include token-sequence** searches the file as in (1) or (2) depending upon the form of directive to which it matches after the token sequence is processed.

22. *Is there any difference that arises if double quotes, instead of angular brackets are used for including the standard header files?*

    If double quotes are used for the inclusion of standard header files instead of angular brackets, the search space unnecessarily increases (in addition to the list of prespecified directories, search will unnecessarily be carried out first in the current working directory), and the time required for the inclusion will be more.

23. *Under what circumstances should the use of quotes be preferred over the use of angular brackets for the inclusion of header files and under what circumstances is the use of angular brackets beneficial?*

    Self-created or user-defined header files should be included with double quotes because the inclusion with double quotes makes the files to be searched first in the current working directory (where the user has kept self-created header files) and then in the prespecified list of directories. If the standard header files are to be included, angular brackets should be used because the standard header files are present in the prespecified list of directories and there is no use in searching them in the current working directory. Usage of double quotes for including the standard header files will work but will take more time.

24. *What is conditional compilation?*

Backward Reference: Refer Section 8.3.4.6 for a description on conditional compilation directives.

25. *What is the role of the* error *directive?*

Backward Reference: Refer Section 8.3.4.4 for a description on error directive.

Suppose the user wants to develop some functionality that is very specific to some applications like Video Graphic Adaptors (VGAs), etc. The user has written the following piece of code:

```
main()
{
    #ifndef VGA
        #error This code is for Video Graphic Adaptors only
    #else
        int hresolution=640, vresolution=480;
        //....code specific to VGA follows
    #endif
}
```

The code on compilation gives 'Fatal error: This code is for Video Graphic Adaptors only' as VGA is not previously defined. If VGA is previously defined using the define directive, the code sets the horizontal and vertical resolution to be 640 and 480, respectively, and the other code statements specific to VGA will be processed.

26. *What is the role of the* pragma *directive?*

Backward Reference: Refer Section 8.3.4.5 for a description on the pragma directive. Also refer Question numbers 27-30 and their answers.

27. *Are nested multi-line comments by default allowed in C? If no, how can the* pragma *directive be used to allow them?*

No, by default the nested multi-line comments are not allowed. Use #pragma option -C to make the nested multi-line comments allowed.

Backward Reference: Refer the description given in Section 8.3.4.5. Also refer Question number 12 (Chapter 1) and its answer.

28. *How can the* pragma *directive be used to suppress* 'Function should return a value' *warning?*

Backward Reference: Refer the description given in Section 8.3.4.5 to answer this question.

29. *By default, a program execution always starts with and terminates with the function* main. *Can I make some other function to execute before or after the execution of the function* main? *If yes, how?*

Yes, the #pragma startup and #pragma exit directives can be used to execute a function before and after the execution of the function main.

Backward Reference: Refer Section 8.3.4.5 for a description on pragma startup and pragma exit.

30. *A compiler can translate a high-level language program into an equivalent low-level language program, i.e. assembly-level language or machine-level language program. Till now, the compiler has been producing a machine-level code. How can I configure the compiler so that it starts producing an assembly-level code?*

Assembly-level code can be generated by using -S option of the Turbo C 3.0 compiler. It should be noted that this option cannot be used with the pragma directive. It should be invoked from the command line only.

Code Snippets

Determine the output of the following code snippets. Assume that the inclusion of the required header files has been made and there is no prototyping error due to them. Also, the trigraph processor is available and is invoked first.

31.
```
??=include<stdio.h>
main()
{
    int arr??(5??)=??<1,2,3,4,5??>;
    printf("The first three elements are: %d %d %d",arr[0],arr[1],arr[2]);
}
```

32.
```
%:include<stdio.h>
main()
<%
    int arr<:5:>=<%1,2,3,4,5%>;
    printf("The first three elements are:\n%d %d %d",arr[0],arr[1],arr[2]);
%>
```

33.
```
main()
{
    printf("Trigraph??/tsequences??/nin string literal");
}
```

34. main()
```
{
    printf("Digraph<:sequences:>");
}
```

35. main()
```
{
    printf("Will it be replaced???/tYes/No?");
}
```

36. main()
```
{
    printf("Hello
Readers!!");
}
```

37 main()
```
{
    printf("Hello \
Readers!!");
}
```

38. main()
```
{
    printf("Hello ""Readers!!");
}
```

39. main()
```
{
    printf("Hello " "Readers!!");
}
```

40. main()
```
{
    char *str="Hello";
    printf(str"Readers!!");
}
```

41. #define PI=3.14
```
main()
{
    int rad=2;
    printf("Circumference of the circle is %f",2*PI*rad);
}
```

42. #define PI 3.14
```
main()
{
    int rad=2;
    printf("Circumference of the circle is %f",2*PI*rad);
}
```

43. #define PI 3.14;
```
main()
```

```
{
    int rad=2;
    printf("Circumference of the circle is %f",2*PI*rad);
}
```

44.
```
#define int char
main()
{
    int var;
    printf("The size of var is %d",sizeof(var));
}
```

45.
```
#define + -
#define * /
main()
{
    int a;
    a=2+3*5;
    printf("The value of a is %d",a);
}
```

46.
```
#define clrscr() 200
main()
{
    printf("This will be printed\n");
    clrscr();
    printf("The value is %d",clrscr());
}
```

47.
```
#define SQUARE(x) x*x
main()
{
    printf("The square value of 2 is %d", SQUARE(2));
}
```

48.
```
#define SQUARE (x) x*x
main()
{
    printf("The square value of 2 is %d",SQUARE(2));
}
```

49.
```
#define SQUARE(x) x*x
main()
{
    int a=20,b;
    b=a/SQUARE(2);
    printf("The value of b is %d",b);
}
```

50.
```
#define SQUARE(x) (x*x)
main()
{
    int a=20,b;
```

```
    b=a/SQUARE(2);
    printf("The value of b is %d",b);
}
```

51.
```
#define SQUARE(x) (x*x)
main()
{
    int a=5,b;
    b=SQUARE(a+2);
    printf("The value of b is %d",b);
}
```

52.
```
#define SQUARE(x) ((x)*(x))
main()
{
    int a=5,b;
    b=SQUARE(a+2);
    printf("The value of b is %d",b);
}
```

53.
```
#define SQUARE(x) ((x)*(x))
main()
{
    int a=2,b;
    b=SQUARE(++a);
    printf("The value of b is %d",b);
}
```

54.
```
#define SQUARE(x) ((x)*(x));
main()
{
    int a=2,b=4;
    if(SQUARE(a)==b)
        printf("Square of a is equal to b");
    else
        printf("Square of a is not equal to b");
}
```

55.
```
#define SWAP(a,b) a^=b; b^=a; a^=b;
main()
{
    int a=20,b=10;
    printf("The values of a and b before swap are %d %d\n",a,b);
    SWAP(a,b)
    printf("The values of a and b after swap are %d %d\n",a,b);
}
```

56.
```
#define SWAP(a,b) a^=b; b^=a; a^=b;
main()
{
    int a=20,b=10;
    printf("Swap the values of a and b only if a is greater than b");
    if(a>b)
```

```
        SWAP(a,b)
    else
        printf("Values are not swapped");
    printf("Resultant values of a and b are %d %d",a,b);
}
```

57. #define SWAP(a,b) a^=b, b^=a, a^=b

```
main()
{
    int a=20,b=10;
    printf("Swap the values of a and b only if a is greater than b\n");
    if(a>b)
        SWAP(a,b);
    else
        printf("Values are not swapped\n");
    printf("Resultant values of a and b are %d %d",a,b);
}
```

58. #define SWAP(a,b) a^=b^=a^=b

```
main()
{
    int a=20,b=10;
    printf("Swap the values of a and b only if a is greater than b\n");
    if(a>b)
        SWAP(a,b);
    else
        printf("Values are not swapped\n");
    printf("Resultant values of a and b are %d %d",a,b);
}
```

59. #define VALUE 100

```
main()
{
    int MAXVALUE=1000;
    printf("The VALUE is %d",MAXVALUE);
}
```

60. #define STR(x) #x

```
main()
{
    printf(STR(Hello Readers!!));
}
```

61. #define STR(x) #x

```
main()
{
    printf(STR(Hello                    Readers!!));
}
```

62. #define STR(x) #x

```
main()
{
    printf(STR(            Hello Readers!!            ));
}
```

63.
```
#define STR(x) #x
main()
{
    printf(STR(Hello "Read"ers!!));
}
```

64.
```
#define STR(x,y,z) #x#y#z
main()
{
    char str1[30]=STR(THE,C,PREPROCESSOR);
    char str2[30]=STR(THE,C,COMPILER);
    puts(str1);
    puts(str2);
}
```

65.
```
#define STR(x) #x
#include STR(stdio.h)
main()
{
    printf("Third form of include directive");
}
```

66.
```
#define PASTE(tk1,tk2) tk1##tk2
main()
{
    int var1=100;
    printf("The value of var1 is %d",PASTE(var,1));
}
```

67.
```
#define PASTE(tk1,tk2) tk1##tk2
main()
{
    int var1=100,var2=200,var3=300;
    int i;
    for(i=1;i<=3;i++)
        printf("The value of var%d is %d\n",i,PASTE(var,i));
}
```

68.
```
#define PASTE(tk1,tk2) tk1##tk2
main()
{
    int var[]={100,200,300};
    int i;
    for(i=0;i<=2;i++)
        printf("The value of var%d is %d\n",i,PASTE(var,[i]));
}
```

69.
```
#define p(x,y,z) x##y##z
main()
{
    int arr[]={ p(2,3,4), p(,5,6), p(6,,7), p(8,9,), p(10,,), p(,11,)},i;
    for(i=0;i<6;i++)
        printf("%d ",arr[i]);
}
```

70.
```
#define CONST 100
#undef CONST
main()
{
    printf("The value of CONST is %d",CONST);
}
```

71.
```
#define CONST 100
#undef VAR
main()
{
    printf("The value of CONST is %d",CONST);
}
```

72.
```
#define CONST 100
main()
{
    printf("The value of CONST is %d",CONST);
    #undef CONST
}
```

73.
```
#define CONST 100
main()
{
    printf("The value of CONST is %d",CONST);
}
#undef CONST
```

74.
```
#define CONST 100
main()
{
    #define CONST 10
    printf("The value of CONST is %d",CONST);
}
```

75.
```
#define VER 1
main()
{
    #ifdef VER
        printf("Place code corresponding to version 1");
    #else
        printf("Place code corresponding to version other than 1");
    #endif
}
```

76.
```
#define VER 1
main()
{
    #ifdef VER
        printf("Place code corresponding to version 1");
    #else
        WILL IT BE A COMPILATION ERROR??
```

```
    #endif
}
```

77.
```
#define VER 1
main()
{
    #if VER==1
        printf("Place code corresponding to version 1");
    #else
        printf("Place code corresponding to version other than 1");
    #endif
}
```

78.
```
#define VER 1
main()
{
    #if VER=1
        printf("Place code corresponding to version 1");
    #else
        printf("Place code corresponding to version other than 1");
    #endif
}
```

79.
```
#define VER 1
main()
{
    int a=1;
    #if a==VER
        printf("Place code corresponding to version 1");
    #else
        printf("Place code corresponding to version other than 1");
    #endif
}
```

80.
```
#define VER 1
main()
{
    const int a=1;
    #if a==VER
        printf("Place code corresponding to version 1");
    #else
        printf("Place code corresponding to version other than 1");
    #endif
}
```

81.
```
main()
{
    #ifdef WINDOWS
        PLACE CODE FOR WINDOWS OPERATING SYSTEM
    #elif defined(LINUX)
        PLACE CODE FOR LINUX OPERATING SYSTEM
    #else
        #error OPERATING SYSTEM IS NOT KNOWN
```

```
    #endif
}
```

82.
```
main()
{
/* The C PREPROCESSOR
/* THERE ARE VARIOUS DIRECTIVES*/
PRAGMA IS ONE OF THEM*/
printf("THE C PREPROCESSOR");
}
```

83.
```
#pragma option -C
main()
{
/* The C PREPROCESSOR
/* THERE ARE VARIOUS DIRECTIVES*/
PRAGMA IS ONE OF THEM*/
printf("THE C PREPROCESSOR");
}
```

84.
```
int req_var_value;
func()
{
    printf("This function setups the prerequisites of function main\n");
    req_var_value=200;
}
#pragma startup func
main()
{
    printf("This is function main\n");
    printf("The requisite value of variable is %d",req_var_value);
}
```

85.
```
#define size_of(data) ((char *)(&data+1)-(char *)(&data))
main()
{
    int INT;
    char CHAR;
    float FLOAT;
    double DOUBLE;
    printf("Size of int: %d\n",size_of(INT));
    printf("Size of char: %d\n",size_of(CHAR));
    printf("Size of float: %d\n",size_of(FLOAT));
    printf("Size of double: %d\n",size_of(DOUBLE));
}
```

Multiple-choice Questions

86. A translator that converts a program written in a high-level language into an equivalent program written in some other high-level language is

    a. Interpreter
    b. Compiler
    c. Assembler
    d. Preprocessor

87. Preprocessing is a phase of translation, which occurs

a. Before compilation
b. After compilation
c. After compilation but before linking
d. None of these

88. Which of the following are replaced even within string literals?

a. Macro names
b. Digraph sequences
c. Trigraph sequences
d. None of these

89. Among function-like macro call and function call, which one is efficient time-wise?

a. Function-like macro call
b. Function call
c. Both take equal time
d. None of these

90. The following piece of code on execution leads to:

```
main(){
puts("Hello","Readers!!"); }
```

a. Compilation error
b. Hello
c. Readers!!
d. None of these

91. The following piece of code on execution leads to:

```
#define puts printf
main(){
puts("Hello","Readers!!"); }
```

a. Compilation error
b. Hello
c. Readers!!
d. None of these

92. The following piece of code on execution leads to:

```
#define int char
main(){
int a=4;
printf("%d",sizeof(a)); }
```

a. Compilation error
b. 1
c. 2
d. None of these

93. The following piece of code on execution leads to:

```
#define sizeof
main(){
int a=4;
printf("%d",sizeof(a)); }
```

a. Compilation error
b. 1
c. 2
d. 4

94. The following piece of code on execution leads to:

```
#define a 10
void fun();
main()
{
   fun();
   printf("%d",a); }
fun()
{
   #undef a
```

```
    #define a 50
}
```

a. Compilation error
b. 10
c. 50
d. None of these

95. If the following piece of code is executed on a 16-bit DOS environment, the output will be

```
#define cp_d char*
typedef char* cp_t;
main(){
cp_t p1,p2;
cp_d p3,p4;
printf("%d %d\n",sizeof(p1), sizeof(p2));
printf("%d %d",sizeof(p3), sizeof(p4));
}
```

a. 2 2
   2 2
b. 2 2
   2 1
c. 2 1
   2 1
d. 2 1
   2 2

Outputs and Explanations to Code Snippets

31. The first three elements are: 1 2 3

    Explanation:

    The source file contains the trigraph sequences like ??=, ??(, ??), ??< and ??>. During the first phase of translation, these trigraph sequences are replaced by their character equivalents #, [,], { and }, respectively, by the Borland trigraph processor TRIGRAPH.EXE.

32. The first three elements are: 1 2 3

    Explanation:

    The digraph sequences are replaced by their character equivalents. The digraph sequences %:, <%, %>, <: and :> are replaced by #, {, }, [and], respectively. Some of the IDEs like GNU provides an integrated digraph processor with a GNU GCC compiler while some of them like Turbo C require a separate digraph processor.

33. Trigraph   sequences
    in string literal

    Explanation:

    Trigraph sequences are replaced even within string literals. The trigraph sequence ??/ in the string literal "Trigraph??/tsequences??/nin string literal" is replaced by the character equivalent \. Hence, the string literal after the trigraph replacement becomes "Trigraph\tsequences\nin string literal". The resultant string when printed produces the mentioned output.

34. Digraph<:sequences:>

    Explanation:

    Backward Reference: Refer to the explanation given in Answer number 4.

    The digraph sequences within string literals are not replaced.

35. Will it be replaced? Yes/No?

Explanation:

Trigraph sequences are replaced within string literals. After processing, the trigraph processor outputs:

```
main
{
    printf("Will it be replaced?\tYes/No?");
}
```

The processed code on execution outputs the above-mentioned result.

36. Compilation error "Unterminated string or character constant"

Explanation:

String literals cannot span multiple lines in this way.

37. Hello Readers!!

Explanation:

Backward Reference: Refer to the explanation given in Section 8.3.2.

During phase 2 of translation, the physical source lines in

```
main()
{
    printf("Hello \
    Readers!!");
}
```

are spliced to form the following logical source lines:

```
main()
{
    printf("Hello Readers!!");
}
```

Logical source lines are processed by the compiler. Hence, on execution, Hello Readers!! is the output.

38. Hello Readers!!

Explanation:

Backward Reference: Refer to the explanation given in Section 8.3.

During phase 6 of translation, adjacent string literal constants are concatenated.

39. Hello Readers!!

Explanation:

Backward Reference: Refer to the explanation given in Section 8.3.

During phase 7 of translation, the white-space characters between two tokens are removed. After the execution of this phase, the white space between the string literal tokens "Hello " and "Readers!!" is removed and they become adjacent to each other. During rescanning and further replacement, these adjacent string literals are concatenated to form "Hello Readers!!".

40. Compilation error

Explanation:

During translation, only the string literals are concatenated. str is not a string literal. A try to concatenate the string pointed to by str with the string literal "Readers!!" leads to the compilation error.

41. Compilation error

Explanation:

The compilation error is due to the erroneous definition of object-like macro PI.

Backward Reference: Refer to the explanation given in Section 8.3.4.1.2.

There shall be a white-space character (blank-space character or horizontal tab-space character) between the macro name and the replacement list in the definition of the object-like macro instead of the character '='.

42. Circumference of the circle is 12.560000

Explanation:

During phase 4 of translation, macro names are replaced by their replacement list. Thus, after phase 4 of translation, the source code becomes:

```
main()
{
    int rad=2;
    printf("Circumference of the circle is %f", 2*3.14*rad);
}
```

The above code on execution outputs the above-mentioned result.

43. Compilation error

Explanation:

After macro expansion, the statement printf("Circumference of the circle is %f",2*PI *rad); becomes printf("Circumference of the circle is %f",2*3.14;*rad);, which is not valid due to the occurrence of the semicolon after 3.14. It is always recommended to avoid the use of semicolon in or at the end of a macro definition.

44. The size of var is 1

Explanation:

It is legal to use a reserve word as a macro name. However, this should be done with utmost care. After the preprocessing stage, the declaration int var; becomes char var;. Since the memory allocation is done by the compiler, to which the type of identifier var is char, it allocates 1 byte to it. Hence, the size of var comes out to be 1.

45. Compilation error "Define directive needs an identifier"

Explanation:

Macro name should be identifiers. Since + and - are not valid identifiers, they cannot be used as macro names.

46. This will be printed
    The value is 200

    Explanation:

    After the macro expansion, the code becomes:
```
main()
{
    printf("This will be printed\n");
    200;
    printf("The value is %d",200);
}
```
    The above code is free from any compilation error and on execution gives the above-mentioned result.

47. The square value of 2 is 4

    Explanation:

Backward Reference: Refer to the explanation given in Section 8.3.4.1.

48. Compilation error "Undefined symbol x in function main"

    Explanation:

    SQUARE in the given piece of code does not become a function-like macro. It becomes an object-like macro due to the white-space character between the macro name SQUARE and left parenthesis. After macro expansion, the given piece of code becomes:
```
main()
{
    printf("The square value of 2 is %d",(x) x*x(2));
}
```
    The preprocessed code on compilation gives 'Undefined symbol x' error because the symbol x has not been declared. Even if x would have been declared, there would still be an error because expression (x) x*x(2) is not well formed.

49. The value of b is 20

    Explanation:

    After the macro expansion, the expression b=a/SQUARE(2) becomes b=a/2*2. Since the division and the multiplication operators have the same precedence and are left-to-right associative, in the given expression division is carried out first and then multiplication is done.

50. The value of b is 5

    Explanation:

    After the macro expansion, the expression b=a/SQUARE(2) becomes b=a/(2*2), which on evaluation assigns 5 to the variable b. The result is different from the result of the execution in Answer number 49 because the replacement list of macro SQUARE has been parenthesized.

51. The value of b is 17

    Explanation:

    After the macro expansion, the expression b=SQUARE(a+2) becomes b=a+2*a+2. Since the multiplication operator has higher precedence as compared to the addition operator, multiplication is carried out first. Hence, the right side of the expression b=5+2*5+2 evaluates to 17, which is then assigned to b.

52. The value of b is 49

Explanation:

After the macro expansion, the expression b=SQUARE(a+2) becomes b=(a+2)*(a+2), which on evaluation assigns 49 to the variable b. The result is different from the result of the execution in Answer number 51 because all the occurrences of the parameters in the replacement list of macro SQUARE has been parenthesized.

53. The value of b is 16

Explanation:

Backward Reference: Refer Section 8.3.4.1.2.3 to answer this question.

54. Compilation error

Explanation:

The semicolon at the end of the macro definition is the cause of the compilation error. After the macro expansion, the if controlling expression becomes ((a)*(a));==b. The expression is ill-formed and on compilation leads to an error.

55. The values of a and b before swap are 20 10
The values of a and b after swap are 10 20

Explanation:

After the expansion of the macro SWAP, the given piece of code becomes:

```
main()
{
    int a=20,b=10;
    printf("The values of a and b before swap is %d %d\n",a,b);
    a^=b; b^=a; a^=b;
    printf("The values of a and b after swap is %d %d\n",a,b);
}
```

The above code swaps the values of a and b.

56. Compilation error "Misplaced else in function main"

Explanation:

When the macro SWAP is replaced by the multiple statements (i.e. a^=b; b^=a; a^=b;), only the first statement (i.e. a^=b;) forms the if body. The other two statements will be considered as the statements next to the if statement. The else clause remains unmatched and leads to 'Misplaced else' error.

57. Swap the values of a and b only if a is greater than b
Resultant values of a and b are 10 20

Explanation:

After the expansion of the macro SWAP, there will be a single statement in the if body. Hence, there will be no error as in Answer number 56.

58. Swap the values of a and b only if a is greater than b
Resultant values of a and b are 10 20

Explanation:

After the expansion of the macro SWAP, there will be a single statement in the if body, which swaps the value of the variables a and b.

59. The VALUE is 1000

Explanation:

No replacement is carried out if a name same as the macro name appears as a part of a string literal constant or as a part of some other name.

60. Hello Readers!!

Explanation:

The stringizing operator # preceding a parameter of a function-like macro converts an argument corresponding to the parameter into a string literal. In the given piece of code, STR(Hello Readers!!) gets converted to a string literal "Hello Readers!!" and is printed.

61. Hello Readers!!

Explanation:

The stringizing operator # converts a sequence of white-space characters between the argument's preprocessing tokens into a single white-space character in the replaced string literal. In the given piece of code, STR(Hello   Readers!!) gets converted to "Hello Readers!!".

62. Hello Readers!!

Explanation:

The stringizing operator # deletes the white-space characters before the first preprocessing token and after the last preprocessing token of the argument. In the given piece of code, STR(Hello Readers!!   ) gets converted to "Hello Readers!!" and is printed.

63. Hello "Read"ers!!

Explanation:

The stringizing operator # inserts backslash character (i.e. \) before every instance of " and \ characters that appears in the argument while converting it into string literal. In the given piece of code, STR(Hello "Read"ers!!) gets converted to "Hello \"Read\"ers!!". This string is printed by the printf function. Hence, the output is Hello "Read"ers!!.

64. THECPREPROCESSOR
    THECCOMPILER

Explanation:

The stringizing operator converts each argument corresponding to a parameter into a string literal, and the adjacent string literals get concatenated.

65. Third form of include directive

Explanation:

The stringizing operator converts stdio.h into "stdio.h". After replacement, the source file inclusion directive becomes #include"stdio.h". This form of include directive is valid and searches the file stdio.h firstly in the current working directory and then in the prespecified list of directories.

66. The value of var1 is 100

Explanation:

In a function-like macro definition, if in the replacement list, a ## preprocessing token appears between two parameters, the parameters are replaced by the corresponding arguments and the arguments are glued and pasted to form one token. In the given piece of code, the arguments var and 1 corresponding to the parameters tk1 and tk2, respectively, are pasted to create one token, i.e. var1. Hence, after preprocessing, the given piece of code becomes:

```
main()
{
    int var1=100;
    printf("The value of var1 is %d",var1);
}
```

This code on execution outputs the mentioned result.

67. Compilation error "Undefined symbol vari in function main"

Explanation:

During the preprocessing stage, the macro PASTE performs the token pasting and gets replaced by vari. During the compilation stage, the name vari is found to be undefined and a compile time error is raised.

68. The value of var0 is 100
The value of var1 is 200
The value of var2 is 300

Explanation:

During the preprocessing stage, the macro PASTE performs the token pasting and gets replaced by var[i]. To C compiler var[i] is a well-formed expression having a subscript operator whose operands are of array type and integer type. Hence, on execution the given code outputs the mentioned result.

69. 234 56 67 89 10 11

Explanation:

The preprocessing tokens ## paste the arguments corresponding to the parameters x, y and z. If any of the argument corresponding to the parameter x, y or z is missing, it will be ignored. After token pasting and macro expansion, p(2,3,4) will be replaced by one token, i.e. 234. Similarly, p(,5,6) will be replaced by 56 as the missing argument corresponding to the parameter x is ignored.

70. Compilation error "Undefined symbol CONST in function main"

Explanation:

The undef directive causes the CONST preprocessor definition to be no longer defined as a macro name. Hence, during the preprocessing stage, no macro expansion is carried out for CONST. After the preprocessing stage, during the compilation stage, there will be a compilation error since the name CONST has not been declared.

71. The value of CONST is 100

Explanation:

It is not erroneous to apply undef to an unknown identifier. Hence, #undef VAR is perfectly valid. Since, VAR has not been previously defined using the define directive, this directive will be ignored without any error or warning message.

72. The value of CONST is 100

Explanation:

At the point of usage of CONST, CONST is defined as a macro with 100 as its replacement list. During the preprocessing stage, macro CONST will be replaced by 100. And when the undef directive is encountered, it causes CONST to be no longer defined as a macro name.

73. The value of CONST is 100

Explanation:

A preprocessor directive can appear anywhere within a program.

74. The value of CONST is 10

Explanation:

A macro can be redefined anywhere in the program. The most recent definition of the macro is considered while expanding the macro. If the redefinition of the macro is not identical, the compiler will issue a warning 'Redefinition of 'macroname' is not identical'.

75. Place code corresponding to version 1

Explanation:

The ifdef directive tests whether a name has been defined as a macro or not. Since VER has already been defined using the define directive, the printf statement that lies between #ifdef-#else will be compiled and later on executed.

76. Place code corresponding to version 1

Explanation:

#ifdef-#else-#endif is a condition compilation directive. The ifdef directive tests whether a name has been defined using the define directive or not. Since VER has already been defined using the define directive, the printf statement that lies between #ifdef-#else will be compiled and later on executed. The text that lies between #else-#endif will not be compiled. Hence, there will be no compilation error.

77. Place code corresponding to version 1

Explanation:

Since, the constant expression (i.e. VER==1) of the if directive evaluates to true, the statements that lie between #if-#else will be compiled and later on executed.

78. Compilation error "L-value required in function main"

Explanation:

The constant expression of the if directive is erroneous. A symbolic constant VER is placed on the left side of the assignment operator, and this leads to a compilation error.

79. Compilation error "Constant expression required in function main"

Explanation:

Only a constant expression can be used with the if directive. Since a is a variable, a==VER is not a constant expression and cannot be used with the if directive.

80. Place code corresponding to version 1

Explanation:

The const qualifier has been used to make a as a qualified constant. Hence, a==VER forms a constant expression and can be used with the if directive.

81. Fatal: Error directive: OPERATING SYSTEM IS NOT KNOWN in function main

    Explanation:

    The defined operator checks whether a given identifier has been defined as a macro or not. It evaluates to 1 if identifier has been defined. Since WINDOWS and LINUX have not been defined, the error directive produces the customized error OPERATING SYSTEM IS NOT KNOWN.

82. Compilation error

    Explanation:

    By default, nested multi-line comments are not allowed in C language.

83. THE C PREPROCESSOR

    Explanation:

    The #pragma option -C has been used to make the nested multi-line comments allowed.

84. This function setups the prerequisites of function main
    This is function main
    The requisite value of variable is 200

    Explanation:

    The #pragma startup is used to make the function func execute before the function main. The function func sets the value of global variable req_var_value to be 200. This value of global variable req_var_value is accessed inside the function main.

85. Size of int: 2
    Size of char: 1
    Size of float: 4
    Size of double: 8

    Explanation:

    The macro size_of implements the functionality of the sizeof operator.

Answers to Multiple-choice Questions

86. d 87. a 88. c 89. a 90. a 91. b 92. b 93. d 94. b 95. b

Programming Exercises

Program 1 | Define a macro to find the greatest of the two given numbers. Illustrate the use of this macro in a program

PE 8-1.c

```
//Macro to find greatest of the two numbers
#include<stdio.h>
#define GREATEST(a,b) (a>b?a:b)
main()
{
int num1, num2;
printf("Enter two numbers:\t");
scanf("%d %d", &num1, &num2);
printf("The greatest of two numbers is %d",GREATEST(num1,num2));
}
```

Output window

```
Enter two numbers:    12 10
The greatest of two numbers is 12
```

(Contd...)

Program 2 | Define a macro to check whether a given number is even or odd. Illustrate the use of this macro in a program

PE 8-2.c

```
//Macro to check whether a given number is even or odd
#include<stdio.h>
#define EVENODD(a) ((a)%2==0?"even":"odd")
main()
{
int num;
printf("Enter a number to be checked:\t");
scanf("%d", &num);
printf("%d is an %s number", num, EVENODD(num));
}
```

Output window

```
Enter a number to be checked: 12
12 is an even number
```

Output window (second execution)

```
Enter a number to be checked: 5
5 is an odd number
```

Program 3 | Define a macro to find the harmonic mean of two numbers. Illustrate the use of this macro in a program

PE 8-3.c

```
//Macro to find the harmonic mean of two numbers
#include<stdio.h>
#define HMEAN(a,b)  ((float)(2*(a)*(b))/((a)+(b)))
main()
{
int num1, num2;
printf("Enter two numbers:\t");
scanf("%d %d", &num1, &num2);
printf("Harmonic mean of %d and %d is %f",num1, num2, HMEAN(num1,num2));
}
```

Output window

```
Enter two numbers:    4 6
Harmonic mean of 4 and 6 is 4.800000
```

Program 4 | Define a macro to swap the contents of two variables. Illustrate the use of this macro in a program

PE 8-4.c

```
//Macro to swap the contents of two variables
#include<stdio.h>
#define SWAP(a,b)  (a^=b^=a^=b)
main()
{
int num1, num2;
printf("Enter two numbers:\t");
scanf("%d %d", &num1, &num2);
printf("Before swapping, the value of num1=%d and num2=%d\n",num1,num2);
SWAP(num1, num2);
printf("After swapping, the value of num1=%d and num2=%d",num1,num2);
}
```

Output window

```
Enter two numbers:    4 6
Before swapping, the value of num1=4 and num2=6
After swapping, the value of num1=6 and num2=4
```

Program 5 | Define a nested macro to find the minimum of three integers. Illustrate the use of this macro in a program

PE 8-5.c

```
//Nested macro to find the minimum of three integers
#include<stdio.h>
#define MIN2(a,b) (a<b?a:b)
#define MIN3(a,b,c) (MIN2(a,b)<c?MIN2(a,b):c)
main()
{
int a, b, c;
printf("Enter three numbers:\t");
scanf("%d %d %d", &a, &b, &c);
printf("Minimum of %d, %d and %d is %d", a, b, c, MIN3(a,b,c));
}
```

Output window

```
Enter three numbers:    4 1 6
Minimum of 4, 1 and 6 is 1
```

Program 6 | Define a macro to check whether a given three-digit number is an Armstrong number or not. Illustrate the use of this macro in a program

PE 8-6.c

```
//Nested macro to check whether a given three digit number is an Armstrong number or not
#include<stdio.h>
#define POW3(x) ((x)*(x)*(x))
#define ARM(n) ((n==POW3(n%10)+POW3(n/10%10)+POW3(n/100%10) ) ? "is":"is not")
main()
{
int num;
printf("Enter a three digit number:\t");
scanf("%d", &num);
printf("%d %s an Armstrong number", num, ARM(num));
}
```

Output window

```
Enter a three digit number:    153
153 is an Armstrong number
```

Output window (second execution)

```
Enter a three digit number:    127
127 is not an Armstrong number
```

Test Yourself

1. Fill in the blanks in each of the following:
   a. A translator that converts a program written in a high-level language into an equivalent program in a machine-level language is known as ____________.
   b. The set of characters available when the source program file is executing is called ____________.
   c. The first two characters of a trigraph sequence are ____________.
   d. The input character sequence `x+++++y` is divided into the following stream of tokens ____________________.
   e. ____________ is a facility provided by a C preprocessor, by which a token can be replaced by the user-defined sequence of characters.
   f. Object-like macros are also known as ____________.
   g. The ____________ directive is used to configure some of the compiler options.
   h. The only directive that has no effect is ____________.
   i. ____________ is the smallest element of the language during the third to sixth phase of translation.
   j. The C tokenizer always tries to create ____________ possible token.

2. State whether each of the following is true or false. If false, explain why.
   a. During the preprocessing stage, each instance of backslash character immediately followed by a new-line character is deleted.
   b. The keywords are not preprocessing tokens. Thus, it is possible to use a keyword as an identifier name in a preprocessor directive, e.g. `#define int char`.
   c. The preprocessor directives are terminated with a semicolon.
   d. The preprocessor directives can only appear before the function `main`.
   e. The concatenation operator (i.e. ##) can appear at the beginning or at the end of the replacement list in a macro definition.
   f. ## is one token and there should be no white-space character between two ## characters.
   g. A predefined macro cannot appear immediately following a `define` directive.
   h. A predefined macro can be undefined using an `undef` directive.
   i. If the identifier specified with the `undef` directive is not currently defined as a macro, there will be a compilation error.
   j. The scope of a macro is the block in which it is defined.
   k. Macro replacement is carried out even within a string literal constant.

3. Programming exercises:
   a. Define a macro to check whether a given year is a leap year or not. Illustrate the use of this macro in a program.
   b. Define a macro to find the sum of digits of a three-digit number. Illustrate the use of this macro in a program.
   c. Define a macro to check whether a given three-digit number is perfect or not. Illustrate the use of this macro in a program.
   d. Define a macro that does not make use of a modulus operator to check whether a given number is even or not. Illustrate the use of this macro in a program.
   e. Define a macro to find the maximum of three integers. Illustrate its use.
   f. Define a macro that does not make use of a bitwise XOR operator to swap the contents of two variables. Illustrate its use.

9

STRUCTURES, UNIONS, ENUMERATIONS AND BIT-FIELDS

Learning Objectives

In this chapter, you will learn about:

- User-defined data types
- Structures
- How to define new data types using structures
- How to declare objects of the newly created structure type
- Various operations that can be applied on the objects of a structure type
- Arrays, pointers, functions and structures used in conjunction
- Creating syntactically convenient name for user-defined types
- Unions
- Difference between structures and unions
- Application of unions in interrupt programming
- Enumerations
- Storing information less than a byte by making use of bit-fields

9.1 Introduction

In previous chapters, you have seen that C language provides a rich set of primitive and derived data types for the efficient storage and manipulation of data. In case these data types do not suit your requirements, C language also provides the flexibility to create new data types. These data types are known as **user-defined data types** and can be created by using structures, unions and enumerations. In chapter 4, you have learnt that arrays can be used for the storage of homogeneous data. However, they cannot be used for the storage of data of different types. The data of different types can be grouped together and stored by making use of structures. One of the similarities between arrays and structures is that both of them contain a finite number of elements. Thus, array types and structure types are collectively known as aggregate types.

Unions are similar to structures in all aspects except the manner in which their constituent elements are stored. In structures, separate memory is allocated to each element, while in unions all the elements share the same memory.

Enumerations help you in defining a data type whose objects can take a limited set of values. These values are referred to by names, known as enumerators, which are more convenient to handle. In this chapter, I will tell you how to define new data types using structures, unions and enumerations. I will also let you know how to declare and manipulate objects of these newly defined data types.

9.2 Structures

A **structure** is a collection of variables under a single name and provides a convenient way of grouping several pieces of related information together. Unlike arrays, it can be used for the storage of heterogeneous data (i.e. data of different types). There are three aspects of working with structures:

1. Defining a structure type, i.e. creating a new type
2. Declaring variables and constants (i.e. **objects**) of the newly created type
3. Using and performing operations on the objects of the structure type

9.2.1 Defining a Structure

The general form of **structure-type definition** (or just **structure definition**) is:

```
[storage_class_specifier][type_qualifier] struct [structure_tag_name]
   {
      type member_name1[, member_name11, ...];
      [type member_name2[, member_name22, ...]];
      .........
   } [variable_name];
```

The important points about structure definition are as follows:

1. The terms enclosed within the square brackets are optional and might not be present in a structure definition statement. However, the terms shown in **bold** are the mandatory parts of the structure definition.
2. A structure definition consists of the keyword struct followed by an optional identifier name, known as **structure tag-name**, and a **structure declaration-list** enclosed within the braces. The examples of the structure definition given in Table 9.1 are valid.

Table 9.1 | Structure definitions with and without tag-name

(a)	(b)

struct book //←Structure tag-name is book
{
    char title [25]; //←Structure declaration-list
    char author[20];
    int pages;
    float price;
};
	struct //←Structure tag-name not present
	{
	    char title[25]; //←Structure declaration-list
	    char author[20];
	    int pages;
	    float price;
	};

3. The structure definition defines a **new type**, known as **structure type**. For example, in Table 9.1(a) the structure type is struct book. After the definition of the structure type, the keyword struct is used to declare its variables.
4. Since the tag-name of a structure is an identifier, all the rules discussed in Section 1.5.1 for writing an identifier name are applicable for writing the structure tag-name. If the tag-name is present, it will act as a **name** for the **newly created data type**.
5. The newly created type (i.e. tag name of the defined structure) is **visible**, after its definition, only in the scope in which it is defined. Hence, it is not possible to declare objects of the defined structure type outside the scope in which it (i.e. its tag name) is visible. The piece of code in Program 9-1 illustrates this fact.

Prog 9-1.c

```
//The defined structure type is visible only in the scope in which it is defined
#include<stdio.h>
func();             //←Declaration of the function func
main()
{
  struct coord  //←The type struct coord is defined in the scope local to the function main
  {
     int x,y;
  };
  struct coord pt1, pt2;  //←Declaring variables pt1 and pt2 of the created type struct coord
//←Other statements in the function main
//← ..............................
}
func()
{
struct coord pt3;    //←The tag name coord is not visible here
//←Other statements in the function func
//← ..............................
}
```

Output window

Compilation errors

"Undefined structure 'coord' in function func()"

"Size of 'pt3' is unknown or zero in function func()"

Remarks:

- Since the structure coord is defined in the function main, it is visible only in the function main
- It is possible to declare the variables of this newly created type in the scope local to the function main, but not outside this scope
- Hence, the declaration of the variable pt3 of type struct coord in the scope local to the function func leads to the compilation error

Program 9-1 | A program to illustrate that a defined structure type is visible only in the scope in which it is defined

6. The newly created type is **incomplete** until the closing brace of the structure declaration-list is encountered. The newly created type is **complete** thereafter.
7. The structure declaration-list consists of declarations of one or more variables, possibly of different types. The variable names declared in the structure declaration-list are known as **structure members** or **fields**. Structure members can be variables of the basic types (e.g. `char`, `int`, `float`, etc.), pointer types (e.g. `char*`, etc.) or **aggregate type** (i.e. arrays or other structure types). They are declared in the same way as normal identifiers are declared.

- An **incomplete type** describes an object but lacks the information needed to determine its size. Due to the lack of information about the size, an object of incomplete type cannot be created.
- **Array type and structure type** are collectively known as **aggregate type**.

8. A structure declaration-list cannot contain a member of `void` type or **incomplete type** or function type. Hence, **a structure definition cannot contain an instance of itself**. However, it may contain a pointer[†] to an instance of itself. Such a structure is known as a **self-referential structure.**
9. In principle, a structure definition can have an infinite number of members. However, practically the number of members in a single structure definition depends upon the translation limits of the compiler.

Forward Reference: Translation limits mentioned in ANSI/ISO specifications (Appendix C).

The interpretation of the above-mentioned rules is shown in Table 9.2.

Table 9.2 | Rules regarding the types of structure members

	Form of data	Structure definition

a.	| a | b | c |
	Types → char int float
		`struct record`
		`{ //← Structure declaration-list consists of variables of different types`
		`char a;`
		`int b;`
		`float c;`
		`};`
		(Valid)
		A structure can have data of different types

(Contd...)

[†]Refer Section 9.3 for a description on pointers to structures.

<table>
<tr><td>b.</td><td>A box contains two boxes
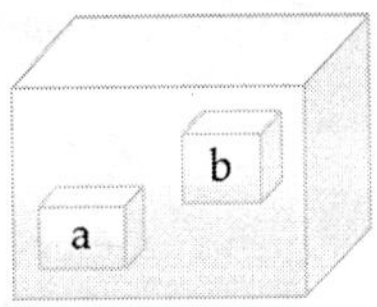</td><td><pre>struct box
{
struct box a; //←Type struct box is incomplete until the closing brace is enco-
struct box b; // -untered. Hence, a member of type struct box cannot be created
};   //← Type struct box is complete this point onwards</pre>(Invalid)
A structure cannot contain an instance of itself</td></tr>
<tr><td>c.</td><td>A name consists of two names: first name and last name.
| first_name | last_name |
A phonebook entry consists of the name of a person and his mobile number.
| person_name | mobile_no |</td><td><pre>struct name
{
   char first_name[20];
   char last_name[20];
};   //←Type struct name is complete now onwards
struct phonebook_entry
{
   struct name person_name; //←Member of complete type struct name
   char mobile_no[10];   //   can be created
};</pre>(Valid)
A structure can contain members of other complete types</td></tr>
<tr><td>d.</td><td>A node of a linked list consists of integer data and a pointer to a node.
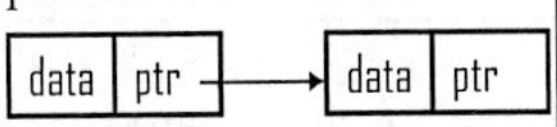Node 1 Node 2
Linked list</td><td><pre>struct node
{
   int data;
   struct node* ptr; //←Structure contains a pointer to an instance of itself.
};   // This is an example of a self-referential structure</pre>(Valid)
A structure can contain a pointer to itself</td></tr>
</table>

10. It is possible to use the shorthand declaration to declare two or more structure members of the same type. The examples of the structure definition given in Table 9.3 are valid.

Table 9.3 | Shorthand declaration used to declare structure members of the same type

<table>
<tr><td><pre>struct book
{
   char title [25], author[20]; //←Shorthand declaration
   int pages;
   float price;
};</pre>(a)</td><td><pre>struct two_dimensional_coordinate
{
   int x,y; //← Shorthand declaration
};</pre>(b)</td></tr>
</table>

11. The name of a structure member can be the same as the structure tag-name without any conflict, since they can always be distinguished from the context. However, the names of two structure members in a structure declaration-list can never be the same.

12. Two different structure types may contain members of the same name without any conflict.
13. It is important to note that a **structure definition does not reserve any space in the memory.**

A structure definition does not reserve any memory space for the structure members in the **data segment** but since structure definition becomes a part of the program code, it takes some space in the **code segment.**

14. Since structure definition does not reserve any memory space for the structure members, it is not possible to initialize the structure members during the structure definition. The structure definitions in Table 9.4 are not valid.

Table 9.4 | Initialization of structure members is not allowed during the structure definition

<table>
<tr>
<td>

```
struct book
{
    char title [30]="India 2020: A Vision for the new millennium ";
    char author[20]="A P J Abdul Kalam";
    int pages=400;
    float price=225.50;
};
```

(a)
</td>
<td>

```
struct two_dimensional_coordinate
{
    int x=0;
    int y;
};
```

(b)
</td>
</tr>
</table>

15. If a structure definition does not contain a structure tag-name, the created structure type is **unnamed**. The unnamed structure type is also known as an **anonymous** structure type. It is not possible to declare its objects (i.e. variables and constants) after its definition. Thus, the objects of unnamed or anonymous structure type should be declared only at the time of structure definition.

    The declaration of the structure variables at the time of unnamed structure definition is given in Table 9.5.

Table 9.5 | Declaration of structure variables at the time of structure definition

<table>
<tr>
<td>

```
struct
{
    char title [25];
    char author[20];
    int pages;
    float price;
} bookl;
//←Declaration of structure variable bookl
```

(a)
</td>
<td>

```
struct
{
    int x;
    int y;
} ptl, pt2; //←Declaration of structure variables ptl, pt2
```

(b)
</td>
</tr>
</table>

The declaration of structure constants at the time of unnamed structure definition is given in Table 9.6.

Table 9.6 | Declaration of structure constants at the time of structure definition

(a)

```
const struct
{
    char title [25];
    char author[20];
    int pages;
    float price;
} book={"Programming C", "Anirudh", 450, 225.50};
//←Creation of qualified constant book
```

(b)

```
struct
{
    char title [25];
    char author[20];
    int pages;
    float price;
} const book={"Programming C", "Anirudh", 450, 225.50};
//←Creation of qualified constant book
```

> *i* It is always better to provide a structure tag-name while creating a structure type. The tag-name is convenient for declaring the variables and constants of the defined structure type later in the program.

16. A structure-type definition can optionally have a storage class specifier and type qualifiers. However, the type qualifiers and storage class specifier (except typedef†) should only be used in a structure definition if the structure objects are also declared at the same time. The piece of code in Program 9-2 illustrates this fact.

Prog 9-2.c

```
//Use of storage class specifier while defining a structure type
#include<stdio.h>
static struct point
{
    int x;
    int y;
};
main()
{
    struct point ptl;
    //←Other statements
}
```

Output window

Compilation error "Storage class 'static' not allowed here".

Remark:

- The storage class specifiers except typedef should not be used in a structure-type definition if the objects are not declared at the time of structure definition

Program 9-2 | A program illustrating that a storage class specifier except typedef should not be used while defining a structure type if its objects are not declared at the same time

17. Since a structure definition is a statement, it must always be terminated with a semicolon.

9.2.2 Declaring Structure Objects

Variables and constants (i.e. objects) of the created structure type can be declared (actually defined) either at the time of structure definition or after the structure definition. The declaration of variables and constants at the time of structure definition has been discussed in Section 9.2.1. Variables and constants of the created structure type can be created after the structure

† Refer Section 9.7 for a description on using typedef storage class specifier in structure definition or with structure object declaration.

definition only if the defined structure type is **named** or **tagged**. The general form of declaring structure objects is:

```
[storage class specifier] [type_qualifier] struct named_structuretype identifier_name [=intialization_list [,...]];
```

The important points about the structure object declaration are as follows:

1. The terms enclosed within the square brackets are optional and might not be present in a structure object declaration statement. The terms shown in **bold** are the mandatory parts of the structure object declaration.
2. A structure object declaration consists of:
   i. The keyword struct for declaring structure variables. It can also be used in conjunction with const qualifier for declaring structure constants.
   ii. The tag-name of the defined structure type.
   iii. Comma-separated list of identifiers (i.e. variable names or constant names). A variable can optionally be initialized by providing an initializer. However, initialization of a constant is must.
   iv. A terminating semicolon.

   The following structure variable declarations are valid:

   ```
   struct book c_book, algorithm_book;  //←Structure type book defined in Table 9.1(a)
   struct phonebook_entry entry;        //←Structure type phonebook_entry defined in Table 9.2(c)
   struct two_dimensional_coordinate pt1={2,3}, pt2; //← Structure type two_dimensional_coordinate de-
                                                     //  fined in Table 9.3(b). The structure vari-
                                                     //  able pt1 //is initialized.
   ```

   The following structure constant declarations are valid:

   ```
   const struct book c_book, algorithm_book={"C Programming", "Anirudh", 450, 225.50};
   const struct phonebook_entry entry={{"Mohit","Virmani"}, "1234567899"};
   const struct two_dimensional_coordinate pt1={2,3}, pt2={4,5};
   ```

3. Note that, in C language, the objects of the defined structure type cannot be declared without using the keyword struct. However, this rigidity is relaxed in C++ language. If it is inconvenient to use the keyword struct every time to declare an object of the defined structure type, use the storage class specifier typedef[§] to create a syntactically convenient alias name for the defined structure type so that the keyword struct need not be used again and again.
4. Upon the declaration of a structure object, the amount of the memory space allocated to it is equal to the sum of the memory space required by all of its members. For example, the amount of memory allocated to a variable of the structure type struct book defined in Table 9.1 (a) is 51 bytes (if the integer takes 2 bytes) or 53 bytes (if the integer takes 4 bytes). The number of bytes of the memory space occupied by an object of the structure type also depends upon how members of the structure object are stored[¶] in the memory. The memory space allocated to a structure object can be determined by using the sizeof operator.
5. The structure members are assigned memory addresses in increasing order, with the first structure member starting at the beginning address of the structure itself. This can be checked by applying address-of operator on a structure object and its members as

§ Refer Section 9.7 for a description on the usage of typedef storage class specifier with structures.

¶ Refer Section 9.2.3.1.3 for a description on the alignment of structure members.

done in Program 9-7 in Section 9.2.3.1.3. Whether structure members are stored in consecutive memory locations or not, depends upon how the members of a structure object are aligned (refer footnote¶ on previous page).

6. **Initializing members of a structure object:** Like variables and array elements, the members of a **structure object** can also be initialized at the compile time. The syntactic rules about structure member initialization are as follows:
   i. The members of a structure object can be initialized by providing an **initialization list**. An initialization list is a comma-separated list of initializers.
   ii. The order of initializers must match the order of structure members in the structure definition.
   iii. The type of each initializer should be the same as the type of corresponding structure member in the structure definition. If the type of an initializer is not the same as the type of the corresponding structure member, implicit type casting will be done if types are compatible. If types are not compatible, there will be a compilation error.
   iv. The number of initializers in an initialization list can be less than the number of members in a structure object and if it happens, the leading structure members (i.e. occurring first) will be initialized with the initializers in the initialization list. The rest of the members will automatically be initialized with 0 (if they are of integer type), 0.0 (if they are of floating point type), '\0' (if they are of char type) and null pointer (if they are of pointer type). This rule is recursively applied to initialize all the elements/members of a structure member (if it is of aggregate type).
   v. Nested structures and arrays can be initialized by using nested braces.

   Examples of structure member initialization are as follows:

```
struct book c_book={"My Life", "C Motilal", 400, 210.50};
struct phonebook_entry entry={{"Rajesh","Kumar"}, "9814000561"};
struct two_dimensional_coordinate pt1={2}, pt2={2,3};
```

> It is important to note that **the structure members cannot be initialized during the structure definition**; however, **the members of a structure object can be initialized by providing an initialization list**.

7. A structure object declaration can optionally have a type qualifier. If the type qualifiers are used while declaring a structure object, they are applied to all the members of the structure object. The piece of code in Program 9-3 illustrates this fact.

Prog 9-3.c

```
//Using type qualifiers while declaring a structure object
#include<stdio.h>
struct point
{
    int x;
    int y;
};
main()
{
```

Output window

Compilation errors "Cannot modify a constant object in function main()"

Remarks:

- To access the members of a structure object, the member access operator, i.e. dot operator is used. Refer Section 9.2.3.1.1 for a description on how to access members of a structure object using the dot operator

(Contd...)

Prog 9-3.c

```
    const struct point pt={2,3};
    pt.x=20;
    pt.y=40;
    //←Other statements...
}
```

Output window

- The type qualifier const is applied to all the members of the structure object. Hence, the type of pt.x and pt.y is const int and thus, it is not possible to place them on the left side of the assignment operator

Program 9-3 | A program that illustrates the use of type qualifiers while declaring a structure object

8. A structure object declaration can optionally have a storage class specifier. The important points about the usage of a storage class specifier in a structure object declaration are as follows:

   i. If a structure object is declared with a storage class specifier other than typedef, the properties resulting from the storage class specifier except with respect to linkage, also apply to the members of the object, and so on recursively for any aggregate member object present in the structure definition. The piece of code in Program 9-4 illustrates this fact.

Prog 9-4.c

```
//Declaring structure object with a storage class specifier other than
//typedef
#include<stdio.h>
struct point
{
    int x;
    int y;
};
main()
{
    struct point pt1;
    static struct point pt2;
    printf("The coordinates of pt1 are %d,%d\n", pt1.x, pt1.y);
    printf("The coordinates of pt2 are %d,%d\n", pt2.x, pt2.y);
}
```

Output window

```
The coordinates of pt1 are 9495,19125
The coordinates of pt2 are 0,0
```

Remarks:

- Since the structure object pt1 is local to the function main and is not initialized, its members contain garbage values
- Since the structure object pt2 is declared with static storage class qualifier, all the properties resulting from it except linkage, are applicable to all the members of the structure object pt2
- Thus, all the members of the structure object pt2 are initialized to zero, since static storage class specifier has been used
- To access the members of a structure object, the member access operator, i.e. dot operator is used. Refer Section 9.2.3.1.1 for a description on how to access members of a structure object using the dot operator

Program 9-4 | A program that illustrates the declaration of a structure object with a static storage class specifier

   ii. The structure objects declared with register storage class specifier are treated as automatic (i.e. auto) objects.

9.2.3 Operations on Structures

The operations that can be performed on an object (i.e. variable or constant) of a structure type are classified into two categories:

1. Aggregate operations
2. Segregate operations

9.2.3.1 Aggregate Operations

An aggregate operation treats an operand as an entity and operates on the entire operand as a whole instead of operating on its constituent members. The four aggregate operations that can be applied on an object of a structure type are as follows:

1. Accessing members of an object of a structure type
2. Assigning a structure object to a structure variable
3. Address of a structure object
4. Size of a structure (i.e. either structure type or a structure object)

9.2.3.1.1 Accessing Members of an Object of a Structure Type

The members of a structure object can be accessed by using:

1. Direct member access operator (i.e. ., also known as **dot operator**).
2. Indirect member access operator[††] (i.e. ->, also known as **arrow operator**).

The important points about the use of a dot operator are as follows:

1. The dot operator accesses a structure member via structure object name while the arrow operator accesses a structure member via a pointer to the structure. The general form of using a dot operator is:

   ```
   structure_object_name.structure_member_name
   ```

2. The dot operator is a binary operator.
3. The first operand of the dot operator should have qualified or unqualified structure type and the second operand should be the name of a member of that type. The piece of code in Program 9-5 illustrates the use of the dot operator.

Line	Prog 9-5.c	Output window
1	//Use of dot operator	Enter values of translation vector:
2	#include<stdio.h>	4 2
3	struct coord //←Definition of type struct coord	After translation, coordinates are:
4	{ //← Creation of new type for 2-D coordinate	Pt1 (8,7)
5	int x,y;	Pt2 (6,5)
6	};	**Remarks:**
7	main()	• In line number 15, the
8	{	first operand of each
9	struct coord pt1={4,5}; //←pt1 is a variable of type struct coord	dot operator is of un-
10	const struct coord pt2={2,3}; //←pt2 is a qualified constant of type struct coord	qualified structure type
11	int tx, ty;	(i.e. struct coord)

(Contd...)

[††] Refer Section 9.3.2 for a description on indirect member access operator.

Line | Prog 9-5.c

```
12     printf("Enter values of translation vector:\n");
13     scanf("%d %d",&tx, &ty);
14     printf("After translation, coordinates are:\n");
15     printf("Pt1 (%d,%d)\n", pt1.x+tx, pt1.y+ty);
16     printf("Pt2 (%d,%d)\n", pt2.x+tx, pt2.y+ty);
17 }
```

Output window

- In line number 16, the first operand of each dot operator is of qualified structure type (i.e. const struct coord)

Program 9-5 | A program to illustrate the use of a direct member access operator

9.2.3.1.2 Assigning a Structure Object to a Structure Variable

Like simple variables, a structure variable can be assigned with or initialized with a structure object (i.e. variable or constant) of the same structure type. The piece of code in Program 9-6 illustrates the assignment and initialization of a structure variable.

Line | Prog 9-6.c

```
1  //Initialization and assignment of a structure variable
2  #include<stdio.h>
3  struct book            //←Structure definition
4  {
5      char title[25];
6      char author[20];
7      int price;
8  };
9  main()
10 {
11     //Initializing a structure variable by providing an initialization list
12     struct book b1={"Cutting Stone", "Abraham", 200};
13     //Initializing a structure variable with another structure variable
14     struct book b2=b1;
15     // Declaring an uninitialized structure variable
16     struct book b3;
17     b3=b2;    //←Assigning a structure variable to a structure variable
18     printf("%s by %s is of Rs. %d rupees\n", b1.title, b1.author, b1.price);
19     printf("%s by %s is of Rs. %d rupees\n", b2.title, b2.author, b2.price);
20     printf("%s by %s is of Rs. %d rupees\n", b3.title, b3.author, b3.price);
21 }
```

Output window

```
Cutting Stone by Abraham is of Rs. 200
Cutting Stone by Abraham is of Rs. 200
Cutting Stone by Abraham is of Rs. 200
```

Remarks:

- In line number 12, the structure variable b1 is initialized by providing an initialization list
- In line number 14, the structure variable b2 is initialized with the structure variable b1
- In line number 17, the structure variable b2 is assigned to the structure variable b3
- The assignment operator copies the values of all the members of a structure object present on its right side to the corresponding members of a structure variable present on its left side
- Hence, printing the values of members of all the three structure variables gives the same result

Program 9-6 | A program that illustrates the initialization and assignment of a structure variable

The important points about the structure variable assignment are as follows:

1. Unlike arrays, a structure variable can be assigned with or initialized with a structure object of the same type. If the type of assigning or initializing structure object is not the

same as the type of structure variable on the left side of the assignment operator, there will be a compilation error. Note that it is not even possible to explicitly type cast a structure type to another structure type.

2. The assignment operator assigns (i.e. copies) values of all the members of the structure object on its right side to the corresponding members of the structure variable on its left side one by one. Hence, the assignment operator, when applied on structure variables performs **member-by-member copy**.
3. The structure assignment does not copy any padding bits.[‡‡]
4. Due to member-by-member copy behavior of the assignment operator on the structure variables, structure objects can be passed to functions[§§] by value and can also be returned from functions.

9.2.3.1.3 Address-of a Structure Object

The address-of operator when applied on a structure object gives its base (i.e. starting) address. It can also be used to find the addresses of the constituting members of a structure object. The piece of code in Program 9-7 illustrates the use of the address-of operator on a structure object and its constituting members.

Prog 9-7.c	Memory contents	Output window

//Address-of operator and structures
#include<stdio.h>
struct complex
{
int re, im;
};
main()
{
struct complex c1={2,3};
const struct complex c2={4,5};
printf("Address of c1 is %p\n",&c1);
printf("Address of its real part is %p\n",&c1.re);
printf("Address of its imaginary part is %p\n",&c1.im);
printf("Address of c2 is %p\n",&c2);
printf("Address of its real part is %p\n",&c2.re);
printf("Address of its imaginary part is %p\n",&c2.im);
}
	c1
	c1.re: 2 (222C)
	c1.im: 3 (222E)
	
	c2
	c2.re: 4 (223C)
	c2.im: 5 (223E)
		Address of c1 is 233F:222C
		Address of its real part is 233F:222C
		Address of its imaginary part is 233F:222E
		Address of c2 is 233F:223C
		Address of its real part is 233F:223C
		Address of its imaginary part is 233F:223E
		Remarks:
		• The memory allocation is purely random, and the result of the execution may vary for executions at different times or on different machines
		• The address of the first structure member is the same as the address of the structure object
		• Thus, the first structure member starts at the beginning address of the structure itself

Program 9-7 | A program that illustrates the use of the address-of operator on structures

The output of the address-of operator depends upon how the members of a structure object are stored in the memory. There are two different ways of storing the members of a structure object:

[‡‡] Refer Section 9.2.3.1.3 for a description on structure padding.

[§§] Refer Section 9.6.2 for a description on passing structure objects to functions by value.

a. **Byte aligned:** If the members of a structure object are byte aligned, then every structure member starts from a new byte (i.e. they can appear at any byte boundary). In byte alignment, the data members are stored next to each other. Storage of members of a structure variable using byte alignment is shown in Figure 9.1.

Definition

```
struct type
{
   char a;
   int b;
   char c;
   float d;
}var;
```

Memory contents

var

a	b		c	d			
1001	1011	1100	1001	1111	1101	1010	1000
2000	2001	2002	2003	2004	2005	2006	2007

In byte alignment, data members are placed next to each other

char takes 1 byte, int takes 2 bytes and float takes 4 bytes in the memory
Note that only 4 bits are shown in the cells above but actually 8 bits are present in each cell

Figure 9.1 | Storage of the members of a structure object using byte alignment

b. **Machine-word boundary aligned:** Most of the machines access objects of certain types faster if they are aligned properly. In order to increase the performance of the code on such machines, the compiler aligns the members of a structure object with the storage boundaries whose **addresses are multiple of their respective sizes.** This is shown in Figure 9.2.

Definition

```
struct type
{
   char a;
   int b;
   char c;
   int d;
}var;
```

Memory contents

var

a		b		c			d
1001	H	1011	1100	1001	H	1111	1101
2400	2401	2402	2403	2404	2405	2406	2407

H represents holes.
char takes 1 byte, int takes 2 bytes and float takes 4 bytes in the memory

Figure 9.2 | Storage of members of a structure object using machine-word boundary alignment

The character members can appear at any byte boundary (since the size of character type is 1). Let us assume that the structure member a of the type struct type (as shown in Figure 9.2) gets allocated at the memory address 2400. Since the size of the integer type is 2, the member b must appear immediately at the next even-byte boundary. Thus, the memory location 2401 is not a valid start location for the structure member b. Hence, it starts from the storage boundary with the memory address 2402. Similarly, the next two members of the structure object var are stored.

The vacant spaces (as shown in Figure 9.2) in between the members of a structure, if they are machine-word boundary aligned, are known as **holes**. The holes contain random bytes known as **padding bytes**. Thus, the process by which the C compiler inserts unused bytes after the structure members to ensure that each member is appropriately aligned is called **structure padding**. Consider another example given in Figure 9.3.

Definition	Memory contents

struct newtype
{
    char a;
    double b;
}var;
	var

a								b							
1001	H	H	H	H	H	H	H	1101	0010	1101	1101	0010	1001	1011	1100
2400	**2401**	**2402**	**2403**	**2404**	**2405**	**2406**	**2407**	**2408**	**2409**	**240A**	**240B**	**240C**	**240D**	**240E**	**240F**

H represents holes.

char takes 1 byte and double takes 8 bytes

Figure 9.3 | Another example of storing a structure object using machine-word boundary alignment

Let us assume that the character member a of the type struct newtype is stored at the memory location 2400. The size of the member b is 8 bytes, since it is of type double. Hence, it can only start from a storage boundary whose address is a multiple of 8. Thus, the structure member b is placed at the memory address 2408 and there are seven holes (i.e. padding bytes) between members a and b.

A character object can be allocated at any memory address and have no alignment requirement. Thus, if in Figure 9.3, the character member a gets allocated at the memory address 2405 instead of the memory address 2400, the number of padding bytes required would have been two and if it gets allocated at 2407, no padding byte would have been required. Does it mean that the number of padding bytes required to store objects of a given structure type is variable?

No, for a given compiler and the underlying hardware configuration, the number of padding bytes required to store objects of a given structure type is fixed. A structure member whose address requirement is a higher multiple than another is said to have **stricter alignment**. Thus, in Figure 9.3, the member b has stricter alignment than the member a. Also, **each structure object must be as strictly aligned as its most strictly aligned member**. Thus, an object of the structure type defined in Figure 9.3 should be as strictly aligned as its member b and can only start from the memory locations that are divisible by 8. Therefore, the objects of the structure type defined in Figure 9.3 can start from memory addresses like 2400, 2408, etc. Hence, if a structure object starts from any of these memory locations, the number of padding bytes required would be 7.

Interestingly, if you think that 7 bytes are too much to be wasted for padding, you can place a limit on the amount of padding that can be done by the compiler. The amount of padding can be restricted by setting[¶¶] a **pack size** value. By default, the pack size in Turbo C 3.0 and 4.5 is 2 and is 4 in MS-VC++ 6.0. Thus, **if the members of a structure object are machine-word aligned, they can appear at the storage boundaries that have addresses that are either multiple of their respective sizes or the pack size, whichever is smallest**. Therefore, if the structure object shown in Figure 9.3 is stored using Turbo C 3.0/4.5, there will be two holes between the members a and b and if it is stored using MS-VC++6.0, there will be four holes (since pack size is 4) instead of 7.

¶¶ Refer Section 9.2.3.1.4 for a description on how to set the pack size.

The important points about structure padding are as follows:

i. The members of a structure object are always stored in the order in which they are declared. They will never be reordered to improve the alignment and save padding.

ii. The padding can only appear in between two structure members (i.e. internal padding) or after the last structure member (i.e. trailing padding). In no case can it appear before the first member of the structure object. The reason behind placing the padding bytes after the last member of the structure object is to enable the alignment in an array of structures. Consider the structure type and an array object defined in Figure 9.4.

Definition

```
struct ntype
{
    int a;
    char b;
}var[2];
```

Memory contents

var

var[0]				var[1]			
a		b		a		b	
1001	1010	0101	H	0100	1110	1100	H
2400	2401	2402	2403	2404	2405	2406	2407

H represents holes.
int takes 2 bytes and char takes 1 byte

Figure 9.4 | Storage of array of structure objects when the members of a structure are machine-word boundary aligned

The member a of the first element of the array var (i.e. first structure object) starts at the even-byte boundary. The member b can be placed at the next byte boundary. Thus, there is no padding between the members a and b of the first structure object. The member a of the second element of the array (i.e. second structure object) must appear at the even-byte boundary. Thus, 2403 is not a valid start location for the member a of the second structure object. Therefore, the compiler places a padding byte at the end of the first structure object so that the second structure object can be aligned properly.

iii. Whether the members of a structure object will be byte aligned or machine-word boundary aligned, depends upon the compiler, its configuration, the working environment and the underlying machine. Some compilers (e.g. Borland TC 3.0 and Borland TC 4.5) use byte alignment by default while some compilers (e.g. MS-VC++ 6.0) by default use machine-word boundary alignment. The pragma directive can also be used to configure[†††] the compiler to use the appropriate alignment scheme for storing the structure members.

9.2.3.1.4 Use of sizeof Operator on Structures

When the sizeof operator is applied to an operand of a structure type, the result is the total number of bytes that an object of such type will occupy in the memory. The important points about the use of a sizeof operator on structures are as follows:

[†††] Refer Section 9.2.3.1.4 for a description on how to configure the compiler to use the appropriate alignment scheme for storing the structure members.

1. The general form of sizeof operator is:
    a. sizeof expression or the sizeof(expression)
    b. sizeof(type i.e structure_type)

The usage of both the forms of sizeof operator on operands of a structure type is given in the code segment listed in Program 9-8.

Prog 9-8.c

```
//sizeof operator & structures
#include<stdio.h>
struct pad
{
    char a;
    int b;
    char c;
    float d;
};
main()
{
struct pad var;
printf("Objects of type struct pad will take %d bytes\n", sizeof(struct pad));
printf("Structure variable var takes %d bytes\n",sizeof var);
}
```

Output window (Borland TC 3.0)

Objects of type struct pad will take 8 bytes
Structure variable var takes 8 bytes

Output window (Borland TC 4.5) (second execution)

Objects of type struct pad will take 8 bytes
Structure variable var takes 8 bytes

Output window (MS-VC++ 6.0) (third execution)

Objects of type struct pad will take 16 bytes
Structure variable var takes 16 bytes

Remarks:

- In Borland Turbo C 3.0/4.5, character takes 1 byte, integer takes 2 bytes and float takes 4 bytes
- Also, in Borland Turbo C 3.0/4.5, structure members are stored using byte alignment. Hence, there is no padding
- Thus, the sizeof operator gives the output as 1+2+1+4=8 bytes in Borland Turbo C 3.0/4.5
- In Microsoft VC++ 6.0, character takes 1 byte, integer takes 4 bytes and float takes 4 bytes
- Also, in Microsoft VC++ 6.0, the structure members are machine-word boundary aligned and the default pack size is of 4 bytes
- Thus, the sizeof operator outputs 4+4+4+4=16 bytes in Microsoft VC++ 6.0

Program 9-8 | A program that illustrates the use of the sizeof operator on structures

2. The result of the sizeof operator when applied on a structure is equal to the sum of the size of all of its members. It also **includes the space taken by internal and trailing padding.** The pragma directive can be used to turn the structure padding on or off. In Borland Turbo C 3.0 and 4.5, the structure padding can be turned on by using #pragma option -a. Another method to turn on the structure padding in TC 4.5 is by invoking the following menu items:

    options>project>advanced compiler>processor>data alignment>word alignment instead of byte alignment.

The piece of code in Program 9-9 illustrates the use of the pragma directive to configure Borland TC 3.0 and 4.5, so that it stores the structure members using the machine-word boundary alignment.

Prog 9-9.c

```
1  //sizeof operator & structures
2  #include<stdio.h>
3  #pragma option -a
4  struct pad
5  {
6      char a;
7      int b;
8      char c;
9      float d;
10 };
11 main()
12 {
13 struct pad var;
14 printf("Objects of type struct pad will take %d bytes\n", sizeof(struct pad));
15 printf("Structure variable var takes %d bytes\n",sizeof var);
16 }
```

Output window (Borland TC 3.0/4.5)

```
Objects of type struct pad will take 10 bytes
Structure variable var takes 10 bytes
```

Remarks:

- In line number 3, the pragma directive is used to store the structure members using machine-word boundary alignment
- In Borland Turbo C 3.0/4.5, the pack size is 2 bytes
- In Borland Turbo C 3.0/4.5, float takes 4 bytes
- Hence, the sizeof operator gives an output as 2+2+2+4=10 bytes

Program 9-9 | A program to illustrate that the result of the sizeof operator includes internal and trailing padding

The pragma option that can be used to turn off the structure padding in Borland Turbo C 3.0 and 4.5 is #pragma option -a-. The #pragma option -a- is, however, not recognized in MS-VC++ 6.0. To specify the pack size for structures, MS-VC++ 6.0 uses #pragma pack(n) directive, where n is the size according to which the packing will be done. The piece of code in Program 9-10 illustrates the structure packing in MS-VC++ 6.0.

Prog 9-10.c

```
//sizeof operator & structures
#include<stdio.h>
#pragma pack(2)
struct pad
{
    char a;
    int b;
    char c;
    float d;
};
main()
{
struct pad var;
printf("Objects of type struct pad will take %d bytes\n", sizeof(struct pad));
printf("Structure variable var takes %d bytes\n",sizeof var);
}
```

Output window (MS-VC++ 6.0)

```
Objects of type struct pad will take 12 bytes
Structure variable var takes 12 bytes
```

Remarks:

- In Microsoft VC++ 6.0, #pragma pack(n) is used to specify the pack size
- #pragma pack(2) specifies the pack size to be 2 bytes
- To store the structure members using byte alignment in MS-VC++ 6.0 #pragma pack(1) is used. #pragma pack(1) specifies that members can be placed at any byte boundaries
- #pragma pack(2) specifies that members of size greater than two can be placed at even-byte boundaries
- In Microsoft VC++ 6.0, integer takes 4 bytes
- Thus, the sizeof operator gives output as 2+4+2+4=12 bytes

(Contd...)

Memory contents

Alignment with machine-word boundaries, pack size is 2 bytes

var

a		b				c		d			
1001	H	1011	1100	1111	1010	1001	H	1111	1101	1010	1000
2000	2001	2002	2203	2004	2005	2006	2007	2008	2009	2010	2011

(a) #pragma pack(2) used

Alignment with byte boundaries, pack size is 1 byte

var

a	b				c	d			
1001	1011	1100	1111	1010	1001	1111	1101	1010	1000
2000	2001	2002	2003	2004	2005	2006	2007	2008	2009

(b) #pragma pack (1) used

Using MS-VC++ 6.0, char takes 1 byte, int takes 4 bytes and float takes 4 bytes in the memory

Program 9-10 | A program that finds the size of a structure object and a structure type after packing the structure members according to the given pack size

9.2.3.1.5 Equating Structure Objects of the Same Type

The use of an equality operator on the operands of a structure type is not allowed and leads to a compilation error. The piece of code in Program 9-11 illustrates this fact.

Line | Prog 9-11.c

```
1  //Equality operator and structures
2  #include<stdio.h>
3  #pragma pack(2)
4  struct pad
5  {
6      char a;
7      int b;
8      char c;
9      float d;
10 };
11 main()
12 {
13 struct pad var1={'A', 2, 'B', 2.5}, var2={'A', 2, 'B', 2.5};
14 if(var1==var2)
15     printf("Structure variables are equal\n");
16 else
17     printf("Structure variables are unequal\n");
18 }
```

Output window (MS-VC++ 6.0)

Compilation error "Invalid structure operation in function main"

Remarks:

- Since the structure members are not always stored in the contiguous memory locations, the use of the equality operator is not allowed on the objects of a structure type
- Thus, the usage of the equality operator on the structure variables in line number 14 leads to the compilation error

Memory contents

var1

a		b				c		d			
A	1011	2				B	1101	2.5			
2000	2001	2002	2003	2004	2005	2006	2007	2008	2009	2010	2011

(Contd...)

Memory contents											
var2											
a		b				c		d			
A	1010	2				B	0001	2.5			
4000	4001	4002	4003	4004	4005	4006	4007	4008	4009	4010	4011

Program 9-11 | A program to illustrate that the application of the equality operator on the structure objects is not allowed

The important points about the application of an equality operator on the objects of a structure type are as follows:

1. Unlike arrays, the members of a structure object may not be stored in contiguous memory locations. If the members of a structure object are machine-word boundary aligned, there may be some holes in the structure. These holes are filled with **padding**, which is random and undefined. As given in Program 9-11, although the values of all the members of both the structure variables are equal, the structures are not equal because the holes do not contain identical padding.
2. Due to the structure padding, the operation of the equality operator on structures is restricted and this is a general rule. Even if byte alignment is used for storing members of a structure object, in which there are no holes between the structure members, the use of the equality operator on structure objects leads to a compilation error.

Forward Reference: Also refer Question number 18 and its answer to find other reasons for why the equality operator does not work on structures.

3. For similar reasons, the application of relational operators like >=, <=, >, < and != is not allowed on structures.
4. Whether two structure objects are equal or not can be determined by comparing all the members of the structure objects separately. The piece of code in Program 9-12 checks the equality of two structure objects.

Prog 9-12.c

```
//Equality operator and structures
#include<stdio.h>
struct pad
{
    char a;
    int b;
    float c;
};
main()
{
struct pad var1={'A', 2, 2.5}, var2={'A', 2, 2.5};
const struct pad var3={'B',3,5.5}, var4={'C',7,9.5};
printf("Checking equality of structure objects:\n");
if(var1.a==var2.a && var1.b==var2.b && var1.c==var2.c)
    printf("Structure variables are equal\n");
```

Output window (MS-VC++ 6.0)

```
Checking equality of structure objects:
Structure variables are equal
Structure constants are unequal
```

Remarks:

- The equality of structure objects can be checked by equating every member of the structure object
- Specify different initializers in the initialization list of the structure variable var2 and then re-execute the code

(Contd...)

```c
else
    printf("Structure variables are unequal\n");
if(var3.a==var4.a && var3.b==var4.b && var3.c==var4.c)
    printf("Structure constants are equal\n");
else
    printf("Structure constants are unequal\n");
}
```

Program 9-12 | A program that illustrates a method of determining whether two structure objects are equal

9.2.3.2 Segregate Operations

A segregate operation operates on the individual members of a structure object. The individual members of a structure object are like normal objects (i.e. variables and constants). Therefore, any operation that is applicable on an object of a particular type can be applied on a structure member of that type. The piece of code in Program 9-13 illustrates segregate operations on the members of a structure variable.

Prog 9-13.c

```c
//Segregate operations
#include<stdio.h>
struct book
{
    char title[25];
    char author[20];
    int pages;
    float price;
};
main()
{
 struct book book1, book2;
 printf("Enter title, author name, pages and price of book1:\n");
 gets(book1.title);
 gets(book1.author);
 scanf("%d %f",&book1.pages,& book1.price);
 flushall();
 printf("Enter title, author name, pages and price of book2:\n");
 gets(book2.title);
 gets(book2.author);
 scanf("%d %f",&book2.pages, &book2.price);
 printf("\nInsecondedition,thepagesofbooksareincreasedby100\n");
 printf("The cost of books is increased by 10%\n\n");
 // Operations on individual members
 book1.pages+=100;
 book2.pages+=100;
 book1.price=book1.price*110/100;
 book2.price=book2.price*110/100;
 printf("In second edition: book1 has %d pages\n",book1.pages);
```

Output window

```
Enter title, author name, pages and price of book1:
The Book of Wisdom
Stephen W. K. Tan
480
225
Enter title, author name, pages and price of book2:
Who moved my cheese?
Dr Spencer Johnson
400
210

In second edition, the pages of books are increased by 100
The cost of books is increased by 10%

In second edition: book1 has 580 pages
The second edition of book1 is of Rs. 247.500000
In second edition: book2 has 500 pages
The second edition of book2 is of Rs. 231.000000
```

(Contd...)

Prog 9-13.c	Output window
printf("The second edition of book1 is of Rs. %f\n",book1.price);	
printf("In second edition: book2 has %d pages\n",book2.pages);	
printf("The second edition of book2 is of Rs. %f\n",book2.price);	
}	

Program 9-13 | A program that illustrates the operations on the individual members of a structure object

9.3 Pointers to Structures

As pointer to any other type can be created, it is possible to create a pointer to a structure type as well. The pointers to structures have the following advantages:

1. It is easier to manipulate the pointers to structures than manipulating structures themselves.
2. Passing a pointer to a structure as an argument to a function‡‡‡ is efficient as compared to passing a structure to a function. The size of a pointer to a structure is generally smaller than the size of the structure itself. Thus, passing a pointer to a structure as an argument to a function requires less data movement as compared to passing the structure to a function.
3. Some wondrous data structures (e.g. linked lists, trees, etc.) use the structures containing pointers to structures. Pointers to structures play an important role in their successful implementation.

9.3.1 Declaring Pointer to a Structure

The general form of declaring a pointer to a structure is:

[storage_class_specifier] [type_qualifier] **struct named_structure_type* identifier_name**[=l-value[,...]];

The important points about declaring a pointer to a structure are as follows:

1. The terms enclosed within the square brackets are optional and might not be present in a declaration statement. The terms shown in **bold** are the mandatory parts of a structure pointer declaration statement.
2. A pointer to a structure type can be declared in a separate declaration statement only if the structure type is named. If the structure type is unnamed, the structure pointer should be created at the time of structure definition as shown in Program 9-14.
3. The declared structure pointer can optionally be initialized with an l-value. The initializing l-value should be of appropriate type, else there will be a compilation error.

The piece of code in Program 9-14 illustrates the declaration of a pointer to a structure.

Prog 9-14.c	Output window (Borland TC 4.5)
//Pointers to structures	Addresses of pt1 and pt2 are 2397:0076 2397:2292
#include<stdio.h>	Addresses of ptr1 and ptr2 are 2397:0D38 2397:228E
struct coord	ptr1 and ptr2 point to 2397:0076 2397:2292
{	Size of type (struct coord) is 6
int x, y,z;	Size of type (struct coord*) is 4

(Contd...)

‡‡‡ Refer Section 9.6.3 for a description on passing a pointer to a structure as an argument to a function.

```
}pt1={2,3,5}, *ptr1;     //←Declaration of structure pointer at the
                         //    time of structure definition
main()
{
struct coord pt2={4,5,6};
struct coord *ptr2=&pt2; //←Declaration of structure pointer in a
                         //    separate declaration statement
ptr1=&pt1;
printf("Addresses of pt1 and pt2 are %p %p\n",&pt1,&pt2);
printf("Addresses of ptr1 and ptr2 are %p %p\n",&ptr1,&ptr2);
printf("ptr1 and ptr2 point to %p %p\n",ptr1,ptr2);
printf("Size of type (struct coord) is %d\n", sizeof(struct coord));
printf("Size of type (struct coord*) is %d\n",sizeof(struct coord*));
printf("pt1 and pt2 take %d bytes\n", sizeof(pt1));
printf("ptr1 and ptr2 take %d bytes\n", sizeof(ptr1));
}
```

pt1 and pt2 take 6 bytes
ptr1 and ptr2 take 4 bytes

Remarks:

- As the memory allocation is purely random, the output may vary for different executions at different times or on different machines
- If executed using Borland Turbo C 3.0, only offset addresses will be printed and the size of struct coord*, ptr1 and ptr2 that gets printed is 2 bytes.

Memory content

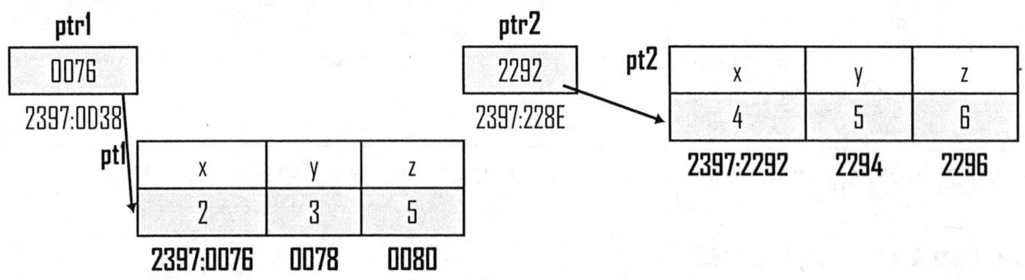

Program 9-14 | A program that illustrates the declarations and the use of pointers to a structure type

9.3.2 Accessing Structure Members Via a Pointer to a Structure

The members of a structure object can be accessed via a pointer to a structure object by using one of the following two ways:

1. By using the dereference or indirection operator and the direct member access operator
2. By using the indirect member access operator (i.e. ->, known as the **arrow operator**)

The important points about accessing the structure members, via a pointer to the structure object are as follows:

1. The general form to access a structure member via a pointer to the structure object using the dereference and dot operator is:

   `(*pointer_to_structure_type).structure_member_name`

2. It is mandatory to parenthesize the dereference operator and the structure pointer because the dot operator has a higher precedence than the dereference operator.
3. The members of a structure object can also be accessed via the pointer to the structure object by using only one operator, known as the **indirect member access operator** or **arrow operator**. The general form of such access is:

   `pointer_to_structure_object->structure_member_name`

4. The arrow operator consists of a hyphen (-) followed by a right arrow (>) with no space in between.
5. The expression `pointer_to_structure_object->structure_member_name` is equivalent to the expression `(*pointer_to_structure_object).structure_member_name`.

The piece of code in Program 9-15 illustrates the structure member access via the pointer to the structure object.

Prog 9-15.c

```
1  //Accessing structure members via pointer to the structure object
2  #include<stdio.h>
3  struct coord
4  {
5  int x, y;
6  };
7  main()
8  {
9  struct coord pt={2,3};
10 struct coord *ptr=&pt;
11 printf("Coordinates of Ptl are (%d,%d)\n",(*ptr).x, (*ptr).y);
12 printf("Coordinates of Ptl are (%d,%d)\n",ptr->x, ptr->y);
13 }
```

Output window

```
Coordinates of Ptl are (2,3)
Coordinates of Ptl are (2,3)
```

Remarks:

- In line number 11, the structure members are accessed via the pointer to the structure object by using the dereference operator and direct member access operator
- In line number 12, the structure members are accessed by using the indirect member access operator

Program 9-15 | A program that illustrates structure member access via structure pointer

9.4 Array of Structures

It is possible to create an array whose elements are of structure type. Such an array is known as an **array of structures**. Consider the structure type `struct book` defined in Program 9-13. The information about the title of the book, author's name, number of pages and its price can be stored in a variable of type `struct book`. We have created the variables `bookl` and `book2` of this type in Program 9-13 to store the specified information about two books. Now, suppose we need to store the information about a number of books available in a library. To store the information about several books, creating a separate variable for each book is not feasible. Here an array of structures provides a convenient way to store the information about the books available in the library. The piece of code in Program 9-16 illustrates the use of array of structures for this purpose.

Prog 9-16.c

```
//Array of structures
#include<stdio.h>
#include<conio.h>
#define MAXBOOKS 10
struct book
{
    char title[30];
    char author[30];
    int pages;
```

Output window (Borland Turbo C 4.5)

```
Enter the information of bookl:
Enter the title of the book:    The law and the lawyer
Enter the author's name:    M K Gandhi
Enter the number of pages in the book:    200
Enter the price of the book:    125
Do you want to enter more(Y/N):    Y
Enter the information of book2:
Enter the title of the book:    Rise and fall of super powers
Enter the author's name:    Paul
```

(*Contd...*)

```
10 float price;
11 };
12 main()
13 {
14 struct book library[MAXBOOKS];
15 int count=0,i;
16 char ch;
17 while(1)
18 {
19     printf("Enter the information of book %d:\n", count+1);
20     printf("Enter the title of the book:\t");
21     gets(library[count].title);
22     printf("Enter the author's name:\t");
23     gets(library[count].author);
24     printf("Enter the number of pages in the book:\t");
25     scanf("%d",&library[count].pages);
26     printf("Enter the price of the book:\t");
27     scanf("%f",&library[count].price);
28     flushall();
29     count++;
30     if(count==MAXBOOKS)
31     {
32         printf("Capacity full\n");
33         break;
34     }
35     else
36     {
37         printf("Do you want to enter more(Y/N):\t");
38         ch=getche();
39         printf("\n");
40         if(ch=='y'||ch=='Y')
41             continue;
42         else
43             break;
44     }
45 }
46 printf("\nFollowing are the books in the library:\n\n");
47 for(i=0;i<count;i++)
48 {
49 printf("%s by %s: %d pages is of Rs. %6.2f\n",
50 library[i].title, library[i].author, library[i].pages,
51 library[i].price);
52 }
53 }
```

```
Enter the number of pages in the book:    250
Enter the price of the book:    150
Do you want to enter more(Y/N):    N

Following are the books in the library:

The law and the lawyer by M K Gandhi: 200 pages is of Rs. 125.00
Rise and fall of great powers by Paul: 250 pages is of Rs. 150.00
```

Remarks:

- In line number 4, macro MAXBOOKS is defined to have value 10
- In line number 5, the structure type struct book is defined
- In line number 14, an array of 10 elements is declared whose element type is struct book
- Elements of this array can be accessed in the same way as the elements of other arrays can be accessed, i.e. by using the subscript operator
- If executed using Borland Turbo C 3.0 or other older compilers, there will be the following error:
  scanf: floating point formats not linked
  Abnormal program termination error

Program 9-16 | A program that illustrates the use of array of structures

The important points about the use of array of structures are as follows:

1. An array of structures is declared in the same way as any other kind of array is declared. The only difference is that the element type of an array of structures is the defined

structure type while the element type of other arrays is either a basic type or a derived type.

2. An array of structures is quite big in size. If it is defined inside the block/local scope without using the `static` storage class specifier (as in Program 9-16), it is placed on the stack. The **stack** is an area of memory that starts out small and grows automatically up to a predefined limit. It is possible that the default size of a stack is too small to accommodate an array of structures. In such a case, there will be stack overflow run-time error. The following solutions can be used to fix this problem:
   a. Reduce the array size. For example, Program 9-16 executes fine till the size of the array `library` is kept 60 (in TC 4.5). If the size of the array is further increased, there will be stack overflow run-time error.
   b. Use the storage class specifier `static` while declaring the array so that it is not stored on the stack.
3. If Program 9-16 is executed using the Borland Turbo C 3.0 compiler, the following error will occur:

   ```
   scanf: floating point formats not linked
   Abnormal program termination
   ```

   The reason behind this error is that older Borland compilers like Borland Turbo C 3.0 for DOS attempt at keeping the size of a program compact by using the smaller versions of the `scanf` function if the program does not use floating point values. However, these compilers get fooled if the floating point values are in an array of structures (as in Program 9-16). The problem can be solved by adding the following lines of code:

   ```
   #include<math.h>
   float dummy= cos(0.0);       //←This statement is an executable statement and should
                                // not be placed in the global scope. It should be placed
                                // in the local scope after the non-executable statements.
   ```

   The piece of code in Program 9-17 illustrates the usage of the above dummy statement to rectify the problem of the `scanf` function in Borland Turbo C 3.0 or other older compilers:

Prog 9-17.c

```
//Array of structures
#include<stdio.h>
#include<conio.h>
#include<math.h>
#define MAXBOOKS 10
struct book
{
    char title[30];
    char author[30];
    int pages;
    float price;
};
main
{
 struct book library[MAXBOOKS];
```

Output window (Borland Turbo C 3.0)

```
Enter the information of bookl:
Enter the title of the book:    The law and the lawyer
Enter the author's name:    M K Gandhi
Enter the number of pages in the book:    200
Enter the price of the book:    125
Do you want to enter more(Y/N):    Y
Enter the information of book2:
Enter the title of the book:    Rise and fall of super powers
Enter the author's name:    Paul Kennedy
Enter the number of pages in the book:    250
Enter the price of the book:    150
Do you want to enter more(Y/N):    N

Following are the books in the library:
```

(Contd...)

```
int count=0,i;
char ch;
float dummy=cos(0.0);
while(1)
{
    printf("Enter the information of book %d:\n", count+1);
    printf("Enter the title of the book:\t");
    gets(library[count].title);
    printf("Enter the author's name:\t");
    gets(library[count].author);
    printf("Enter the number of pages in the book:\t");
    scanf("%d",&library[count].pages);
    printf("Enter the price of the book:\t");
    scanf("%f",&library[count].price);
    flushall();
    count++;
    if(count==MAXBOOKS)
    {
        printf("Capacity full\n");
        break;
    }
   else
    {
        printf("Do you want to enter more(Y/N):\t");
        ch=getche();
        printf("\n");
        if(ch=='y'||ch=='Y')
            continue;
        else
            break;
    }
}
printf("\nFollowing are the books in the library:\n\n");
for(i=0;i<count;i++)
{
printf("%s by %s: %d pages is of Rs. %6.2f\n",
library[i].title, library[i].author, library[i].pages,
library[i].price);
}
}
```

```
The law and the lawyer by M K Gandhi: 200 pages is of Rs. 125.00
Rise and fall of great powers by Paul Kennedy: 250 pages is of Rs. 150.00
```

Remarks:

- The dummy statement `float dummy=cos(0.0);` is used to load the floating point version of the `scanf` function
- Addition of this statement removes the problem of the `scanf` function associated with the usage of floating point values in an array of structures in older compilers like Borland Turbo C 3.0

Program 9-17 | A program that solves the problem of the scanf function associated with the usage of floating values in an array of structures in older compilers like Borland Turbo C 3.0

9.5 Structures within a Structure (Nested Structures)

A structure can be nested within another structure. Nested structures are used to create complex data types. Consider the example of structure type phonebook_entry created in Table 9.2(c). A record in a phone book consists of the fields: name of a person and his mobile number. The field 'name of a person' is a composite field that further consists of a person's first name and his last name. To construct such a type, which consists of composite fields, nested structures are used. The program segment in Program 9-18 illustrates the use of nested structures.

Line | Prog 9-18.c

```
1  //Nested structures
2  #include<stdio.h>
3  #include<conio.h>
4  struct name
5  {
6      char first_name[20];
7      char last_name[20];
8  };
9  struct phonebook_entry
10 {
11     struct name person_name;
12     char mobile_no[15];
13 };
14 main()
15 {
16     struct phonebook_entry p1, p2;
17     printf("Enter the details of the first person:\n");
18     printf("Enter the first name of the person:\t");
19     gets(p1.person_name.first_name);
20     printf("Enter the last name of the person:\t");
21     gets(p1.person_name.last_name);
22     printf("Enter the mobile number:\t");
23     gets(p1.mobile_no);
24 
25     printf("Enter the details of the second person:\n");
26     printf("Enter the first name of the person:\t");
27     gets(p2.person_name.first_name);
28     printf("Enter the last name of the person:\t");
29     gets(p2.person_name.last_name);
30     printf("Enter the mobile number:\t");
31     gets(p2.mobile_no);
32 
33     printf("\nRecords in the phone book are:\n");
34     printf("-----------------------------------\n");
35     printf("%s %s:\t%10s\n",p1.person_name.first_name,
36     p1.person_name.last_name, p1.mobile_no);
37     printf("%s %s:\t%10s\n",p2.person_name.first_name,
38     p2.person_name.last_name, p2.mobile_no);
39 }
```

Output window

```
Enter the details of the first person:
Enter the first name of the person:     Parul
Enter the last name of the person:      Sood
Enter the mobile number:    9882687681
Enter the details of the second person:
Enter the first name of the person:     Rajini
Enter the last name of the person:      Bansal
Enter the mobile number: 9412345980

Records in the phone book are:
----------------------------------------
Parul Sood :      9882687681
Rajini Bansal:    9412345980
```

Remark:

- As the structure member `person_name` is of type `struct name`, the dot operator is applied twice to access its members (as shown in line numbers 35-38)

Program 9-18 | A program that illustrates the use of nested structures

The important points about nested structures are as follows:

1. The nested structures contain the members of other structure types. The structure types used in the structure definition should be complete.

2. It is even possible to define a structure type within the declaration-list of another structure-type definition. The piece of code in Program 9-19 illustrates this fact.

Prog 9-19.c

```
//A structure type defined within another structure type definition
#include<stdio.h>
struct phone_entry
{
    struct name
    {
        char fnam[20];
        char lnam[20];
    } pnam;
    char mno[10];
};
main()
{
struct phone_entry per1={{"Anil","Kumar"}}, per2={{"Anand"}};
printf("Enter the mobile number of %s %s\n",per1.pnam.fnam, per1.pnam.lnam);
gets(per1.mno);
 printf("Enter the mobile number of %s %s\n",per2.pnam.fnam, per2.pnam.lnam);
gets(per2.mno);
printf("\nPhone book entries are:\n");
printf("------------------------\n");
printf("%s %s:\t%s\n", per1.pnam.fnam, per1.pnam.lnam, per1.mno);
printf("%s %s:\t%s\n", per2.pnam.fnam, per2.pnam.lnam, per2.mno);
}
```

Output window

```
Enter the mobile number of Anil Kumar
9814456767
Enter the mobile number of Anand
9888852525

Phone book entries are:
------------------------
Anil Kumar    9814456767
Anand    9888852525
```

Remark:

- The structure type struct name is defined within the declaration-list of the structure type struct phone_entry

Program 9-19 | A program illustrating that it is allowed to define a structure type within the structure definition-list of another structure-type definition

3. The member access operator is used to access the members of structure members, e.g. in Program 9-19, the member fnam of the structure member pnam of the structure variable per1 can be assessed by writing per1.pnam.fnam.
4. In principle, structures can be nested infinitely. However, practically the number of levels of nested structure definitions in a single structure definition list depends upon the translation limits➲ of the compiler.

➲ **Forward Reference:** Translation limits mentioned in ANSI/ISO specifications (Appendix C).

9.6 Functions and Structures

In Chapter 5, you have learnt about functions. You have seen that the flexibility of functions can be increased by passing arguments to functions. In the previous chapters, you have learnt about how to pass variables, arrays and pointers to functions. In this section, I will tell you how to pass structures to a function. The three ways of passing a structure object to a function are as follows:

1. Passing each member of a structure object as a separate argument
2. Passing the entire structure object by value
3. Passing the structure object by address/reference

9.6.1 Passing Each Member of a Structure Object as a Separate Argument

A structure object can be passed to a function by passing each member of the structure object. The members of the structure object can be passed by value or by address/reference. The piece of code in Program 9-20 illustrates the passing of structure objects by the means of passing each of its members by value and by address/reference.

Line | Prog 9-20.c

```
1  //Passing structure objects by passing their structure members
2  #include<stdio.h>
3  struct complex
4  {
5      int re;
6      int im;
7  };
8  add_complex(int, int, int, int);
9  mult_complex(int*,int*,int*,int*);
10 main()
11 {
12     struct complex no1, no2;
13     printf("Enter the real and imaginary parts of 1st number:\t");
14     scanf("%d %d",&no1.re, &no1.im);
15     printf("Enter the real and imaginary parts of 2nd number:\t");
16     scanf("%d %d",&no2.re, &no2.im);
17     add_complex(no1.re, no1.im, no2.re, no2.im);
18     mult_complex(&no1.re, &no1.im, &no2. re, &no2.im);
19 }
20 add_complex(int a, int b, int c, int d)
21 {
22 if(b+d<0)
23     printf("The result of their addition is %d%di\n",a+c,b+d);
24 else
25     printf("The result of their addition is %d+%di\n",a+c,b+d);
26 }
27 mult_complex(int* a, int* b, int* c, int*d)
28 {
29 int re, im;
30 re=*a * *c-*b * *d;
31 im=*a * *d + *b * *c;
32 if(im<0)
33     printf("The result of their multiplication is %d%di\n",re, im);
34 else
35     printf("The result of their multiplication is %d+%di\n",re, im);
36 }
```

Output window

```
Enter the real and imaginary parts of 1st number:  2 -3
Enter the real and imaginary parts of 2nd number:  4  5
The result of their addition is 6+2i
The result of their multiplication is 23-2i
```

Output window (second execution)

```
Enter the real and imaginary parts of 1st number:  -2 -3
Enter the real and imaginary parts of 2nd number:  4 -5
The result of their addition is 2-8i
The result of their multiplication is -23-2i
```

Remarks:

- In line number 17, each member of the structure objects no1 and no2 is passed by value to the function add_complex
- In line number 18, each member of the structure objects no1 and no2 is passed by address/reference to the function mult_complex

Program 9-20 | A program that illustrates the method of passing a structure object by passing its members

The observable points about passing a structure object by the means of passing its members are as follows:

1. This method of passing a structure object to a function is highly inefficient, unmanageable and infeasible if the number of members in a structure object to be passed is large.
2. This method of passing a structure to a function is suited if the structure contains only a few members. Also, the members must be of basic types or derived types but not of structure type (i.e. nested structures).
3. The members of the structure object can be passed by value or by address/reference.

9.6.2 Passing a Structure Object by Value

The member-by-member copy behavior of the assignment operator when applied on structures makes it possible to pass a structure object to, and return a structure object from a function by value. The piece of code in Program 9-21 illustrates the passing of a structure object to a function by value.

Prog 9-21.c

```
//Passing and returning structure objects by value
#include<stdio.h>
struct complex
{
    int re;
    int im;
};
struct complex add_complex(struct complex, struct complex);
main()
{
    struct complex no1, no2, no3;
    printf("Enter the real and imaginary parts of 1st number:\t");
    scanf("%d %d",&no1.re, &no1.im);
    printf("Enter the real and imaginary part of 2nd number:\t");
    scanf("%d %d",&no2.re, &no2.im);
    no3=add_complex(no1,no2);
    if(no3.im<0)
    printf("The result of their addition is %d%di\n",no3.re, no3.im);
    else
    printf("The result of their addition is %d+%di\n",no3.re, no3.im);
}
struct complex add_complex(struct complex a, struct complex b)
{
    struct complex temp;
    temp.re=a.re+b.re;
    temp.im=a.im+b.im;
    //It is invalid to write temp=a+b
    return temp;
}
```

Output window

```
Enter the real and imaginary parts of 1st number:   2 -3
Enter the real and imaginary parts of 2nd number:   4 5
The result of their addition is 6+2i
```

Output window (second execution)

```
Enter the real and imaginary parts of 1st number:   -2 -3
Enter the real and imaginary parts of 2nd number:   4 -5
The result of their addition is 2-8i
```

Remarks:

- The structure objects no1 and no2 are passed to the function add_complex by value
- This passing is possible because of member-by-member copy behavior of the assignment operator when applied on structures

Program 9-21 | A program that illustrates the passing of a structure object to a function by value

The observable points about passing structure objects to a function by value are as follows:

1. This method of passing a structure object to a function is better (i.e. manageable) than the previous method of the structure passing in which each member of the object is passed individually.
2. In this method, all the members of a structure object are passed together instead of being passed individually.
3. If the number of members in a structure object is quite large, this method involves large data movement. In such a case, the method of passing structure object via the pointer (as discussed in Section 9.6.3) will be more efficient.
4. As the structure objects are passed by value, the changes made in the formal parameters in the called function are not reflected back to the calling function. The piece of code in Program 9-22 illustrates this fact.

Prog 9-22.c

```
//Taking reflection of a point about a line inclined at 45° to the x-axis
#include<stdio.h>
struct point
{
    int x;
    int y;
};
reflectpoint(struct point);
main()
{
    struct point pt;
    printf("Enter the x and y coordinates of the point:\t");
    scanf("%d %d",&pt.x, &pt.y);
    reflectpoint(pt);
    printf("The x and y coordinates of the reflected point: (%d,%d)",pt.x, pt.y);
}
reflectpoint(struct point pt)
{
    int temp;
    temp= pt.x;
    pt.x=pt.y;
    pt.y=temp;
}
```

Output window

```
Enter the x and y coordinates of the point:    4 7
The x and y coordinates of the reflected point: (4,7)
```

Remark:

- The changes made in the structure object in the called function reflectpoint are not reflected back to the calling function main

Program 9-22 | A program to illustrate the usage of passing the structure objects by value

9.6.3 Passing a Structure Object by Address/Reference

If the number of members in a structure object is quite large, it is beneficial to pass the structure object by address/reference. This method of passing the structure object requires fixed data (i.e. equal to the size of a pointer) movement irrespective of the size of the structure object. The piece of code in Program 9-23 illustrates the method of passing the structure objects to a function by address/reference.

Line | Prog 9-23.c

```
1  //Passing and returning structure objects by address/reference
2  #include<stdio.h>
3  struct complex
4  {
5      int re;
6      int im;
7  };
8  struct complex mult_complex(struct complex*, struct complex*);
9  main()
10 {
11     struct complex no1, no2, no3;
12     printf("Enter the real and imaginary parts of Ist number:\t");
13     scanf("%d %d",&no1.re, &no1.im);
14     printf("Enter the real and imaginary parts of 2nd number:\t");
15     scanf("%d %d",&no2.re, &no2.im);
16     no3=mult_complex(&no1,&no2);
17     if(no3.im<0)
18     printf("The result of their multiplication is %d%di\n",no3.re, no3.im);
19     else
20     printf("The result of their multiplication is %d+%di\n",no3.re, no3.im);
21 }
22 struct complex mult_complex(struct complex* a, struct complex* b)
23 {
24     struct complex temp;
25     temp.re=a->re*b->re-a->im*b->im;
26     temp.im=a->re*b->im+a->im*b->re;
27     //It is invalid to write temp=a*b
28     return temp;
29 }
```

Output window

```
Enter the real and imaginary parts of Ist number:   2 -3
Enter the real and imaginary parts of 2nd number:   4 5
The result of their multiplication is 23-2i
```

Output window (second execution)

```
Enter the real and imaginary parts of Ist number:   -2 -3
Enter the real and imaginary parts of 2nd number:   4 -5
The result of their multiplication is -23-2i
```

Remark:

- In line number 16, the structure objects no1 and no2 are passed by address/reference to the function mult_complex

Program 9-23 | A program that illustrates the passing of a structure object to a function by address/reference

The observable points about passing the structure objects to a function by address/reference are as follows:

1. This method of passing a structure object to a function is better (i.e. efficient) than the previous method of passing a structure object by value.
2. In this method of passing a structure object, instead of passing the entire structure object, only the address of a structure object is passed. Hence, this method of structure passing requires less data movement.
3. Since a structure object is passed by address, the changes made in the objects pointed to by the formal parameters in the called function are reflected back to the calling function. The piece of code in Program 9-24 illustrates this fact.

Line | Prog 9-24.c

```
//Taking reflection of a point about a line inclined at 45° to the x-axis
#include<stdio.h>
struct point
{
```

Output window

```
Enter the x and y coordinates of the point:   4 7
The x and y coordinates of the reflected point: (7,4)
```

(Contd...)

Prog 9-24.c

```
    int x;
    int y;
};
reflectpoint(struct point*);
main()
{
    struct point pt;
    printf("Enter the x and y coordinates of the point:\t");
    scanf("%d %d",&pt.x, &pt.y);
    reflectpoint(&pt);
printf("The x and y coordinates of the reflected point: (%d,%d)",pt.x, pt.y);
}
reflectpoint(struct point* pt)
{
    int temp;
    temp= pt->x;
    pt->x=pt->y;
    pt->y=temp;
}
```

Output window

Remark:

- The changes made in the structure object in the called function reflectpoint are reflected back to the calling function main

Program 9-24 | A program to illustrate the usage of passing the structure objects by address/reference

9.7 typedef and Structures

In Section 9.2.2, we have seen that a structure object can be declared by using the keyword struct followed by the tag-name of the defined structure type and the identifier name of the object to be declared. The usage of the keyword struct while declaring a structure object sometimes proves to be a bit inconvenient. In Chapter 7, we have seen that the storage class specifier typedef can be used for creating syntactically convenient names (i.e. aliases). Thus, it can be used to create an alias for the defined structure type so that the keyword struct is not required repeatedly to declare the structure objects. The piece of code in Program 9-25 illustrates the use of the typedef storage class specifier along with structures.

Prog 9-25.c

```
//Use of typedef to create an alias for a structure type
#include<stdio.h>
typedef struct name
{
    char first_name[20];
    char last_name[20];
} NAME;
struct phonebook_entry
{
    NAME person_name;
    char mobile_no[11];
};
typedef struct phonebook_entry PH_ENTRY;
main()
```

Output window

```
Enter the details of the first person:
Enter the first name of the person:    Sam
Enter the last name of the person:    Mine
Enter the mobile number:    9870096971
Enter the details of the second person:
Enter the first name of the person:    Mani
Enter the last name of the person:    Kumar
Enter the mobile number:    9922134654

Records in the phone book are::
-----------------------------------
Sam Mine:    9870096971
Mani Kumar:    9922134654
```

(Contd...)

```
15 {
16     PH_ENTRY p1, p2;
17     printf("Enter the details of the first person:\n");
18     printf("Enter the first name of the person:\t");
19     gets(p1.person_name.first_name);
20     printf("Enter the last name of the person:\t");
21     gets(p1.person_name.last_name);
22     printf("Enter the mobile number:\t");
23     gets(p1.mobile_no);
24
25     printf("Enter the details of the second person:\n");
26     printf("Enter the first name of the person:\t");
27     gets(p2.person_name.first_name);
28     printf("Enter the last name of the person:\t");
29     gets(p2.person_name.last_name);
30     printf("Enter the mobile number:\t");
31     gets(p2.mobile_no);
32
33     printf("\nRecords in the phone book are::\n");
34     printf("------------------------------------\n");
35     printf("%s %s:\t %10s\n",p1.person_name.first_name,
36     p1.person_name.last_name, p1.mobile_no);
37     printf("%s %s:\t %s\n",p2.person_name.first_name,
38     p2.person_name.last_name, p2.mobile_no);
39 }
```

Remarks:

- The storage class specifier typedef is used to name a new type or to rename an old type
- In line number 3, it is used to name a new type
- In line number 13, it is used to rename the already defined type struct phonebook_entry

Program 9-25 | A program that illustrates the use of the storage class specifier typedef to name and rename a structure type

A typedef name, i.e. the created alias name can be the same as the structure name. The piece of code in Program 9-26 illustrates this fact.

Prog 9-26.c

```
//Alias name can be same as structure name
#include<stdio.h>
struct name
{
    char first_name[20];
    char last_name[20];
};
typedef struct name name; //←typedef name is same as structure tag-name
main()
{
name person;
printf("Enter the first name and the last name of the person:\n");
scanf("%s %s",person.first_name, person.last_name);
printf("The name of the person is %s %s",person.first_name, person.last_name);
}
```

Output window

```
Enter the first name and the last name of the person:
Arvind Mishra
The name of the person is Arvind Mishra
```

Remarks:

- In C, it is not allowed to declare an object of the defined structure type by using the tag-name of the defined structure type without using the keyword struct
- However, in C++, this rigidity was relaxed

Program 9-26 | A program that illustrates the use of the storage class specifier typedef

9.8 Unions

Just like structures, unions are used to create user-defined types. A **union** is a collection of one or more variables, possibly of different types. All the major aspects of union, like defining a union type, declaring objects of a union type, using and performing operations on objects of a union type are the same as that of structures. The only difference between them is in the terms of storage of their members. In structures, a separate memory is allocated to each member, while in unions, all the members of an object share the same memory.

A union object is used only if one of its constituting members is to be used at a time. In such a situation, it proves to be memory efficient as compared to structures. The important points about unions are as follows:

1. **Defining a union type:** A union type is defined in the same way as a structure type, with the only difference that the keyword `union` is used instead of the keyword `struct` to define the union type.
2. **Declaring union objects:** Objects of a union type can be declared either at the time of union type definition or after the union type definition in a separate declaration statement. Objects of the union type can be created after the union definition only if the defined union type is named or tagged.

The general form of declaring a union object is:

[storage_class_specifier] [type_qualifier] **union named_union_type identifier_name** [=intialization_list [,...]];

The important points about a union object declaration are as follows:

1. The terms enclosed with the square brackets are optional and might not be present in a union variable declaration statement. The terms shown in **bold** are the mandatory parts of a union object declaration statement.
2. A union object declaration consists of:
   a. The keyword `union` for declaring union variables. It can also be used in conjunction with `const` qualifier for declaring a union constant.
   b. The tag-name of the defined union type.
   c. Comma-separated list of identifiers. The variables can optionally be initialized by providing initialization lists. However, the initialization of constants is must.
   d. A terminating semicolon.
3. **Size of a union object or union type:** Upon the declaration of a union object, the amount of memory allocated to it is the amount necessary to contain its largest member. It can be checked by using the `sizeof` operator. The piece of code in Program 9-27 illustrates the use of the `sizeof` operator on a union object.

Prog 9-27.c	Output window

<pre>//Unions and sizeof operator
#include<stdio.h>
union variables
{
    char a;
    int b;</pre>
	Objects of type union variables will take 8 bytes
	Union variable var takes 8 bytes
	Remarks:
	• The sizeof operator when applied on unions returns the size of its largest member

(Contd...)

```
    float c;
    double d;
};
main()
{
union variables var;
printf("Objects of type union variables will take %d bytes\n",sizeof(union variables));
printf("Union variable var takes %d bytes\n", sizeof(var));
}
```

- Since in the union type union variables, the size of the largest member (i.e. d of type double) is 8, the sizeof operator when applied on the union type union variables or on the objects of this type, outputs 8

Program 9-27 | A program that illustrates the use of the sizeof operator on unions

4. **Address-of a union object:** The members of a union object are stored in the memory in such a way that they overlap each other. All the members of a union object start from the same memory location, which in fact, is the same as the starting address of the union object. This can be checked by applying the address-of operator to the union object as well as to its constituting members. The application of the address-of operator on a union object and its constituent members is illustrated in Program 9-28.

Prog 9-28.c

```
//Address-of operator and unions
#include<stdio.h>
union variables
{
    char a;
    int b;
    float c;
};
main()
{
  union variables var;
  printf("Starting address of var is %p\n",&var);
  printf("Starting address of 1st member is %p\n",&var.a);
  printf("Starting address of 2nd member is %p\n",&var.b);
  printf("Starting address of 3rd member is %p\n",&var.c);
  printf("Starting address of 4th member is %p\n",&var.d);
}
```

Memory contents

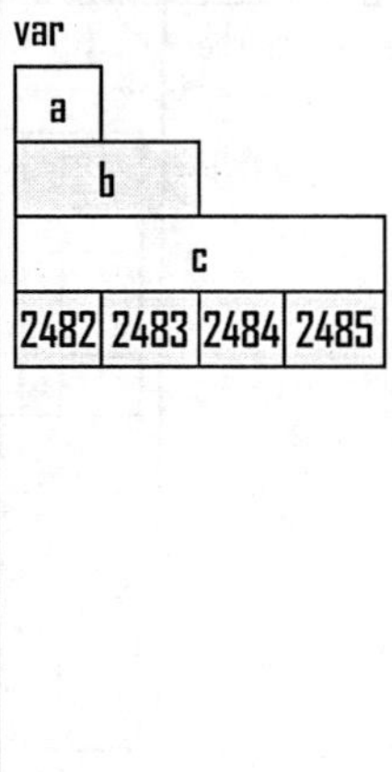

Output window

```
Starting address of var is 1A5F:2482
Starting address of 1st member is 1A5F:2482
Starting address of 2nd member is 1A5F:2482
Starting address of 3rd member is 1A5F:2482
```

Remark:

- In the defined type union variables, the first byte (lower order) is shared by all the three members a, b and c. The second byte is shared by the members b and c. The third and the fourth bytes are exclusively owned by the member c

Program 9-28 | A program illustrating that all the members of a union object start from the same memory location

5. **Initialization of a union object:** Since the members of a union object share the same memory, the union object can hold the value of only one of its member at a time. Hence, while initializing a union object, it is allowed to initialize its first member only. The piece of code in Program 9-29 illustrates this fact.

Line	Prog 9-29.c
1	//Initialization of union objects
2	#include<stdio.h>
3	union variables
4	{
5	char a;
6	int b;
7	float c;
8	};
9	main()
10	{
11	union variables var={'A', 2, 2.5};
12	printf("The values of the members are %c %d %f", var.a, var.b, var.c);
13	}

Output window

Compilation error "Declaration syntax error in function main()"

Remarks:

- The initialization of all the members of the union object var, in line number 11 gives a compilation error
- To remove this error, initialize only the first member of the union object var and then re-execute the code

Program 9-29 | A program illustrating that only the first member of a union object can be initialized

Since the members of a union object share the memory in an overlapped fashion, only one member at a time can be assigned a value. Accessing the value of this member gives a meaningful result, while accessing the value of any other member gives a garbage value as a result. The piece of code in Program 9-30 illustrates this fact.

Trace	Prog 9-30.c
	//Access only the lastly assigned member of a
	//union object
	#include<stdio.h>
	union variables
	{
	char a;
	int b;
	};
1	main()
	{
2	union variables var={'A'};
3	printf("First member is %c\n",var.a);
4	var.b=300;
5	printf("First member now is %c\n",var.a);
6	printf("Second member is %d\n",var.b);
7	var.a='A';
8	printf("First member now is %c\n",var.a);
9	printf("Second member now is %d\n",var.b);
10	}

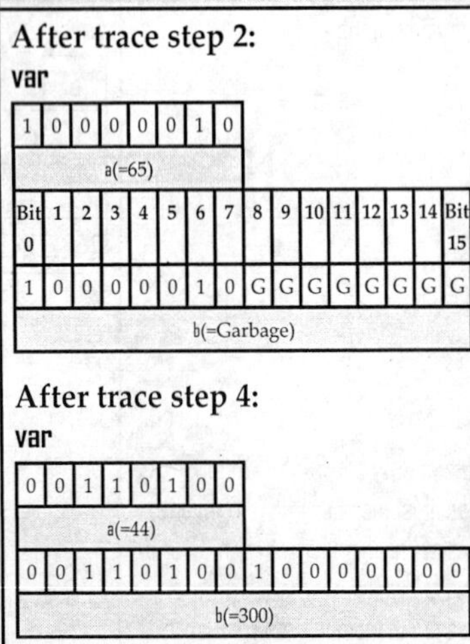

Note that in the above illustrations, the bit 0, i.e., LSB is present on the left-hand side

Output window

First member is A
First member now is ,
Second member is 300
First member now is A
Second member now is 321

Remarks:

- After trace step 2, the member a of the union variable var is initialized with the character constant 'A', i.e. 65
- This also initializes the lower order byte of the member b, while its upper order byte still contains garbage value
- After trace step 4, the value assigned to member b, i.e. 300 completely modifies the content of the member a

(*Contd...*)

			• Hence, the value of member a becomes 44 (i.e. 00101100 in binary number system) • After trace step 7, when the value 'A' i.e. 65 is placed in the member a, the lower order byte of the member b is modified and becomes 65 • Hence, the value of the entire member b comes out to be 65+256=321

Program 9-30 | A program illustrating that accessing only the lastly assigned member gives a meaningful result

One of the potential pitfalls in using the unions is the possibility of accidentally retrieving the value currently stored in the union through an inappropriate member. For example, in Program 9-30, if the last assignment is to the member a and the programmer accidentally retrieves the value of the member b, the result will be a garbage value.

3. **Operations on union objects:** All the operations on union objects are applied in the same way as they are applied on the structure objects. For example, the members of a union object can be accessed in the same way as the members of a structure object can be assessed, i.e. by using a member access operator.

   Similar to structures, the following operations are feasible on unions:

   a. Assigning a union object to a union variable of the same type.
   b. Passing a union object or a pointer to a union object as a function argument.
   c. Returning a union object from a function, etc.

9.9 Practical Application of Unions

In the previous chapters, you have used printf, scanf, getch and other library functions a number of times. These library functions perform rudimentary operations like printing an output on the screen, reading input from the keyboard, etc. In other words, these functions interact with the hardware of the machine. However, if you delve deeper into the technical details of how these functions interact with the hardware, you will come to know that these functions do not have any direct interaction with the hardware. The process through which the library functions interact with the hardware of the machine is shown in Figure 9.5.

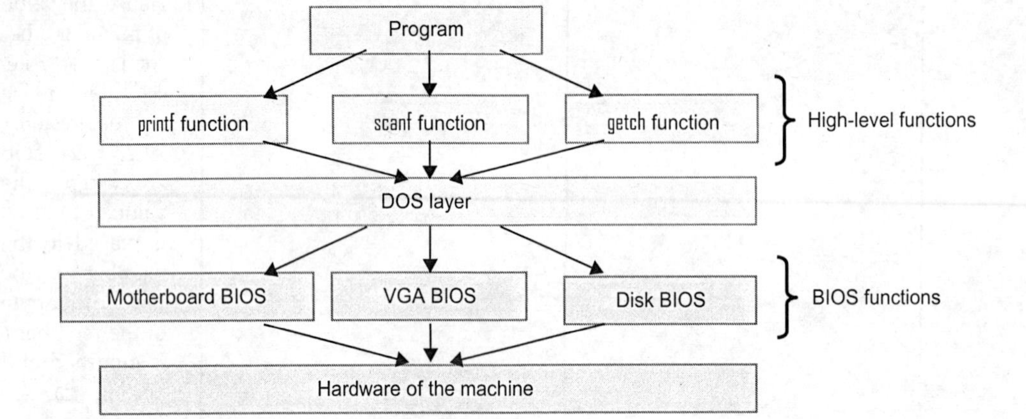

Figure 9.5 | Hardware interaction

The important points about the mechanism through which hardware interaction is performed are as follows:

1. The interaction with the hardware of the machine is done by calling the low-level machine specific code routines, generally provided by the hardware manufacturers. These routines are known as **B**asic **I**nput **O**utput **S**ystem (**BIOS**) routines.
2. There are several different BIOSes. For example, the motherboard BIOS performs the initial hardware detection and system booting. The Video Graphic Adaptor (VGA) BIOS handles all the screen manipulation functions. The Disk BIOS manages disk input–output and other disk operations.
3. These BIOSes are generally placed in the **R**ead **O**nly **M**emory (**ROM**) to ensure that they are always available and are not affected by the disk failures. Thus, they are also known as **ROM-BIOS**es.
4. There is a layer of Disk Operating System (DOS) software, which sits on the top of these lower-level BIOSes and provides a common access to these lower-level BIOSes in a form that is easier to use in the programs.
5. A call to a library function generates a DOS call, which may in turn call an appropriate BIOS routine to interact with the hardware.
6. Thus, a task performed by a library function can also be performed by directly calling DOS or by calling the lower-level BIOS routines to perform the task.

9.9.1 Calling DOS and BIOS Functions

DOS and BIOS functions can be called by generating **interrupts**. An **interrupt** is a signal to the **microprocessor** or just the **processor** of the computer informing that an event has occurred and it needs an immediate attention. When the processor receives an interrupt signal, it suspends the execution of the current program and executes a specific routine (DOS or BIOS routine) known as **Interrupt Service Routine (ISR)**. An interrupt signal can be generated either by hardware or a software function call. When it is generated by hardware (e.g. key press), it is known as **hardware interrupt**. If it is generated by giving a call to the software functions like `int86`, `int86x`, `intdos`, `intdosx`, etc., it is called **software interrupt**. In this section, we will look at how to generate the software interrupts using the functions `int86` and `intdos`.

The prototype of the function int86 is int int86(int intno, union REGS* inregs, union REG* outregs);. and the function intdos is intdos(union REGS* inregs, union REGS* outregs);.

The important points about the usage of the functions int86 and intdos are as follows:

1. Calling ISRs (DOS or BIOS routines) is not as simple as calling the high-level functions because ISRs are not named. These are stored at the specific locations in the memory and can be executed by transferring the program control to those memory locations. It is very cumbersome to remember the starting address of every ISR. Thus, to abbreviate the problem, an index table, known as **Interrupt Vector Table** (**IVT**) is provided. The IVT is stored in the first 1024 bytes of the memory, i.e. from the memory address 0x0000-0x03FF. There are 256 entries in IVT and each entry is of 4 bytes, which specifies the complete (i.e. segment and offset) address of the interrupt service routine.
2. To call a BIOS service routine, an integer number is provided as an argument to the function int86. This integer argument is an index of an IVT entry, where the address of the specific ISR is stored. From IVT, the address of the ISR is retrieved and the control is transferred to the starting memory location of the ISR. The mentioned procedure is shown in Figure 9.6.

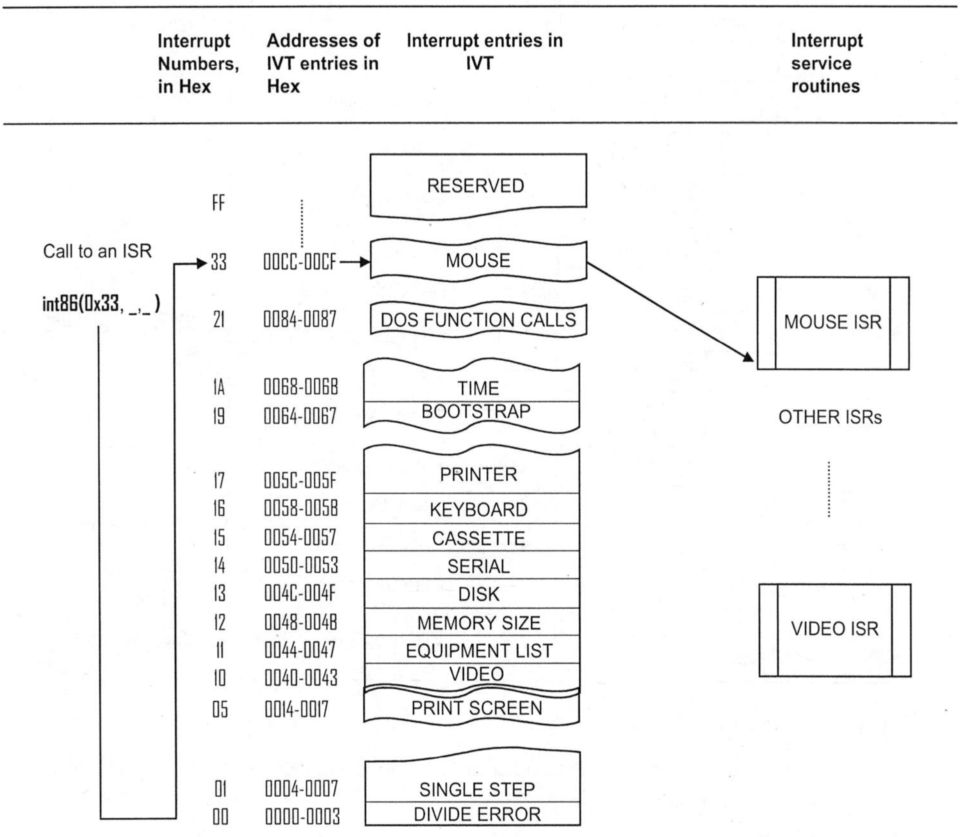

Figure 9.6 | Interrupt vector table and its use

3. To call a DOS service routine, the functions intdos and intdosx are used. The DOS services are grouped together under the interrupt number 0x21. The functions intdos and intdosx execute interrupt 0x21 to invoke the specified DOS function. Since these functions always execute interrupt 0x21, the interrupt number is not given as an input to them.
4. Like arguments are given to the functions, similarly inputs are given to ISRs, which determine their behavior. The inputs to ISRs are given by placing the values in the CPU's (i.e. microprocessor's) registers. The CPU register is a sort of memory, which is internal to it, provides direct and very fast data access as compared to the external memories like cache, **R**andom **A**ccess **M**emory (RAM) and hard disk. The number of registers in a CPU and their size depends upon the architecture of a microprocessor. The registers available in 8086 microprocessor and its family are shown in Figure 9.7.

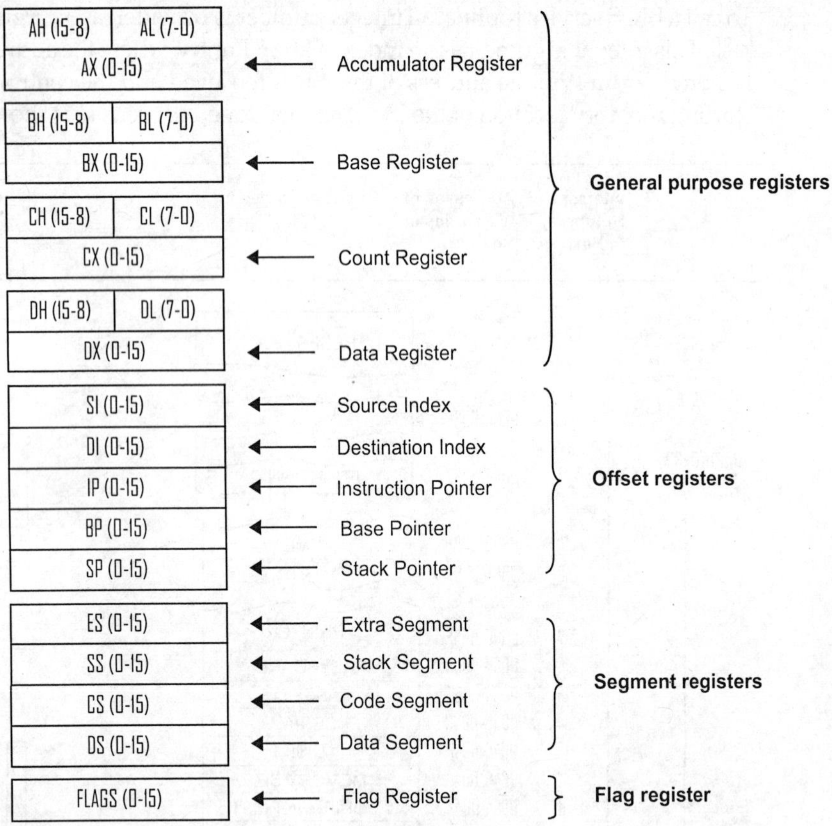

Figure 9.7 | Registers available in 8086 microprocessor and their classification

As shown in Figure 9.7, the registers available in 8086 microprocessor are classified as:

1. General-purpose registers
2. Offset registers
3. Segment registers
4. Flag register

The general-purpose registers, i.e. Accumulator register, Base register, Count register and Data register are 16-bit registers and are referred to as AX, BX, CX and DX, respectively. It is also possible to individually access the lower and the higher bytes of these registers. The lower and the higher bytes of these registers are referred to as AL, AH, BL, BH, CL, CH, DL and DH, respectively. The other registers can be accessed in totality, i.e. all the 16 bits at a time. In Borland Turbo C 3.0/4.5, a type union REGS has been defined in the header file dos.h, which helps in passing the information to and from the functions int86 and intdos.

The important points about the predefined type union REGS are as follows:

1. The type union REGS has been defined in the header file dos.h as:
```
union REGS
{
    struct WORDREGS x;
    struct BYTEREGS h;
};
```
   The types struct WORDREGS and struct BYTEREGS have also been defined in the header file dos.h as:
```
struct WORDREGS
{
    unsigned int ax, bx, cx, dx;
    unsigned int si, di, cflag, flags;
};
struct BYTEREGS
{
    unsigned char al, ah, bl, bh;
    unsigned char cl, ch, dl, dh;
};
```
2. The objects of the type union REGS can be declared as:
   union REGS identifier_names; e.g. union REGS inregs, outregs;
3. The 16-bit members (i.e. ax, bx, cx, etc.) are accessed through the member x, and 8-bit members (i.e. al, ah, bl, bh, etc.) are accessed through the member h of the declared objects of the union type union REGS. For example, if the object iregs is defined to be of the union type union REGS. The 16-bit member bx is accessed as iregs.x.bx while its higher and lower parts, i.e. bh and bl are accessed as iregs.h.bh and iregs.h.bl, respectively.
4. An input to the interrupt service routine can be given by setting the values of the specific members of the declared objects of the type union REGS and by passing them by address/reference to the functions int86 and intdos. The value of a member of a declared object of the type union REGS can be set as:
```
inregs.x.ax=1;   //←Setting the value of the member ax to be 1
inregs.h.ch=2;   //←Setting the value of the member ch to be 2
```

9.9.2 Interrupt Programming

Examples of interrupt programming are given in Programs 9-31 to 9-36. The elaborated interrupt list is given in Appendix D for reference. The exhaustive interrupt list may run up to thousands of pages and such a listing is beyond the scope of this book.

Prog 9-31a.c
Using library function

```
//Printing text at specific location using the function gotoxy
#include<stdio.h>
#include<conio.h>
main()
{
int row, col;
clrscr();
printf("Enter the row and column number in which you want\
to print the text\t");
scanf("%d %d",&row, &col);
gotoxy(row,col);
printf("Hello Readers");
}
```

Prog 9-31b.c
Using interrupt programming

```
//Implementing function gotoxy using interrupt programming
#include<stdio.h>
#include<conio.h>
#include<dos.h>
void mygotoxy(int, int);
main()
{
int row, col;
clrscr();
printf("Enter the row and column in which you want\
to print the text\t");
scanf("%d %d",&row, &col);
mygotoxy(row,col);
printf("Hello Readers");
}
void mygotoxy(int x, int y)
{
union REGS inregs, oregs;
inregs.h.ah=2;
inregs.h.bh=0;
inregs.h.dh=x;
inregs.h.dl=y;
int86(0x10, &inregs, &oregs);
}
```

Output window (Turbo C 3.0)

```
Enter the row and column number in which you want to print the text:    4 5


    Hello Readers
```

Remarks:

- The program calls a ROM-BIOS function that positions the cursor in the desired row and column
- The associated interrupt has number 0x10 in hexadecimal (i.e. 16 in decimal)
- There are a number of services available under this interrupt like positioning the cursor on the screen, changing the size of the cursor, plotting a pixel on the screen, etc
- These service routines have a service number associated with them. The associated service number is to be placed in the AH register before the interrupt is being called
- Refer Appendix D for an elaborated description of ROM-BIOS services
- The function call `int86(0x10, &inregs, &oregs);` can also be written as `int86(16, &inregs, &oregs);`
- Generally, interrupts are numbered in hexadecimal and thus, the first method of calling the function is preferred
- All the programs making the use of interrupts work with Turbo C 3.0 compiler for DOS but not with Turbo C 4.5 and MS-VC++ 6.0 compilers for Windows. These compilers work with 32-bit environment (i.e. Windows) and create 32-bit programs, whereas interrupts work only with 16-bit programs

Program 9-31 | A program that illustrates the usage and the implementation of the function gotoxy

Prog 9-32a.c
Using library function

```
//Reading a character using the function getche
#include<stdio.h>
#include<conio.h>
main()
{
char ch;
clrscr();
printf("Enter a character:\t");
ch=getche();
printf("\nThe character that you entered is %c",ch);
}
```

Prog 9-32b.c
Using interrupt programming

```
//Implementing the function getche using the interrupt programming
#include<stdio.h>
#include<conio.h>
#include<dos.h>
char mygetche();
main()
{
char ch;
clrscr();
printf("Enter a character:\t");
ch=mygetche();
printf("\nThe character that you entered is %c",ch);
}
char mygetche()
{
union REGS inregs, oregs;
inregs.h.ah=1;
intdos(&inregs, &oregs);
return oregs.h.al;
}
```

Output window (Turbo C 3.0)

```
Enter a character:    H
The character that you entered is H
```

Remarks:

- The program calls a DOS routine that reads a character from the standard input with echo
- The DOS routines are grouped together under the interrupt number 0x21 in hexadecimal (i.e. 16 in decimal)
- There are a number of services available under this interrupt like read a character, write a character on the screen, write a character to the printer, get machine name, create directory, rename directory, delete file, etc.
- These service routines have a service number associated with them. The associated service number is to be placed in the AH register before the interrupt is called
- Refer Appendix D for an elaborated description of DOS services
- The function call `intdos(&inregs, &oregs);` can also be written as `int86(0x21, &inregs, &oregs);`

Program 9-32 | A program that illustrates the usage and the implementation of the function getche

Prog 9-33a.c
Using library function

```
//Printing the character using the function putch
#include<stdio.h>
#include<conio.h>
main()
{
char ch;
```

Prog 9-33b.c
Using interrupt programming

```
//Implementing the function putch using the interrupt programming
#include<stdio.h>
#include<conio.h>
#include<dos.h>
myputch();
main()
```

(Contd...)

Prog 9-33a.c
Using library function

```
clrscr();
printf("The character is:\t");
putch('A');
}
```

Prog 9-33b.c
Using interrupt programming

```
{
char ch;
clrscr();
printf("The character is:\t");
myputch();
}
myputch()
{
union REGS inregs, oregs;
inregs.h.ah=2;
inregs.h.dl='A';
intdos(&inregs, &oregs);
}
```

Output window (Turbo C 3.0)

```
The character is:	A
```

Remarks:

- The program calls a DOS routine to implement the functionality of the putch function
- The routine that writes a character onto the screen has service number 2
- The service number is placed in the AH register by assigning 2 to inregs.h.ah before the interrupt is called
- Refer Appendix D to see that the character to be written is placed in the DL register
- In the given code, the character 'A' is placed in the DL register by assigning 'A' to inregs.h.dl

Program 9-33 | A program that illustrates the usage and the implementation of the function putch

Prog 9-34.c
Using library function

```
//Printing a string on the screen by using the interrupt programming
#include<stdio.h>
#include<conio.h>
#include<dos.h>
main()
{
union REGS inregs, oregs;
char *ch="Interrupt Programming$";
clrscr();
inregs.h.ah=9;
inregs.x.dx=(unsigned int)ch;
intdos(&inregs,&oregs);
}
```

Output window (Turbo C 3.0)

```
Interrupt Programming
```

Remarks:

- The service number of the DOS routine that prints a string on to the screen is 9. It is to be placed in the AH register before the interrupt is called, thus 9 is assigned to inregs.h.ah
- The segment:offset address of the string that is to be printed is to be placed in the DX register
- ch points to the base address of the string that is to be printed
- Thus, ch is assigned to inregs.x.dx. But, since ch is of type char*, it has to be explicitly type casted to unsigned int before assigning to inregs.x.dx
- The program prints a string on the screen without using the printf and puts function

Program 9-34 | A program that illustrates the usage and the implementation of the function puts

Prog 9-35.c
Using library function

```
//Getting the machine name using the interrupt programming
#include<stdio.h>
#include<conio.h>
#include<alloc.h>
#include<dos.h>
char* machinename();
main()
{
clrscr();
printf("The name of the machine is %s", machinename());
}
char* machinename()
{
union REGS inregs, oregs;
char *ch=(char*)malloc(16);
inregs.h.ah=0x5E;
inregs.x.dx=(unsigned int)ch;
intdos(&inregs,&oregs);
return ch;
}
```

Output window (Turbo C 3.0)

```
The name of the machine is COMP2
```

Remarks:

- The service number of the DOS routine that get the machine name is 5E
- Thus, the hexadecimal value 5E is placed in the AH register by assigning the value to inregs.h.ah
- The service routine also expects the base address of a 16-byte buffer (i.e. character array) in which the machine name will be placed to be assigned to the DX register
- Instead of the function call intdos(&inregs, &oregs); the function call int86(0x21, inregs, oregs); can also be used

Program 9-35 | A program that illustrates the usage of the interrupt programming to get the machine name

Prog 9-36.c
Using library function

```
//Mouse Programming using interrupt programming
#include<stdio.h>
#include<conio.h>
#include<dos.h>
initmouse();
showmouseptr();
union REGS iregs, oregs;
main()
{
    clrscr();
    printf("Developing the mouse support\n");
    initmouse();
    getch();
}
initmouse()
{
    iregs.x.ax=0;
    int86(0x33, &iregs, &oregs);
    if(oregs.x.ax==0)
        printf("Mouse not supported by the system");
    else
        showmouseptr();
}
```

Output window (Turbo C 3.0)

```
Developing the mouse support
```

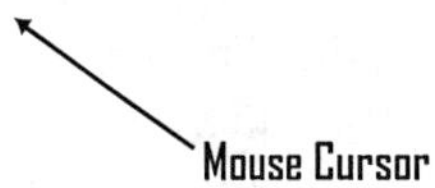

Remarks:

- The interrupt number for developing the mouse support is 0x33
- The program implements only two services, i.e. initialize the mouse support and show the mouse pointer

(Contd...)

Prog 9-36.c Using library function	Output window (Turbo C 3.0)

showmouseptr()
{
    iregs.x.ax=1;
    int86(0x33,&iregs,&oregs);
}
	• Refer Appendix D and implement other services to read the position and button status of the mouse, to define the horizontal and the vertical cursor range, to change the shape of the cursor, etc

Program 9-36 | A program that illustrates the usage of the interrupt programming to provide mouse support

9.10 Enumerations

In C language, **enumerations** provide another way to create user-defined types. An enumeration type is designed for the objects that can have a limited set of values. For example, consider an application in which we want a variable to hold a Boolean value. We can create an enumeration type BOOL that have two values FALSE and TRUE. The values FALSE and TRUE are known as **enumeration constants.** The variables of type BOOL can either have value FALSE or TRUE (i.e. Boolean value). Note that the values FALSE and TRUE are not the strings, but are integer constants. The compiler internally associates an integer value each with the names FALSE and TRUE. Thus, any operation that is applicable on an integer constant can be applied on them and any operation that is applicable on a variable of integer type can be applied on a variable of type BOOL. Since the integer values are represented by the names, the enumeration type helps in making the programs more readable. The important points about enumerations are as follows:

1. **Definition of an enumeration type:** The general form of an enumeration-type definition is:

   [storage_class_specifier][type_qualifier] **enum** [tag-name] **{enumeration-list}**[identifier=initializer[,...]];

   The important points about the definition of an enumeration type are as follows:

   i. The terms enclosed within the square brackets are optional and might not be present in the definition of an enumeration type. The terms shown in **bold** are mandatory parts of an enumeration definition.
   ii. An enumeration definition consists of a keyword enum, followed by an optional identifier name known as **enumeration tag-name** and a comma-separated list of **enumerators** enclosed within braces. All the enumerators present in the enumeration list forms an **enumeration set.**
   iii. An **enumerator** is an identifier that can hold an integer value. It is also known as the **enumeration constant**. An integer value can optionally be assigned to an enumerator, e.g. in the enumeration-type definition enum BOOLEAN {true=1, false=0};, the integer constants 1 and 0 are assigned to the enumerators true and false, respectively.
   iv. The names of the enumerators in the enumeration list must be unique.
   v. The values assigned to enumerators in the enumeration list need not be unique, e.g. the enumeration definition enum COLORS {red=2, green=1, yellow=1}; is perfectly valid.
   vi. Each enumeration constant has a scope that begins just after its appearance in the enumeration list. Due to this rule, the enumeration definition enum COLORS {red=2, green=red, yellow=green}; is perfectly valid.
   vii. Each enumerator in an enumeration list names a value. The enumeration constants are like symbolic constants except that their values are set automatically. By default, the first enumerator has the value 0. Each subsequent enumerator, if not

explicitly assigned a value, has a value 1 greater than the value of the enumerator that immediately precedes it. The piece of code in Program 9-37 illustrates the interpretation of this rule.

Prog 9-37.c

```
//If not explicitly specified, values to the enumeration constants are
//automatically assigned
#include<stdio.h>
enum CARS {alto, omni, esteem=3, wagonR, swift=1, dzire};
main()
{
 printf("The value of various enumeration constants are:\n");
 printf("%d %d %d %d %d %d", alto, omni, esteem, wagonR, swift, dzire);
}
```

Output window

```
The values of various enumeration constants are:
0 1 3 4 1 2
```

Remarks:

- The first enumerator, i.e. alto is automatically initialized with 0
- Each subsequent enumerator, if not explicitly assigned a value, has a value 1 greater than the value of the enumerator that immediately precedes it. Thus, the enumeration constant omni will have the value 1
- The enumeration constant esteem is explicitly given a value 3
- The enumeration constant wagonR will have the value 3+1=4
- Similarly, the enumeration constants swift and dzire will have the values 1 and 2, respectively

Program 9-37 | A program to illustrate that the values of enumeration constants are set automatically

viii. The enumeration definition can optionally have the storage class specifier and type qualifiers. However, they should be used in an enumeration-type definition statement only if the objects of the defined enumeration type are declared at the same time.

ix. The enumeration definition is a statement and must be terminated with a semicolon.

2. **Declaring objects of an enumeration type:** There are two ways to declare variables of an enumeration type:

   a. **At the time of enumeration-type definition:** Objects of an enumeration type can be declared at the time of enumeration-type definition. The variable declarations of the defined enumerated type given in Table 9.7 are valid.

Table 9.7 | Declaration of enumeration variables at the time of the enumeration-type definition

enum BOOL {false, true} flag1, flag2; (a)	enum {false, true} flag1, flag2; (b)

The declarations of the constants of the defined enumerated type given in Table 9.8 are valid.

Table 9.8 | Declaration of the enumeration constants at the time of enumeration-type definition

enum BOOL {false, true} const flag1=true, flag2=false; (a)	const enum BOOL {false, true} flag1=true, flag2=false; (b)
enum {false, true} const flag1=true, flag2=false; (c)	const enum {false, true} flag1=true, flag2=false; (d)

b. **After enumeration-type definition in a separate declaration statement**: Objects of an enumeration type can be created after its definition only if it is named or tagged. The keyword `enum` is used to declare the variables of the defined enumeration type. It is used in conjunction with the `const` qualifier to create the constants of the newly created type. The general form of declaring the objects of the defined enumeration type is:

[storage_class_specifier][type_qualifier]**enum named_eumeration_type identifier_name**[=initializer[,...]];

The important points about the declaration of an object of the defined enumeration type are as follows:

i. The terms enclosed within the square brackets are optional and might not be present in an enumeration object declaration. The terms shown in **bold** are the mandatory parts of the enumeration object declaration.

ii. An enumeration object declaration consists of:

   a. The keyword `enum` for declaring the enumeration variables. The keyword `enum` in conjunction with the `const` qualifier for declaring the constant of the defined enumeration type.
   b. The tag name of the defined enumeration type.
   c. Comma-separated list of identifiers (i.e. variable names and constant names). A variable can optionally be initialized by providing an initializer. However, the initialization of a constant is must.
   d. An object of an enumeration type can be initialized with another object of the same enumeration type or with one of the enumerators present in the enumeration list or with an integer value. The piece of code in Program 9-38 illustrates this fact.

Prog 9-38.c

```
//Initialization of an object of the enumeration type
#include<stdio.h>
enum SWITCH {off, on};
main()
{
    enum SWITCH s1=on;
    enum SWITCH s2=s1, s3=0;
    printf("The value of enumeration object s1 is %d\n",s1);
    printf("The value of enumeration object s2 is %d\n",s2);
    printf("The value of enumeration object s3 is %d\n",s3);
}
```

Output window

```
The value of enumeration object s1 is 1
The value of enumeration object s2 is 1
The value of enumeration object s3 is 0
```

Warnings(2):

Initializing SWITCH with int in function main()
Function should return a value in function main()

Remarks:

- Enumerations behave like integers, but it is common for a compiler to issue a warning message when an object of an enumeration type is initialized with something other than one of its constants or an expression of its type
- When the enumeration objects are initialized with integers, the compiler will not check that whether the initialized value is valid for such an enumeration or not
- Thus, it is even possible to initialize `s3` with `-8`, `9` or any other integer value

Program 9-38 | A program that illustrates the initialization of an enumeration object

3. **Operations on the objects of an enumeration type:** The following operations can be performed on the object of an enumeration type:

   a. **Size of an enumeration object or enumeration type**: An enumeration object holds an enumerator, which in fact is an integer constant. Thus, when the sizeof operator is applied on an enumeration object or an enumeration type, it outputs the size of an integer. The piece of code in Program 9-39 illustrates this fact.

Prog 9-39.c

```
//Size of an enumeration object or enumeration type
#include<stdio.h>
enum SWITCH {off, on};
main()
{
    enum SWITCH s=on;
    printf("The size of the enumeration type SWITCH is %d\n",sizeof(enum SWITCH));
    printf("The size of the enumeration object s is %d\n",sizeof(s));
}
```

Output window

```
The size of the enumeration type SWITCH is 2
The size of the enumeration object s is 2
```

Remarks:

- The size of the enumeration type or an enumeration object is the same as the size of an integer object
- If executed using MS-VC++ 6.0, it outputs 4

Program 9-39 | A program that illustrates the use of the sizeof operator on an enumeration type and an enumeration object

   b. **Address-of an enumeration object**: The address-of operator can be applied on an enumeration object to find the address of the memory space allocated to it. The piece of code in Program 9-40 illustrates the application of the address-of operator on an enumeration object.

Prog 9-40.c

```
//Address-of operator and structures
#include<stdio.h>
enum SWITCH {off, on};
main()
{
    enum SWITCH s=on;
    printf("Address of memory space allocated to s is %p\n",&s);
}
```

Output window

```
Address of memory space allocated to s is 249F:220C
```

Remarks:

- As the memory allocation is purely random, the printed address may vary for executions at different times or on different machines
- The definition of an enumeration type does not take any space in the memory, i.e. data segment. However, since it becomes a part of the code, it occupies some space in the code segment
- Hence, it is possible to apply the address-of operator on an enumeration type

Program 9-40 | A program that illustrates the use of the address-of operator on an object of enumeration type

   c. **Assignment of an enumeration object to an enumeration variable:** A variable of an enumeration type can be assigned with another object of the same enumeration type or with one of the enumerators present in the enumeration list or with an integer value.

d. **Behavior of equality operator on the objects of an enumeration type:** The equality operator can be applied to check the equality of two objects of an enumeration type.

The piece of code in Program 9-41 illustrates the use of an assignment operator and the equality operator on the objects of an enumeration type.

Prog 9-41.c

```
//Equality of enumeration objects
#include<stdio.h>
enum SWITCH {off, on};
main()
{
    enum SWITCH s1=on, s2;
    s2=s1;          //←Assignment to an enumeration variable
    if(s1==s2)   //←Testing the equality of two enumeration variables
        printf("Both the switches are in ON state\n");
    else
        printf("Switches are in different states\n");
}
```

Output window

```
Both the switches are in ON state
```

Remarks:

- An integer can also be assigned to an enumeration type
- When the enumeration objects are assigned with integers, the compiler will not check whether the assigned value is valid for such an enumeration or not. However, it will issue a warning message
- It is possible to equate the enumeration objects of the same enumeration type
- It is even possible to equate the enumeration object with an integer constant or an integer variable

Program 9-41 | A program that illustrates the use of the equality operator on the objects of an enumeration type

e. **Other operators**: All the operators that work on integer objects can be applied on the objects of an enumeration type and those that can be applied on integer constants can be applied on enumerators. The piece of code in Program 9-42 illustrates the use of logical operators on the objects of enumeration types.

Prog 9-42.c

```
//Enumerations and logical operators
#include<stdio.h>
enum COMBINATION {series=1, parallels=2};
enum SWITCH {OFF, ON};
main()
{
    enum COMBINATION ckt;
    enum SWITCH s1, s2;
    printf("Enter the configuration of the circuit:\n");
    printf("(Press 1 for series and 2 for parallel)\n");
    scanf("%d",&ckt);
    printf("Enter the status of the switches:\n");
    printf("(Press 0 for OFF state and 1 for ON state)\n");
    scanf("%d %d",&s1,&s2);
    if(ckt==series)
    {
     if(s1==ON && s2==ON)
         printf("The bulb will glow");
```

Series configuration

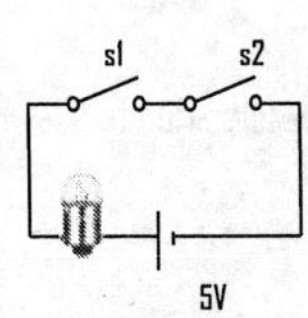

Parallel configuration

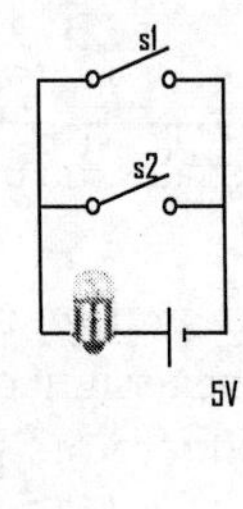

Output window

```
Enter the configuration of the circuit:
(Press 1 for series and 2 for parallel)
1
Enter the status of the switches:
(Press 0 for OFF state and 1 for ON state)
1 1
The bulb will glow
```

Output window (second execution)

```
Enter the configuration of the circuit:
(Press 1 for series and 2 for parallel)
1
Enter the status of the switches:
(Press 0 for OFF state and 1 for ON state)
1 0
Circuit is not complete, bulb will not glow
```

(Contd...)

```
    else
        printf("Circuit is not complete, bulb will not glow");
    }
    else
    {
     if(s1==ON || s2==ON)
        printf("The bulb will glow");
     else
        printf("Circuit is not complete, bulb will not glow");
    }
}
```

Output window (third execution)

```
Enter the configuration of the circuit:
(Press 1 for series and 2 for parallel)
2
Enter the status of the switches:
(Press 0 for OFF state and 1 for ON state)
1 0
The bulb will glow
```

Output window (fourth execution)

```
Enter the configuration of the circuit:
(Press 1 for series and 2 for parallel)
2
Enter the status of the switches:
(Press 0 for OFF state and 1 for ON state)
0 0
Circuit is not complete, bulb will not glow
```

Program 9-42 | A program that illustrates the use of logical operators on the objects of the enumeration type

f. **Type conversions**: The objects of the enumeration type can participate in the expressions and can be passed as arguments to functions. Whenever necessary, an enumeration type is automatically promoted to an arithmetic type. The piece of code in Program 9-43 illustrates this fact.

Prog 9-43.c

```
 1  //Enumerations and Type conversion
 2  #include<stdio.h>
 3  enum shapes {triangle=3, quadrilateral, pentagon, hexagon};
 4  main()
 5  {
 6      enum shapes s1=triangle, s2=quadrilateral, s3;
 7      printf("The number of vertices in s1 are %d\n", s1);
 8      printf("The number of vertices in s2 are %d\n",s2);
 9      printf("Total number of vertices in s1 and s2 are %d\n",s1+s2);
10      printf("\nNo. of vertices in s3 are twice the no. of vertices in s1\n");
11      s3=2*s1;
12      printf("The number of vertices in s3 are %d\n",s3);
13  }
```

Output window

```
The number of vertices in s1 are 3
The number of vertices in s2 are 4
Total number of vertices in s1 and s2 are 7

No. of vertices in s3 are twice of the no. of vertices in s1
The number of vertices in s3 are 6
```

Remarks:

- Whenever objects of an enumeration type participate in an expression, they are promoted to arithmetic type, if required
- In line number 11, the enumeration type `enum shapes` is initially promoted to an integer type and then later demoted back to the enumeration type `enum shapes`

Program 9-43 | A program that illustrates the implicit-type conversion of an enumeration object

g. **Limitation of enumeration type:** The only limitation of an enumeration type is that it is not possible to print the value of an enumeration object in the symbolic form. The value of an enumeration object is always printed in the integer form. However, a debugger may be able to print the values of enumeration objects in the symbolic form. The piece of code in Program 9-44 illustrates this fact.

Prog 9-44.c

```
//Limitation of an enumeration type
#include<stdio.h>
main()
{
enum BOOLEAN {false, true} var;
var=true;
printf("The value of var is %d",value);
//printf("The value of var is %s",value);
}
```

Output window

The value of var is 1

Watch window

After trace step-3:

a: 1 /*true*/

Remarks:

- It is not possible to print the value of an enumeration object in the symbolic form
- As shown in the watch window, a debugger prints the value of an enumeration object both in the symbolic form and the integer form

Program 9-44 | A program illustrating that the value of an enumeration object cannot be printed in the symbolic form

9.11 Bit-fields

From the knowledge that you have imbibed till now, the smallest amount of information that you can store in the memory is 1 byte, i.e. in the form of character objects. However, most of the computer applications need to process the information smaller than a byte. For example, in data communication, the receiver application needs to check the parity of the received data. The parity of the received data can either be even or odd. Only 1 bit of information is sufficient to specify the parity, i.e. bit will be 0 if the parity is even and 1 otherwise. The receiver also needs to know whether the data communication will be synchronous or asynchronous. Again, this information can be stored using 1 bit, i.e. bit will be 0 if data communication is synchronous and 1 otherwise. If the data communication is asynchronous, the receiver has to explicitly synchronize itself with the sender. For this purpose, the sender sends start bits to the receiver, before sending the actual data. The number of start bits that a sender sends can be 0, 1, 2 or 3. The receiver can store this information by using 2 bits.

> **Parity** checking is one of the simplest error-checking techniques. Parity refers to the number of bits with the value of one in a given set of bits. Parity can be either even or odd. If the number of 1's in the given set of bits is even, the parity is said to be even. In odd parity, the number of 1's in the given set of bits is odd.

The receiver applications need to be very compact in size (i.e. memory efficient) as they have to be used in mobile devices. When it is required to make smaller applications, where every bit of the memory space is precious, the memory cannot be wasted by storing the information that takes 1 or 2 bits into separate bytes.

Here, the application of bit-fields comes into the real picture. Bit-fields help in packing several objects into a single unit. They can only be declared as a part of a structure or a union.

In a structure or a union declaration-list, it is possible to specify for a member, the number of bits that it will take in the memory. Such a member is called a **bit-field**. The general form of a bit-field declaration is:

```
struct|union [tag_name]
{
    type member_name : integer_constant_expression;
    [type member_name : integer_constant_expression;]
    ..............
}[variable_name];
```

The important points about the bit-field declaration are as follows:

1. The terms shown in square brackets are optional and might not be present. The terms shown in **bold** are mandatory parts of the declaration. The symbol | stands for OR, i.e. either struct or union should be present.
2. A bit-field declaration can only appear within a structure or a union declaration-list.
3. Bit-fields must be of integral type. Thus, the type that can be specified in the bit-field declaration can be char, int or unsigned int.
4. A compile time integer constant expression specifies the width of the bit-field in bits. It must be non-negative and should not be greater than the number of bits available in an object of the type used in the bit-field declaration. The piece of code in Program 9-45 illustrates this fact.

Prog 9-45.c	Output window

//The size of a bit-field
#include<stdio.h>
struct receiver
{
    unsigned int parity: 22;
    unsigned int mode: 1;
    unsigned int start_bits:2;
    int data;
};
main()
{
//←Statements...
}
	Compilation error "Bit field too large"
	Remarks:
	• The number of bits specified for a bit-field should not be more than the number of bits available in an object of the type used in the bit-field declaration
	• Thus, it is not possible to specify the size of the bit-field parity to be 22, as the number of bits in an object of the type unsigned int is 16

Program 9-45 | A program that demonstrates a constraint about the size of a bit-field

5. If the value of the constant expression specifying the number of bits in a bit-field is 0, then the declaration should have no declarator (i.e. name of the bit-field). A bit-field having 0 width is known as an **unnamed bit-field**. Unnamed bit-fields cannot be referenced as their content at the run time is unpredictable. They are used as dummy fields for the alignment purposes. The piece of code in Program 9-46 illustrates this fact.

Line | Prog 9-46.c

```
1  //Unnamed bit-fields
2  #include<stdio.h>
3  struct receiver
4  {
5      unsigned int parity: 1;
6      unsigned int mode: 0;
7      unsigned int start_bits:2;
8      int data;
9  };
10 main()
11 {
12 //←Statements...
13 }
```

Output window

Compilation error "Bit field must contain at least one bit"

Remarks:

- If the value of constant expression specifying the number of bits in a bit-field is 0, then the declaration should have no declarator
- If the bit field is named, then it must contain at least 1 bit
- Thus, the specification of the declarator mode in line number 6 leads to the compilation error
- Remove the declarator name mode and re-compile the code

Program 9-46 | A program illustrating that if the size of a bit-field is 0, the bit-field should be unnamed

The operations that can be performed on the bit-fields are as follows:

1. **Referencing a bit-field:** As bit-fields are a part of a structure or a union object, they are referenced in the same way as other structure or union members are referenced. The piece of code in Program 9-47 illustrates this fact.

Prog 9-47.c

```
//Referencing a bit-field
#include<stdio.h>
struct receiver
{
    unsigned int parity: 1;
    unsigned int mode: 1;
    unsigned int start_bits: 2;
    int data;
};
main()
{
struct receiver mobile_receiver={1, 1, 2, 200};
if(mobile_receiver.parity==0)
    printf("The receiver works with even parity\n");
else
    printf("The receiver works with odd parity\n");
if(mobile_receiver.mode==0)
    printf("The receiver supports synchronous data transmission\n");
else
{
    printf("The receiver supports asynchronous data transmission\n");
    printf("There should be %d start bits\n", mobile_receiver.start_bits);
}
}
```

Output window

The receiver works with odd parity
The receiver supports asynchronous data transmission
There should be 2 start bits

Remark:

- Bit-fields can be referenced in the same way as other members of structure or union type are referenced, i.e. by using a direct member access operator or an indirect member access operator

Program 9-47 | A program that illustrates how to access the bit-fields

2. **Other operations:** Bit-field behave like an integer object and can participate in expressions in exactly the same way as an object of the integer type would do, regardless of how many bits are there in the bit-field.

   The following operations cannot be performed on bit-fields:

   1. **Address-of a bit-field:** It is not possible to obtain the address of a bit-field member. Unary address-of operator cannot be applied to a bit-field object. Thus, it is not possible to have an array of bit-fields or pointers to bit-fields. The piece of code in Program 9-48 illustrates this fact.

Prog 9-48.c

```
1  //Address-of a bit-field member
2  #include<stdio.h>
3  struct receiver
4  {
5      unsigned int parity: 1;
6      unsigned int mode: 1;
7      unsigned int start_bits: 2;
8      int data;
9  };
10 main()
11 {
12 struct receiver mobile_receiver={1, 1, 2, 200};
13 printf("The memory address of object mobile_receiver is %p\n", &mobile_receiver);
14 printf("The memory address of bit-field parity is %p\n",&mobile_receiver.parity);
15 //←Other statements...
16 }
```

Output window

Compilation error "illegal to take address of bit-field in function main()"

Remarks:

- It is not allowed to take the address of a bit-field member
- Hence, line number 14 is erroneous and leads to a compilation error
- Comment line number 14 and re-execute the code to see that it is possible to take the address of a structure object that contains bit-fields

Program 9-48 | A program to illustrate that it is not possible to take the address of a bit-field

   2. **Size-of a bit-field:** Like the address-of operator, it is not possible to apply the sizeof operator on a bit-field object. The piece of code in Program 9-49 illustrates this fact.

Prog 9-49.c

```
1  //sizeof a bit-field member
2  #include<stdio.h>
3  struct receiver
4  {
5      unsigned int parity: 1;
6      unsigned int mode: 1;
7      unsigned int start_bits: 2;
8      int data;
9  };
10 main()
11 {
12 struct receiver mobile_receiver={1, 1, 2, 200};
13 printf("The size of bit-field object parity is %d\n",sizeof(mobile_receiver.parity));
14 //←Other statements...
15 }
```

Output window

Compilation error "sizeof may not be applied to a bit-field in function main()"

Remarks:

- It is not allowed to apply the sizeof operator to a bit-field object
- Hence, line number 13 is erroneous and leads to a compilation error

Program 9-49 | A program illustrating that it is not possible to apply the sizeof operator on bit-fields

The important points about the application of the sizeof operator on bit-fields are as follows:

1. An implementation may allocate an addressable storage unit large enough to hold a bit-field. If enough space remains, a bit-field that immediately follows another bit-field in a structure shall be packed into adjacent bits of the same unit. If insufficient space remains, whether a bit-field that does not fit is put into the next unit or overlaps adjacent units is implementation defined.
2. An unnamed bit-field (i.e. bit-field with width 0) indicates that no further bit-field is to be packed in the unit in which the previous bit-field (if any) is placed. The piece of code in Program 9-50 illustrates this fact.

Prog 9-50.c

```
//sizeof structure having unnamed bit-field
#include<stdio.h>
struct receiver
{
    unsigned int parity: 1;
    int :0;                    //←Unnamed bit-field
    unsigned int mode: 1;
    unsigned int start_bits: 2;
    int data;
};
main()
{
struct receiver mobile_receiver;
printf("The size of object mobile_receiver is %d\n", sizeof(mobile_receiver));
//←Other statements...
}
```

Output window (Turbo C 4.5)

```
The size of object mobile_receiver is 6
```

Remarks:

- The unnamed bit-field is used for alignment purposes
- An unnamed bit-field indicates that no further bit-field is to be packed in the unit in which the previous bit-field is placed
- Thus, the bit-fields, i.e. mode and start_bits are placed in the unit next to the unit in which the bit-field parity is placed
- The structure member data takes 2 bytes
- Thus, the total size occupied by the structure object mobile_receiver is 2+2+2= 6 bytes

Program 9-50 | A program that illustrates the use of an unnamed bit-field for alignment purpose

9.12 Summary

1. C language also provides the flexibility to create new types, known as user-defined types.
2. User-defined types can be created by using structures, unions and enumerations.
3. Unlike arrays, the data of different types can be grouped together and stored by making use of structures.
4. A structure is a collection of variables under a single name and provides a convenient way of grouping several pieces of related information together.
5. The structure definition defines a new type, known as structure type.
6. The structure declaration-list in a structure definition consists of declarations of one or more variables, possibly of different types.
7. A structure declaration-list cannot contain a member of void type or incomplete type or function type.
8. A structure definition cannot contain an instance of itself.
9. A structure definition may contain a pointer to an instance of itself. Such a structure is known as self-referential structure.

10. Structure definition does not reserve any space in memory.
11. It is not possible to initialize the structure members during the structure definition.
12. The structure members cannot be initialized during the structure definition, but the members of a structure object can be initialized by providing an initialization list.
13. An unnamed structure type is also known as an anonymous structure type.
14. The member of a structure object can be accessed by using: direct member access operator or indirect member access operator.
15. A structure object can be assigned to a structure variable of the same type.
16. An assignment operator when applied on structure variables performs member-by-member copy.
17. The members of a structure object can be byte aligned or machine-word boundary aligned.
18. If the members of a structure object are machine-word boundary aligned, the padding bytes can appear in between two structure members or after the last structure member.
19. The `sizeof` operator when applied on a structure object includes the space taken by internal and trailing padding.
20. The use of the equality operator on operands of a structure type is not allowed.
21. An operation that is applicable on an object of a particular type can be applied on a structure member of that type.
22. Like a pointer to any other type, it is possible to create a pointer to a structure type as well.
23. It is possible to define a structure type within the declaration-list of another structure-type definition.
24. Unions are similar to structures except that memory is shared among all the members.
25. The amount of memory allocated to a union object is the amount necessary to contain its largest member.
26. Only the first member of a union object can be initialized.
27. Unions are extensively used in interrupt programming.
28. Enumerations provide another way to create a user-defined type. An enumeration type is designed for variables that can have a limited set of values.
29. In a structure or a union declaration-list, it is possible to specify for a member, the number of bits that it will take in the memory. Such a member is called a bit-field.
30. Bit-fields help in packing several objects into a single unit.

Exercise Questions

Conceptual Questions and Answers

1. *I know that C language provides a rich set of primitive and derived data types for the efficient storage and manipulation of the data. Unfortunately, none of the primitive or derived data types suit my requirements. What should I do so that I can efficiently store and manipulate the data?*

   C language provides a rich set of primitive and derived data types for the efficient storage and manipulation of the data. Even then, in case these data types do not suit your requirements, you can define new data types. These new data types are known as user-defined data types. In C language, the user-defined data types can be created by using structures, unions and enumerations.

Functions are created for the operations allowed on these data types. These user-defined data types along with the defined functions can be used for the efficient storage and manipulation of the data.

2. *What are aggregate types?*

   Aggregate types represent multiple values of the same type or of different types. Aggregate types include arrays and structures. Arrays are used to represent multiple values of the same type, while structures are used to represent multiple values of the same type or of different types.

3. *Like structure type, union type also contains a number of members, possibly of different types. Then, why does the aggregate type not include union type?*

   Aggregate type does not include a union type because an object of a union type can contain only one member at a time.

4. *What are anonymous structures?*

   Unnamed structures are known as anonymous structures. The tag-names are not specified while defining anonymous structures.

5. *Consider the following piece of code:*

```
struct complex
{
    int re;
    int im;
}
main()
{
    struct complex no1={2,3}, no2={4,5};
    printf("The sum of complex numbers is %d+%di",no1.re+no2.re, no1.im+no2.im);
}
```

   We know that the structure-type definition is a statement and must be terminated with a semicolon. However, Turbo C 3.0 compiler on compiling the above-mentioned code gives no error, although the structure-type definition is not terminated with a semicolon. Why? Can it be avoided to terminate a structure definition with a semicolon?

   The Turbo C 3.0 compiler does not show any error because it interprets the structure-type definition as a return type of the function main. This does not mean that the structure definition should not be terminated with a semicolon. The missing semicolon at the end of a structure definition would lead to a compilation error in the following cases:

   1. Some compilers (e.g. Borland Turbo C 4.5) do not allow the return type of the function main to be any other type except int. In such cases, the mentioned piece of code on compilation gives an error. Hence, the mentioned piece of code will not work with all the compilers.
   2. If there is some declaration statement present after the structure definition with a missing terminating semicolon (as shown below), there will be a compilation error even if it is compiled with a Borland Turbo C 3.0 compiler.

```
struct complex
{
    int re;
    int im;
}                   //←The missing semicolon will lead to a compilation error
int somevariable;  //←Declaration statement
main()
```

```
{
...//←Statements
}
```

6. *I have written the following piece of code:*

```
struct type
{
    char a;
    int b;
    float c;
};
type variable;
```

The mentioned piece of code does not work and gives a compilation error. Why? How can I rectify it?

In C language it is not allowed to declare an object of the defined structure type only by using its tag-name without using the keyword struct. Hence, the statement type variable; is erroneous. There are two ways to rectify this problem:

1. **Using the keyword struct:** Use the keyword struct to declare the object variable of the defined structure type. Hence, the statement type variable; should be written as struct type variable;.
2. **Using the storage class specifier typedef:** Use the storage class specifier typedef to construct a syntactically convenient alias name for the defined structure type and then declare an object using the alias name. The storage class specifier typedef can be used either at the time of the structure definition or after the structure definition in a separate statement as shown below:

<table>
<tr>
<td><pre>typedef struct type
{
    char a;
    int b;
    float c;
}type;
type variable; //←Object declaration</pre></td>
<td><pre>struct type
{
    char a;
    int b;
    float c;
};
typedef struct type type;
type variable;   //←Object declaration</pre></td>
</tr>
<tr>
<td>(a) typedef used at the time of structure definition</td>
<td>(b) typedef used after the structure definition in a separate statement</td>
</tr>
</table>

7. *I know that a function cannot be defined within the body of another function. However, can I define a structure type within another structure-type definition?*

Yes, a structure type can be defined within another structure-type definition. For example, the structure definitions struct registers, struct word_registers, struct byte_registers shown below are perfectly valid:

```
struct registers
{
    struct word_registers {unsigned int ax, bx, cx, dx, si, di, cflags, flags;} x;
    struct byte_registers {unsigned char al, ah, bl, bh, cl, ch, dl, dh;} h;
};
```

8. *Why does a structure not have an instance of itself?*

Backward Reference: Refer Section 9.2.1 to answer this question.

9. *Can a structure have a pointer to itself?*

   Yes, a structure can have a pointer to an instance of itself. Such a structure is known as a self-referential structure.

10. *I know that the* sizeof *operator when applied on the structures returns the total memory space required by all of its members. I have applied the* sizeof *operator on an object of the following structure type:*

```
struct fields
{
    char a;
    int b;
    char c;
    float d;
};
```

   The sizeof *operator is returning a size larger than the sum of size of all the fields. Why? How can I rectify this problem?*

   A structure may have internal and trailing padding to align the structure members with the machine-word boundaries. The sizeof operator counts these internal and trailing padding bytes as well. Thus, the sizeof operator returns a size larger than the sum of size of all the fields of the structure. This problem can be rectified by byte aligning of the members of the structure so that there is no padding. The members of a structure can be byte aligned by using #pragma option -a- (if working with Borland Turbo C 3.0/4.5) or #pragma pack(1) (if working with MS-VC++ 6.0) .

11. *I have defined two structure types* struct type1 *and* struct type2 *as given below.*

```
struct type1                struct type2
{                           {
    long a;                     char c;
    short b;                    long a;
    char c;                     short b;
};                          };
```

   Both the types have the same members but listed in a different order. Would the sizeof *operator return the size of both the types to be same?*

   No, the sizeof operator would not necessarily return the same size for both the defined structure types. If the members of the structure types are machine-word boundary aligned, the structure members may have the padding in between or at the end. The padding depends upon the order in which of the members of a structure are placed in the structure-type definition. For example, if MS-VC++ 6.0 compiler is used and the pack size is 4 bytes, an object of the type struct type1 will be stored in the memory as:

a				b		c	
1001	1000	0101	0010	0000	1111	1011	H
2400	2401	2402	2403	2404	2405	2406	2407

   An object of the structure type struct type2 will be stored in the memory as:

c				a				b			
1011	H	H	H	1001	1000	0101	0010	0000	1111	H	H
2400	2401	2402	2403	2404	2405	2406	2407	2408	2409	2410	2411

The structure member c of the structure type struct type2 can start from any byte boundary. The structure member a can only start from a storage boundary that has an address, which is multiple of 4, i.e. size of type long. Hence, the structure member a cannot start from the memory location 2401, since it is not multiple of 4. It can be placed at memory address 2404 and thus there are 3 padding bytes in between the member c and a. The structure member b can start from memory location 2408, since the memory address is a multiple of 2, i.e. size of type short.
The compiler also places 2 padding bytes after the member b because it wants to ensure the alignment constraints on the next structure object, if there is any. Suppose the compiler does not pad at the end and the member c of the next structure object starts from the memory location 2410. It is a valid start location for the member c since it is of char type. Then, the compiler places 3 padding bytes as it did in the previous object and places the member a at the memory location 2414. However, the memory address 2414 is not divisible by 4, i.e. size of the member a. Hence, it is not a valid start location for the member a. Thus, the compiler cannot enforce alignment constraints by starting the second structure object from the memory location 2410.
Now, suppose the compiler pad places 2 bytes at the end of the first structure object and starts placing the members of the next structure object from the memory location 2412. The member c of the second structure object is placed at the memory location 2412. There will be 3 padding bytes in between the structure members c and a and the member a starts from the memory location 2416. It is a valid start location for the member a, since the address is divisible by 4. Thus, the compiler is able to enforce alignment constraints.

Thus, if the members of the structure objects are machine-word boundary aligned, an object of the type struct type1 will take 8 bytes while an object of the type struct type2 will take 12 bytes. If the members of the structure objects are byte aligned, objects of both the types struct type1 and struct type2 will take the same number of bytes because in byte alignment there is no padding.

12. *Some of the precious memory space can be saved if the members of a structure type are judiciously arranged. Would the compiler do this task for me and rearrange the members of the defined structure type in a manner that requires less padding?*

    No, the members of a structure object are always stored in the order in which they are declared in the structure-type definition. The compiler will never reorder them to improve the alignment and save padding.

13. *Is the following definition of the structure type syntactically correct?*

```
struct car
{
    char* make;
    char* model;
    enum color colour;
};
enum color {red, green, blue};
```

    No, the given definition of the structure type struct car is erroneous. The scope of the enumeration tags begins just after the appearance of the tag in a type specifier that declares the tag (i.e. enumeration tags cannot be used before they are defined). Thus, the usage of the enumeration tag color in the declaration-list of the struct car leads to the compilation error ''color' must be a previously defined enumeration tag'. The code can be rectified by defining enumeration type enum color before the definition of the structure type struct car.

14. *Is the following piece of code syntactically correct? If yes, what would its output be?*

```
struct complex
{
```

```
    int re;
    int im;
};
struct complex con(struct complex);
main()
{
    struct complex num={2,3};
    printf("After conjugation, the real and imaginary parts are %d and %d",con(num).re, con(num).im);
}
struct complex con(struct complex num)
{
    num.im=-num.im;
    return num;
}
```

Yes, the given piece of code is syntactically correct and on execution outputs:

```
After conjugation, the real and imaginary parts are 2 and -3
```

If f is a function returning a structure or a union, and x is a member of that structure or union, then f().x is a valid expression. Thus, con(num).re and con(num).im are valid expressions and evaluates to 2 and -3, respectively.

15. *Like array name and function name, does a structure name point to the base address of the structure?*

    No, like array name and function name (i.e. function designator), the structure name does not point to the base address of the structure. A structure name refers to the entire structure.

16. *Like for arrays, can it be said with certainty that the members of a structure object are stored in contiguous memory locations?*

    No, like arrays it cannot be said with certainty that the members of a structure object are stored in contiguous memory locations. Members of a structure object may have padding in between.

17. *Given the following type definition and object declarations:*

    ```
    struct t { int i; const int ci;};
    struct t t;
    const struct t ct;
    ```

    What would be the type of the following expressions?

    1. t.i
    2. t.ci
    3. ct.i
    4. ct.ci

    The given expressions are of the following types:

    1. t.i int
    2. t.ci const int
    3. ct.i const int
    4. ct.ci const int

18. *Why does the equality operator (==), inequality operator (!=) and other relational operators not work on structures?*

    The equality operator, inequality operator and relational operators do not work on structures because there is no way for a compiler to implement structure comparison. A simple byte-by-byte comparison would fail while comparing the random bits present in the internal padding.

A member-by-member comparison might require unacceptable amounts of repetitive code for large structures. Also, any compiler-generated comparison would not compare the members appropriately in all cases, e.g. the members of the type char* should be compared with the strcmp function instead of being compared with equality (==) operator.

Backward Reference: Refer Section 9.2.3.1.5 for more details.

Forward Reference: Refer Question numbers 40 and 41 and their answers.

19. *How can I find the byte offset of a member within a structure?*

The byte offset of a member within a structure can be found by using offsetof macro defined in the header file stddef.h. The offsetof macro accepts the name of the structure type as the first argument and the name of member whose offset is to be found as the second argument. It returns the byte offset of the member as an integer value. The following piece of code illustrates the use of the offsetof macro to find the offset of a member:

```
#include<stddef.h>
struct type
{
    char a;
    int b;
    char c;
    float d;
};
main()
{
printf("The offset of member a is %d\n",offsetof(struct type, a));
printf("The offset of member b is %d\n",offsetof(struct type, b));
printf("The offset of member c is %d\n",offsetof(struct type, c));
printf("The offset of member d is %d\n",offsetof(struct type, d));
}
```

The mentioned piece of code on execution using Borland Turbo C 3.0/4.5 outputs:

```
The offset of member a is 0
The offset of member b is 1
The offset of member c is 3
The offset of member d is 4
```

The important points about the usage of the offsetof macro are as follows:

1. The output of the offsetof macro depends upon how the structure members are aligned (i.e. byte aligned or machine-word boundary aligned). Make the structure members machine-word boundary aligned in the above-mentioned code by using #pragma option -a and then re-execute the above-mentioned code and look at the output.
2. If the macro is not previously defined, define it as:

```
#define offsetof(s_name, m_name) (size_t)&(((s_name*)0)->m_name)
```

20. *How is the declaration* struct type {.......}; *different from* typedef struct {........} type;?

The differences between the two declaration statements are as follows:

struct type{.....};	typedef struct {......} type;
1. This declaration statement declares a structure tag name (i.e. type) 2. The keyword struct is to be used while declaring objects of the defined type (e.g. struct type objects;) 3. The requirement of using the keyword struct to declare the instances of the defined structure type is a bit inconvenient	1. This declaration statement declares a typedef name (i.e. an alias name) 2. The objects can be declared just by using the typedef name (e.g. type objects;). There is no need to use the keyword struct 3. This form of declaration is slightly more abstract. For example, from the declaration statement type objects; the user does not come to know that type refers to a structure type as the keyword struct is not used

21. *I have heard that a structure can have a pointer to itself but the mentioned piece of code is not working and is giving a compilation error. Why?*

```
typedef struct
{
    int data;
    NODE* link;
} NODE;
```

The storage class specifier typedef creates a new name (i.e. an alias name) for a type. We can define a new structure type and create a typedef name (i.e. alias name) for it at the same time. However, a typedef name cannot be used until it is defined. In the given question, the typedef name NODE is used before it is defined. This leads to a compilation error. There are two ways to rectify this problem:

1. Instead of defining an unnamed type, define a named type by giving a tag name to the structure (e.g. struct node). Then declare the field link as struct node* link;. The rectified code is mentioned below:

```
typedef struct node
{
    int data;
    struct node* link;
} NODE;
```

2. Disentangle the typedef definition from the structure definition and place it before the structure definition as shown below:

```
typedef struct node NODE;
struct node
{
    int data;
    NODE *link;
};
```

22. *Is the definition of the following union type syntactically correct? If yes, what would be the size of an object of the following union type?*

```
union numbers
{
    struct {char a[10];} one;
    struct {int a[10];} two;
    struct {float a[10];} three;
};
```

Yes, the definition of the union type union numbers is syntactically valid. The amount of the memory allocated to a union object is equal to the size of its largest member. Since the largest member in the given union type union numbers is three (i.e. of 4×10=40 bytes), the size of an object of the union type union numbers would be 40.

23. *Is the following piece of code syntactically correct? If yes, what would its output be?*

```
typedef struct error
{
    int warning, error, exception;
} error;
main()
{
    error err;
    err.error=2;
    switch(err.error)
    {
        case 1:  printf("Some warnings are there\n"); break;
        case 2: printf("Some error occurred\n"); break;
        case 3: printf("Some exception is there\n");
    }
}
```

Yes, the following piece of code is syntactically correct and on execution outputs 'Some error occurred'. Based upon the context, the compiler can distinguish between the different usages of the name error. For example, in the statement error err; the usage of error is treated as the typedef name. In the statement err.error=2; the usage of error is treated as the member name. If there would have been a statement like struct error err; the usage of error would have been treated as the structure tag name.

24. *How can I keep track of which field of a union is in use?*

There is no automatic way to keep a track of which union field is in use. However, we can create a type with an additional member, which keeps a record of the union field currently in use. The following code segment illustrates the definition of such type:

```
struct trackedunion
{
    enum {UNKNOWN, CHAR, INT, FLOAT, LONG, DOUBLE} code;
    union
    {
        char a;
        int b;
        float c;
        long d;
        double e;
    } u;
};
```

Initially the value of code is set to UNKNOWN, because it is not known that which union field is in use. After that, whenever a value is assigned to a union field, the code field is set appropriately. Thus, the code field keeps a track of which union field is being last written to.

25. *What are the differences between a symbolic constant and an enumeration constant?*

The important differences between symbolic constants and enumeration constants are as follows:

Symbolic constants	Enumeration constants
1. Symbolic constants are created with the help of define directive	1. Enumeration constants are created as a part of enumeration type definition
2. The symbolic constants have global scope. They can be used throughout the translation unit (i.e. file) after their definition	2. The enumeration constants have the local scope. They can only be used in the scope in which the enumeration type has been defined
3. Symbolic constants do not have any type associated with them	3. Enumeration constants are of integer type
4. The values of the symbolic constants are to be mentioned explicitly	4. The values of the enumeration constants are set automatically. By default, the first enumeration constant has value 0

26. *Instead of printing the values of the enumeration constants, I want to print them symbolically. How can I do that?*

    The only limitation of an enumeration type is that it is not possible to print the value of an enumeration object in their symbolic form. By default, the value of an enumeration object is always printed in the integer form. However, you can write your own function to map an enumeration value into a string. The following piece of code illustrates one such function map that maps an enumeration value into a string:

```
#include<stdio.h>
enum BOOLEAN {FALSE, TRUE};
char* map(enum BOOLEAN);
main()
{
   enum BOOLEAN a, b;
   a=FALSE;
   b=TRUE;
   printf("The values of a and b in integer form are %d and %d\n", a, b);
   printf("The values of a and b in symbolic form are %s and %s",map(a), map(b));
}
char* map(enum BOOLEAN a)
{
   switch(a)
   {
      case 0:
         return "FALSE";
      case 1:
         return "TRUE";
   }
}
```

    The above-mentioned piece of code on execution outputs:

```
The values of a and b in integer form are 0 and 1
The values of a and b in symbolic form are FALSE and TRUE
```

27. *Is the following piece of code syntactically correct? If yes, what would its output be?*

```
typedef enum error {warning, error, exception} error;
main()
```

```
{
    error err;
    err=error;
    switch(err)
    {
        case 1: printf("Some warnings are there\n"); break;
        case 2: printf("Some error occurred\n"); break;
        case 3: printf("Some exception is there\n");
    }
}
```

No, the mentioned piece of code is syntactically incorrect and on compilation leads to 'Multiple declarations for 'error'' error. The compiler shows an error because based upon the context, it is not able to distinguish between the use of error as an alias name in the declaration statement error err; and error as an enumeration constant in the assignment statement err=error;.

28. *What is the efficient way to store flag values?*

Flag refers to one or more bits that are used to store a value that has an assigned meaning. Flags are generally used to control or indicate the outcome of different operations. For example, the carry flag of microprocessor is set to 1 if an addition operation generates a carry out of the most significant bit position. Similarly, the zero flag is set to 1 when the result of an operation is zero (e.g. subtraction of two equal numbers). Flags can be efficiently stored by making the use of bit fields.

Backward Reference: Refer Section 9.11 for more details.

29. *What are unnamed bit-fields? Why are they used?*

Bit-fields with length 0 are known as unnamed bit-fields. Unnamed bit-fields are used for the alignment purposes. An unnamed bit-field indicates that the next field should be placed in a separate unit and not with the previous field in the same unit.

30. *'Use of standard library functions increase the size of the executable file but the use of interrupt functions does not increase the size of the executable file'. Is this statement true?*

No. This statement is false. The Turbo C library functions also use the interrupts and were written by programmers. The only difference between the library functions and the interrupts is in the ease of usage. The library functions are easier to use and are more flexible as compared to interrupts.

Code Snippets

Determine the output of the following code snippets. Assume that the inclusion of the required header files has been made and there is no prototyping error due to them.

31.
```
struct book
{
    char title[20];
    char author[20];
    int pages;
    float price;
};
main()
```

```
{
    book Cbook;
    printf("The size of object Cbook is %d bytes", sizeof(Cbook));
}
```

32.
```
struct book
{
    char title[20];
    char author[20];
    int pages;
    float price;
};
main()
{
    struct book Cbook;
    Cbook.title="The power of positive attitude";
    Cbook.author="P Subramanyam";
    Cbook.pages=400;
    Cbook.price=225.50;
    printf("%s by %s is of %f rupees", Cbook.title, Cbook.author, Cbook.price);
}
```

33.
```
struct book
{
    char *title;
    char *author;
    int pages;
    float price;
};
main()
{
    struct book Cbook;
    Cbook.title="The power of positive attitude";
    Cbook.author="P Subramanyam";
    Cbook.pages=400;
    Cbook.price=225.50;
    printf("%s by %s is of %f rupees", Cbook.title, Cbook.author, Cbook.price);
}
```

34.
```
struct car
{
    struct engine e;
    struct chassis c;
};
struct engine
{
    int hp;
    int cc;
};
struct chassis
```

```
{
    int length;
    int width;
};
main()
{
    struct car yourcar={{68, 1400}, {3200, 2358}};
    if(yourcar.e.cc<1400)
        printf("It is a small segment car\n");
    else if(yourcar.e.cc>=1400 && yourcar.e.cc<1600)
        printf("It is a middle segment car\n");
    else
        printf("It is a big segment car\n");
}
```

35.
```
struct car
{
    struct engine {int hp; int cc;} e;
    struct chassis {int length; int width;} c;
};
main()
{
    struct car yourcar={{68, 1400}, {3200, 2358}}, mycar={{52, 1000},{3500,2500}};
    if(yourcar.c.length>mycar.c.length)
        printf("Your car is lengthier than mine\n");
    else
        printf("My car is lengthier than yours\n");
}
```

36.
```
//Assuming the compiler used is Borland Turbo C 4.5
struct car
{
    char *make;
    char *model;
    char *reg_no;
    struct {int hp; int cc;} e;
    struct {int length; int width; char* color;} c;
    float cost;
};
main()
{
    struct car mycar;
    printf("The size of type struct car is %d\n",sizeof(struct car));
    printf("The objects of type struct car will take %d bytes of memory\n", sizeof(mycar));
}
```

37.
```
struct car
{
    char *manufacturer="Maruti";
    char *make;
};
```

```
main()
{
    struct car mycar, yourcar;
    mycar.make="Swift";
    yourcar.make="Dzire";
    printf("We own %s and %s cars manufactured by %s", mycar.make, yourcar.make, mycar.manufacturer);
}
```

38. struct car

```
{
    char *make;
    char *model;
};
main()
{
    struct car mycar={"Maruti", "Dzire"};
    struct car yourcar=mycar;
    strupr(yourcar.make);
    strupr(yourcar.model);
    printf("Your car is %s-%s\n",yourcar.make, yourcar.model);
    printf("My car is %s-%s\n",mycar.make, mycar.model);
}
```

39. struct car

```
{
    char *make;
    char *model;
};
main()
{
    struct car mycar={"Maruti", "Dzire"}, yourcar={"Maruti", "Dzire"};
    if(mycar==yourcar)
        printf("Both of us own car of same make and model");
    else
        printf("We own different types of cars");
}
```

40. struct car

```
{
    char *make;
    char *model;
};
main()
{
    struct car mycar={"Maruti", "Dzire"}, yourcar={"Maruti", "Dzire"};
    if(mycar.make==yourcar.make && mycar.model==yourcar.model)
        printf("Both of us own car of same make and model");
    else
        printf("We own different types of cars");
}
```

41.
```
struct car
{
    char *make;
    char *model;
};
main()
{
    struct car mycar={"Maruti", "Dzire"}, yourcar={"Maruti", "Dzire"};
    if(strcmp(mycar.make,yourcar.make)==0 && strcmp(mycar.model, yourcar.model)==0)
        printf("Both of us own cars of same make and model");
    else
        printf("We own different types of cars");
}
```

42.
```
struct 3Dpoints
{
    int x;
    int y;
    int z;
};
main()
{
    struct 3Dpoints pt1, pt2;
    pt1.x=pt2.x=20;
    pt1.y=10; pt2.y=30;
    printf("Points in xy plane are:\n");
    printf("Pt1(%d %d)\n", pt1.x, pt1.y);
    printf("Pt2(%d %d)\n",pt2.x,pt2.y);
}
```

43.
```
struct complex
{
    int re;
    int im;
};
main()
{
    struct complex number={2,3};
    int *ptr1=&number.re, *ptr2=&number.im;
    if(ptr2>ptr1)
        printf("The imaginary part is stored towards the right of real part in the number object\n");
    else if(ptr1>ptr2)
        printf("The real part is stored towards the right of imaginary part in the number object\n");
    else
        printf("Both the real part and imaginary part overlap\n");
}
```

44.
```
struct point
{
    int x, y;
};
```

```
main()
{
    struct point origin;
    printf("The coordinates of origin are %d,%d", origin.x, origin.y);
}
```

45.
```
struct point
{
    int x, y;
};
main()
{
    struct point origin={0};
    printf("The coordinates of origin are %d,%d", origin.x, origin.y);
}
```

46.
```
struct point
{
    int x, y;
};
main()
{
    static struct point origin;
    printf("The coordinates of origin are %d,%d", origin.x, origin.y);
}
```

47.
```
#include<alloc.h>
struct node
{
    int data;
    struct node *link;
};
main()
{
    struct node* ptr, *temp;
    ptr=(struct node*)malloc(sizeof(struct node));
    ptr->data=10;
    temp=(struct node*)malloc(sizeof(struct node));
    ptr->link=temp;     temp->data=20;
    temp=(struct node*)malloc(sizeof(struct node));
    ptr->link->link=temp;     temp->data=30;
    temp->link=NULL;
    temp=ptr;
    while(temp!=NULL)
    {
        printf("%d\t",temp->data);
        temp=temp->link;
    }
}
```

48.
```
struct complex
{
    int re;
    int im;
};
main()
{
    struct complex no={2,3};
    struct complex* cptr=&no;
    printf("The real and imaginary parts of complex number are %d and %d", *cptr.re, *cptr.im);
}
```

49.
```
struct complex
{
    int re;
    int im;
};
main()
{
    struct complex no={2,3};
    struct complex* cptr=&no;
    printf("The real and imaginary parts of complex number are %d and %d\n", (*cptr).re, (*cptr).im);
    printf("The real and imaginary parts of complex number are %d and %d", cptr->re, cptr->im);
}
```

50.
```
union contactno
{
    char mobileno[10];
    char landlineno[10];
    char pagerno[10];
};
main()
{
    union contactno electrician={"9416234213", "5356785", "941-998856"};
    printf("The mobile number of my electrician is %s\n", electrician.mobileno);
    printf("You can also contact him on his landline number %s", electrician.landlineno);
}
```

51.
```
union coordinates
{
    int x;
    int y;
};
main()
{
    union coordinates point;
    point.x=20;
    point.y=30;
    printf("The coordinates of point are %d,%d", point.x, point.y);
}
```

52.
```
#define struct union
struct type
{
    char a;
    int b;
    float c;
};
main()
{
    printf("The size of defined structure type is %d", sizeof(struct type));
}
```

53.
```
typedef struct union;
struct type
{
    char a;
    int b;
    float c;
};
main()
{
    printf("The size of defined structure type is %d", sizeof(struct type));
}
```

54.
```
enum color {red, green, blue};
main()
{
    printf("The values of enumeration constants are %d %d %d", red, green, blue);
}
```

55.
```
enum color {red, green=red, blue=green};
main()
{
    printf("The values of enumerations constants are %d %d %d", red, green, blue);
}
```

56.
```
enum values {a, b=32767, c};
main()
{
    printf("Values of enumeration constants are %d %d %d", a, b, c);
}
```

57.
```
enum values {a=2, b=3, c};
main()
{
    int var=7, res1, res2;
    res1=var%b;
    res2=res1%res2;
    printf("The values of res1 and res2 are %d and %d",res1, res2);
}
```

58.
```
main()
{
    int bitfield: 2;
    bitfield=3;
    printf("The value of bitfield is %d",bitfield);
}
```

59.
```
int parity=1;
struct dataobject
{
    int paritybits: parity;
    int data;
};
main()
{
    int i, count=0;
    struct dataobject obj={0, 2, 23};
    while(obj.data!=0)
    {
        if(obj.data%2==1)
            count++;
        obj.data=obj.data>>1;
    }
    if(count%2==0)
    {
        obj.paritybits=0;
        printf("The data has even parity");
    }
    else
    {
        obj.paritybits=1;
        printf("The data has odd parity");
    }
}
```

60.
```
struct dataobject
{
    int paritybits: 1;
    int data;
};
main()
{
    int i, count=0;
    struct dataobject obj={0, 2, 23};
    while(obj.data!=0)
    {
        if(obj.data%2==1)
            count++;
        obj.data=obj.data>>1;
    }
```

```
    if(count%2==0)
    {
        obj.paritybits=0;
        printf("The data has even parity");
    }
    else
    {
        obj.paritybits=1;
        printf("The data has odd parity");
    }
}
```

Multiple-choice Questions

61. User-defined types can be created by using
    a. Structures
    b. Unions
    c. Enumerations
    d. All of these

62. A structure declaration-list cannot contain a member of
    a. `void` type
    b. Incomplete type
    c. Function type
    d. All of these

63. Objects of the defined structure type can be created
    a. At the time of structure declaration
    b. After the structure declaration
    c. Either at the time of structure declaration or after the structure declaration
    d. None of these

64. A member of a structure object can be accessed through the structure object name by using
    a. Direct member access operator
    b. Indirect member access operator
    c. Arrow operator
    d. None of these

65. A member of a structure object can be accessed through a pointer to the structure object by using
    a. Direct member access operator
    b. Indirect member access operator
    c. Dereference operator
    d. None of these

66. Which of the following operators is not applicable on an object of a structure type?
    a. Equality operator
    b. Assignment operator
    c. Address-of operator
    d. `sizeof` operator

67. Nested structure contains members of
    a. Same structure type
    b. Other defined structure types
    c. Incomplete structure types
    d. None of these

68. The maximum number of members in a structure declaration-list
    a. Can be two
    b. Can be infinite
    c. Depends upon the translation limits of the compiler
    d. None of these

69. Which of the following method of passing a structure object to a function is most efficient?
    a. Passing each member of a structure object as a separate argument
    b. Passing a structure object by value
    c. Passing a structure object by address/reference
    d. None of these

70. The amount of the memory allocated to a union object is
    a. The amount of memory necessary to contain its largest member
    b. The amount of memory necessary to contain its smallest member
    c. The sum of memory requirement of all of its members
    d. None of these

71. Which member(s) of a union object can be initialized?
    a. Only first member
    b. Only last member
    c. All members
    d. None of these

72. An enumeration constant is of
    a. char type
    b. int type
    c. float type
    d. None of these

73. The width specifier of a bit field should be a
    a. Variable
    b. Constant
    c. Compile time constant expression of integer type
    d. None of these

74. The value of a constant expression specifying the width of a bit field cannot be
    a. 0
    b. 1
    c. Greater than the number of bits available in an object of the type used in bit field declaration
    d. None of these

75. A bit-field of which of the following types cannot be created
    a. int
    b. unsigned int
    c. char
    d. float

Outputs and Explanations to Code Snippets

31. Compilation error "Undefined symbol 'book' in function main"

    Explanation:

    In C language, it is not allowed to declare an object of the defined structure type by using its tag-name without using the keyword struct. Hence, the declaration statement book Cbook; is erroneous and leads to the compilation error. To rectify the code, use the keyword struct in the declaration statement and write it as struct book Cbook; or use the storage class specifier typedef to create book as an alias name for the structure type struct book.

32. Compilation error "L-value required in function main"

    Explanation:

    Both the expressions Cbook.title and Cbook.author are of type char[20] (i.e. array type) and do not have an l-value. Hence, they cannot be placed on the left side of the assignment operator. Placement of these expressions on the left side of the assignment operator leads to the specified compilation error.

33. The power of positive attitude by P Subramanyam is of 225.500000 rupees

    Explanation:

    The expressions Cbook.title and Cbook.author are of type char* and have l-values. Hence, they can be assigned the base addresses of the strings.

34. Compilation errors
"Undefined structure 'engine'"
"Undefined structure 'chassis'"
"Size of the type is unknown or zero"

Explanation:

Structure tags have the scope that begins just after the appearance of the tag in a type specifier that declares the tag. The usage of the structure tag-names engine and chassis in the declaration-list of the structure type struct car leads to 'Undefined structure 'engine'' and 'Undefined structure 'chassis' errors because the structure tags have not yet been defined. Also, a structure definition cannot contain a member of the incomplete type. A structure type is said to be incomplete until the closing brace of its declaration-list is encountered. An incomplete type lacks the information needed to determine the size of its object. Hence, the usage of incomplete types struct engine and struct chassis in the declaration-list of struct car leads to the 'Size of the type is unknown' error. To rectify the code, define the structure types struct engine and struct chassis before the definition of the structure type struct car.

35. My car is lengthier than yours

Explanation:

It is allowed to define a structure type within another structure-type definition. Hence, the definitions of the structure types struct engine and struct chassis in the declaration-list of struct car are perfectly valid. Also, the members e and c are of the complete type because before their occurrence the closing brace of their respective structure types, i.e. struct engine and struct chassis has already been seen by the compiler. The length member of the member c of the objects yourcar and mycar is initialized with the values 3200 and 3500, respectively. Hence, the expression yourcar.c.length>mycar.c.length evaluates to false and "My car is lengthier than yours" gets printed.

36. The size of type struct car is 28
The objects of type struct car will take 28 bytes of memory

Explanation:

The specified result is the result of the execution in Turbo C 4.5.

Backward Reference: Refer Section 9.2.3.1.4 to answer this question.

37. Compilation error

Explanation:

Since the structure definition does not reserve any memory space for the structure members, it is not possible to initialize the structure members during the structure definition. Hence, the initialization of the structure member manufacturer with the string literal "Maruti" during the structure definition is erroneous and leads to the compilation error.

38. Your car is MARUTI-DZIRE
My car is MARUTI-DZIRE

Explanation:

Suppose the structure object mycar gets allocated at the memory location 2000. The make and the model members of the structure object mycar are initialized with the string literals "Maruti" and "Dzire" (say located at memory locations 4000 and 6000, respectively). Thus, they point to the base addresses of the strings. Another structure object yourcar, say gets allocated at the memory location 8000. Since the structure object yourcar is initialized with the structure object mycar, all the members of mycar are copied one by one to the corresponding members of yourcar. Thus, the make and model members of the structure object yourcar also start pointing to the strings located at the memory locations 4000 and 6000, respectively. This is shown in the figure below:

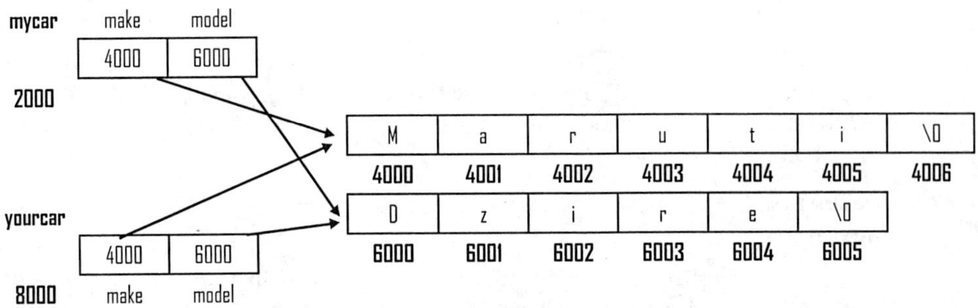

As the corresponding members of the structure objects mycar and yourcar point to the same memory locations (i.e. same strings), the changes made in the strings through yourcar.make and yourcar.model will also be available through mycar.make and mycar.model.

39. Compilation error "Illegal structure operation in function main"

Explanation:

The use of the equality operators on the structures is not allowed. Hence, the expression mycar==yourcar is erroneous and leads to a compilation error.

Backward Reference: Refer Section 9.2.3.1.5 for more details.

40. We own different types of cars

Explanation:

Suppose the structure objects mycar and yourcar get allocated at the memory locations 2000 and 6400, respectively. The members of these structure objects point to the string literals as shown in the figure given below:

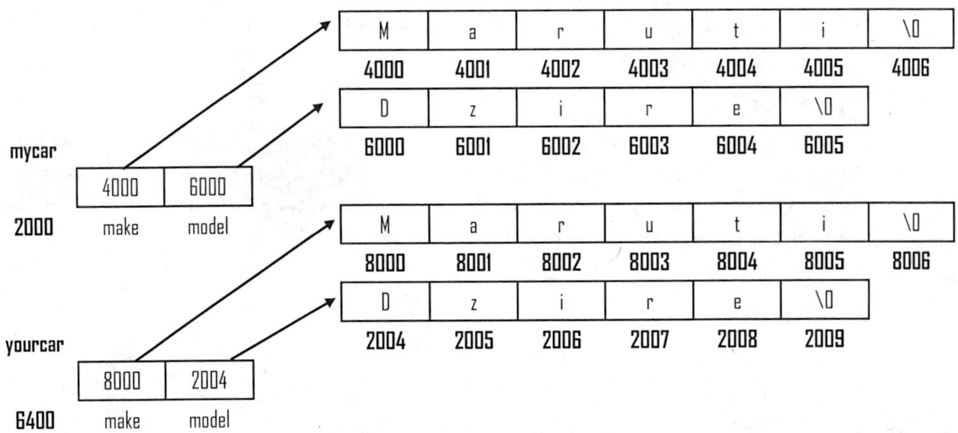

The sub-expression mycar.make==yourcar.make compares the value 4000 with 8000 and hence evaluates to false. Similarly, the sub-expression mycar.model==yourcar.model also evaluates to false. Thus, the if expression evaluates to false and the printf statement present in the else body gets executed.

The specified code gives the unexpected output because the equality operator compares the pointers instead of the strings pointed to by the pointers.

41. `Both of us own cars of same make and model`

Explanation:

In the given code, the `strcmp` function is used to compare the strings pointed to by the pointers. Since the strings compare equal, the `if` expression evaluates to `true` and the `printf` statement present in the `if` body gets executed.

42. `Compilation error`

Explanation:

The tag-name of a structure is an identifier and must start with a letter or an underscore. `30points` is not a valid identifier name and hence cannot form a structure tag-name.

43. `The imaginary part is stored towards the right of real part in the number object`

Explanation:

If the objects pointed are the members of the same structure object, pointers to the structure members declared later compare greater than the pointers to the members declared earlier in the structure. Thus, `ptr2>ptr1` evaluates to `true`.

44. `The coordinates of origin are 7903,19125`

Explanation:

Since the structure object `origin` is defined inside the body of the function `main`, it has local scope. Thus, its members will not be automatically initialized and will contain garbage values.

45. `The coordinates of origin are 0,0`

Explanation:

If the number of initializers in the initialization list is less than the number of structure members in a structure object, the leading structure members (equal to the number of initializers in the initialization list) are initialized with the initializers in the initialization list and the rest of the structure members will automatically be initialized with `0`. Thus, in the given code, the member `y` of the structure object `origin` automatically gets initialized to `0`.

46. `The coordinates of origin are 0,0`

Explanation:

If a structure object is declared with a storage class specifier, the properties resulting from the storage class specifier (except with respect to linkage) apply to all the members of the object. Thus, as the structure object `origin` is declared with the storage class specifier `static`, all the members of the structure object will automatically be initialized to `0`.

47. `10   20   30`

Explanation:

The code creates a linked list of three nodes. The data fields of the nodes are assigned the values `10`, `20` and `30`, respectively. The `while` loop is used to traverse the list and print the values of the data field.

48. `Compilation error "Structure required on the left side of . in function main"`

Explanation:

The dot operator has higher precedence than the dereference operator. Hence, the expression `*cptr.re` is interpreted as `*(cptr.re)`. The dot operator on its left side expects a structure name. Since in the interpreted expression pointer to a structure is present on the left side of the dot operator instead of a structure name, there is a compilation error.

49. The real and imaginary parts of complex number are 2 and 3
    The real and imaginary parts of complex number are 2 and 3

    Explanation:

    The members of a structure object can be accessed via the pointer to the structure object by using one of the following two ways:
    1. By using a dereference or indirection operator and dot operator
    2. By using an arrow operator

50. Compilation error

    Explanation:

    It is not allowed to initialize all the members of a union object. Only the first member of the union object can be initialized.

51. The coordinates of point are 30,30

    Explanation:

    In the union object point, both the members x and y share the memory locations. Changing the value of a member will change the value of the other member too. Thus, assignment of the value 30 to the member y will also change the value of the member x from 20 to 30.

52. The size of defined structure type is 4

    Explanation:

    During the preprocessing stage, the macro struct is text replaced by the replacement string union wherever it appears in the program code. Thus, after the preprocessing stage, the code becomes

```
union type
{
    char a;
    int b;
    float c;
};
main()
{
    printf("The size of defined structure type is %d", sizeof(union type));
}
```

    When the sizeof operator is applied on a union type, it outputs the size of its largest member. Thus, sizeof(union type) returns 4.

53. Compilation error

    Explanation:

    The storage class specifier typedef is used for creating a synonym name or alias for a known type. The syntax of the typedef declaration is:

    typedef type_name synonym_name;

    The type_name should be a defined type. Since in the given declaration, struct is not a defined type, the statement is erroneous and on compilation shows an error '{ expected'. The compiler expects structure declaration-list after the keyword struct. Also, the synonym_name should be a valid identifier name. In the given declaration statement, synonym name is union, which is a keyword and not a valid identifier name. This also leads to an error.

54. The values of enumeration constants are 0 1 2

Explanation:

The values of the enumeration constants are set automatically. The first enumerator has the value 0. Each subsequent enumerator, if not explicitly assigned a value, has a value 1 greater than the value of the enumerator that immediately precedes it. Thus, the enumeration constant red will have the value 0, green will have the value 1 and blue will have the value 2.

55. The values of enumeration constants are 0 0 0

Explanation:

Each enumeration constant has a scope that begins just after its appearance in an enumeration list. Thus, it is possible to initialize the enumerator green with the enumerator red and the enumerator blue with the enumerator green.

56. Compilation error "The value for 'c' is not within the range of an int"

Explanation:

An enumerator can hold an integer value. Also, each subsequent enumerator in an enumeration list, if not explicitly assigned with a value, has a value 1 greater than the value of the enumerator that immediately precedes it. Thus, the enumerator c will have the value 32767+1, i.e. 32768. Since the value of the enumerator c falls outside the range of the integer type, there will be a compilation error.

57. The value of res1 and res2 are 1 and 1

Explanation:

All the operators that work on an integer type can be applied on objects of an enumeration type and the operators applicable on integer constants can be applied on enumerators. Thus, the application of the modulus operator on the objects of enumeration type res1 and res2 and enumerator b is perfectly valid.

58. Compilation error

Explanation:

A bit-field declaration can only appear within a structure or a union declaration-list.

59. Compilation error "Constant expression required"

Explanation:

The width specifier of a bit-field can be a constant expression of the integer type. In the given piece of code, the variable parity is used to specify the width of the bit-field paritybits. This is erroneous and leads to the specified compilation error.

60. The data has even parity

Explanation:

The while loop is used to count the number of 1's in the data member of the structure object obj. After the termination of the while loop, the value of the variable count is equal to the number of 1's in the data member. If the value of variable count is even, the bit-field paritybits of the object obj is set to 0 else it is set to 1. A message indicating the parity of data is also printed.

Answers to Multiple-choice Questions

61. d 62. d 63. c 64. a 65. b 66. a 67. b 68. c 69. c 70. a 71. a 72. b 73. c 74. c 75. d

Programming Exercises

Program 1 | Define a data type for storing complex numbers and implement addition, subtraction, multiplication, conjugate and modulus operations for the defined type

PE 9-1.c

```
//Definition of complex data type and various operations applicable on it
#include<stdio.h>
#include<math.h>
#include<string.h>
struct complex
{
    int re;
    int im;
};
typedef struct complex COMP;
COMP add(COMP, COMP);
COMP sub(COMP*, COMP*);
COMP mult(COMP, COMP);
COMP conjugate(COMP);
float modulus(COMP);
void print(char* opr, COMP result, char* no='\0');
void printmod( char*, float);
main()
{
    COMP no1, no2, result;
    float mod;
    printf("Enter the real and imaginary part of first complex number:\n");
    scanf("%d %d", &no1.re, &no1.im);
    printf("Enter the real and imaginary part of second complex number:\n");
    scanf("%d %d", &no2.re, &no2.im);
    result=add(no1, no2);
    print("addition", result);
    result=sub(&no1, &no2);
    print("subtraction", result);
    result=mult(no1, no2);
    print("multiplication", result);
    result=conjugate(no1);
    print("conjugate", result, "no1");
    mod=modulus(no1);
    printmod("no1",mod);
}
COMP add(COMP no1, COMP no2)
{
    COMP result;
    result.re=no1.re+no2.re;
    result.im=no1.im+no2.im;
    return result;
}
```

Output window

```
Enter the real and imaginary part of first complex number:
2 3
Enter the real and imaginary part of second complex number:
4 5
The result of addition is 6+8i
The result of subtraction is -2-2i
The result of multiplication is -7+19i
The result of conjugate of no1 is 2-3i
The result of modulus of no1 is 3.605551
```

(Contd...)

PE 9-1.c

```
COMP sub(COMP* no1, COMP* no2)
{
    COMP result;
    result.re=no1->re-no2->re;
    result.im=no1->im-no2->im;
    return result;
}
COMP mult(COMP no1, COMP no2)
{
    COMP result;
    result.re=no1.re*no2.re – no1.im*no2.im;
    result.im=no1.re+no2.im + no1.im* no2.re;
    return result;
}
COMP conjugate(COMP no)
{
    COMP result;
    result.re=no.re;
    result.im=-no.im;
    return result;
}
float modulus(COMP no)
{
    float result;
    result=pow((no.re*no.re+no.im*no.im), 0.5);
    return result;
}
void print(char* opr, COMP res, char* no)
{
    if(strcmp(opr, "conjugate")==0)
    {
      if(res.im<0)
        printf("The result of conjugate of %s is %d%di\n",no,res.re,res.im);
      else
        printf("The result of conjugate of %s is %d+%di\n",no,res.re,res.im);
    }
    else
    {
        if(res.im<0)
            printf("The result of %s is %d%di\n",opr, res.re,res.im);
        else
            printf("The result of %s is %d+%di\n",opr, res.re,res.im);
    }
}
void printmod(char* no, float result)
{
    printf("The result of modulus of %s is %f\n", no, result);
}
```

Output window

Program 2 | Develop a phonebook application. It should be able to store, modify and list entries present in the phonebook. A phonebook entry consists of the name of a person and his contact information. The name of a person consists of his first name and family name. The contact information consists of the landline number and the mobile number of the person

PE 9-2.c

```
#include<stdio.h>
#include<string.h>
#include<stdlib.h>
#include<conio.h>
typedef struct name          //←Definition of struct type name
{
    char fname[20];
    char lname[20];
}NAM;                        //←struct type name is aliased as NAM
typedef struct contact       //← Definition of struct type contact
{
    char landline[12];
    char mobile[12];
}CON;                        //←struct type contact is aliased as CON
typedef struct phoneentry   //←Definition of struct type phoneentry
{
    NAM pname;
    CON pcontact;
}PENT;                       //←struct type phoneentry is aliased as PENT

void printmenu()             //←Function printmenu prints various options
{
    printf("****************************************\n");
    printf("1. Press 1 to add records in phone book\n");
    printf("2. Press 2 to delete a record\n");
    printf("3. Press 3 to list available records\n");
    printf("4. Press 4 to search a record\n");
    printf("5. Press 5 to exit\n");
    printf("*****************************************\n\n");
}

void addrecord(PENT book[], int* count)     //←Function addrecord adds a record in phone book and increments the count
{
    char ch;
    clrscr();
    printf("                ****************\n");
    printf("                 ADD RECORDS\n");
    printf("                ****************\n");
    printf("Enter the first name of the person:\t");
    gets(book[*count].pname.fname);
    printf("Enter the last name of the person:\t");
    gets(book[*count].pname.lname);
    printf("Enter the landline number:\t");
    gets(book[*count].pcontact.landline);
    printf("Enter the mobile number:\t");
    gets(book[*count].pcontact.mobile);
    (*count)++;
```

(Contd...)

PE 9-2.c

```
printf("Record entered successfully\n\n");
    flushall();
    printf("Do you want to enter more records(Y/N):\t");
    scanf("%c",&ch);
    flushall();
    if(ch=='Y'||ch=='y')
        addrecord(book, count);
    else
        return;
}

void listrecords(PENT book[],int count)     //←Function listrecords lists all the records available in the phone book
{
    int i=0;
    clrscr();
    printf("                    ********************\n");
    printf("                      LISTING RECORDS\n");
    printf("                    ********************\n");
    printf("\n%-4s %-20s%-20s%-12s %-12s\n","S.No","First name","Last name","Landline No.", "Mobile No.");
    printf("---------------------------------------------------------------------------\n");
    while(i<count)
    {
        printf("%4d. %-20s%-20s%-12s %-12s\n" ,i+1,book[i].pname.fname,book[i].pname.lname, book[i].pcontact.landline,
        book[i].pcontact.mobile);
            i++;
    }
    printf("---------------------------------------------------------------------------\n");
    printf("\n%d record(s) available\n",count);
    printf("Press any key to return to main menu...\n");
    getch();
}

void searchrecord(PENT book[], int count)     //←Function searchrecord searches a record according to various criteria
{
    int ch,i=0, found=0, no=0;
    char key[25];
    clrscr();
    printf("                    ****************\n");
    printf("                     SEARCH RECORDS\n");
    printf("                    ****************\n");
    printf("1. Press 1 to search by first name\n");
    printf("2. Press 2 to search by last name\n");
    printf("3. Press 3 to search by mobile number\n");
    printf("4. Press any other key to return to main menu\n");
    flushall();
    printf("Enter your choice:\t");
    scanf("%d",&ch);
    switch(ch)
    {
        case 1:
            printf("\n\nEnter the first name of the person\n");
```

(Contd...)

```
            flushall();
            gets(key);
            while(i<count)
            {
                if(strcmp(book[i].pname.fname,key)==0)
                {
                    if(no==0)
                        printf("\n%-4s %-20s%-20s%-12s %-12s\n","S.No","First name","Last name","Landline No.", "Mobile No.");
                    found=1; no++;
                    printf("%4d. %-20s%-20s%-12s %-12s\n", no, book[i].pname.fname, book[i].pname.lname, book[i].pcontact.landline,
                    book[i].pcontact.mobile);
                }
                i++;
            }
            if(found==0)
                printf("No record found\n");
            else
            printf("\n%d record(s) found\n",no);
            printf("Press any key to continue...\n");
            getch();
            break;
        case 2:
            printf("\n\nEnter the last name of the person\n");
            flushall();
            gets(key);
            while(i<count)
            {
                if(strcmp(book[i].pname.lname,key)==0)
                {
                    if(no==0)
                        printf("\n%-4s %-20s%-20s%-12s %-12s\n","S.No","First name","Last name","Landline No.", "Mobile No.");
                    found=1; no++;
                        printf("%4d. %-20s%-20s%-12s %-12s\n", no,book[i].pname.fname, book[i].pname.lname,
                        book[i].pcontact.landline, book[i].pcontact.mobile);
                }
                i++;
            }
            if(found==0)
                printf("No record found\n");
            else
                printf("\n%d record(s) found\n",no);
            printf("Press any key to continue...\n");
            getch();
            break;
        case 3:
            printf("\n\nEnter the mobile number of the person\n");
            flushall();
            gets(key);
            while(i<count)
            {
                if(strcmp(book[i].pcontact.mobile,key)==0)
                {
                    if(no==0)
```

(Contd...)

PE 9-2.c

```
                    printf("\n%-4s %-20s%-20s%-12s %-12s\n","S.No","First name","Last name","Landline No.", "Mobile No.");
                found=1; no++;
            printf("%4d.%-20s%-20s%-12s %-12s\n", no, book[i].pname.fname, book[i].pname.lname, book[i].pcontact.landline,
                book[i].pcontact.mobile);
            }
        i++;
        }
        if(found==0)
            printf("No record found\n");
        else
        printf("\n%d record(s) found\n",no);
    }
    printf("Press any key to continue....\n");
    getch();
}

deleterecord(PENT book[], int* count)     //←Function deleterecords deletes a record with particular S.NO in the list
{
    int sno, i;
    clrscr();
    printf("                    *****************\n");
    printf("                        RECORD DELETION\n");
    printf("                    *****************\n");
    printf("\n\nEnter the S.No of the record that you want to delete:\t");
    scanf("%d",&sno);
    i=sno-1;
    if(sno<=0||sno>*count)
        printf("Not a valid S.No\n");
    else
    {
        while(i<*count)
        {
            book[i]=book[i+1];
            i++;
        }
        *count=*count-1;
        printf("Record successfully deleted\n");
    }
    printf("Press any key to return to main menu...\n");
    getch();
}

main()
{
    int ch, count=0;
    PENT book[50];
    clrscr();
    while(1)
    {
        printf("        PHONE BOOK            \n");
        printmenu();
        printf("Enter the choice:\t");
```

(*Contd...*)

```
        scanf("%d",&ch);
        flushall();
        switch(ch)
        {
            case 1:
                addrecord(book,&count);
                break;
            case 2:
                deleterecord(book, &count);
                break;
            case 3:
                listrecords(book, count);
                break;
            case 4:
                searchrecord(book, count);
                break;
            case 5:
                exit(1);
                break;
            default:
                printf("Invalid option\n");
                getch();
                exit(1);
        }
        clrscr();
    }
}
```

Output window (screen 1)

```
        PHONE BOOK
*******************************************
1. Press 1 to add records in phone book
2. Press 2 to delete a record
3. Press 3 to list available records
4. Press 4 to search a record
5. Press 5 to exit
*******************************************

Enter the choice:    1
```

Output window (screen 2)

```
        ****************
            ADD RECORDS
        ****************
Enter the first name of the person:    Arvind
Enter the last name of the person:    Kakria
Enter the landline number:    2576898
Enter the mobile number:    9878776856

Do you want to enter more records(Y/N): y
```

(Contd...)

Output window (screen 3)

```
        ****************
          ADD RECORDS
        ****************
Enter the first name of the person:    Mohit
Enter the last name of the person:     Bansal
Enter the landline number:    2576897
Enter the mobile number:    9888566892

Do you want to enter more records(Y/N): n
```

Output window (screen 4)

```
      PHONE BOOK
********************************************
1. Press 1 to add records in phone book
2. Press 2 to delete a record
3. Press 3 to list available records
4. Press 4 to search a record
5. Press 5 to exit
********************************************

Enter the choice:    3
```

Output window (screen 5)

```
        *****************
          LISTING RECORDS
        *****************
S.No  First Name          Last Name            Landline No.     Mobile No.
--------------------------------------------------------------------------
  1.  Arvind              Kakria               2576898          9878776856
  2.  Mohit               Bansal               2576897          9888566892
--------------------------------------------------------------------------

2 record(s) available
Press any key to return to main menu...
```

Output window (screen 6)

```
      PHONE BOOK
********************************************
1. Press 1 to add records in phone book
2. Press 2 to delete a record
3. Press 3 to list available records
4. Press 4 to search a record
5. Press 5 to exit
********************************************

Enter the choice:    2
```

(Contd...)

Output window (screen 7)

```
        *****************
         RECORD DELETION
        *****************

Enter the S.NO of the record that you want to delete:    1
Record successfully deleted
Press any key to return to main menu...
```

Output window (screen 8)

```
      PHONE BOOK
******************************************
1. Press 1 to add records in phone book
2. Press 2 to delete a record
3. Press 3 to list available records
4. Press 4 to search a record
5. Press 5 to exit
******************************************

Enter the choice:   3
```

Output window (screen 9)

```
        *****************
         LISTING RECORDS
        *****************
S.No  First Name          Last Name          Landline No.      Mobile No.
---------------------------------------------------------------------------
  1.  Mohit               Bansal             2576897           9888566892
---------------------------------------------------------------------------

1 record(s) available
Press any key to return to main menu...
```

Output window (screen 10)

```
      PHONE BOOK
******************************************
1. Press 1 to add records in phone book
2. Press 2 to delete a record
3. Press 3 to list available records
4. Press 4 to search a record
5. Press 5 to exit
******************************************

Enter the choice:   5
```

Test Yourself

1. Fill in the blanks in each of the following:
   a. Structures can be used for the storage of data of __________ type.
   b. A structure that contains a pointer to an instance of itself is known as __________.
   c. __________ and __________ are collectively known as aggregate type.
   d. Unnamed structure types are also known as __________.
   e. Like elements of an array are accessed by their indices, the elements of a structure are accessed by their __________.
   f. Elements of a structure type can be accessed faster if they are __________ aligned.
   g. The members of a structure object can be accessed via a pointer to the structure object by using __________ operator.
   h. The precedence of the direct member access operator is __________ than the dereference operator.
   i. The memory allocated to a union object is the amount necessary to contain its __________ member.
   j. The __________ can be used to create an alias for a previously defined type.

2. State whether each of the following is true or false. If false, explain why.
   a. The variables of the defined structure type can only be declared in the scope in which the defined structure type is visible.
   b. A structure declaration-list cannot contain a member of `void`, function or incomplete type.
   c. Structure, unions and enumerations are collectively known as aggregate type.
   d. A structure that contains an instance of itself is known as a self-referential structure.
   e. The name of a structure member can be the same as the structure tag-name.
   f. A structure definition does not reserve any space in the memory.
   g. Structure members can be initialized during the structure definition.
   h. In C language, an object of a structure type can be created by just using its tag-name.
   i. Like an array name, the name of a structure refers to its base address.
   j. The assignment operator copies all the members of a structure object to a structure variable along with the padding bytes.
   k. Structure padding can appear anywhere within a structure object.
   l. Unlike functions, a structure can be defined within another structure-type definition.
   m. The keyword `typedef` is used to create a new data type.
   n. Unions can be initialized in the same way as structures are initialized.

3. Programming exercise:
   a. Define a structure data type called `DATE` for storing dates. The type contains three integer members: day, month and year. Implement the following operations for the defined data type:
      i. `Isvalid`: Checks whether the entered date is valid or not, e.g. 31-2-2009 is not a valid date since February does not have 31 days.
      ii. `Nextdate`: Finds the next date, e.g. if the current data is 31-1-2009, then the result of `Nextdate` operation is 1-2-2009.
      iii. `Datediff`: Finds the difference between two dates.
   b. Define a structure data type `TRAIN_INFO`. The type contains:
      i. Train No: integer type
      ii. Train name: string
      iii. Departure time: aggregate type `TIME`
      iv. Arrival time: aggregate type `TIME`

v. Start station: string
vi. End station: string

The structure type TIME contains two integer members: hour and minute. Maintain a train timetable and implement the following operations:

1. List all the trains (sorted according to train number) that depart from a particular station.
2. List all the trains that depart from a particular station at a particular time.
3. List all the trains that depart from a particular station within the next one hour of a given time.
4. List all the trains between a pair of start station and end station.

10

FILES

Learning Objectives

In this chapter, you will learn about:

- Files
- C's approach to perform file input–output
- Streams
- How to create, read, write and update files
- Sequential access files
- Random access files

10.1 Introduction

In the previous chapters, we have used functions such as `scanf` and `printf` to read and write data. These are console input–output (I/O) functions that read data from or write data to the terminal, i.e. keyboard and screen, respectively. The console I/O is preferred in interactive programs where the amount of data in I/O is small. If a program deals with I/O of large volume of data, the console I/O is not convenient and consumes a lot of time. Moreover, the entered data are stored in variables and arrays. These data are lost when either the program is terminated or the computer is turned off or power goes off. Upon re-execution of the program, the entire data need to be entered again. You might have faced such inconvenience while executing Program 9-2 in the last chapter. Every time the program is executed, all the records in the phonebook are to be entered again. It is therefore required to enter the data and store (i.e. save) it on disk so that it can be read by a program whenever required. This prevents one from entering the data again and again. Data can be stored on a disk by using files.

In this chapter, I will tell you about files and how to perform basic file operations such as creating a file, writing data to a file, reading data from a file, copying content of one file to another, etc. I will also make you delve deeper into the technical details of how C language performs file I/O. You will see that C adopts a device-independent model of input and output. Input and output whether from physical devices such as terminals (e.g. printer, screen, keyboard, etc.) or from files on the disks are performed in the same way.

10.2 Files

Most programs do either input or output or most frequently both in order to perform a meaningful task. The input or output is performed using peripheral devices attached to the system. The devices may include I/O devices like printer, screen, keyboard, etc. or they may include mass storage devices like magnetic disks, optical disks, magnetic tapes, etc. To perform I/O in a device-independent form, C treats each of them in the same way. C treats each of them as a **file**. Thus, a **file** can be a data set that can be read or written repeatedly (such as a disk file), or a stream of bytes received from or sent to a peripheral device (such as a keyboard or display). The latter are known as **interactive files** or **device files**.

In order to perform operations like reading from a file or writing to a file, some mechanism is required to refer to the file. All the files (including the device files) have names that are strings. The name of a file generally has two parts: file name and extension name. The constraints on the file name are dictated by the underlying operating system. For example, in MS-DOS, a file name can be up to eight characters long and can be in uppercase or lowercase letters. File extensions consist of a period (i.e. dot) followed by up to three characters. Extensions are optional, but it is a good idea to use them since they are useful for describing the content of a file. For example, the **.h** extension in **stdio.h** helps you in quickly identifying that it is a header file. Similarly, the extensions **.exe** means **executable file**, **.com** means **command file**, **.c** means **C program file**, **.cpp** means **cplusplus program file**, **.txt** means **text file**, **.dat** means **data file**, etc.

A file must be opened before any operation can be performed on it. Opening a file associates a connection or a communication channel with it. The connection to an open file is represented either as a **stream** or as a **file descriptor**. **File descriptors** provide a primitive, low-level interface for performing input and output operations on files. **Streams** provide a high-level interface, layered on the top of primitive file descriptor facilities, for performing file I/O. Since streams are implemented in terms of file descriptors, the file descriptor can be extracted from a stream. It is also possible to open a connection as a file descriptor and then associate a stream with it.

The I/O on a file can be performed either by using streams or file descriptors. However, the C library functions for performing I/O using streams are much richer and more powerful than the corresponding counterparts for the file descriptors. Thus, input and output using the streams are more flexible and more convenient than using the file descriptors. Therefore, it is advisable to perform input and output operations using the streams rather than using the file descriptors. The file descriptors should only be used to perform low-level control operations for which there are no equivalent stream operations.

10.3 Streams

Input and output, whether to or from physical devices such as terminals (e.g. screen, keyboard, printer) or files supported on mass storage devices (e.g. hard disk) are mapped into **logical data streams**, whose properties are more uniform than their associated files. A **stream** can be thought of as a buffer to which bytes flow from a device (e.g. keyboard, disk, network connection, etc.) during an input operation and during an output operation, bytes from the stream are made available to the device (e.g. printer, screen, disk, network connection, etc.). Thus, a stream is a fairly abstract, high-level concept representing a communication channel to a data file or a device. Figure 10.1 illustrates the mechanism adopted by C language to perform input and output.

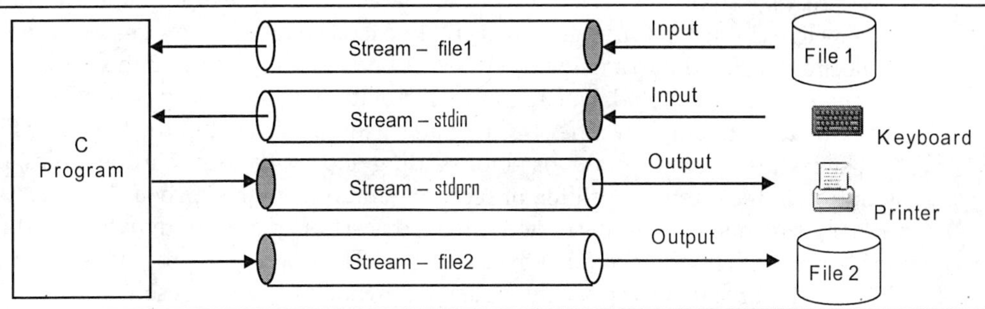

Figure 10.1 | Input and output using streams

The important points about streams are as follows:

1. Before data can be read from, or written to a file, the file must be opened (which may involve creating a new data file). Opening a file associates (opens) a stream with it.
2. When a program is executed, five **standard streams** namely stdin, stdout, stderr, stdaux and stdprn are already open and available for use. The stream stdin is associated with keyboard for reading the input. The streams stdout and stderr are associated with the screen for writing the output and the errors, respectively. The stream stdprn is associated with the printer (i.e. parallel port LPT1) and the stream stdaux is associated with an auxiliary port (i.e. serial port COM1).
3. It is possible to associate more than one stream with a file (e.g. both the streams stdout and stderr are associated with the screen), but it is not possible to associate a stream with two files at a time.
4. A stream can be opened for input (i.e. read), output (i.e. write) or both (i.e. update).

5. A stream associated with a file is represented by an object of the type FILE defined in the header file stdio.h as:

```
typedef struct
{
    short level;                //←fill/empty buffer level
    unsigned flags;             //←File status flags
    char fd;                    //←File descriptor
    unsigned char hold;         //←ungetc character if no buffer
    short bsize;                //←Buffer size
    unsigned char *buffer;      //←Data transfer buffer
    unsigned char *curp;        //← Current active pointer
    unsigned int istemp;        //←Temporary file indicator
    short token;                //←Used for validity checking
} FILE;
```

6. An object of type FILE contains† all the information needed to control a stream, including its file position indicator (i.e. current active pointer), a pointer to its associated buffer (if any), an error indicator that records whether a read/write error has occurred and an end of file indicator that records whether the end of file has reached.
7. Input from, or output to, a file can be performed either in **text mode** or **binary mode**. Accordingly, the corresponding associated stream can be a **text stream** or a **binary stream**. A text stream is an ordered sequence of the characters composed into lines, terminated by a new line character. Carriage return and line feed character combinations present in the file are translated into a new line character before being placed in the stream. Thus, text streams are interpreted. Due to this interpretation, what the program sees (i.e. data within the text stream) can differ from what is actually present in the file (refer Figure 10.2). Text streams are typically used for reading and writing standard text files, printing output to the screen or printer, or receiving input from the keyboard.

   Binary streams are un-interpreted. They consists of one or more bytes of arbitrary information with no translation of the characters. Thus, what the program sees (i.e. data within the binary stream) is exactly the same as what is actually present in the file (refer Figure 10.2). Binary streams are typically used for reading and writing binary files (such as graphics files, word processing files, etc.), or reading and writing to the modem.

   Figure 10.2 illustrates the difference between the text view and binary view of a file.
8. A stream can be **unbuffered, line buffered** or **fully buffered**. If a stream is un-buffered, the characters written to the stream are immediately transmitted to the program (during an input operation) or to the file (during an output operation). Since the I/O operations on a file (i.e. disk or some other peripheral device) are generally slow and time consuming, the data are read from or written to the file in the form of data blocks instead of a single character at a time. The data block read from, or to be written to, the file is kept in a stream, which acts as a buffer. When the program requires an input, it reads it from the stream. When the stream gets empty, the next data block from the file is read into it. During an output operation, the characters to be written to the file are accumulated in the stream and transmitted to the file as a block. When the accumulated block will be

† Refer Section 10.5 for a description on the FILE type.

transmitted to the file depends upon whether the stream is line buffered or fully buffered. If a stream is line buffered, the characters are transmitted to the file when a new line character is encountered. If a stream is fully buffered, the characters are transmitted to the file when the stream buffer is full (i.e. completely filled).

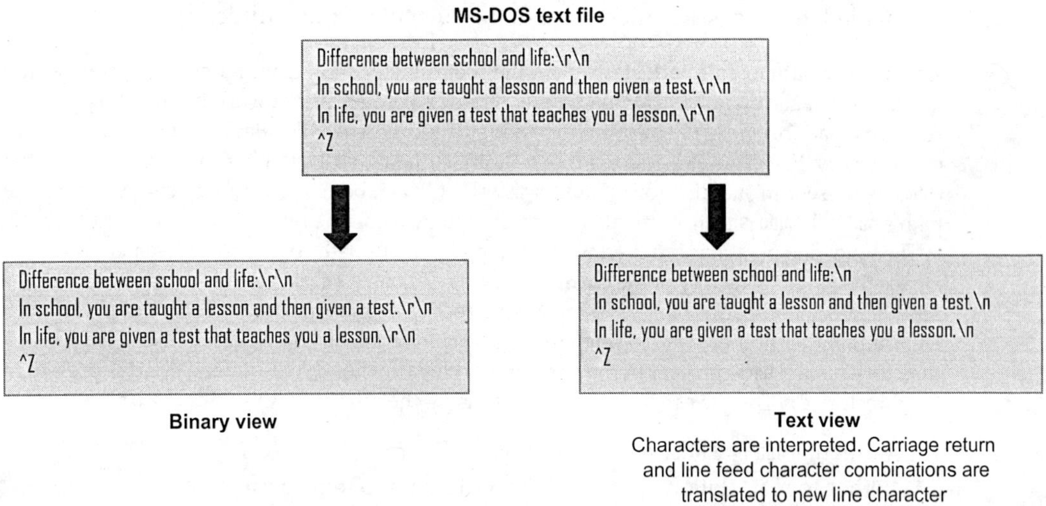

Figure 10.2 | Binary and text views of a file

9. The association between a file and the stream can be broken by closing the stream. Before a stream is disassociated from the file, any unwritten buffer content is transmitted to the file (i.e. the stream is flushed). All the streams are automatically closed (i.e. flushed) when the program terminates successfully (i.e. program does not get terminated abnormally).

10.4 I/O Using Streams

C language provides a number of library functions for reading and writing files using streams. Most of the functions accept an object of the type FILE* as an argument. The object of the type FILE*, sometimes known as **file pointer**, represents a **pointer to a stream.** This argument provides the information about the stream and its associated file on which the operations are to be performed. It is advisable to manipulate FILE objects (i.e. streams) by using the input/output library functions rather than manipulating them directly. The library functions described in the following sections are used for creating the streams and performing the input and output operations on them.

10.4.1 Opening a Stream

To perform an operation on a file, the file must be opened. The file can be opened by using the function fopen. Opening a file with the function fopen creates a new stream and establishes a connection between the file and the stream. The function fopen is declared in the header file stdio.h as:

```
FILE* fopen(const char* filename, const char* mode);
```

The important points about the usage of the function fopen are as follows:

1. The function fopen opens a file whose name is the string pointed to by the argument filename and associates a stream with it. The argument string filename may also include the path information. The path specifies the drive and the directory where the file is located. The path can be an **absolute path** or a **relative path**. If path information is not provided, the file is assumed to be in the current working directory.

> An **absolute path** or **full path** starts from the root directory (i.e. drive name) and provides the information regarding the location of a file regardless of the current working directory.
> A **relative path** provides the information about the location of a file relative to the current working directory. For example, assume that **c:\tc\bin** is the current working directory and the file **stdio.h** is present in the directory **c:\tc\include**. The file can be referred to by using the absolute path as **c:\tc\include\stdio.h**. It can also be referred to by using the relative path as **..\include\stdio.h**.
> The following notations are used while writing a relative path: Two consecutive periods (i.e. ..) means the parent directory of the current working directory, single period (i.e. .) means the current directory and backslash (i.e. \) means the root directory (in case of DOS and WINDOWS environment). Another way to refer the file **stdio.h** can be **\tc\include\stdio.h**. Now, suppose a directory named **dir** is present in the current working directory. A file named **file.txt** is present in the directory **dir**. The file can be referred to by using the relative path as **.\dir\file.txt**.

2. The argument mode is a string that specifies:
   a. Whether to read data from the file or write data to it, or perform both.
   b. Whether to generate new contents for the file or leave the existing contents in place.
   c. Whether write operations to a file can alter the existing contents or can only append bytes at the end of the file.
   d. Whether file is opened in text mode or binary mode.

   The above-mentioned options for a file can be specified by providing an appropriate string (listed in Table 10.1) as an argument mode to the function fopen.

Table 10.1 | Various modes for opening a file

Mode string	Description
"r"	Opens an existing file in the text mode for reading only
"w"	Opens a file in the text mode for writing only. If the file already exists, it is truncated to zero length (i.e. all the contents will be overwritten). If it does not exist, a new file is created
"a"	Opens a file in the text mode for append access (i.e. writing at the end of the file). If the file already exists, its contents are unchanged and the output to the stream is appended at the end of the file. Otherwise, a new empty file is created
"rb"	Opens an existing file in the binary mode for reading only
"wb"	Opens a file in the binary mode for writing only. If the file already exists, it is truncated to zero length. If it does not exist, a new file is created
"ab"	Opens a file in the binary mode for append access, i.e. writing at the end of the file. If the file already exists, its contents are unchanged and the output to the stream is appended at the end of the file. Otherwise, a new empty file is created

(Contd...)

"r+"	Opens an existing file in the text mode for update (i.e. reading and writing). The initial contents of the file are unchanged and the file position indicator is at the beginning of the file
"w+"	Opens a file in the text mode for update (i.e. reading and writing). If the file already exists, it is truncated to zero length. If it does not exist, a new file is created
"a+"	Opens or creates a file in the text mode for both reading and appending. If the file exists, its initial contents are unchanged. Otherwise, a new file is created. The initial file position for reading is at the beginning of the file, but the output is always appended at the end of the file
"r+b" or "rb+"	Opens an existing file in the binary mode for update (i.e. reading and writing). The initial contents of the file are unchanged and the initial file position is at the beginning of the file
"w+b" or "wb+"	Opens a file in the binary mode for update (i.e. reading and writing). If the file already exists, it is truncated to zero length. If it does not exist, a new file is created
"a+b" or "ab+"	Opens or creates a file in the binary mode for both reading and appending. If the file already exists, its initial contents are unchanged. Otherwise, a new file is created. The initial file position for reading is at the beginning of the file, but the output is always appended at the end of the file

3. The function fopen returns a pointer to the object controlling the stream. If the open operation fails, it returns a NULL pointer. The open operation may fail under the following circumstances:
   a. Opening a file with the read mode fails if the file does not exist or cannot be read.
   b. Opening a file with the write mode fails if the file cannot be created. It cannot be created if the disk is write-protected, if there is not enough space on the disk for creating the file, etc.
4. When a file is opened with the update mode (i.e. for reading and writing), both the input and output operations can be performed on the associated stream. However, the output should not be directly followed by an input without flushing‡ the stream and the input should not be immediately followed by an output without an intervening call to a file-positioning§ functions like fseek or fsetpos.
5. When opened, a stream is fully buffered if and only if it does not refer to an interactive device. The buffering of a stream can be set by using the functions setbuf and setvbuf¶.

10.4.2 Closing Streams

An open stream can be closed by using the function fclose. It is declared in the header file stdio.h as:

```
int fclose(FILE* stream);
```

The important points about the use of the function fclose are as follows:

1. A successful call to the function fclose causes the stream pointed to by the argument stream and the associated file to be closed.

---

‡ Refer Section 10.4.13 for a description on how to flush a stream.

§ Refer Section 10.4.5 for a description on file positioning.

¶ Refer Section 10.4.13 for a description on stream buffering.

2. Before the stream is closed, any unwritten data present in the stream buffer are written to the file (i.e. stream is flushed). Any unread buffered data are discarded.
3. A call to the function fclose disassociates the stream from the file and any buffer set by the functions setbuf or setvbuf is disassociated from the stream. The memory allocated to the buffer[††] is deallocated, if it was allocated automatically.
4. After the stream is closed, the link between the stream and the file is broken. No further I/O can be performed from the file unless the stream is reopened.
5. The function fclose returns zero if the stream is closed successfully and EOF [‡‡] if an error occurs. For instance, an error occurs if the disk gets full, when the function fclose flushes the remaining buffered data to the file before closing the stream.

The piece of code in Program 10-1 illustrates the usage of the function fclose.

Line | Prog 10-1.c

```
1  //The function fclose
2  #include<stdio.h>
3  #include<conio.h>
4  main()
5  {
6      printf("File your tax return on time\n");
7      fclose(stdout);
8      printf("Let the country progress");
9  }
```

Output window

File your tax return on time

Remarks:

- The function fclose in line number 7 closes the standard stream stdout
- After the stream stdout is closed, the link between the stream and the file (i.e. screen) is broken. No further output can now take place via the stream stdout
- Thus, the string "Let the country progress" in line number 8 does not get printed on the screen

Program 10-1 | A program that illustrates the use of the function fclose

The function fclose closes a specific stream. However, if the number of streams is more, all the user-defined streams can be closed in a single function call by using the function fcloseall. The function fcloseall closes all the open streams except the standard streams, i.e. stdin, stdout, stderr, stdaux and stdprn. The function fcloseall is declared in the header file stdio.h as:

```
int fcloseall(void);
```

The important points about the function fcloseall are as follows:

1. The function fcloseall closes all the open streams (except the standard streams) and the corresponding files.
2. The association between all the streams (except the standard streams) and their corresponding files is broken. Any buffered unwritten data present in the stream are written to the corresponding files, and the buffered unread data are discarded.
3. The function fcloseall returns zero if all the streams are closed successfully and EOF if an error is detected.
4. It is better to close each stream separately so that the problems with the individual streams can be identified.
5. All open streams are automatically closed when the program terminates successfully. When the program terminates abnormally either due to a call to the function abort or

[††]Refer Section 10.4.13 for a description on the usage of automatic and explicit buffers used by the streams for I/O buffering.

[‡‡]Refer Section 10.4.6 for a description on EOF.

due to some runtime error (e.g. division by zero, floating point formats not linked, etc.), whether the open streams will be closed or not is implementation defined.

The piece of code in Program 10-2 illustrates that the function fcloseall does not close the standard streams like stdout.

Line	Prog 10-2.c	Output window
1	//The function fcloseall does not close the standard streams	File your tax return on time Let the country progress **Remarks:** • The function fcloseall does not close the standard streams • Thus, the call to the function fcloseall in line number 7 does not close the standard stream stdout • Therefore, the call to the function printf in line number 8 prints the string "Let the country progress" on the screen
2	#include<stdio.h>	
3	#include<conio.h>	
4	main()	
5	{	
6	printf("File your tax return on time\n");	
7	fcloseall();	
8	printf("Let the country progress");	
9	}	

Program 10-2 | A program to illustrate that the function fcloseall does not close the standard streams

10.4.3 Character Input

The function fgetc and the macro getc are used to read a character from a stream. The function fgetc is declared in the header file stdio.h as:

```
int fgetc(FILE* stream);
```

The important points about the usage of fgetc and getc are as follows:

1. The function fgetc reads the next character from the stream pointed to by the argument stream as unsigned char, converts it into int and returns its value.
2. After the character is read, the associated file position indicator[§§] for the stream pointed to by the argument stream is incremented.
3. If the end of file has been encountered or read error occurs, EOF is returned. Whether end of file has been encountered or a read error has occurred can be distinguished by using the functions feof and ferror[¶¶].
4. The macro getc is just like the function fgetc, except that it is implemented[†††] as a macro. The macro getc is defined in the header file stdio.h as:

```
#define getc(f) ((--((f)->level) >=0 )? (unsigned char)(*(f)-> curp++): fgetc(f))
```

5. The macro getchar is used to read the next character from the input stream stdin. It is defined in the header file stdio.h as:

```
#define getchar getc(stdin)
```

The piece of code in Program 10-3 illustrates the use of the functions fopen and fgetc to read the content of a file.

---

§§ Refer Section 10.4.5 for a description on file position indicator.

¶¶ Refer Section 10.4.6 for a description on the functions feof and ferror.

††† Refer Section 10.5 for a description on the implementation of the macro getc.

Line | Prog 10-3.c

```
1  //Read the content of a file
2  #include<stdio.h>
3  #include<conio.h>
4  #include<stdlib.h>
5  main()
6  {
7      FILE *fp;
8      char ch;
9      fp=fopen("abc.txt","r");
10     if(fp==NULL)
11     {
12         printf("Unable to read the file\n");
13         getch();
14         exit(1);
15     }
16     else
17     {
18         while((ch=fgetc(fp))!=EOF)
19         {
20             printf("%c",ch);
21         }
22         fclose(fp);
23     }
24 }
```

abc.txt

If you file your waste paper basket for fifty years, you have a public library

Output window

If you file your waste paper basket for fifty years, you have a public library

Remarks:

- The prototype of the function exit is available in the header file stdlib.h
- The function fopen opens the data file abc.txt in read mode
- Since no path information is provided and only file name is given, the data file is assumed to be present in the current working directory
- If the data file is present there, it is successfully opened and a stream is associated with it. The pointer to the stream is assigned to the variable fp
- If the data file is not found, the function fopen fails and returns a NULL pointer
- The if statement in line number 10 checks whether the file is successfully opened or not
- If the file is successfully opened, the while loop in the else body reads and prints all the characters till end of file, i.e. EOF character is encountered
- It is important to note that the expression ch=fgetc(fp) must be parenthesized since the logical negation operator (i.e. !=) has higher precedence than the assignment (i.e. =) operator
- The macro getc can also be used in place of the function fgetc
- In line number 22, the function fclose closes the stream and dissociates it from the file

Program 10-3 | A program that reads the content of a file and displays it on the screen

10.4.4 Character Output

The function fputc and the macro putc are used to write a character to the stream. The function fputc is declared in the header file stdio.h as:

```
int fputc(int c, FILE* stream);
```

The important points about the usage of fputc and putc are as follows:

1. The function fputc writes the character specified by the argument c to the output stream pointed to by the argument stream at the position indicated by the associated file position indicator for the stream.
2. The file position indicator is advanced appropriately.
3. The function fputc firstly converts the character c to the type unsigned char and writes it to the stream stream.
4. The function fputc returns the character written. If a write error occurs, the error indicator for the stream is set and the function fputc returns EOF.

5. The macro putc is just like the function fputc, except that it is implemented[‡‡‡] as a macro. The macro putc is defined in the header file stdio.h as:

```
#define putc(c,f) ((++((f)->level) < 0 )? (unsigned char)(*(f)-> curp++=(c)): fputc((c),f))
```

6. The macro putchar is used to output a character to the stream stdout. It is defined in the header file stdio.h as:

```
#define putchar putc((c),stdout)
```

The code segment in Program 10-4 illustrates the use of the function fputc to write a string to a file.

Line | Prog 10-4.c

```
1  //Write a string to a file
2  #include<stdio.h>
3  #include<conio.h>
4  #include<stdlib.h>
5  main()
6  {
7      FILE *fp;
8      char str[255];
9      int i=0;
10     fp=fopen("abc.txt","w");
11     if(fp==NULL)
12     {
13         printf("Unable to create the file\n");
14         getch();
15         exit(1);
16     }
17     else
18     {
19         printf("Enter the string that you want to write the file:\n");
20         gets(str);
21         while(str[i]!='\0')
22         {
23             fputc(str[i++],fp);
24         }
25         fclose(fp);
26     }
27 }
```

Ouput window

```
Enter the string you want to write to the file:
UNIX has its weak points but its file system is not one of them.
```

abc.txt (after the execution of the program)

```
UNIX has its weak points but its file system is not one of them.
```

Remarks:

- The function fopen opens the data file abc.txt in the write mode
- Since no path information is provided and only file name is given, the file is assumed to be present in the current working directory
- If the data file is present there, the data file will be overwritten. If it is not present, data file will be created
- In line number 23, the function fputc writes the characters present in the string str to the stream pointed to by fp iteratively
- Note that till this point, characters are written to the stream and not to the data file abc.txt
- In line number 25, the function fclose closes the stream pointed to by fp and disassociates it from the file. Before this disassociation occurs, the characters available in the stream are actually written to the data file
- The macro putc can be used in place of the fputc in line number 23
- Note that there is no need to explicitly place EOF character at the end of file like null character (i.e. '\0') is placed at the end of strings

Program 10-4 | A program that writes a string to a file

[‡‡‡] Refer Section 10.5 for a description on the implementation of the macro putc.

The code segment in Program 10-5 illustrates the use of the functions fgetc and fputc to copy content of one file to another.

Line | Prog 10-5.c

```
1  //Copy content of one file to another file
2  #include<stdio.h>
3  #include<conio.h>
4  #include<stdlib.h>
5  main()
6  {
7      FILE *fp1, *fp2;
8      char ch;
9      fp1=fopen("c:\\tc\\abc.txt","r");
10     fp2=fopen("..\\new.txt","w");
11     if(fp1==NULL || fp2==NULL)
12     {
13         printf("Problem in reading or writing a file\n");
14         printf("Unable to continue\n");
15         getch();
16         exit(1);
17     }
18     else
19     {
20         while((ch=fgetc(fp1))!=EOF)
21         {
22             fputc(ch,fp2);
23         }
24         fcloseall();
25     }
26 }
```

c:\tc\abc.txt (before the execution of the program)

Desolation is a file, and the endurance of darkness is preparation for great light.

Current working directory: c:\tc\bin
c:\tc\new.txt (after the execution of the program)

Desolation is a file, and the endurance of darkness is preparation for great light.

Remarks:

- The content of a file can be copied to another file by iteratively copying all the characters present in it
- Let us assume that the current working directory is c:\tc\bin
- In line number 9, the absolute path and the file name are given to the function fopen. It will open the data file abc.txt present in the directory (folder in Windows) c:\tc in read mode and associates a stream pointed to by fp1 with it
- Note that double slashes are used while writing the path name because a single slash forms an escape sequence, e.g. \t is an escape sequence
- In line number 10, the relative path and the file name are given to the function fopen. It will look for the file new.txt in the parent directory of c:\tc\bin, i.e. in c:\tc
- If the file is present, it will be overwritten else a new file will be created
- The while loop in line number 20 reads character from the stream pointed to by fp1 and writes it to the stream pointed to by fp2. All the characters are read and written iteratively
- The function fcloseall closes all the open streams. Before the streams are closed, they are flushed. Thus, the execution of this function actually writes the characters available in the stream pointed to by fp2 to the file new.txt

Program 10-5 | A program that copies the content of one file to another

The code segment in Program 10-6 appends the content of a file at the end of another file.

Line | Prog 10-6.c

```
//Copy content of one file at the end of another file
#include<stdio.h>
#include<conio.h>
#include<stdlib.h>
```

abc.txt (before the execution of the program)

I am still learning.

new.txt (before the execution of the program)

We learn by doing.

(Contd...)

```
main()
{
    FILE *fp1, *fp2;
    char ch;
    fp1=fopen("abc.txt","r");
    fp2=fopen("new.txt","a");
    if(fp1==NULL || fp2==NULL)
    {
        printf("Problem in reading or writing a file\n");
        printf("Unable to continue\n");
        getch();
        exit(1);
    }
    else
    {
        while((ch=fgetc(fp1))!=EOF)
        {
            fputc(ch,fp2);
        }
        fcloseall();
    }
}
```

new.txt (after the execution of the program)

We learn by doing. I am still learning.

Remarks:

- The function fopen opens the data file abc.txt in the read mode and the data file new.txt in the append mode
- Since only the names of the files are mentioned, they are supposed to be present in the current working directory
- The while loop reads the content of the data file associated with the stream pointed to by fp1 (i.e. abc.txt) and appends it to the data file associated with the stream pointed to by fp2 (i.e. new.txt)

Program 10-6 | A program that appends the content of one file at the end of another file

10.4.5 File Position Indicator

When a file is opened, a stream is associated with it. The file position indicator for the associated stream indicates where the stream is currently reading or writing in the file.

The important points about the file position indicator are as follows:

1. The file position indicator is represented as a long integer, which counts the number of bytes from the beginning of the file.
2. The initial value of the file position indicator depends upon the mode in which the file is opened. If the file is opened in the read mode or the write mode, the file position indicator is at the beginning of the file and will have value zero. If the file is opened in the append mode, the initial value of the file position indicator is implementation defined.
3. Every successful I/O operation on the stream associated with the file, advances the file position indicator through the file. Each time a character is read or written, the file position indicator is incremented.
4. The current location (i.e. value) of the file position indicator for the stream can be determined by using the functions ftell and fgetpos.

   a. **The function ftell**: The function ftell is declared in the header file stdio.h as:

   ```
   long int ftell(FILE *stream);
   ```

   The important points about the function ftell are as follows:

   i. A successful call to the function ftell returns the current value of the file position indicator for the stream pointed to by the argument stream.

   ii. On failure, the function ftell returns -1L.

b. **The function fgetpos**: The function fgetpos is declared in the header file stdio.h as:

`int fgetpos(FILE *stream, fpos_t* pos);`

The important points about the function fgetpos are as follows:

i. The function fgetpos stores the current value of the file position indicator for the stream pointed to by the argument stream, in the object pointed to by the argument pos.
ii. fpos_t is a typedef name defined in the header file stdio.h as:

`typedef long fpos_t;`

iii. If successful, the function fgetpos returns zero. On failure, it returns a non-zero value.

The piece of code in Program 10-7 illustrates the use of functions ftell and fgetpos to determine the value of file position indicator.

Line	Prog 10-7.c

```
1  //Use of the functions ftell and fgetpos to determine the
2  //current value of the file position indicator
3  #include<stdio.h>
4  #include<conio.h>
5  #include<stdlib.h>
6  main()
7  {
8      FILE *fp1, *fp2;
9      char ch;
10     long int loc1, loc2;
11     fp1=fopen("abc.txt","r");
12     fp2=fopen("cde.txt","a");
13     if(fp1==NULL||fp2==NULL)
14     {
15         printf("Unable to read the file\n");
16         printf("Unable to continue\n");
17         getch();
18         exit(1);
19     }
20     else
21     {
22         loc1=ftell(fp1);
23         loc2=ftell(fp2);
24         printf("Initially, indicators are located at %ld %ld\n",loc1, loc2);
25         ch=fgetc(fp1);
26         fputc('!',fp2);
27         loc1=ftell(fp1);
28         loc2=ftell(fp2);
29         printf("After I/O, indicators move to the location %ld %ld\n",loc1,loc2);
30         ch=fgetc(fp1);
31         fputc('!',fp2);
```

abc.txt (before execution of the program)

Strength is life!!

cde.txt (before execution of the program)

Weakness is death

Output window

Initially, indicators are located at 0 0
After I/O, indicators move to the location 1 18
Finally, indicators are at the location 2 19

cde.txt (after execution of the program)

Weakness is death!!

Remarks:

- The file abc.txt is opened in the read mode and the file cde.txt is opened in the append mode
- The initial values of the file position indicators are zero
- Every successful input–output operation on stream advances the file position indicator
- Since in append mode, the characters are added at the end of the file, after the first write operation (i.e. in line number 26) the value of file position indicator will be the number of characters previously present in the file plus one, i.e. 18

(Contd...)

```
        fgetpos(fp1,&loc1);
        fgetpos(fp2,&loc2);
        printf("Finally, indicators are at the location %ld %ld\n",loc1,loc2);
    }
    fcloseall();
}
```

Program 10-7 | A program that illustrates the use of the functions ftell and fgetpos

5. For some files (e.g. disk files) the location (i.e. value) of the file position indicator can also be changed so that data can be read from or written to any portion of the file. Files that allow changing the value of the file position indicator are known as **random access files.** Some files do not allow the file position indicator to be changed. Such files are known as **sequential access files** (e.g. printers). The value of the file position indicator in random access files can be changed with the help of functions fseek, fsetpos and rewind.

   a. **The function fseek**: The function fseek is declared in the header file stdio.h as:

   ```
   int fseek(FILE *stream, long int offset, int whence);
   ```

   The important points about the function fseek are as follows:

   i. The function fseek sets the file position indicator for the stream pointed to by the argument stream.

   ii. The whence value indicates whether the offset is relative to the beginning of the file, the current file position or the end of the file. The value of whence must be one of the symbolic constants (macros) or their corresponding values listed in Table 10.2. The symbolic constants are defined in the header file stdio.h.

Table 10.2 | Possible values of whence argument

S.No	whence	Value	File location
1.	SEEK_SET	0	Seek from the beginning of the file
2.	SEEK_CUR	1	Seek from the current position
3.	SEEK_END	2	Seek from the end of the file

   iii. The offset is the difference in bytes between the file position indicated by the argument whence and the new location of file position indicator. If the value of offset is negative, the new location will be before (i.e. towards the left of) the whence position. If it is positive, the new location will be after (i.e. towards the right of) the whence position, and if it is zero, the new location will be the same as the whence position.

   iv. Before the file indicator position is set to new location, the function fseek flushes (i.e. writes) any unwritten buffered data to the file. After flushing, the file position indicator is changed to the new location.

   v. A successful call to the function fseek clears the end-of-file indicator for the stream and undoes any effect of the function ungetc[§§§] on the stream.

   vi. On success (i.e. if the file position indicator is successfully moved) the function fseek returns a zero value. On failure, it returns a non-zero value.

---

§§§ Refer Section 10.5 for a description on the function ungetc.

The piece of code in Program 10-8 illustrates the use of the function fseek on an update stream.

Line | Prog 10-8.c

```
1  //Use of the function fseek on an update stream
2  #include<stdio.h>
3  #include<conio.h>
4  #include<stdlib.h>
5  main()
6  {
7     FILE *fp;
8     char ch;
9     fp=fopen("abc.txt","r+");
10    if(fp==NULL)
11    {
12       printf("Unable to open the file\n");
13       printf("Unable to continue\n");
14       getch();
15       exit(1);
16    }
17    else
18    {
19       fseek(fp, -10L, SEEK_END);
20       fputc('1',fp);
21       fseek(fp,0L, SEEK_SET);
22       while((ch=fgetc(fp))!=EOF)
23          putchar(ch);
24    }
25    fclose(fp);
26 }
```

abc.txt (before the execution of the program)
I will file nomination papers for assembly elections at 10:00 AM.

Output window
I will file nomination papers for assembly elections at 11:00 AM.

abc.txt (after the execution of the program)
I will file nomination papers for assembly elections at 11:00 AM.

Remarks:

- The file abc.txt is opened in the "r+" mode, i.e. update mode
- The content of the stream pointed to by fp as it appears to the C program will be

I will file nomination papers for assembly elections at 10:00 AM.\n^Z

- The fseek function in line number 19 positions the file position indicator 10 characters towards the left of SEEK_END whence position. This is shown as:

New Position ↓ SEEK_END ↓

I will file nomination papers for assembly elections at 10:00 AM.\n^Z

- The function fputc writes the character '1' to the stream fp at the position indicated by the file position indicator. The character '1' overwrites the character '0' present in the stream
- **Note that till now, the character '1' has overwritten the character '0' in the stream only and not in the file, because the data of the stream have not yet been flushed to the file**
- **Observe this fact by tracing the program and checking the content of the file abc.txt after the execution of the statement in line number 20 but before the execution of the statement in line number 21**
- The call to the function fseek in line number 21 position the file position indicator at the beginning of the file. Before repositioning, the unwritten buffered data are written to the file
- **After execution of the statement in line number 21, check the content of the file to see that '1' actually overwrites '0' in the file**
- The while loop prints all the characters present in the file

Program 10-8 | A program that illustrates the use of the function fseek

b. **The function fsetpos**: The function fsetpos is declared in the header file stdio.h as:

```
int fsetpos(FILE *stream, fpos_t* pos);
```

The important points about the function fsetpos are as follows:

i. The function fsetpos sets the file position indicator for the stream pointed to by the argument stream according to the value of the object pointed to by the argument pos.
ii. A successful call to the function fsetpos clears the end-of-file indicator for the stream and undoes any effect of the function ungetc on the stream.
iii. On success (i.e. if the file position indicator is successfully moved), the function fsetpos returns a zero value. On failure, it returns a non-zero value.

The piece of code in Program 10-9 illustrates the use of the function fsetpos on an update stream.

Line | Prog 10-9.c

```
1  //Use of the function fsetpos on an update stream
2  #include<stdio.h>
3  #include<conio.h>
4  #include<stdlib.h>
5  main()
6  {
7      FILE *fp;
8      char ch;
9      fpos_t location;
10     fp=fopen("abc.txt","r+");
11     if(fp==NULL)
12     {
13         printf("Unable to open the file\n");
14         printf("Unable to continue\n");
15         getch();
16         exit(1);
17     }
18     else
19     {
20         fgetpos(fp,&location);
21         location+=18;
22         fsetpos(fp,&location);
23         fputs("25",fp);
24         location=0;
25         fsetpos(fp,&location);
26         while((ch=fgetc(fp))!=EOF)
27             putchar(ch);
28     }
29     fclose(fp);
30 }
```

abc.txt (before the execution of the program)

Bring file number 18

Output window

Bring file number 25

abc.txt (after the execution of the program)

Bring file number 25

Remarks:

- The file abc.txt is opened in the "r+" mode, i.e. the update mode
- The initial value of file position indicator for the stream pointed to by fp will be zero
- The function fgetpos in line number 20 stores the current value of the file position indicator for the stream pointed to by fp in the object pointed to by its second argument (i.e. in the object location)
- Thus, after the execution of the statement in line number 20, the value of location would be 0
- The expression in line number 21 manipulates the value of the object location and makes it 18
- The function fsetpos in line number 22 sets the position of the file position indicator for the stream pointed to by fp according to the value of the object pointed to by its second argument (i.e. 18 characters after the start position)
- The function fputs writes the string "25" in the stream pointed to by fp at the location indicated by the file position indicator
- Thus, the string "25" overwrites the string "18". Till now, "25" has been written in the stream pointed to by fp and not physically to the file abc.txt
- The call to the function fsetpos in line number 25 flushes the content of the stream and sets the file position indicator to the beginning of the file
- The while loop prints the content of the file

Program 10-9 | A program that illustrates the use of the function fsetpos

c. **The function rewind**: The function rewind is declared in the header file stdio.h as:

```
void rewind(FILE *stream);
```

The important points about the function rewind are as follows:

i. The function rewind sets the file position indicator for the stream stream to the beginning of the file.

ii. It is equivalent to (void) fseek(stream, 0L, SEEK_SET); except that the error indicator¶¶¶ for the stream is also cleared.

iii The function rewind returns no value.

10.4.6 End of File and Errors

Like strings are terminated by the null character, i.e. '\0' and lines are terminated by the new line character, i.e. '\n', files are terminated by a special character known as **end-of-file character**. Different operating systems use different special characters to mark the end of the file. For example, DOS and WINDOWS use Ctrl+Z character to mark the file's end while the UNIX operating system uses Ctrl+D character for it.

C provides a number of library functions like fgetc, etc. to read characters from a file. While reading, when these functions encounter the end of the file, they return **EOF** character, irrespective of the character used by the operating system to mark the end of the file. The EOF, commonly known as **end-of-file character**, is a macro defined in the header file stdio.h. The important points about EOF are as follows:

1. EOF is an end-of-file indicator. It indicates that end of file has been reached and no more data can be read from the stream associated with the file. It is a macro (symbolic constant) defined in the header file stdio.h as:

```
#define EOF (-1)
```

2. The actual value of EOF is a system-dependent negative number, but the most common choice for EOF is -1. It is guaranteed that the EOF value compare unequal to any valid character code because the ASCII value of valid characters spans from 0 to 255.
3. File access and I/O functions also return EOF character in case they encounter some error while performing the operation.

If EOF is used to indicate both the end of file and error, then how can it be determined whether end of file has been reached or an error has occurred?

The C language provides an answer to this question by providing the functions feof and ferror. Whether end of file is encountered or an error has occurred can be distinguished by using the functions feof and ferror:

1. **The function feof:** The function feof is declared in the header file stdio.h as:

```
int feof(FILE* stream);
```

The important points about the function feof are as follows:

a. The function feof tests the end-of-file indicator†††† flag for the stream pointed to by the stream.

¶¶¶ Refer Section 10.5 for a description on error indicator flag.

†††† Refer Section 10.5 for a description on end-of-file indicator flag.

b. The function feof returns a non-zero value (i.e. true) if the end-of-file indicator flag for the stream is set (i.e. end of file has been reached).

Consider the code to copy content of one file to another listed in Program 10-5. The mentioned code checks the EOF character to determine whether end of file has been reached. As discussed, looking for EOF is not the best way to determine the end-of-file condition because EOF can also be returned by a file I/O function if some error occurs. Thus, the code listed in Program 10-5 is rewritten in Program 10-10 by using the function feof to determine the end-of-file condition.

Line | Prog 10-10.c

```
1  //Copy content of one file to another file
2  #include<stdio.h>
3  #include<conio.h>
4  #include<stdlib.h>
5  main()
6  {
7      FILE *fp1, *fp2;
8      char ch;
9      fp1=fopen("abc.txt","r");
10     fp2=fopen("new.txt","w");
11     if(fp1==NULL || fp2==NULL)
12     {
13         printf("Problem in reading or writing a file\n");
14         printf("Unable to continue\n");
15         getch();
16         exit(1);
17     }
18     else
19     {
20         while(!feof(fp1))
21         {
22             ch=fgetc(fp1);
23             fputc(ch,fp2);
24         }
25         fcloseall();
26     }
27 }
```

abc.txt

Desolation is a file, and the endurance of darkness is preparation for great light.

new.txt (after the execution of the program)

Desolation is a file, and the endurance of darkness is preparation for great light.
ÿ

Remarks:

- The file abc.txt is opened in the read mode and the stream pointed to by fp1 is associated with it
- The file new.txt is opened in the write mode and the stream pointed to by fp2 is associated with it
- If the function fopen successfully opens the files, the program will proceed else the program will be terminated by the call to the function exit
- The while loop reads all the characters from the stream fp1 and writes them to the stream fp2
- The function fcloseall closes all the opened streams and flushes the characters present in the buffer of the streams, if any
- **Observe the presence of the character ÿ at the end of the file new.txt. It is an end-of-file character.**
- The reason behind its presence in the file new.txt is that the function feof return true only when the end-of-file condition has been reached and the end-of-file indicator flag is set
- Refer Section 10.5. for a description on the end-of-file indicator flag
- Thus, in line number 22, the function fgetc reads the end-of-file character from the stream fp1. In line number 23, the function fputc writes the read end-of-file character to the stream fp2 and then the while expression evaluates to false and the loop terminates
- Change the statement written in line number 23 to **if(!feof(fp1)) fputc(ch,fp2);** so that the end-of-file character does not get written to the file new.txt

Program 10-10 | A program that copies the content of a file to another

2. **The function ferror:** The function ferror is declared in the header file stdio.h as:

   int ferror(FILE* stream);

   The important points about the function ferror are as follows:

   a. The function ferror tests the error indicator flag for the stream pointed to by the stream.
   b. The function ferror returns a non-zero value (i.e. true) if the error indicator flag for the stream is set (i.e. an error has occurred).

10.4.7 Line Input

The function fgetc is used to read a character from a stream. However, many programs interpret input on the basis of lines. These programs require the use of the functions that can read a line of text from a stream. The C library has the function fgets that can read a line of text from a stream. It is declared in the header file stdio.h as:

char* fgets(char* s, int n, FILE* stream);

The important points about the usage of function fgets are as follows:

1. The function fgets reads characters from the stream pointed to by stream into the array pointed to by s. It stops either by reading n-1 characters or a new line character.
2. The file position indicator is moved appropriately.
3. The new line character is retained and the null character is appended to mark the end of the string.
4. The function fgets returns s if successful.
5. If end of file (i.e. EOF) is encountered and no character has been read into the array, the content of the array remain unchanged and a null pointer is returned.
6. If a read error occurs, the content of array s are indeterminate and a null pointer is returned.

The piece of code in Program 10-11 illustrates the above-mentioned points.

Line	Trace	Prog 10-11.c
1		//Use of the function fgets
2		#include<stdio.h>
3	1	main()
4		{
5		FILE *fp;
6		char str[50],*p;
7	2	fp=fopen("abc.txt","r");
8	3	p=fgets(str, 35, fp);
9	4	printf(str);
10	5	p=fgets(str, 15, fp);
11	6	printf(str);
12	7	p=fgets(str, 15, fp);
13	8	printf(str);
14	9	p=fgets(str, 50, fp);
15	10	printf(str);
16	11	p=fgets(str, 10, fp);
17	12	printf(str);
18	13	}

After trace step 2: abc.txt

```
Nostalgia is a file that\n
removes the rough\n
edges from the good old days\n^Z
```

str="¥ÄÇÈÌÜßäö\xl\BJ|\xl" i.e. Garbage
p=""

After trace step 3: abc.txt

```
Nostalgia is a file that\n
removes the rough\n
edges from the good old days\n^Z
```

str="Nostalgia is a file that\n"
p=" Nostalgia is a file that\n"

After trace step 5: abc.txt

```
Nostalgia is a file that\n
removes the rough\n
edges from the good old days\n^Z
```

Output window

```
Nostalgia is a file that
removes the rough
edges from the good old days
edges from the good old days
```

Remarks:

- The function fgets in line number 8 terminates after reading the '\n' character from the stream pointed to by fp. The '\n' character is retained. This can be confirmed by looking at the contents of str after trace step 3
- The function fgets in line number 10 terminates after reading 14 (i.e. 15-1) characters from the stream pointed to by fp

(Contd...)

			str="removes the ro" p="removes the ro" **After trace step 7:** **abc.txt** Nostalgia is a file that\n removes the rough\n edges from the good old days\n^Z str="ugh\n" p="ugh\n" **After trace step 9:** **abc.txt** Nostalgia is a file that\n removes the rough\n edges from the good old days\n^Z str="edges from the good old days\n" p="edges from the good old days\n" **After trace step 11:** **abc.txt** Nostalgia is a file that\n removes the rough\n edges from the good old days\n^Z str="edges from the good old days\n" p=NULL	• The function fgets in line numbers 12 and 14 terminates after reading the '\n' character from the stream pointed to by fp • The function fgets in line number 16 encounters end of file and no character has been read. Thus, the contents of the character array str remain the same. This can be confirmed by looking at the contents of str after trace steps 9 and 11 • Also, the function fgets on encountering end of file returns a null pointer. Look at the value of p after trace step 11

Program 10-11 | A program that illustrates the use of the fgets function

10.4.8 Line Output

A line of text can be written to a stream by using the function fputs. The function fputs is declared in the header file stdio.h as:

```
int fputs(char *s, FILE* stream);
```

The important points about the usage of the function fputs are as follows:

1. The function fputs writes the string pointed to by the pointer s to the stream pointed to by stream.
2. The terminating null character (i.e. '\0') of the string is not written to the stream.
3. The successful execution of the function fputs returns a non-negative value. If a write error occurs, EOF is returned.

The piece of code in Program 10-12 illustrates the usage of the function fputs.

Line	Prog 10-12.c	Output window
1	//Usage of fputs function	The value returned by the function fputs is 111
2	#include<stdio.h>	**abc.txt (after the execution of the program)**
3	#include<conio.h>	Hello Readers
4	#include<stdlib.h>	**Remarks:**
5	main()	• The function fputs in line number 18 writes the string "Hello Readers" to the stream pointed to by fp
6	{	
7	FILE *fp;	
8	int i;	

(Contd...)

Line	Prog 10-12.c	Output window
9	fp=fopen("abc.txt","w");	• The successful execution of the function fputs returns a non-negative value • The value returned by the function fputs is printed by the statement in line number 19
10	if(fp==NULL)	
11	{	
12	printf("Unable to create the file\n");	
13	getch();	
14	exit(1);	
15	}	
16	else	
17	{	
18	i=fputs("Hello Readers", fp);	
19	printf("The value returned by the function fputs is %d\n", i);	
20	}	
21	fclose(fp);	
22	}	

Program 10-12 | A program that illustrates the use of the function fputs

10.4.9 Formatted Input

The function fscanf is used to read formatted input from a stream like the function scanf is used to read formatted input from the keyboard (i.e. the stream stdin). The function fscanf is declared in the header file stdio.h as:

```
int fscanf(FILE* stream, char* format, ...);
```

The important points about the usage of the function fscanf are as follows:

1. The function fscanf reads input from the stream pointed to by the argument stream.
2. The input will be taken according to the format specifiers present in the format string pointed to by the argument format.
3. The arguments of the fscanf function following the format string should denote l-values.
4. The function fscanf can be used to read string from a file by using %s specifier. All the rules discussed in Section 6.4 for reading strings using the scanf function are applicable.
5. The function fscanf returns EOF if an error occurs before the first item is read. Otherwise, it returns the number of items successfully read.

10.4.10 Formatted Output

The function fprintf is used to write output to a stream like the function printf is used to write output to the screen (i.e. the stream stdout). The function fprintf is declared in the header file stdio.h as:

```
int fprintf(FILE *stream, char *format, ...);
```

The important points about the usage of the function fprintf are as follows:

1. The function fprintf writes the output to the stream pointed to by the argument stream.
2. The values of the arguments present after the format string pointed to by the argument format, will be written to the stream according to the format specifiers present in the format string.
3. On successful execution, the function fprintf returns the number of characters written to the stream. On error, it returns a negative value.

Program 10-13 provides a solution to the following problem and illustrates the use of the functions fprintf and fscanf.

The number of students present in a class and the marks secured by them in computing end-term examination is present in a file named marks.txt. The number of students and their marks are line separated (i.e. number of students are written in the first line and their marks are written in the next line). The marks of students are blank space separated. Sort the marks of the students and write the sorted list in the file at the end.

Line | Prog 10-13.c

```
1  //The functions fscanf and fprintf
2  #include<stdio.h>
3  #include<conio.h>
4  #include<stdlib.h>
5  selectionsort(int num[], int noe)
6  {
7      int i, j, min, temp;
8      for(i=0;i<noe-1;i++)
9      {
10         min=i;
11         for(j=i+1;j<noe;j++)
12             if(num[j]<num[min])
13                 min=j;
14         {
15             temp=num[min];
16             num[min]=num[i];
17             num[i]=temp;
18         }
19     }
20 }
21 main()
22 {
23     FILE *fp;
24     char str[50],*p;
25     int i, noe, num[50];
26     fp=fopen("marks.txt","r");
27     if(fp==NULL)
28     {
29         printf("Unable to open the file\n");
30         getch();
31         exit(1);
32     }
33     fscanf(fp,"%d",&noe);
34     for(i=0;i<noe;i++)
35         fscanf(fp,"%d",&num[i]);
36     fclose(fp);
37     selectionsort(num, noe);
38     fp=fopen("marks.txt","a");
39     if(fp==NULL)
40     {
41         printf("Problem in accessing the file\n");
```

marks.txt (before the execution of the program)

```
10
23 12 89 73 45 65 22 90 78 67
```

marks.txt (after the execution of the program)

```
10
23 12 89 73 45 65 22 90 78 67
List of marks in sorted order is:
12 22 23 45 65 67 73 78 89 90
```

Remarks:

- The file marks.txt is opened in read mode
- The function fscanf in line number 33 reads the number of entries present in the file
- The iterative use of the fscanf function in line number 35 reads all the entries into the array num
- The function selectionsort is used to sort all the elements of the array
- In line number 36 the file is closed and in line number 38 it is reopened in the append mode
- The iterative use of the function fprintf in line number 47 appends the elements of the sorted array num to the file
- Note that instead of closing the file and then reopening it again in the append mode, it can initially be opened in the "r+" mode for reading and writing

(Contd...)

Prog 10-13.c	

```
        printf("Unable to continue");
        exit(1);
    }
    fprintf(fp,"List of marks in sorted order is:\n");
    for(i=0;i<noe;i++)
        fprintf(fp,"%d ",num[i]);
    fclose(fp);
}
```

Program 10-13 | A program that illustrates the use of the functions fscanf and fprintf

10.4.11 Block Input

Binary files as well as text files can be efficiently read by using block input, which reads data in terms of fixed size blocks instead of reading it by characters or by lines. The block input can be done by using the function fread. The function fread is declared in the header file stdio.h as:

```
size_t fread(void *data, size_t size, size_t n, FILE* stream);
```

The important points about the usage of the function fread are as follows:

1. The function fread reads up to n elements of size size into the memory block (i.e. array) pointed to by the argument data from the stream pointed to by the argument stream.
2. The function fread returns the number of elements read successfully, which may be less than n if a read error occurs or if end of file (i.e. EOF) is encountered.
3. If the argument size or n is zero (i.e. no data are to be read), the function returns zero, and the contents of the block and the state of the stream remain unchanged.

10.4.12 Block Output

Fixed size blocks of data can be written to a stream by using the function fwrite. The function fwrite is declared in the header file stdio.h as:

```
size_t fwrite(void *ptr, size_t size, size_t n, FILE* stream);
```

The important points about the usage of the function fwrite are as follows:

1. The function fwrite writes up to n elements of size size from the memory block (i.e. array) pointed to by the argument data to the stream pointed to by the argument stream.
2. The function fwrite returns the number of elements successfully written, which may be less than n only if a write error occurs.
3. If the argument size or n is zero (i.e. no data is to be written), the function returns zero, and the state of the stream remains unchanged.

The piece of code in Program 10-14 illustrates the use of the functions fread and fwrite to perform block input and output.

Prog 10-14.c

```
//Use of fread and fwrite functions
#include<stdio.h>
#include<conio.h>
#include<stdlib.h>
struct name
```

Output window

```
Enter the details of a person:
Enter the first name of the person:    Jane
Enter the last name of the person:    Ramon
Enter the mobile number:    9988700323
Do you want to enter more records(Y/N)  Y
```

(*Contd...*)

```
{
    char first_name[20];
    char last_name[20];
};
struct phonebook_entry
{
    struct name person_name;
    char mobile_no[15];
};
main()
{
    FILE* fp;
    char ch;
    struct phonebook_entry p;
    fp=fopen("phonebook.txt","wb+");
    if(fp==NULL)
    {
        printf("Some problem occurred\n");
        printf("Unable to continue\n");
        exit(1);
    }
    while(1)
    {
        printf("Enter the details of a person:\n");
        printf("Enter the first name of the person:\t");
        gets(p.person_name.first_name);
        printf("Enter the last name of the person:\t");
        gets(p.person_name.last_name);
        printf("Enter the mobile number:\t");
        gets(p.mobile_no);
        fwrite(&p, sizeof(p),1, fp)
        printf("Do you want to enter more records(Y/N)\t");
        scanf("%c",&ch);
        fflush(stdin);
        if(ch!='Y' && ch!='y')
            break;
    }
    rewind(fp);
    printf("\n\nPhonebook entries present in file are:\n");
    printf("%-20s %-20s %-15s\n","First Name", "Last Name", "Mobile \
    Number");
    printf("---------------------------------------------------\n");
    while(!feof(fp))
    {
        fread(&p, sizeof(p), 1, fp);
        if(feof(fp))
            break;
        else
```

```
Enter the first name of the person:    Sandoor
Enter the last name of the person:     Fekete
Enter the mobile number:    9889900099
Do you want to enter more records(Y/N)    N


Phonebook entries present in the file are:
First Name          Last Name          Mobile Number
----------------------------------------------------
Jane                Ramon              9988700323
Sandoor             Fekete             9889900099
```

Remarks:

- The function call fflush(stdin) is used to flush the buffer associated with the stream stdin
- Refer Section 10.4.13 for a description on the function fflush

(Contd...)

Prog 10-14.c	Output window
`printf("%-20s %-20s %-15s\n", p.person_name.first_name,`	
`p.person_name.last_name, p.mobile_no);`	
`}`	
`fclose(fp);`	
`}`	

Program 10-14 | A program that illustrates the use of the functions fread and fwrite

10.4.13 Stream Buffering and Flushing the Streams

In the previous sections, we have discussed various functions used to read characters from, or write characters to, a stream. However, how these characters are transmitted to the program (during an input operation) or to the file (during an output operation) depends upon the stream buffering. Three common choices for stream buffering are: **no buffering, line buffering** and **full buffering.** Accordingly, the streams are: **unbuffered, line buffered** or **fully buffered**.

If a stream is unbuffered, the characters written to the stream are immediately transmitted to the program (during an input operation) or the file (during an output operation). If the stream is line buffered, the characters present in the stream are transmitted to the destination when a new line character is encountered. When the stream is fully buffered, the characters present in the stream are transmitted to the destination when the stream gets full (i.e. in block of size equal to the buffer size).

It is very important to properly understand stream buffering while designing a user interface for a program. Otherwise, the output may not appear when it is desired or it might appear when it is not intended. The important points about stream buffering are as follows:

1. When opened, a stream by default is fully buffered if and only if it is not connected to an interactive device.
2. If an opened stream is connected to an interactive device, by default it is line buffered.
3. For a buffered stream, the buffer to be used for I/O buffering is automatically allocated. However, the functions setvbuf and setbuf can be used to specify a buffer that should be used by the stream for I/O buffering.
4. By default, the size of the automatically allocated buffer for a buffered stream is given by the macro BUFSIZ, defined in the header file stdio.h. The macro BUFSIZ expands to an integer constant 512. Thus, by default the size of the automatically allocated buffer for a buffered stream is 512.
5. The streams can be configured to have a behavior that differs from the default behavior. Whether an opened stream should be unbuffered, line buffered or fully buffered, which buffer is to be used for I/O buffering and what should the size of the buffer be, can be explicitly specified by using the functions setvbuf and setbuf.

    a. **The function setvbuf**: The function setvbuf is declared in the header file stdio.h as:

    ```
    int setvbuf(FILE* stream, char *buf, int mode, size_t size);
    ```

    The important points about the usage of the function setvbuf are as follows:

    i. The function setvbuf may be used only after the stream pointed to by stream has been associated with a file and before any operation is performed on the stream.

ii. The argument mode determines how stream will be buffered. The argument mode can be one of the symbolic constants (macros) or their corresponding values listed in Table 10.3. The symbolic constants are defined in the header file stdio.h.

Table 10.3 | Possible values of the mode argument

S.No	mode	Value	Description
1.	_IOFBF	0	Input/output will be fully buffered
2.	_IOLBF	1	Input/output will be line buffered
3.	_IONBF	2	Input/output will be un-buffered

iii If the argument buf is not a null pointer, the array pointed to by it will be used as a buffer for I/O buffering instead of the automatically allocated buffer. The array pointed to by buf should be a character array with a size of at least size. The space allocated for the array pointed to by buf should not be freed till the stream is open and the array remains its buffer.

iv If the argument buf is a null pointer, the function setvbuf function automatically allocates a buffer to be used for I/O buffering. The buffer is allocated by using malloc. The size of the allocated buffer will be equal to size. The memory used by the automatically allocated buffer is automatically freed when the stream is closed.

v The setvbuf function returns zero on success, or non-zero if an invalid value is given for mode or on failure.

The piece of code in Program 10-15 illustrates the use of the function setvbuf.

Line	Trace	Prog 10-15.c	Tracing	Output window

1
2
3
4
5
6
7
8
9
10
11
12
13
	
	1
	
	2
	3
	4
	5
	6
	7
	8
		//Function setvbuf
		#include<stdio.h>
		#include<conio.h>
		main()
		{
		char arr[30];
		setvbuf(stdout, arr, _IOFBF, 30);
		puts("Fairways are narrow");
		fflush(stdout);
		puts("you have to walk down");
		puts("them in a single file");
		fclose(stdout);
		}
			After trace step 3:
			arr="Fairways are narrow\n"
			Output Window:
			Blank
			After trace step 4:
			arr="Fairways are narrow\n"
			Output Window:
			Fairways are narrow
			After trace step 5:
			arr="you have to walk down\n"
			Output Window:
			Fairways are narrow
			After trace step 6:
			arr="a single file\n"
			Output Window:
			Fairways are narrow
			you have to walk down
			them in
				Fairways are narrow
				you have to walk down
				them in a single file
				Remarks:
				• The function setvbuf in line number 7, changes the buffering properties of the standard stream stdout
				• After the successful execution of the statement in line number 7, the stream stdout will be fully buffered, the character array arr will be used as the buffer for the stream and the buffer size will be 30
				• The function puts writes to the stream stdout

(Contd...)

Line	Trace	Prog 10-15.c	Tracing	Output window
			After trace step 7: arr="a single file\n" **Output Window:** Fairways are narrow you have to walk down them in a single file	• After trace step 3, there will be No Output on the screen because stdout is now buffered and neither the buffer has got full nor it is flushed • After trace step 4, the string will be printed onto the screen because the buffer is flushed by using the function fflush • After trace step 5, the string "you have to walk down\n" is placed in the buffer and will not be transmitted to the screen • While executing trace step 6, by placing the characters "them in", the buffer got full, hence it is flushed • Thus, after the execution of trace step 6, the buffer i.e. arr contents are "a single file"

Program 10-15 | A program that illustrates the use of the function setvbuf

b. **The function setbuf**: The function setbuf is declared in the header file stdio.h as:

```
void setbuf(FILE* stream, char *buf);
```

The important points about the usage of the function setbuf are as follows:

i. If the argument buf is not a null pointer, the function setbuf specifies that the I/O will be fully buffered and an array pointed by buf will be used for I/O buffering. The size of the array pointed to by buf must be BUFSIZ.
ii. If the argument buf is a null pointer, I/O will be unbuffered.
iii. The function setbuf returns no value.
iv. Thus, except that it returns no value, the function setbuf is equivalent to the function setvbuf invoked with the values _IOFBF for mode and BUFSIZ for size, or if buf is a null pointer, with the value _IONBF for mode.

6. As seen in Program 10-15, the characters from a buffered output stream are transmitted to the file when the buffer gets full (in the case of fully buffered streams) or when new line character is encountered (in the case of line-buffered streams). However, even if these conditions are not met, the characters from a stream can be transmitted to the file by flushing the buffer associated with the stream. Similarly, for a buffered input stream, the characters present in the stream can be cleared by flushing the buffer associated with the stream. The buffers associated with the streams can be flushed by using the library functions fflush and flushall.

a. **The function fflush**: The function fflush is declared in the header file stdio.h as:

```
int fflush(FILE* stream);
```

The important points about the function fflush are as follows:

i. If the stream pointed to by stream is an input stream, the function fflush clears the buffer associated with it.

ii. If the stream pointed to by stream is an output stream, the function fflush transmits the characters present in the buffer associated with the stream to the file.

iii. If the stream is a NULL pointer, the function fflush performs the flushing action on all open streams.

iv. The function fflush sets the error indicator for the stream stream and returns EOF if an error occurs, otherwise it returns zero.

b. **The function flushall**: The function flushall is declared in the header file stdio.h as:

```
int flushall(void);
```

The important points about the function flushall are as follows:

i. The function flushall clears all buffers associated with the open input streams and writes all buffers associated with open output streams to the respective files.

ii. Any read operation following the call to the function flushall reads new data into the buffers from the input files.

iii. The function flushall returns an integer that is equal to the number of open input and output streams.

10.5 File Type

In the previous sections, we have seen that streams provide an efficient and convenient interface to perform file I/O. Streams are objects of the type FILE defined in the header file stdio.h. Since streams are so important it is worth exploring the inner details of the structure type FILE.

The definition of the structure type FILE is as follows:

```
typedef struct
{
    short level;                    //←fill/empty buffer level
    unsigned flags;                 //←File status flags
    char fd;                        //←File descriptor
    unsigned char hold;             //←ungetc character if no buffer
    short bsize;                    //←Buffer size
    unsigned char *buffer;          //←Data transfer buffer
    unsigned char *curp;            //← Current active pointer
    unsigned int istemp;            //←Temporary file indicator
    short token;                    //←Used for validity checking
} FILE;
```

The structure FILE contains several pieces of information like: a pointer to a buffer, so that the file can be read in large chunks; a count to the number of characters left in the buffer; a pointer to the next character position in the buffer; the file descriptor; and flags describing read/write mode, error status and end-of-file indication, etc.

The descriptions of the various members of the structure type FILE are as follows:

1. **Buffer level**: The member level is of short int type. It describes the number of characters left in the buffer that are not yet read.

   Program 10-16 uses the level member of the FILE type to illustrate that new line character is left in the standard input stream stdin when a string is read by using the function scanf, while no character is left in the stream if the string is read by using the function gets.

Prog 10-16.c

```
//Different ways to read a string
#include<stdio.h>
#include<conio.h>
main()
{
    char str1[20], str2[20];
    printf("Two different ways to read a string\n");
    printf("Enter string 1:\t");
    scanf("%s",str1);
    printf("No. of characters left after using scanf is %d\n",stdin->level);
    fflush(stdin);
    printf("Enter string 2:\t");
    gets(str2);
    printf("No. of characters left after using gets is %d\n",stdin->level);
    printf("The strings entered are:\n");
    printf("%s %s", str1, str2);
}
```

Output window

```
Two different ways to read a string
Enter string 1:    Member
No. of characters left after using scanf is 1
Enter string 2:    Level
No. of characters left after using gets is 0
The strings entered are:
Member Level
```

Remarks:

- The scanf function does not remove the new line character present at the end of the string entered by the user
- Thus, one character is left in the buffer associated with the stream stdin. Thus, the value of stdin->level is 1
- The function gets removes all the characters including the new line character from the stream stdin
- Thus, the value of stdin->level is 0

Program 10-16 | A program that illustrates the application of the level member

2. **File status flags**: The member flags is of unsigned int type. It indicates the current status of the stream. Table 10.4 lists the definition of flag bits along with their description.

Table 10.4 | File status flags

S.No	File status flags	Description
1.	#define _F_RDWR 0x0003	File is opened for reading/writing
2.	#define _F_READ 0x0001	File is opened for reading only
3.	#define _F_WRIT 0x0002	File is opened for writing only
4.	#define _F_BUF 0x0004	Stream is fully buffered
5.	#define _F_LBUF 0x0008	Stream is line buffered
6.	#define _F_ERR 0x0010	Error indicator flag for the stream
7.	#define _F_EOF 0x0020	End-of-file indicator flag for the stream
8.	#define _F_BIN 0x0040	Stream is opened in binary mode
9.	#define _F_IN 0x0080	Data are incoming
10.	#define _F_OUT 0x0100	Data are outgoing
11.	#define _F_TERM 0x0200	File is a terminal

Program 10-17 uses the end-of-file indicator flag to determine whether the end of file has been reached or not instead of using the macro EOF or the function feof.

Prog 10-17.c

```
1  //Copy content of one file to another file
2  #include<stdio.h>
3  #include<conio.h>
4  #include<stdlib.h>
5  main()
6  {
7      FILE *fp1, *fp2;
8      char ch;
9      fp1=fopen("abc.txt","r");
10     fp2=fopen("cde.txt","w");
11     if(fp1==NULL || fp2==NULL)
12     {
13         printf("Problem in reading or writing a file\n");
14         printf("Unable to continue\n");
15         getch();
16         exit(1);
17     }
18     else
19     {
20         while((fp1->flags & _F_EOF) != _F_EOF)
21         {
22             ch=fgetc(fp1);
23             if((fp1->flags & 0x0020) != 0x0020)
24                 fputc(ch,fp2);
25         }
26     }
27     fcloseall();
28 }
```

abc.txt

File Management

cde.txt (after the execution of the program)

File Management

Remarks:

- The code presents a third way to check for the end-of-file condition
- The other two ways are:
  i. Use of EOF character
  ii. Use of the function feof
- The macro _F_EOF has the value 0x0020
- Hence, both of them can be interchangeably used as in line numbers 20 and 23

Program 10-17 | A program that illustrates the use of the EOF flag bit of the flag member

Similarly, other flag bits can also be checked to infer the information about the configuration and the status of the stream. Program 10-18 checks the flag bits to determine whether the stream is opened for reading, writing or update.

Prog 10-18.c

```
//Check whether a stream/ file is opened for reading, writing or update
#include<stdio.h>
main()
{
    FILE* fp;
    fp=fopen("abc.txt","r");
    if((fp->flags & _F_RDWR) == _F_RDWR)
        printf("File is opened for update\n");
    else
```

Output window

File is opened for reading

Remark:

- Change the mode string used in the function fopen to "a" and "w" and then re-execute the code

(Contd...)

Prog 10-18.c

```
        if((fp->flags & _F_READ) == _F_READ)
            printf("File is opened for reading\n");
        else
            if((fp->flags & _F_WRIT) == _F_WRIT)
                printf("File is opened for writing\n");
    fclose(fp);
}
```

Output window

Program 10-18 | A program that checks various bits of the member flag to determine the configuration of the stream

3. **File descriptor**: File descriptor is a unique non-negative integer used to identify an open file. The value of a file descriptor can range from 0 to FOPEN_MAX. FOPEN_MAX is a macro defined in the header file stdio.h. It describes the maximum number of files that a process (i.e. a program in execution) can open simultaneously. The file descriptor values for the standard streams have already been defined and are shown in Table 10-5.

Table 10.5 | File descriptor values for standard streams

S.No	Standard stream	File descriptor value
1.	stdin	0
2.	stdout	1
3.	stderr	2
4.	stdaux	3
5.	stdprn	4

4. **Hold character**: The member hold holds the character returned by the ungetc function, if there is no buffer. The function ungetc is declared in the header file stdio.h as:

```
int ungetc(int c, FILE* stream);
```

The important points about the function ungetc are as follows:

i. The function ungetc pushes the character specified by c back on the input stream pointed to by stream.
ii. The ANSI C standard guarantees pushback of only one character at a time.
iii. The ungetc function returns the character pushed back or EOF if the operation fails.

Suppose it is required to read the characters from a stream up to (but not including) the next colon. The function fgetc can be used to read characters until a colon is read and then function ungetc can be used to push the colon back onto the stream. Program 10-19 illustrates such use of the function ungetc.

Prog 10-19.c

```
//Use of the function ungetc
#include<stdio.h>
#include<conio.h>
#include<stdlib.h>
main()
```

abc.txt

Segment:Offset

Output window

Segment
The character that is pushed back is :

(Contd...)

```
6  {
7      FILE* fp;
8      char ch;
9      char str[20];
10     fp=fopen("abc.txt","r");
11     setbuf(fp, NULL);
12     ch=fgetc(fp);
13     while(ch!=':')
14     {
15         printf("%c",ch);
16         ch=fgetc(fp);
17     }
18     ungetc(ch, fp);
19     printf("\nThe character that is pushed back is %c\n",fp->hold);
20     fgets(str, 20, fp);
21     printf("The characters present in the stream buffer are:\n");
22     puts(str);
23 }
```

The characters present in the stream buffer are:
:Offset

Remarks:

- By default, the opened streams are buffered and the buffer size is 512
- The function setbuf in line number 11 is used to make the stream pointed to by fp unbuffered
- The while loop reads the character from the stream fp, till the colon is read
- The function ungetc in line number 18, pushes the character ':' back on to the stream fp
- The member hold holds the ungetc character. Thus, ':' is printed by the function printf in line number 19
- Note that the member hold holds the character, if the stream is unbuffered
- Comment the function setbuf in line number 11 and then check the result

Program 10-19 | A program that illustrates the use of the function ungetc

5. **Buffer size**: The member bsize is of type short int. It specifies the size of the buffer used by the stream. Program 10-20 uses the member bsize to illustrate that the standard output stream stdout is unbuffered if not redirected, and by default the size of the buffer used for a buffered stream is 512.

Prog 10-20.c

```
//The size of buffer
#include<stdio.h>
main()
{
    FILE* fp;
    fp=fopen("abc.txt","r");
    printf("Buffer size for the stream stdout is %d\n", stdout->bsize);
    printf("Buffer size for the stream fp is %d\n", fp->bsize);
    fclose(fp);
}
```

Output window

Buffer size for the stream stdout is 0
Buffer size for the stream fp is 512

Remarks:

- The stream stout is unbuffered, if not redirected
- Thus, the buffer size for the stream stdout is 0
- User-defined streams by default are buffered and the buffer size is 512
- Thus, the buffer size for the stream fp is 512

Program 10-20 | A program that illustrates the use of the member bsize

6. **Buffer**: The member buffer is a character pointer to data buffer used by the stream for I/O buffering.
7. **Current active pointer:** The member curp is a pointer to the next character position in the buffer. The macros getc and putc use curp to read and write the character to the stream. The description of the definitions of the macros getc and putc is as follows:

   i. **The macro getc**: The macro getc is defined in the header file stdio.h as:

   ```
   #define getc(f) ((--((f)->level) >=0 )? (unsigned char)(*(f)-> curp++): fgetc(f))
   ```

The getc macro reduces the buffer level and compares it to be greater than equal to zero. If it evaluates to true, it returns the character pointed to by curp and advances the pointer curp else if the level becomes negative, it calls the function fgetc to replenish the buffer.

ii. **The macro putc**: The macro putc is defined in the header file stdio.h as:

```
#define putc(c,f) ((++((f)->level) < 0 )? (unsigned char)(*(f)-> curp++=(c)): fputc((c),f))
```

The macro putc places character c in the buffer at the location pointed to by curp and then advances the pointer.

10.6 Files and Command Line Arguments

Program 10-5 copies the content of one file to another file. Every time the program is executed, it copies the content of file **abc.txt** to the file **new.txt**. Thus, the program is inflexible. We require a program that can copy the content of any given source file to any destination file. This can be done by getting the names of the source and destination files at the run time instead of hard coding them in the program. One way to get the names of the source file and destination file at the run time is by using the command line arguments. Program 10-21 illustrates the use of the command line argument in the development of the general file copy application.

Prog 10-21 filecopy.c

```
//File copy program that makes use of command line arguments
#include<stdio.h>
#include<conio.h>
#include<stdlib.h>
main(int argc, char* argv[])
{
    FILE *fp1, *fp2;
    char ch;
    if(argc<3)
    {
        printf("Usage: filecopy sourcefile destinationfile");
        getch();
        exit(1);
    }
    fp1=fopen(argv[1], "r");
    fp2=fopen(argv[2], "w");
    if(fp1==NULL || fp2==NULL)
    {
        printf("Some problem occurred\n");
        printf("Unable to continue");
        getch();
        exit(1);
    }
    while(!feof(fp1))
    {
        ch=fgetc(fp1);
```

Command window

```
c:\tc\bin>filecopy source.txt destination.txt
```

source.txt (before the execution of the program)

Confidence is as vital to success as oxygen is to the body.

destination.txt (after the execution of the program)

Confidence is as vital to success as oxygen is to the body.

Remark:

- Instead of file names, argv[1] and argv[2] are given as arguments in the calls to the function fopen

(Contd...)

```
        if(!feof(fp1)) fputc(ch, fp2);
    }
    fcloseall();
}
```

Program 10-21 | A program to copy the content of one file to another

10.7 Summary

1. The console input–output is preferred in interactive programs where the amount of data input–output is small.
2. If a program deals with input–output of a large volume of data, file input–output is convenient and less time consuming as compared to console input–output.
3. C performs the input–output in a device-independent form by treating each physical device as a file.
4. A file can be a data set that can be read or written repeatedly (such as a disk file), or a stream of bytes received from or sent to a peripheral device (such as a keyboard or display).
5. In C, files are referred to by their file names.
6. A file must be opened before any operation can be performed on it.
7. The connection to an open file is represented either as a stream or as a file descriptor.
8. Streams provide a high-level interface to perform file input–output.
9. Files can be opened by using the function fopen. Opening a file associates a stream with it.
10. Five standard streams namely stdin, stdout, strerr, stdaux and stderr are already open when a program is executed and are available for use. These streams need not be opened or closed.
11. A stream can be opened for input, output or both.
12. A file can be opened in a text mode or a binary mode. Accordingly, the corresponding associated stream can be a text stream or a binary stream.
13. Text streams are interpreted while binary streams are uninterpreted.
14. A stream can be unbuffered, line buffered or fully buffered.
15. Streams are objects of the type FILE. Generally, they are manipulated by using objects of the type FILE*, i.e. pointer to a stream.
16. A stream can be closed by using the function fclose. Closing a stream breaks the association between the stream and the file.
17. The function fcloseall closes all the open streams except the standard streams.
18. Input from a stream can be taken by using the functions: fgetc, fgets, fscanf, fread, etc.
19. Output to a stream can be given by using the functions: fputc, fputs, fprintf, fwrite, etc.
20. The file position indicator for the associated stream indicates where in the file the stream is currently reading or writing.
21. The current location of a file position indicator can be determined by using the functions: ftell or fgetpos.
22. The value of the file position indicator can be changed by using the functions: fseek, fsetpos or rewind.
23. Streams can be flushed using the functions: fflush or flushall.

Exercise Questions

Conceptual Questions and Answers

1. *What is a stream?*

   A **stream** is a continuous series of bytes that flows into or out of a program. Input and output from physical devices or from disk files are handled with streams.

Backward Reference: Refer Section 10.3 for a description on streams.

2. *What are standard streams?*

   When a program is executed, the streams that are already open and are available to the program for use are known as **standard streams**. The C language provides the following five standard streams:

Standard stream	Description	Associated file
stdin	Standard input	Keyboard
stdout	Standard output	Screen
stderr	Standard error	Screen
stdaux	Standard auxiliary	COM1: port
stdprn	Standard printer	LPT1: port

   Note that the streams stdaux and stdprn are not always defined because LPT1 and COM1 have no meaning under certain operating systems. However, the streams stdin, stdout and stderr are always defined. These streams need not be opened or closed.

3. *What is meant by stream redirection?*

   Changing the source file or the target file of an open stream is known as **stream redirection**. Stream redirection is useful for changing the file attached to the standard streams stdin, stdout or stderr. A stream can be redirected by using the function freopen. The function freopen is declared in the header file stdio.h as:

```
FILE* freopen(const char* filename, const char* mode, FILE* stream);
```

   The important points about the function freopen are as follows:

   1. The function freopen opens the file whose name is the string pointed to by the argument filename and associates the stream pointed to by stream with it. The role of the argument mode is the same as in the function fopen.
   2. If filename is a null pointer, the function freopen attempts to change the mode of the stream to that specified by the argument mode. The file associated with the stream remains the same.
   3. The function freopen first attempts to close the file associated with the stream. Failure to close the stream is ignored. The error indicator flag and the end-of-file indicator flag for the stream are cleared (i.e. reset).

4. *By default, the stream* stdout *writes characters to the screen. Can I make the stream* stdout *be printed somewhere other than the screen?*

   Yes, the stream stdout can be printed somewhere other than screen by redirecting it. The following piece of code illustrates the redirection of the stream stdout:

```
#include<stdio.h>
main()
```

```
{
    freopen("abc.txt","w",stdout);
    printf("Where will this gets printed?");
}
```

The mentioned piece of code on execution prints the string "Where will this gets printed?" to the file **abc.txt** instead of printing it on the screen because the stream stdout has been redirected.

5. *What is file handle?*

   The file descriptor of a stream is also known as the **file handle**. It is a non-negative integer that can completely describe the stream. The file handle (i.e. file descriptor) of a stream can be determined by using the function fileno. The function fileno is defined in the header file stdio.h as:

   ```
   int fileno(FILE* stream);
   ```

   The important points about the function fileno are as follows:

   1. The fileno is actually a macro defined in the header file stdio.h as:

      ```
      #define fileno(f) ((f)->fd)
      ```

   2. It returns the integer file handle associated with the stream.

   The following piece of code illustrates the use of the function fileno to retrieve the file handles of the standard streams stdin and stdout:

   ```
   #include<stdio.h>
   main()
   {
       printf("File handle of the standard input stream is %d\n",fileno(stdin));
       printf("File handle of the standard output stream is %d",fileno(stdout));
   }
   ```

   The mentioned code on execution outputs

   ```
   File handle of the standard input stream is 0
   File handle of the standard input stream is 1
   ```

6. *How can I restore a redirected stream?*

   The following steps should be followed to redirect a stream and restore it back:

   1. Duplicate the file handle of the stream before redirecting it by using the function dup. The function dup is declared in the header file IO.h as int dup(int handle);. It takes the handle of the stream as an input for which a duplicate handle is to be created.
   2. Redirect the stream by using the function freopen.
   3. Work with the redirected stream and close it after the use by using the function fclose.
   4. Restore the original stream back by using the function fdopen. The function fdopen opens a stream that has been duplicated with the function dup.

   The following piece of code illustrates the redirection and restoration of the standard stream stdout:

   ```
   #include<stdio.h>
   #include<IO.h>
   main()
   {
       int dup_handle;
       dup_handle=dup(fileno(stdout));              //Duplicating the file handle of the stream stdout
       printf("Writing to original stdout stream\n");
       printf("This will be printed on the screen\n");
       freopen("abc.txt","w", stdout);              //Redirecting the stream
   ```

```
    printf("Writing to the redirected stdout stream\n");
    printf("This will be printed in the file\n");
    fclose(stdout);
    fdopen(dup_handle, "w");                    //Restoring the stream
    printf("Writing back to the original stdout stream\n");
    printf("This will appear again on the screen");
}
```

7. *What are the differences between a text stream and a binary stream?*

Text stream	Binary stream
1. Text streams are interpreted 2. Carriage return and line feed character combinations are translated to new line character and vice versa	1. Binary streams are uninterpreted 2. No translation of characters takes place
3. Text streams are typically used for reading and writing standard text files, printing output to screen or printer, or receiving input from the keyboard	3. Binary streams are typically used for reading and writing binary files such as graphics file or word processing file, or reading and writing to the modem

8. *I have written the following statement to open a file:*

```
FILE* fp=fopen("file.dat", 'r');
```

Why does the mentioned statement not work?

The mentioned statement does not work because the argument `mode` in call to the function `fopen` should be a string and not a character. The rectified statement can be written as:

```
FILE* fp=fopen("file.dat","r");
```

9. *I have written the following statement to open the file* `file.txt` *present in* `c:\tc\bin` *directory:*

```
FILE* fp=fopen("c:\tc\bin\file.txt","r");
```

Why does the mentioned statement not work?

The mentioned statement does not work because the backslash character appearing in the string literal given as an argument to the function `fopen` begins an escape sequence and gives a special meaning to the character following it. The characters '\t', '\b' and '\f' present in the string literal are treated as tab, backspace and form feed character. These escape sequences manipulate the file name. The file with this manipulated file name probably does not exist. Thus, the function `fopen` fails and returns `NULL` pointer.

The mentioned problem can be rectified by using one of the following two ways:

1. Use double backslashes instead of a single backslash in order to override escape sequences. The rectified file name can be written as "c:\\tc\\bin\\file.txt".
2. In MS-DOS, forward slashes are also accepted as directory separators. Thus, replace the backward slashes in the string literal `filename` by the forward slashes in order to eliminate escape sequences. The rectified file name can be written as "c:/tc/bin/file.txt".

10. *A program reads a character from the keyboard until* `EOF`. *How do I enter* `EOF` *from the keyboard to terminate the input?*

Different operating systems use different special characters to mark the end of a file. DOS and WINDOWS use the Ctrl+Z character to mark file's end while UNIX uses Ctrl+D for it. Thus, to enter the end-of-file character from the keyboard, enter the Ctr+Z character if working in DOS or WINDOWS environment and enter the Ctrl+D character if working in UNIX environment.

The C language defines a symbolic constant EOF, which is returned by the library functions when the end of file is encountered, irrespective of the character used to mark the file's end. Execute the following piece of code using Turbo C 3.0/4.5 to see that the input gets terminated by the Ctrl+Z character:

```
#include<stdio.h>
main()
{
    char ch;
    while((ch=getchar())!=EOF)
        putchar(ch);
}
```

11. *A file consists of the following sequence of numbers:*

    -6 -5 -4 -3 -2 -1 0 1 2 3 4 5 6

    A loop is used to read numbers from the file till EOF *is encountered. So does the loop terminate after reading all the number or does it terminate after reading* -1 *as* EOF *has the value* -1*?*

    The loop will terminate after reading all the numbers and not after reading -1. -1 is not a character but is made up of two characters '-' and '1'. Also, their ASCII codes (i.e. 45 and 49) are not equal to the defined value of EOF (i.e. -1). In fact, none of the valid characters compare equal to the EOF character because the ASCII codes of valid characters are non-negative and spans from 0 to 255.

12. *What is the difference if the function* fwrite *is used to output an integer value* 12345 *to a file instead of the function* fprintf*?*

    When the function fprintf is used to write the integer value 12345 to the file, it writes the binary codes of the characters '1', '2', '3', '4' and '5' (i.e. 49, 50, 51, 52 and 53) to the file. Thus, the data that are written to the file are

00110001	00110010	00110011	00110100	00110101

    When the function fwrite is used to write the integer value 12345 to the file, it writes the binary code for the value 12345 to the file. Thus, the data written to the file are:

00110000	00111001

13. *How is the file opened with the "r" mode different from the file opened with the "r+" mode?*

    The file opened with the "r" mode can only be used for reading, while the file opened with the "r+" mode can be used for reading as well as writing (i.e. update).

14. *Both the "r+" and "w+" modes are used to open a file for update. Then, what is the difference between them?*

    Both the "r+" mode and the "w+" mode open a file for update. If the "r+" mode is used and the file does not exist, the function fopen will fail and returns a NULL pointer. However, if the "w+" mode is used and the file does not exist, a new file will be created. If the "r+" mode is used and the file already exists, the content of the file will remain unchanged. However, if the "w+" mode is used and the file already exists, the file is truncated to zero length.

15. *Both the "w+" and "a+" modes are used to open a file for update. Also, if the file does not exist, a new file is created in both the modes. Then, what is the difference between them?*

    Both the "w+" and "a+" modes are used to open a file for update. Also, if the file does not exist, a new file is created in the both the modes. However, if the file already exists, in the "w+" mode it is truncated to zero length while in the "a+" mode its initial content remain unchanged.

16. *If I use the function* scanf *with* %c *format specifier to read a* Y/N *response, the latter input gets skipped. Why? How can I rectify this problem?*

This problem occurred because the new line character is left in the standard input stream stdin after reading the Y/N response. The problem can be rectified by flushing the stream stdin after reading the Y/N response using the function call fflush(stdin).

Backward Reference: Refer Question number 15 and its answer in Chapter 6 for a similar problem.

17. *How can I check whether a given stream is associated with a terminal?*

Whether a stream is associated with a terminal or a data file can be determined by checking the _F_TERM flag of the member flags of the stream. The following piece of code illustrates such a test:

```
#include<stdio.h>
main()
{
    FILE *fp=fopen("abc.txt","w");
    if((fp->flags & _F_TERM) == _F_TERM)
        printf("Stream fp is associated with a terminal\n");
    else
        printf("Stream fp is not associated with a terminal\n");
    if((stdout->flags & _F_TERM) == _F_TERM)
        printf("Stream stdout is associated with a terminal\n");
    else
        printf("Stream stdout is not associated with a terminal\n");
}
```

The mention piece of code on execution outputs:

```
Stream fp is not associated with a terminal
Stream stdout is associated with a terminal
```

18. *I have written the following piece of code to determine whether the standard error stream* stderr *is associated with a terminal or not:*

```
#include<stdio.h>
main()
{
    if(stderr->flags & _F_TERM == _F_TERM)
        printf("The stream stderr is associated with a terminal");
    else
        printf("The stream stderr is not associated with a terminal");
}
```

The mentioned piece of code on execution outputs "The stream stderr is not associated with a terminal", *although the stream* stderr *is associated with the terminal (i.e. screen). Why?*

This problem occurred because the precedence of the bitwise AND operator (&) and the equality operator (==) has not been taken into consideration. The equality operator has a higher precedence than bitwise AND operator. Thus, the equality operator operates first and the expression _F_TERM==_F_TERM evaluates to true (i.e. 1). Now, the expression stderr->flags & 1 is evaluated and it evaluates to false because the LSB of the member flags of the stream stderrr is 0 since it an output stream. The problem can be rectified by parenthesizing the sub-expression stderr->flags & _F_TERM. The rectified expression can be written as (stderr->flags & _F_TERM)==_F_TERM.

19. *Can I use the function* fprintf *to display output on screen?*

    Yes, the function fprintf can be used to display the output on the screen by providing stdout as the argument stream to it. The function call fprintf(stdout, ...) is equivalent to the function call printf(...) and displays the output on the screen.

20. *When a program terminates abnormally, the last few lines of its output are often lost. Why?*

    When a program terminates abnormally, the last few lines of its output are often lost because the open streams are not flushed in case of abnormal termination.

Code Snippets

Determine the output of the following code snippets. Assume that the inclusion of the required header files has been made and there is no prototyping error due to them. The content of the referred file is shown alongside.

21.
```
main()
{
    FILE* fp=fopen("abc.txt", 'r');
    while(!feof(fp))
        printf("%c",fgetc(fp));
}
```

abc.txt
You are only young once,
and if you work it right,
once is enough.

22.
```
main()
{
    FILE* fp=fopen("abc.txt", "r");
    while(!feof(fp))
    {
        printf("%c",fgetc(fp));
        fseek(fp,-1,SEEK_CUR);
    }
}
```

abc.txt
You are only young once,
and if you work it right,
once is enough.

23.
```
main()
{
    int streams;
    streams=flushall();
    printf("Number of opened streams are %d",streams);
}
```

24.
```
main()
{
    FILE *fp=fopen("abc.txt","r");
    printf("%d",fp->fd);
}
```

abc.txt
Never bet on sure things
unless
you can afford to lose

25.
```
main()
{
    FILE* fp1, *fp2;
    int count1=0, count2=0;
    fp1=fopen("abc.txt", "r");
    fp2=fopen("abc.txt","rb");
    while(fgetc(fp1)!=EOF)
            count1++;
```

abc.txt
Never bet on sure things
unless
you can afford to lose

```
    while(fgetc(fp2)!=EOF)
        count2++;
    printf("The number of characters in text stream is %d\n", count1);
    printf("The number of characters in binary stream is %d", count2);
}
```

26.
```
main()
{
    FILE* fp;
    unsigned char ch;
    fp=fopen("abc.txt","r");
    while((ch=fgetc(fp))!=EOF)
        printf("%c",ch);
    fclose(fp);
}
```

abc.txt
Doing easily what others find difficult is talent; doing what is impossible for talent is genius

27.
```
main()
{
    FILE* fp1, fp2;
    char ch;
    fp1=fopen("abc.txt", "r");
    fp2=fopen("cde.txt","w");
    while((ch=fgetc(fp1))!=EOF)
        fputc(ch, fp);
}
```

abc.txt
The world is divided into: the people who do things and, the people who get the credit. Try, if you can, to belong to the first group. There's less competition.

28.
```
main()
{
    FILE* fp1, *fp2;
    char ch;
    fp1=fopen("abc.txt","r");
    fp2=fopen("cde.txt","w");
    while((ch=fgetc(fp1))!=EOF)
        fputc(ch, fp2);
    fclose(fp1, fp2);
}
```

abc.txt
Doing easily what others find diffucult is talent; doing what is impossible for talent is genious.

29.
```
main()
{
    FILE *fp1, *fp2;
    fp1=fopen("abc.txt","r");
    fp2=fopen("cde.txt","r+b");
    printf("%x %x", fp1->flags, fp2->flags);
}
```

abc.txt, cde.txt
Doing easily what others find diffucult is talent; doing what is impossible for talent is genious.

30.
```
main()
{
    if(stdin->flags & _F_TERM == _F_TERM)
        printf("The stream stdin is associated with a terminal");
    else
        printf("The stream stdin is not associated with a terminal");
}
```

Multiple-choice Questions

31. File input–output in C can be performed by using
    a. Only streams
    b. Only file descriptors
    c. Both streams and file descriptors
    d. None of these

32. By default, the stream stdout is
    a. Unbuffered
    b. Line buffered
    c. Fully buffered
    d. None of these

33. If a stream is fully buffered, the stream buffer is flushed when
    a. New line character is encountered
    b. EOF is encountered
    c. Buffer gets full
    d. None of these

34. The size of the buffer for a stream can be set by using the function
    a. setvbuf
    b. setbuf
    c. fsetpos
    d. None of these

35. If a file is to be opened for an update operation, the value of the argument mode in a call to the function fopen should be
    a. "r"
    b. "u"
    c. "a"
    d. "r+"

36. Which of the following functions does not manipulate the value of the file position indicator
    a. fputc
    b. fseek
    c. ftell
    d. fgetc

37. Which of the following functions can be used to close the standard stream?
    a. fclose
    b. fcloseall
    c. feof
    d. None of these

38. Streams are objects of the type
    a. FILE*
    b. FILE
    c. int
    d. int*

39. Only for positioning purpose, a call to the function rewind on the stream pointed to by s is equivalent to the function call
    a. fseek(s, 0L, SEEK_SET);
    b. fseek(s, 0L, SEEK_CUR);
    c. fseek(s, 0L, SEEK_END);
    d. None of these

40. The file descriptor value of the stream stdin is
    a. 0
    b. 1
    c. 2
    d. None of these

Outputs and Explanations to Code Snippets

21. Compilation error

    Explanation:

    The argument mode of the function fopen should be a string and not a character. Hence, it is erroneous to use 'r' instead of "r" as an argument in the call to the function fopen.

22. YYYYYY...infinite times

Explanation:

The function fgetc reads the first character, i.e. Y from the text stream pointed to by the argument fp and increments the file position indicator. The printf function prints the character read by the function fgetc. The function fseek repositions the file position indicator back to the beginning of the file. Hence, during the next iteration of the loop, the function fgetc reads the character Y again. In this way, iterations of the loop read the character Y and print it. The end of the file will never be reached and hence, the loop turns out to be an infinite loop.

23. Number of opened streams are 5

Explanation:

The function flushall returns the number of open input and output streams. Since the five standard streams are already open when a program is executed, the function flushall returns 5.

24. 5

Explanation:

When a program is executed, five standard streams are already open and are available for use. The file descriptors of these standard streams range from 0 to 4. Thus, the file descriptor for the stream pointed to by fp will be the next integer value, i.e. 5.

25. The number of characters in text stream is 55
The number of characters in binary stream is 58

Explanation:

Text streams are interpreted. The carriage return and line feed character combinations present at the end of the line are translated into new line characters. However, no such interpretation takes place for binary streams. Thus, the number of characters shown by the binary stream is more than the number of characters shown by the text stream. The file **abc.txt** in the text mode and the binary mode appears as:

```
abc.txt
Never bet on sure things\r\n
unless\r\n
you can afford to lose\r\n
^Z
```

MS-DOS file abc.txt

```
abc.txt
Never bet on sure things\n
unless\n
you can afford to lose\n
^Z
```

Text mode

```
abc.txt
Never bet on sure things\r\n
unless\r\n
you can afford to lose\r\n
^Z
```

Binary mode

26. Doing easily what others find difficult is talent;
doing what is impossible for talent is genius.

Explanation:

The mentioned piece of code on execution prints the content of the file abc.txt on the screen but it will enter an infinite loop and the program will not terminate. The function fgetc returns -1 upon encountering the end of the file. The returned value is stored in the unsigned char ch. Hence, on comparison it will always be unequal to EOF and thus the while loop becomes infinite.

27. Compilation error

Explanation:

In the declaration statement, the variable fp is declared to be of type FILE and not FILE*. Hence, it cannot be used to hold the value returned by the function fopen, since the function fopen returns a value of type FILE*. Moreover, the conversion from the type FILE* to the type FILE is not a standard conversion and cannot be carried out by the compiler implicitly. Hence, there will be a compilation error.

28. Compilation error

Explanation:

The function fclose can have only one argument of type FILE*. Hence, the function call fclose(fp1, fp2) is erroneous and leads to 'Extra parameter in call to fclose in function main' error.

29. 5 47

Explanation:

The following file status macros are defined in the header file stdio.h:

S.No	File status flags	Description
1.	#define _F_RDWR 0x0003	File is opened for reading/writing
2.	#define _F_READ 0x0001	File is opened for reading only
3.	#define _F_WRIT 0x0002	File is opened for writing only
4.	#define _F_BUF 0x0004	Stream is fully buffered
5.	#define _F_LBUF 0x0008	Stream is line buffered
6.	#define _F_ERR 0x0010	Error indicator flag for the stream
7.	#define _F_EOF 0x0020	End-of-file indicator for the stream
8.	#define _F_BIN 0x0040	Stream is opened in binary mode
9.	#define _F_IN 0x0080	Data are incoming
10.	#define _F_OUT 0x0100	Data are outgoing
11.	#define _F_TERM 0x0200	File is a terminal

Since the file abc.txt is opened in read mode and as by default the stream is fully buffered, the flags _F_READ and _F_BUF for the stream are set. Thus, the value of fp1->flags will be equal to 0x0001 + 0x0004, i.e. 0x0005. Similarly, since the file cde.txt is opened in the binary update mode (i.e. read and write), the value of fp2->flags will be 0x0003 + 0x0004 + 0x0040, i.e. 0x0047.

30. The stream stdin is associated with a terminal

Explanation:

Although the expression stdin->flags & _F_TERM is not parenthesized, it still prints "The stream stdin is associated with a terminal" because the LSB of stdin->flags is 1 (since the stream stdin is opened for reading only).

Answers to Multiple-choice Questions

31. c 32. a 33. c 34. a 35. d 36. c 37. a 38. b 39. a 40. a

Programming Exercises

Program 1 | Count the number of characters present in a file

PE 10-1.c

```
#include<stdio.h>
#include<conio.h>
#include<stdlib.h>
main()
{
    FILE* fp;
    char name[50];
    int count=0;
    printf("Enter the name of the file:\t");
    gets(name);
    fp=fopen(name, "r");
    if(fp==NULL)
    {
        printf("File cannot be opened\n");
        printf("Unable to continue\n");
        getch();
        exit(1);
    }
    while(fgetc(fp)!=EOF)
        count++;
    printf("The number of characters present in the file are %d", count);
}
```

abc.txt

```
Hello Readers
```

cde.txt

```
File
Management
```

Output window (first execution)

```
Enter the name of the file:    abc.txt
The number of characters present in the file are 14
```

Output window (second execution)

```
Enter the name of the file:    cde.txt
The number of characters present in the file are 16
```

Remarks:

- At the end of the line, carriage return and line feed character combinations are present
- As the file is opened in text mode, these characters are interpreted as new-line character
- Hence, at the end of the lines new-line characters are present

Program 2 | Count the number of words present in a file

Word is defined as any sequence of characters that does not contain a blank, tab or new line character.

PE10-2.c

```
#include<stdio.h>
#include<conio.h>
#include<stdlib.h>
main()
{
    FILE* fp;
    char name[50], ch;
    int count=0;
    printf("Enter the name of the file:\t");
    gets(name);
    fp=fopen(name, "r");
    if(fp==NULL)
    {
        printf("File cannot be opened\n");
        printf("Unable to continue\n");
        getch();
        exit(1);
    }
    while((ch=fgetc(fp))!=EOF)
        if(ch==' ' || ch='\t' || ch=='\n')
            count++;
    printf("The number of words present in the file are %d", count);
}
```

abc.txt

```
Laziness may appear attractive, but work gives satisfaction.
```

cde.txt

```
The harder you work,
the luckier you get.
```

Output window (first execution)

```
Enter the name of the file:    abc.txt
The number of words present in the file are 8
```

Output window (second execution)

```
Enter the name of the file:    cde.txt
The number of characters present in the file are 8
```

Remarks:

- Two words may be separated by a blank space, tab, or a new line character
- The last line in the file has an extra new line character
- Thus, the total number of words in a file is equal to count and not count+1

Program 3 | Compare content of two files to determine whether they are the same or not

PE10-3.c

```
#include<stdio.h>
#include<conio.h>
#include<stdlib.h>
main()
{
    FILE* fp1, *fp2;
    char file1[50], file2[50], ch1, ch2;
    int flag_unequal=0;
    printf("Enter the name of the file 1:\t");
    gets(file1);
    printf("Enter the name of the file 2:\t");
    gets(file2);
    fp1=fopen(file1, "r");
    fp2=fopen(file2,"r");
    if(fp1==NULL|| fp2==NULL)
    {
        printf("Files cannot be opened. Some problem occurred\n");
        printf("Unable to continue\n");
        getch();
        exit(1);
    }
    while((ch1=fgetc(fp1))!=EOF && (ch2=fgetc(fp2))!=EOF)
        if(ch1!=ch2)
        {
            flag_unequal=1;
            break;
        }
    if(flag_unequal==1)
        printf("File content differs");
    else
        printf("File content is same");
}
```

abc.txt

```
Belief is the death of intelligence
```

cde.txt

```
Belief is the death of intelligence
```

Output window

```
Enter the name of the file 1:    abc.txt
Enter the name of the file 2:    cde.txt
File content is same
```

Program 4 | Check whether a given word exist in a file or not. If it exists, find the number of times it occurs

PE 10-4.c

```
#include<stdio.h>
#include<conio.h>
#include<stdlib.h>
main()
{
    FILE* fp;
    char file[50], word[50], temp[50], ch;
    int count=0, i=0;
    printf("Enter the name of the file:\t");
    gets(file);
    fp=fopen(file, "r");
    if(fp==NULL)
```

abc.txt

```
All men who have achieved great things have been great dreamers.
```

Output window

```
Enter the name of the file:    abc.txt
Enter the word, you want to look for:    have
The number of words present in the file are 2
```

(Contd...)

PE 10-4.c

```
    {
        printf("File cannot be opened\n");
        printf("Unable to continue\n");
        getch();
        exit(1);
    }
    printf("Enter the word, you want to look for:\t");
    gets(word);
    while((ch=fgetc(fp))!=EOF)
    {
    if(ch==' ' || ch=='\n')
    {
        temp[i]='\0';
        if(strcmp(word,temp)==0)
            count++;
        i=0;
    }
    else
    {
        temp[i++]=ch;
    }
    printf("The number of words present in the file are %d", count);
}
```

Output window

Program 5 | Search for a given word in the file and if it exists, replace it by its reversal

PE10-5.c

```
1  #include<stdio.h>
2  #include<string.h>
3  #include<conio.h>
4  #include<stdlib.h>
5  main()
6  {
7      FILE* fp;
8      char file[50], word[50], temp[50], ch;
9      int count=0,i=0, length;
10     printf("Enter the name of the file:\t");
11     gets(file);
12     fp=fopen(file, "r+");
13     if(fp==NULL)
14     {
15         printf("File cannot be opened\n");
16         printf("Unable to continue\n");
17         getch();
18         exit(1);
19     }
20     printf("Enter the word, you want to look for:\t");
21     gets(word);
22     while((ch=fgetc(fp))!=EOF)
```

abc.txt (before the execution of program)

He who does not understand your silence will probably not understand your words.

Output window

```
Enter the name of the file:     abc.txt
Enter the word, you want to look for:     understand
The number of replacements done in the file are 2
```

abc.txt (after the execution of program)

He who does not dnatsrednu your silence will probably not dnatsrednu your words.

Remarks:

- The call to function fseek in line number 34 is very important
- Remember that when file is opened for updation, the input should not be immediately followed by the output without an intervening call to a file-positioning function

(Contd...)

```
{
    if(ch==' ' || ch=='\n' || ch=='\t')
    {
        temp[i]='\0';
        if(strcmp(word,temp)==0)
        {
            count++;
            length=strlen(temp);
            fseek(fp,-1*length-1, SEEK_CUR);
            strrev(temp);
            fprintf(fp,"%s",temp);
            fseek(fp,1L,SEEK_CUR);
        }
        i=0;
    }
    else
    {
        temp[i++]=ch;
    }
}
printf("The number of replacements done in the file is %d",count);
}
```

Test Yourself

1. Fill in the blanks in each of the following:
   a. The connection to an open file is represented either as a ____________ or as a ____________.
   b. Five standard streams are _____, _____, _____, _____ and _____.
   c. The streams stdout and stderr are associated with the ____________ for writing the output and the errors.
   d. An object of the type ____________ contains all the information required to control the stream.
   e. ____________ stream is an ordered sequence of the characters composed into lines, terminated by a new-line character.
   f. If a stream is fully buffered, the characters are transmitted to the file when ____________.
   g. The mode string used to open an existing file in the text mode for update is ____________.
   h. When the end of the file is encountered, the function fgetc returns ____________.
   i. The current location of the file position indicator for the stream can be determined by using the functions ____________ and ____________.
   j. The function call rewind(stream) is equivalent to the function call (void) fseek(stream, 0L, ____).
   k. By default, the size of a buffer for a fully buffered stream is ____________.
   l. If the argument buf in a call to the function setbuf is a null pointer, I/O will be ____________.

2. State whether each of the following is true or false. If false, explain why.
   a. Standard streams are always present and need not be opened or closed.
   b. In binary streams, any carriage return character that appears before a line feed character is dropped.
   c. The standard streams stdaux and stdprn are not always defined.
   d. By default, the stream stdout by default is line buffered.
   e. The default buffer size for a stream is 512 and can be varied by using the function setvbuf.
   f. The function ftell is used to position the file position indicator within the file and to report the new location of the file position indicator.
   g. A file must be opened before it is used.
   h. It is possible to associate more than one stream with a file but not a stream with two files at a time.
   i. All open streams must be explicitly closed before the successful termination of the program.
   j. The mode string "rb+" is the same as the mode string "r+b".

3. Programming exercise:
   a. Write a C program to count the number of lines present in a file.
   b. Write a C program to count the number of occurrences of a given word in a file.
   c. Write a C program to copy content of a file to another file, replacing each string of one or more blanks by a single blank.
   d. Write a C program to reverse the content of a file. Use command line arguments to get the name of the file. Using a temporary file is allowed.
   e. Write a C program to reverse the content of a file without using any temporary file. Use command line arguments to get the name of the file.

Appendix A

NUMBER SYSTEMS

A.1 Number systems

A **number system**, also known as the **numeral system**, is a system for naming or representing numbers. Each number system is characterized by a value known as **base** or **radix**. A number system with base, or radix, r is a system that uses distinct symbols for r digits. The first digit in every number system starts from 0. For example, a number system with base 2 contains two digits: 0 and 1; base 8 contains eight digits: 0–7. If the base of a number system exceeds 10, the additional digits use the letters of the alphabet, beginning with an A. Numbers are represented by a string of digit symbols. Table A.1 lists some of the available number systems along with their base and the digits they use to represent numbers.

Table A.1 | Number systems

S.No	Number system	Base/Radix	Symbols/Digits
1.	Binary	2	0, 1
2.	Ternary	3	0,1,2
3.	Quaternary	4	0,1,2,3
4.	Quinary	5	0,1,2,3,4
5.	Senary	6	0,1,2,3,4,5
6.	Septenary	7	0, 1, 2, 3, 4, 5, 6
7.	Octonary or Octal	8	0, 1, 2, 3, 4, 5, 6, 7
8.	Nonary	9	0, 1, 2, 3, 4, 5, 6, 7, 8

(Contd...)

S.No	Number system	Base/Radix	Symbols/Digits
9.	Decimal	10	0, 1, 2, 3, 4, 5, 6, 7, 8, 9
10.	Undenary	11	0, 1, 2, 3, 4, 5, 6, 7, 8, 9, A
11.	Dudoenary	12	0, 1, 2, 3, 4, 5, 6, 7, 8, 9, A, B
12.	Hexadecimal	16	0, 1, 2, 3, 4, 5, 6, 7, 8, 9, A, B, C, D, E, F

Out of these number systems, four number systems, namely **binary**, **octal**, **decimal** and **hexadecimal number systems** are the most commonly used. The decimal number system is familiar to us. We use it to process any numerical quantity in day-to-day activities. However, the computers do not use the decimal number system. They can only understand the binary number system and work with binary digits, i.e. 0 and 1. The octal and hexadecimal number systems are derived from the binary number system and are used to represent the binary numbers in a compressed form.

The important points about the number systems are as follows:

1. A number in a number system is a string of digits allowed in the number system. For example, 10101 is a valid binary number but 1012 is not, because the digit 2 does not exist in the binary number system.
2. It is not possible to determine the value of a number just by looking at it. For example, it is not possible to determine the value represented by the number 101. It can be a valid binary number and represents 5 in the decimal number system. It can also be a valid octal number and represents 65 in the decimal number system. Thus, just by looking at the number 101, we cannot determine whether it represents 5 or 65 in the decimal number system. To determine the exact value represented by a number, we must have information about its number system. This information can be provided by specifying the base of the number system as a subscript to the number enclosed within parentheses. For example, 101 in the binary number system is represented as $(101)_2$ and in the octal number system as $(101)_8$.
3. Each digit in a number has a **place value**. The right-most digit of a number has a place value of 0. The place value of the other digits is one more than the place value of the digit towards its right. For example, in a decimal number 483, the place value of the digit 3 is 0, the digit 8 is 1 and the digit 4 is 2.
4. Each number system is **weighted,** which means that some weight is associated with each digit of a number. For a number in a number system with base r, the weight associated with the digit of the number having a place value of p is equal to r^p. For example, in a decimal number 483, the weight associated with the digit 3 is 10^0, the digit 8 is 10^1 and the digit 4 is 10^2.
5. Since the weight associated with the right-most digit is the least, it is known as the **least significant digit** (**LSD**) and as the weight associated with the left-most digit is the most, it is known as the **most significant digit** (**MSD**). For example, in a decimal number 483, digit 3 is the least significant digit and digit 4 is the most significant digit.
6. For a number in a number system, it is always possible to find an equivalent number in other number systems. An equivalent number in other number systems can be found by applying number system conversions.

A.2 Number System Conversions

Number system conversions are applied to find equivalent numbers in other number systems. Number system conversions are classified as:

1. Conversion from the decimal number system to any other number system.
2. Conversion from any number system to the decimal number system.
3. Conversion from the binary number system to the octal and hexadecimal number system.
4. Conversion from the octal and hexadecimal number system to the binary number system.

A.2.1 Conversion from Decimal Number System to Any Other Number System

A decimal number can be converted to another number system with base or radix *r*, by using the procedure given below:

1. Divide the given decimal number by the radix *r* of the desired number system to get a quotient and a remainder.
2. Successively keep on dividing the obtained quotients with the radix *r* till 0 is obtained as the quotient.
3. Preserve the remainders obtained during each division and write them in reverse order (i.e. the remainder obtained first becomes the LSD and the remainder obtained last becomes MSD) to form the equivalent binary number.

For example, the conversion of a decimal number 23 to the binary, the octal and the hexadecimal number systems is shown in Table A.2.

Table A.2 | Conversion from the decimal to the binary, octal and hexadecimal number systems

Binary	Octal	Hexadecimal
2 | 23 2 | 11 r = 1 ↑LSB 2 | 5 r = 1 2 | 2 r = 1 2 | 1 r = 0 | 0 r = 1 MSB $(23)_{10} = (10111)_2$	8 | 23 8 | 2 r = 7 ↑LSB | 0 r = 2 MSB $(23)_{10} = (27)_8$	16 | 23 16 | 1 r = 7 ↑LSB | 0 r = 1 MSB $(23)_{10} = (17)_{16}$

A.2.2 Conversion from Any Other Number System to Decimal Number System

A number given in any number system can be converted to the decimal number system by multiplying each digit of the number with its associated weight and then by summing up the results of all the multiplications.

For example, conversion from the binary, octal and hexadecimal number systems to the decimal number system is shown in Table A.3.

Table A.3 | Conversion from the binary, octal and hexadecimal number systems to the decimal number system

Binary to decimal	Octal to decimal	Hexadecimal to decimal
$(1011)_2 \rightarrow (?)_{10}$ $1\times2^3+0\times2^2+1\times2^1+1\times2^0$ $=8+0+2+1=11$ $(1011)_2 \rightarrow (11)_{10}$	$(726)_8 \rightarrow (?)_{10}$ $7\times8^2+2\times8^1+6\times8^0$ $=448+16+6=470$ $(726)_8 \rightarrow (470)_{10}$	$(AB)_{16} \rightarrow (?)_{10}$ $10\times16^1+11\times16^0$ $=160+11=171$ $(AB)_{16} \rightarrow (171)_{10}$

A.2.3 Conversion from Binary Number System to Octal and Hexadecimal Number System

Octal and hexadecimal number systems are used to represent the binary numbers in a compressed form. Thus, the conversions from and to the binary, octal and hexadecimal number systems are very important.

A binary number can be converted to an octal number by using the following procedure:

1. The binary number is partitioned into groups of 3 bits each. The group size is kept as three because 3 bits can represent all the 8 combinations (0–7) present in the octal number system (since $2^3=8$).
2. Start creating groups from the right side of the number. If the left-most group remains incomplete, complete it by appending 0's on the left.
3. For each group of bits assign the corresponding octal equivalent.
4. The string of octal digits so obtained gives the octal equivalent of the binary number.

Conversion from the binary to the octal number system is shown in Table A.4.

Table A.4 | Conversion from the binary to the octal number system

Binary to octal	Binary to octal
$(101001)_2 \rightarrow (?)_8$ 1 0 1 | 0 0 1 5 | 1 $(101001)_2 \rightarrow (51)_8$	$(1011101)_2 \rightarrow (?)_8$ 1 | 0 1 1 | 1 0 1 The left-most group is incomplete. Complete the group by appending 0's on the left and assign an octal equivalent to each group. 0 0 1 | 0 1 1 | 1 0 1 1 | 3 | 5 $(1011101)_2 \rightarrow (135)_8$

Conversion from the binary to the hexadecimal number system is similar except that the bits are divided into groups of four. The group size is kept as four because 4 bits can represent all the 16 combinations (0–F) present in the hexadecimal number system. The equivalent hexadecimal digit for each group of four digits is written. The string of the hexadecimal digits so obtained gives the hexadecimal equivalent of the binary number.

Conversion from the binary to the hexadecimal number system is shown in Table A.5.

Table A.5 | Conversion from the binary to the hexadecimal number system

Binary to hexadecimal	Binary to hexadecimal
$(11101001)_2$ → $(?)_{16}$ 1 1 1 0 1 0 0 1 E 9 $(11101001)_2$ → $(E9)_{16}$	$(1011101)_2$ → $(?)_{16}$ 1 0 1 1 1 0 1 The leftmost group is incomplete. Complete the group by appending 0's on the left and assign a hexadecimal equivalent to each group. 0 1 0 1 1 1 0 1 5 D $(11101001)_2$ → $(5D)_{16}$

A.2.4 Conversion from Octal and Hexadecimal Number System to Binary Number System

The conversions from the octal and hexadecimal number system to the binary number system are the reverse of the binary to the octal and hexadecimal number system conversions. To convert a given octal number to the binary number system, for each octal digit write the equivalent three-digit binary code. Similarly, to convert a given hexadecimal number to the binary number system, for each hexadecimal digit write the equivalent four-digit binary code.

Conversions from the octal and hexadecimal number systems to the binary number system are given in Table A.6.

Table A.6 | Conversion from the octal and hexadecimal number systems to the binary number system

Octal to binary	Hexadecimal to binary
$(45)_8$ → $(?)_2$ 4 5 1 0 0 1 0 1 $(45)_8$ → $(100\ 101)_8$	$(CD)_{16}$ → $(?)_{10}$ C D 1 1 0 0 1 1 0 1 $(CD)_{16}$ → $(1100\ 1101)_{16}$

Appendix B

ALGORITHMS AND FLOWCHARTS

B.1 Algorithm

The study of algorithms, sometimes called **algorithmics**, is one the fundamental areas of Computer Science. **Algorithmics** is concerned with discovering efficient algorithms and representing them so that they can be understood by the computers. In this brief introduction to algorithms, I will tell you about what defines an algorithm and how to represent algorithms.

Algorithm is a fundamental notion in Computer Science. Therefore, it deserves a precise description. An **algorithm** can be described as 'A finite set of instructions, which if followed, accomplishes a particular task'. In addition, every algorithm must satisfy the following criteria:

1. **Input:** An algorithm may have zero or more quantities that are externally supplied as the input. An algorithm with zero input is rigid and performs the same type of task. Inputs are provided to increase the flexibility of the algorithm and help in developing generic algorithms.
2. **Output:** An algorithm must produce at least one output.
3. **Definiteness:** Each instruction must be clear and unambiguous. For example, an instruction like 'add 2 or 3 to x' is not allowed.
4. **Finiteness:** An algorithm must have a finite number of instructions, i.e. it always terminates. This is one of the most important differences between an algorithm and a program. An algorithm always terminates while a program may or may not terminate.
5. **Effectiveness:** Every instruction of an algorithm must be feasible. It should be possible to carry out the instructions of the algorithm.

Thus, an algorithm can be formally described as 'a well-ordered finite collection of unambiguous and effectively computable operations that when executed produces a result'.

There are a number of choices for writing algorithms. One option is to write an algorithm in a natural language like **plain English**. Although, plain English seems to be a good choice for writing algorithms, the following are some inherent problems associated with the specification of an algorithm in plain English:

1. Algorithms written in plain English are verbose. An algorithm written in plain English includes many words that contribute to correct grammar or style but do nothing to communicate the algorithm.
2. Instructions written in plain English are generally ambiguous. Often an English sentence can be interpreted in many different ways.

The above-mentioned problems make plain English a poor choice for specifying algorithms. Another option for writing algorithms is using **programming languages. Programming languages** avoid the problems of being wordy and ambiguous however, there are some other disadvantages that make them undesirable for writing algorithms. The specification of an algorithm in a programming language requires learning special syntax and symbols that are not a part of plain English language. Also, an algorithm written in a programming language is difficult to read and understand especially if one is not conversant with the programming language in which it is written. The dependence of algorithm specification on programming languages can be eliminated by using a **pseudocode**. A **pseudocode** is used to express algorithms in a manner that is independent of a particular programming language. The prefix pseudo is used to emphasize that this code is not meant to be compiled or executed on a computer. Using the pseudocode, one can convey the basic ideas about an algorithm without worrying about how the algorithm will be implemented. The pseudocode basically consists of C and Pascal constructs and English-like phrases. The conventions commonly used in a pseudocode are as follows:

1. Two forward slashes // are used to indicate that the remaining line should be treated as a comment.
2. An identifier begins with a letter. The data types of variables are not explicitly declared. The types will be clear from the context.
3. There are two Boolean values, **true** and **false**. In order to produce these values, the logical operators **and**, **or** and **not**, and the relational operators <, <=, >, >=, != are provided.
4. Elements of multi-dimensional arrays are accessed using square brackets. For example, if M is a two-dimensional array, the $(i,j)^{th}$ element of the array is denoted as $M[i,j]$. Array indices start at 0.
5. Assignment statements have the form $x{:=}e$, which assigns the value of expression e to the variable x. Multiple assignments can be performed in one statement; for example, $x{:=}y{:=}e$ assigns the value of expression e to variables x and y.
6. Loop constructs can be specified by using one of the three forms:

   for *variable:= value1* to *value2* **do** in steps of *increment*
       loop statements

   while *conditional expression* **do**
       loop statements

   do
       statements
   while *conditional expression*

7. A conditional statement has the following forms:
   if *condition* **then** *statement*
   if *condition* **then** *statement1* **else** *statement2*
8. Input and output are done using the instructions **read** and **write**. No format specifiers are used to specify the size of input or output quantities.
9. There is only one type of procedure: **Algorithm**. A pseudocode procedure is specified by giving its name, followed by a parameter list and then the sequence of steps in the procedure. The inclusion of the parameter list in procedures increases the flexibility of procedures and allows more generic procedures to be developed.

Another way to express algorithms is using structured English, which combines the familiarity of plain English with the structure and order of programming languages and pseudocode. In this approach, English is used to write operations. Each operation in the algorithm is written on a separate line so that they are easily distinguished from others. The operations are grouped by indenting and numbering lines.

In Table B.1, an algorithm to add *n* numbers is described by using the above-discussed notations.

Table B.1 | Different notations used to specify an algorithm to add *n* numbers

Plain English	**Programming language 'C'**

First, read the numbers to be added. Initialize a resultant value to 0. Now, add all the numbers to this resultant value one by one. If all the numbers have been added, output the resultant value.	int add(int a[], int n)
	{
	  int i, s=0;
	  for(i=0;i<n;i++)
	    s=s+a[i];
	  return s;
	}

Pseudocode	**Structure English**

Algorithm add(a, n)
{
  s:=0.0;
  for i:=1 to n do
    s:=s+a[i];
  return s;
}
	Step 1: Start
	Step 2: Initialize sum(*s*) and number of numbers read(*i*) to 0
	Step 3: Read the number of numbers to be added. Let it be *n*
	Step 4: Read a number to be added and let it be *a*.
	Step 5: *s*=*s*+*a* and *i*=*i*+1
	Step 6: If *i*<*n*, go to Step 4 else go to step 7.
	Step 7: Output the value of sum(*s*)
	Step 8: Stop

B.2 Flowcharts

A **flowchart** is a graphical representation of an algorithm. It is a diagrammatic representation that illustrates the sequence of operations to be performed to get a solution to a problem. Flowcharts are generally drawn in the early stages of formulating a computer solution to the problem.

The American National Standard Institute (ANSI) defines a flowchart as 'A graphical representation for defining and analyzing solution to a problem in which standard symbols are used to represent operation, data flow or equipment'. Flowcharts are drawn according to the defined rules and using standard symbols prescribed by ANSI. The symbols prescribed by ANSI are given in Table B.2.

Table B.2 | Flowchart symbols

S.No	Symbol	Name	Description
1.	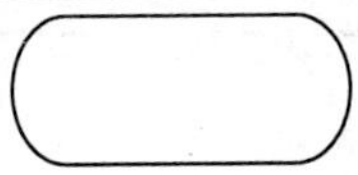	Terminator	A start or stop point in a process
2.	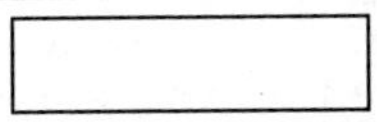	Process	A computation step or an operation
3.	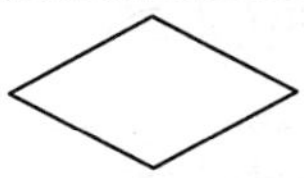	Decision	Decision making or branching
4.	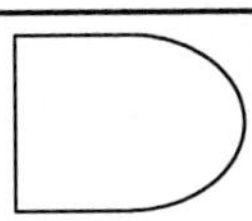	Delay	A waiting period
5.	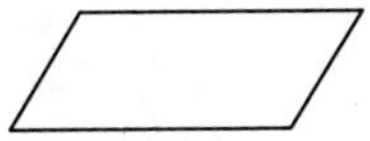	Data I/O	Input or output operation
6.	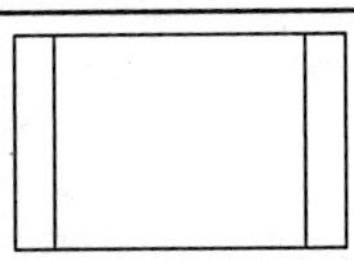	Predefined process	A formally defined sub-process
7.	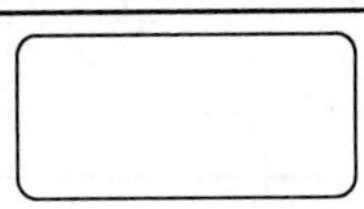	Alternate process	An alternate to the normal process step
8.	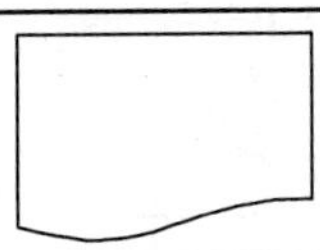	Document	A document or a report
9.	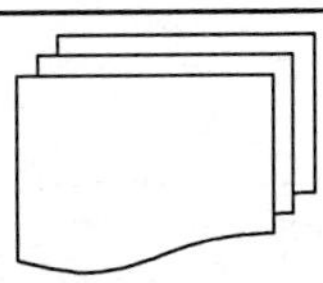	Multi-document	Multiple documents
10.	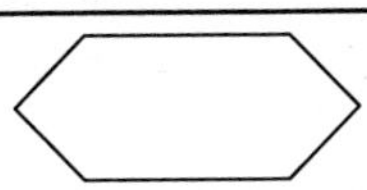	Preparation	A preparation or set-up process step
11.	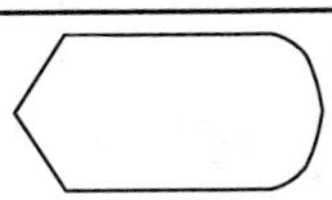	Display	A machine display
12.		Manual input	Manual input to a system

(Contd...)

S.No	Symbol	Name	Description
13.	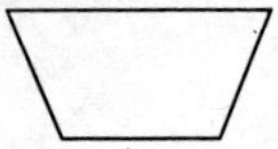	Manual operation	A process step that is not automated
14.		Card	Punch card I/O
15.	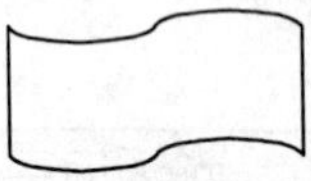	Punched tape	Punch tape I/O
16.	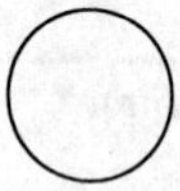	On-page connector	Connector for joining two parts of a program. Should exist in a pair on a page
17.		Off-page connector	Continuation onto another page
18.		Logical OR	Logical OR operation
19.		Summing junction	Logical AND operation
20.	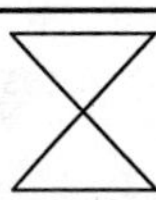	Collate	Organizing data into a standard format or arrangement
21.	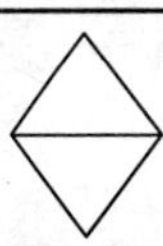	Sort	Sort data in some predefined order
22.	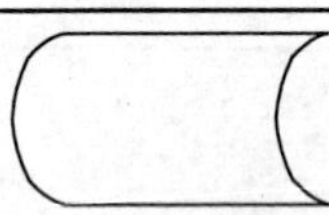	Stored data	General data storage
23.		Magnetic disk	Data storage on magnetic disk
24.	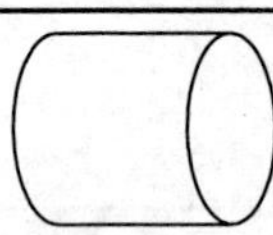	Direct access storage	Storage on a hard drive

(Contd...)

25.	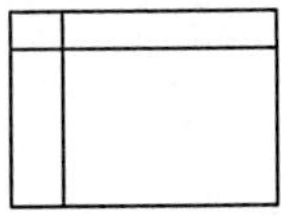	Internal storage	Data stored in main memory (RAM)
26.		Magnetic tape	Data storage on magnetic tape
27.		Flow lines	Indicates the direction of flow of information
28.	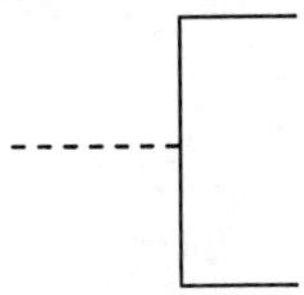	Annotation	Used for comment writing

Creating flowcharts is more of an art than a science. There is no unique correct flowchart for solving a given problem. Each programmer can come up with his or her own flowchart, provided the formal rules for drawing flowcharts are observed. Though there are no hard and fast rules, the guidelines for drawing flowcharts are as follows:

1. Every flowchart should begin with a terminator labeled 'Start' and end with a terminator labeled 'Stop'. These merely indicate the physical starting and terminating points of the flowchart.
2. Symbols in the flowchart are connected by lines with arrowheads to define the direction of flow from step to step. The default direction of flow is from top to bottom of the page and from left to right. Arrowheads should be used to show the direction of the flow, especially if it is other than top to bottom or left to right.
3. Lines should never cross. In certain circumstances, a programmer may find it difficult to avoid crossing a line or to prevent drawing a long and jagged line between the symbols. In such circumstances, the connector symbols can be used to keep the flowchart simple. The connector symbol indicates a transfer of flow and thus, always appears in pairs. An arrowhead leading into the connector indicates that the control is to be transferred to the point at which that connector's counterpart appears. An arrowhead leading from a connector indicates the point at which the control re-enters the flowchart.
4. Only one flow line should come out from a process symbol.
5. Only one flow line should enter a decision symbol, but two or three should come out of it. Labels should be placed on flow lines coming out of the decision symbol to indicate the decision.
6. Write within symbols briefly. Additional necessary information to describe data or computational steps can be provided by using the annotation symbol.
7. The symbols may be drawn of any size, only the shape is standard.

Figure B.1 illustrates a flowchart to add *n* numbers.

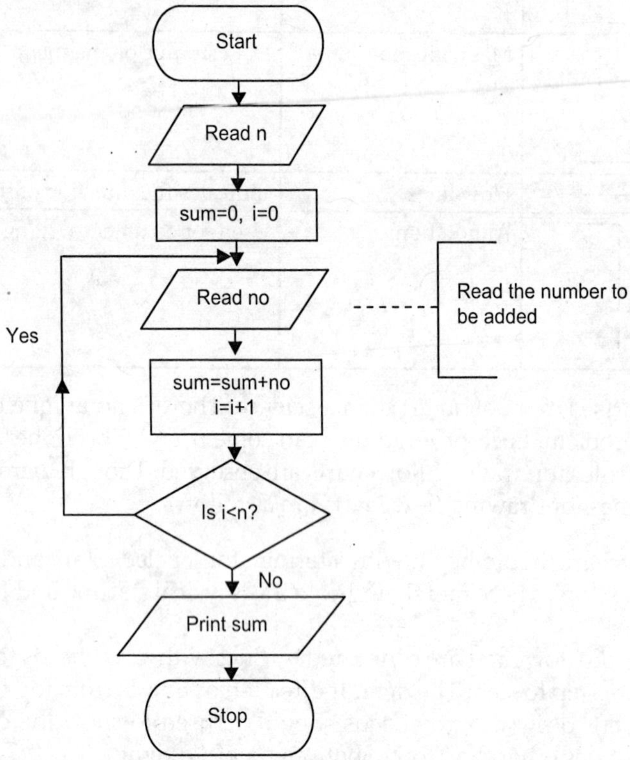

Figure B.1 | Flowchart to add *n* numbers

Appendix C

TRANSLATION LIMITS

According to ANSI/ISO standard, each compiler conforming to the standard should be able to translate and execute a program that contains constructs subject to the following limits:

- 127 nesting levels of blocks
- 63 nesting levels of conditional inclusion
- 12 pointer, array and function declarators (in any combinations) modifying an arithmetic, structure, union or incomplete type in a declaration
- 63 nesting levels of parenthesized expressions within a full expression
- 63 significant characters in an internal identifier (i.e. with internal linkage) or a macro name
- 31 significant characters in an external identifier (i.e. external linkage)
- 4095 external identifiers in one translation unit (i.e. file)
- 511 identifiers with block scope declared in one block
- 4095 macro identifiers simultaneously defined in one preprocessing translation unit
- 127 parameters in one function definition
- 127 arguments in one function call
- 127 parameters in one macro definition
- 127 arguments in one macro invocation

- 4095 characters in a logical source line
- 4095 characters in a character string literal
- 15 nested levels for #included files
- 1023 case labels for a switch statement (excluding those for any nested switch statements)
- 1023 members in a single structure or union
- 1023 enumeration constants in a single enumeration
- 63 levels of nested structure or union definition in a single structure definition-list

Appendix D

ROM–BIOS AND DOS SERVICES

Table D.1 presents an elaborate interrupt list along with the values to be placed in the input registers before calling the interrupts and the values returned by them. The exhaustive interrupt list may run up to thousands of pages and listing it is beyond the scope of this book.

Table D.1 | Interrupt list

S.No	int No.	Purpose	Service	Inputs	Returns	Notes
1.	0x05	Print screen	-	-	Nothing	Sends screen contents to printer. Works in text mode
2.	0x10	Video				
i.		Set video mode	0	AH=0x00 AL=Desired Video mode	Nothing	The value of AL and corresponding video modes are: 0x0: 40×25 text, 16 grey 0x1: 40×25 text, 16/8 color 0x2: 80×25 text, 16 grey 0x3: 80×25 text, 16/8 color 0x4: 320×200 graphics, 4 color 0x5: 320×200 graphics, 4 grey 0x6: 640×200 graphics, mono 0x7: 80×25 text, mono 0x8: 160×200 graphics, 16 color 0x9: 320×200 graphics, 16 color 0xA: 640×200 graphics, 4 color 0xD: 320×200, 16 color EGA, VGA 0xE: 640×200, 16 color EGA, VGA 0xF: 640×350, mono EGA, VGA

(Contd...)

S.No	int No.	Purpose	Service	Inputs	Returns	Notes
						0x10: 640×350, 4 or 16 color EGA, VGA 0x11: 640×480 graphics, 2 color 0x12: 640×480 graphics, 16 color, VGA 0x13: 320×200 graphics, 256 color, VGA
ii.		Set cursor size-text mode	1	AH=0x01 CH=cursor start scan line and options CL=bottom scan line containing cursor	Nothing	Bits of the CH register and corresponding options: Bit(s) Description 7 should be zero 6,5 cursor blink (00=normal, 01=invisible, 10=erratic, 11=slow) (00=normal, other=invisible on EGA/VGA) 4-0 topmost scan line containing cursor
iii.		Set cursor position	2	AH=0x02 BH=page number DH=row (00 is top) DL=column (00 is left)	Nothing	
iv.		Get cursor position	3	AH=0x03 BH=page number	CH=start scan line CL=end scan line DH=row DL=column	
v.		Select active display page	5	AH=0x05 AL=new page number	Nothing	Specify which of the multiple display pages will be visible
vi.		Scroll window up	6	AH=0x06 AL=number of lines by which to scroll up BH=attribute used to write blank lines at the bottom of the window CH, CL= row, column of window's upper left corner DH, DL=row, column of window's lower right corner	Nothing	Affects only the current active page
vii.		Scroll window down	7	AH=0x07 AL=number of lines by which to scroll down	Nothing	Affects only the current active page

(*Contd...*)

				BH=attribute used to write blank lines at the top of the window CH, CL= row, column of window's upper left corner DH, DL=row, column of window's lower right corner		
viii.		Set color palette	B	AH=0x0B BH=palette color ID BL=color to be used with the palette	Nothing	Works for CGA/EGA/VGA only
ix.		Display pixel	C	AH=0x0C AL=pixel value CX= pixel column DX=pixel row BH=page number	Nothing	
x.		Read pixel	D	AH=0x0D CX=pixel column DX=pixel row BH=page number	AL=pixel value	
xi.		Get current video mode	F	AH=0x0F	AH=number of character columns on screen AL=display mode BH=active page number	
3.	0x11	Get equip-ment list	-	Nothing	AX=equipment list	Bits of AX represents: Bit(s) Description 0 disk drive present/absent (0: absent, 1: present) 1 math coprocessor pres-ent/absent (0: absent, 1: present) 2-3 RAM in 16Kb blocks 4-5 initial video mode 00= unused 01=40×25 color 10=80×25 color 11=80×25 mono 6-7 Number of disk drives 8 DMA present/absent (0: absent, 1: present) 9-11 Number of serial ports 12 Game port (0: absent, 1: present) 13 serial printer 14-15 number of printers

(Contd...)

S.No	int No.	Purpose	Service	Inputs	Returns	Notes
4.	0x12	Get memory size	-	Nothing	AX=memory size in Kb	
5.	0x13	Disk services				
i.		Reset disk controller	0	AH=0x00 DL=disk 0x00-7F floppy disk (bit 7 is reset) 0x80-FF hard disk (bit 7 is set)	Nothing	
ii.		Get disk status	1	AH=0x01 DL=disk 0x00-7F floppy disk 0x80-FF hard disk	AL= status code	Status code values in AL are AL=0: no error AL=1: bad command AL=2: address mark not found AL=3: write attempt to write protected disk-F AL=4: sector not found AL=5: reset failed-H AL=6: floppy disk removed-F AL=7: bad parameter table-H AL=8: DMA overrun-F AL=9: DMA across 64Kb boundary AL=A: bad sector flag-H AL=B: bad track flag-H AL=C: media type not found-F AL=D: invalid number of sectors on format-H AL=E: control data address mark detected-H AL=F: DMA arbitration level out of range-H AL=10: bad CRC AL=11: ECC corrected data error-H AL=20: NEC controller failure AL=40: seek failed AL=80: time out (failed to respond) AL=AA: drive not ready-H AL=BB: undefined error-H AL=CC: write fault-H AL=E0: status register error-H AL=FF: sense operation failed-H -F: Floppy disk only -H: Hard disk only

(Contd...)

iii.		Read disk sectors	2	AH=0x02 AL=number of sectors CH=track number CL=sector number DH=head number DL=disk 0x00-7F floppy disk 0x80-FF hard disk ES:BX=pointer to buffer	If successful: Carry Flag=clear AH=0x00 AL=number of sectors read If unsuccessful: Carry Flag=set AH= status code	For status code, refer interrupt no. 0x13, service number 1
iv.		Write disk sectors	3	AH=0x03 AL=number of sectors CH=track number CL=sector number DH=head number DL=disk 0x00-7F floppy disk 0x80-FF hard disk ES:BX=pointer to buffer	If successful: Carry Flag=clear AH=0x00 AL=number of sectors written If unsuccessful: Carry Flag=set AH= status code	For status code, refer interrupt no. 0x13, service number 1
v.		Verify disk sectors	4	AH=0x04 AL=number of sectors CH=track number CL=sector number DH=head number DL=disk 0x00-7F floppy disk 0x80-FF hard disk ES:BX=pointer to buffer	If successful: Carry Flag=clear AH=0x00 AL=number of sectors verified If unsuccessful: Carry Flag=set AH= status code	For status code, refer interrupt no. 0x13, service number 1
vi.		Format disk track	5	AH=0x05 AL=number of sectors CH=track number CL=sector number DH=head number DL=disk 0x00-7F floppy disk 0x80-FF hard disk ES:BX=pointer to 4-byte address fields containing of -byte 0=track -byte 1=head -byte 2=sector -byte 3=bytes/sector 0- if 128 bytes per sector	If successful: Carry Flag=clear AH=0x00 AL=number of sectors verified If unsuccessful: Carry Flag=set AH= status code	

(Contd...)

S.No	int No.	Purpose	Service	Inputs	Returns	Notes
				1- if 256 bytes per sector 2- if 512 bytes per sector 3- if 1024 bytes per sector		
vii.		Get drive parameters	8	AH=0x08 DL=disk 0x00-7F floppy disk 0x80-FF hard disk	If successful: Carry Flag=clear BL=drive type CH=low eight bits of maximum cylinder number DH=maximum head number DL=number of drives ES:DI= drive parameter table (floppies only) If unsuccessful: Carry Flag=set AH=status code	For status code, refer interrupt no. 0x13, service number 1 BL specifies values for diskette drive types: 0x01- 360K, 40 track, 5.25″ 0x02- 1.2M, 80 track, 5.25″ 0x03- 720K, 80 track, 3.5″ 0x04- 1.44M, 80 track, 3.5″
viii.		Initialize two fixed disk base tables	9	AH=0x09 DL=disk 0x80-FF hard disk	If successful: Carry Flag=clear AH=0x00 If unsuccessful: Carry Flag=set AH=status code	For status code, refer interrupt no. 0x13, service number 1
ix.		Read long	A	AH=0x0A AL=number of sectors DL=disk 0x80-FF hard disk DH=head number CH=cylinder number CL=sector number ES:BX=pointer to buffer	If successful: Carry Flag=clear AH=0x00 AL=number of sectors read If unsuccessful: Carry Flag=set AH=status code	For status code, refer interrupt no. 0x13, service number 1 This service is supported for hard disks only. The upper 2-bits of 10-bit cylinder number are placed in the upper 2 bits of CL register
x.		Write long	B	AH=0x0B AL=number of sectors DL=disk 0x80-FF hard disk DH=head number CH=cylinder number	If successful: Carry Flag=clear AH=0x00 AL=number of sectors written	For status code, refer interrupt no. 0x13, service number 1 This service is supported for hard disks only. The upper 2-bits of 10-bit cylinder number are placed in the upper 2 bits of CL register

(Contd...)

				CL=sector number ES:BX=pointer to buffer	If unsuccessful: Carry Flag=set AH=status code	
xi.		Seek to cylinder	C	AH=0x0C CH=lower 8 bits of cylinder CL=upper 2 bits of cylinder in bits 6-7 DH=head number DL= disk 0x80-FF hard disk	If successful: Carry Flag=clear AH=0x00 AL=number of sectors written If unsuccessful: Carry Flag=set AH=status code	For status code, refer interrupt no. 0x13, service number 1 This service is supported for hard disks only
xii.		Reset fixed disk system	D	AH=0x0D DL= disk 0x80-FF hard disk	If successful: Carry Flag=clear AH=0x00 AL=number of sectors written If unsuccessful: Carry Flag=set AH=status code	For status code, refer interrupt no. 0x13, service number 1 This service is supported for hard disks only.
xiii.		Test for drive ready	10	AH=0x10 DL= disk 0x80-FF hard disk	If successful: Carry Flag=clear AH=0x00 AL=number of sectors written If unsuccessful: Carry Flag=set AH=status code	For status code, refer interrupt no. 0x13, service number 1 This service is supported for hard disks only
xiv.		Reca-librate drive	13	AH=0x11 DL= disk 0x80-FF hard disk	If successful: Carry Flag=clear AH=0x00 AL=number of sectors written If unsuccessful: Carry Flag=set AH=status code	For status code, refer interrupt no. 0x13, service number 1 This service is supported for hard disks only
xv.		Control-ler diag-nostics	14	AH=0x14	If successful: Carry Flag=clear	For status code, refer interrupt no. 0x13, service number 1

(Contd...)

S.No	int No.	Purpose	Service	Inputs	Returns	Notes
					AH=0x00 AL=number of sectors written If unsuccessful: Carry Flag=set AH=status code	This service is supported for hard disks only
xvi.		Get disk type	15	AH=0x15 DL=disk 0x00-7F floppy disk 0x80-FF hard disk	If successful: Carry Flag=clear AH=disk-type code CX:DX= number of 512 byte sectors when AH=3 If unsuccessful: Carry Flag=set AH=status code	For status code, refer interrupt no. 0x13, service number 1 This service is not supported for PC or PC/XT. Disk-type codes are: AH=0: disk non-existent AH=1: disk, no change detection present AH=2: disk change detection present AH=3: fixed disk
xvii.		Get disk change status	16	AH=0x16	DL=drive that had disk change 0x00-7F floppy disk AH=disk change status	This service is not supported on PC or PC/XT. Status code in AH are: 00= no disk change 01= disk changed
xviii.		Set disk type	17	AH=0x17 AL= floppy disk-type code 0x00 not used 0x01 320/360Kb floppy disk in 360Kb drive 0x02 320/360Kb floppy disk in 1.2Mb drive 0x03 1.2Mb floppy disk in 1.2Mb drive 0x04 720Kb floppy disk in 720Kb drive DL= disk 0x00-7F floppy disk	If successful: Carry Flag=clear AH=0x00 AL=number of sectors written If unsuccessful: Carry Flag=set AH=status code	For status code, refer interrupt no. 0x13, service number 1 This service is not supported for floppy disks on PC or PC/XT. Disk-type codes for AL are: AL=00: no disk AL=01: regular disk, regular drives AL=03: high-capacity disk in high capacitydrives
xix		Set media type for format	18	AH=0x18 CH=number of cyliners CL=sectors per track DL= disk 0x00-7F floppy disk	If successful: Carry Flag=clear AH=0x00 ES:DI=segment: offset of disk	For status code, refer interrupt no. 0x13, service number 1

(Contd...)

					parameter table for media type If unsuccessful: Carry Flag=set AH=status code	
6.	0x16	Key-board				
i.		Read keyboard character	0	-	AH=scan code AL=ASCII code	
ii.		Report whether character ready	1	AH=0x01	zero flag=0 character available to be received zero flag=1 no character in keyboard buffer AH=scan code AL=ASCII code	
iii.		Get shift status	2	AH=0x02	AL key status	The bits of AL register signifies: Bit Description Bit 0=1 Right shift key depressed Bit 1=1 Left shift key depressed Bit 2=1 Control key depressed Bit 3=1 Alt key depressed Bit 4=1 Scroll Lock ON Bit 5=1 Num Lock ON Bit 6=1 Caps Lock ON Bit 7=1 Insert ON
7.	0x017	Printer				
i.		Send one byte to printer	0	AH=0x00 AL=character DX=printer number 0- LPT1 1- LPT2 2- LPT3	AH=success/ failure code	The bits of AH register signifies: Bit Description Bit 0=1 Time out Bit 3=1 I/O error Bit 4=1 Printer selected Bit 5=1 Out of paper Bit 6=1 Printer Acknowledge Bit 7=1 Printer not busy
ii.		Initialize printer	1	AH=0x01 AL=character DX=printer number 0- LPT1 1- LPT2 2- LPT3	AH=success/ failure code	The status code is same as for service 0x01

(Contd...)

S.No	int No.	Purpose	Service	Inputs	Returns	Notes
iii.		Get printer status	2	AH=0x02 AL=character DX=printer number 0- LPT1 1- LPT2 2- LPT3	AH=success/ failure code	The status code is same as for service 0x01
8.	0x19	Boot-strap Loader	-	-	Nothing	Reboots the system
9.	0x1A	Time				
i.		Read contents of the clock tick counter	0	AH=0x00	AL=midnight signal, 0x00 if midnight passed since last read, non-zero otherwise CX=tick count, high portion DX=click count, low portion	
ii.		Set value in clock tick counter	1	AH=0x01 CX=tick count, high portion DX=click count, low portion	Nothing	
iii.		Get current time from CMOS time/date chip	2	AH=0x02	CH=hours in Binary Coded Decimal (BCD) CL=minutes in BCD DH=seconds in BCD DL=1 if daylight saving time, 0 if standard time	Applies to AT and later only
iv.		Set time in CMOS time/date chip	3	AH=0x03 CH=hours in Binary Coded Decimal (BCD) CL=minutes in BCD DH=seconds in BCD DL=1 if daylight saving time, 0 if standard time	Nothing	Applies to AT and later only
v.		Read date from CMOS time/date chip	4	AH=0x04	DL=day in BCD DH=month in BCD CL=year in BCD	

(Contd...)

					CH=century in BCD	
vi.		Set date in CMOS time/date chip	5	AH=0x05 DL=day in BCD DH=month in BCD CL=year in BCD CH=century in BCD	Nothing	
vii.		Set alarm in CMOS time/date chip	6	AH=0x06 CH=hours in BCD CL=minutes in BCD DH=seconds in BCD	If successful: Carry flag is clear If unsuccessful: Carry flag is set	
viii.		Reset alarm	7	AH=0x07	Nothing	
10.	0x21	DOS services				
i.		Terminate program	0	AH=0x00 CS=PSP segment address	Nothing	
ii.		Read character from standard input, with echo	1	AH=0x01	AL=character read	Waits for keyboard input from STDIN and echoes to STDOUT
iii.		Write character to standard output	2	AH=0x02 DL=character to write	AL=last character output	Outputs character to STDOUT
iv.		Read character from STDAUX	3	AH=0x03	AL=character read	Wait for character and reads from STDAUX
v.		Write character to STDAUX	4	AH=0x04 DL=character to write	Nothing	Sends character in DL to STDAUX. It waits until STDAUX is available
vi.		Write character to printer	5	AH=0x05 DL=character to print	Nothing	Sends character in DL to STDPRN i.e. standard print stream. It waits until STDPRN device is ready before output
vii.		Direct console I/O	6	AH=0x06 DL=(0-FE) character to output. =FF if console input request	AL=input character if console input request	Reads from or writes to the console device depending upon the value of DL

(*Contd...*)

S.No	int No.	Purpose	Service	Inputs	Returns	Notes
					Zero flag=0 if console request character available in AL =1 if no character is ready and request was console input	Cannot output character FF as FF indicates read operation For console read, no echo is produced
viii.		Direct console input without echo	7	AH=0x07	AL=character from STDIN	Waits for keyboard input until keystroke is ready Character is not echoed to STDOUT
ix.		Console input without echo	8	AH=0x08	AL=character from STDIN	
x.		Print string	9	AH=0x09 DS:DX=pointer to the string ending in '$'	Nothing	Outputs character string to STDOUT up to '$'
xi.		Buffered keyboard Input	A	AH=0x0A DS:DX=pointer to input buffer of the format	Nothing	
xii.		Check standard input status	B	AH=0x0B	AL=00 if no character available =FF if character is available	Checks STDIN for available characters. The available character is not returned
xiii.		Clear keyboard buffer and invoke keyboard function	C	AH=0x0C AL=0x01, 0x06, 0x07, 0x08, 0x0A	See return values of services with AH value 0x01, 0x06, 0x07, 0x08, 0x0A	The main function is to clear the input buffer and specific 0x21 interrupt routine
xiv.		Disk reset	D	AH=0x0D	Nothing	All file buffers are flushed to disk
xv.		Select disk	E	AH=0x0E DL=zero based, drive number (0-A:, 1-B:……etc.)	AL=one based, total number of logical drives including hardfiles	
xvi.		Get allocation table information	1B	AH=0x1B	AL=sectors per cluster CX=bytes per sector	Retrieves information on capacity and format of default drive DS:BX can be used to determine if drive is RAMDISK or removable

(Contd...)

					DX= clusters on disk DS:BX= Segment offset of media descriptor 0xF8-Hard disk 0xFC- 5.25 inch single sided, 9 sector 0xFD- 5.25 inch double sided, 9 sector 0xFE- 5.25 inch single sided, 8 sector 0xFF- 5.25 inch double sided, 8 sector	
xvii.		Get allocation table information for specified drive	1C	AH=0x1C CL=drive number (0-default, 1-A:, 26-Z:)	AL=sectors per cluster CX=bytes per sector DX=clusters on disk DS:BX= Segment offset of media descriptor (Refer service AH=0x1B)	Retrieves information on capacity and format of default drive DS:BX can be used to determine if drive is RAMDISK or removable
xviii.		Get disk free space	36	AH=0x36 DL=drive number (0-default, 1-A:, 26-Z:)	AX=sectors per cluster=FFFF if drive is invalid BX=number of available clusters CX=number of bytes per sector DX=number of clusters per drive	Used to determine available space on specified disk
xiv.		Create directory	39	AH=0x39 DS:DX= segment: offset address of directory name	If successful: carry flag is clear If unsuccessful: carry flag is set AX=error	

(Contd...)

S.No	int No.	Purpose	Service	Inputs	Returns	Notes
xx.		Remove directory	3A	AH=0x3A DS:DX= segment: offset address of directory name	If successful: carry flag is clear If unsuccess-ful: carry flag is set AX=error	Allows deletion of directory if it is empty
xxi.		Change directory	3B	AH=0x3B DS:DX= segment: offset address of directory name	If successful: carry flag is clear If unsuccess-ful: carry flag is set AX=error	
xxii.		Delete file	41	AH=0x41 DS:DX= segment: offset address of the filename	If successful: carry flag is clear If unsuccess-ful: carry flag is set AX=error	Wild characters not allowed in file name
xxiii.		Get file attribute	43	AH=0x43 AL=0 DS:DX=segment: offset address of the file name	If successful: carry flag is clear If unsuccessful: carry flag is set AX=error	File attributes are bit encoded. The bits of CX register signifies: Bit Description Bit 0=1 Read only Bit 1=1 Hidden Bit 2=1 System Bit 3=1 Volume label entry Bit 4=1 Sub-directory entry Bit 5=1 Archive bit Bit 6=1 Unused Bit 7=1 Unused
xxiv.		Set file attri-butes	43	AH=0x43 AL=1 DS:DX=segment: offset address of the file name	If successful: carry flag is clear If unsuccessful: carry flag is set AX=error	File attributes are bit encoded. The bits of CX register signifies: Bit Description Bit 0=1 Read only Bit 1=1 Hidden Bit 2=1 System Bit 3=1 Volume label entry Bit 4=1 Sub-directory entry Bit 5=1 Archive bit Bit 6=1 Unused Bit 7=1 Unused
xxv.		Get current directory	47	AH=0x47 DL=Drive number (0-default, 1-A:, 2-B:...etc.) DS:DI=segment: offset address of buffer where DOS places the current directory name	If successful: carry flag=clear and buffer is filled with full pathname from root of current directory.	Returns the current directory relative to the root directory. The leading slash '\' and drive designator are omitted

(Contd...)

					If unsuccessful: Carry flag=set AX=error code	
xxvi.		Find first matching file	4E	AL=0x4E DS:DX=segment: offset address of file name. File name can contain wild card characters. CX= file attributes used while searching	If successful: carry flag=clear Disk transfer area is setup with the file information. The file information is 43 bytes long and contains following details: 0-20 reserved bytes 21 file attributes 22-23 time of creation/ modification 24-25 date of creation/ modification 26-30 file size 31-422 file name If function unsuccessful: Carry flag=set AX=error code	File attributes are bit encoded. The bits of CX register signifies: Bit Description Bit 0=1 Read only Bit 1=1 Hidden Bit 2=1 System Bit 3=1 Volume label entry Bit 4=1 Sub-directory entry Bit 5=1 Archive bit Bit 6=1 Unused Bit 7=1 Unused
xxvii.		File next matching file	4F	AH=0x4F Assumes that DTA points to buffer used by previous successful interrupt 0x21, function 0x4E	If successful: Carry flag=clear Disk transfer area is set up with the file information. The file information is 43 bytes long and contains detail given in service 0x4E If unsuccessful: Carry flag=set AX=error code	This service is useful for write own DIR command
xxviii.		Rename file	56	AH=0x56 DS:DX=segment: offset address of file to be renamed. Wild	If successful: carry flag=clear If unsuccessful:	Supports full pathnames and allows renaming files across directories. In DOS version 3.0 and later, this function can be used to rename directories

(Contd...)

S.No	int No.	Purpose	Service	Inputs	Returns	Notes
				card characters are not allowed. ES:DI: segment: offset address of new name of file. Wild card characters are not allowed.	Carry flag=set AX=error code	
11.	0x33	Mouse				
i.		Reset mouse and get status	0	AX=0x00	AX=0xFFFF is mouse support is available AX=0 if mouse support is not available BX-number of buttons	Resets mouse to default driver values. Mouse is positioned to screen centre. Mouse cursor is reset and hidden
ii.		Show mouse cursor	1	AX=0x01	Nothing	
iii.		Hide mouse pointer	2	AX=0x02	Nothing	
iv.		Get mouse posi-tion and button status	3	AX=0x03	CX=horizontal x position (0-639) DX=vertical y position (0-199) BX=Button status	The bits of BX signifies: Bit(s) Description 0 Left button pressed 1 Right button pressed 2 Center button pressed
v.		Set mouse cursor position	4	AX=0x04 CX=horizontal position DX=vertical position	Nothing	Default cursor position is at the screen center. The position must be within the range of the current video mode. The position may be rounded to fit screen mode resolution
vi.		Set mouse horizon-tal Min/Max position	7	AX=0x07 CX=maximum horizontal position DX=maximum horizontal position	Nothing	Restricts mouse horizontal movement to window. If minimum value is greater than the maximum value, the values are swapped
vii.		Set mouse vertical Min/Max position	8	AX=0x08 CX=maximum vertical position DX=maximum vertical position	Nothing	Restricts mouse vertical movement to window. If minimum value is greater than the maximum value, the values are swapped

Appendix E

GRAPHICS PROGRAMMING

E.1 Computer Graphics

These days, computers have invaded the field of art. They have been used in many graphical applications such as interior designing, architectural planning, flight simulation, virtual museums, pencil drawings, caricature generation, video games, animations, etc. The journey of computer graphics formally began in 1963, when Ivan Sutherland, the father of Computer Graphics, demonstrated the use of computers for the interactive design of line drawings. Sutherland developed a system, called Sketchpad, for man–machine interactive picture generation that made people aware of the potential capabilities of the computers that can be used in the field of graphics. His work gave a boost to the developments in the field of computer graphics, and by the end of 1970, a large number of algorithms existed for scan conversion, hidden line/surface removal, shading and rendering. These developments were sufficient for computer graphics to be adopted as an efficient, powerful and economical tool by engineers, scientists, designers, illustrators and artists.

This appendix provides a basic introduction about graphics programming using Turbo C 3.0. However, if you are passionate about graphics programming and want to develop some real-time graphical applications, I suggest you learn and use Open Graphics Library (OpenGL). OpenGL consists of over 250 standard library functions that can be used to draw two-dimensional and three-dimensional scenes, which are as realistic as photographs.

E.2 Initializing Graphics Mode in Turbo C 3.0

The first step in graphics programming is to initialize the graphics mode. In Turbo C 3.0, the graphics mode can be initialized by calling the function `initgraph`. The prototype of the function `initgraph` is `void initgraph(int *graphdriver, int *graphmode, char *pathtodriver);` and is available in the header file `graphics.h`. The important points about the use of the function `initgraph` are as follows:

1. The function initgraph accepts three arguments: the graphics driver, the graphics mode and the path to the driver.
2. The argument *graphdriver is an integer that specifies the graphics driver to be used. The graphics driver constants enumerated in the header file graphics.h are listed in Table E.1.

Table E.1 | Graphics driver constants and their values

Graphics driver constant	Value
DETECT	0
CGA	1
MCGA	2
EGA	3
EGA64	4
EGAMONO	5
IBM8514	6
HERCMONO	7
ATT400	8
VGA	9
PC3270	10

   The graphics driver can be detected automatically by using the macro DETECT. The macro DETECT, defined in the header file graphics.h, requests the function initgraph to automatically determine which graphics driver to load in order to switch to the highest resolution graphics mode.
3. The argument *graphmode is an integer that specifies the graphics mode. If the macro DETECT has been used to determine the graphics driver, the function initgraph sets *graphmode to the highest resolution available for the detected driver.
4. The argument pathtodriver is a string that specifies the directory path where the function initgraph initially looks for the graphics driver (.BGI files). **BGI** stands for Borland Graphics Interface. If the drivers are not present in the listed directory, the drivers are searched in the current working directory. If the BGI files are present in the current working directory, an empty string, i.e. "" can be given as an argument for this parameter.
5. The function initgraph loads the graphics driver from the disk and initializes the graphics mode. Once the graphics mode is initialized, the coordinate system (with the resolution depending upon the given graphics mode) is established and the screen is cleared. The origin of the established coordinate system is at the top left corner. The x-coordinates increase towards the right and the y-coordinates increase in the downward direction.
6. The initgraph function also resets all graphics settings (color, palette, current position, viewport, etc.) to their defaults. Whether the function initgraph has successfully initialized the graphics mode or not can be determined by checking the value returned by the function graphresult. The function graphresult returns 0 if the graphics mode is successfully initialized, otherwise it returns a negative value ranging from -1 to -18 to indicate a graphics error. Various graphics error constants along with their values have been enumerated in the header file graphics.h.

7. Another way to check whether the graphics mode has been successfully initialized or not is by looking at the screen. When the graphics mode is successfully initialized, there will be no cursor blinking on the screen as it blinks in the text mode. This is one of the major differences between the text mode and the graphics mode.

E.3 Drawing Basic Shapes

After the graphics mode has been successfully initialized, the basic shapes can be drawn by using the standard library functions like `line`, `circle`, `rectangle`, `ellipse`, `sector`, `drawpoly`, etc. The complex two-dimensional and three-dimensional scenes can also be created by making use of these primitive functions in an intelligent manner. This section describes how to draw basic shapes using these primitive functions.

E.3.1 Simple Line Drawing

The functions `line`, `linerel` and `lineto` can be used to draw the lines according to the current color, line style and thickness settings. The prototypes of these functions are available in the header file `graphics.h`. The important points about the line-drawing functions available in the graphics library are as follows:

1. The prototype of the function `line` is `void line(int x1, int y1, int x2, int y2);`. It draws a line from the coordinate (x1,y1) to the coordinate (x2,y2) using the current color, line style and thickness. It does not update the value of the current position (CP).
2. The prototype of the function `linerel` is `void linerel(int dx, int dy);`. It draws a line from the coordinate position described by CP to the coordinate that is relative distance (dx,dy) apart from CP. The value of CP is advanced by (dx,dy).
3. The prototype of the function `lineto` is `void lineto(int x, int y);`. It draws a line from the coordinate position described by CP to the coordinate (x,y). The value of CP becomes (x,y).

Program E.1 illustrates the use of the line-drawing functions to draw a triangle.

Line | Prog E-1.c

```
1  //Line drawing functions
2  #include<stdio.h>
3  #include<conio.h>
4  #include<graphics.h>
5  main()
6  {
7      //request auto detection
8      int gdriver=DETECT, gmode, errcode;
9      //initialize the graphics mode
10     initgraph(&gdriver, &gmode, "d:\\tc\\bgi");
11     //read the result of initialization
12     errcode=graphresult();
13     //terminate if graphics mode is not properly initialized
14     if(errcode!=0)
15     {
```

Output window

Remarks:

- The third argument to the `initgraph` function is the path of the directory where .BGI files are present. The path of the directory containing .BGI files may be different on your system
- The `initgraph` function resets all the graphics settings
- The value of CP is set to (0,0) and the color is set to white
- The function `moveto` in line number 22 sets the value of CP
- The prototype of the function `moveto` is `void moveto(int x, int y);`. It moves the current position to (x,y)

(Contd...)

Prog E-1.c

```
        printf("Graphics error: %s\n", grapherrormsg(errcode));
        printf("Cannot continue. Press any key to terminate");
        getch();
        exit(1);
    }
    line(100,100,50,150);
    moveto(50,150);     //See remarks for explanation
    linerel(100,0);
    lineto(100,100);
    outtextxy(110,100,"(100,100)");     //See remarks for explanation
    outtextxy(20,155,"(50,150)");
    outtextxy(120,155,"(150,150)");
    getch();
    closegraph();
    return 0;
}
```

Output window

- A variant of the function moveto that can be used to manipulate the value of CP is moverel. The function moverel moves the CP by a relative distance. The prototype of the function moverel is void moverel(int dx, int dy);
- A string in a graphics mode can be printed by using the function outtextxy. The prototype of the function outtextxy is void outtextxy(int x, int y, char *string);. It prints the string string with the default text characteristics (i.e. font, direction and character size) at the coordinate position (x,y)
- The text characteristics can be set by using the function settextstyle
- The function closegraph closes the graphics mode. It then restores the screen to the mode it was in before the function initgraph was called
- BGI graphics is not supported under Windows. Therefore, the code will not work with Turbo C 4.5 and MS-VC++ 6.0
- If there is a linker error, switch on the graphics library by going to Option menu>Linker>Libraries

Screenshot

Program E-1 | A program that illustrates simple line drawing using standard library functions

E.3.2 Stylish Line Drawing

Architectural, engineering and other graphical applications generally require the lines of different styles (like dashed, center, dotted, etc.), thickness and colors to be drawn. For example, an engineering drawing may require dashed lines to indicate the hidden edges of an object or center lines to indicate axes of a hollow cylinder. The style and the thickness of the line can be set by using the function setlinestyle, and the color of a drawing can be set by using the function setcolor. After setting the line style and color, the functions line, linerel and lineto can be used to draw lines. These functions draw lines according to the current color, style and the thickness settings.

E.3.2.1 Setting the Pattern and Thickness of the Line

The function setlinestyle can be used to set the line style and its thickness. The prototype of the function setlinestyle is void setlinestyle(int linestyle, unsigned pattern, int thickness); and is present in the header file graphics.h. The important points about the function setlinestyle are as follows:

1. The function setlinestyle sets the style for all the lines drawn by the functions line, lineto, linerel, rectangle, drawpoly, etc.
2. The parameter linestyle specifies the line style. Various line style constants enumerated in the header file graphics.h are listed in Table E.2.

Table E.2 | Line style constants and their values

Line style constant	Value
SOLID_LINE	0
DOTTED_LINE	1
CENTER_LINE	2
DASHED_LINE	3
USERBIT_LINE	4

3. The second parameter pattern is applicable only for the user-defined lines, i.e. if the first parameter is USERBIT_LINE or its equivalent value.
4. The thickness parameter can be one of the two enumerated constants NORM_WIDTH having a value of 1 or THICK_WIDTH having a value of 3. The former corresponds to line thickness of one pixel (normal lines) while the latter corresponds to line thickness of three pixels (thick lines).
5. If invalid inputs are given to the function setlinestyle, the function graphresult returns -11 and the current line style remains unchanged.

E.3.2.2 Setting the Color

The current drawing color can be set by using the function setcolor. The prototype of the function setcolor is void setcolor(int color);. The important points about the function setcolor are as follows:

1. The function setcolor sets the current drawing color to color.
2. The parameter color can be one of the enumerated color constants or its equivalent value listed in Table E.3.

Table E.3 | Color constants and their values

Color constant	Value
BLACK	0
BLUE	1
GREEN	2
CYAN	3
RED	4
MAGENTA	5
BROWN	6
LIGHTGRAY	7
DARKGRAY	8
LIGHTBLUE	9
LIGHTGREEN	10
LIGHTCYAN	11
LIGHTRED	12
LIGHTMAGENTA	13
YELLOW	14
WHITE	15

Program E.2 illustrates the stylish line drawing.

Prog E-2.c

```
//Stylish line drawing
#include<stdio.h>
#include<conio.h>
#include<graphics.h>
main()
{
    //request auto detection
    int gdriver=DETECT, gmode, errcode, pattern=0xA;
    //initialize the graphics mode
    initgraph(&gdriver, &gmode, "d:\\tc\\bgi");
    //read the result of initialization
    errcode=graphresult();
    //terminate if graphics mode is not properly initialized
    if(errcode!=0)
    {
        printf("Graphics error: %s\n", grapherrormsg(errcode));
        printf("Cannot continue. Press any key to terminate");
        getch();
        exit(1);
    }
```

Output window

Remarks:

- The function getmaxx() and getmaxy() returns the maximum x and y coordinates, respectively
- The function rectangle draws a rectangle. It is declared as void rectangle(int left, int top, int right, int bottom); in the header file graphics.h
- The function rectangle draws the rectangle in the current line style, thickness and line color

(Contd...)

```
    rectangle(0, 0, getmaxx(), getmaxy());   //See remarks for explanation
    setlinestyle(SOLID_LINE, pattern, 3);
    setcolor(RED);
    line(40, 40, 40, 240);
    outtextxy(10,250,"Solid Thick");
    setlinestyle(DOTTED_LINE, pattern, 1);
    setcolor(MAGENTA);
    line(170, 40, 170, 240);
    outtextxy(130,250,"Dotted Thin");
    setlinestyle(CENTER_LINE, pattern, 1);
    setcolor(YELLOW);
    line(300, 40, 300, 240);
    outtextxy(250,250,"Center Thin");
    setlinestyle(DASHED_LINE, pattern, 1);
    setcolor(BLUE);
    line(430, 40, 430, 240);
    outtextxy(380,250,"Dotted Thin");
    setlinestyle(USERBIT_LINE, pattern, 1);
    setcolor(GREEN);
    line(560, 40, 560, 240);
    outtextxy(500,250,"Userdefined Thin");
    getch();
    closegraph();
    return 0;
}
```

Screenshot

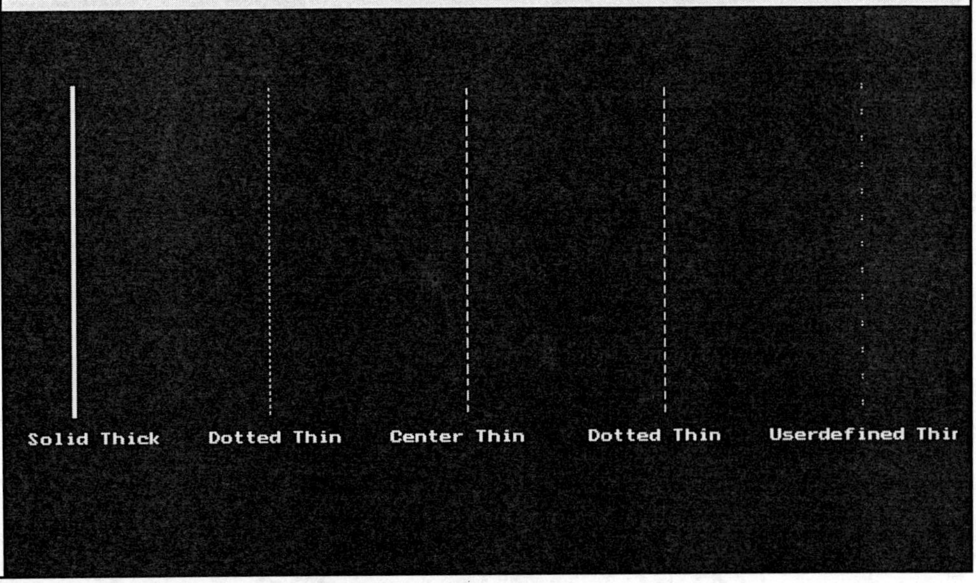

Program E-2 | A program that illustrates stylish line drawing

E.3.3 Drawing Other Basic Shapes

Basic shapes other than line such as circle, rectangle, ellipse, polygon, arc, sector, pie, etc. can be drawn by using the functions circle, rectangle, ellipse, drawpoly, arc, sector, pieslice, respectively. Program E.3 illustrates the use of these functions.

Line | Prog E-3.c

```
1  //Drawing other basic shapes
2  #include<stdio.h>
3  #include<conio.h>
4  #include<graphics.h>
5  main()
6  {
7      //request auto detection
8      int gdriver=DETECT, gmode, errcode;
9      int poly[12]={350,450,350,410,430,400,350,350,300,430,350,450};
10     //initialize the graphics mode
11     initgraph(&gdriver, &gmode, "d:\\tc\\bgi");
12     //read the result of initialization
13     errcode=graphresult();
14     //terminate if graphics mode is not properly initialized
15     if(errcode!=grOK)
16     {
17         printf("Graphics error: %s\n", grapherrormsg(errcode));
18         printf("Cannot continue. Press any key to terminate");
19         getch();
20         exit(1);
21     }
22     rectangle(0, 0, getmaxx(), getmaxy());
23     circle(100,100,50);
24     outtextxy(75,170, "Circle");
25     rectangle(200,50,350,150);
26     outtextxy(240, 170, "Rectangle");
27     ellipse(500, 100,0,360, 100,50);
28     outtextxy(480, 170, "Ellipse");
29     arc(100,270,0,110,40);
30     outtextxy(95,280,"Arc");
31     pieslice(375,270,0,180,40);
32     outtextxy(345,280,"Pieslice");
33     sector(150, 400, 30, 300, 100,50);
34     outtextxy(120, 460, "Sector");
35     drawpoly(6, poly);
36     outtextxy(340, 460, "Polygon");
37     getch();
38     closegraph();
39 }
```

Output window

Remarks:

- The function circle draws a circle in the current color. The prototype of the function circle is void circle(int x, int y, int radius);
- The prototype of the function ellipse is void ellipse(int x, int y, int stangle, int endangle, int xradius, int yradius);. It draws an elliptical arc with xradius as the radius of major axes and yradius as the radius of minor axes. The elliptical arc extends from stangle to endangle
- The prototype of the function arc is void arc(int x, int y, int stangle, int endangle, int radius);. It draws a circular arc with radius radius and the arc extends from stangle to endangle
- The function pieslice draws and fills a circular pieslice. It is declared as void pieslice(int x, int y, int stangle, int endangle, int radius);.
- The function sector draws and fills an elliptical pieslice. It is declared as void sector(int x, int y, int stangle, int endangle, int xradius, int yradius);
- The function drawpoly is declared as void drawpoly(int numpoints, int *polypoints);. It draws a polyline with numpoint-1 edges. The parameter polypoints should have 2*numpoint entries, which are x and y coordinate pairs of the vertices of the polyline
- The closed polygon can be drawn by providing the last coordinate pair entry the same as the first coordinate pair entry in polypoints
- Refer the coordinate sequence given in line number 9. The last coordinate pair 350, 450 is the same as the first coordinate pair. Thus, the figure drawn in the output is a closed polygon

(Contd...)

	Screenshot
	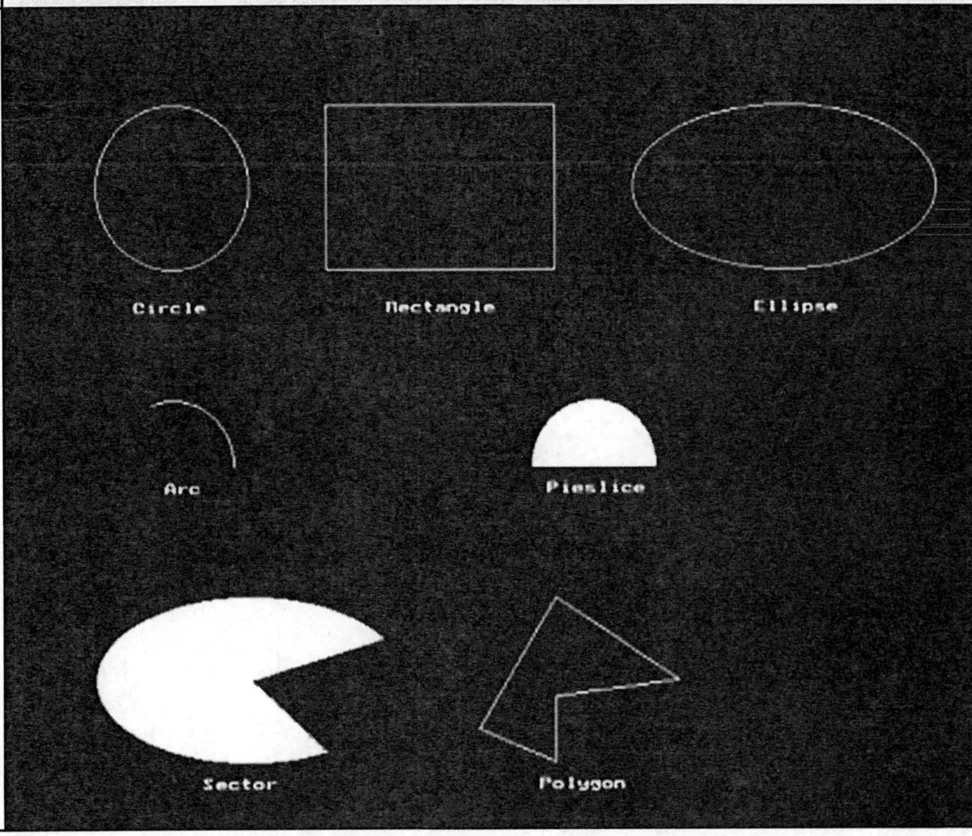

Program E-3 | A program that illustrates the basic shape drawing

E.4 Region Filling

Many graphical applications like bar charts, pie charts, depth maps, etc. require the generation of the filled regions. Closed regions like circle, ellipse, rectangle, polygon, etc. (bounded by a single color solid boundary) can be filled by using the functions like fillellipse, fillpoly, floodfill, etc. Filled rectangles can also be generated by using the functions bar and bar3d. Program E.4 illustrates the use of the bar function to generate a bar chart of runs scored in a cricket match.

Prog E-4.c	Output window

//Bar chart
#include<stdio.h>
#include<conio.h>
#include<graphics.h>
main()
{
    //request auto detection
    int gdriver=DETECT, gmode, errcode,i;
	Remarks:
	• The function settextstyle is used to set the text font, the direction and the size of the characters

(Contd...)

Prog E-4.c

```
    int scores[10]={10,22,5,12,14,8,12,17,2,9};
    //initialize the graphics mode
    initgraph(&gdriver, &gmode, "d:\\tc\\bgi");
    //read the result of initialization
    errcode=graphresult();
    //terminate if graphics mode is not properly initialized
    if(errcode!=0)
    {
        printf("Graphics error: %s\n", grapherrormsg(errcode));
        printf("Cannot continue. Press any key to terminate");
        getch();
        exit(1);
    }
    settextstyle(TRIPLEX_FONT,0,2);
    outtextxy(230,10,"BAR CHART");
    line(200,400,400,400);
    line(200,100,200,400);
    settextstyle(SMALL_FONT,0,4);
    outtextxy(270,410,"OVERS");
    settextstyle(SMALL_FONT,1,4);
    outtextxy(180,240,"SCORES");
    for(i=0;i<9;i++)
    {
        bar(210+20*i, 400-scores[i]*10, 220+20*i,400);
    }
    getch();
    closegraph();
}
```

Output window

- The prototype of the function settextstyle is void settextstyle(int font, int direction, int charsize);.
  The parameter font can be one of the font names DEFAULT_FONT, TRIPLEX_FONT, SMALL_FONT, SANS_SERIF_FONT, GOTHIC_FONT enumerated in the header file graphics.h
- The parameter direction can be one of the enumerated constants HORIZ_DIR, i.e. 0 or VERT_DIR, i.e. 1
- The size of each character can be magnified by using the parameter charsize
- The function bar draws a two-dimensional filled-in rectangular two-dimensional bar. Its prototype is void bar(int left, int top, int right, int bottom);
- The bar is filled using the current fill pattern and fill color. The generated bar will not have any outline
- The outlined bars can be generated by using the function bar3d

Screenshot

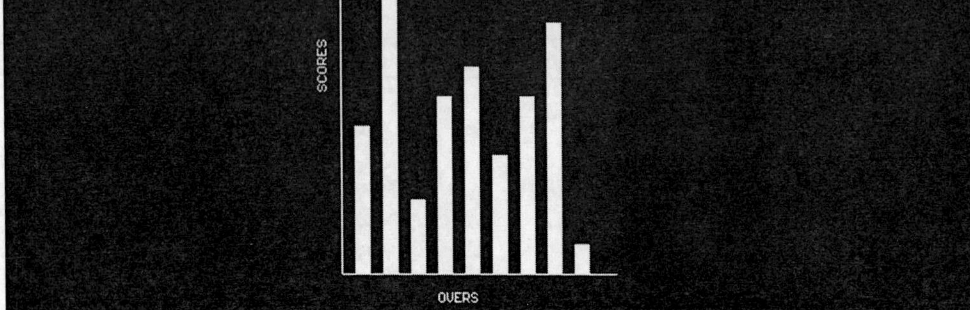

Program E-4 | A program that illustrates the use of the function bar

E.4.1 Filling Regions with Different Patterns and Colors

The functions fillellipse, fillpoly and floodfill fill the region with the standard fill pattern and the set color. The filling pattern and the color of the filling can be changed by using the function setfillstyle. The prototype of the function setfillstyle is void setfillstyle(int pattern, int color);. The important points about the function setfillstyle are as follows:

1. The function setfillstyle sets the current fill pattern and fill color.
2. The parameter pattern can be one of the enumerated fill pattern constants listed in Table E.4.

Table E.4 | Fill pattern constants and their values

Fill pattern constant	Value	Fills with
EMPTY_FILL	0	Background color
SOLID_FILL	1	Solid fill
LINE_FILL	2	---
LTSLASH_FILL	3	///
SLASH_FILL	4	///, thick lines
BKSLASH_FILL	5	\\\, thick lines
LTBKSLASH_FILL	6	\\\
HATCH_FILL	7	Light hatch
XHATCH_FILL	8	Heavy crossed hatch
INTERLEAVE_FILL	9	Interleaving lines
WIDE_DOT_FILL	10	Widely spaced dots
CLOSE_DOT_FILL	11	Closely spaced dots
USER_FILL	12	User-defined fill pattern

3. If the pattern is EMPTY_FILL or its equivalent value, the region will be filled with the current background color, otherwise the region will be filled with the pattern in the current drawing color. The background color can be set by using the function setbkcolor and the drawing color can be set by using the function setcolor.
4. If invalid input is passed to the function setfillstyle, the function graphresult returns -11, and the current fill pattern and the color remain unchanged.

Program E.5 illustrates the use of the function setfillstyle in filling the regions with different patterns.

Prog E-5.c

```
//Filling regions with different patterns
#include<stdio.h>
#include<conio.h>
#include<graphics.h>
char *patternnames[]=
{
"EMPTY_FILL", "SOLID_FILL", "LINE_FILL", "LTSLASH_FILL", "SLASH_FILL",
"BACKSLASH_FILL", "LTBACKSLASH_FILL", "HATCH_FILL", "XHATCH_FILL",
"INTERLEAVE_FILL"
};
main()
{
    int gdriver=DETECT, gmode, errcode;
    int xinitial, yinitial, xcent, ycent, xinc, yinc, xl, yl, xr, yr, pttrn=0, i, j;
    initgraph(&gdriver, &gmode, "d:\\tc\\bgi");
    errcode=graphresult();
    if(errcode!=0)
    {
        printf("Graphics error: %s\n", grapherrormsg(errcode));
        printf("Cannot continue. Press any key to terminate");
        getch();
        exit(1);
    }
    xinc=getmaxx()/5; yinc=getmaxy()/2;
    for(i=0; i<2; i++)
    {
        xinitial=0; yinitial=i*yinc;
        for(j=0; j<5; j++)
        {
            xl=xinitial+j*xinc; yl=yinitial;
            xr=xl+xinc; yr=yl+yinc;
            xcent=(xl+xr)/2; ycent=(yl+yr)/2;
            rectangle(xl, yl, xr, yr);
            setfillstyle(pttrn, BLUE);
            floodfill(xcent, ycent, WHITE);
            outtextxy(xl+5, ycent, patternnames[pttrn]);
            pttrn++;
        }
    }
    getch();
    closegraph();
    return 0;
}
```

Output window

Remarks:

- The function floodfill fills a bounded region according to the pattern and the color set by the function setfillstyle
- If the function setfillstyle is not used to set the filling pattern and color, the function floodfill fills the region with the default pattern, i.e. SOLID_FILL and the current drawing color
- It is declared as
  `void floodfill(int x, int y, int border);`
- The (x, y) is the coordinate of the seed point from where the flood fill function starts filling. The third parameter border is the color of the boundary enclosing the region
- If the seed point is within the enclosed region, the inside will be filled
- If the seed point is outside the enclosed region, the exterior will be filled
- If the boundary is not closed, the entire area will be filled

(Contd...)

	Screenshot
	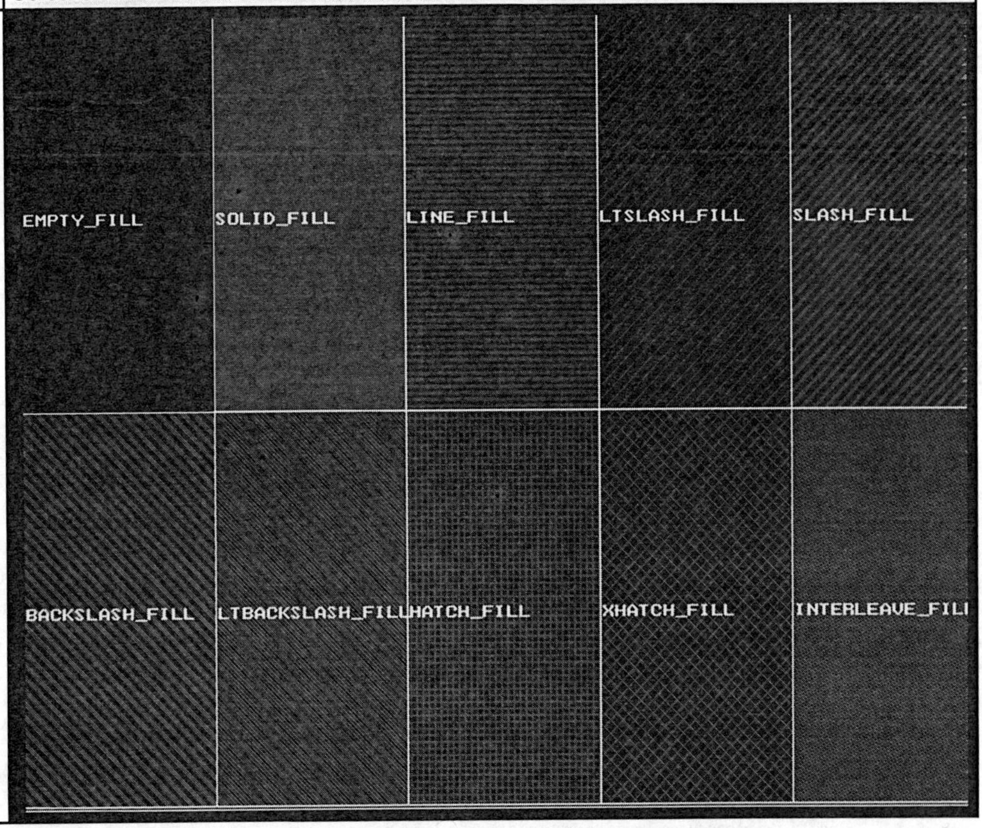

Program E-5 | A program that illustrates the region filling with different patterns

E.5 Pattern Drawing Based on Regular Polygons

Some of the patterns commonly encountered in computer graphics can be drawn by making use of regular polygons. A polygon is said to be **regular** if it is simple (i.e. no two edges cross each other), all of its edges are of equal length and all of its interior angles are equal. An **n-gon** is a regular polygon with **n** sides. The code snippet listed in Program E.6 draws n-gons for various values of **n**.

Prog E-6.c	Output window
//Drawing n-gons #include<stdio.h> #include<conio.h> #include<graphics.h> #include<math.h> #define PI 3.14159265 #define N 30	**Remarks:** • The user-defined type struct point is defined to store x and y coordinates of a point

(Contd...)

Prog E-6.c

```
struct point
{
    int x;
    int y;
};
typedef struct point POINT;
drawnpoly(int R, int n, int xc, int yc)
{
    POINT pts[N];
    int i, j;
    for(i=0; i<n; i++)
    {
        pts[i].x=xc+R*cos(2*PI*i/n);
        pts[i].y=yc+R*sin(2*PI*i/n);
    }
    for(i=0; i<n; i++)
        line(pts[i].x, pts[i].y, pts[(i+1)%n].x, pts[(i+1)%n].y);
}

main()
{
    int gdriver=DETECT, gmode, errcode;
    initgraph(&gdriver, &gmode, "d:\\tc\\bgi");
    errcode=graphresult();
    if(errcode!=0)
    {
        printf("Graphics error: %s\n", grapherrormsg(errcode));
        printf("Cannot continue. Press any key to terminate");
        getch();
        exit(1);
    }
    drawnpoly(30, 3, 30, 60);
    outtextxy(10, 100, "n:");
    outtextxy(30, 100, "3");
    drawnpoly(30, 4, 120, 60);
    outtextxy(120, 100, "4");
    drawnpoly(30, 5, 210, 60);
    outtextxy(210, 100, "5");
    drawnpoly(30, 6, 300, 60);
    outtextxy(300, 100, "6");
    drawnpoly(30, 8, 390, 60);
    outtextxy(390, 100, "8");
    drawnpoly(30, 12, 480, 60);
    outtextxy(475, 100, "12");
    drawnpoly(30, 30, 560, 60);
    outtextxy(555, 100, "30");
    getch();
```

Output window

- The coordinates of a vertex of a polygon can be generated by substituting the value of **a** as **0** in the equation mentioned in the following figure:

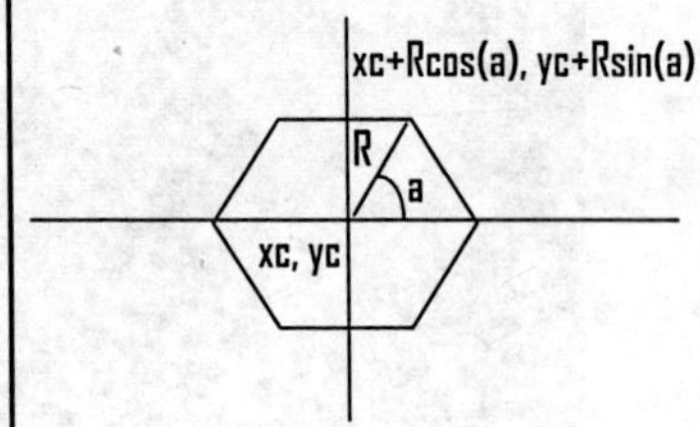

- The coordinates of other vertices of the polygon can be determined by successively incrementing the value of **a** by **2π/n**, where n is the number of the vertices, and substituting the value of **a** in the equation mentioned in the above figure

(Contd...)

```
    closegraph();
    return 0;
}
```

Screenshot

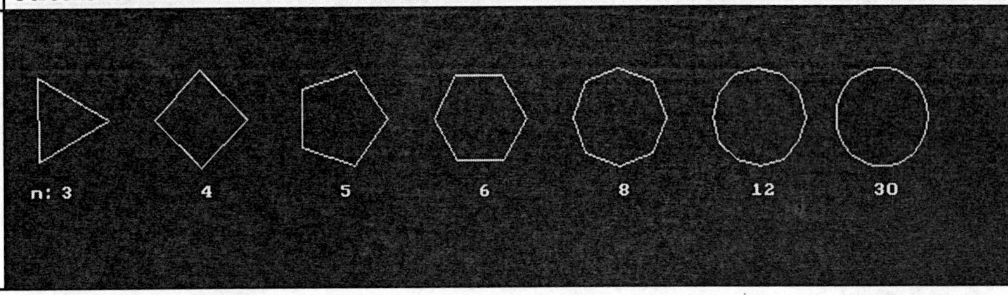

Program E-6 | A program that illustrates n-gon drawing

E.5.1 Drawing Rosettes

A **rosette** is an n-gon with each vertex joined to every other vertex. Rosettes can be easily drawn by drawing n-gons and connecting each vertex to every other vertex. Program E.7 presents rosette drawing.

Prog E-7.c | **Output window**

```
//Drawing rosettes
#include<stdio.h>
#include<conio.h>
#include<math.h>
#include<graphics.h>
#define PI 3.14159265
struct point
{
    int x;
    int y;
};
typedef struct point POINT;
rosette(int R, int n, int xc, int yc)
{
POINT pts[30];
int i, j;
for(i=0;i<n;i++)
{
    pts[i].x=R*cos(2*PI*i/n)+xc;
    pts[i].y=R*sin(2*PI*i/n)+yc;
}
for(i=0;i<n;i++)
    for(j=i+1; j<n; j++)
    {
        moveto(pts[i].x, pts[i].y);
```

(Contd...)

Prog E-7.c

```
        lineto(pts[j].x, pts[j].y);
    }
}
main()
{
    int gdriver=DETECT, gmode, errcode;
    initgraph(&gdriver, &gmode, "d:\\tc\\bgi");
    errcode=graphresult();
    if(errcode!=0)
    {
        printf("Graphics error: %s\n", grapherrormsg(errcode));
        printf("Cannot continue. Press any key to terminate");
        getch();
        exit(1);
    }
    settextstyle(DEFAULT_FONT, 0, 0);
    rosette(40, 5, 100, 200);
    outtextxy(30, 250, "5-Rosette: size 40");
    rosette(60, 11, 250, 200);
    outtextxy(180, 270, "11-Rosette: size 60");
    rosette(120, 21, 480, 200);
    outtextxy(400, 330, "21-Rosette: size 120");
    getch();
    closegraph();
    return 0;
}
```

Output window

Screenshot

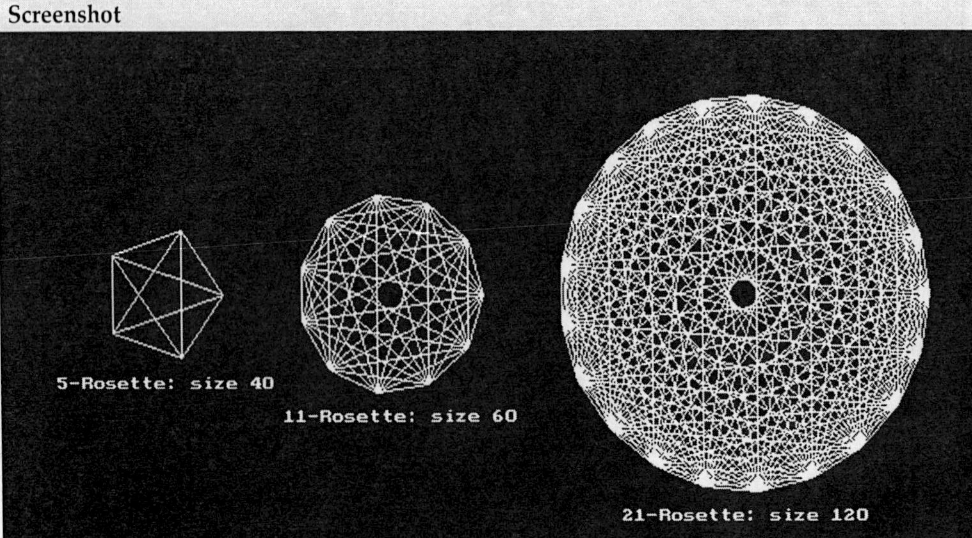

Program E.7 | A program that illustrates rosette drawing

E.5.2 Swirling Polygons

Interesting patterns can be drawn by **swirling polygons**. Program E.8 illustrates pattern generation by polygon swirling.

Prog E-8.c

```
//Swirling polygons
#include<stdio.h>
#include<conio.h>
#include<math.h>
#include<graphics.h>
#define PI 3.14159265
swirlingpoly(int n, float xc, float yc, float R, float rangle)
{
    double angle=rangle*PI/180;
    double angleinc=2*PI/n;
    int i;
    moveto(R*cos(angle)+xc, R*sin(angle)+yc);
    for(i=0; i<n; i++)
    {
        angle+=angleinc;
        lineto(R*cos(angle)+xc, R*sin(angle)+yc);
    }
}
main()
{
    int gdriver=DETECT, gmode, errcode;
    int i;
    initgraph(&gdriver, &gmode, "d:\\tc\\bgi");
    errcode=graphresult();
    if(errcode!=0)
    {
        printf("Graphics error: %s\n", grapherrormsg(errcode));
        printf("Cannot continue. Press any key to terminate");
        getch();
        exit(1);
    }
    for(i=0; i<50; i++)
        swirlingpoly(6,180,200, i*3,i*2);
    outtextxy(110, 360, "Swirling Hexagon");
    for(i=0; i<50; i++)
        swirlingpoly(8,480,200, i*3,i*2);
    outtextxy(410, 360, "Swirling Octagon");
    getch();
    closegraph();
    return 0;
}
```

Output window

(Contd...)

Screenshot

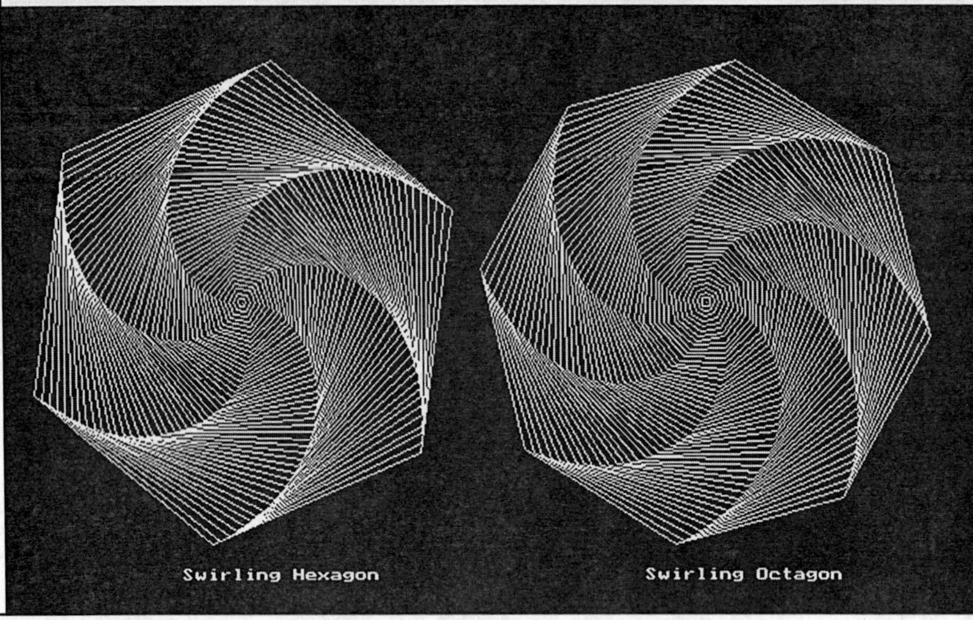

Program E.8 | A program that generates swirling polygons

E.6 Motif and Tiling

Laying copies of the same pattern side by side to cover the region is called **tiling**. The pattern that is replicated and copied at different positions is known as a **motif**. Program E.9 illustrates tiling.

Prog E-9.c

```
//Motif and Tiling
#include<stdio.h>
#include<conio.h>
#include<graphics.h>
motif(int x,int y,int size)
{
    rectangle(x,y,x+size,y+size);
    arc(x,y+size,0,90,size);
    arc(x+size,y+size,90,180,size);
    arc(x+size,y,180,270,size);
    arc(x,y,270,360,size);
}
main()
{
    int gdriver=DETECT, gmode, errcode;
    int i, j, xinitial=150, yinitial=150;
    int rows=3, cols=5, size=60;
```

Output window

(Contd...)

```
    initgraph(&gdriver, &gmode, "d:\\tc\\bgi");
    errcode=graphresult();
    if(errcode!=0)
    {
        printf("Graphics error: %s\n", grapherrormsg(errcode));
        printf("Cannot continue. Press any key to terminate");
        getch();
        exit(1);
    }
    motif(30,30,50);
    outtextxy(35,85, "Motif");
    //Tiling
    for(i=0;i<rows;i++)
    {
        xinitial=200;
        for(j=0; j<cols;j++)
            motif(xinitial+j*size,yinitial,size);
        yinitial=yinitial+size;
    }
    outtextxy(320,335,"Tiling");
    getch();
    closegraph();
    return 0;
}
```

Screenshot

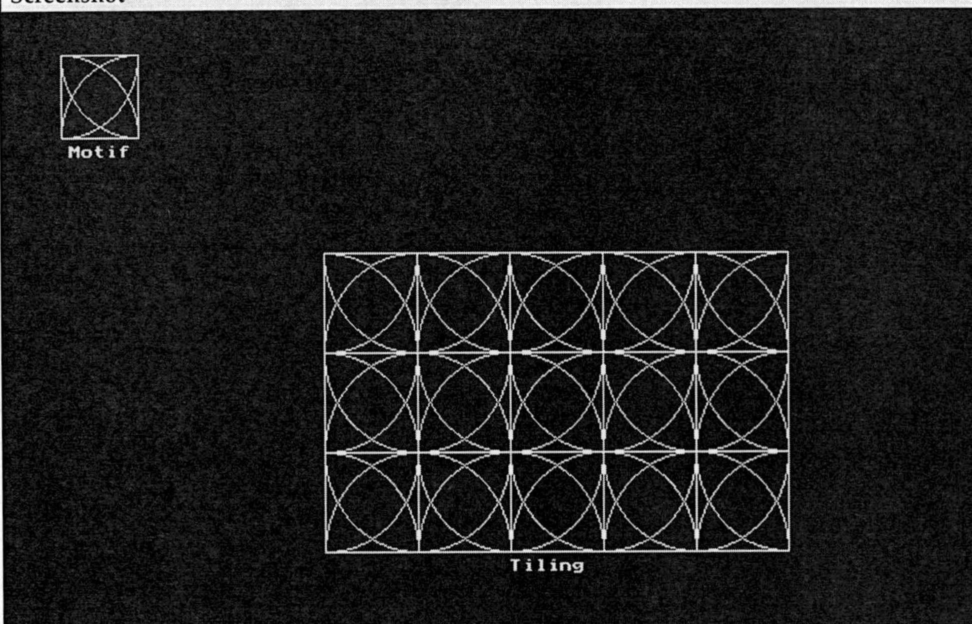

Program E.9 | A program that illustrates tiling

E.7 Viewport and clipping

A viewport specifies a rectangular area on a display device for graphical output. The viewport can be set by using the function setviewport. The prototype of the function setviewport is void setviewport(int left, int top, int right, int bottom, int clip);. The important points about the function setviewport are as follows:

1. The function setviewport establishes a new viewport for the graphical output.
2. The viewport's coordinates are given in absolute screen coordinates by (left, top) and (right, bottom).
3. The function setviewport sets the CP to (0,0) in the viewport.
4. The parameter clip determines whether the drawings are clipped at the current viewport boundaries. If it is a non-zero value, all the drawings will be clipped against the current viewport boundaries.
5. If the function setviewport is not used to change the view settings, the entire screen area is the default viewport.
6. If invalid input is passed to the function setviewport, the function graphresult returns -11 and the current view settings remain unchanged.

Program E.10 illustrates the use of the function setviewport for viewport setting.

Prog E-10.c | **Output window**

```
//Setting viewport
#include<stdio.h>
#include<conio.h>
#include<math.h>
#include<graphics.h>
#define PI 3.14159265
#define CLIP_ON 1
swirlingpoly(int n, float xc, float yc, float R, float rangle)
{
    double angle=rangle*PI/180;
    double angleinc=2*PI/n;
    int i;
    moveto(R*cos(angle)+xc, R*sin(angle)+yc);
    for(i=0; i<n; i++)
    {
        angle+=angleinc;
        lineto(R*cos(angle)+xc, R*sin(angle)+yc);
    }
}
main()
{
    int gdriver=DETECT, gmode, errcode;
    int i;
    initgraph(&gdriver, &gmode, "d:\\tc\\bgi");
    errcode=graphresult();
    if(errcode!=0)
```

(*Contd...*)

```
    {
        printf("Graphics error: %s\n", grapherrormsg(errcode));
        printf("Cannot continue. Press any key to terminate");
        getch();
        exit(1);
    }
    setviewport(200, 100, 400, 300, CLIP_ON);
    for(i=1; i<100; i++)
        swirlingpoly(9, 100, 100, i*2, i*5);
    getch();
    closegraph();
    return 0;
}
```

Screenshot

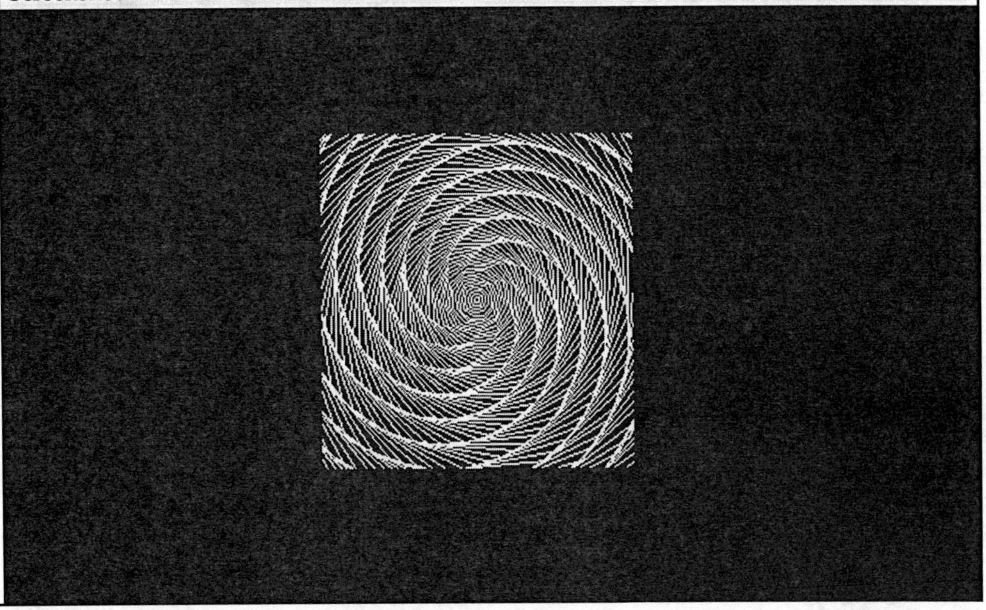

Program E.10 | A program that illustrates the use of the function setviewport for making viewport settings

Appendix F

ANSWERS TO TEST YOURSELF QUESTIONS

Chapter 1: Data Types, Variables and Constants

1. a. Dennis Ritchie; b. letter or an underscore; c. data type; d. definition; e. l-value; f. modifiable l (ell); g. `const`; h. escape sequences; i. string; j. `double`; k. functions; l. semicolon; m. format specifiers, format string; n. `sizeof`; o. l-value.

2. a. True.
   b. True.
   c. True.
   d. False. Comments are to increase the readability of the program. They are not processed by the compiler.
   e. True.
   f. False. It is an example of shorthand declaration.
   g. False. Type modifier modifies the base type to yield a new type.
   h. False. Constants do not have a modifiable l-value. In general, we say that constants do not have an l-value and have only r-value.
   i. True. A character constant can have two characters enclosed within single quotes e.g. '\n', '\t', etc.
   j. False. The function `scanf` can read more than one value at a time.

3. a. Valid; b. Valid; c. Valid; d. Valid; e. Invalid. + is a special character and cannot be a part of an identifier.; f. Valid; g. Invalid. An identifier name cannot start with a digit.; h. Valid; i. Invalid. & is a special character and cannot be a part of an identifier.; j. Valid; k. Valid.

4. a. Valid; b. Valid; c. Invalid. It is an identifier name.; d. Invalid. Comma is not allowed.; e. Valid; f. Invalid. Exponent cannot have a decimal point.; g. Invalid. G is not a valid hexadecimal digit.; h. Valid; i. Valid; j. Valid; k. Valid.

5. a. `int a=10; int b=20;`
   b. `int a=10; float b=2.5;`
   c. `int a=23u, b=0x2f;`
   d. Cannot modify constant object. Remove statement `number=500;`
   e. `printf("%d %d %d",1,2,3);`
   f. `printf("To err is human");`
   g. `printf("%d %d", no1, no2);`
   h. `printf("Humans learn by making mistakes");`
   i. `scanf("%d %d", &no1, &no2);`
   j. `sum_of_values=first_value+second_value;`

Chapter 2: Operators and Expressions

1. a. operand; b. simple expression; c. right to left; d. integer; e. Boolean constant; f. higher; g. precedence, associativity; h. type conversion; i. `sizeof`; j. Comma.

2. a. True.
   b. True.
   c. False. It depends only upon the sign of the numerator.
   d. False. The knowledge of associativity is also required.
   e. False. It is a ternary operator.
   f. True.
   g. True.
   h. True.
   i. False. It cannot be assigned a value, but it can be initialized with a value.
   j. True.

3. a. 1; b. 1; c. 0; d. 2; e. 1; f. 1; g. 1; h. 0; i. -6; j. -1.600000

4. a. Invalid. l-value required error. The r-value cannot be placed on the left side of assignment operator.
   b. Valid. The expression evaluates to `0` and the values of `a` and `b` after evaluation of expression are `0` and `15`, respectively.
   c. Invalid. l-value required error. The r-value cannot be placed on the left side of the assignment operator.
   d. Invalid. The operand of the modulus operator must of integer type.
   e. Invalid. l-value required error. The r-values cannot be placed on the left side of the assignment operator.
   f. Invalid. The operands of the bitwise operator must be of `char`, `short`, `int` or `long` type.
   g. Invalid. l-value required error. The expression `a+++++b` will be interpreted as `a++ ++ +b`, which is an erroneous expression.

h. Invalid. The operator ~ is a unary operator.
i. Valid. The expression evaluates to 15 and the values of a and b after the evaluation of expression are 15 and 5, respectively.
j. Invalid. Two binary operators cannot come next to each other without having any operand in between.

Chapter 3: Statements

1. a. statement; b. semicolon; c. block; d. identifier-labeled, case-labeled and default-labeled statements; e. integral; f. definite repetition looping; g. sentinel value; h. indefinite repetition loop; i. non-executable statements; j. flow control; k. continue; l. expression; m. do-while; n. break; o. dangling else.

2. a. True.
   b. True.
   c. True.
   d. False. An exit-controlled loop is executed at least once. The body of an entry-controlled loop will not be executed even once if the loop-controlling expression is initially false.
   e. False. An identifier-labeled statement does not alter the flow of control.
   f. False. A continue statement can appear inside, or as a loop body but not inside, or as a switch body.
   g. True.
   h. False. A break statement is used to terminate the loop.
   i. False. A switch selection expression must be of integral type.
   j. True.

3. a. `if(count>10) printf("Count is greater than 10);`
   b. `a=b=c=10;`
   c. `stud=var+=10;`
   d. `(num&1)==1?a=10:a=20;`
   e. `for(fact=1,i=1;i<=n;i++) fact*=i;`

Chapter 4: Arrays and Pointers

1. a. homogenous; b. zero; c. contiguous; d. integral; e. subscript; f. dereference; g. `*(*(arr+5)+4)`; h. direct indexing; i. address; j. 1.

2. a. True.
   b. False. It can also be zero.
   c. True.
   d. True.
   e. False. A void pointer cannot be assigned to a pointer variable without explicit type casting.
   f. False. The name of the array refers to the address of the first element of the array.
   g. True.

h. False. It is imperative that one mentions the size specifier if the array is not explicitly initialized.
i. False. Multi-dimensional arrays in C are stored the memory using row major order of storage.
j. False. The declaration statement `int* a[10];` declares `a` as an array of 10 integer pointers.

Chapter 5: Functions

1. a. Functions; b. `main`; c. actual arguments; d. by value, by address/reference; e. formal parameters; f. `char*`; g. `double`; h. an array type or a function type; i. Tail recursion; j. `int`; k. activation record; l. stack; m. winding of recursion.

2. a. True.
   b. False. `main` is a user-defined function.
   c. False. There can be any number of `return` statements within a function body, but only one `return` statement will get executed.
   d. True.
   e. True.
   f. False. The `return` statement is used to terminate the execution of a function, and the `exit` function is used to terminate the execution of a program.
   g. False. A function cannot be defined within the body of another function.
   h. False. Indirectly recursive functions are known as mutually recursive functions.
   i. True.
   j. True.
   k. True.
   l. True.
   m. True.

Chapter 6: Strings and Character Arrays

1. a. empty string; b. a null character; c. 1 byte; d. `char*`; e. double quotes; f. concatenated; g. `%s`; h. `strcmpi`; i. ^ (caret); j. `getch`; k. command line arguments.

2. a. True.
   b. False. The length of the empty string literal constant is zero.
   c. True.
   d. False. The number of bytes required to store a string literal constant is one more than the number of characters present in it.
   e. True.
   f. True.
   g. True.
   h. True.
   i. False. The first argument of the `printf` function must be of `const char*` type.
   j. False. The string library function `strrev` reverses all the characters of a string except the terminating null character.

k. False. A character array can be initialized with a string literal constant. For example, `int a[10]="Hello";` is a valid declaration statement.
l. True.

Chapter 7: Scope, Linkage, Lifetime and Storage Classes

1. a. scope; b. Label name; c. `extern`; d. each object must have only one definition in a scope; e. definition of an identifier in the immediate scope shadows/supersedes the definitions of the identifier present in the enclosing scope; f. Name resolution; g. external; h. `static`; i. no; j. internal, external, no; k. lifetime; l. automatic; m. dynamic memory allocation; n. `auto`; o. `typedef`;

2. a. True.
   b. False. Function scope terminates with the closing brace of the function definition. Function prototype scope terminates with the end of the function declaration.
   c. False. It is possible to declare an identifier with a same name and type more than once in the same scope.
   d. True.
   e. False. It is not allowed to declare identifiers with a same name but different types in different scopes. However, it is possible to define identifiers with a same name but different types in different scopes.
   f. True.
   g. False. The variables declared with `auto` storage class specification are not implicitly initialized. The variables declared with `static` storage class specification are implicitly initialized.
   h. True.
   i. True.
   j. True.
   k. False. The value of an `auto` variable ceases to exist when control moves out of a function. However, the value of a `static` variable persists between the function calls as it has a global lifetime.
   l. False. `size_t` is not a type. It is a synonym for the type `unsigned int`.
   m. False. The value of the memory space allocated by using the `malloc` function is not initialized to zero. However, all the bits in the memory space allocated using the function `calloc` are initialized to zero.
   n. False. Careless allocation of the memory at the run time leads to memory leak.

Chapter 8: The C Preprocessor

1. a. compiler; b. execution character set; c. `??`; d. `x ++ ++ + y`; e. Macro; f. symbolic constants; g. `pragma`; h. null directive; i. Preprocessing token; j. biggest.

2. a. True.
   b. True.
   c. False. A new line character ends the preprocessor directive.
   d. False. A preprocessor directive can appear anywhere within a program.

e. False. The concatenation operator must appear between two tokens.
f. True.
g. True.
h. False. A predefined macro cannot be undefined using the undef directive.
i. False. If the identifier specified with the undef directive is not currently defined as a macro, the statement will be ignored and will have no effect.
j. False. The identifier defined as macro can be used from the point of its definition till a corresponding undef directive is encountered or till the end of the translation unit.
k. False. No macro replacement is carried out if a name same as the macro name appears as a part of a string literal constant or as a part of some other name.

Chapter 9: Structures, Unions, Enumerations and Bit-fields

1. a. heterogeneous; b. self-referential structure; c. Arrays, structures; d. anonymous structure; e. names; f. machine-word boundary; g. arrow; h. higher; i. largest j. typedef.

2. a. True.
   b. True.
   c. False. Arrays and structures are collectively known as aggregate type.
   d. False. A structure cannot have an instance of itself. A structure that contains a pointer to an instance of itself is known as a self-referential structure.
   e. True.
   f. True.
   g. False. Structure members cannot be initialized during the structure definition since no memory is allocated at that time.
   h. False. In C, the keyword struct along with the tag-name of the defined structure type is used to create an object of the structure type.
   i. False. The name of a structure does not refer to its base address. It refers to the entire structure.
   j. False. Padding bytes are not copied.
   k. False. The padding can only appear in between two structure members or after the last structure member.
   l. True.
   m. False. The typedef can only be used to create an alias name for the defined type.
   n. False. Only the first member of a union can be initialized, while in structures all the members can be initialized.

Chapter 10: Files

1. a. stream, file descriptor; b. stdin, stdout, stderr, stdaux and stdprn; c. screen; d. FILE; e. Text; f. the stream buffer gets full; g. "r+"; h. EOF; i. ftell, fgetpos; j. SEEK_SET; k. 512; l. unbuffered.
2. a. True.
   b. False. Binary streams are uninterpreted. It happens in text streams.
   c. True.

d. False. By default, the stream stdout is un buffered.
e. True.
f. False. The function ftell cannot be used to position the file position indicator within the file.
g. True.
h. True.
i. False. The open streams are automatically closed when the program terminates successfully.
j. True.

Index

__cplusplus macro 493
__DATE__ macro 491
__FILE__ macro 491
__FILE__ macro 496
__LINE__ macro 491
__LINE__ macro 496
__STDC__ macro 492
__TIME__ macro 492

A

absolute path 634
abstract parameter declaration 261
accumulator register 323, 575
activation 287
activation record 286, 287
active 287
actual arguments 268
addition operator 50
address-of operator 20, 64, 194, 202, 545, 569, 583, 589
advantages of arrays 211
aggregate operations 543
aggregate types 536, 592
alias 431
alias name 566
American National Standard Institute *see* ANSI 2
American Standard Code for Information Interchange *see* ASCII 38
angular brackets 23
anonymous structure type 538
ANSI 2
argument count 373
argument vector 373
arguments with a side-effect 486
arithmetic operators 50
arithmetic statement 106
arithmetic type(s) 62, 194
arithmetic-type conversion 51
Armstrong number 173, 530
array index out-of-bound check 189
array of character pointers 371
array of function pointers 295
array of pointers 209
array of strings 370
array of structures 556
array subscripting 203
array type derivation 189
array type *see* arrays 184
arrays 184
arrays of arrays *see* multi-dimensional arrays 203
arrow operator 555
ASCII 480
assembler 479
assembly-level code 510
assignment 60, 139, 442
assignment operators 50, 60
assignment statement 106, 107
associativity 49
auto storage class 426
auxiliary parameters 284

B

backspace character 39
backward jump 124
base case 283
base register 575
Basic Combined Programming Language *see* BCPL 2
basic data types
  character *also* char 6
  double precision floating point *also* double integer *also* int 6
  single-precision floating point *also* float 6
  void 6
Basic Input Output System *see* BIOS 572
BCPL 2
binary files 652
binary mode 632
binary number system 24, 25
binary operators 50
binary recursion 287
binary search 335
binary stream 632, 666
binary tree 288
BIOS 572
bit-field 587, 586
bitwise operators 50
block 109
block input 652
block scope 412, 413
block-structured language 2
body of a function 16, 263
bottom-up development 258
braces 16
branching statements 107, 113, 114
  conditional branching 114
  unconditional branching 114
break statement 124, 134

bubble sort 243
buffer 347, 661
buffer level 658
buffer size 661
buffered input functions 347, 348
byte alignment of structure members 546
byte offset of a member 597

C

C character set
  execution character set 3
  source character set 3
C program file 630
C-style character strings 341
C.A.R Hoare partitioning strategy 333
call by address *see also* pass by address 274
call by reference *see also* pass by address 274
call by value *see also* pass by value 273
called function 265
calloc function 433
case label 112
case-labeled statements 111, 112
case-sensitive language 2, 23
character arrays 342
character input 637
character literal constant
  non-printable character literal constants 12
  printable character literal constants 12
character output 638
character pointers 341
character set 480
character stuffing 39
closing streams 635
code redundancy 259
code reuse 259
code segment 227, 292, 538
codeblocks 440
column major order of storage 208
column size specifier 204, 209
comma operator 62, 268
command file 630
command line arguments 281, 373, 662
command line 373
command prompt 373
comments 15, 27
  multi-line comment 15
  single-line comment 15
common macro pitfalls 484
common type 51
compilation 503
compile-time initialization 442
compiler 478, 479
compiling a program 17
complete parameter declaration 261
complete type 536
composing a function *see* function definition 302
compound expression 48
compound statement 109
concatenation 490
concatenation operator 490
conditional branching *see* selection statements 114
conditional compilation directives 482, 500
conditional operator 62
console input-output 630
constants 11, 54
  literal constants 11
  qualified constants 11
  symbolic constants 11
const qualifier 214
constant declarations 107
continue Statement 125, 136
count register 575
cplusplus program file 630
CPU registers
  flag register 574
  general-purpose registers 574
  offset registers 574
  segment registers 574
C standards
  ANSI C/Standard C/C89 Standard 2
  C99 Standard 2
  ISO C/C90 Standard 2
  Kernighan & Ritchie (K&R) C Standard 2
current active pointer 661

D

dangling else problem 118
data file 630
data object *also* object 9
data register 575
data segment 227, 443, 538
data structure 185
data type 6, 25
debugging 259, 265
declaration of a function pointer 293
declaration of a single-dimensional array 186
declaration of a three-dimensional array 209
declaration of a two-dimensional array 204
declaration of array of strings 370
declaration of library functions 297
declaration statement 5, 110
declaring objects of an enumeration type 581
declaring pointer to a structure 554
declaring structure objects 539
declaring union objects 568
decrement operator 50, 54
default arguments 278
default-labeled statements 111, 113
define directive 14, 483
defining a structure 534
defining a union type 568
definition of an enumeration type 580
definition repetition loops *see* counter-controlled loops 126
definition statement 7, 110
delay function 144
demotion 52

dereference operator 195
dereferencing a pointer 194
derived data types 189, 212
derived data types
- array type 6
- function type 6
- pointer type 6

determination of scope of an identifier 412
device files 630
digraph sequences 504, 520
direct indexing 211, 445
direct member access operator *also* dot operator 543
direct recursion 282
directive handling 479
Disk Operating System *see* DOS 572
divide-and-conquer strategy 258, 330, 333, 335
division operator 50, 54
do clause 131
DOS 572
do-while body 131
do-while statement 131
dummy operator 95
dup function 665
dynamic array 470
dynamic link 287
dynamic memory allocation 425, 432, 444
dynamically allocated array 448

E

EBCDIC 480
element type 185
ellipses 301
else body 116
else clause 116
empty string 341
end of file 646
end-of-file character 646, 666
entry-controlled loops 147
enumeration constants 580, 600
enumeration set 580
enumeration tag-name 580
enumerators 580
EOF character 646
EOF macro 493
equivalent types 414
error directive 482, 496
escape sequences 12, 479
evaluating arithmetic expressions 51
executable file 630
executable statements 16, 107, 263
executing a program 17
execution character set 480
execution of C program 265
exit-controlled loops 147
explicit initialization 442
explicit type casting 200
explicit-type conversion 67, 68
exponent 30
expression 48
expression statement 106, 110
expression syntax error 70
extern storage class specifier 420, 425
extern storage class 430
external identifier 412
external linkage 420
extra segment 227, 443

F

far pointer 227
fdopen function 665
feof function 646
ferror function 648
fflush function 657
fgetc function 637
fgetpos function 642
fgets function 648
Fibonacci series 174, 285, 472
fields *see* structure members 536
file descriptor 630, 660
file handle 665
file I/O 630
file pointer 633
file position indicator 638, 641
file scope 412, 413
file status flags 658
file type 657
fileno function 665
files 630
fixed argument functions 299
floating point literal constant 11
floating point mode arithmetic 52
floating point number 30
flow control statements 113
- branching statements 113
- selection statements 113
- jump statements 113
- iteration statements 113

Floyd's triangle 178
flushall function 657
flushing the streams 654
for body 127
for header 127
for statement 127
formal parameters 268
format specifier(s) 18, 19, 28
format string 18
formatted input 650
formatted output 650
forward jump 124
fprintf function 650
fputc function 638
fputs function 648
fread function 652
free function 436
free-flow language 2
freopen function 665
fscanf function 650
fseek function 643
fsetpos function 644
ftell function 641
full expression 66, 85
full path *see* absolute path 634
fully buffered stream 632
function call operator 265
function call *see* function invocation 264, 265
function call statement 107, 265
function declaration 260, 263
function designator 194, 261, 294
function implementation *see* function definition 263
function invocation *see* function call statements 110, 264

function pointer 293
function prototype scope 412, 414
function prototype *see* function declaration 261
function scope 412, 414
function type 293
function type derivation 293
function use *see* function invocation 264
function with inputs and no output 267
function with inputs and one output 269
function with inputs and outputs 273
function with no input-output 264
function-like macros 483, 484, 507
functions 14, 258, 507
fwrite function 652

G

garbage value 28
Gauss-Jordan elimination method 251
general-purpose language 2
generic pointer 200
getc macro 637, 661
getchar function 346
gets function 346
global declaration 14, 15
global identifier 412
global namespace pollution problem 449
global scope 412
global variable 107
goto statement 123
Greedy Tokenizer 86

H

harmonic mean 529
header of a function 16, 263
heap 436, 443
heterogenous data 215
high-level language 2
hold character 660
holes 546
homogeneous data 184
huge pointer 227

I

I/O using streams 633
identifier-labeled statement 111
identifiers 4, 54
IEEE 754 30
if-else statement 116
if body 114, 116
if controlling expression 114
if header 114
if ladder 118
if statement 114
if-else controlling expression 116
if-else header 116
illegal pointer operations 200
implicit initialization 442
implicit-type conversion 51, 68
improved maintainability 259
inactive 287
include directive 22, 495
incomplete type 536
increment operator 50, 53
indefinite repetition loops *see* sentinel-controlled loops 132
index *see also* subscript 185
indexed variable *see also* subscripted variables 185
indirect member access operator *also* arrow operator 543, 555
indirect recursion 282
indirection operator 195
infinite recursion 283, 327
information hiding 259
initialization 60, 442
initialization list 139, 187, 541
initializer 187
insertion sort 240
Institute of Electrical and Electronics Engineers *see* IEEE 30
Instruction Pointer *see* IP 312
integer literal constant 11
integer mode arithmetic 51
integral data type 25, 38
Integrated Development Environment *see* IDE 23
inter-segment access 227
interactive files 630
internal linkage 422
internal padding 549, 596
International Organization for Standardization *see* ISO 2
interpreter 479
interrupt programming 575
interrupts
  hardware interrupt 572
  software interrupt 572
Interrupt Service Routine *see* ISR 572
Interrupt Vector Table *see* IVT 573
intra-segment access 227
inverted search set 345
invertible matrix 251
ISO 646 480
ISO8859 480
ISO8859-1 480
ISO8859-2 480
ISO8859-16 480
ISR 572
iteration statements
  do-while statement 126
  for statement 126
  while statement 126
IVT 573

J

jump statement 109, 114, 123
  break statement 123
  continue statement 123
  goto statement 123
  return statement 123
jumping *see* unconditional branching

K

keywords *also* reserved words 5, 146

L

L-value
  modifiable l-value 9
  non-modifiable l-value 9
L-value required error 53, 69
label name 111
labeled statements 111
Least Significant Bit *see* LSB 169
length of a string 341
length of a data type 8
lexical analyzer 86
library functions 297
library of mathematical functions 298
library of standard input/output functions 299
library of string processing functions 299
lifetime 424, 425
  allocated 425
  automatic *also* local 425
  static *also* global 425
limitation of enumeration type 586
limitations of arrays 211
line buffered stream 632, 654
line directive 482, 496
line input 648
line output 648
line splicing 39, 479, 481
linear arrays *see* one-dimensional arrays 186
linear recursion 286
linear search 239
linkage
  external linkage 420
  internal linkage 420
  no linkage 420
linked list 537, 554
linking 503
list of strings 369
literal constant
  character literal constant 11
  floating point literal constant 11
  integer literal constant 11
  string literal constant 11
little-endian format 92
loading 503
local declaration 412
local scope 412
local variables 287
logical AND 57
logical data streams 631
logical NOT 57
logical operators 50
logical OR 57
logical source lines 481
longhand declaration 6
loop counter 126
looping statement 107
lower triangular matrix 250

M

machine code 137
machine-word boundary alignment of structure members 546
macro 483
macro expansion 479, 484, 505
macro name 483
macro replacement directive 482, 483
magic number 30
magical white space 484
malloc function 432
mantissa 30
matrix *see* two-dimensional arrays 203
matrix addition 246
matrix inverse 251
matrix multiplication 246
matrix transpose 248
member-by-member copy 545
memory allocation 8
memory leak 436
memory representation of multi-dimensional arrays
  column major order of storage 208
  row major order of storage 208
merge sort 330
miscellaneous operators 50, 61
  address-of operator 61
  array subscript operator 61
  comma operator 61
  conditional operator 61
  function call operator 61
  indirection operator 61
  member select operator 61
  direct member access operator *also* dot operator 61
  indirect member access operator *also* arrow operator 61
  sizeof operator 61
mixed mode arithmetic 52
modifiable l-value 53
modularization 258
modulus operator 50, 55, 169
Most Significant Bit *see* MSB 24
mouse programming 579
multi-line comments 27, 510
multiplication operator 50
mutually recursive functions 282

N

n-ary recursion 291
n-D array 203
name resolution 418, 419
named structure type 540
near pointer 227
negative integral numbers 24
nested if statement 118
nested if-else statement 118
nested loop 134, 146, 207
nested structures 560
new line character 39
newly created data type 535
no linkage 424
non-executable statements 16, 107, 263
non-printable character literal constant 12
non-tail recursion 284
NULL 201
null character 340, 351
null directive 482, 502
null macro 493

null pointer 196, 201
null statement 109, 110

O

object-like macros 483
offset address 195
offsetof macro 597
one definition rule 416
one's complement 24, 97
opening a stream 633
operand 48
operations on structures
  aggregate operations 543
  segregate operations 543
operations on void pointer 200
operator 48, 54
operator precedence problems 485
out-of-bound index 189

P

pack size 547
padding 552
padding bytes 546
palindrome 172, 404
parameter list 261
parameter-type list 261
parameters 287
parentheses 18
parity 586
parity checking 586
partitioning 333
pass by address 273
pass by value 273
passing a structure object to a function 561
passing arrays to functions 275
passing one-dimensional arrays to functions 276
passing two-dimensional arrays to functions 277
perfect number 172
phases of translation 479
phonebook application 619
physical source lines 481
pivot element 333
plane size specifier 209
pointer 192
pointer arithmetic 197
pointer subtraction 198
pointer to a pointer 193, 210
pointer to a stream 633
pointer to an array 210
pointer type *see* pointer 184
pointers to functions 292
pointers to structures 554
portable language 2
post-decrement operator 54
post-increment operator 53
practical application of unions 571
pragma directive 482, 497, 550
#pragma exit 499
#pragma option 497
#pragma startup 499
#pragma warn 498
pre-decrement operator 54
pre-defined functions *see* library functions 297
pre-increment operator 53
precedence 49
precision specifier 37
predefined macros 491
preprocessing 503
preprocessing token 481
preprocessor 478, 479
preprocessor directive(s) 14, 15, 107, 478, 482
primitive data types *see* basic data types 6
principal diagonal elements 248
printable character literal constant 12
printf function 349
printing strings on the screen 349
procedural language 2
processor *see* microprocessor 572
programmer-defined functions *see* user-defined functions 259
promoted 51
putc macro 638, 662

Q

qualified constants 13, 60, 96
qualifiers *see* type qualifier 7
quick sort 333

R

R-value 9
random access files 643
range 8, 26
Read Only Memory *see* ROM 572
readability 259
reading strings from the keyboard 343
realloc function 434
recurrence relation 283
recursion 282
recursive case 283
recursive function 282
reference type 192, 194
referencing a bit-field 588
referencing operation 194
register storage class 428
registers 312
register window 323
relational operators 50, 56
  equal to operator 56
  greater than operator 56
  greater than or equal to operator 56
  less than operator 56
  less than or equal to operator 56
  not equal to operator 56
relationship between arrays and pointers 202
relative path 634
reserved word(s) 5, 54, 146
return expression 270
return statement 126, 270
rewind function 646
role of ellipses 301
role of header files 297
row major order of storage 208
row size specifier 204, 209
run-time initialization 442

S

same scope 414
saved state 287
scalar types 62
scope 412
scope of macro definitions 494
search set 344
segment address 195
segregate operations 553
selection *see* conditional branching 114
selection sort 242
selection statements
  if-else statement 114
  if statement 114
  switch statement 114
self-referential structure 536
sentinel value 132
separators 54, 81, 82
sequence point 487
sequential access files 643
setbuf function 656
setvbuf function 654
shadowing 418
shorthand assignment operators 60
shorthand declaration 6, 261
side-effect 486
sign-two's complement representation 24
simple expression 48, 108
single-dimensional array *see also* one-dimensional array 186
single subscripted variables *see* one-dimensional arrays 186
size specifier(s) 187, 204, 209
sizeof operator 21, 63, 202, 548, 568, 583, 589
sleep function 144
solution to dangling else problem 118
source character set 480
source file inclusion directive 482, 495
source language 478
splicing 481
stack 287, 443, 558
stack segment 443
standard input streams 381
standard streams 631, 664
statement 106
static array 470
static local variable 439
static memory allocation 425, 444
static storage class specifier 422
static storage class 429
statically allocated array 448
stepwise refinement 258
storage classes 425
storage class specifiers
  auto 425
  extern 425
  register 425
  static 425
  typedef 425
storage duration 424
storing flag values 601
strcat function 354
strchr function 361
strcmp function 355
strcmpi function 357
strcpy function 353
stream 380, 630, 631, 664
stream buffering
  full buffering 654
  line buffering 654
  no buffering 654
stream redirection 664, 665
stricter alignment 547
strictly aligned member 547
strictly upper triangular matrix 250
string library functions 352
string literal *see* string literal constant 340
string literal constant 13, 340
string type 341
string variable 343
stringification 488
stringizing operator 488
strlen function 353
strlwr function 358
strncat function 365
strncmp function 367
strncmpi function 368
strncpy function 364
strnset function 369
strongly typed language 304
strrchr function 362
strrev function 358
strset function 360
strstr function 363
struct BYTEREGS 575
struct WORDREGS 575
structure declaration-list 534
structure members 536
structure object 541
structure of a C program 14
structure padding 546
structure programming language 123
structure tag-name 534
structure type 535
structured-type definition *see* structure definition 534
structures 534
strupr function 359
sub-expression 66, 85
subtraction operator 50
subscript 189
subscript operator 189
subscripting 191
switch body 118, 119
switch header 118
switch selection expression 118
switch statement 118
symbolic constants *see also* object-like macro 14, 483, 600
symmetric matrix 249

T

tab character 39
tagged structure type 540
tail recursion 284
target language 478
temporary storage 287
termination of scope of an identifier 413
terminator 82, 109
testing 259
text file(s) 630, 652
text mode 632

text stream 632, 666
three-dimensional arrays 208
token 54, 481
tokenization 479, 481
tokenizer 86, 481
token concatenation 490
token pasting 490
token replacement 488
top-down design 258
Tower of Hanoi problem 288
tracing 265, 323
tracking union field 599
trailing padding 549
translation limits 536
translation unit 413
translators 478, 503
trigraph replacement 479, 480
trigraph sequence(s) 480, 504, 520
truncation 52
two's complement 24, 89, 97
two-dimensional arrays 203
type *see* data type 6
  basic data types 6
  derived data types 6
  user-defined data types 6
type cast operator 67, 97
type checking 262, 301
type modifiers
  long 7
  short 7
  signed 7
  unsigned 7
typedef storage class specifier 540, 566
typedef storage class 431
type qualifiers
  const qualifier 7
  volatile qualifier 7

U

unary minus operator 50, 52
unary operators 50
unary plus operator 50, 52, 95
unbuffered input functions 347, 348
unbuffered stream(s) 632, 654
unconditional branching *see* jump statements 114
undef directive 492, 493
undesirable semicolon 487
union REGS 575
unions 568
unnamed bit-field 587, 590, 601
unnamed structure type 538
unstructured jumping 123
unwinding of recursion 287
upper triangular matrix 250
usage of a two-dimensional array 205
usage of single-dimensional array 188
use of library functions 298
user-defined data types 534
  enumeration 7
  structure 7
  union 7
user-defined functions 259

V

value-at operator 195
variable argument functions 300, 301
variables 10
va_arg 300
va_end 300
va_start 300
vectors *see* one-dimensional arrays 186
visibility of an identifier 417
void functions 265
void pointer 197, 200

W

warning 307
while body 129
while clause 131
while controlling expression 129
while header 129
while statement 129
white space characters 67
  blank space character 4
  carriage return 4
  form feed character 4
  horizontal tab space character 4
  new line character 4
width specifiers 36
winding of recursion 286
wrap around 26, 37